CONTENTS

PREFACE

Consider Ethics: Theory, Readings, and Contemporary Issues, Third Edition, is aimed at promoting careful thought about ethics. It covers competing ethical theories and a variety of ethical issues, including the relation of scientific inquiry to ethics, the nature of virtue, the role of both feelings and reason in ethics, the relation between religion and ethics, and the question of moral responsibility. Though the focus of the book is ethical theory, the issues raised are illustrated and debated through discussions of such practical ethical questions as capital punishment, abortion, terrorism, drug-enhanced athletic performance, homosexuality, and limits on legitimate police inquiry. The style is conversational, inviting the reader to actively engage with the most important ethical theorists of the past and present.

Consider Ethics is an open inquiry into intriguing and disputed issues: readers consider a variety of perspectives and reach their own judgments. Ethics involves questions that are inherently fascinating, and *Consider Ethics* is a relaxed and conversational book that encourages readers to think more carefully and in greater depth about questions concerning the nature of ethics itself: how ethical principles can be known (if indeed they can be known at all), how ethical systems might be constructed, the nature and existence of free will, and the relation of free will to value questions. These questions have many interconnections, and the response to early questions will influence conclusions concerning later issues, while later conclusions may prompt reexamination of earlier views. Drawing out those implications—encouraging readers to think carefully about how their earlier answers are related to later questions—is a major goal of the text. Each position examined—from utilitarianism to Kantian ethics to care ethics—is presented in its strongest form, and readers draw their own conclusions concerning the most plausible positions and the strongest arguments.

SPECIAL FEATURES OF THE TEXT

- Readings from a wide variety of sources, including philosophers from many periods up to the present, as well as works from primatology, biology, anthropology, and law.
- Twenty chapters covering a wide range of ethical theory along with several topics of popular debate.
- Readings from major philosophers, from Aristotle to Martha Nussbaum, allow students to examine key ethical positions through primary texts.
- Examination of major philosophical work on ethical theory, as well as a wide range of research in biology, psychology, sociology, anthropology, and law that has major implications for our understanding of ethics.
- The text covers a wide range of competing ethical theories, noting arguments for and against each, and allows students to make their own judgments of the most plausible.
- Special boxed inserts within each chapter provide points of clarification as well as specific short passages giving a flavor of the arguments presented by both advocates and critics of the positions discussed.
- Exercises at the end of each chapter raise provocative open questions concerning the strengths, weaknesses, and implications of each position; these can be adapted for classroom discussion and/or written assignments.
- The text is conversational in tone, inviting students to consider arguments, join in the inquiry, and engage in the continuing debate.
- Additional reading suggestions at the end of each chapter offer both Web-based and printed resources for further inquiry.

SUPPORT FOR INSTRUCTORS AND STUDENTS

- **myethicskit** is an online resource that offers a wealth of tools to help student learning and comprehension, including practice quizzes, videos, primary source readings and more. MyEthicsKit also includes a rich array of interactive tools enhanced with audio and video to engage students in learning. For more information please see your Pearson sales representative or visit www.myethicskit.com
- Instructor's Manual with Tests (0-205-01777-0) For each chapter in the text, this valuable resource provides a detailed outline, list of objectives, discussion questions, and suggested readings and videos. In addition, test questions in multiple-choice, true/false, fill-in-the-blank, and short answer formats are available for each chapter. For easy access, this manual is available at www.pearsonhighered.com/irc.
- MyTest (0-205-01776-2) This computerized software allows instructors to create their own personalized exams, edit any or all of the existing test questions, and add new questions. Other special features of this program include random generation of test questions, creation of alternate versions of the same test, scrambling question sequence, and test preview before printing. For easy access, this software is available at www.pearsonhighered.com/irc.
- PowerPoint Presentation Slides (0-205-01775-4) These PowerPoint slides display text for each chapter to help instructors convey philosophical principles in a clear and engaging way. For easy access, they are available at www.pearsonhighered.com/irc.

NEW TO THIS EDITION

- New exercises added to every chapter are designed to encourage readers to reach their own conclusions concerning the strengths and weaknesses of the various theoretical views, to explore comparisons and disputes and connections among those views, and consider the practical implications of the various theoretical perspectives
- New boxed examples and special quotations are scattered throughout every chapter.
- A new section on sentimentalism explores both the history and the contemporary development of the sentimentalist view of ethics, from Francis Hutcheson and Adam Smith to contemporary writers such as Simon Blackburn.
- The chapter on utilitarian theory adds an examination of Michael Slote's "satisficing" version of the theory.
- There is a new section on value pluralism, together with new readings by Susan Wolf and Catherine Wilson on that question.
- There are new essays or excerpts from James Rachels, Bishop Joseph Butler, Adam Smith, Jonathan Bennett, Bernard Williams, Martha Nussbaum, and (anthropologist) Elvin Hatch.
- There are two new "applied" chapters: one examining the use of deceit in police investigations (with essays by law professors Christopher Slobogin and Margaret L. Paris), and a second debating the use of performance-enhancing drugs in athletics (with essays by Robert L. Simon and W. M. Brown).

ACKNOWLEDGMENTS

I am indebted to many people who helped with various elements and the several editions of this book. My colleagues in the Department of Philosophy and Religious Studies have been a constant source of ideas, energy, encouragement, and friendship; special thanks to Chris Bache, Walter Carvin, Stephanie Dost-Barnhizer, Jeff Limbian, Brendan Minogue, Mustansir Mir, Deborah Mower, Bernard Oakes, Gabriel Palmer-Fernandez, Charles Reid, Tom Shipka, Donna Sloan, Arnold Smith, J-C Smith, Andrew Stypinski, Linda "Tess" Tessier, Alan Tomhave, Mark Vopat, and Victor Wan-Tatah. I am also grateful to many others. Mark Shutes, until his untimely death, was a rich source of information about political ethics as well as about issues in anthropology and politics and pretty much everything else. Nawal Ammar has stimulated and improved my thinking on cultural differences in ethics. John White frequently gave me articles and ideas that proved very helpful. Homer Warren has been a wise guide through the tangles of many difficult contemporary social and ethical debates. Robert Weaver has discussed many of these ideas with me at various times, and has been a very valuable resource in understanding issues in biomedical ethics. Lauren Schroeder has offered fascinating ideas on a wide range of subjects, particularly in the area of environmental ethics. Charles Singler has been a rich source of topics and ideas in contemporary social and political ethics. Lia Ruttan has provided very helpful comments on rough drafts, and I have learned a great deal from her concerning ethical systems in other cultures, as well as the ethics of cultural research. Richard White has been a wonderful source of ideas and insights, ranging from juvenile justice to bioethics. Richard Double has been a special source of encouragement and inspiration, has informed me of much valuable material I should otherwise have missed, and has kindly shared with me his deep insights into the tangle of questions involving free will and moral responsibility. George Graham has broadened my philosophical outlook on many issues, especially on questions related to abnormal psychology and philosophy of mind. Robert Kane's books and conversations have forced me to think much harder and more carefully about many questions related to free will. Stephen Flora has been a very valuable resource in the area of contemporary behavioral psychology. Fred Alexander has taught me a great deal about ethics, to my joy; and also a great deal about poker, to my sorrow. Jack Raver has been a marvelous stimulus on many contemporary ethical issues, and his unadulterated joy in ethical and social debates both inspires and invigorates. Robyn Repko, a philosopher at the beginning of her philosophical career, has been a source of many interesting ideas, both in psychology and philosophy. Joan Bevan, who managed our department for many years, is genuinely remarkable: she does a staggering amount of work with such joyful efficiency that it looks almost easy. Whatever the problem—from computer malfunctions to dealing with painfully slow responses to permission requests—Joan invariably fixed it, and the first edition of the book would *never* have been completed without her help. She was assisted ably and cheerfully by our student worker, Justina Rachella. Following Joan's retirement, her place was filled by one of the very few people who could have lived up to her standard: Mary Dillingham stepped in, took over the reins, and never missed a beat. My years as department chair would have been utter disaster without their amazing fortitude, hard work, and organizational skill. Both Joan and Mary have the wonderful ability to stay cheerful, calm, and utterly efficient in the constant chaos of an academic department filled with philosophers and religious studies scholars. Our student worker during the transition, Hannah Detec, was incomparable; without her, the entire department would have crashed and burned during that difficult period between Joan's retirement and Mary's arrival. James Hamilton also provided very able student support during that period, and our current student worker, the cheerfully hard-working Gina Ponzio, has proved more than worthy of continuing in this long line of exceptional talent. The librarians at YSU have for many years been remarkably effective at finding any book or article, no matter how obscure; and they have been an important part of everything I have written. Special thanks to Karen and Sherry at the Beat Coffee Shop, who brew the world's best coffee and always serve it with a smile.

My editor for the first edition, Priscilla McGeehon, offered a great variety of very valuable suggestions for improving the text, constantly encouraged and appropriately prodded, and answered every question and smoothed every rough spot in the bumpy process of finishing a book. Eric Stano, editor for the second edition, made excellent suggestions for improving the text. The current editor, Nancy Roberts, and the special assignment editor who worked on this text, Kate Fernandes, have been helpful and supportive throughout the development of this edition. The editors of each edition were especially good at finding reviewers who made detailed examinations of the text and offered superb ideas for changes and improvements. My project manager for the third edition, Shiny Rajesh, has been careful, thorough, and highly professional in turning a rough draft into a polished final product. Special thanks for the excellent suggestions of the following persons who reviewed the work in progress: Mary Alexander, Ashford University; Amy Beaudry, Quinsigamond Community College; Phillip Cronce, Chicago State University; Kevin Sweeney, Southern Maine Community College; Jayne Tristan, University of North Carolina at Charlotte; Edwin Aiman, University of Houston; Fritz Allhoff, University of California, Santa Barbara; Lisa Bellatoni, Quincy University; Sheryl Breen, St. Olaf College; Jeff Broome, Arapahoe Community College; Stephen R. Brown, University of Oklahoma; Andrei Buckareff, University of Rochester; Maria Carl, Seattle University; John Draeger, Syracuse University; Howard Ducharme, University of Akron; George Griffith, Chadron State College; Maurice Hamington, Lane Community College; Kenneth D. Hines, Penn State Worthington Scranton; Aaron Meskin, Texas Tech

University; Chris Meyers, Southern Methodist University; Jeffrey Morgan, University College of the Fraser Valley; Lawrence Nelson, Santa Clara University; Dave Raymond, Northern Maine Technical College; Franklin E. Robinson, Murray State University; Phil Schneider, Coastal Carolina University; Daniel Silber, Florida Southern University; E. Ssekasozi, Lincoln University of Missouri; Les Sutter, International College; Martin Tracey, Benedictine University; John Wadhams, Eastfield College; Stevens F. Wandmacher, University of Michigan-Flint; David Whitford, Claflin University; and Diane Wilkinson, University of South Florida.

My wife, Mary Newell Waller, has not only discussed many of these questions with me but also provided much help in the area of contemporary clinical psychology. My sons, Russell and Adam, have been a rich source of ideas and comments, a great source of joy and pride, and have often been a sounding board for trying out ideas. It's not easy trying to eat your morning cereal when your father is quizzing you about whether someone who rejects moral responsibility could offer a sincere apology; but they suffered such queries with both good cheer and real insight. The book is much better for their suggestions, including their clear guidance on what sections did *not* work.

Finally, my students at Youngstown State University have tried out many sections of the book, and working with them over the past two decades was the inspiration for writing this text. My students at Youngstown State are the children of immigrants from every corner of the globe, whose parents often arrived penniless to work in the steel mills. Their parents and grandparents struggled—and some died—to establish and protect the rights of working men and women in this country. Their children, my students, grew up through the hard times of mill closings in the Mahoning Valley. Those students, gathered from the widest range of ethnic backgrounds, now study together and learn from one another in mutual respect and friendship. And those students—frequently the first in their family to attend college—work full-time jobs, care for families (often including children as well as aging parents or grandparents), take substantial course loads, and still approach their studies with energy, enthusiasm, insight, and good cheer. Sometimes they are students who have devoted decades to difficult and dangerous industrial work; lost their jobs, their pensions, and their health care; and are standing up and starting over and heading off to college. Their remarkable fortitude, warmth, intelligence, and enthusiasm have been a constant source of inspiration, and it is to the students of Youngstown State University that I dedicate this book.

BRUCE N. WALLER

1
Thinking About Ethics

ETHICS AND CRITICAL THINKING

This is an invitation to think carefully about the nature of ethics and ethical inquiry. You've no doubt already thought carefully about a good many ethical issues, such as abortion, capital punishment, environmental ethics, academic honesty, and animal rights. We'll be looking at some of those issues, and others besides. But we'll also do something that's not quite so common—we'll be thinking about the nature of ethics itself: how do we have knowledge of ethical principles? Is knowledge of ethics similar to knowledge of physics? *Can* we have knowledge of ethical principles? Are ethical principles fixed or changing? Are they absolute or circumstantial? These are sometimes called *meta*ethical questions, that is, questions about the nature and concepts of ethics. Thinking carefully about those questions may help in thinking more carefully about such issues as economic justice, abortion, and treatment of animals. In any case, it may help us gain a clearer perspective.

Thinking carefully about ethics involves, rather obviously, thinking *carefully*. So it will be useful to start with some consideration of *how* to think carefully, critically, and effectively, and how to avoid some common errors. Some people maintain that ethics is *not* based on reasoning, but is instead built on emotions and feelings, or on intuitions. In fact, some maintain that ethics is not a matter of finding truth at all: there are no objectively true ethical principles, and thus there are no true ethical principles to be discovered through reasoning (nor by any other means). Those are interesting positions, and you may ultimately conclude that ethics is not based on reasoning. But even if that is your conclusion, it is still useful to start with some considerations about critical thinking, since in order to reach such a conclusion you will have to use careful reasoning. We will examine several readings by people who argue *against* reason-based ethics, as well as several readings arguing that reason is the foundation of ethics. Regardless, all of them give *arguments* for their views, and those arguments must be critically examined.

What's the Question?

Perhaps the first and most crucial step in critical thinking is the most obvious, but also the most neglected: be clear on exactly what is at issue. That is, when examining an argument, think first about *precisely* what the argument is supposed to be proving; get clear on the *conclusion* of the argument. "Ladies and gentlemen of the jury, this was the most vicious crime I have ever come across in all my years as district attorney. It was cruel, callous, heartless, and brutal," the district attorney insists in her argument to the jury. Is the district attorney's argument *relevant?*

That depends. It depends on what *conclusion* she is arguing for. Suppose she is arguing that the defendant is guilty of a brutal murder, but the question at issue is whether the defendant is the guilty party (the defense claims this is a case of mistaken identity). In that case, the district attorney's argument is *irrelevant* to that conclusion. Everyone agrees the crime was awful; the question is whether the defendant did it. (Incidentally, relevance is not determined by whether the claim is true or false, but by whether it *matters* if the claim is true or false. It may be true that the crime was brutal, but it remains irrelevant to the defendant's guilt. And on the other hand, a *false* claim may be relevant: if an unreliable eyewitness *falsely* claims to have seen the defendant commit the murder, that claim will certainly be *relevant* to the question of whether the defendant is guilty. It's *relevant* because *if* it were true, it would be strong proof of the defendant's guilt: it's relevant because it *matters* whether it is true or false). Suppose now that the defendant has already been found guilty, and since this is a capital case the trial has moved on to the sentencing phase. In that case, exactly the same argument ("this was a brutal and heartless crime") will be *relevant* to the question of whether the person who did the crime should receive the death penalty. Of course the argument may be *relevant* without being completely convincing; the jury might decide that the crime was indeed brutal, but other mitigating factors (such as the age of the defendant) count more heavily *against* capital punishment.

When an arguer uses an *irrelevant* point in support of a conclusion, we say that the arguer has committed the *fallacy* (or argument error) of *irrelevant reason*. It is sometimes called the *red herring* fallacy. When fox hunters would send the hounds out to chase a fox, and then ride their horses across the fields in pursuit of the fox and hounds, they would eventually tire of the "sport," and wish to go back to the lodge for tea and scones. But the dogs would still be chasing the fox, and thus be difficult to collar. So the handler of the dogs would drag a bag of oily cooked herring (herring turns red and becomes very oily when cooked) across the trail of the fox. When the dogs ran into the smelly oil from the red herring, they would lose the scent of the fox, mill around aimlessly, and thus be easy to catch. So that's where we get the name for the "red herring fallacy": the fallacy "drags a red herring," drags a distraction, across the trail of the argument, and thus takes listeners off the track. We get so worked up about the red herring of what a brutal murder it was, we forget that the real issue is whether the defendant is guilty.

Red herrings are a common argument trick. When the Bush administration was arguing for an attack on Iraq, they spent a lot of time talking about the importance of fighting terrorism. Of course everyone is legitimately concerned about terrorism, but the real question was not whether we should fight terrorism, but whether Iraq was engaged in terrorism. By dragging the terrorism red herring across the trail of the argument, it was easy to distract people from the more difficult issue, for which proof was very thin: the question of whether Iraq was supporting terrorist activities or providing weapons of mass destruction to terrorists.

So the first step in evaluating arguments is to be clear on *exactly* what's at issue, exactly what the conclusion is. If I'm the defendant in a burglary trial, the prosecutor must prove every element of the crime beyond a reasonable doubt. But my defense attorney does *not* have to prove that I *didn't* do it; instead, he only needs to show that there is a *reasonable doubt* of my guilt. If you evaluate the defense attorney's arguments as if they were designed to prove innocence, then you will evaluate them badly.

Ad Hominem Fallacy

There are many argument fallacies in addition to the red herring fallacy, but one of the most important in the study of ethics is the *ad hominem* fallacy. An ad hominem argument is an argument "to the person"; that is, an ad hominem argument is an attack on the person. And an ad hominem *fallacy* is an attack on the *source of an argument*. If someone gives an argument, we must evaluate the argument on its own merits, not on the merits of the person giving the argument. Suppose you come into your ethics classroom and discover an argument written on the blackboard, say, an argument against the death penalty. In order to evaluate that argument, you don't need to know anything at all about who wrote the argument on the board. Suppose you read the argument and decide it is a strong and convincing argument, and then you find it was written by Bill Clinton, the politician you most despise. That would not change the argument. Then you learn that a mistake had been made, and the argument was written by Mother Teresa, one of your moral heroes. That does not change one word of the argument. So if you are evaluating *arguments*, the *source* of the argument is irrelevant. And if you attack the source of the argument in order to discredit the argument, you have committed the *ad hominem fallacy*.

It is especially important to keep that in mind when discussing ethics, because ethics discussions can get intensely personal and downright hostile. If you don't believe me, have a nice discussion of the abortion question with someone who holds a view diametrically opposed to your own. Such "discussions" often generate more heat than light, and one reason is because they often degenerate into ad hominem abuse: the pro-choice advocate is branded a "baby killer," and the pro-life side is called a "neanderthal." Difficult as it may be to discuss such issues without sliding into fallacious ad hominem arguments, it is essential if there is to be serious ethical inquiry. One way to avoid such abusive arguments is to keep in mind that the character of the arguer is irrelevant to the quality of the argument. When arguing about ethics—or anything else— you can attack *arguments* as vigorously as you wish, but attacking *arguers* is fallacious. To see why, consider this example. Spring break is approaching, and at the end of class I give you an *argument* for why you should not drink and drive: drinking and driving can be easily avoided if you plan in advance, it places others at unfair risk, and the negative consequences for you—if you are in an accident, or get arrested—can be very severe, certainly out of all proportion to any benefits you might derive from drinking and driving. Is that a good argument against drinking and driving? Not a very original one, but it does give some legitimate reasons to avoid drinking and driving. Now suppose later this evening you see me stagger out of the tavern, fumble around for my keys, finally get my car started, and weave away down the street, taking out three side-view mirrors and one fender in the process. If you now say, "Well, there goes Bruce, totally plastered, driving merrily away. And just this afternoon he was arguing against drinking and driving. Any argument that sleazy hypocrite makes against drinking and driving must be pure rubbish." That would be an ad hominem fallacy. True enough, I'm a sleazy hypocrite who argues for one thing and then does another. But that does not change my *argument*. It's still the same argument, whether I'm a sleazy hypocrite or a paragon of virtue. Suppose you learn that it was my evil twin brother you saw coming out of the tavern and driving away. Would that suddenly rehabilitate my argument? Of course not. It's the very same argument, and it must stand or fall on its own merits, and it doesn't matter whether the arguer is drunk or sober, hypocritical or sincere, vicious or virtuous.

Ad hominem attacks on arguers commit the ad hominem fallacy. But not all ad hominem arguments are fallacious. Some may be perfectly legitimate. Think back to the O.J. Simpson trial. One of the key witnesses for the prosecution was police officer Mark Fuhrman (he was the first officer to arrive at the Simpson residence, and he found the famous glove—the one that didn't fit when Simpson tried it on). He testified under oath that he never used racial slurs, and that he held no prejudice against blacks. But he lied. It turned out that the man could hardly open his mouth without spewing out racial hatred (he once said that he would like to round up all African Americans and burn them), and he particularly despised interracial couples (like O.J. and Nicole) and often harassed them. This key prosecution witness was a lying, vicious racist. The defense made an *ad hominem* attack on Mark Fuhrman, but it was perfectly legitimate. Mark Fuhrman was giving testimony, not argument, and in order to evaluate his testimony you need to know if he is truthful, unbiased, and objective—or that he is *not*. If Mark Fuhrman were giving *argument* instead of testimony, then his vile character would be irrelevant: you would have to hold your nose and evaluate his arguments on their own merits. If I give *testimony* that I have seen extraterrestrials ("Take my word for it, I saw them with my own eyes, they're here"), then you need to know about my drinking habits, my history of drug use, my mental stability, and my reputation for integrity. But if I give an *argument* for the existence of extraterrestrial intelligence ("Think of the billions and billions of stars in our galaxy, and all their planets and moons, and how many opportunities there would be for life to develop in other solar systems"), then my character, habits, and mental state are *irrelevant* to the quality of my argument. So when you are arguing about ethics, you can attack one another's arguments with all the energy and ingenuity you can muster, but to avoid committing the ad hominem fallacy you must resist attacking the arguer.

The Principle of Charity and the Strawman Fallacy

One other principle of critical thinking is especially important in thinking critically about ethics: the *principle of charity*. That is simply the principle of being *charitable* or *generous* toward the positions and arguments we oppose. In other words, you should interpret opposing views and arguments as generously, fairly, and honestly as you can. That doesn't mean you can't attack opposing views; by all means, subject them to the closest scrutiny and the fiercest criticism—and be willing to have your own views subjected to the same criticism. After all, that's one of the best ways of separating the wheat from the chaff when we examine ethical issues. But resist the temptation to score cheap points and win false victories by misrepresenting opposing views. When someone distorts or misrepresents a position in order to make it easier to attack, that is called the *strawman* fallacy. It's easier to knock down a strawman than a real man, and it's easier to defeat a distorted version of a position than the real thing. In both cases, it's not much of a victory. Following the principle of charity—always represent opposing views in their strongest and most plausible form—is the best way of avoiding strawman fallacies, and it is also essential if you are to have any chance of convincing your opponents that your own view is more plausible. If you attack and defeat a distorted and inaccurate representation of my position, I am not likely to be convinced that your arguments are effective.

Strawman fallacies are depressingly common in ethical debate. Think again of the abortion controversy. If I am pro-life, I may accuse my opponents of believing that it is morally acceptable to kill infants up to age one. In fact, there *are* a few people who do hold that view. But obviously that is not the view of most pro-choice advocates, who favor elective abortion but vigorously oppose infanticide. If I represent my opponents as favoring infanticide of one-year-old children, then I am attacking a *strawman*. I may win that argument against the strawman position, but I'm not likely to convince those pro-choicers whose views I have misrepresented. Likewise, suppose I am pro-choice. I then accuse my pro-life opponents of wanting to outlaw not only abortion but also all forms of artificial contraception—there would be no birth control pills or condoms. Again, some of the opponents of legal abortion *do* take that view, but it is an extreme view, and certainly not the view of most persons who are pro-life. It is a much easier position to attack, and so I may easily defeat this strawman version of the pro-life position, but again, such a strawman "victory" is not likely to convince many people.

Consistency

One last point concerning thinking critically about ethics. A key question in examining ethical views is whether they are internally *consistent,* and whether they are consistent with our other beliefs. Suppose I oppose elective abortion but support the death penalty, and you accuse me of being inconsistent in my principles. I will respond that my views are *not* inconsistent: I oppose abortion because it is the taking of an innocent life, but those who are executed are *not* innocent. Or suppose the argument goes the other way: I oppose capital punishment, but support the right to elective abortions, and you accuse me of inconsistency. I will respond that abortion kills a fetus, but a fetus is not a full person; capital punishment is carried out against persons. Or I might say that in the case of the fetus, the mother's right to control of her own body takes precedence; in contrast, when an imprisoned person is executed there is no question of interference with a woman's control of her own body.

Those may or may not be adequate answers to the charge of inconsistency; that will be a much debated question. However, I cannot simply accept inconsistencies in my ethical views. That is, I cannot legitimately say: Okay, so I have views that are in conflict and beliefs that contradict each other; so what? I can't legitimately make that response, because allowing contradictions within my views makes it possible to prove *anything,* and thus makes careful reasoning impossible. Think about it for a moment. Suppose that you allow me both of these contradictory premises: "The sky is blue," *and* "The sky is not blue." Then I can "prove" anything at all. What follows from "The sky is blue"? Well, it follows that *either* the sky is blue *or* anything you like. (It's true that I am a human; therefore, it is also true that *either* I am a human *or* I am the richest person on Earth, and it is also true that either I am a human *or* Oprah Winfrey is an extraterrestrial, and it is also true that I am a human *or* there is no corn in Iowa.) So it follows that the sky is blue *or* genocide is good. But remember, we also have the contradictory premise: The sky is *not* blue. So let's put them together: Either the sky is blue *or* genocide is good, *and* the sky is not blue. (That's like saying "Either Brendan is in the library or he's at the tavern, and he's not at the library.") It follows that genocide is good. We could use the same reasoning to "prove" that Miami is in Maine, or that the Pacific Ocean does not exist, or *anything else*. If you allow a contradiction, then you can "prove" anything. And that makes accurate reasoning impossible. If your views contain contradictions, you have to deal with those contradictions (either by rejecting one of the conflicting views or by finding a way to reconcile them); you can't just let them fester.

There is a well-known saying by American transcendentalist philosopher Ralph Waldo Emerson: "Consistency is the hobgoblin of little minds." People sometimes use that slogan to defend sloppy thinking: to defend thinking that includes contradictions and does not insist on consistency. But that's not what Emerson meant. Emerson knew the danger of internal contradictions. What he meant was simply that it is alright for your ideas and beliefs to *change*. Beliefs that you now hold don't have to be held forever; it's *okay* to change your mind. Maybe some of your beliefs, perhaps even some of your ethical beliefs, cannot survive careful scrutiny. If so, perhaps you should discard them and replace them with new ones. As Emerson suggested, it's nice to keep an open mind. But it shouldn't be so open that it allows internal contradictions.

STUDYING ETHICS

If you take a course in geography, you expect that the course will make you a better geographer. If you take a course in creative writing, you anticipate that the course will improve your creative writing. And it is reasonable to hope that a course in chemistry will make you a better chemist. So when you take a course in ethics, what should you expect? That you will learn more about ethics? That seems a minimum expectation. But should you also expect that you will become more ethical, more virtuous, and a better person?

Before we go too far in exploring whether a course in ethics is likely to make you a morally better person, perhaps we should agree on what would count as moral improvement. And there's the rub. It's not so easy to decide what makes a morally superior person. That is the sort of thing we'll explore: how do we decide—and *can* we decide—what counts as moral virtue and as morally good behavior? There are many different views on that question, and the purpose of this book is *not* to tell you which view is correct. Rather, this book will help you explore a wide range of distinctive and often conflicting accounts of ethics, and the focus will be on helping you decide where your own views fit. Perhaps in the course of examining these views and where your own ideas fit along this wide spectrum, you may decide that some of your ethical opinions should change. But that's not the purpose of the book. There are plenty of moral self-help books, and there are plenty of books that will tell you in no uncertain terms what you *ought* to believe about ethics. This is not one of them. This book is designed to give you an opportunity to think more carefully about some major issues in metaethics (that is, about the nature of ethics itself), some specific ethical questions, and how your own views fit. Nothing more—but also nothing less, and those are substantial goals.

The Nature of Ethical Principles

Should you expect studying ethics to make you ethically better, the way you expect studying math to make you a better mathematician? Some people say yes, and others say no. That's one of the questions we'll examine. But there are lots of questions in ethics. After all, ethics is a vast subject, with a long and remarkable history. There are many good places to start an examination of ethics, but among the most basic (and disputed) questions in ethics is this one: do ethical truths have to be eternal verities, not really part of this world of decay, known through some special power; or are they more mundane, ordinary facts, part of the standard furniture of our world, and known through ordinary means? (Of course there is another option: ethical truths don't exist at all, anywhere; we'll set that possibility aside for the moment, but we'll return to it.) When you seek ethical guidelines, what characteristics must they have? It's hard to know if you've found them unless you know what to look for. What would count as an ethical guide, an ethical principle? "If you want to be trusted and prosperous, practice honesty." Benjamin Franklin thought that was really all the justification needed—and perhaps all the justification possible—for honesty: it *pays*, long term. Contrast that with the starkly unconditional form of the Hebrew commandment: "Thou shalt not bear false witness." Of course you could read this as: If you don't want to get into trouble with God then don't bear false witness. But most people interpret it not as some arbitrary rule that you must follow to retain God's favor, but rather as a basic moral principle that God (in His moral wisdom) recognizes and puts in the form of a commandment.

"What counts as ethics?" is a question worth pondering. Think for a minute about what ethical principles would have to look like, in your own view—not whether you think abortion is right or wrong, whether it is wrong to cheat on your taxes or your lover, whether you have an obligation to help the impoverished or prevent global warming or protest human rights abuses, and not the question of whether you believe there actually *are* objectively true moral principles. Instead, think about what you would be willing to *count* as a genuine moral principle. (If you deny that such principles exist, or that such principles are objectively *true*, you must have some sense of what it is that you are denying the existence of: you can't claim that a jabberwocky doesn't exist if you have no idea what a jabberwocky is.)

The first reason to consider what counts as a moral principle is to avoid talking past one another. Suppose I think that genuine moral principles must be absolutes like "Never lie," and I deny that there are any true moral absolutes of that sort. You believe that moral principles are much more modest: "If you want to promote trust and harmony, then you should be truthful in your dealings with others," and you insist that we have good reason to believe that there are such moral principles. We may suppose that we are in basic conflict—"There are no genuine moral principles," I shout; "There certainly are," you reply—when perhaps we really agree. You might agree with me that there are no moral absolutes, and I might agree with you that more modest moral principles make perfectly good sense. Or maybe not. Perhaps we really do have a fundamental difference in our views. But we won't know that until we look carefully at exactly what each of us counts as a moral principle.

There is another important reason to look carefully at what you count as a moral principle. It may tell you a lot about yourself, and some of your basic beliefs and assumptions. Those assumptions and beliefs may be so deep and influential that you hardly know they are there. Like wearing tinted contact lenses through which you view everything you see, such assumptions color the way you see the world without you even being aware of them. Perhaps you think real moral principles exist, perhaps not. That is a question you have probably thought about already. But what do you count as real moral principles? (Not the question of whether real moral principles exist: I don't think unicorns exist, but I know what I would count as a unicorn.)

For many people, genuine moral principles must be very special indeed. Plato, the ancient Greek philosopher, believed they are eternal truths known only through pure reason: reason that sees through the illusions of the senses and discovers the fixed and absolute and immutable truth. Moses found moral truths on a mountaintop, in the awesome presence of God, permanent moral truths carved into enduring stone. Descartes, a French philosopher of the seventeenth century, believed that God implants moral principles in our minds as innate ideas. And in the eighteenth century, Immanuel Kant discovered the basic governing principle of morality through rigorous reason, an absolute and unconditional moral truth that filled him with awe: "Two things fill the mind with ever new and increasing admiration and awe, the oftener and more steadily they are reflected on: the starry heavens above me and the moral law within me."[1]

In contrast, others have considered moral principles to be much simpler and more mundane. Aristotle, one of Plato's students, regarded moral principles as basic guides to living the good life. Thomas Hobbes, a British philosopher who lived in the seventeenth century, thought moral principles were devised by humans to bring order and peace to society. Jeremy Bentham, in late-eighteenth- and early-nineteenth-century Britain, asserted that the basic moral principle is simple and obvious: maximize pleasure and minimize suffering for everyone. David Hume, a British philosopher of the eighteenth century, insisted that morality is rooted in the simple affection that human social animals feel for one another.

There are many more examples of this fundamental conflict between those who regard morality as consisting in special absolute principles, and those who see moral rules as a more ordinary phenomenon based in natural affections or devised rules of order. And obviously there is enormous variation among those on both sides. For example, Plato thinks absolute moral rules are discovered by Reason, while Moses thinks they are ordered by God. On the other side, Hume thinks moral rules are based in natural animal affections, while Hobbes traces them to social agreement. Those differences within the two camps notwithstanding, it is worth noting the basic contrast between the two perspectives—and worth thinking about where your own sympathies lie in this basic conflict. For this contrast involves considerably more than the nature of moral principle. If moral principles are universal, absolute, and eternal principles—as Plato, Moses and Kant believe—then we can't discover them by taking surveys. Nor can we find them through psychological or biological study, no matter how carefully and thoroughly we try. And we cannot create them by social agreement. Instead, such universal principles will require special ways of knowing. They are discovered, but they are not discovered the way we discover new elements or a new species of beetle or the Loch Ness Monster.

Knowing Ethical Principles

If at last we drag some reclusive beast out of the depths of Loch Ness, then we will discover that some species we had thought long extinct still survives. Maybe such creatures exist—probably not. Unconditional, absolute moral principles are different. Those who believe in them believe that they *must* exist. They don't exist only if we like them, or happen to recognize them, or choose to adopt them. Rather, they are universal, eternal moral principles that are unconditionally true whether anyone recognizes them or not. There might have been a Loch Ness Monster; it happens there is not. But eternal moral principles have no such contingency. They are absolute truths, not discovered by fishing in Loch Ness nor by any other form of observation or experiment. So not only are there special universal moral principles but we also require special powers or capacities to recognize them. The sensory powers that reveal a new beetle species are not adequate for this task.

What powers must we have to recognize such absolute moral truths? That varies, depending on what the absolute moral truths are. Some claim the truths are dictated by God, and are given to us by special revelation. Others hold that each of us has a special innate moral capacity—a conscience, or a moral sense—that implants in us the basic moral truths. Philosophers such as Plato and Kant maintain that the special power that reveals such eternal moral truths is the power of Reason—not the ordinary reason that enables you to select a horse to wager on in the eighth race at Belmont, but a power of Reason that enables you to see beyond mere appearances and surface features and discern deep, underlying moral truths. But whatever the means by which we discover absolute moral principles—whether by God's special revelation, or some remarkable innate intuitive power, or through sublime Reason—this is not a natural capacity like sight or hearing that we share with other animals. Rather, this is a special power that sets us apart from the natural world: a power that makes us almost godlike.

If you think of moral principles as more mundane, conditional matters, then you are likely to have a more modest account of how those moral principles are recognized. Moral principles aren't written in the heavens, nor are they special absolute truths. Since they are not extraordinary, they require no extraordinary powers for their understanding, and they do not set moral humans apart as unique and special. If morality is based in feelings of sympathy and social concern, then morality requires no special powers or esoteric capacities. For example, Darwin believed that morality is simply a natural result of social sympathy:

> The following proposition seems to me in a high degree probable—namely, that any animal whatever, endowed with well-marked social instincts, the parental and filial affections being here included, would inevitably acquire a moral sense or conscience, as soon as its intellectual powers had become as well, or nearly as well developed, as in man.[2]

Natural Morality Versus Transcendent Morality

So, when you think of morality, what is your image of the subject? Is morality something that rises *above* the natural world, something that *transcends* the natural world? Or is morality a more natural process: based on our emotions, perhaps, or on rules we draw up for promoting social harmony? We might call it, for convenience, the contrast between *natural* morality and *transcendent* morality, or between contingent morality and absolute morality.

This is an issue people feel strongly about. Richard Halverson, the former chaplain of the U.S. Senate, insisted that there can be no morality other than absolute morality:

> Abandoning an absolute ethical moral standard leads irresistibly to the absence of ethics and morality. Each person determines his own ethical/moral code. That's anarchy. Humans become their own gods and decide, each in his own way, what is good and what is evil. Evil becomes good—good becomes evil. Upside down morality! Good is ridiculed! Evil is dignified![3]

So, only absolute moral standards can keep us from anarchy. Give up absolute moral standards, and soon murder and mayhem will be celebrated as virtue, and we will have no moral guidance whatsoever. Those who oppose absolute ethics have little patience with the transcendent absolutism favored by Chaplain Halverson. Ethics requires no mysteries or miracles, they would insist, and denying transcendent moral absolutes does not lead to moral anarchy. After all, humans come equipped with social sympathies and common needs and interests, and we don't require absolute God-approved moral principles to recognize that some types of behavior undermine society and others enhance the social welfare for all. Whether bond traders in Manhattan, cattle traders in the Sudan, or spice merchants in India, the value and benefits of cooperation and honesty are obvious enough, and require neither divine sanction nor special insight.

GOD'S COMMANDMENTS AND ETHICS

Let's start by looking at some views that champion *absolute* moral principles: moral principles are eternal, universal, fixed truths. Like the stars, they exist whether we discover them or not, and they offer steady points of light for reliable moral navigation. Among such absolutist views we obviously find some religious doctrines. One religious version of absolutism goes by the name *theological voluntarism*. That's just a classy name for a very common view: Moral principles are set by God, God commands them; and God neither changes nor makes exceptions, so God's commandments are fixed, eternal, and absolute. What is right is *whatever God commands*, or *whatever God chooses*. God doesn't condemn murder because murder is wrong; rather, murder is wrong *because* God condemns murder.

> Theological voluntarism is so named because it makes ethical principles dependent on what *God wills*. Something is good because God *wills* that it be so, not because God recognizes it to be good. It is sometimes called the *Divine Command* theory of ethics: Good is whatever God commands, and *only* what God commands is good. On this view, God's will or God's command is the whole of ethics. A law or principle is right *if and only if* it is willed (commanded) by God.

Many people turn to religion for ethical guidance. Indeed, there are some who adamantly insist that their personal religious beliefs provide the only acceptable ethical standards: "The Bible says it, I believe it, that settles it," is an example of such an approach. But even for those who have unwavering faith in the pronouncements of their own religion or religious leaders or sacred texts, ethical issues can sometimes pose quandaries. For example, one may insist on the importance of the commandment that "Thou shalt not bear false witness," and then when faced with a difficult situation—you are hiding escaped slaves from slave catchers—your obligation to "Do unto others as you would have them do unto you" might lead you to protect these escapees from capture, torture, and enslavement and thus lead you to "bear false witness": "No, I have not seen any escaped slaves."

And the problems can get even thornier. In the very same chapter in which God orders "Thou shalt not kill," God also commands the slaughter of whole cities—men, women, and children—who have the misfortune of living on the land that God assigns to the children of Israel. "Put to the sword every inhabitant, and spare not one" is hard to reconcile with "Thou shalt not kill"; so what should we do?

Ethical Principles as Divine Commandments

This raises serious questions concerning the relation between ethics and religion. Perhaps the most basic of these troubling questions are these: Is an ethical guideline (or law) right because God commands it? Or does God command it because it is right? That is, do ethical principles exist only because God affirms them? Or does God affirm these ethical principles because (in His or Her wisdom) God *recognizes* the truth of these ethical laws? If you are religious, you might wish to take a moment to think about your answer to that question, for your answer makes a big difference in the way you think of ethics.

Does God command us to be honest because honesty is good? Or is honesty good because God approves of honesty? This may seem a strange, perhaps even a disturbing question. The question exposes a tension between two fundamentally incompatible sources that the Western religious tradition has struggled to combine: the religious views of ancient Greek philosophy, particularly the views of Aristotle; and the religion of the ancient Hebrews, of Abraham and Moses. Aristotle's God is a God of reason. In fact, Aristotle's

God is perfect, completely self-sufficient, and absolutely unchanging. He wants for nothing, and passes eternity thinking about thinking. Since He is omniscient, He can't try to discover new truths: He knows everything already. And since He is already perfect, He can't engage in any self-improvement projects. Obviously, Aristotle had little sympathy with the popular Greek notions of the gods Zeus and Diana and Triton: gods who plotted, lied, changed their minds, appearances, and affections, and generally seemed to fall a good deal short of perfection. Since God (Aristotle's God) is perfect, He must be changeless: if a perfect God changed, then any change would have to be for the worse and would result in imperfection.

Contrast Aristotle's conception of God with the traditional Hebrew notion. The God of Abraham changes His mind more often than some undergraduates change majors. He creates humankind, then becomes disgusted and resolves to destroy them all; but He finds one good man, so He changes his mind and saves Noah and his family to make a new start. God works out a special deal with the children of Israel, then becomes angry at them and sends them into bondage in Egypt. He eventually rescues them and gives them a new set of rules to follow, but then discovers them worshiping a golden calf and His wrath is kindled and He resolves to destroy them all. Again He changes his mind, and instead kills several thousands. Trying to combine this hot-tempered Hebrew God with the perfect unchanging calm of Aristotle's God is no easy task, and one place the tension comes into play is in considering God's relation to the principles of ethics. Aristotle's God knows all and reasons perfectly and thus knows and understands the true ethical principles. He recognizes true ethical principles because He is infinitely wise, not because He makes them. The Hebrew God, by contrast, wills a set of moral laws: the children of Israel must follow those laws because they are God's commandments, and what makes them ethical principles is that God commands them. Whatever God commands is right, *because* it is God's commandment. God does not recognize what is morally good; rather, the commandments are moral principles *because* God commands them.

If you believe that ethical principles exist *only* because God commands them (the position we called theological voluntarism), then the study of ethics is for you a rather limited exercise. It consists entirely of trying to discover what ethical principles God wills, and there is no room whatsoever to reason about or critically examine ethical questions. There are people who hold such a view, but it obviously requires powerful faith. After all, on this view you cannot examine the ethical principles pronounced by God in terms of their reasonableness or justice or fairness. If God says that it is good to be kind to others, that is *not* because God recognizes that kindness is good; rather, it is strictly because God *pronounces* that kindness is good. Had God pronounced cruelty good, then cruelty would be good, and there would be nothing more to say about it.

> "I do not feel obliged to believe that the same God who has endowed us with sense, reason, and intellect has intended us to forgo their use." *Galileo Galilei*.

Problems with Theological Voluntarism

Those who adopt such a view hold one absolute principle: if God says it then that settles it. If God commands being kind to children, then being kind to children is good. If God commands torturing children, then torturing children is good. Those who believe in an austere and majestic and incomprehensible God often find this view appealing. It is motivated by the fear that *if* there were a moral law independent of God, then God would be *constrained* (by His perfect goodness) to follow that moral law. But God should not be constrained by anything, not even goodness. So God makes morality by His will, rather than following a moral law that He recognizes as true. Adopting this theological voluntarist view (good is whatever God wills it to be) requires a rather reckless leap of faith, for there is no way to critically evaluate such moral principles. You cannot say—if you adopt this view of morality—that you believe in this religion or this account of God because it is morally attractive: such an evaluation would require a standard of morality independent of what God pronounces. It is certainly possible to hold such a theological voluntarist view, and some people seem quite content with it, but it leaves little space for the critical study of ethics.

When they consider it, most religious people favor the other answer. It is not God's pronouncement or commandment that makes murder wrong; rather, God condemns murder because He (in God's great wisdom) recognizes the wrongfulness of murder. Such an approach leaves considerably more room for careful thought about ethics. If you hold religious beliefs, think for a moment about *why* you hold those beliefs. Surely your reason for holding your particular religious views is not merely because "my parents were Muslims" or "I was raised as a Christian" or "all my friends are Jewish." Your religious beliefs are a serious part of your life, and you have thought carefully about them. (Of course you may regard your religion as just part of your culture—you attend services on the High Holy days, and you enjoy assembling with your friends and community to perform various rituals, but you don't take the doctrines of the religion very seriously. In that case, you probably don't turn to your religion for your moral principles. You may find yourself in agreement with the moral principles promoted by your religion, but that is not because they are taught by your religion, and certainly not because you believe they were pronounced true by God.)

So—if you are seriously religious—*why* do you hold the religious beliefs you hold? There may be lots of different reasons for holding your particular religious beliefs, but among the most prominent is this: the religion I follow promotes sound moral principles. (If you have converted from one religion to another, it is not unlikely that one of the main motives for your conversion was dissatisfaction with the moral teachings of your old religion.) That is, one of my reasons for believing in this religion is that its moral principles seem just, fair, and reasonable. If you offer that as grounds for your belief, you must have *some* standard of what counts as just and fair that is independent of your religious belief. ("Why did you convert from religion X?" "Because religion X taught that women are inferior to men and should be subservient to men, and I simply cannot believe that a just God would approve of such vile moral principles." In order to draw such a conclusion, you must have a standard of justice that is independent of God's pronouncements. You believe justice requires equal treatment of women, and therefore you count any claim that God approves of unequal treatment as false, because you believe God adheres to what is just; not the other way around, that *whatever* God wills *is* just.) If you take this view, then your religion certainly is not irrelevant to your ethics, but your critical examination of ethics is not hamstrung by your religious beliefs.

God's Law and Punishment

There is another way God's laws might be relevant to ethics. In some religious traditions, God metes out very severe punishments to those who transgress against His laws, and substantial rewards to those who follow the rules. Such punishments and rewards might give one a strong *motive* for obeying God's commandments, but in themselves they provide no *justification* for believing that God's commandments are just and good. When the Fugitive Slave Act was passed in the United States, aiding escaped slaves became a criminal act, and those who helped runaway slaves could be subjected to imprisonment. During the Nazi era, Germans and citizens in the occupied countries were forbidden to help Jews, and those hiding Jews were often punished by death. In both cases, one would certainly have a prudent motive for following the rules: turning Jews over to the Gestapo and slaves to the slave catchers was the best way to escape punishment. That certainly did not establish that the laws requiring such behavior were ethically legitimate and morally just. Likewise, if God's rules are backed by powerful punishments and rewards, that in itself is no reason to think the rules are ethically sound.

This point is beautifully expressed by a wise Islamic teacher from the Sufi tradition, a woman named Rabi'a. One day Rabi'a rushed through the marketplace, carrying a flaming torch in one hand and a jug of water in the other. When people inquired why she was carrying the torch and the water, she replied that she was going to burn Paradise and quench the fires of Hell so that people would do morally good acts from love of doing the good and not from hope of gain or fear of punishment.[4] Rabi'a's point is clear: the rewards and punishments might motivate people to follow God's laws, but they do not give good reasons to suppose those laws are morally right. Even if the divine laws *are* right, when you follow the divine laws only from hope of reward or fear of punishment it is very doubtful you have acted morally.

RELIGION AND ETHICS

If we reject theological voluntarism, that by no means implies the rejection of religious considerations in our inquiries into ethics. Martin Luther King's campaign for civil rights had special power and broad appeal because it drew heavily on the language and symbols of God leading the children of Israel out of bondage: a powerful story that is common to the Jewish, Christian, and Muslim religious traditions. Religious parables and traditions have often stimulated reform movements, and sometimes encouraged us to look more closely at our lives, habits, and assumptions. Furthermore, organized religions have often contained groups of people who devoted intense systematic study to questions of theology as well as questions of ethics, and the results of their careful deliberations will merit our attention in later chapters.

So if ethics is not based on God's will or God's punishments, then what is the basis of ethics? Supposing that ethical laws are simply willed by God is certainly one type of transcendent, absolutist ethics, but it is by no means the only one. Plato rejected theological voluntarism, but he firmly believed in transcendent, absolute ethical standards. And one of the strongest and most uncompromising advocates of absolutist ethics is Immanuel Kant, who believed that absolute, universal ethical principles could be discovered through the meticulous use of higher Reason. Kant's rationalist approach to ethics will be dealt with in Chapter 4.

⇒⊱ GOD AND HUMAN ATTITUDES ⊰⇐

James Rachels

James Rachels (1941–2003) develops a powerful critique of theological voluntarism/divine command ethics. In fact, he argues that theological voluntarism cannot be an *ethical* theory at all, because theological voluntarism requires that we renounce all critical ethical deliberation and slavishly follow orders, and thus anyone who followed the demands of theological voluntarism would no longer be an ethical actor. Anyone who embraces such a role, Rachels claims, would no longer be autonomous; and if you are not autonomous, you cannot be a moral agent. This essay is from "God and Human Attitudes," *Religious Studies*, volume 7 (1971).

Kneeling down or grovelling on the ground, even to express your reverence for heavenly things, is contrary to human dignity.

Kant

1. It is necessarily true that God (if He exists) is worthy of worship. Any being who is not worthy of worship cannot be God, just as any being who is not omnipotent, or who is not perfectly good, cannot be God. This is reflected in the attitudes of religious believers who recognize that, whatever else God may be, He is a being before whom men should bow down. Moreover, He is unique in this; to worship anyone or anything else is blasphemy. In this paper I shall present an *a priori* argument against the existence of God which is based on the conception of God as a fitting object of worship. The argument is that God cannot exist, because no being could ever *be* a fitting object of worship.

However, before I can present this argument, there are several preliminary matters that require attention.

The chief of these, which will hopefully have some independent interest of its own, is an examination of the concept of worship. In spite of its great importance this concept has received remarkably little attention from philosophers of religion; and when it has been treated, the usual approach is by way of referring to God's awesomeness or mysteriousness: to worship is to 'down in silent awe' when confronted with a being that is 'terrifyingly mysterious'. But neither of these notions is of much help in understanding worship. Awe is certainly not the same thing as worship; one can be awed by a performance *of King Lear*, or by witnessing an eclipse of the sun or an earthquake, or by meeting one's favourite film-star, without worshiping any of these things. And a great many things are both terrifying and mysterious that we have not the slightest inclination to worship—I suppose the Black Plague fits that description for many people. The account of worship that I will give will be an alternative to those which rely on such notions as awesomeness and mysteriousness.

2. Consider McBlank, who worked against his country's entry into the Second World War, refused induction into the army, and was sent to jail. He was active in the 'ban the bomb' movements of the fifties; he made speeches, wrote pamphlets, led demonstrations, and went back to jail. And finally, he has been active in opposing the war in Vietnam. In all of this he has acted out of principle; he thinks that all war is evil and that no war is ever justified. I want to make three observations about McBlank's pacifist commitments. (*a*) One thing that is involved is simply his recognition that certain facts are the case. History is full of wars; war causes the massive destruction of life and property; in war men suffer on a scale hardly matched in any other way; the large nations now have weapons which, if used, could destroy the human race; and so on. These are just facts which any normally informed man will admit without argument. (*b*) But of course they are not *merely* facts, which people recognise to be the case in some indifferent manner. They are facts that have special importance to human beings. They form an ominous and threatening backdrop to people's lives—even though for most people they are a backdrop only. But not so for McBlank. He sees the accumulation of these facts as having radical implications for his conduct; he behaves in a very different way from the way he would behave were it not for these facts. His whole style of life is different; his conduct is altered, not just in its details, but in its pattern. (*c*) Not only is his overt behaviour affected; so are his ways of thinking about the world and his place in it. His *self-image* is different. He sees himself as a member of a race with an insane history of self-destruction, and his self-image becomes that of an active opponent of the forces that lead to this self-destruction. He *is* an opponent of militarism just as he is a father or a musician. When some existentialists say that we 'create ourselves' by our choices, they may have something like this in mind.

Thus, there are at least three things that determine McBlank's role as an opponent of war: first, his recognition that certain facts are the case; second, his taking these facts as having important implications for his conduct; and third, his self-image as living his life (at least in part) in response to these facts. My first thesis about worship is that the worshiper has a set of beliefs about God which function in the same way as McBlank's beliefs about war.

First, the worshiper believes that certain things are the case: that the world was created by an all-powerful, all-wise being who knows our every thought and action; that this being, called God, cares for us and regards us as his children; that we are made by him

in order to return his love and to live in accordance with his laws; and that, if we do not live in a way pleasing to him, we may be severely punished. Now these beliefs are certainly not shared by all reasonable people; on the contrary, many thoughtful persons regard them as nothing more than mere fantasy. But these beliefs are accepted by religious people, and that is what is important here. I do not say that this particular set of beliefs is definitive of religion in general, or of Judaism or Christianity in particular; it is meant only as a sample of the sorts of belief typically held by religious people in the West. They are, however, the sort of beliefs about God that are required for the business of worshiping God to make any sense.

Second, like the facts about warfare, these are not merely facts which one notes with an air of indifference; they have important implications for one's conduct. An effort must be made to discover God's will both for people generally and for oneself in particular; and to this end, the believer consults the church authorities and the theologians, reads the scripture, and prays. The degree to which this will alter his overt behaviour will depend, first, on exactly what he decides God would have him do, and second, on the extent to which his behaviour would have followed the prescribed pattern in any case.

Finally, the believer's recognition of these 'facts' will influence his self-image and his way of thinking about the world and his place in it. The world will be regarded as made for the fulfilment of divine purposes; the hardships that befall men will be regarded either as 'tests' in some sense or as punishments for sin; and most important, the believer will think of himself as a 'Child of God' and of his conduct as reflecting either honour or dishonour upon his Heavenly Father. . . .

3. Worship is something that is *done*; but it is not clear just *what* is done when one worships. Other actions, such as throwing a ball or insulting one's neighbour, seem transparent enough. But not so with worship: when we celebrate Mass in the Roman Catholic Church, for example, what are we doing (apart from eating a wafer and drinking wine)? Or when we sing hymns in a protestant church, what are we doing (other than merely singing songs)? What is it that makes these acts acts of *worship*? One obvious point is that these actions, and others like them, are ritualistic in character; so, before we can make any progress in understanding worship, perhaps it will help to ask about the nature of ritual.

First we need to distinguish the ceremonial form of a ritual from what is supposed to be accomplished by it. Consider, for example, the ritual of investiture for an

English Prince. The Prince kneels; the Queen (or King) places a crown on his head; and he takes an oath: 'I do become your liege man of life and limb and of earthly worship, and faith and trust I will bear unto thee to live and die against all manner of folks.' By this ceremony the Prince is elevated to his new station; and by this oath he acknowledges the commitments which, as Prince, he will owe the Queen. In one sense the ceremonial form of the ritual is quite unimportant: it is possible that some other procedure might have been laid down, without the point of the ritual being affected in any way. Rather than placing a crown on his head, the Queen might break an egg into his palm (that could symbolise all sorts of things). Once this was established as the procedure to be followed, it would do as well as the other. It would still be the ritual of investiture, so long as it was understood that by the ceremony a Prince is created. The performance of a ritual, then, is in certain respects like the use of language: in speaking, sounds are uttered and, thanks to the conventions of the language, something is said, or affirmed, or done, etc.: and in a ritual performance, a ceremony is enacted and, thanks to the conventions associated with the ceremony, something is done, or affirmed, or celebrated, etc.

How are we to explain the point of the ritual of investiture? We might explain that certain parts of the ritual symbolise specific things, for example that the Prince kneeling before the Queen symbolises his subordination to her (it is not, for example, merely to make it easier for her to place the crown on his head). But it is essential that, in explaining the point of the ritual as a whole, we include that a Prince is being created, that he is henceforth to have certain rights in virtue of having been made a Prince, and that he is to have certain duties which he is now acknowledging, among which are complete loyalty and faithfulness to the Queen, and so on. If the listener already knows about the complex relations between Queens, Princes, and subjects, then all we need to tell him is that a Prince is being installed in office; but if he is unfamiliar with this social system, we must tell him a great deal if he is to understand what is going on.

So, once we understand the social system in which there are Queens, Princes, and subjects, and therefore understand the role assigned to each within that system, we can sum up what is happening in the ritual of investiture in this way: someone is being made a Prince, and he is accepting that role with all that it involves. (Exactly the same explanation could be given, *mutatis mutandis*, for the marriage ceremony.)

The question to be asked about the ritual of worship is what analogous explanation can be given of it. The ceremonial form of the ritual may vary according to the customs of the religious community; it may involve singing, drinking wine, counting beads, sitting with a solemn expression on one's face, dancing, making a sacrifice, or what-have-you. But what is the point of it?

As I have already said, the worshiper thinks of himself as inhabiting a world created by an infinitely wise, infinitely powerful, perfectly good God; and it is a world in which he, along with other men, occupies a special place in virtue of God's intentions. This gives him a certain role to play: the role of a 'Child of God'. My second thesis about worship is that in worshipping God one is acknowledging and accepting this role, and that this is the primary function of the ritual of worship. Just as the ritual of investiture derives its significance from its place within the social system of Queens, Princes, and subjects, the ritual of worship gets its significance from an assumed system of relationships between God and men. In the ceremony of investiture, the Prince assumes a role with respect to the Queen and the citizenry; and in worship, a man affirms his role with respect to God.

Worship presumes the superior status of the one worshiped. This is reflected in the logical point that there can be no such thing as mutual or reciprocal worship, unless one or the other of the parties is mistaken as to his own status. We can very well comprehend people loving one another or respecting one another, but not (unless they are misled) worshiping one another. This is because the worshiper necessarily assumes his own inferiority; and since inferiority is an asymmetrical relation, so is worship. (The nature of the 'superiority' and 'inferiority' involved here is of course problematic; but on the account I am presenting it may be understood on the model of superior and inferior positions within a social system. More on this later.) This is also why *humility* is necessary on the part of the worshiper. The role to which he commits himself is that of the humble servant, 'not worthy to touch the hem of His garment'. Compared to God's gloriousness, 'all our righteousnesses are as filthy rags' (Isaiah 64: 6). So, in committing oneself to this role, one is acknowledging God's greatness and one's own relative worthlessness. This humble attitude is not a mere embellishment of the ritual: on the contrary, worship, unlike love or respect, *requires* humility. Pride is a sin, and pride before God is incompatible with worshiping him.

On the view that I am suggesting, the function of worship as 'glorifying' or 'praising' God, which is usually taken to be its primary function, may be regarded as derivative from the more fundamental nature of worship as commitment to the role of God's Child. 'Praising' God is giving him the honour and respect due to one in his position of eminence, just as one shows respect and honour in giving fealty to a King.

In short, the worshiper is in this position: He believes that there is a being, God, who is the perfectly good, perfectly powerful, perfectly wise Creator of the Universe; and he views himself as the 'Child of God,' made for God's purposes and responsible to God for his conduct. And the ritual of worship, which may have any number of ceremonial forms according to the customs of the religious community, has as its point the acceptance of, and commitment to, one's role as God's Child, with all that this involves. If this account is accepted, then there is no mystery as to the relation between the act of worship and the worshiper's other activity. Worship will be regarded not as an isolated act taking place on Sunday morning, with no necessary connection to one's behaviour the rest of the week, but as a ritualistic expression of and commitment to a role which dominates one's whole way of life.

4. An important feature of roles is that they can be violated; we can act and think consistently with a role, or we can act and think inconsistently with it. The Prince can, for example, act inconsistently with his role as Prince by giving greater importance to his own interests and welfare than to the Queen's; in this case, he is no longer her 'liege man'. And a father who does not attend to the welfare of his children is not acting consistently with his role as a father (at least as that role is defined in our society), and so on. The question that I want to raise now is, What would count as violating the role to which one is pledged in virtue of worshiping God?

In *Genesis* there are two familiar stories, both concerning Abraham, that are relevant here. The first is the story of the near-sacrifice of Isaac. We are told that Abraham was 'tempted' by God, who commanded him to offer Isaac as a human sacrifice. Abraham obeyed without hesitation: he prepared an alter, bound Isaac to it, and was about to kill him until God intervened at the last moment, saying 'Lay not thine hand upon the lad, neither do thou any thing unto him; for now I know that thou fearest God, seeing thou hast not withheld thy son, thine only son from me' (Genesis 22: 12). So Abraham passed the test. But how could he have failed? What was his 'temptation'? Obviously, his temptation was to disobey God; God had ordered

him to do something contrary to both his wishes and his sense of what would otherwise be right and wrong. He could have defied God; but he did not—he subordinated himself, his own desires and judgments, to God's command, even when the temptation to do otherwise was strongest.

It is interesting that Abraham's record in this respect was not perfect. We also have the story of him bargaining with God over the conditions for saving Sodom and Gomorrah from destruction. God had said that he would destroy those cities because they were so wicked; but Abraham gets God to agree that if fifty righteous men can be found there, then the cities will be spared. Then he persuades God to lower the number to forty-five, then forty, then thirty, then twenty, and finally ten. Here we have a different Abraham, not servile and obedient, but willing to challenge God and bargain with him. However, even as he bargains with God, Abraham realises that there is something radically inappropriate about it: he says, 'Behold now, I have taken upon me to speak unto the Lord, which am but dust and ashes . . . O let not the Lord be angry . . . ' (Genesis 18: 27, 30).

The fact is that Abraham could not, consistently with his role as God's subject, set his own judgment and will against God's. The author of Genesis was certainly right about this. We cannot recognise any being *as God*, and at the same time set ourselves against him. The point is not merely that it would be imprudent to defy God, since we certainly can't get away with it; rather, there is a stronger, logical point involved— namely, that if we recognise any being *as God*, then we are committed, in virtue of that recognition, to obeying him.

To see why this is so, we must first notice that 'God' is not a proper name like 'Richard Nixon' but a title like 'President of the United States' or 'King'. Thus, 'Jehovah is God' is a nontautological statement in which the title 'God' is assigned to Jehovah, a particular being— just as 'Richard Nixon is President of the United States' assigns the title 'President of the United States' to a particular man. This permits us to understand how statements like 'God is perfectly wise' can be logical truths, which is highly problematic if 'God' is regarded as a proper name. Although it is not a logical truth that any particular being is perfectly wise, it nevertheless is a logical truth that if any being is God (i.e. if any being properly holds that title) then that being is perfectly wise. This is exactly analogous to saying: although it is not a logical truth that Richard Nixon has the authority to veto congressional legislation, nevertheless it is a logical truth that if Richard Nixon is President of the United States then he has that authority.

To bear the title 'God', then, a being must have certain qualifications. He must, for example, be all-powerful and perfectly good in addition to being perfectly wise. And in the same vein, to apply the title 'God' to a being is to recognise him as one to be obeyed. The same is true, to a lesser extent, of 'King'—to recognise anyone as King is to acknowledge that he occupies a place of authority and has a claim on one's allegiance as his subject. And to recognise any being as God is to acknowledge that he has *unlimited* authority, and an unlimited claim on one's allegiance. Thus, we might regard Abraham's reluctance to defy Jehovah as grounded not only in his fear of Jehovah's wrath, but as a logical consequence of his acceptance of Jehovah *as God*. Camus was right to think that 'From the moment that man submits God to moral judgment, he kills Him in his own heart'. What a man can 'kill' by defying or even questioning God is not the being that (supposedly) *is* God, but *his own conception of that being as God*. That God is not to be judged, challenged, defied, or disobeyed, is at bottom a truth of logic; to do any of these things is incompatible with taking him as One to be worshiped.

5. So the idea that any being could be *worthy* of worship is much more problematical than we might have at first imagined. For in admitting that a being is worthy of worship we would be recognising him as having an unqualified claim on our obedience. The question, then, is whether there could be such an unqualified claim. It should be noted that the description of a being as all-powerful, all-wise, etc., would not automatically settle the issue; for even while admitting the existence of such an awesome being we might still question whether we should recognise him as having an unlimited claim on our obedience.

In fact, there is a long tradition in moral philosophy, from Plato to Kant, according to which such a recognition could never be made by a moral agent. According to this tradition, to be a moral agent is to be an autonomous or self-directed agent; unlike the precepts of law or social custom, moral precepts are imposed by the agent upon himself, and the penalty for their violation is, in Kant's words, 'self-contempt and inner abhorrence'. The virtuous man is therefore identified with the man of integrity, i.e. the man who acts according to precepts which he can, on reflection, conscientiously approve in his own heart. Although this is a highly individualistic approach to morals, it is not thought to invite anarchy because men are regarded as more or less reasonable and as desiring what we would normally think of as a decent life lived in the company of other men.

On this view, to deliver oneself over to a moral authority for directions about what to do is simply incompatible with being a moral agent. To say 'I will follow so-and-so's directions no matter what they are and no matter what my own conscience would otherwise direct me to do' is to opt out of moral thinking altogether; it is to abandon one's role as a moral agent. And it does not matter whether 'so-and-so' is the law, the customs of one's society, or God. This does not, of course, preclude one from seeking advice on moral matters, and even on occasion following that advice blindly, trusting in the good judgment of the adviser. But this is to be justified by the details of the particular case, e.g. that you cannot in that case form any reasonable judgment of your own due to ignorance or inexperience in dealing with the types of matters involved. What is precluded is that a man should, while in possession of his wits, adopt this style of decision-making (or perhaps we should say this style of *abdicating* decision-making) as a general strategy of living, or abandon his own best judgment in any case where he can form a judgment of which he is reasonably confident.

What we have, then, is a conflict between the role of worshiper, which by its very nature commits one to total subservience to God, and the role of moral agent, which necessarily involves autonomous decision-making. The point is that the role of worshiper takes precedence over every other role which the worshiper has—when there is any conflict, the worshiper's commitment to God has priority over any other commitments which he might have. But the first commitment of a moral agent is to do what in his own heart he thinks is right. Thus the following argument might be constructed:

a. If any being is God, he must be a fitting object of worship.
b. No being could possibly be a fitting object of worship, since worship requires the abandonment of one's role as an autonomous moral agent.
c. Therefore, there cannot be any being who is God

. . .

The argument . . . will probably not persuade anyone to abandon belief in God—arguments rarely do—and there are certainly many more points which need to be worked out before it can be known whether this argument is even viable. Yet it does raise an issue which is clear enough. Theologians are already accustomed to speaking of theistic belief and commitment as taking the believer 'beyond morality', and I think they are right. The question is whether this should not be regarded as a severe embarrassment.

EXERCISES

1. Do you expect this study of ethics—that you are now undertaking—to make you more virtuous, less virtuous, or to have no effect on your moral character?

2. John has been found guilty of academic dishonesty by the student-faculty review board. He plagiarized a history paper (he bought it off the Web) and was caught with a cheat sheet during a chemistry exam. Assume that we all agree that such academic dishonesty is wrong. What would you recommend as the best way of reforming John's dishonest behavior and character? Would your proposed reform process include a course in ethics?

3. The university has decided to develop a special ethics course for students who have been found guilty of violations of the honor code. First-time offenders can take the class, and if they pass the class they will have the academic dishonesty conviction removed from their permanent record. Is that a good idea?

   Set aside your answer to that question: don't worry about whether the course is a good idea or not. Whatever you think about such a course, you have been given the job of designing the course honor code violators will take. What would you include in such a course? Are there any novels you would assign? Movies you would show? Field trips you would make?

4. One of your high school friends has a deep-rooted prejudice against homosexuals. You would like to help your friend get over this prejudice. What would you do? Do you think it would help if your friend took a course in ethics? If you were designing the course, what would you include?

5. I have come into possession of a small but lovely drawing by Michelangelo. (Never mind how I came to possess this drawing. Let's just agree that I own it fair and square, and that I did not gain possession of it by theft, deceit, or fraud. The drawing is legitimately my own.) I have decided to paste the drawing over my dartboard, and use it as a target. You may think this quite stupid (even if I don't care for the drawing, it is obviously worth an enormous sum of money). That's not the issue. The question is this: Would I be doing anything *morally wrong* by destroying the drawing in this frivolous manner?

6. If a movie wins an Oscar, that obviously increases its box office appeal and results in greater profits for the producer. Not surprisingly, there have often been intense campaigns to persuade members of the Academy to vote for a particular picture. The Academy of Motion Picture Arts and Sciences (the folks who are in charge of the Academy Awards, or Oscars) have become disturbed about the amount of campaigning and lobbying for the awards. Producer Sid Ganis, who headed an Academy committee to look into the issue, said, "In the last number of years, there has been verbose campaigning, along with the press' depiction of studios vying against each other for Oscars, leading to a sense that Oscars could be bought with a lot of money." As a result of their study, Ganis's committee developed a set of guidelines in an effort to curtail such campaigning for Academy Awards. The guidelines note that recently there have been "an unfortunate series of manipulative and excessive Academy Awards 'campaigns,'" and the guidelines "set out some standards for ethical conduct where Academy Awards are concerned." But is this an *ethical* issue? If a film producer throws lavish parties and pays a public relations firm to run a campaign to have his film win the Academy Award for "best picture," has the producer done something *unethical?* (Of course if the producer bribes some of the Academy voters to vote for his picture, that raises ethical issues; but is campaigning for an Academy Award itself an *ethical* issue?)[5]

7. Oral sex was once widely regarded as a moral wrong (in some religious traditions it still is); indeed, in many U.S. states engaging in oral sex was a criminal act until just a few years ago. Today, most people in Western cultures regard consensual oral sex as not a moral issue at all. What standard would you use for determining whether something *counts* as a moral question?

8. I find the idea of cannibalism repulsive. But is it a moral issue? Suppose that some small religious sect in this country included in their death rituals the eating of a small portion of flesh from the deceased, and regarded that as a very important part of their religious practices and an important part of honoring their dead. Should such practices be legally prohibited? Would such practices be *morally wrong?*

9. We can divide and subdivide ethical views along a number of different cuts. This may be thought of as a preview of some of the issues we'll examine. You might use it to locate your own ethical perspective (your perspective for the moment, at least; you may change—and you may find it useful to compare your ethical views at the end of the class with those you hold now).

   A. Do you think ethics is a matter of natural processes, or is it transcendent (divinely given, or perhaps enshrined in a transcendent realm)? You might believe that ethical truths are special truths, not derived by observation of this world—transcendent truths—even if you doubt or deny the existence of God.

   B. Are ethical principles *made* or *discovered?*

    C. Is ethics objective or nonobjective? (Are there actual objective facts in ethics, or is it all just a matter of opinion? Can I be dead wrong about one of my ethical beliefs, the same way I am simply wrong if I believe that Venus is the largest planet in our solar system?)

    D. Is ethics a matter of protecting the individual, or enhancing the welfare of all? That is, is ethics basically individualistic or in some way communitarian? Another way of thinking about this: If you were marooned on a small isolated tropical island, and would never see another sentient being (you will have to subsist on bananas, nuts, and berries), would ethics still be important for you?

    E. Is ethics known more through reason or by experience of some sort (including intuitions)? Even those who *deny* there are objective ethical truths can split on this question ("*If* there were ethical facts, they would have to be known by pure reason").

    F. Is ethics universal or more local or even individual? (If people from a different culture have different ethical rules from our own, must at least one set of rules be *wrong?*)

    G. Saul Smilansky divides views of morality into two categories: the *laudatory* and the *deprecatory*. He distinguishes them thus: "*Laudatory* views hold moral behavior to be the highest achievement of civilization, the hallmark of humanity's superiority over other species, the measure of one's personal worth . . . . *Deprecatory* views of morality, by contrast, perceive morality as a burden, at best an unfortunate social necessity that obstructs the pursuit of more interesting and important matters." (*10 Moral Paradoxes* [Oxford: Blackwell Publishing, 2007]) Is your own view of morality laudatory, or is it deprecatory?

10. Go back to your own answers to Question 9, and think about how they are connected. For example, if you changed your mind about your answer to the first question, would that also lead you to revise your answer to some of the other questions? Of the questions in Question 9, which one would you select as the most *basic* question in ethics?

11. Suppose that we could build a society in which everyone naturally and happily and eagerly behaved in a morally virtuous manner; that is, suppose that acting morally required no effort whatsoever, that doing the morally right thing was always attractive and pleasant. (This is not a society filled with zombies or automatons; you still *choose* to do the right thing, it's just that the choice is always easy and pleasant.) Would that be a desirable or undesirable way of structuring society? (This question is inspired by Saul Smilansky's "Morality and Moral Worth," in *10 Moral Paradoxes* [Oxford:Blackwell Publishing, 2007]).

12. The story of Joshua, in the Hebrew Bible, tells of Joshua following God's commandment and destroying entire nations of people: all the men, women and children in every city:

> And Joshua returned, and all Israel with him, to Debir; and fought against it; and he took it, and the king thereof, and all the cities thereof; and they smote them with the edge of the sword, and utterly destroyed all the souls that were therein; he left none remaining: as he had done to Hebron, so he did to Debir, and the king thereof; as he had done also to Libnah, and to her king.
>
> So Joshua smote all the country of the hills, and of the south, and of the vale, and of the springs, and all their kings; he left none remaining, but utterly destroyed all that breathed, as the Lord God of Israel commanded. Joshua 11, 38–41.

Suppose someone says: God's commandment to kill all those people was *morally wrong*. Is that a denial of the existence of God (or at least a denial that the God depicted in the book of Joshua is really God)?

    Suppose that—in response to that account in the book of *Joshua*—someone says: the Israelis must have gotten it wrong. Perhaps they thought that God ordered such genocidal slaughter, but they were mistaken, because God would never order such a cruel bloodbath. Would that response be a rejection of theological voluntarism?

13. In Plato's *Euthyphro*, Socrates puts the following question to Euthyphro:

> We are agreed that the gods love piety because it is pious, and that it is not pious because they love it. Is this not so?

    To phrase a similar question in more contemporary terms, we might say: "We are agreed that God loves just acts because they are just, and they are not just simply because God loves them, right?" If you agree that God's love of justice is determined by the goodness of justice (rather than God's will determining what counts as just), does that in any way diminish the power or majesty of God?

14. The eighteenth-century French philosopher Denis Diderot wrote a dialogue in which he argued that a just God would never condemn nonbelievers to eternal torment: perhaps God would punish, but would then pardon. After all, if a child does something wrong and asks forgiveness, a loving father does not banish the child forever, but eventually pardons the child and welcomes the child back into his care; a loving

God would do the same for His wayward children. In the dialogue, the person speaking with Diderot disputes that claim: God's justice is not our justice, and we cannot understand the ways of God. Diderot responds that either the same concept of justice must apply to all of us, as well as to God, "or I no longer know what justice means, and I am completely ignorant of what will please or displease God." Is Diderot right? If it were true that "God's justice is not our justice," would that make the concept of justice unintelligible?

15. If you adopt a theological voluntarist view of ethics—you hold that you are morally obligated to do *whatever* God commands you to do—would you still count as an autonomous person?

16. The classic case of theological voluntarism is the story of Abraham and Isaac, told in the 22nd Chapter of *Genesis*: God commands Abraham to kill Isaac, Abraham's beloved son, as an offering to God; and without questioning, Abraham obeys God's command: "Abraham built an altar there, and laid the wood in order, and bound Isaac his son, and laid him on the altar upon the wood. And Abraham stretched forth his hand, and took the knife to slay his son." Thus, if God commands Abraham to kill Isaac, then killing Isaac becomes morally good—at least from the theological voluntarism perspective. However, Søren Kierkegaard—a Danish theologian/philosopher of the mid-nineteenth century—interprets the story differently: Abraham, in *choosing* to follow God's terrible command, moves *beyond* all considerations of ethics, beyond all understanding, beyond reason: he *transcends* ethics. Thus (according to Kierkegaard), Abraham does not adopt an ethic of theological voluntarism, but instead moves beyond ethics altogether through his act of faith. Is that a more plausible interpretation of the story?

ADDITIONAL READING

There are many excellent guides to critical thinking. Among them are S. Morris Engel, *With Good Reason*, 6th ed. (New York: St. Martin's, 2000); Theodore Schick, Jr., and Lewis Vaughn, *How to Think About Weird Things*, 4th ed. (Boston, MA: McGraw Hill, 2004); and Bruce N. Waller, *Critical Thinking: Consider the Verdict*, 6th ed. (Upper Saddle River, NJ: Pearson, 2011).

On the subject of the relation between ethics and religion, Plato's *Euthyphro* (available in a number of translations and editions) remains the classic source for the argument against theological voluntarism. Kai Nielsen, *Ethics Without God* (London: Pemberton Press, and Buffalo, NY: Prometheus Books, 1973), is perhaps the best and clearest contemporary argument against basing ethics on religion. A very sophisticated and interesting opposing view—which argues for the importance of religious considerations in ethics—can be found in George N. Schlesinger, *New Perspectives on Old-Time Religion* (Oxford: Clarendon Press, 1988). A brief argument for how ethics might be based on religion is given by Jonathan Berg, "How Could Ethics Depend on Religion?" in Peter Singer, editor, *A Companion to Ethics* (Oxford: Blackwell, 1991). Philip L. Quinn develops a detailed and sophisticated defense of theological voluntarism in "Divine Command Theory," in Hugh LaFollette, editor, *The Blackwell Guide to Ethical Theory* (Oxford: Blackwell Publishers, 2000).

There are two excellent anthologies on the subject: P. Helm, editor, *Divine Commands and Morality* (Oxford: Oxford University Press, 1981); and G. Outka and J. P. Reeder, Jr., editors, *Religion and Morality: A Collection of Essays* (Garden City, NY: Anchor/Doubleday, 1973). An excellent online discussion of theological voluntarism is an essay by Mark Murphy in the online *Stanford Encyclopedia of Philosophy*; go to *http://plato.stanford.edu/entries/voluntarism-theological/*. Lawrence M. Hinman offers a very interesting presentation in his "Divine Command Theories of Ethics." Go to *http://ethics.sandiego.edu/* and click on "Religion and Ethics.".

Søren Kierkegaard's interpretation of the story of Abraham and Isaac can be found in his *Fear and Trembling: A Dialectical Lyric*, which Kierkegaard wrote under the pseudonym Johannes de Silentio. An interesting book on Kierkegaard's ethical views is C. Stephen Evans, *Kierkegaard's Ethic of Love* (New York: Oxford University Press, 2004).

Among general works, Peter Singer's edited work, *A Companion to Ethics* (Oxford: Blackwell Publishers, 1991), is a superb guide to many topics in ethical theory as well as applied ethics. An excellent collection of readings is edited by Hugh LaFollette, *The Blackwell Guide to Ethical Theory* (Oxford: Blackwell Publishers, 2000). Another collection of outstanding contemporary articles is Stephen Darwall, Allan Gibbard, and Peter Railton, editors, *Moral Discourse and Practice* (Oxford: Oxford University Press, 1997).

For an examination of some key contemporary debates in ethics and ethical theory, see Bruce N. Waller, editor, *You Decide! Current Debates in Ethics* (New York: Pearson Longman, 2006); and James Dreier, editor, *Contemporary Debates in Moral Theory* (Malden, MA: Blackwell Publishing, 2006).

NOTES

[1] Immanuel Kant, *The Critique of Practical Reason and Other Writings in Moral Philosophy*, trans. L. W. Beck (Chicago, IL: University of Chicago Press, 1949), p. 259. First published in 1788.

[2] Charles Darwin, *The Descent of Man*, 2nd ed. (London: John Murray, 1875), p. 99. First published in 1871.

[3] Quoted (with strong approval) on July 7, 2002, by Cal Thomas, syndicated columnist.

[4] For more on Rabi'a, see Margaret Smith, *Studies in Early Mysticism in the Near and Middle East* (Oxford: Oneworld Publications, 1995); and Margaret Smith, *Rabi'a: The Life and Work of Rabi'a and Other Women Mystics in Islam* (Oxford: Oneworld Publications, 1995).

[5] This case is based on a report by Gregg Kilday in *The Toronto Star,* September 5, 2003.

2
Egoism and Relativism

Ethical egoism and cultural relativism are very different ethical theories, but it may be useful to consider them together. In some ways, cultural relativism is a bit like ethical egoism writ large. The ethical egoist maintains that whatever benefits *me* is the right thing to do. The cultural relativist says that whatever my *culture* approves is what I should do. Advocates of both views tend to present themselves as tough-minded and scientifically oriented: the egoist claiming to start from stark psychological facts, and the cultural relativist from the hard facts of sociology and anthropology. Both tend to share a reductionist orientation: whatever else you might romantically or idealistically imagine ethics to be, what *really* is involved in ethics is just seeking one's own good (the egoist says) or following the customs of one's culture (the cultural relativist claims). Both views are interesting, both views are admirable in their attempt to integrate scientific and empirical considerations into ethics, and both views are worth considering.

EGOISM

Egoism comes in two varieties. First is *psychological egoism*: the view that—as a matter of empirical psychological fact—all our behavior is selfish, or self-interested. Second is *ethical egoism,* which is the very different claim that we *ought* to always act in a way that is self-interested. Though often run together, they are very different positions. Sam could be a psychological egoist while fervently rejecting ethical egoism. That is, Sam could believe that we are psychologically constructed to always behave selfishly; but Sam might also believe that is an ethical disaster, since selfishness is bad. And Sandra could be an ethical egoist, who believes that we *ought* to act selfishly, but also believe that our psychological makeup is such that we often fail to act selfishly (according to ethical egoist Sandra, we sometimes behave altruistically rather than selfishly, and those altruistic acts are morally wrong). If one is both a psychological and an ethical egoist, then one is in the fortunate position of believing that everyone always and inevitably does right: selfishness is virtue, and we cannot avoid acting selfishly, and thus we cannot avoid acting virtuously.

Psychological Egoism

Psychological egoism has great appeal for many people, and psychological egoists are typically confident of the irrefutable wisdom and plain truth of the position they hold. From the right perspective, psychological egoism seems clear and unassailable truth. Why did you buy a cup of coffee? Because you want a cup of coffee, obviously; you have a selfish interest in enjoying a delicious, rich cup of coffee. But why did you give money to a drought relief fund? Because I want to enjoy the reputation of a generous and public-spirited person; it's in my selfish interest to have such a reputation. But why did you make a secret anonymous donation last week? Because it made me feel good to think I was helping others: I received more satisfaction from spending the money that way than by any other use I could have found for the money. So even that "generous act" was actually selfish. But what about when your dear old mother rose from her bed and interrupted her own much needed rest, in order to hold a cool cloth to your fevered brow and bring you medicine and comfort? Was that a selfish act? Yes, that too was selfish. She gained greater pleasure from ministering to her child than she could have derived from resting. She did it, ultimately, for her own selfish pleasure.

Criticisms of Psychological Egoism

Psychological egoism begins to sound seductively convincing. No matter what case one proposes—the generous anonymous donor, the selfless loving mother—the psychological egoist easily shows it to have been a selfish act. But perhaps too easily. After all, psychological egoism is supposed to be an *empirical* claim. It is not based on logic, or pure reasoning, or definition, but based instead on empirical observation and testing. But if it is an empirical claim, then it must be possible to tell what sort of empirical evidence would count against the claim. Since psychological egoists believe that psychological egoism is empirically true, obviously they need not provide evidence that it is false. If it is to be an empirical truth, however, they must be able to tell us what *would* count as evidence that it is false. Suppose I claim that all moose are brown, and I assert that as an empirical truth based on long observation of moose. If it is an empirical truth, then I have to be able to say what would count *against* it. Easy enough. If you show me a purple moose, and I investigate to make sure the moose has not been dyed a different color, and this purple moose is a DNA match to brown moose, and its mother and father were perfectly respectable moose, then I will admit that I was empirically mistaken: it's not true that all moose are brown. (If I insist that this purple animal is not a moose, since all moose *must* be brown, I am proposing a new definition of moose, rather than making an empirical claim about the moose species.) So if psychological egoism is an empirically based claim that all behavior is selfishly motivated, what would count as proving the claim wrong?

That's the problem. Not even the most generous, selfless, noble act escapes the clutches of egoistic selfishness. You plunge into icy water, at great risk to your own life, to rescue a small child to whom you are not related. No one else is around, so there is no hope of reward or recognition. The child is a thoroughly obnoxious and ungrateful wretch, who is more likely to kick you in the shins than thank you for your heroic efforts. Even then, the egoist categorizes this as selfish, self-interested behavior: you take pleasure in the rescue, and you avoid the suffering of watching a small child perish. But this makes the claim empty: *nothing* could count as an unselfish act, since every purposeful act has some motivation, and the egoist is redefining all motivations as selfish. The claim is true, but it is reduced to a tautology: all selfishly motivated acts are selfishly motivated acts. But the psychological egoist is supposed to be giving us a genuine psychological claim, not a claim that is rendered true on the basis of a special definition.

The persuasiveness of psychological egoism rests on a special and all-inclusive meaning of "selfishness." If we are short of food, and you make a greedy secret raid on our limited food supply, then that is a selfish act. If you offer to take the smallest share, but you know that we are only minutes from being rescued and supplied with abundant food, and your only motive is to win honor and praise for your pretended generosity, then your behavior hardly counts as a shining example of generosity. But if you offer a portion of your food simply because you are concerned about the welfare of another member of your party, and you have no ulterior motives other than the benefit of that person, then that is a genuinely generous and unselfish act. If the act brings you satisfaction, that does *not* transform it into a selfish act. After all, finding genuine satisfaction and joy in the good of others is the hallmark of a generous person, one who is *not* acting for his or her own selfish goals. Furthermore, even when we do act for self-interested motives, those motives need not squeeze out all generous motivation. You want to do well in your calculus class, for self-interested reasons. You also want your friend to do well in calculus, and you unselfishly provide tutoring to help him reach that goal. By tutoring your friend, you may learn the material better yourself; but that doesn't transform your motivation into something selfish. When in high school you did volunteer work at an extended care facility for the elderly, you may have had a selfish interest in how attractive such volunteer work would appear on your college application; but that does not mean that you could not also have a genuine and unselfish motive as well: the motive of bringing comfort and joy to the people with whom you worked.

Far from selfish egoism being a universal truth, the fact is that we can find examples of unselfish generosity not only among humans but in other species as well. Charles Darwin cites examples of blind helpless birds that were fed by their companions. Whatever one thinks of unselfish behavior in other species, there seems to be abundant evidence of it in our own—mixed in, of course, with a substantial amount of cruelty, selfishness, and callousness. But the presence of *some* level of unselfish behavior is sufficient to undercut the claims of psychological egoism.

Ethical Egoism

If we do sometimes act unselfishly, then the next question emerges: *should* we act unselfishly? Or should we instead, as the ethical egoist insists, always act for our own benefit?

Individual Ethical Egoism   Actually, there are at least two different versions of ethical egoism: *individual* ethical egoism and *universal* ethical egoism. The individual ethical egoist maintains that everyone ought to do what benefits *me*. If Susan is an individual ethical egoist, then Susan believes that everyone, Susan included, ought to aim at the benefit of Susan. *Universal* ethical egoism is the position of extreme rugged individualism: everyone ought to aim exclusively at his or her own benefit, and should neither give, ask, nor receive help from others.

By its very nature, individual ethical egoism has few advocates. That is not to say that individual ethical egoism is a rare position. To the contrary, judging by the behavior of some corporate executive officers who enrich themselves at the expense of employees and investors and stockholders, one suspects that individual ethical egoism is alive and flourishing. But individual ethical egoists are unlikely to publicly promote their views. If Ken is a dedicated individual ethical egoist, who firmly believes that everyone should be working for the benefit of Ken (and that no other ethical rules apply), then Ken may attempt to create the impression that he is dedicated to the welfare of all and eager to help others. After all, if everyone else *should* be striving for *my* benefit, then the best way to accomplish that is to convince them that their work will benefit everyone, including themselves. That being the case (and since an individual ethical egoist will have no moral reluctance to tell lies, though he will of course think it wrong for *you* to lie to *him*), it is very difficult to tell how many individual ethical egoists there really are.

It is sometimes suggested that individual ethical egoism is self-contradictory, because advocating such a system is self-defeating: by openly asserting that you are only interested in yourself, and you believe that others should sacrifice everything for your benefit, you are likely to become an outcast. People will be reluctant to associate with you, much less devote themselves to promoting your welfare. But what this shows is not that individual ethical egoism is inherently contradictory, but only that the individual ethical egoist would be wise not to publicize her ethical views; or to speak plainly, the individual ethical egoist would be wise to lie about her ethical views (a policy she can adopt with no ethical qualms).

Is there any way to convince the individual ethical egoist to change her views? That's a difficult question. If it's possible, it won't be easy. After all, the genuine individual ethical egoist thinks no one else really matters. If we point out that other people are hurt by her actions, that will be a matter of indifference to her. We might point out to her how profoundly isolated she is: she can never really reveal herself to anyone, can never be open with others, cannot have any friends for whom she feels real affection and deep bonds of shared honesty. Individual ethical egoism begins to look like a rather lonely, loveless, and uneasy life. But if that is the sort of life one wants—a life lived with narrow and exclusive concern for oneself—then perhaps that will not be disturbing. In short, if you regard a totally self-centered life as a real and attractive possibility, then it is difficult to offer you good reasons not to adopt individual ethical egoism. Of course we can give good reasons for *appearing* to take a larger view, in order to gain the social benefits that accrue to that appearance; but it is much more difficult to give reasons why you should genuinely pursue a moral life, rather than a fraud that takes every possible exploitative advantage. Noting the implications of individual ethical egoism, however, is likely to severely limit its appeal. Few would wish to live a life of constant deception, a life cut off from genuine intimacy, friendship, concern for others, and mutual affection. Individual ethical egoism looks more like a path to psychopathology than to happiness.

Why Care for Others? If we seek self-interested reasons that can answer "Why be concerned for others?" we encounter other problems. There are traditional attempts to prove that a calculating egoist would not be happy: your conscience will bother you, your life will require constant deception, you will cut yourself off from any genuine relations (you hide your real motives, so no one can care for you as you actually are). But if you are the sort of person who can genuinely consider a life of systemic selfishness as an attractive "lifestyle," then probably such concerns will not weigh heavily on you.

> "I'm a philosopher, not a rat-catcher, and I don't see it as my job to dig vermin out of such burrows as individual egoism." *Brian Medlin, "Ultimate Principles and Ethical Egoism,"* Australasian Journal of Philosophy, *1957.*

Individual ethical egoism is a difficult position to refute. Some people take that as evidence of its strength. But it may instead be because the position starts from such an alien perspective—a perspective of absolutely no concern for others—that it is difficult to find any common ground for discussion. It is perfectly reasonable and morally legitimate to have a healthy regard for one's own interests. In fact, without at least some degree of self-respect, it is difficult to imagine having satisfactory relations with others. But exclusive concern for oneself, coupled with indifference to the needs and interests of others, is not likely to strike many people as a desirable or fulfilling perspective on the world.

Universal Ethical Egoism Universal ethical egoism—*everyone* should pursue what is to his or her individual self-interested advantage—does at least have the advantage of being a position one can openly advocate. And it has had some champions. Some people argue that universal ethical egoism is simply nature's way: we all struggle for our own selfish purposes, the strong survive, the weak and unfit are eliminated, and thus we evolve and get better. It's harsh, but that's just the way it is. And if we want to be successful, we have to follow nature's plan.

Universal ethical egoism is red-blooded, two-fisted ethics. Unfortunately, it is based on a crude and distorted view of evolutionary science. Natural evolution doesn't have a plan, and it certainly has no goal or purpose. The evolutionary survivors aren't superior, morally or otherwise; rather, they are simply better suited for the particular environment in which they happen to land. In any case, the paved ground, polluted air, and shopping malls in which we now function, the bioengineered and heavily processed foods we eat, and the high-tech medical treatments we receive make talk of "natural" processes a bit strained. Even if we set all that aside, the old "every man for himself" stuff is more suited to Hollywood action movies than our own evolutionary history. Rather than rugged individualists, we are a profoundly social species. Due to our extraordinarily long and vulnerable infancy, humans form strong family and social bonds. This has great advantages for our species—otherwise it would not have been a successful evolutionary strategy. Mutual affection and concern and cooperation are essential to making that strategy work. The notion of humans as rugged individuals is an artificial contrivance, while cooperation and affection come naturally to members of our deeply social species.

A second version of universal ethical egoism is based in economic considerations: we will all prosper if everyone seeks his or her individual benefit, without worrying about others. Unfettered laissez-faire capitalism (as opposed to regulated capitalism with an extensive social welfare component) will promote everyone's ultimate good. But while that is often voiced as a timeless truth, the evidence for it is very weak. Of all the industrialized nations, the United States comes closest to that ideal of unfettered capitalism (having the least regulation, the lowest taxes, and the most meager social welfare support), and the U.S. economy has been successful in enriching a large number of people (though whether that is a result of an effective economic system or the power to exploit the workers and resources of other countries might be a debated point). But in any case, whatever the success of such a universal egoist economic system in producing wealth for a small segment of society, it is hard to say that it has benefitted everyone. After all, the United States leads the industrialized world in number of homeless, homicide rate, atmospheric pollution, number of people without health care, number of people in prison, number of children living in poverty, infant mortality rate, and—though I'm not sure anyone is keeping a careful count—probably enjoys a substantial lead in criminal enterprises by chief executive and chief financial officers. Whatever its virtues, it is difficult to maintain that unfettered capitalism (based on "every man for himself") has resulted in the maximum possible benefit for everyone. In sum, if the claim is that everyone pursuing their own selfish interests will result in the greatest possible benefit for everyone, it is difficult to find any empirical grounds—biological, economic, or otherwise—for that universal egoistic article of faith.

RELATIVISM

Relativism. It's a term used in a variety of ways and disciplines, ranging from physics to anthropology to ethics. So, it's important to be clear on what we're talking about. "Ethical relativism" is the thesis that what is right is *relative* to each culture. That is, there are no absolute or fixed principles of ethics, but only the ethical systems of various cultures. What is right in Canada is not the same as what is right in Indonesia. And what was right in ancient Rome is not what is right in contemporary Rome.

Sociological Relativism and Cultural Relativism

If relativism is simply the claim that different cultures have different ethical systems, that is an interesting claim but not very controversial. If you travel from Pakistan to Scotland, you will find different languages, religions, climates, cultures, and moral codes. That differing cultures have differing customs, standards, and moral codes is an empirical observation made by sociologists and anthropologists. That thesis might be called *sociological relativism*, and it is well supported by social scientific study. In contrast, *cultural relativism* is the claim that not only do differing ethical codes exist, but ethical judgments can only be made *relative to* a given culture: ethical principles have objective force only within a given culture. On this view, capital punishment is wrong in France, and right in Saudi Arabia; in the United States, abortion was wrong in 1950 and right in 2000. According to the cultural relativist, it makes no sense to say that capital punishment is always or absolutely wrong, for right and wrong are strictly relative to culture.

> " . . . a mild form of relativism is expressed by 'when in Rome do as the Romans do'. I must say that this piece of advice has always seemed to me very bad. For one thing, some things done by Romans—perhaps not so much now, but in earlier times—were pretty beastly. Even apart from that, the Romans may not like you doing what they do. Moreover, you may not be very good at it. But the relevant point is something that these comments illustrate, that this maxim is not an expression of relativism at all. It is an absolute principle applying to everyone, telling them how to behave in certain circumstances: either, narrowly taken, when they are in Rome, or more broadly, when they are away from home.
>
> Another thing that is not relativism is the thesis that the expression or application of a given value may be different in different circumstances. This is simply common sense and known to everyone. To take a perfectly obvious example, what counts as showing respect or insulting someone differs from place to place, but that does not mean that the value of respect for others is itself relative." *Bernard Williams, "Relativism, History, and the Existence of Value," pp. 106–107 in Joseph Raz,* The Practice of Value, *edited by R. Jay Wallace (Oxford: The Clarendon Press, 2003).*

Cultural relativism is *not* the view that ethical principles are relative to circumstances. That would fit the utilitarian perspective, not the cultural relativist. Utilitarians hold that we should do whatever—in those circumstances—would produce the best consequences (the greatest balance of pleasure over suffering) for everyone. So in specific instances we must consider the particular circumstances, but there is still a basic utilitarian principle that is cross-culturally true: you should always act in such a way that your act will produce the greatest balance of pleasure over pain for everyone. For utilitarians that principle is just as true in Australia as it is in Egypt. In contrast, cultural relativists do not believe that there are any universal ethical principles. Ethical principles are relative to cultures. In one culture, it might be right to be a utilitarian; in another culture, utilitarian ethics would be wrong.

Benefits of Cultural Relativism

Cultural relativism has some good points. Perhaps the most important is to shake us out of our ethical provincialism, and remind us that other cultures may have values that are not the same as our own, and that does not always mean theirs are wrong. Before we conclude that a different cultural ethic is mistaken, or even barbaric and evil, we should strive to understand how those values actually function in the culture. And as anthropologists constantly remind us, that is likely to be a much more complicated matter than we thought. For example, among some of the Aboriginal peoples of the Canadian Northwest, the basic ethical concept of "justice" is quite different from that in the rest of Canada as well as in the United States. Instead of focusing on who deserves punishment for a crime, and what degree of punishment should be meted out, they concentrate on how unity and harmony can be restored to the community, and on how both the harmed and those who did the harm can be restored to the community as a whole. If a young person breaks the law, this is seen as a symptom of something wrong in the community, and the goal is to restore the entire community to health. This leads to a very different concept of justice and a very different system of justice in that culture, but it is far from clear that it is an ethically inferior system. Even if we do not think it would work as a system of justice in our larger and more diverse culture, it may be a very good ethical system for a culture of closely united villages and deep family ties that interconnect almost all members. In any case, imposing the Western adversarial system of justice, with its punitive emphasis and atmosphere of confrontation and hostility, might well cause cultural disintegration and harmful repercussions we can hardly anticipate. And cultural destruction is a very serious danger. As Kate Brown and Andrew Jameton note:

> One reason for respecting cultural diversity rests on the observation that community membership, participation, and shared symbolism are important sources of human happiness and health, apart from any validity of the symbols with reference to science or to reality.[1]

Thus, even if we conclude that the ethics of a particular culture doesn't entirely meet with our approval—or would not work in our system—we should exercise great caution in attempting reforms. It is easy to cause more harm than good, even with the best intentions.

Speaking of good intentions, it is worth noting that not infrequently the intentions of "cultural reformers" are not quite as good as they would have us believe. Some Europeans claimed they were coming to the "New World" to carry out "cultural reform" and convert the natives to the true religion. Judged by their actions, the "cultural reform" served only as a thin justification for plundering the wealth of the cultures they discovered, and then killing or enslaving the people they found. A good example can be found in the "explanation" of why in 1832 the Seminoles were forcibly removed from their Florida homeland and moved to Oklahoma: it was the result of "the solicitude manifested by the President of the United States for the improvement of their condition, by recommending a removal to a country more suitable to their habits and wants."[2] Such "improvement in condition" and "cultural reform" often accompanies the theft of land. The blessings of "cultural reform" the United States brought to Central America often consisted in driving subsistence farmers and their families off their lands so U.S. corporations could have large plantations and cheap labor to grow pineapples or sugarcane for profitable export. Currently, some people suspect that the announced desire of some American politicians to bring cultural reform (and the "blessings of democracy") to countries in the Middle East is motivated more by love of oil than by love of reform. This does not imply that there is never room for "cultural reform," but the sordid history of such "reforms" reminds us to look closely at the actual motives of the reformers.

Criticisms of Cultural Relativism

Cultural relativism may broaden our understanding of other cultures and promote tolerance, and may prompt us to examine carefully both the motives and the consequences of promoting cultural reform. Notwithstanding those benefits, cultural relativism also faces some serious problems. The first is one that arises in the example previously cited. What culture does an Aboriginal Canadian youth belong to? She is a member of a tribal culture, such as the Dene. She is also part of the larger Aboriginal culture, comprised of many different tribes with distinct cultures and traditions. She is a Canadian citizen and a member of that culture as well. The norms of those cultures may not always coincide. As noted before, the Canadian principles of justice may conflict with Aboriginal principles. This creates a problem for the ethical theory of cultural relativism: as a member of several different cultures, with conflicting norms, how can we decide what this Dene woman *should* do? That problem is very common. If you live in Pittsburgh, you are a member of that culture (you probably have deep affection for the Steelers, you spend at least one summer day at Kennywood Park, and you drink Iron City beer); but you are also a member of a distinctive neighborhood culture, which may be distinguished by ethnicity, religious affiliation, and a local tavern; and a member of the larger American culture as well. If what is right is set by the rules of your culture, you may find yourself pulled in several different directions by the conflicting rules of your several cultures. In the culture of small-town north Louisiana, dancing and drinking are regarded as sinful and immoral. When young people from those communities find oil field jobs along the south Louisiana coast, they find that an evening of drinking wine, playing music, and dancing is considered a wholesome exercise of family and community values. Thus, cultures are not as distinct and isolated as cultural relativism seems to require.

A second, and perhaps even more serious, problem for cultural relativism is the problem of ethical reform. Or perhaps we should say the problem of the *impossibility* of ethical reform. If whatever my culture treats as right *is* right, then "reform" must always be wrong. In that case, when the U.S. culture approved of slavery, the abolitionists were mistaken; when women pushed for the right to vote and other basic rights (in a culture that denied such rights), then they were also wrong. Indeed, all our most revered reformers— Frederick Douglass, Susan B. Anthony, Mahatma Gandhi, Martin Luther King—would not only be wrong, but *morally* wrong: they fiercely opposed the moral and cultural norms of their societies, and by the principles of cultural relativism they were therefore opposing what was *right* in the societies in which they lived. Discrimination against homosexuals is a widespread cultural norm in the United States, but thankfully there seems to be gradual progress in overcoming that prejudice. Cultural relativism would stop such movements in their tracks.

Third, cultural relativism seems to weaken and trivialize our ethical concerns. The southern rural farm culture in which I grew up ate a large meal (which we called dinner) at noon and a light "supper" in the evening. In my present culture, we eat a light lunch at noon, and the large dinner meal is served in the evening. No problem. That's analogous to "I like apple pie and you prefer cherry." We can both have what we prefer, it's just a difference in tastes; we can live with the disagreement. Cultural relativism invites us to treat moral issues in the same manner. In our culture women are regarded as persons with full and equal rights; in your culture women are the property of fathers or husbands, and have no rights whatsoever. That's okay. You follow your cultural practices and we'll follow ours. But in this case, that solution is not so attractive. I may find your food too spicy and your dress too drab and the games in your culture a bit strange, but there is nothing morally offensive in them. But if you treat women as property, that's not just a difference in tastes, and I cannot comfortably "tolerate" such practices as if they were merely taste preferences. That was the attitude taken by some "states' rights" advocates during the civil rights era: in our state blacks have no right of equal protection under the law, no right to vote, no right to be safe from brutal racist attacks; if you want to have such rights in your state, that's fine, but leave us alone to follow our own cultural heritage. But tolerating racism and brutality and injustice is not like tolerating a preference for grits instead of potatoes with your scrambled eggs. If you believe that racism is *morally wrong,* you cannot just dismiss it as a cultural quirk. Your family likes the beach, mine prefers to vacation in the mountains, and that's fine with you. But if your family believes that children should be treated with care and affection, and my family favors brutal child abuse, that is *not* a difference you can quietly tolerate. To do so would mean denying the importance and strength of your moral convictions.

Cultural relativists legitimately remind us that at least *some* of our notions of what is morally right or wrong have no basis other than cultural tradition. That reminder is useful in preventing us from condemning— or "reforming"—the practices and norms of other cultures simply because they differ from those with which we are more familiar. But frankly, that is a service that is probably performed better by teachers of cultural anthropology than by those who espouse the ethics of cultural relativism. Beyond that limited virtue, it is difficult to see many advantages to cultural relativist ethics. In fact, it is difficult to see any real basis for cultural relativist ethics. Certainly cultures are complex, and they develop in ways that allow them to perform useful functions. But there is no better reason to suppose that every culture is good than to suppose that every individual is good.

The Nazi culture may have "kept order," but the order it kept was brutal, repressive, and murderous. The culture of the antebellum American South no doubt had some charming features: respect for elders, commitment to honesty and integrity, and loyalty to friends and family. But its virtues were heavily weighted with a system that was built on slavery and brutality, promoted a rigid caste system, treated women as mere ornaments and not as full persons in their own right, and regarded labor with contempt. Any ethical theory that makes it impossible to intelligently critique a culture—including one's *own* culture—blocks consideration of some of the most important ethical issues we face.

Grounds for Cultural Relativism

The ethics of cultural relativism can be constructed on two very different foundations. First, one might adopt cultural relativism on the grounds that when it comes to cultures, "whatever is, is right." That is, cultures always develop in such a manner that they are the best they could possibly be in that situation: every culture is the optimum fit for its circumstances. Thus, colonial New England culture would not be a good fit for us, but it was the ideal culture for those who lived in New England during that period. The caste system would not work in twenty-first-century Montreal, but it was perfect for India in 1900. The culture of ancient Rome would not be right for today's Minneapolis, but it was just right for ancient Rome. But that requires faith that cultures always "evolve" or develop in such a way that they work as well as they possibly could. That faith has no foundation in empirical fact. There is no evidence of a guiding hand that shapes every culture to be the best it could possibly be. Indeed, there is abundant evidence that cultures can be and often are repressive and harmful and cruel, and far from the best possible culture that could have developed in those settings. Consider, for example, certain European cultures of the sixteenth century, cultures that busied themselves by killing infidels, torturing heretics, burning witches, stifling dissent, blocking free inquiry, and maintaining a rigid hierarchy of caste and privilege. It is easy to imagine how such a culture could be improved, and of course reformers have brought many such improvements to pass. Indeed, it is more difficult to imagine how you could make that culture worse than to imagine how you might have made it better. So if the ethics of cultural relativism is based on belief that whatever culture exists is always the best it could be, then it is based on a very weak foundation.

As noted earlier, we should be very cautious in concluding that a cultural practice is wrong: it may have a more complicated function and more complex relation to the larger conditions of that culture than we can readily appreciate. We can find an appropriate analogy in environmental studies. Often we discover that the destruction of an animal or insect "pest" that we thought useless or harmful has consequences for the entire ecosystem, and consequences we had neither anticipated nor desired. Still, it does not follow that when we look at cultural practices, whatever is must be the best possible. It may well be that cultural practices that were once somewhat beneficial have been preserved by the force of custom or law or religious sanction to a time when they have long outlived their usefulness. And it is quite possible that some cultural practices that developed out of superstition or oppression survived though they were detrimental to most members of the culture. After all, cultures that were once successful often become inflexible, and perish because they cannot change and adapt. That being the case, it is hard to maintain that whatever cultural practices a culture is currently maintaining must be *right* for that culture.

But there is a second possible grounds for cultural relativism: the belief that there are no good grounds for ethical claims, and therefore no basis for criticizing any existing cultural practice. But this second path to cultural relativism seems no smoother than the first. If there are no grounds for any ethical judgments, then there are no grounds for supposing that the norms of each culture *should* be accepted as good. On this approach to cultural relativism, attacking cultural practices would be as legitimate as supporting them. "There is no reason to think the norms of our culture are right. Therefore we should accept them without criticism." Somehow, that argument seems less than compelling.

In short, it is difficult to find reasonable grounds for cultural relativism as an ethical theory. It is surely desirable to have people understand and appreciate other cultures, and it is a good thing to get beyond the biased provincialism that leads one to suppose that any culture that deviates from our own cultural norms and traditions must therefore be inferior or even morally depraved. But there are much better ways to accomplish that laudable goal than by adopting the implausible ethics of cultural relativism.

OTHER FORMS OF ETHICAL RELATIVISM

Cultural relativism is perhaps the best known relativist theory of ethics, but it is by no means the only one. The problem is that when philosophers speak of ethical relativism, they often mean very different things. For example, there are "methodological relativists," "metaethical relativists," and "moral judgment relativists"; and to further complicate things, the advocates of these positions do not always define those categories in precisely the same way. We can't explore all those issues and distinctions here. However, one view that is sometimes classified—or misclassified—as ethical relativism will come in for more detailed examination. That is the view that ethical truths (like *all* truths) are not truths that "correspond to reality" or copy the world as it actually is. Instead, truths (including truths of ethics) are theories or beliefs that *work well*, that *lead us effectively*, and that *function efficiently*. What is *true*—whether in ethics or physics or engineering—is what works best for us. Though people who take this view are sometimes described as (and less often describe themselves as) *relativists*, their views are very different from the "cultural relativism" discussed in this chapter. For example, Richard Rorty, a leader of this "relativist" view (though he strongly rejects the relativist title), clearly opposes cultural relativism: "Truth is, to be sure, an absolute notion, in the following sense: 'true for me but not for you' and 'true in my culture but not in yours' are weird, pointless locutions."[3] To avoid confusing this with the many questions surrounding relativism, we'll call that view ethical *pragmatism*. It will be examined in Chapter 6.

⇌ SECOND SERMON UPON HUMAN NATURE ⇌
Bishop Joseph Butler

Joseph Butler (1692–1752) was a priest in the Church of England, ultimately becoming a bishop. Many of his sermons were collected and published as books of essays, including the sermon from which the following reading is excerpted. Butler worked to develop a moral system based on human nature. He acknowledged the strong human feeling of self-love that Hobbes and Mandeville emphasized, but argued that humans have other strong affections as well, including a natural affection for others; and with the aid of the judgments of the human conscience, we are capable of living sound moral lives that are not dominated by narrow self-interest. In this essay from *Fifteen Sermons upon Human Nature* (1726) Butler attempts to establish the existence of a natural feeling of benevolent concern for others: a natural benevolent affection that refutes the claims of egoism.

Every man hath a general desire of his own happiness; and likewise a variety of particular affections, passions, and appetites to particular external objects. The former proceeds from, or is self-love; and seems inseparable from all sensible creatures, who can reflect upon themselves and their own interest or happiness, so as to have that interest an object to their minds: what is to be said of the latter is, that they proceed from, or together make up that particular nature, according to which man is made. The object the former pursues is somewhat internal, our own happiness, enjoyment, satisfaction; whether we have, or have not, a distinct particular perception what it is, or wherein it consists: the objects of the latter are this or that particular external thing, which the affections tend towards, and of which it hath always a particular idea or perception. The principle we call self-love never seeks anything external for the sake of the thing, but only as a means of happiness or good: particular affections rest in the external things themselves. One belongs to man as a reasonable creature [reflecting upon his own interest or happiness]. The other, though quite distinct from reason, are as much a part of human nature.

That all particular appetites and passions are towards *external things themselves*, distinct from the *pleasure arising from them*, is manifested from hence; that there could not be this pleasure, were it not for that prior suitableness between the object and the passion: there could be no enjoyment or delight from one thing more than another, from eating food more than from swallowing a stone, if there were not an affection or appetite to one thing more than another.

Every particular affection, even the love of our neighbour, is as really our own affection, as self-love; and the pleasure arising from its gratification is as much my own pleasure, as the pleasure self-love would have, from knowing I myself should be happy some time hence, would be my own pleasure. And if, because every particular affection is a man's own, and the pleasure arising from its gratification his own pleasure, or pleasure to himself, such particular affection must be called self-love; according to this way of speaking, no creature whatever can possibly act but merely from self-love; and every action and every affection whatever is to be resolved up into this one principle. But then this is not the language of mankind; or if it were, we should want words to express the difference, between the principle of an action, proceeding from cool consideration that it will be to my own advantage; and an action, suppose of revenge, or of friendship, by which a man runs upon certain ruin, to do evil or good to another. It is manifest the principles of these actions are totally different, and so want different words to be distinguished by: all that they agree in is, that they both proceed from, and are done to gratify an inclination in a man's self. But the principle or inclination in one case is self-love; in the other, hatred or love of another. There is then a distinction between the cool principle of self-love, or general desire of our happiness, as one part of our nature, and one principle of action; and the particular affections towards particular external objects, as another part of our nature, and another principle of action. How much soever therefore is to be allowed to self-love, yet it cannot be allowed to be the whole of our inward constitution; because, you see, there are other parts or principles which come into it.

Further, private happiness or good is all which self-love can make us desire, or be concerned about: in having this consists its gratification: it is an affection to ourselves; a regard to our own interest, happiness, and private good: and in the proportion a man hath this, he is interested, or a lover of himself. Let this be kept in mind; because there is commonly, as I shall presently have occasion to observe, another sense put upon these words. On the other hand, particular affections tend towards particular external things: these are their objects; having these is their end: in this consists their gratification: no matter whether it be, or be not, upon the whole, our interest or happiness. An action done from the former of these principles is called an interested action. An action proceeding from any of the latter has its denomination of passionate, ambitious, friendly, revengeful, or any other, from the particular appetite or affection from which it proceeds. Thus self-love as one part of human nature, and the several particular principles as the other part, are, themselves, their objects and ends, stated and shewn.

From hence it will be easy to see, how far, and in what ways, each of these can contribute and be subservient to the private good of the individual. Happiness does not consist in self-love. The desire of happiness is no more the thing itself, than the desire of riches is the possession or enjoyment of them. People may love themselves with the most entire and unbounded affection, and yet be extremely miserable. Neither can self-love any way help them out, but by setting them on work to get rid of the causes of their misery, to gain or make use of those objects which are by nature adapted to afford satisfaction. Happiness or satisfaction consists only in the enjoyment of those objects, which are by nature suited to our several particular appetites, passions, and affections. So that if self-love wholly engrosses us, and leaves no room for any other principle, there can be absolutely no such thing at all as happiness, or enjoyment of any kind whatever; since happiness consists in the gratification of particular passions, which supposes the having of them. Self-love then does not constitute *this* or *that* to be our interest or good; but, our interest or good being constituted by nature and supposed, self-love only puts us upon obtaining and securing it. Therefore, if it be possible, that self-love may prevail and exert itself in a degree or manner which is not subservient to this end; then it will not follow, that our interest will be promoted in proportion to the degree in which that principle engrosses us, and prevails over others. Nay further, the private and contracted affection, when it is not subservient to this end, private good, may, for anything that appears, have a direct contrary tendency and effect. And if we will consider the matter, we shall see that it often really has. *Disengagement* is absolutely necessary to enjoyment; and a person may have so steady and fixed an eye upon his own interest, whatever he places it in, as may hinder him from *attending* to many gratifications within his reach, which others have their minds free and open to. Over-fondness for a child is not generally thought to be for its advantage: and, it there be any guess to be made from appearances, surely that character we call selfish is not the most promising for happiness. Such a temper may plainly be, and exert itself in a degree and manner which may give unnecessary and useless solicitude and anxiety, in a degree and manner which may prevent obtaining the means and materials of enjoyment, as well as the making use of them. Immoderate self-love does very ill consult its own interest: and, how much soever a paradox it may appear, it is certainly true, that even from self-love we should endeavour to get over all inordinate regard to, and consideration of ourselves. Every one of our passions and affections hath its natural stint and bound, which may easily be exceeded; whereas our enjoyments can possibly be but in a determinate measure and degree. Therefore such excess of the affection, since it cannot procure any enjoyment, must in all cases be useless; but is generally attended with inconveniences, and often is downright pain and misery. This holds as much with regard to self-love as to all other affections. The natural degree of it, so far as it sets us on work to gain and make use of the materials of satisfaction, may be to our real advantage; but beyond or besides this, it is in several respects an inconvenience and disadvantage. Thus it appears, that private interest is so far from being likely to be promoted in proportion to the degree in which self-love engrosses us, and prevails over all other principles; that the contracted affection may be so prevalent as to disappoint itself, and even contradict its own end, private good.

⬥ THE GOOD SIDE OF RELATIVISM ⬥
Elvin Hatch

Elvin Hatch is an anthropologist in the Department of Anthropology, University of California—Santa Barbara, specializing in cultural anthropology and the study of small communities. Among his many works is the book *Culture and Morality: The Relativity of Values in Anthropology* (New York: Columbia University Press, 1983). In this essay—"The Good Side of Relativism," *Journal of Anthropological Research*, volume 53, 1997—Hatch does not actually defend cultural relativism, but instead disputes some of the claims of those who condemn cultural relativism; that is (in the phrase of the distinguished cultural anthropologist Clifford Geertz), rather than being pro-cultural relativist, Hatch is an anti-antirelativist. Hatch counsels that understanding evolving cultures is a complicated process and that while some cultural practices are worthy of condemnation, we should resist the temptation to condemn any practice different from our own. Cultural practices that involve the mistreatment of women are changing, and that is a positive development; but too often the "reform" agenda also includes imposing a radically individualist Western economic pattern that undercuts social support systems, destroys effective subsistence economic practices, and leaves many of the poorest indigenous groups vulnerable to economic exploitation. The recognition of universal human rights is a positive good, but it is also important—Hatch argues—to recognize the genuine and enormously complicated problems that are involved in transforming cultures and cultural practices.

The efflorescence of ethical relativism among American anthropologists took place in the 1930s and 1940s, when Benedict and Herskovits were its most notable proponents.... Their relativism combined two principles. The first was an attitude of skepticism in relation to Western values, for they held that Western standards with respect to such matters as sexuality and work are historically conditioned and do not warrant elevation to the status of universal principles. The second was the value of tolerance, inasmuch as they held that people everywhere ought to be free to live as they choose.

Opposition to this form of relativism was evident almost from the start, however . . . , and by the 1950s some of the leading anthropologists in this country were speaking out against it. World War II stimulated some of this reaction, for it was difficult for people in the United States not to think in terms of universal or ultimate values in the face of the events taking place then. The intellectual climate for nearly two decades following the war also included a number of powerful images which seemed to speak against relativism. These were images about the end of colonialism, opportunities for economic development in underdeveloped countries, and the seemingly universal desirability of Western technology. Thus during the postwar years, such leading figures in anthropology as Ralph Linton, Robert Redfield, and Alfred Kroeber were critical of moral relativism, while a variety of philosophers underlined the flaws in the ethical reasoning of Benedict and Herskovits.... Strong opposition has continued to the present, and today ethical relativism is more often attacked than embraced; I am not sure that anyone now is willing fully to endorse the version of relativism that was articulated by its major proponents in American anthropology in the 1930s.

It is in this context that I want to offer a defense of ethical relativism. This will be a very limited defense, and I do not propose reinstating the theories of either Benedict or Herskovits. But I believe that in our rush to distance ourselves from the moral and philosophical difficulties of their ideas, we may give up too much, and, indeed, we may fail to see the legacy of their thought continuing in other ethical theories today. In any event, it is important for us to keep sight of the issues that they were concerned with.

I need to be clear that I accept that there are situations in which ethical relativism is untenable, for it may lead to moral neutrality and inaction in situations that are intolerable. Ethical relativism is mistaken when it calls for us to be nonjudgmental in relation to such issues as political executions, genocide, genital mutilations, honor killings, and the like. The recent executions of Ken Saro-Wiwa and others in Nigeria, which received international attention at the time this essay was first drafted, are a case in point. A strict relativist might argue that a moral response by the West is ethically unwarranted, yet how can we not respond? Again, how can we not express value judgments in regard to the reports of rape and mass killing in parts of the former Yugoslavia? But ethical relativism is not a simple, unitary scheme that can be dismissed by a single argument, for it is a complex notion made up of a variety of features which need to be evaluated individually. A corollary is that most anthropologists are ethical relativists in some respects and nonrelativists in others.

Underlying my defense of relativism—or my interest in looking on its good side—is my recognition that at the time of writing, the United States seems to be experiencing a cultural shift to the right, or at least the cultural right has gained significant ground in the national political arena. We see concerted attacks on multiculturalism in the schools and universities, for example, and on multilingualism, immigrants, and affirmative action. These pressures—which have never been absent in the United States, but which appear to be stronger now than they have been in recent memory—stimulate us to take another look at relativism. The philosophical questions raised by it do not exist independently of a context of real-world affairs, and as those affairs change, we see the elements making up that complex of features called relativism in a different light. Put simply, our judgments about ethical relativism are historically situated.

THE PARADOX OF ETHICAL RELATIVISM

The place to begin is with what I will call the paradox of ethical relativism. On one hand, the theory is mistaken to the extent that it denies the very possibility of making moral judgments across cultures or of

developing a framework of human rights; but on the other hand, the problems that the relativists of the Boasian tradition were concerned with have not gone away. One of these is the problem of establishing reasonable and general grounds for making moral judgments about the actions of others, and another is a strong tendency among the more powerful peoples of the world to use their own standards, or standards favorable to them, in their relations with others. What standards are appropriate for us to use, how do we defend them, and how can we know that they will hold up to the scrutiny of those who do not share our perspective, now or in the future? No moral theory that has been advanced in opposition to relativism has been sufficiently convincing that it clearly stands above the rest as the winning alternative; consequently we cannot forge ahead with confidence in making moral judgments or establishing universal standards and a body of human rights. Whenever a set of standards is proposed, I feel myself being pulled back by a nagging sense of doubt. I have yet to see a general ethical theory that I personally find convincing. The paradox of ethical relativism is that we can't live with it, but it isn't clear how to avoid the skepticism which underlies it.

This paradox has helped structure the debate over the question of moral judgments and human rights, which is suggested by the fact that ethical relativism occupies such a prominent place in the literature on universal standards. Much of this literature takes relativism as its starting point or as its main foil. The present set of essays is illustrative: these grew out of a session on "Human Rights: Universalism versus Relativism" at the 1995 meetings of the American Anthropological Association. It is as if we cannot conceive the one—the search for general moral principles or human rights (whether they are based on utilitarian principles, Kantian rights-based theory, or any other ground)—outside the context of the other. Adapting a Derridian argument, the question of human rights and general standards of ethical judgment are never a mere "presence," something to be established in their own right, but exist only in relation to their opposite, which is relativism.

I have mentioned my sense of skepticism about attempts to establish general moral standards, and the ethical relativism that underlies the paradox that I cite *is* a form of skepticism. What is more, the moral theories of such Boasians as Benedict and Herskovits had an important skeptical component . . . , although not all forms of relativism in the anthropological literature did so. For example, skepticism seems to have played no part in the relativism of Malinowski, whose position rested on the principle that other cultures are successful or functional, which in turn assumed a universal standard of good. For example, his analysis of magic contained the message that missionaries and colonial administrators should not undermine the magical beliefs of other peoples because these rituals enabled the individual to cope with his or her anxieties and therefore to be more effective with the task at hand. Malinowski's relativism rested not on a form of skepticism, but on a version of utilitarian theory whereby the practical benefits of institutions served as a standard for making value judgments. For Malinowski, the institutions of non-Western societies are appropriate given the conditions in which those peoples live, and Western values regarding such matters as sexuality and marriage do not constitute universal standards.

The relativism that was incubated in Boasian anthropology adopted a skeptical attitude toward cross-cultural standards of all kinds, including Malinowski's utilitarianism. The Boasians would have been justified in accusing Malinowski of accepting this standard uncritically: it needed better philosophical grounding than he provided, and one even wonders how much care he gave to these matters. And this problem is still with us: the failure to arrive at a moral theory that is generally accepted and that will serve as an intellectual basis for universal human rights is notable.

I disagree with Benedict and Herskovits to the extent that they held that warrantable judgments across cultural boundaries can never be made, if only because the failure to act is itself an action that may have unacceptable consequences for other people—consequences which are unacceptable to us. But I agree with Benedict's and Herskovits's version of relativism on several other counts. The first is their basic skepticism: we do not have a set of moral principles that are rationally warranted, generally acceptable among those who are informed on these issues, and universally applicable. While there are situations in which we are compelled to take a moral stand, the grounds which warrant our doing so will necessarily be ad hoc and limited. I also agree with the connection that they made between skepticism and tolerance: when we do not find good reason to make judgments about the actions or ways of life of other people, we ought to show tolerance toward them, and we should do so on the basis of the moral principle that people ought to be free to live as they choose. One might argue that any ethical theory might call for tolerance in situations in which it lacks adequate reasons to respond otherwise. And it seems to me that, to the extent that it does, that theory *incorporates* relativism. Ethical relativism is espoused even among the ethical theorists who reject it. But my

argument goes even further, for I am suggesting that, at this point at least, no ethical theory which seeks to establish general standards of value is fully compelling. Consequently we are faced with the paradox of relativism: we have no moral theory to replace it with, yet there are situations in which the failure to take a moral stand other than tolerance is clearly unacceptable.

THE ISSUE OF CULPABILITY

Relativism may have at least a tacit presence even in cases in which we decide that moral judgments are warranted, for to judge that the actions of the Other are intolerable is to raise the additional question of what went wrong: who or what was responsible for the actions that we find objectionable? To put this another way, moral judgments may take place at two levels. The first concerns the events that we want to evaluate, and here the issue is to find adequate grounds for making value judgments about those events; the second concerns the human agents involved, and here the question is their responsibility for these matters. It is important that relativism is an issue at both levels. I turn here to the second level, the question of culpability, and the work of Edward Tylor is illustrative.

Tylor was not a relativist at the first level, of course, for he ranked human societies by reference to degrees of moral perfection, and, in principle, evaluations were to be made on the basis of how effective the institutions were in promoting human happiness and physical well-being. . . . Yet a form of relativism appeared at the second level, for he argued that savage societies should not be judged according to European standards of thought. Savages were not as intelligent as Europeans— they did not have the intellectual capacity to draw the same moral conclusions from experience that Europeans did; hence their institutions should be understood according to their standards of reason and not one's own. The implication was that the people of the lower societies were not culpable for their moral mistakes. Like children, they didn't know better. This was a form of relativism in that a society's standards of justice, say, were relative to the level of the people's intelligence, and institutions that were appropriate for societies at one level, that of the Tasmanians, say, were not appropriate for societies at another level, such as Britain. To state this another way, while Tylor faulted the institutions of lower societies, he held that the individual's actions should not be judged by reference the standards of a higher civilization.

We find a similar division between the two levels of moral judgment in the work of Ruth Benedict. What stimulated Elgin Williams's criticism of her *Patterns of Culture* in 1947 was that Penguin had just issued a new, twenty-five-cent edition of her book, making it readily accessible, as Williams said, to the common man. The book was now available on book racks in drug stores and dime stores across the country. Williams showed that while the formal argument of Benedict's book was one of relativism and tolerance—she explicitly argued that all cultures were equally valid—in another sense the book was profoundly nonrelativistic, for it offered a plethora of value judgments. And Williams applauded her for it. For example, Benedict described war as an asocial, destructive trait; she preferred the nonviolent marital relations of the Zuni to the jealous outbursts of the Plains; and she favored the lack of a sense of sin among the Zuni to the guilt complexes that were associated with Puritanism.

We find similar departures from relativism elsewhere in Benedict's work, including her discussions of what she called the bereavement situation. . . , or the cultural patterns associated with a person's death. She distinguished between realistic and non-realistic ways of handling death and grief. . . . The Pueblo peoples of the Southwest, she said, handled death in a realistic fashion, for the individual's behavior was directed toward the loss itself and toward getting past the trauma with as little disruption as possible. By contrast, the Navajo were nonrealistically preoccupied with contamination. They had a strong fear of pollution from the dead and of the dangers posed by the possibility of the ghost's return.

These cases reveal Benedict abandoning her relativism, but it reappeared at another level. For example, while she looked unfavorably on Plains warfare and while she regarded Navajo reactions to death as nonrealistic, an implicit message was that the people themselves should not be faulted. Yet her grounds for denying their culpability were different from those that underlay Tylor's thinking. It was not that the people didn't know better, but that they adhered to cultural traditions which largely governed their lives: to a significant degree, the individual's actions were a product of cultural conditioning. While Tylor granted agency to other peoples but absolved them of culpability because of their low intelligence, Benedict held that all people were equally intelligent but denied their blameworthiness on the grounds of enculturation. In other words, the individual's culpability should not be judged by reference to standards that derive from outside his or her culture.

This reveals how our assumptions about culture, society, and human behavior influence the kinds of value judgments we make, and it suggests the critical importance of being clear about these matters in our own minds when developing moral judgments. This also reveals the importance of separating the two levels of moral evaluation. Consider the recent executions in Nigeria. It is one thing to condemn the Nigerian government's actions, but quite another to assign moral responsibility. Ethical, political, and legal judgments may be made at both levels, but the reasoning is different in the two cases, and the paradox of relativism applies to both. It is conceivable that one could favor the imposition of sanctions against the Nigerian government in order to bring about a change in its policies, while still accepting that the people who were behind the executions were not morally culpable since they were acting reasonably given the cultural meanings that underlay their behavior.

It is not only ethical relativism that operates at both levels, for other ethical theories do so as well, such as when they take into account, say, what Benedict referred to as cultural conditioning. And when they absolve the individual of blame on these grounds, then they are employing the relativistic principle whereby the individual's actions should be judged by reference to the historically variable standards within the culture, not by external ones.

TOLERANCE AND SKEPTICISM

The Boasian relativists may be faulted for being less critical than they should have been with regard to the question of making moral arguments. . . . First, they were patently inconsistent. On one hand, they held that moral standards are historically conditioned, the same as pottery designs or folk tales—like all cultural features, values differ from society to society, and therefore we are not justified in making cross-cultural judgments. But on the other hand, the Boasians proceeded to do exactly what they asserted should not be done, which was to advance a universal moral standard. This was the standard of tolerance, whereby we ought not be judgmental about cultural differences; we ought to allow people to live as they choose.

Second, it was a mistake for them to assume that the means for arriving at universally valid moral principles should be by a comparative study of cultures. The question of values is a philosophical matter and not an empirical one. True, judgments of reality (as distinct from judgments of value) do enter legitimately into the application of value standards, inasmuch as the empirical facts of the case need to be understood before a standard of value may be applied to a given situation. But the process of arriving at value standards is a rational and not an empirical matter and cannot be approached by a comparative study of cultures. Indeed, if the Boasians had been consistent about using the comparative method, then surely they would have had to give up the call for tolerance, since intolerance is more likely the norm around the world.

Yet in spite of its difficulties, there is something to recommend the call for tolerance, which is grounded on the notion that people ought to be free to live as they choose. But the idea needs to be framed differently from the way the Boasians conceptualized it. In place of the straightforward principle that we ought to be tolerant of other ways of life, we should substitute the more limited principle that we ought to do so in the absence of persuasive arguments that would enable us to make moral judgments. Tolerance ought to constitute the default mode of thought governing our ethical judgments today. For example, we ought to be nonjudgmental in relation to culinary styles and modes of dress and about people's life goals and their treatment of one another—we should, that is, unless we see persuasive reasons to react otherwise. If we are not tolerant in such situations, then our actions necessarily will be arbitrary and will contravene the moral principle of freedom, whereby people should be able to live as they choose. This notion of relativism as default is crucial: the nonjudgmentalism that we associate with relativism is an attitude that does not come easily to most Americans, perhaps to most people throughout the world. Certainly it does not come easily to the religious right in the United States or to many members of the present U.S. Congress.

If we retain the Boasian call for tolerance as our default, what about Boasian skepticism? How may we fit that into our thinking? The Boasian relativists were not as consistently skeptical as it might appear, as Elgin Williams's criticisms of Benedict reveal. The principle that we should extract from Benedict—a principle that she herself was not very careful with, as Williams has shown—is the importance of maintaining a highly critical attitude in relation to the standards that we use in making value judgments. We need not remain skeptical to the point of denying the possibility of making any valid judgments, but we should submit our evaluations to severe scrutiny. And we do not need to resort to such obvious examples as the moral beliefs of the religious right to make this case, for anthropology itself provides illustrations. This point is crucial: even well-meaning, sympathetic, and informed people may be faulted for their failure to be as cautiously skeptical as they should.

I appreciate that it doesn't take relativism to make us aware of unwarranted judgments about other people, for surely any scholarly ethical theory today recognizes the subtleties of ethnocentrism. Yet the limited form of relativism that I urge suggests that an attitude of skepticism should be our first reflex in the face of moral judgments. I want to illustrate the subtleties of ethnocentrism and the importance of a basic skepticism in relation to moral judgments by examining the work of the late Ernest Gellner. His *Reason and Culture* . . . is about rationality, not ethics, but the central argument of the book has important implications for ethical relativism. At one level, he rejected universal rationality, for he accepted that reason does not stand outside of culture. . . . And he held that in an important sense, modern science is an irrational endeavor, as criticisms of the Popperian philosophy of science have shown. . . . But Gellner accepted universal rationality at another level, for Western thought, he argued, is demonstrably better than that of other peoples. What sets Western rationality apart is that it gets better results, regardless of its truth-value. He wrote,

> The astonishing and unquestionable power of the [Western] technology born of [Western] rational inquiry is such that the majority of mankind—and in particular those men eager to increase their wealth and/or power—are eager to emulate it.

What are the characteristics of this new, Western form of thought, this rationally unwarranted rationality which is conquering the world? It is a fusion of two seemingly contradictory philosophical theories, Western rationalism and Western empiricism. This form of thought is empiricist in that it takes experience as the arbiter of competing ideas, but this empiricism is under the control of rationalism. . . .

Drawing on Weber's analysis of the history of Western society, Gellner . . . went on to describe Western rationality as a way of life, or lifestyle, which permeates much of Western society and culture. For example, it is manifest in the modern economy, which operates according to judgments about efficiency and cost-effectiveness. Gellner is clear that not all spheres of society or culture are fully dominated by the rationalist ideal, for in many spheres—etiquette might be one example—rules "have no rhyme or reason" . . . . Even more to the point, morality itself, he said . . . cannot be justified by pragmatic considerations the way science and economic production can.

Gellner's valorization of Western rationality stopped short of defending Western values in general, but I suggest that his privileging of Western rationality helps to normalize certain forms of thinking, and in doing so may have harmful ethical consequences. An example would be the use of highly rational, highly empirical, but highly value-laden economic models derived from the West for development programs in other parts of the world. Gellner's response to this criticism might be that it ignores a key part of his argument, which is the importance of the judgments of non-Western peoples. It is *their* demand for the products of Western rationality—medicines, new crop forms, tape recorders, television, rifles, missiles—that confirms the universality of Western forms of thought. And if an economic order is imposed on them that they do not want, then their judgments should be respected. Yet it is extremely difficult to circumscribe those things which are genuinely desired by the Other and to distinguish them from the things that are forced upon them because of asymmetries of privilege, prestige, and power. Gellner's thinking was insufficiently skeptical.

Consider the case of Appalachia. The Tennessee Valley Authority was created by an act of Congress in 1933, and its initial purpose was the planning and development of the entire Tennessee River Basin, which was considered underdeveloped and poverty-stricken. Dams would be built to improve navigation and flood control and to produce hydroelectric power, conservation programs would be implemented, and both agricultural and industrial development would be introduced. According to David Whisnant . . . , the TVA began as a progressive, idealistic, democratic, comprehensive effort to improve the region. Its idealistic goals were soon subverted by powerful business interests, particularly after the dams were completed in 1944. But even if the original goals had not been subverted, Whisnant argues, the TVA would have been destructive. The leading figures in the organization believed that by instituting rational, apolitical, disinterested economic and social engineering, the project would succeed in improving the lives of these backward people. . . . In brief, the project was founded on a set of cultural assumptions of the dominant society, assumptions about development and the virtues of bringing a people with an aberrant way of life into the mainstream. Whisnant . . . writes,

> Beneath the vast technological superstructure of TVA I perceived a substructure of cultural values and assumptions that controlled the agency more surely than the geomorphology of the Tennessee River Valley itself.

This kind of normalization is manifest in another characteristic of the relationship between Appalachia and the larger society, which is the tendency of the latter to perceive the Appalachian people as backward and impoverished. It is unquestionable that the people of that region do suffer impoverishment, which is evident, for example, in the figures on health care and education. But granting that, nevertheless, the *perception,* by mainstream, middle-class Americans, of the Appalachians' backwardness and impoverishment is a result of something else as well. For one thing, there has been a "systematic denigration" of the local population as a way to justify such programs as the TVA. . . . The portrayal of Appalachia as backward has served the interests of certain individuals and agencies of the dominant society. For another, and more to the point here, some Appalachian patterns are seen as backward from the point of view of mainstream, middle-class America. The emotional forms of religious service among the congregations that proliferate in Appalachia . . . are illustrative. These are perceived by the dominant society as manifestations of a gullible people. Similarly, one Appalachian pattern is a form of economic life whereby the people depend heavily on the informal economic sector (such as subsistence gardening and labor and food exchanges); they are jacks of all trades, and they tend to avoid long-term job commitments and regular employment. . . . Tom Plaut . . . argues that while there are many studies of the culture of Appalachia, very little work has been done on the "rationalist, achievement-oriented, 'scientific' culture" that is overwhelming the region. This "scientific" culture "has levelled, bleached, and bled out a rich variety of human ways of being that have stood in its path". . . . Plaut sees the way of life of the Appalachians as meritorious in its own right.

Earlier I said that it is sometimes difficult to distinguish between those features of Western society which the Other truly wants and those which are forced on them. I suggest that one aspect of this problem is that mainstream Westerners tend to engage in a kind of metonymic thinking in conceiving the relationship between Us and the Other, for technology serves as a trope for representing a more general relationship among societies. For example, the success of such Western forms of technology as tape recorders, electric guitars, and rifles provides a model for thinking about the relationship between the Western economy and that of the Other. We tend to elide the distinction between specific forms of technology and, say, the value of economic efficiency and the work ethic. The theme of skepticism that we find in the work of Benedict and Herskovits retains its significance today.

CONCLUSION

The emergence of relativism at about the turn of this century was associated with a Copernican shift in both the Western worldview and the Western sense of self-identity. Western thought about where our civilization stood in the total gamut of human societies underwent profound change, and this took place in part in the context of Boasian anthropology and was one aspect of the emerging relativistic perspective. Whereas earlier, anthropologists imagined their own societies to be at the pinnacle of development, the Boasian worldview had it that the West occupied a very equivocal position, for while it may have enjoyed greater material power than other peoples, it did not enjoy moral superiority. This facet of relativism was crucial, and it remains a central legacy, regardless of how we may feel about the possibility of establishing general ethical standards or universal human rights. What is more, the efforts today to develop a warranted body of human rights are framed by this principle, for we now assume that the views of non-Western peoples ought to weigh as heavily as the views of Westerners in establishing general standards. So the very search for universal human rights today rests upon a relativistic foundation. Even the ethical theories which reject relativism reflect the Copernican shift that the Boasians helped to achieve.

EXERCISES

1. Kant's ideal moral individual is one who feels no compassion for others, but helps them out of a pure sense of duty. Suppose that such a Kantian moralist lost her belief in rationally known objective moral truth. Would that person become an egoist? An amoralist? Or something else?

2. In Plato's *Republic,* Socrates considers a person who has been given a magical ring—the ring of Gyges—that makes him invisible. This person will be able to carry out all manner of crimes with no risk of being caught. Socrates attempts to show that a person who took advantage of such magic would end up miserable, rather than genuinely happy. Do you think Socrates could succeed in showing that?

3. In the criticism of psychological egoism, we said the psychological egoist claims her position is an empirical truth (everyone always seeks his or her own selfish interests). But that doesn't work as an empirical claim, the criticism goes; it is actually a self-sealing, definitional claim, because the psychological egoist cannot tell what would count *against* it. Is that a legitimate criticism? *Could* a psychological egoist give an example of what selfless behavior would be like?

4. The Western culture in which most of us live generally approves of eating meat. But many persons within that culture belong to groups that oppose eating at least some forms of meat: Jainists oppose all meat-eating, Muslims and Jews abhor pork. If I am a relativist living in Texas, and am also a Jainist, and I refuse to eat barbecued ribs, have I done something wrong? Would I be doing something wrong—from a cultural relativist perspective—whether I refused ribs or not?

5. In the United States, abortion was once widely condemned, and was also illegal. Now abortion is widely accepted (though of course a minority fiercely opposes elective abortion). If you were a dedicated cultural relativist, at what point would you think abortion has changed from wrong to right? When a majority of U.S. citizens favored legalized abortion? When the Supreme Court ruled on *Roe* v. *Wade?* Or when?

6. In Canada, there are recently established tribal courts and tribal justice systems that deal with criminal offenses among tribal members. These courts generally have a more *restorative* approach to justice, in which the goal is to restore the crime victim's well-being and dignity (to the greatest degree possible), to reform and restore the offender to the community, and to restore the harmony and wholeness of the community. This is a very different orientation from other Canadian court procedures, which take a more retributive approach to criminal justice. Is this a case of cultural relativism?

7. In the United States, Great Britain, and (most of) Canada, the criminal justice system operates on the "adversarial" model: the defendant is represented by an attorney who strives to protect the defendant and prevent conviction and cast doubt on the charges against the defendant, while the state is represented by a district attorney who endeavors to win a conviction against the defendant. The process is a battle between two "adversaries" (the district attorney or prosecutor, and the counsel for the defense). The criminal defendant has several clear rights, including the right (through an attorney) to cross-examine all prosecution witnesses, the right to exclude "hearsay" testimony, and the right to refuse to answer any questions (the right against "self-incrimination"). In several European countries—France is a good example—the system of justice is quite different. Called an "inquisitorial" system, the trial is dominated by the judge, who conducts most of the inquiry and asks most of the questions (the lawyers have a much more limited role). In the inquisitorial system, hearsay evidence is admitted, and defendants do not have a right to refuse to answer

questions. Is this difference in systems of justice simply an innocent cultural difference (like tastes in food or clothing styles) that should be respected? Or must we conclude that rights are violated and wrongs committed by the inquisitorial system?

8. If I insist that every culture has the basic right to self-determination, is that a relativist or an absolutist position?

9. Elvin Hatch asserts that "the very search for universal human rights today rests upon a relativistic position." Does Hatch's claim *undercut* or *support* the effort to establish universal human rights?

10. Execution of juveniles is almost universally condemned as a severe violation of human rights: it is legally permitted only in Somalia and the United States. Would it be legitimate for other countries to exert pressure on the United States to reform its cultural practice of execution of juveniles? Would such pressure be effective?

ADDITIONAL READING

Psychological egoism was defended by Thomas Hobbes in *Leviathan*, and was promoted by Bernard de Mandeville in *The Fable of the Bees, or Private Vices, Public Benefits* (London, 1723). Mandeville's book is better written and more cogently argued than the more popular contemporary defense of ethical egoism by the novelist Ayn Rand in *The Virtue of Selfishness* (New York: New American Library, 1961). The classic critique of egoism is by Bishop Joseph Butler, *Fifteen Sermons upon Human Nature, 1726* (which is excerpted earlier). Another excellent critique (among many) of psychological egoism is C. D. Broad, "Egoism as a Theory of Human Motives," in *Ethics and the History of Philosophy* (New York: Humanities Press, 1952). Hugh LaFollette has a very good online discussion of psychological egoism in "The Truth in Psychological Egoism," at www.etsu.edu/philos/faculty/hugh/egoism.htm. Good brief accounts of egoism are Kurt Baier, "Egoism," in Peter Singer, editors, *A Companion to Ethics* (Oxford:Basil Blackwell, 1991); and Elliott Sober, "Psychological Egoism," in Hugh LaFollette, editor, *The Blackwell Guide to Ethical Theory* (Oxford: Blackwell, 2000). For arguments against ethical egoism, see (among many) Laurence Thomas, "Ethical Egoism and Psychological Dispositions," *American Philosophical Quarterly*, Volume 17 (1980); Christine Korsgaard, "The Myth of Egoism," *The Lindley Lectures* (Lawrence:University of Kansas Press, 1999); Kurt Baier, *The Moral Point of View* (Ithaca, NY: Cornell University Press, 1958); and James Rachels, "Two Arguments Against Ethical Egoism," *Philosophia*, Volume 4 (1974). Thomas Nagel's superb book, *The Possibility of Altruism* (Oxford: Clarendon Press, 1970), might also be useful in this context. Jesse Kalin defends ethical egoism in "Two Kinds of Moral Reasoning," *Canadian Journal of Philosophy*, Volume 5 (1975). There are also two good anthologies devoted to ethical egoism: *Morality and Rational Self-Interest*, edited by David Gauthier (Englewood Cliffs, NJ:Prentice-Hall, 1970); and *Egoism and Altruism*, Ronald D. Milo, editor (Belmont, CA:Wadsworth, 1973).

The anthropologist Ruth Benedict, in *Patterns of Culture* (New York: Penguin, 1934), was a major advocate of cultural relativism. Mary Midgley, *Heart and Mind* (New York: St. Martin's Press, 1981), offers a well-crafted critique of cultural relativism. For a more sophisticated version of relativism, and a defense of that view, see Gilbert Harman, *Explaining Value and Other Essays in Moral Philosophy* (Oxford: Clarendon Press, 2000). For a clear and fascinating debate on moral relativism versus moral objectivism, by two outstanding contemporary philosophers, see Gilbert Harman and Judith Jarvis Thomson, *Moral Relativism and Moral Objectivity* (Oxford: Blackwell, 1996). Russ Shafer-Landau includes a clear critique of egoism and relativism in *Whatever Happened to Good and Evil?* (Oxford: Oxford University Press, 2004); another extensive critique of relativism is offered by John. J. Tilley in "Cultural Relativism," *Human Rights Quarterly*, Volume 22 (2000). Hugh LaFollette defends "rational relativist ethics" in "Moral Disagreement and Moral Relativism," *Social Philosophy and Policy*, Volume 20 (1994). For very interesting anthropological examinations of relativism, see Elvin Hatch, *Culture and Morality: The Relativity of Values in Anthropology* (New York: Columbia University Press, 1983); and an excellent article by Clifford Geertz, "Anti-Anti-Relativism," *American Anthropologist*, Volume 86, Number 2 (June 1984), as well as his *Available Light: Anthropological Reflections on Philosophical Topics* (Princeton, NJ: Princeton University Press, 2000). Steven Lukes, professor of sociology, New York University, has written a very clear and insightful small book on the subject: *Moral*

Relativism (New York: Picador, 2008). Good anthologies on relativism include Michael Krausz, *Relativism: Interpretation and Conflict* (Notre Dame, IN: University of Notre Dame Press, 1989); and Paul K. Moser and Thomas L. Carson, *Moral Relativism: A Reader* (New York: Oxford University Press, 2001).

NOTES

[1]K. Brown and A. Jameton, "Culture, Healing, and Professional Obligations: Commentary," *Hastings Center Report* (1993), 17.

[2]Jim Carnes, "Us and Them: A History of Intolerance in America," published by Teaching Tolerance, a project of the Southern Poverty Law Center (1995), p. 16. I discovered this passage in a quotation included in Judith A. Boss, *Ethics for Life* (Mountain View, CA: Mayfield Publishing, 1998).

[3]Richard Rorty, *Truth and Progress: Philosophical Papers*, Volume 3 (Cambridge: Cambridge University Press, 1998), p. 2.

3

Ethics, Emotions, and Intuitions

FOLLOW YOUR REASON OR FOLLOW YOUR HEART?

Christina and Dekisha are juniors at Beverwyck College. They have been close friends since the spring semester of their freshman year, when they suffered together through Professor Stewart's terminally boring Introduction to Philosophy class. They are also dedicated, effective, and tireless volunteers in a local homeless shelter. They work long hours at the shelter, provide care and comfort to the residents, and they are apparently equally effective in their work and equally poplar with the residents. Dekisha and Christina have spent their spring break working night and day at the shelter, and on the last day of spring break they are taking a late-night coffee break and talking together. "This has been the most wonderful spring break I have ever had," Christina says. "I can't think of anything that would have brought me more satisfaction and joy than working with these people, giving them a bit of hope and encouragement, and seeing their sorrows turn into smiles." Dekisha shakes her head. "Not me. I can think of lots of things that would bring me more joy: just to name one, sitting on a warm beach of sugary sand, soaking up sunshine and margaritas, and snuggling with my sweetie. In fact, I would rather be almost anywhere than here. But these people are suffering, and I'm good at helping them, and I have an opportunity to relieve their suffering—so I believe I have a duty to help. It's the right thing for me to do, it's what I should do, and what I must do. But it's certainly not what I would prefer to do." Leave aside for a moment the question of how effectively Dekisha and Christina work at the shelter. Suppose that both are equally effective, equally comforting, and equally kind. The question is simply this: Which of the two, dutiful Dekisha or joyful Christina, would you consider the most *morally* upstanding? (Dekisha and Christina are the two finalists for Morally Outstanding Junior at Beverwyck College, and you are on the selection committee; whom would you choose?)

The correct answer is Dekisha. Christina was merely following her inclinations. Fortunately her inclinations are generous, but that's just a matter of good luck. Her acts of kindness were not really moral acts at all, since they were not done out of deliberate duty. Dekisha wins. It's not even close. (That would be Kant's answer, and perhaps also your answer.)

But on the other hand, maybe Christina should be our winner. She doesn't need rules or duties to do the right thing; instead, her acts of kindness come from deep within her, from her own deep sense of care and affection, and she doesn't have to stop and think before doing the right thing. Dekisha may follow moral rules, but the real moral acts stem from Christina's loving heart. Christina wins.

So which is the best path to morality, Dekisha's rationalist, rule-governed, and duty-driven approach, or Christina's heartfelt commitments?

This question has stirred debate for many centuries. The debate takes many shapes, but it basically turns on this question: To act ethically, is it essential to overcome one's feelings and suppress sentiments in order to follow true rational moral principles that transcend our grubby, earthly, animal natures? Or is ethics rooted in our sentiments, in our feelings of warmth and kindness and compassion and affection—feelings that are not derived from reason and that we share with other animals?

> "The great secret of morals is love; or a going out of our own nature, and an identification of ourselves with the beautiful which exists in thought, action, or person not our own. . . . The great instrument of moral good is the imagination. . . . " *Percy Bysshe Shelley*, A Defense of Poetry, *1821*.

Reason or Feelings: History of the Conflict

This fundamental conflict can be traced through the great religious traditions. One strong element of Jewish tradition is adherence to the divine law in all its majesty and detail, with the path to virtue passing through careful scrutiny of texts and commentaries and the scrupulous keeping of every law. In contrast, in Micah 6:12, the Jewish prophet Micah counsels that living a good life does not require such rigorous rationalistic study, but instead comes easy: "What doth the Lord require of thee, but to do justly, and to love mercy, and to walk humbly with thy God?" In the Christian tradition, Jesus taught the virtues of living simply, with more emphasis on feeding the hungry and caring for the sick and loving your neighbor, and less worry about the law and rules and reason and riches. With St. Paul, the pendulum swings to the other side: Paul emphasizes a precise formula for gaining salvation, and the path is straight, narrow, and difficult. The same marked contrast can be seen between the stern rationalism of St. Thomas Aquinas and the warm natural feelings St. Francis of Assisi found in birds, beasts, and humans. In Islam, the Sufi tradition emphasizes following one's God-given inner feelings (though this requires a process of discipline and purification), while such great Muslim theologians as Ibn Rushd celebrate reason as a legitimate pathway to God and to a virtuous life. Mencius, an ancient Chinese Confucian philosopher, believed that humans are naturally good out of a deep innate sense of compassion. It is this deep natural feeling of compassion rather than rational reflection or strict rules that guides humans to act virtuously:

> If you let people follow their feelings (original nature), they will be able to do good. This is what is meant by saying that human nature is good. If man does evil, it is not the fault of his natural endowment. The feeling of commiseration is found in all men, the feeling of shame and dislike is found in all men; the feeling of respect and reverence is found in all men; and the feeling of right and wrong is found in all men. . . . Humanity, righteousness, propriety, and wisdom are not drilled into us from outside. We originally have them with us.[1]

In contrast, Thomas Hobbes, the seventeenth-century British philosopher, regarded the natural state of humanity as a "war of all against all" in which life is "nasty, brutish, and short." According to Hobbes, the dominating natural sentiments are greed and self-protection, sentiments that can be held in check only by a "great leviathan" who rules through force and fear.

So if you wish to carefully examine your own view of ethics, one good starting point is the tension between duty and sentiment. Is ethics rooted in natural sentiments of affection and generosity and sympathy? Or is ethics primarily a matter of following duty and reason, and combating our natural tendencies of selfishness and greed?

Affection and Duty: The Case of Huck Finn

Here's another case to consider.[2] Huck Finn is floating along the river on a raft, accompanied by his friend Jim, an escaped slave. Life is good, as the two friends while away the leisurely days talking and fishing. As the raft moves farther north, Jim becomes more and more excited: soon he will cross over into free territory, and be a free man. He intends to work hard and save his money, and eventually buy his wife and children out of slavery. If their owner refuses to sell them, Jim plans to steal them. Jim is deeply grateful to Huck: Huck is helping him escape, and Jim regards Huck as his best friend, indeed "the only friend old Jim's got now." But as they move closer to Jim's freedom, Huck becomes despondent. He is helping Jim escape, and Huck regards that as no better than stealing. He is stealing the rightful property of Miss

Watson, who owns Jim, and who always treated Huck well. Huck's conscience starts to bother him: "What did that poor old woman do to you, that you could treat her so mean?" Eventually Huck resolves to do his duty: Huck's moral code requires turning Jim in to prevent his escape. So Huck sets off with that purpose, but his resolve fails him, and when he has the opportunity he can't bring himself to betray his friend. Huck believes that he has done wrong, and that he's no better than a thief, but he can't bring himself to do "his moral duty."

Of course we think that Huck did the *right* thing. It was right to help Jim escape from slavery, and it would have been egregiously wrong for Huck to betray his friend to the slave catchers. But Huck believes he has done wrong. His moral code demanded that he turn Jim in, but his sentiments—his affection for Jim—prevented him from doing his duty. Did Huck perform a morally good act when he acted against his moral code and helped Jim escape? if you perform an act that you believe is morally wrong, can you still be morally right in your behavior? Suppose Huck had feared that if he turned Jim in, Jim might escape and kill him, and so he decides not to turn Jim in (though he still believes he *should*). Is he performing a morally good act? A morally bad act?

In Western philosophy, most ethicists have favored Dekisha. The best path to morality is through duty, through following moral principles, through ignoring or suppressing our feelings, and seeking the guidance of reason and moral law and moral principle. Our feelings tempt us to go astray, distract us from our duty. (Of course reason and duty can also go wrong, as illustrated by Huck's belief in his duty to return an escaped slave. But even though our reason is not infallible, it is still our best guide to ethical principles.) In any case, our feelings are too variable and inconstant to serve as a reliable moral guide.

Hume Versus Kant

In contrast, some writers on ethics have advocated the primacy of feelings over reason as a guide to ethics. Among that group David Hume stands out. Hume was a Scottish philosopher who spent most of his adult life in France. Though he was a contemporary of Kant (born in 1711, 13 years before Kant), they were millennia apart in philosophical views as well as in temperament, and much of what Kant writes is an effort to refute Hume's position. It was Hume's work, Kant said, that "awakened me from my dogmatic slumber" and revealed the profound challenge awaiting anyone who favors rational ethical objectivity.

Kant spent most of his life as a philosophy professor at the University of Konigsberg, in the city of his birth, and he never ventured outside East Prussia. A man of simple, even austere habits, legend has it that the locals set their clocks by his daily walk. Though he was a famous person in his later years—in eighteenth-century Europe, philosophers could gain a substantial measure of renown—Kant continued to live quietly, pursue his writing, and deliver his lectures. David Hume, in contrast, traveled extensively from his Edinburgh birthplace (he returned in his later years, and is buried there), and felt most at home in the exciting and fashionable world of Paris. Eighteenth-century Paris was abuzz with revolutionary ideas—ideas that stimulated the American Revolution and later the French Revolution, radical ideas concerning religion, debates over evolution, and endless discussion of the implications of Newtonian science. Hume delighted in such debates, and was a charming and welcome guest at the most fashionable parties; indeed, his French friends nicknamed him "Le bon David."

Both Kant and Hume were profoundly influenced by the Newtonian scientific revolution, but Newton's theory pushed them in opposite directions. Kant, impressed by the precision and power of Newtonian physics, resolved to forge an ethical system based on a few principles that can be known through pure reason: a system that will set rational beings apart from the deterministic physical world of Newtonian science. Hume, also impressed by Newton's system, had no wish to set humans apart from the natural determinist world. For Hume, that is the only world there is, and we are thoroughly part of it. Kant believed there was no way of establishing universal principles of ethics on the basis of scientific observations, and so ethics must be established through the powers of pure abstract reasoning. Hume agrees that empirical science cannot offer us ethical truths, but neither can pure reason. That leaves Hume's ethics in the realm of feelings and passions. But since for Hume the only genuine knowledge comes from pure mathematics or empirical science, that excludes ethics from the realm of knowledge altogether. Feelings are important, and they are the basis for ethics, but feelings cannot provide an objective foundation for ethics. If we want objective truth, we must look to the sciences, and to the truths of mathematics and geometry that we know through reason. But reason cannot give us ethical truths. Not because reason is flawed, but rather because basic ethical preferences are the proper realm of the feelings, and reason does not operate there. Hume states his position unequivocally:

> 'Tis not contrary to reason to prefer the destruction of the whole world to the scratching of my finger.[3]

Most of us would find this a strange preference indeed. But if it does not involve any false judgment—such as the belief that a scratch on my finger would doom my immortal soul, or the belief that scratching my finger would cause prolonged agony for millions of people, or the belief that I would die from a scratch on my finger but survive the destruction of the world—then (according to Hume) reason cannot refute it. If you believe that smoking contributes to good health and improves your athletic performance, or that you are immune from any health risks from smoking, then reason may be used to change your views. But if you know the severe risks of smoking, but you really consider the pleasures of smoking sufficiently valuable to outweigh the perils of cancer and emphysema, then reason cannot touch your preferences. Our basic preferences, values, and desires do not come from reason, but instead they *use* reason to find means of gaining satisfaction. According to Hume,

> Reason is, and ought only to be the slave of the passions, and can never pretend to any other office than to serve and obey them.[4]

When it comes to *basic* ethical views, there is no truth of the matter for Hume. If you want truth, look to science or mathematics. Ethics is ultimately based on our feelings, and that is not an area where truth and falsity apply. That does not imply that Hume regarded either feelings or ethics as unimportant. To the contrary, Hume regards our feelings of sympathy and benevolence as essential to social order and human cooperation; and he suggests that nature was wise to place something of such great significance in our natural feelings, rather than in our feeble rationality.

OBJECTIVE AND SUBJECTIVE FEELINGS

Some people view feelings differently. Hume insists that ethics is based on feelings, and feelings aren't subject to reason. But others insist that feelings can be a source of truth, and so ethics can ultimately be based on feelings and still be objective truth. Not all truths come from reason and empirical scientific observation, and the truths of ethics are the prime example of such nonrational (not *irrational*) truths. This *objectivist* interpretation of our feelings agrees with a famous saying from Pascal: "The heart has its reasons that the reason knows not."

If we think of ethics as based on feelings, as Hume does, can we also believe that some ethical claims are actually true? Or is ethics more like our tastes?—you like white wine and I prefer red, and there's no question of who is "objectively right." Suppose we ask Christina and Dekisha. You remember Christina and Dekisha, who spend many hours working at the homeless shelter: Christina because she takes great joy in helping those who need help, and Dekisha because she believes it to be her moral duty. Dekisha, being a good Kantian, has no doubts about the matter. There is indeed a moral right and wrong; it is known through pure reason, and it is perfectly objective. Suppose Dekisha is challenged by her friend George. "You know, spending all this time at the homeless shelter is wrong; everyone should think only of themselves, and not worry about others who are less fortunate." Dekisha will have a clear answer: "You are profoundly mistaken. Since each of us needs help at times, we could not will that ignoring the needs of others should be a universal law. When I am in need of help, I think people should help me; after all, I'm a person, not just some object you can ignore or discard. And there is nothing morally special about me that does not apply to other people as well. So rational consistency demands that I acknowledge the universal principle that there is an obligation to help those in need."

Subjective Feelings

How would *Christina* answer George's challenge? That's a more complicated question. There are two very different sorts of answers Christina might give. *Subjective* Christina might say: "Wow, we really feel differently about this. I gain such joy and satisfaction from helping these desperately unfortunate people, it's almost hard for me to believe that you feel it's not worthwhile. But then, I also love Jackson Pollock's paintings, and I know some people who can't stand them. It's not that I'm right and you're wrong, but I do wish your feelings about this were more similar to mine, because this is very important to me. It bothers me more that you feel this way about the homeless than that you don't like Jackson Pollock." *Subjective* Christina cannot say that George is mistaken, and she cannot give rational arguments to refute George's opposing perspective. But she does have other resources. She might do various things to develop such feelings in her friend George: have him read John Steinbeck's *Grapes of Wrath* or give George the opportunity to meet a warm and fascinating homeless person who has suffered a series of terrible misfortunes (because George may have the notion that all homeless people are lazy bums who are exploiting the system, and when George understands the facts of how some good hardworking people wind up in such misfortune, his feelings about them may change). But if George has no factual delusions—"I know that some of the homeless are good and decent people, whose misfortune is not their own fault; still, it's not my problem, and I don't really care what happens to them"—and his feelings cannot be modified by imagination or literature, then there is nothing more for *Subjective* Christina to say.

Objective Feelings

But Christina may have a very different view. *Objective* Christina has strong feelings about the value of helping the homeless, but she does not think such feelings are just a matter of taste or preference. Instead, *Objective* Christina maintains that her feelings—the distress she feels over the suffering of the homeless, and the warm satisfaction she feels when providing help—are a reliable guide to moral truth. She does not believe that George's callous view can be refuted by reason, but she does believe George is *morally* wrong, and *objectively* wrong, to feel that we should not help the homeless. Some people see the world of science and mathematics and reason as the world of objective facts, and the realm of poetry and music and art and tastes and feelings as a subjective nonfactual realm. Objective Christina regards that as a false dichotomy. Of course science is objective, and a preference for tennis over bowling is subjective. But our sentiments regarding ethical issues are not like game preferences. They aren't ultimately based on reason, but why suppose that reason is the only way to know objective truths?

So Objective Christina believes there is wisdom in our feelings. That doesn't imply, of course, that every feeling is a path to truth. Some feelings may be rejected as leading us astray—just as some scientific theories may also be flawed. Objective Christina acknowledges that feelings are not an *infallible* guide to ethics. But she denies that feelings are merely distractions on the path to ethical truth, and she believes feelings can be the source of ethical insight.

SENTIMENTALISM

Both versions of Christina—the objective and the subjective—are ethical *sentimentalists*. While many sentimentalists are on the objective side (maintaining that our feelings and sentiments can guide us to objective ethical truth), other sentimentalists reject the belief that feeling-based ethics is objective. (David Hume is usually understood as rejecting ethical objectivity, though a few philosophers read him as an objectivist.)

When we speak of "sentimentalism" in ethics, we are speaking of a broad movement in ethical theory. This is *not* "sentimentalism" in the standard sense of that term: when ethicists talk about sentimentalism, they are *not* talking about getting teary-eyed when singing *Auld Lang Syne* or when reminiscing about old friends. In ethical theory, *sentimentalism* is the view that feelings/sentiments are vital to ethics and to the proper understanding of ethics: without the right kinds of feelings, ethics would be impossible.

Ethical sentimentalism comes in many shapes and sizes, but the easiest way to get a larger perspective on sentimentalism is to contrast it with some *non*sentimentalist views; and the clearest contrast is with Kant's rationalist ethics. Kant, you may recall, believes that ethics must be a purely rational process: legitimate ethical deliberation resembles mathematical reasoning. Kant can be moved by it: "Two things fill the mind with ever new and increasing admiration and awe, the oftener and the more steadily we reflect on them: the starry heavens above and the moral law within." When we step back and consider the pure and austere process of rational ethical deliberation, we may have a *feeling* of awe—just as we might be awed and inspired and moved by a particularly deep and impressive physics theory or mathematical proof. But when we are *doing* the ethical deliberations, and *willing* ourselves to follow the rational moral law, then feelings play no role whatsoever; to the contrary, they get in the way. For Kant, when our ethical decisions and behavior are motivated by *feelings*, they lose their ethical value—indeed, if our acts are guided by feelings, then Kant refuses to consider them *ethical* at all (they may be pleasant and agreeable, but they have no genuine ethical content). Though sentimentalists have many disagreements among themselves, they all agree that Kant's pure rationalism is the *wrong* approach to ethics. For sentimentalists, feelings are an essential element of ethical decision making and ethical behavior: without feelings, humans could not be ethical actors. Of course, sentimentalists don't deny the *importance* of reason in ethics: it's just that they insist that feelings *also* play an *essential* role in our ethical lives. Even Hume—who insisted that "Reason is, and ought only to be, the slave of the passions"—believed that after the passions/feelings had set the goal, reason would still be important in finding the best path to that goal.

Sentimentalism is in stark conflict with rationalist ethics; and another contrast with sentimentalism is *utilitarian* ethics. Utilitarian ethics (which will be discussed in more detail in Chapter 5) holds that the right act is the act that produces the best possible overall consequences, and the important consequences are pleasure and suffering. At first glance, it might seem strange to contrast sentimentalism with utilitarianism. After all, Bentham's classical utilitarian theory counsels that calculating the *right* act means calculating which act would produce the greatest balance of *pleasure* over *pain* for all involved; and pleasure and pain are certainly feelings. Thus, utilitarians typically insist on the importance of *weighing* feelings and weighing the goodness or badness of an act on the basis of what *feelings* result from that act. But a good utilitarian ethical calculator need not *experience* those feelings in order to make sound utilitarian ethical judgments. Suppose that I am personally immune to all feelings: I never feel pleasure, and I never suffer pains. If I carefully calculate what act would produce the greatest overall balance of pleasure over pain (for those who *do* have such feelings) and act accordingly, I would still be a good utilitarian. In contrast, the sentimentalist maintains that one who never experienced feelings could not really recognize and understand the true nature of ethical life and behavior: feelings are an essential element of the moral life. It's not just that one devoid of all feeling would have no *motivation* for acting ethically (though sentimentalists generally believe that's true); rather, such a person could not enter into the world of ethics. Star Trek's Mr. Spock could be a very good utilitarian and a rationalist ethical superstar, but he would be hopeless as a sentimentalist.

Finally—the last point in saying what sentimentalism is *not*—sentimentalism is not the same as intuitionism (which will be discussed later in this chapter). Intuitionists insist that what is intuited is *not* a *feeling*; rather, it is a direct *insight* which is immediately *known*. Think of your knowledge of geometry: when straight lines intersect, the opposite angles that are formed are identical; when you think about that carefully, you immediately (intuitively) *recognize* that truth. Of course you must be in the right setting, and in the right frame of mind: drunken besotted revelry is not the ideal context for intuitively recognizing geometrical truths. But in the right setting, when you think carefully, you immediately recognize the geometrical truth; and likewise, in the right context, thinking carefully, unburdened by bias, you immediately and intuitively *recognize* that (for example) it is morally right to keep your promises. You don't have an agreeable *feeling* about promise keeping (indeed, you may find your obligation to keep promises burdensome); rather than *feeling* that promise keeping is right, you intuitively recognize the rightness of keeping promises. So intuitionists would insist that their view is not a version of sentimentalism. And sentimentalists agree: our feelings may be very important in our ethical lives, but our feelings are not intuitive flashes of deep insight into ethical truth.

Sentimentalism starts from a *rejection* of the belief that we are inherently selfish, and that self-interest is our controlling motivation. One of the great sentimentalists was Adam Smith (who thought of himself as a philosopher and ethicist, though he is now best known for his work in economics). Smith's great work on sentimentalist ethics was *The Theory of Moral Sentiments*; and in the opening lines of that book, Smith pronounces a fundamental principle of sentimentalist ethics:

> However selfish man may be supposed, there are evidently some principles in his nature, which interest him in the fortune of others, and render their happiness necessary to him, though they derive nothing from it except the pleasure of seeing it.

Smith (and other sentimentalists) does not deny that we are often motivated by narrow self-interest; in fact, when we look at the policies of some Wall Street firms that enrich themselves while impoverishing many others, we might well conclude that there are some people who are motivated by nothing other than selfishness. But sentimentalists insist that *most* people have some strong sentiments of a more generous nature: we can feel pleasure and approval at the good of others even when we gain nothing from it. Smith claims that such sentiments are *evident* and obvious, and it would be difficult to deny it. Miners are trapped by an explosion, and millions of us watch and fervently hope for their rescue and feel great pleasure at their deliverance (or sincere sorrow at their deaths) even though we "derive nothing from it" except the joy of their rescue: the pleasure we feel at their good fortune.

Exactly what role *do* feelings play in sentimentalist ethical theory? Almost all sentimentalists would agree that feelings are important to our *motivation*: it is feelings that *move* us and motivate us to do the right thing, and without such feelings the essential mainspring of ethical motivation is missing. Kant believes that we can follow the moral law through sheer *will power*, and no emotional motivation is required (for Kant, to the degree that emotions provide the motivation for an act, the act loses its genuine ethical value). Sentimentalists generally disagree: Without the emotional motivation, ethical behavior doesn't get started.

But beyond the motivational force of the emotions, do our feelings have any key role? Can they not only *motivate* us (sometimes) to do the right thing but also *guide* us in determining what *is* right? Most sentimentalists answer affirmatively (though their affirmative answers take many shapes). Some sentimentalists would insist that if you deny that feelings give guidance to ethical *truth*, then you can't really be a sentimentalist: if you believe that feelings are our basic motivations, but neither reason nor feelings can guide us to ethical truth (because there is no ethical truth to find, or at least we have no way of finding it), then you are not a sentimentalist but simply a *nonobjectivist*. However, there are a number of ethicists who seem to count themselves as both sentimentalists and nonobjectivists. Whether a *real* sentimentalist must believe in some form of ethical objectivism is an interesting terminological issue, but we'll leave that dispute for others. In any case, we'll discuss nonobjectivism in another chapter; and here, we'll take up those varieties of sentimentalism that favor some degree of ethical objectivity.

Simon Blackburn is a contemporary sentimentalist (though he refers to his own theory as "expressivism") who rejects any independent objective standard for ethical truth and regards the search for such an independent and conclusive objective standard as a search for an ethical "Holy Grail": a futile search for something we don't really need anyway.

> We sentimentalists do not like our good behavior to be hostage to such a search. We don't altogether approve of Holy Grails. We do not see the need for them. We are not quite on all fours with those who do. And we do not see why, even if by some secret alchemy a philosopher managed to glimpse one, it should ameliorate his behavior, let alone that of other people. We think instead that human beings are ruled by passions, and the best we can do is to educate people so that the best passions are also the most forceful. We say of rationalistic moral philosophy what Hume says of abstract reasonings in general, that when we leave our closet, and engage in the common affairs of life, its conclusions seem to vanish, like the phantoms of the night on the appearance of the morning. *Simon Blackburn, "Must We Weep for Sentimentalism" in James Dreier, editor,*Contemporary Debates in Moral Theory *(Oxford: Blackwell Publishing, 2006).*

So *if* our feelings can guide us to ethical truth—or at least provide guidance to which ethical paths and judgments are better or worse—then how does that happen? The first basic question to ask is this: do our feelings *point* to some ethical truth independent of our feelings (that is, are our feelings useful as indications or guides to ethical truths that exist whether we or anyone else has those feelings)? Or are our feelings themselves what *make* a belief or action ethically legitimate? That is, are our ethically relevant feelings *guides* to independent ethical truths, or are they somehow *constitutive* of those ethical truths?

When you (in the right circumstances) *feel* that an act is wrong, shameful, or vile, does that in itself *make* the act wrong, or does it only *inform* you that the act is wrong?

Moral sense theory is one version of ethical sentimentalism. Moral sense theorists believe that our feelings and sentiments are *guides* to an objective moral truth: my *feeling* of shame at an act doesn't *make* the act a morally bad act; but the moral sense of shame *informs* me that my act was morally bad. When I touch a hot stove, I feel pain; the feeling of pain warns me that I touched something I shouldn't have touched. Feelings of shame are moral warnings against doing wrong, and feelings of pride or satisfaction may inform me that I am on the right ethical path. This moral sense is not an *intuition*; rather, the moral sense is analogous to our physical senses: by our moral experience of moral "sensations" or feelings, we learn what is right and wrong; just as by our physical experience, we learn that fire is hot, rocks are hard, sugar is sweet, and flamingoes are pink. Our sensation of pinkness is not what makes flamingoes pink, but it informs us that flamingoes are pink; likewise, our moral sense of shame is not what makes lying bad, but instead the moral sense of shame informs us that telling lies is in itself a bad act. Ethical intuitionists might say that you *know* intuitively it is right to keep your promises: look carefully at promising, and you immediately know that it is wrong to break promises, even if you have never actually engaged in promise keeping or promise breaking at all. Moral sense theorists believe that our moral knowledge comes not from pure intuitions, but from our lived experience of moral sensations/feelings/sentiments.

The idea of an effective universal *moral sense* of right and wrong is ancient, and has long been a key element of the Confucianist philosophy. The great fourth-century BC Confucian master Mencius describes this moral sense thus:

> Why do I say that all people possess within them a moral sense that cannot bear the suffering of others? Well, imagine now a person who *all of a sudden* sees a small child on the verge of falling down into a well. *Any* such person would experience a sudden sense of fright and dismay. This feeling would not be one which they summoned up in order to establish good relations with the child's parents. They would not purposefully feel this way in order to win the praise of their friends and neighbors. Nor would they feel this way because the screams of the child would be unpleasant.

Mencius, 2A.6

Mencius emphasizes a feature of moral sense experience accepted by almost all moral sense theorists: your moral sense experience is not something you *choose* to feel, but is instead immediate and powerful. When you see a child in danger, you feel a sudden sense of dismay; when you observe someone treating a child cruelly, you feel a sense of moral disgust; when you observe an act of kindness or benevolence, you immediately feel strong moral approval.

In making the case for the moral sense, moral sense theorists often rely on analogies with the *aesthetic* sense: analogies with the sense of beauty and with feelings/judgments of taste. That may strike you as a strange strategy: if you are trying to find objective truth in the moral sentiments (where there appear to be significant disagreements), why would you start from sentiments of *taste* and sense of beauty, where there are even greater disagreements? Some tastes run to blues, others to bluegrass; some love hip-hop, and others listen only to "that old-time rock and roll"; some love Mozart, others live for Motown. Even so, there do seem to be some fairly reliable aesthetic standards. I like music, but I recognize that my musical tastes are uneducated and rather crude; and that my son, who has spent many years studying and performing music, hears and appreciates musical subtleties that are beyond my grasp, and beyond my level of appreciation; and I recognize that his musical tastes and sentiments are better than mine. Suppose that you and I are standing in the Sistine Chapel gazing at Michelangelo's magnificent frescoes; you find Michelangelo's work so breath-takingly beautiful you can hardly speak, while my loud comment is that "It's okay, I guess, but I still prefer my black velvet portrait of Elvis." Would you have any doubt that my artistic tastes are inferior, even flawed? Imagine being at the Grand Canyon, watching wonderstruck as the sunset paints the cliffs purple, red, and gold, and your friend is completely indifferent; wouldn't you think your friend sadly lacking in sense of beauty? I like wine: give me a minimally decent cabernet, and I'm perfectly satisfied; indeed, anything better would be wasted on me. But I know people who can appreciate wonderful subtleties of flavor I cannot detect, and I acknowledge that their tastes in wine are superior to mine. Without your aesthetic sense—your "sense of beauty"—you could not appreciate Michelangelo's paintings, or the sublime grace of the Taj Mahal, or the glories of the Grand Canyon; and likewise (so the moral sense theorists might insist) it is your moral sense that guides your appreciation of virtue and your detestation of vice. Francis Hutcheson makes the comparison with the sense of beauty a key element of his case for the moral sense:

> . . . there is some Sense of Beauty natural to men. . . . We find as great an agreement of men in their relishes of forms, as in their external senses which all agree to be natural; and . . . pleasure or pain, delight or aversion, are naturally joined to their perceptions. If the reader be convinced of such determinations of the mind to be pleased with forms, proportions, resemblances, theorems, it will be no difficult matter to apprehend another superior sense, natural also to men, determining them to be pleased with actions, characters, affections. This is the moral sense. . . . (The Preface)

Comparison with the aesthetic sense may help us gain some idea of what the moral sense is; but there will still be a major question for moral sense theory: How do we know that our moral senses are reliable? That is, how can I be sure that my sense of shame (or some other moral emotion) is not mistaken, or illusory? For some of the major moral sense theorists of the Enlightenment era—Anthony Ashley Cooper (Lord Shaftesbury, 1671–1713) and Francis Hutcheson (1694–1746)—the guarantee of the moral sense was easy and obvious: the moral sense is given to us by God, and God would not instill in us a faulty moral sense. You can damage your moral sense by neglecting its admonitions, just as you can damage your visual and auditory senses through misuse. But so long as we use our moral sense carefully, and without denying or ignoring its counsel, we can be confident that this gift from a loving and just God will not lead us astray. As Francis Hutcheson states:

> . . . Human Nature was not left quite indifferent in the affair of virtue, to form to itself observations concerning the advantage, or disadvantage of actions, and accordingly to regulate its conduct. The weakness of our reason, and the avocations arising from the infirmity and necessities of our nature, are so great, that very few men could ever have form'd those long deductions of reason, which show some actions to be in whole advantageous to the agent, and their contraries pernicious. The Author of Nature has much better furnish'd us for a virtuous conduct, than our moralists seem to imagine, by almost as quick and powerful instructions, as we have for the preservation of our bodies. He has made virtue a lovely form, to excite our pursuit of it; and has given us strong affections to be the springs of each virtuous action. (From *The Preface of An Inquiry into the Original of Our Ideas of Beauty and Virtue*, 1726)

That is, our moral sense is designed by God so that we perceive virtuous acts as lovely and attractive. Lord Shaftesbury offers an even more elaborate account of the divine origins of our moral sense: Everything—including humans and human senses and sentiments—must be understood in terms of its *purpose*; more specifically, how it fits into God's divine design of the universe. Thus, something is *good*—whether animal, plant, human, or human emotion—to the extent that it contributes to the well-being or right order of the overall system. Only humans are capable of being motivated by virtuous affections, for those affections are *higher-order* reflective affections: the capacity, through reflection, to feel approval and disapproval of our desires (I desire to accumulate wealth at the expense of others, but that is not a desire that I can *reflectively* feel as worthy; my desire to help others, on the other hand, is a feeling I experience as positive and that I also approve of upon careful reflective examination of that feeling). Because only humans (alone in God's creation) are capable of genuine virtuous action motivated by reflectively approved feelings, clearly our proper role in the overall design is to act virtuously and benevolently. Thus, genuine virtuous behavior is behavior that promotes the well-being of the human species, and ultimately the well-being and proper functioning of the entire system. Reflectively approved sentiments are the motivating force that enables humans to properly fulfill our role in the divinely designed system. A well-ordered human moral sense recognizes and promotes the well-being of the human species and the right order of God's design. (Shaftesbury regarded any suggestion of the innate *depravity* of human kind as abhorrent, and contrary to the proper understanding of the goodness of the divine order. Indeed, Shaftesbury regarded the view that humans are fundamentally evil and depraved as a more harmful and pernicious doctrine than atheism.)

Thus, for Shaftesbury and Hutcheson, there is no question that our moral sense guides us to ethical truths that lie beyond our moral sentiments; for they lead us to truths embodied in God's moral perfection. Consider acts of benevolence (one of Hutcheson's favorite examples): whether observing the benevolence of someone else, or our own benevolent acts, we find that awareness of such acts gives us pleasure; the opposite—grasping stinginess—brings a sense of displeasure. When we observe the cruel miserliness of Scrooge, we feel disturbed; when (transformed by the ghostly visitations) Scrooge becomes generous, we take pleasure in Scrooge's newly awakened benevolence. This is a common emotional reaction—how else could we account for the continuing wide popularity of Dickens' *A Christmas Carol*? Hutcheson maintains that such perceptions by our moral sense guide us toward virtue and give us understanding of true ethical values.

Shaftesbury and Hutcheson could appeal to the basic belief that God *designed* a well-ordered universe (including human moral sentiments) to promote the highest good. But when the design view is called into question, there are serious questions about why we should believe that our "moral sense"—or any of our sentiments and feelings—are a reliable moral guide. David Hume was a trenchant critic of the divine design model, arguing against the belief (common before Hume) that from our observations of our well-ordered world, we could conclude that it must have been produced by a divine designer. The most famous advocate of that position was William Paley, who developed the "watchmaker" argument for the existence of a designer God:

> But suppose I had found a watch upon the ground, and it should be inquired how the watch happened to be in that place. . . . There must have existed, at some time, and at some place or other, an artificer or artificers, who formed [the watch] for the purpose which we find it actually to answer; who comprehended its construction, and designed its use. . . . Every indication of contrivance, every manifestation of design, which existed in the watch, exists in the works of nature. . . . William Paley, *Natural Theology* (1802)

Hume used a dialogue to critique that design argument, casting Cleanthes in the role of the advocate of the design account, and answering that argument in the voice of Philo:

> Now, Cleanthes, said Philo, . . . mark the consequences. First, By this method of reasoning, you renounce all claim to infinity in any of the attributes of the Deity. For, as the cause ought only to be proportioned to the effect, and the effect, so far as it falls under our cognizance, is not infinite; what pretensions have we, upon your suppositions, to ascribe that attribute to the Divine Being? . . .
>
> But were this world ever so perfect a production, it must still remain uncertain, whether all the excellences of the work can justly be ascribed to the workman. If we survey a ship, what an exalted idea must we form of the ingenuity of the carpenter who framed so complicated, useful, and beautiful a machine? And what surprize must we feel, when we find him a stupid mechanic, who imitated others, and copied an art, which, through a long succession of ages, after multiplied trials, mistakes, corrections, deliberations, and controversies, had been gradually improving? Many worlds might have been botched and bungled, throughout an eternity, ere this system was struck out; much labour lost, many fruitless trials made; and a slow, but continued improvement carried on during infinite ages in the art of world-making. In such subjects, who can determine, where the truth; nay, who can conjecture where the probability lies, amidst a great number of hypotheses which may be proposed, and a still greater which may be imagined? . . .
>
> In a word, Cleanthes, a man who follows your hypothesis is able perhaps to assert, or conjecture, that the universe, sometime, arose from something like design: but beyond that position he cannot ascertain one single circumstance; and is left afterwards to fix every point of his theology by the utmost license of fancy and hypothesis. This world, for aught he knows, is very faulty and imperfect, compared to a superior standard; and was only the first rude essay of some infant deity, who afterwards abandoned it, ashamed of his lame performance: it is the work only of some dependent, inferior deity; and is the object of derision to his superiors: it is the production of old age and dotage in some superannuated deity; and ever since his death, has run on at adventures, from the first impulse and active force which it received from him. (pp. 167–169)

Hume (and—a century later—Darwin's evolutionary explanation for biological "fitness") posed a powerful challenge for the claim that our "moral sense" is implanted as part of God's harmonious design. But if our sentiments/feelings—and our moral sense—are not implanted by God, then what reason is there to believe that our sentiments are a reliable moral guide?

David Hume was a sentimentalist who rejected any theological underpinnings for the moral sense and who believed that sentiments are the vital mainspring for all our behavior, including moral behavior; but whether he thought those sentiments gave any sort of *objective* moral truth or *accurate* moral guidance is another question altogether, and deeply disputed. Many read Hume as one who rejects all *objective* ethical standards: Ethics is "merely" a matter of feelings, and there's no truth of the matter in ethics at all. But others regard Hume as believing that the sentiments can guide us to *correct* ethical behavior. On this reading, our sentiments/feelings can guide us toward good behavior, but not because they are divinely implanted; instead, their reliability must be based on less exalted grounds. Trying to establish those grounds has long been a major task for moral sense theorists, and even Shaftesbury and Hutcheson (who ultimately placed their faith in divine design) offered more mundane arguments for the reliability of the moral sense. Contemporary moral sense theorists, such as Annette Baier and Martha Nussbaum, offer naturalistic justifications for the moral sense. (Many—though certainly not all—who favor feminist or care ethics views are also moral sense theorists; but their accounts of the moral sense and its origins are generally quite different from those offered by Shaftesbury and Hutcheson.)

> Achieving and maintaining trusting, caring relationships is quite different from acting in accord with rational principles, or satisfying the individual desires of either self or others. Caring, empathy, feeling with others, being sensitive to other's feelings, all may be better guides to what morality requires in actual contexts than may abstract rules of reason, or rational calculation, or at least they may be necessary components of any adequate morality." *Virginia Held, "Feminist Transformations of Moral Theory,* Philosophy and Phenomenological Research, *vol. 50, 1990.*

Whether shaped in us by God or nature, our moral sense motivates us to act in ways that are beneficial to others, to our social communities, and to our fellow humans. Whatever the origins of humans, we are a profoundly social species, having strong ties to others in our group. Our young have a very long period of vulnerable dependency, and they are best protected by larger groups. Our ancestors soon discovered that defending themselves against attack was more effective if they banded together, and that—being rather slow, and having neither fangs nor claws—hunting was more successful in packs than individually. But maintaining social groups required that we share the dangers and the benefits. A hunter who made a kill and refused to share was despised; a hunter who willingly shared and who bravely defended the group against attack was admired. Maintaining good cooperative social relationships is vital to the success of human social animals, whether we are Chippewa hunter-gatherers, Ashanti traders, a Mardi Gras Krewe, or the Penn State sociology faculty. Morality is essential for such successful cooperation: indeed, some moral sense theorists maintain that morality *consists* in positive support for acts and feelings which promote group cooperation and affection, and discouragement of those that threaten social cooperation. The social sentiments—the sense of positive pleasure at acts of benevolence and kindness, the immediate sense of disgust at acts of selfishness and cruelty—provide motivation that makes the cooperative moral system work. On this view, both the rationalists and the social contract theorists get things exactly backward: It is not rational deliberation that gives us our moral system, nor is it the drawing up of contracts that make morality possible; instead, morality has its origins in the family group, with its affections and feelings (*not* in voluntary cooperative agreements— you don't *choose* your family, nor do you *choose* to feel affection and concern for your children or your parents or your siblings). Morality then moves outward into larger groups that are held together by similar feelings. Contracts and rational rules come much later, if at all, and require a solid foundation of cooperative groups and shared sentiments. On this view, how do we know that our moral sense is *reliable*? We know that our moral sense (that sharing is good) is reliable because it *works*: it promotes social cohesiveness and cooperation. Don't ask whether such moral sentiments correspond to some external moral reality; rather, ask whether they are effective in promoting social cooperation, and whether we can reflectively *approve* of them. Our moral sentiments are not *produced* by rational reflection; but when we do reflect on them, we find that we give them our rational approval.

Sentimentalism bases ethics on our experience of feelings and sentiments (analogously to the way that science is based on sensory experience), rather than on pure reason. Scientists recognize that our sensory experience can be deceptive: the Sun certainly *looks* as if it is circling around us every day, and the stars appear to be far away but not *that* far away. Many medical experiments are done as *double-blind* experiments, in which *both* the test subjects and the person who actually gives the experimental drugs to the test subjects do not know who is getting the real drug and who is receiving a placebo; and researchers use double-blind experiments because they realize that their own biases, hopes, and expectations may influence what they see (if you fervently *hope* that your new drug will have a positive effect, you are more likely to *see* that effect even when it's not there). In order to make accurate observations, scientists must prepare carefully, avoiding biases and preconceptions. Sentimentalists believe the same point applies to our ethically essential experience of feelings and sentiments: we must avoid biases, examine our feelings honestly and objectively, and be sure that we have an accurate understanding of the situation or circumstances that evoke the feelings.

Sentimentalism requires more than just raw feeling; an adequate sentimentalist theory must offer some way of *evaluating* feelings. After all, some feelings do *not* guide us well (as anyone knows who has followed his or her feelings in pursuit of a false manipulative lover): the feeling is strong, and seems right; but it guides your ship onto the rocks rather than into a morally satisfactory channel. Sentimentalists often recommend a *spectator's* perspective on feelings as a means of gaining a better appreciation of which feelings are good moral guides. Our *sympathetic* feelings for others require that we be able—as spectators—to imagine what another is experiencing, even when we are not having that feeling ourselves; perhaps even when we have never had quite that experience ourselves (even if you have never suffered the death of a close friend, you can sympathize with one who has that sad experience by considering how you would feel in that situation). Adam Smith emphasizes that because we have learned how (as spectators) to imagine ourselves in another's circumstances, we can go a valuable step further and take a *spectator's* perspective on our own behavior. When we step back from our own experience, and consider how our behavior would appear to a disinterested spectator, we gain a clearer perspective on our own feelings and motives. In *Four Quartets*, T. S. Eliot writes of the pain of recognizing, too late, one's false motives:

> the shame
> Of motives late revealed, and the awareness
> Of things ill done and done to others' harm
> Which once you took for exercise of virtue.

Gaining a somewhat detached perspective on our own feelings—the perspective of the "impartial spectator"—may help us in making a better moral evaluation of those feelings, and of their moral legitimacy. Self-deception is a major problem when we are immersed in our own feelings and desires; looking at ourselves and our feelings from a more detached perspective may help us recognize the narrow selfishness of our behavior, though we had deceived ourselves into believing that our motives were purely benevolent ("I'm generously taking my best friend's fiancé out for dinner, so she won't be lonely while my friend is studying abroad; what a caring and concerned friend I am").

Contemporary versions of sentimentalism are often classified as "neosentimentalism"; and while they follow the basic principles of sentimentalism (they agree that feelings are the basic elements of morality and of moral motivation), the neosentimentalists place great emphasis on the *evaluation* of feelings. David Hume, a classical sentimentalist, would agree with that emphasis: moral evaluation and motivation are rooted in our sentiments, but careful thought and preparation are essential if those sentiments are to guide us effectively:

> But in order to pave the way for such a sentiment and give a proper discernment of its object, it is often necessary . . .
> that much reasoning should precede, that nice distinctions be made, just conclusions drawn, distant comparisons
> formed, complicated relations examined, and general facts fixed and ascertained. (David Hume, *An Enquiry
> Concerning the Principles of Morals*)

So we cannot just follow whatever feelings move us; rather, we must put ourselves in the right position so that the appropriate feelings can motivate us. To take an obvious example, seeing an infant crying after being stuck with a needle might immediately and unreflectively move us to feel moral disgust at those causing the infant such suffering; but when we examine the relevant facts and understand that the child is being given an injection that will prevent a severe disease or cure an existing one, then we are moved by very different feelings.

Neosentimentalists, taking their cue from Hume, emphasize that we cannot draw legitimate moral guidance and conclusions from whatever feelings we happen to have; rather, we must carefully consider whether those feelings are *appropriate*, whether they are *justified*, and whether the feelings are feelings we can genuinely *endorse* when we reflect upon them. Thus, on the neosentimentalist view, feelings retain their fundamental importance for ethics; but feelings must themselves come under scrutiny and evaluation

> Though Hume counsels that "much reasoning should precede" our reliance on our feelings and sentiments, there is no question that the ultimate moral source is the sentiments: "But after every circumstance, every relation is known, the understanding has no further room to operate, nor any object on which it could employ itself. The approbation or blame which then ensues cannot be the work of the judgment, but of the heart, and is not a speculative proposition or affirmation, but an active feeling of sentiment." (David Hume, *An Enquiry Concerning the Principles of Morals*).

before we accept them as good moral guides. Growing up in a racist or homophobic culture, one may *feel* disgust at an interracial or same-sex couple; but careful reflection shows that there is no basis for such feelings other than narrow prejudice, and the feelings are then recognized as inappropriate: as paths to bias and moral wrongness rather than as legitimate moral guides. A woman who is raised in a profoundly sexist society—in which women are taught subservience, and always to follow the guidance of men (they must honor and *obey* their husbands)—may *feel* guilt at her beliefs in her own independence and competence; but reflection guides her to repudiate that feeling and *endorse* her felt desire for the recognition and exercise of her own abilities and rights. When taking moral guidance from your feelings, the key question is not what you *are* feeling, but what you *would* feel if you were fully informed, if you were not bound by prejudice, not overwhelmed by such powerful feelings as the desire for vengeance, and not misled by narrow self-interest and subtle self-deception. It is still, for sentimentalists, the *feelings*—perhaps the "moral sense"—that guide us; indeed, sentimentalists believe that our ultimate motivation *must* come from our feelings. But feelings are a powerful engine, and it is essential that we look carefully and thoughtfully in every direction to be sure that the right feelings are guiding us effectively.

In sum, sentimentalism is not a simplistic "if it feels good, it *is* good" theory; and being a good sentimentalist does not mean getting overwhelmed by the first tide of feelings that sweeps over you. There is no question that, for better or worse, we are *motivated* by our feelings. Ultimately the question is whether sentiments/feelings can provide legitimate ethical direction. Whether such sophisticated sentimentalist theories *work*, or work better than the opposing views, is a question you will have to think about (or maybe feel about) for yourself.

INTUITIONISM

We'll return in later chapters to questions about feelings, and what they do or do not contribute to ethics. But there is another view about ethics that must be distinguished from the position favored by Objective Christina, with her emphasis on the wisdom of feelings. This other view, which may sound superficially similar to Objective Christina's position, is called *intuitionism*. Intuitionists believe that reason is not the source of basic ethical truths, but neither are feelings. Rather, we *know* the basic truths of ethics by a special power of *intuition*. It is not just a matter of how we *feel* about something, but of what we intuitively recognize. If I find a lost wallet containing several hundred dollars, my *feelings* might be joy at my good fortune, but my *intuition* that I must return the money is something quite different. My power of ethical intuition is not like reason, but neither is it a feeling. Instead it is analogous to my power of vision. When I am in the right place and my vision is clear, I can *see* a mountain. And in the right circumstances, I can also *see* what is right and what is wrong. But making accurate intuitive observations cannot be done easily or carelessly: it requires careful attention to detail, clear conceptual understanding of the language of morality, openness to our moral experiences, and unbiased consideration of all relevant factors.

Where does this intuitive power come from? Some intuitionists answer that it is implanted in us by God, a special power that distinguishes us from beasts. Other intuitionists suggest other sources. But however we come by this power, it is a power we all have, and if we are receptive to it and honest about it, we cannot deny its existence. "How can I be sure this is an intuition of wrongness, and not just the effects of the sauerkraut pizza I had for lunch?" Our intuitive ethical insights are of a special nature and power. When you have a genuine intuition of rightness or wrongness, you cannot help recognizing that it is an ethical truth. Having the ethical intuition without recognizing it as an ethical truth would be like seeing a circle without seeing that it is round. "But I don't have such powers of intuition. I don't get these powerful intuitive ethical insights." Most likely you really do, but you are deceiving yourself because you don't want to acknowledge them. "No, I really don't have them." In that case, you are a moral monster. You have lived such a morally depraved life, and ignored so consistently the ethical prompting from your ethical intuition, that you have finally become ethically blind. But your failure to recognize ethical intuitions shows only the depth of your wickedness, not that such intuitions do not exist.

What Do We Intuit?

That is a rough outline of intuitionism. But once we get beyond that general outline, we soon discover a variety of views marching under the intuitionist banner. Perhaps the most controversial question for intuitionists is the nature of what is intuited. When you consult your ethical intuitions, what do you discover? This question is not just a question of whether we all share the same ethical intuitions. At a deeper level, it is first of all a question of what *types* of intuitions we have. Do we intuit a single basic ethical principle, from which all other principles may be derived (perhaps something like "treat others as you would wish to be treated")? Or do we intuit a number of ethical principles ("tell the truth" and "return favors" and "do not kill")? Or do we perhaps intuit some property of *goodness* that we recognize as an irreducible fact? Maybe instead we intuit the rightness or wrongness of specific acts ("it is wrong to deceive Brenda about the bad brakes on the car I am trying to sell her"). Or possibly we intuit a general property of goodness, as well as general principles, and also the rightness or wrongness of specific acts. But most intuitionists are reluctant to claim such a rich variety of intuitions. Instead, intuitionists usually insist that we have a specific type of intuition that guides our ethical behavior. At the most general level, we might intuit some principle that would form the single overarching rule for all our behavior, and the truth of that principle would be immediately and intuitively evident. In contrast, an intuitionist might insist that rather than a general principle, we intuit the rightness of a specific act. For example, Henry Prichard counsels that we must examine each act we are considering as carefully and fully as we can, and then we will intuit the rightness or the wrongness of the act. Of course we might still make mistakes. But if we consider carefully and keep our intuitions in good working order, that is the best guide we can have to right and wrong.

Somewhere between these two views falls the intuitionist approach of W. D. Ross, who holds that we intuitively know *several* principles. We know, intuitively and immediately and objectively, that it is wrong to break promises. Likewise, we intuitively know that it is right to relieve suffering. These are direct and undeniable moral truths that "come to be self-evident to us just as mathematical axioms do."[5] The hard questions arise when those simple principles come into conflict. What should I do if I have promised to meet you at noon to take you to lunch, but on my way I encounter someone with a broken leg who needs a ride to the hospital? I have a duty to keep my promise, but also a duty to relieve suffering, and I can't do both. So what should I do? Ross would answer: that's a tough question. In such cases of conflict, it's often difficult to be sure what the stronger duty is. That's not surprising. After all, no one should suppose that making the right ethical decision is always easy. But though we face uncertainty in trying to determine what we should do in specific cases, that uncertainty does not infect the general principles. I *know* that I have a duty to keep my promises, and I *know* that I have a duty to relieve suffering. Depending on the situation, one of those duties may be stronger than the other, and knowing what I should do requires careful thought about all the duties I have and the details of my specific situation. But when I reflect carefully, my knowledge that I have a duty to keep my promises and a duty to relieve suffering is immediately and intuitively obvious.

Questions about Intuitionism

Suppose we push intuitionists to tell us more about these special intuitions. How do we know our intuitions are sources of truth? How do we distinguish intuitions from mere feelings? The answers we get are rather limited: you just *know* intuitions when you experience them, and the truth of the intuitions is self-evident. No further explanation is possible, but neither is further explanation needed. Reflect carefully, and you will recognize the intuitive truth that it is wrong to lie.

The intuitionism of W. D. Ross has a solid commonsense appeal. Don't get tangled up in ethical theory and confused by moral speculation: you *know* what's right and wrong. Still, on closer scrutiny, certain aspects of his rule intuitionism may be troubling. After all, there are many cases of "obvious intuitions" we have come to reject—for example, that slavery is just, that women should have no rights, that persons who do not share our religious doctrines should be killed. Why should we regard our ethical intuitions as any more reliable than our immediate conviction that the Sun is traveling over our heads? There is no doubt that we have strong feelings about right and wrong, and that these feelings have a distinctive force. I feel disgusted when June pours chocolate sauce over her broccoli, but my disgust is of a different order when Liz tells a racist joke or steals money from a blind fruit vendor. But the question of whether we have "ethical intuitions" that are sources of objective ethical truth remains a difficult issue.

Which Intuitions Should We Trust?

As a young boy growing up on a farm, Joe has a strong sense—some would call it a strong feeling, others might classify it as a moral intuition—that it is wrong to inflict suffering on farm animals in raising them for slaughter. Joe sees a young calf pulled from his mother, then placed in an isolated stall with little room to move, and then fattened to produce the delicacy of pale veal. Both the calf and his mother appear to suffer significant distress. Joe watches young calves and lambs being castrated so they will be less troublesome and grow more rapidly; they certainly do not seem to enjoy the experience. These observations cause Joe significant distress. He *feels* that what is being done to the animals is wrong. Or some would say he *intuited* that treating animals in this manner is morally wrong.

As Joe grows older, he is taught that treating animals in this way is simply part of the way farming is done, and that the suffering of animals is not something he should worry about. When he sees farm animals suffer, it still bothers Joe, but gradually it bothers him less and less. Learning to ignore animal suffering is part of becoming an adult in Joe's farm culture. Since he wants to be accepted as an adult, he eventually learns to ignore the suffering. It no longer disturbs him, and he no longer considers it morally problematic. "We don't intentionally cause the animals to suffer," Joe now says, "but when you raise farm animals for slaughter, they do sometimes suffer. However, farm animals aren't really moral beings, and so their suffering is not a moral issue. Oh, sure, when I was a child I thought that causing the suffering of farm animals was morally wrong. But I'm more mature now, and I don't feel that way anymore. Those childish feelings were mistaken."

This example brings up the question of animal rights, and often people have *very* strong opinions on that issue. That's not the question here. We'll be discussing it, but not quite yet. For the moment, focus on what is happening to Joe. He has one sort of feeling (or intuition) early in his life, and very different feelings now. Those who believe raising animals for slaughter is morally wrong might say that Joe's early intuitions were correct, and that his culture corrupted or destroyed those moral intuitions. Those who believe raising animals for slaughter is morally legitimate will say that Joe's childish feelings were just mistaken: like feeling you have been wronged when asked to share your toys with a playmate. The feeling is certainly strong, but growing older you realize that such a feeling is not a useful moral guide. Set aside for a moment your own view about who is right and who is wrong about treatment of farm animals. Focus instead on the question of *how* one would try to resolve that question. Clearly, different people can have different feelings (or conflicting intuitions) about moral issues. Indeed, the same person may have conflicting feelings at different times. If intuitions are to serve as moral guides, *how* can we decide which intuitions we should trust, and which ones we should reject (they were not *real* intuitions)?

Intuitionist W. D. Ross has an answer.

> We have no more direct way of access to the facts about rightness and goodness and about what things are right or good, than by thinking about them; the moral convictions of thoughtful and well-educated people are the data of ethics just as sense perceptions are the data of a natural science. Just as some of the latter have to be rejected as illusory, so have some of the former; but as the latter are rejected only when they are in conflict with other more accurate sense perceptions, the former are rejected only when they are in conflict with other convictions which stand better the test of reflection. The existing body of moral convictions of the best people is the cumulative product of the moral reflection of many generations, which has developed an extremely delicate power of appreciation of moral distinctions; and this the theorist cannot afford to treat with anything other than the greatest respect. The verdicts of the moral consciousness of the best people are the foundation on which he must build. . . . [6]

But his solution raises almost as many issues as it settles. How do we recognize "the best people" whose moral verdicts form the foundation of ethics? If we asked that question in the antebellum South, most whites would have pointed to the slave-holding owners of the great plantations. They were, after all, the leaders of the society and the best-educated people of the region (many plantation owners sent their children to top New England universities). Now they strike us as prime examples of moral blindness. The well-educated leaders of our society—the lawyers and doctors, politicians and journalists, professors and accountants, CEOs and CFOs of major corporations—are probably not the people who leap to mind when you think of persons with deep moral wisdom. In fact, there is a long tradition that the best source of moral wisdom is small farmers, who live close to the soil, earn their bread by the honest sweat of their brows, and are uncorrupted by the artificial contrivances of fashion and fad. That was a very popular view in the eighteenth and nineteenth centuries—Thomas Jefferson was one of its champions—and it is represented today by the writings of poet and essayist (and farmer) Wendell Berry. Philosophy professors tend to be well educated and rather reflective, but in all truth, I would not put them at the top of my list of "morally best people." So recognizing the "best people" (whose intuitions are supposed to be most worthy of trust) is a daunting task. And note that we cannot identify the "best people" as those who hold the right moral intuitions, for that would just spin us in a tight circle.

So *if* there are disputes concerning moral intuitions, the disputes may be difficult to settle. But intuitionists still insist on the ethical importance of intuitions. After all, you know, clearly and intuitively, that it is wrong to lie. That's all the proof you can have, but that's all the proof you need.

CONCLUSION

The proper role of the emotions is one of the most difficult and contentious questions in ethics (and it is an issue we shall return to in later chapters). Plato and Kant insist that acting ethically requires vigorously *suppressing* the emotions, relying instead on the dispassionate power of reason. In contrast, Hume believes ethics is rooted in our emotions: without emotions, ethics would not exist. Some think ethics is based on emotions, and so *cannot* be objective. Others believe our emotions *are* a source of objective moral truth. And intuitionists maintain we have special objective intuitive powers distinct from our emotional reactions. You will have to make your own decision about which view is most plausible. But you need not make that decision yet. There are more options and more arguments to come.

✦ A TREATISE OF HUMAN NATURE ✦
David Hume

David Hume was born in Edinburgh, Scotland, in 1711. He wrote several major philosophical works, but was also known during his lifetime for his writings on history, political theory, and economics. Greatly influenced by Isaac Newton's experimental method and by British empiricist philosophy, he endeavored to apply Newton's method to the study of the human mind. A gracious, sociable, and generous person, he had many friends both in Scotland and in France. After spending much of his adult life in Paris, Hume died in Edinburgh in 1776. The following passage was originally published in 1738.

SECTION III. OF THE INFLUENCING MOTIVES OF THE WILL

Nothing is more usual in philosophy, and even in common life, than to talk of the combat of passion and reason, to give the preference to reason, and to assert that men are only so far virtuous as they conform themselves to its dictates. Every rational creature, 'tis said, is oblig'd to regulate his actions by reason; and if any other motive or principle challenge the direction of his conduct, he ought to oppose it, 'till it be entirely subdu'd, or at least brought to a conformity with that superior principle. On this method of thinking the greatest part of moral philosophy, ancient and modern, seems to be founded; nor is there an ampler field, as well for metaphysical arguments, as popular declamations, than this suppos'd pre-eminence of reason above passion. The eternity, invariableness, and divine origin of the former have been display'd to the best advantage: The blindness, unconstancy, and deceitfulness of the latter have been as strongly insisted on. In order to shew the fallacy of all this philosophy, I shall endeavour to prove first, that reason alone can never be a motive to any action of the will; and secondly, that it can never oppose passion in the direction of the will.

The understanding exerts itself after two different ways, as it judges from demonstration or probability; as it regards the abstract relations of our ideas, or those relations of objects, of which experience only gives us information. I believe it scarce will be asserted, that the first species of reasoning alone is ever the cause of any action. As its proper province is the world of ideas, and as the will always places us in that of realities, demonstration and volition seem, upon that account, to be totally remov'd, from each other. Mathematics, indeed, are useful in all mechanical operations, and arithmetic in almost every art and profession: But 'tis not of themselves they have any influence. Mechanics are the art of regulating the motions of bodies *to some design'd end or purpose;* and the reason why we employ arithmetic in fixing the proportions of numbers, is only that we may discover the proportions of their influence and operation. A merchant is desirous of knowing the sum total of his accounts with any person: Why? but that he may learn what sum will have the same *effects* in paying his debt, and going to market, as all the particular articles taken together. Abstract or demonstrative reasoning, therefore, never influences any of our actions, but only as it directs our judgment concerning causes and effects; which leads us to the second operation of the understanding.

'Tis obvious, that when we have the prospect of pain or pleasure from any object, we feel a consequent emotion of aversion or propensity, and are carry'd to avoid or embrace what will give us this uneasiness or satisfaction. 'Tis also obvious, that this emotion rests not here, but making us cast our view on every side, comprehends whatever objects are connected with its original one by the relation of cause and effect. Here then reasoning takes place to discover this relation; and according as our reasoning varies, our actions receive a subsequent variation. But 'tis evident in this case, that the impulse arises not from reason, but is only directed by it. 'Tis from the prospect of pain or pleasure that the aversion or propensity arises towards any object: And these emotions extend themselves to the causes and effects of that object, as they are

pointed out to us by reason and experience. It can never in the least concern us to know, that such objects are causes, and such others effects, if both the causes and effects be indifferent to us. Where the objects themselves do not affect us, their connexion can never give them any influence; and 'tis plain, that as reason is nothing but the discovery of this connexion, it cannot be by its means that the objects are able to affect us.

Since reason alone can never produce any action, or give rise to volition, I infer, that the same faculty is as incapable of preventing volition, or of disputing the preference with any passion or emotion. This consequence is necessary. 'Tis impossible reason cou'd have the latter effect of preventing volition, but by giving an impulse in a contrary direction to our passion; and that impulse, had it operated alone, wou'd have been able to produce volition. Nothing can oppose or retard the impulse of passion, but a contrary impulse; and if this contrary impulse ever arises from reason, that latter faculty must have an original influence on the will, and must be able to cause, as well as hinder any act of volition. But if reason has no original influence, 'tis impossible it can withstand any principle, which has such an efficacy, or ever keep the mind in suspence a moment. Thus it appears, that the principle, which opposes our passion, cannot be the same with reason, and is only call'd so in an improper sense. We speak not strictly and philosophically when we talk of the combat of passion and of reason. Reason is, and ought only to be the slave of the passions, and can never pretend to any other office than to serve and obey them. As this opinion may appear somewhat extraordinary, it may not be improper to confirm it by some other considerations.

A passion is an original existence, or, if you will, modification of existence, and contains not any representative quality, which renders it a copy of any other existence or modification. When I am angry, I am actually possest with the passion, and in that emotion have no more a reference to any other object, than when I am thirsty, or sick, or more than five foot high. 'Tis impossible, therefore, that this passion can be oppos'd by, or be contradictory to truth and reason; since this contradiction consists in the disagreement of ideas, consider'd as copies, with those objects, which they represent.

What may at first occur on this head, is, that as nothing can be contrary to truth or reason, except what has a reference to it, and as the judgments of our understanding only have this reference, it must follow, that passions can be contrary to reason only so far as they are *accompany'd* with some judgment or opinion. According to this principle, which is so obvious and natural, 'tis only in two senses, that any affection can be call'd unreasonable. First, When a passion, such as hope or fear, grief or joy, despair or security, is founded on the supposition of the existence of objects, which really do not exist. Secondly, When in exerting any passion in action, we chuse means insufficient for the design'd end, and deceive ourselves in our judgment of causes and effects. Where a passion is neither founded on false suppositions, nor chuses means insufficient for the end, the understanding can neither justify nor condemn it. 'Tis not contrary to reason to prefer the destruction of the whole world to the scratching of my finger. 'Tis not contrary to reason for me to chuse my total ruin, to prevent the least uneasiness of an *Indian* or person wholly unknown to me. 'Tis as little contrary to reason to prefer even my own acknowledg'd lesser good to my greater, and have a more ardent affection for the former than the latter. A trivial good may, from certain circumstances, produce a desire superior to what arises from the greatest and most valuable enjoyment; nor is there any thing more extraordinary in this, than in mechanics to see one pound weight raise up a hundred by the advantage of its situation. In short, a passion must be accompany'd with some false judgment, in order to its being unreasonable; and even then 'tis not the passion, properly speaking, which is unreasonable, but the judgment.

The consequences are evident. Since a passion can never, in any sense, be call'd unreasonable, but when founded on a false supposition, or when it chuses means insufficient for the design'd end, 'tis impossible, that reason and passion can ever oppose each other, or dispute for the government of the will and actions. The moment we perceive the falshood of any supposition, or the insufficiency of any means our passions yield to our reason without any opposition. I may desire any fruit as of an excellent relish; but whenever you convince me of my mistake, my longing ceases. I may will the performance of certain actions as means of obtaining any desir'd good; but as my willing of these actions is only secondary, and founded on the supposition, that they are causes of the propos'd effect; as soon as I discover the falshood of that supposition, they must become indifferent to me.

Those who affirm that virtue is nothing but a conformity to reason; that there are eternal fitnesses and unfitnesses of things, which are the same to every rational being that considers them; that the immutable measures of right and wrong impose an obligation, not only on human creatures, but also on the Deity himself: All these systems concur in the opinion, that morality, like truth, is discern'd merely by ideas, and by their juxta-position and comparison. In order, therefore, to judge of these systems, we need only consider, whether it be possible, from reason alone, to distinguish betwixt moral good and evil, or whether there must concur some other principles to enable us to make that distinction.

If morality had naturally no influence on human passions and actions, 'twere in vain to take such pains to inculcate it; and nothing wou'd be more fruitless than that multitude of rules and precepts, with which all moralists abound. Philosophy is commonly divided into *speculative* and *practical;* and as morality is always comprehended under the latter division, 'tis supposed to influence our passions and actions, and to go beyond the calm and indolent judgments of the understanding. And this is confirm'd by common experience, which informs us, that men are often govern'd by their duties, and are deter'd from some actions by the opinion of injustice, and impell'd to others by that of obligation.

Since morals, therefore, have an influence on the actions and affections, it follows, that they cannot be deriv'd from reason; and that because reason alone, as we have already prov'd, can never have any such influence. Morals excite passions, and produce or prevent actions. Reason of itself is utterly impotent in this particular. The rules of morality, therefore, are not conclusions of our reason.

But can there be any difficulty in proving, that vice and virtue are not matters of fact, whose existence we can infer by reason? Take any action allow'd to be vicious: Wilful murder, for instance. Examine it in all lights, and see if you can find that matter of fact, or real existence, which you call *vice.* In whichever way you take it, you find only certain passions, motives, volitions and thoughts. There is no other matter of fact in the case. The vice entirely escapes you, as long as you consider the object. You never can find it, till you turn your reflexion into your own breast, and find a sentiment of disapprobation, which arises in you, towards this action. Here is a matter of fact; but 'tis the object of feeling, not of reason. It lies in yourself, not in the object. So that when you pronounce any action or character to be vicious, you mean nothing, but that from the constitution of your nature you have a feeling or sentiment of blame from the contemplation of it. Vice and virtue, therefore, may be compar'd to sounds, colours, heat and cold, which, according to modern philosophy, are not qualities in objects, but perceptions in the mind: And this discovery in morals, like that other in physics, is to be regarded as a considerable advancement of the speculative sciences; tho', like that too, it has little or no influence on practice. Nothing can be more real, or concern us more, than our own sentiments of pleasure and uneasiness; and if these be favourable to virtue, and unfavourable to vice, no more can be requisite to the regulation of our conduct and behaviour.

I cannot forbear adding to these reasonings an observation, which may, perhaps, be found of some importance. In every system of morality, which I have hitherto met with, I have always remark'd, that the author proceeds for some time in the ordinary way of reasoning, and establishes the being of a God, or makes observations concerning human affairs; when of a sudden I am surpriz'd to find, that instead of the usual copulations of propositions, *is*, and *is not*, I meet with no proposition that is not connected with an *ought*, or an *ought not*. This change is imperceptible; but is, however, of the last consequence. For as this *ought*, or *ought not*, expresses some new relation or affirmation, 'tis necessary that it shou'd be observ'd and explain'd; and at the same time that a reason should be given, for what seems altogether inconceivable, how this new relation can be a deduction from others, which are entirely different from it. But as authors do not commonly use this precaution, I shall presume to recommend it to the readers; and am persuaded, that this small attention wou'd subvert all the vulgar systems of morality, and let us see, that the distinction of vice and virtue is not founded merely on the relations of objects, nor is perceiv'd by reason.

⇒ THEORY OF MORAL SENTIMENTS ⇒
Adam Smith

Adam Smith (1723–1790) was a close friend of David Hume. Their sentimentalist views have much in common, but the differences between them are very important. In particular, Smith was more interested in the specific nature of the moral sense and in how that sense might yield objective knowledge of ethics. Adam Smith is best known today for his writings on economics, especially *The Wealth of Nations*. However, during his own lifetime, his work in ethics may have been even more famous, and his first writings as well as his early university appointments were in the area of ethics. *Theory of Moral Sentiments*, published in 1759, was a very influential work; the following excerpt is from that book.

PART I
Of the Propriety of Action
Consisting of Three Sections

SECTION I
Of the Sense of Propriety

CHAPTER I
Of Sympathy

1. How selfish soever man may be supposed, there are evidently some principles in his nature, which interest him in the fortune of others, and render their happiness necessary to him, though he derives nothing from it except the pleasure of seeing it. Of this kind is pity or compassion, the emotion which we feel for the misery of others, when we either see it, or are made to conceive it in a very lively manner. That we often derive sorrow from the sorrow of others, is a matter of fact too obvious to require any instances to prove it; for this sentiment, like all the other original passions of human nature, is by no means confined to the virtuous and humane, though they perhaps may feel it with the most exquisite sensibility. The greatest ruffian, the most hardened violator of the laws of society, is not altogether without it.

2. As we have no immediate experience of what other men feel, we can form no idea of the manner in which they are affected, but by conceiving what we ourselves should feel in the like situation. Though our brother is upon the rack, as long as we ourselves are at our ease, our senses will never inform us of what he suffers. They never did, and never can, carry us beyond our own person, and it is by the imagination only that we can form any conception of what are his sensations.

Neither can that faculty help us to this any other way, than by representing to us what would be our own, if we were in his case. It is the impressions of our own senses only, not those of his, which our imaginations copy. By the imagination we place ourselves in his situation, we conceive ourselves enduring all the same torments, we enter as it were into his body, and become in some measure the same person with him, and thence form some idea of his sensations, and even feel something which, though weaker in degree, is not altogether unlike them. His agonies, when they are thus brought home to ourselves, when we have thus adopted and made them our own, begin at last to affect us, and we then tremble and shudder at the thought of what he feels. For as to be in pain or distress of any kind excites the most excessive sorrow, so to conceive or to imagine that we are in it, excites some degree of the same emotion, in proportion to the vivacity or dulness of the conception.

3. That this is the source of our fellow-feeling for the misery of others, that it is by changing places in fancy with the sufferer, that we come either to conceive or to be affected by what he feels, may be demonstrated by many obvious observations, if it should not be thought sufficiently evident of itself. When we see a stroke aimed and just ready to fall upon the leg or arm of another person, we naturally shrink and draw back our own leg or our own arm; and when it does fall, we feel it in some measure, and are hurt by it as well as the sufferer. The mob, when they are gazing at a dancer on the slack rope, naturally writhe and twist and balance their own bodies, as they see him do, and as they feel that they themselves must do if in his situation. Persons of delicate fibres and a weak constitution of body complain, that in looking on the sores and ulcers which are exposed by beggars in the streets, they are apt to feel an itching or uneasy sensation in the correspondent part of their own bodies. The horror which they conceive at the misery of those wretches affects that particular part in themselves more than any other; because that horror arises from conceiving what they themselves would suffer, if they really were the wretches whom they are looking upon, and if that particular part in themselves was actually affected in the same miserable manner. The very force of this conception is sufficient, in their feeble frames, to produce that itching or uneasy sensation complained of. Men of the most robust make, observe that in looking upon sore eyes they often feel a very sensible soreness in their own, which proceeds from the same reason; that organ being in the strongest man more delicate, than any other part of the body is in the weakest.

4. Neither is it those circumstances only, which create pain or sorrow, that call forth our fellow-feeling. Whatever is the passion which arises from any object in the person principally concerned, an analogous emotion springs up, at the thought of his situation, in the breast of every attentive spectator. Our joy for the deliverance of those heroes of tragedy or romance who interest us, is as sincere as our grief for their distress, and our fellow-feeling with their misery is not more real than that with their happiness. We enter into their gratitude towards those faithful friends who did not desert them in their difficulties; and we heartily go along with their resentment against those perfidious traitors who injured, abandoned, or deceived them. In every passion of which the mind of man is susceptible, the emotions of the by-stander always correspond to what, by bringing the case home to himself, he imagines should be the sentiments of the sufferer.

5. Pity and compassion are words appropriated to signify our fellow-feeling with the sorrow of others. Sympathy, though its meaning was, perhaps, originally the same, may now, however, without much impropriety, be made use of to denote our fellow-feeling with any passion whatever.

CHAPTER II

Of the Pleasure of mutual Sympathy

1. But whatever may be the cause of sympathy, or however it may be excited, nothing pleases us more than to observe in other men a fellow-feeling with all the emotions of our own breast; nor are we ever so much shocked as by the appearance of the contrary. Those who are fond of deducing all our sentiments from certain refinements of self-love, think themselves at no loss to account, according to their own principles, both for this pleasure and this pain. Man, say they, conscious of his own weakness, and of the need which he has for the assistance of others, rejoices whenever he observes that they adopt his own passions, because he is then assured of that assistance; and grieves whenever he observes the contrary, because he is then assured of their opposition. But both the pleasure and the pain are always felt so instantaneously, and often upon such frivolous occasions, that it seems evident that neither of them can be derived from any such self-interested consideration. A man is mortified when, after having endeavoured to divert the company, he looks round and sees that nobody laughs at his jests but

himself. On the contrary, the mirth of the company is highly agreeable to him, and he regards this correspondence of their sentiments with his own as the greatest applause.

2. Neither does his pleasure seem to arise altogether from the additional vivacity which his mirth may receive from sympathy with theirs, nor his pain from the disappointment he meets with when he misses this pleasure; though both the one and the other, no doubt, do in some measure. When we have read a book or poem so often that we can no longer find any amusement in reading it by ourselves, we can still take pleasure in reading it to a companion. To him it has all the graces of novelty; we enter into the surprise and admiration which it naturally excites in him, but which it is no longer capable of exciting in us; we consider all the ideas which it presents rather in the light in which they appear to him, than in that in which they appear to ourselves, and we are amused by sympathy with his amusement which thus enlivens our own. On the contrary, we should be vexed if he did not seem to be entertained with it, and we could no longer take any pleasure in reading it to him. It is the same case here. The mirth of the company, no doubt, enlivens our own mirth, and their silence, no doubt, disappoints us. But though this may contribute both to the pleasure which we derive from the one, and to the pain which we feel from the other, it is by no means the sole cause of either; and this correspondence of the sentiments of others with our own appears to be a cause of pleasure, and the want of it a cause of pain, which cannot be accounted for in this manner. The sympathy, which my friends express with my joy, might, indeed, give me pleasure by enlivening that joy: but that which they express with my grief could give me none, if it served only to enliven that grief. Sympathy, however, enlivens joy and alleviates grief. It enlivens joy by presenting another source of satisfaction; and it alleviates grief by insinuating into the heart almost the only agreeable sensation which it is at that time capable of receiving.

CHAPTER III

Of the manner in which we judge of the propriety or impropriety of the affections of other men, by their concord or dissonance with our own

1. When the original passions of the person principally concerned are in perfect concord with the sympathetic emotions of the spectator, they necessarily appear to this last just and proper, and suitable to their objects; and, on the contrary, when, upon bringing the case home to himself, he finds that they do not coincide with what he feels, they necessarily appear to him unjust and improper, and unsuitable to the causes which excite them. To approve of the passions of another, therefore, as suitable to their objects, is the same thing as to observe that we entirely sympathize with them; and not to approve of them as such, is the same thing as to observe that we do not entirely sympathize with them. The man who resents the injuries that have been done to me, and observes that I resent them precisely as he does, necessarily approves of my resentment. The man whose sympathy keeps time to my grief, cannot but admit the reasonableness of my sorrow. He who admires the same poem, or the same picture, and admires them exactly as I do, must surely allow the justness of my admiration. He who laughs at the same joke, and laughs along with me, cannot well deny the propriety of my laughter. On the contrary, the person who, upon these different occasions, either feels no such emotion as that which I feel, or feels none that bears any proportion to mine, cannot avoid disapproving my sentiments on account of their dissonance with his own. If my animosity goes beyond what the indignation of my friend can correspond to; if my grief exceeds what his most tender compassion can go along with; if my admiration is either too high or too low to tally with his own; if I laugh loud and heartily when he only smiles, or, on the contrary, only smile when he laughs loud and heartily; in all these cases, as soon as he comes from considering the object, to observe how I am affected by it, according as there is more or less disproportion between his sentiments and mine, I must incur a greater or less degree of his disapprobation: and upon all occasions his own sentiments are the standards and measures by which he judges of mine.

2. To approve of another man's opinions is to adopt those opinions, and to adopt them is to approve of them. If the same arguments which convince you convince me likewise, I necessarily approve of your conviction; and if they do not, I necessarily disapprove of it: neither can I possibly conceive that I should do the one without the other. To approve or disapprove, therefore, of the opinions of others is acknowledged, by every body, to mean no more than to observe their agreement or disagreement with our own. But this is equally the case with regard to our approbation or disapprobation of the sentiments or passions of others. . . .

PART III

Of the Foundation of our Judgments concerning our own Sentiments and Conduct, and of the Sense of Duty

CHAPTER I

Of the Principle of Self-approbation and of Self-disapprobation

2. . . . The principle by which we naturally either approve or disapprove of our own conduct, seems to be altogether the same with that by which we exercise the like judgments concerning the conduct of other people. We either approve or disapprove of the conduct of another man according as we feel that, when we bring his case home to ourselves, we either can or cannot entirely sympathize with the sentiments and motives which directed it. And, in the same manner, we either approve or disapprove of our own conduct, according as we feel that, when we place ourselves in the situation of another man, and view it, as it were, with his eyes and from his station, we either can or cannot entirely enter into and sympathize with the sentiments and motives which influenced it. We can never survey our own sentiments and motives, we can never form any judgment concerning them; unless we remove ourselves, as it were, from our own natural station, and endeavour to view them as at a certain distance from us. But we can do this in no other way than by endeavouring to view them with the eyes of other people, or as other people are likely to view them. Whatever judgment we can form concerning them, accordingly, must always bear some secret reference, either to what are, or to what, upon a certain condition, would be, or to what, we imagine, ought to be the judgment of others. We endeavour to examine our own conduct as we imagine any other fair and impartial spectator would examine it. If, upon placing ourselves in his situation, we thoroughly enter into all the passions and motives which influenced it, we approve of it, by sympathy with the approbation of this supposed equitable judge. If otherwise, we enter into his disapprobation, and condemn it.

3. Were it possible that a human creature could grow up to manhood in some solitary place, without any communication with his own species, he could no more think of his own character, of the propriety or demerit of his own sentiments and conduct, of the beauty or deformity of his own mind, than of the beauty or deformity of his own face. All these are objects which he

cannot easily see, which naturally he does not look at, and with regard to which he is provided with no mirror which can present them to his view. Bring him into society, and he is immediately provided with the mirror which he wanted before. It is placed in the countenance and behaviour of those he lives with, which always mark when they enter into, and when they disapprove of his sentiments; and it is here that he first views the propriety and impropriety of his own passions, the beauty and deformity of his own mind. To a man who from his birth was a stranger to society, the objects of his passions, the external bodies which either pleased or hurt him, would occupy his whole attention. The passions themselves, the desires or aversions, the joys or sorrows, which those objects excited, though of all things the most immediately present to him, could scarce ever be the objects of his thoughts. The idea of them could never interest him so much as to call upon his attentive consideration. The consideration of his joy could in him excite no new joy, nor that of his sorrow any new sorrow, though the consideration of the causes of those passions might often excite both. Bring him into society, and all his own passions will immediately become the causes of new passions. He will observe that mankind approve of some of them, and are disgusted by others. He will be elevated in the one case, and cast down in the other; his desires and aversions, his joys and sorrows, will now often become the causes of new desires and new aversions, new joys and new sorrows: they will now, therefore, interest him deeply, and often call upon his most attentive consideration. . . .

6. When I endeavour to examine my own conduct, when I endeavour to pass sentence upon it, and either to approve or condemn it, it is evident that, in all such cases, I divide myself, as it were, into two persons; and that I, the examiner and judge, represent a different character from that other I, the person whose conduct is examined into and judged of. The first is the spectator, whose sentiments with regard to my own conduct I endeavour to enter into, by placing myself in his situation, and by considering how it would appear to me, when seen from that particular point of view. The second is the agent, the person whom I properly call myself, and of whose conduct, under the character of a spectator, I was endeavouring to form some opinion. The first is the judge; the second the person judged of. But that the judge should, in every respect, be the same with the person judged of, is as impossible, as that the cause should, in every respect, be the same with the effect.

7. To be amiable and to be meritorious; that is, to deserve love and to deserve reward, are the great characters of virtue; and to be odious and punishable, of vice. But all these characters have an immediate reference to the sentiments of others. Virtue is not said to be amiable, or to be meritorious, because it is the object of its own love, or of its own gratitude; but because it excites those sentiments in other men. The consciousness that it is the object of such favourable regards, is the source of that inward tranquillity and self-satisfaction with which it is naturally attended, as the suspicion of the contrary gives occasion to the torments of vice. What so great happiness as to be beloved, and to know that we deserve to be beloved? What so great misery as to be hated, and to know that we deserve to be hated?

⇒ THE CONSCIENCE OF HUCKLEBERRY FINN ⇒
Jonathan Bennett

Jonathan Bennett (born 1930) taught philosophy at the University of Cambridge, the University of British Columbia, and Syracuse University. He has written important philosophical works in a wide variety of areas, including history of philosophy, logic, philosophy of language, and ethics. The paper reprinted here, "The Conscience of Huckleberry Finn," was originally published in *Philosophy*, Volume 49 (1974): 123–134. It contains wonderful cases, is very readable, and offers a very insightful analysis of the challenges involved in weighing sympathies against moral principles.

In this paper I shall present not just the conscience of Huckleberry Finn but two others as well. One of them is the conscience of Heinrich Himmler. He became a Nazi in 1923; he served drably and quietly, but well, and was rewarded with increasing responsibility and power. At the peak of his career he held many offices and commands, of which the most powerful was that of leader of the S.S.—the principal police force of the Nazi regime. In this capacity, Himmler commanded the whole concentration-camp system, and was responsible for the execution of the so-called 'final solution of the Jewish problem'. It is important for my purposes that this piece of social engineering should be thought of not abstractly but in concrete terms of Jewish families being marched to what they think are bath-houses, to the accompaniment of loud-speaker renditions of extracts from *The Merry Widow* and *Tales of Hoffman*, there to be choked to death by poisonous gases. Altogether, Himmler succeeded in murdering about four and a half million of them, as well as several million gentiles, mainly Poles and Russians.

The other conscience to be discussed is that of the Calvinist theologian and philosopher Jonathan Edwards. He lived in the first half of the eighteenth century, and has a good claim to be considered America's first serious and considerable philosophical thinker. He was for many years a widely-renowned preacher and Congregationalist minister in New England; in 1748 a dispute with his congregation led him to resign (he couldn't accept their view that unbelievers should be admitted to the Lord's Supper in the hope that it would convert them); for some years after that he worked as a missionary, preaching to Indians through an interpreter; then in 1758 he accepted the presidency of what is now Princeton University, and within two months died from a smallpox inoculation. Along the way he wrote some first-rate philosophy: his book attacking the notion of free will is still sometimes read. Why I should be interested in Edwards' conscience will be explained in due course. I shall use Heinrich Himmler, Jonathan Edwards and Huckleberry Finn to illustrate different aspects of a single theme, namely the relationship between *sympathy* on the one hand and *bad morality* on the other.

All that I can mean by a 'bad morality' is a morality whose principles I deeply disapprove of. When I call a morality bad, I cannot prove that mine is better; but when I here call any morality bad, I think you will agree with me that it is bad; and that is all I need. There could be dispute as to whether the springs of someone's actions constitute a morality. I think, though, that we must admit that someone who acts in ways which conflict grossly with our morality may nevertheless have a morality of his own—a set of principles of action which he sincerely assents to, so that for him the problem of acting well or rightly or in obedience to conscience is the problem of conforming to those principles. The problem of conscientiousness can arise as acutely for a bad morality as for any other: rotten principles may be as difficult to keep as decent ones. As for 'sympathy': I use this term to cover every sort of fellow-feeling, as when one feels pity over someone's loneliness, or horrified compassion over his pain, or when one feels a shrinking reluctance to act in a way which will bring misfortune to someone else. These feelings must not be confused with moral judgments. My sympathy for someone in distress may lead me to help him, or even to think that I ought to help him; but in itself it is not a judgment about what I ought to do but just a feeling for him in his plight. We shall get some light on the difference between feelings and moral judgments when we consider Huckleberry Finn.

Obviously, feelings can impel one to action, and so can moral judgments; and in a particular case sympathy and morality may push in opposite directions. This can happen not just with bad moralities, but also with good ones like yours and mine. For example, a small child, sick and miserable, clings tightly to his mother and screams in terror when she tries to pass him over to the doctor to be examined. If the mother gave way to her sympathy, that is to her feeling for the child's misery and fright, she would hold it close and not let the doctor come near; but don't we agree that it might be wrong for her to act on such a feeling? Quite generally, then, anyone's moral principles may apply to a particular situation in a way which runs contrary to the particular thrusts of fellow-feeling that he has in that situation. My immediate concern is with sympathy in relation to bad morality, but not because such conflicts occur only when the morality is bad.

Now, suppose that someone who accepts a bad morality is struggling to make himself act in accordance with it in a particular situation where his sympathies pull him another way. He sees the struggle as one between doing the right, conscientious thing, and acting wrongly and weakly, like the mother who won't let the doctor come near her sick, frightened baby. Since we don't accept this person's morality, we may see the situation very differently, thoroughly disapproving of the action he regards as the right one, and endorsing the action which from his point of view constitutes weakness and backsliding. Conflicts between sympathy and bad morality won't always be like this, for we won't disagree with every single dictate of a bad morality. Still, it can happen in the way I have described, with the agent's right action being our wrong one, and vice versa. That is just what happens in a certain episode in chapter 16 of *The Adventures of Huckleberry Finn*, an episode which brilliantly illustrates how fiction can be instructive about real life. Huck Finn has been helping his slave friend Jim to run away from Miss Watson, who is Jim's owner. In their raft-journey down the Mississippi River, they are near

to the place at which Jim will become legally free. Now let Huck take over the story:

> Jim said it made him all over trembly and feverish to be so close to freedom. Well, I can tell you it made me all over trembly and feverish, too, to hear him because I begun to get it through my head that he was most free—and who was to blame for it? Why, me. I couldn't get that out of my conscience, no how nor no way. . . . It hadn't ever come home to me, before, what this thing was that I was doing. But now it did and it stayed with me, and scorched me more and more. I tried to make out to myself that I warn't to blame, because I didn't run Jim off from his rightful owner; but it warn't no use, conscience up and say, every time: 'But you knowed he was running for his freedom, and you could a paddled ashore and told somebody.' That was so—I couldn't get around that, no way. That was where it pinched. Conscience says to me: 'What had poor Miss Watson done to you, that you could see her nigger go off right under your eyes and never say one single word? What did that poor old woman do to you, that you could treat her so mean? . . . ' I got to feeling so mean and so miserable I most wished I was dead.

Jim speaks of his plan to save up to buy his wife, and then his children, out of slavery; and he adds that if the children cannot be bought he will arrange to steal them. Huck is horrified:

> Thinks I, this is what comes of my not thinking. Here was this nigger which I had as good as helped to run away, coming right out flat-footed and saying he would steal his children—children that belonged to a man I didn't even know; a man that hadn't ever done me no harm. I was sorry to hear Jim say that, it was such a lowering of him. My conscience got to stirring me up hotter than ever, until at last I says to it: 'Let up on me—it ain't too late, yet—I'll paddle ashore at first light, and tell.' I felt easy, and happy, and light as a feather, right off. All my troubles was gone.

This is bad morality all right. In his earliest years Huck wasn't taught any principles, and the only ones he has encountered since then are those of rural Missouri, in which slave-owning is just one kind of ownership and is not subject to critical pressure. It hasn't occurred to Huck to question those principles. So the action, to us abhorrent, of turning Jim in to the authorities presents itself clearly to Huck as the right thing to do.

For us, morality and sympathy would both dictate helping Jim to escape. If we felt any conflict, it would have both these on one side and something else on the other—greed for a reward, or fear of punishment. But Huck's morality conflicts with his sympathy, that is, with his unargued, natural feeling for his friend. The conflict starts when Huck sets off in the canoe towards the shore, pretending that he is going to reconnoitre, but really planning to turn Jim in:

> As I shoved off, [Jim] says: 'Pooty soon I'll be a-shout'n for joy, en I'll say, it's all on accounts o' Huck I's a free man . . . Jim won't ever forgit you, Huck; you's de bes' fren' Jim ever had; en you's de only fren' old Jim's got now.'
>
> I was paddling off, all in a sweat to tell on him; but when he says this, it seemed to kind of take the tuck all out of me. I went along slow then, and I warn't right down certain whether I was glad I started or whether I warn't. When I was fifty yards off, Jim says: 'Dah you goes, de ole true Huck; de on'y white genlman dat ever kep' his promise to ole Jim.' Well, I just feJt sick. But I says, I got to do it—I can't get out of it.

In the upshot, sympathy wins over morality. Huck hasn't the strength of will to do what he sincerely thinks he ought to do. Two men hunting for runaway slaves ask him whether the man on his raft is black or white:

> I didn't answer up prompt. I tried to, but the words wouldn't come. I tried, for a second or two, to brace up and out with it, but I warn't man enough—hadn't the spunk of a rabbit. I see I was weakening; so I just give up trying, and up and says: 'He's white.'

So Huck enables Jim to escape, thus acting weakly and wickedly—he thinks. In this conflict between sympathy and morality, sympathy wins.

One critic has cited this episode in support of the statement that Huck suffers 'excruciating moments of wavering between honesty and respectability'. That is hopelessly wrong, and I agree with the perceptive comment on it by another critic, who says:

> The conflict waged in Huck is much more serious: he scarcely cares for respectability and never hesitates to relinquish it, but he does care for honesty and gratitude—and both honesty and gratitude require that he should give Jim up. It is not, in Huck, honesty at war with respectability but love and compassion for Jim struggling against his

conscience. His decision is for Jim and hell; a right decision made in the mental chains that Huck never breaks. His concern for Jim is and remains irrational. Huck finds many reasons for giving Jim up and none for stealing him. To the end Huck sees his compassion for Jim as a weak, ignorant, and wicked felony.

That is precisely correct—and it can have that virtue only because Mark Twain wrote the episode with such unerring precision. The crucial point concerns reasons, which all occur on one side of the conflict. On the side of conscience we have principles, arguments, considerations, ways of looking at things:

> 'It hadn't ever come home to me before what I was doing'
> 'I tried to make out that I warn't to blame'
> 'Conscience said "But you knowed . . . "—I couldn't get around that'
> 'What had poor Miss Watson done to you?'
> 'This is what comes of my not thinking
> '. . . children that belonged to a man I didn't even know'.

On the other side, the side of feeling, we get nothing like that. When Jim rejoices in Huck, as his only friend, Huck doesn't consider the claims of friendship or have the situation 'come home' to him in a different light. All that happens is: 'When he says this, it seemed to kind of take the tuck all out of me. I went along slow then, and I warn't right down certain whether I was glad I started or whether I warn't.' Again, Jim's words about Huck's 'promise' to him don't give Huck any reason for changing his plan: in his morality promises to slaves probably don't count. Their effect on him is of a different kind: 'Well, I just felt sick.' And when the moment for final decision comes, Huck doesn't weigh up pros and cons: he simply *fails* to do what he believes to be right—he isn't strong enough, hasn't 'the spunk of a rabbit'. This passage in the novel is notable not just for its finely wrought irony, with Huck's weakness of will leading him to do the right thing, but also for its masterly handling of the difference between general moral principles and particular unreasoned emotional pulls.

Consider now another case of bad morality in conflict with human sympathy, the case of the odious Himmler. Here, from a speech he made to some S.S. generals, is an indication of the content of his morality:

> What happens to a Russian, to a Czech, does not interest me in the slightest. What the nations can offer in the way of good blood of our type, we will

take, if necessary by kidnapping their children and raising them here with us. Whether nations live in prosperity or starve to death like cattle interests me only in so far as we need them as slaves to our *Kultur*; otherwise it is of no interest to me. Whether 10,000 Russian females fall down from exhaustion while digging an antitank ditch interests me only in so far as the antitank ditch for Germany is finished.

But has this a moral basis at all? And if it has, was there in Himmler's own mind any conflict between morality and sympathy? Yes there was. Here is more from the same speech:

> . . . I also want to talk to you quite frankly on a very grave matter . . . I mean . . . the extermination of the Jewish race. . . . Most of you must know what it means when 100 corpses are lying side by side, or 500, or 1,000. To have stuck it out and at the same time—apart from exceptions caused by human weakness—to have remained decent fellows, that is what has made us hard. This is a page of glory in our history which has never been written and is never to be written.

Himmler saw his policies as being hard to implement while still retaining one's human sympathies—while still remaining a 'decent fellow'. He is saying that only the weak take the easy way out and just squelch their sympathies, and is praising the stronger and more glorious course of retaining one's sympathies while acting in violation of them. In the same spirit, he ordered that when executions were carried out in concentration camps, those responsible 'are to be influenced in such a way as to suffer no ill effect in their character and mental attitude'. A year later he boasted that the S.S. had wiped out the Jews

> without our leaders and their men suffering any damage in their minds and souls. The danger was considerable, for there was only a narrow path between the Scylla of their becoming heartless ruffians unable any longer to treasure life, and the Charybdis of their becoming soft and suffering nervous breakdowns.

And there really can't be any doubt that the basis of Himmler's policies was a set of principles which constituted his morality—a sick, bad, wicked morality. He described himself as caught in 'the old tragic conflict between will and obligation'. And when his physician Kersten protested at the intention to destroy the Jews, saying that the suffering involved

was 'not to be contemplated', Kersten reports that Himmler replied:

> He knew that it would mean much suffering for the Jews. . . . 'It is the curse of greatness that it must step over dead bodies to create new life. Yet we must . . . cleanse the soil or it will never bear fruit. It will be a great burden for me to bear.'

This, I submit, is the language of morality.

So in this case, tragically, bad morality won out over sympathy. I am sure that many of Himmler's killers did extinguish their sympathies, becoming 'heartless ruffians' rather than 'decent fellows'; but not Himmler himself. Although his policies ran against the human grain to a horrible degree, he did not sandpaper down his emotional surfaces so that there was no grain there, allowing his actions to slide along smoothly and easily. He did, after all, bear his hideous burden, and even paid a price for it. He suffered a variety of nervous and physical disabilities, including nausea and stomach-convulsions, and Kersten was doubtless right in saying that these were 'the expression of a psychic division which extended over his whole life'.

This same division must have been present in some of those officials of the Church who ordered heretics to be tortured so as to change their theological opinions. Along with the brutes and the cold careerists, there must have been some who cared, and who suffered from the conflict between their sympathies and their bad morality.

In the conflict between sympathy and bad morality, then, the victory may go to sympathy as in the case of Huck Finn, or to morality as in the case of Himmler.

Another possibility is that the conflict may be avoided by giving up, or not ever having, those sympathies which might interfere with one's principles. That seems to have been the case with Jonathan Edwards. I am afraid that I shall be doing an injustice to Edwards' many virtues, and to his great intellectual energy and inventiveness; for my concern is only with the worst thing about him—namely his morality, which was worse than Himmler's. According to Edwards, God condemns some men to an eternity of unimaginably awful pain, though he arbitrarily spares others—'arbitrarily' because none deserve to be spared:

> Natural men are held in the hand of God over the pit of hell; they have deserved the fiery pit, and are already sentenced to it; and God is dreadfully

provoked, his anger is as great towards them as to those that are actually suffering the executions of the fierceness of his wrath in hell . . . ; the devil is waiting for them, hell is gaping for them, the flames gather and flash about them, and would fain lay hold on them . . . ; and . . . there are no means within reach that can be any security to them. . . . All that preserves them is the mere arbitrary will, and uncovenanted unobliged forbearance of an incensed God.

Notice that he says 'they have deserved the fiery pit.' Edwards insists that men *ought* to be condemned to eternal pain; and his position isn't that this is right because God wants it, but rather that God wants it because it is right. For him, moral standards exist independently of God, and God can be assessed in the light of them (and of course found to be perfect). For example, he says:

They deserve to be cast into hell; so that . . . justice never stands in the way, it makes no objection against God's using his power at any moment to destroy them. Yea, on the contrary, justice calls aloud for an infinite punishment of their sins.

Elsewhere, he gives elaborate arguments to show that God is acting justly in damning sinners. For example, he argues that a punishment should be exactly as bad as the crime being punished: God is infinitely excellent; so any crime against him is infinitely bad; and so eternal damnation is exactly right as a punishment—it is infinite, but, as Edwards is careful also to say, it is 'no more than infinite.'

Of course, Edwards himself didn't torment the damned; but the question still arises of whether his sympathies didn't conflict with his *approval* of eternal torment. Didn't he find it painful to contemplate any fellow-human's being tortured for ever? Apparently not:

The God that holds you over the pit of hell, much as one holds a spider or some loathsome insect over the fire, abhors you, and is dreadfully provoked; . . . he is of purer eyes than to bear to have you in his sight; you are ten thousand times so abominable in his eyes as the most hateful venomous serpent is in ours.

When God is presented as being as misanthropic as that, one suspects misanthropy in the theologian. This suspicion is increased when Edwards claims that 'the saints in glory will . . . understand how terrible the sufferings of the damned are; yet . . . will not be sorry for

[them].' He bases this partly on a view of human nature whose ugliness he seems not to notice:

The seeing of the calamities of others tends to heighten the sense of our own enjoyments. When the saints in glory, therefore, shall see the doleful state of the damned, how will this heighten their sense of the blessedness of their own state. . . . When they shall see how miserable others of their fellow-creatures are . . . ; when they shall see the smoke of their torment, . . . and hear their dolorous shrieks and cries, and consider that they in the mean time are in the most blissful state, and shall surely be in it to all eternity; how they will rejoice!

I hope this is less than the whole truth! His other main point about why the saints will rejoice to see the torments of the damned is that it is *right* that they should do so:

The heavenly inhabitants . . . will have no love nor pity to the damned. . . . [This will not show] a want of a spirit of love in them . . . ; for the heavenly inhabitants will know that it is not fit that they should love [the damned] because they will know then, that God has no love to them, nor pity for them.

The implication that of course one can adjust one's feelings of pity so that they conform to the dictates of some authority—doesn't this suggest that ordinary human sympathies played only a small part in Edwards' life?

Huck Finn, whose sympathies are wide and deep, could never avoid the conflict in that way; but he is determined to avoid it, and so he opts for the only other alternative he can see—to give up morality altogether. After he has tricked the slave-hunters, he returns to the raft and undergoes a peculiar crisis:

I got aboard the raft, feeling bad and low, because I knowed very well I had done wrong, and I see it warn't no use for me to try to learn to do right; a body that don't get started right when he's little, ain't got no show—when the pinch comes there ain't nothing to back him up and keep him to his work, and so he gets beat. Then I thought a minute, and says to myself, hold on—s'pose you'd a done right and give Jim up; would you feel better than what you do now? No, says I, I'd feel bad— I'd feel just the same way I do now. Well, then, says I, what's the use you learning to do right, when it's troublesome to do right and ain't no trouble to do wrong, and the wages is just the same? I was stuck.

I couldn't answer that. So I reckoned I wouldn't bother no more about it, but after this always do whichever come handiest at the time.

Huck clearly cannot conceive of having any morality except the one he has learned—too late, he thinks—from his society. He is not entirely a prisoner of that morality, because he does after all reject it; but for him that is a decision to relinquish morality as such; he cannot envisage revising his morality, altering its content in face of the various pressures to which it is subject, including pressures from his sympathies. For example, he does not begin to approach the thought that slavery should be rejected on moral grounds, or the thought that what he is doing is not theft because a person cannot be owned and therefore cannot be stolen.

The basic trouble is that he cannot or will not engage in abstract intellectual operations of any sort. In chapter 33 he finds himself 'feeling to blame, somehow' for something he knows he had no hand in; he assumes that this feeling is a deliverance of conscience; and this confirms him in his belief that conscience shouldn't be listened to:

> It don't make no difference whether you do right or wrong, a person's conscience ain't got no sense, and just goes for him anyway. If I had a yaller dog that didn't know no more than a person's conscience does, I would pison him. It takes up more room than all the rest of a person's insides, and yet ain't no good, nohow.

That brisk, incurious dismissiveness fits well with the comprehensive rejection of morality back on the raft. But this is a digression.

On the raft, Huck decides not to live by principles, but just to do whatever 'comes handiest at the time'—always acting according to the mood of the moment. Since the morality he is rejecting is narrow and cruel, and his sympathies are broad and kind, the results will be good. But moral principles are good to have, because they help to protect one from acting badly at moments when one's sympathies happen to be in abeyance. On the highest possible estimate of the role one's sympathies should have, one can still allow for principles as embodiments of one's best feelings, one's broadest and keenest sympathies. On that view, principles can help one across intervals when one's feelings are at less than their best, i.e. through periods of misanthropy or meanness or self-centredness or depression or anger.

What Huck didn't see is that one can live by principles and yet have ultimate control over their content.

And one way such control can be exercised is by checking of one's principles in the light of one's sympathies. This is sometimes a pretty straightforward matter. It can happen that a certain moral principle becomes untenable—meaning literally that one cannot hold it any longer—because it conflicts intolerably with the pity or revulsion or whatever that one feels when one sees what the principle leads to. One's experience may play a large part here: experiences evoke feelings, and feelings force one to modify principles. Something like this happened to the English poet Wilfred Owen, whose experiences in the First World War transformed him from an enthusiastic soldier into a virtual pacifist. I can't document his change of conscience in detail; but I want to present something which he wrote about the way experience can put pressure on morality.

The Latin poet Horace wrote that it is sweet and fitting (or right) to die for one's country—*dulce et decorum est pro patria mori*—and Owen wrote a fine poem about how experience could lead one to relinquish that particular moral principle. He describes a man who is too slow donning his gas mask during a gas attack—'As under a green sea, I saw him drowning,' Owen says. The poem ends like this:

> In all my dreams, before my helpless sight
> He plunges at me, guttering, choking, drowning.
> If in some smothering dreams you too could pace
> Behind the wagon that we flung him in,
> And watch the white eyes writhing in his face,
> His hanging face, like a devil's sick of sin;
> If you could hear, at every jolt, the blood
> Come gargling from the froth-corrupted lungs,
> Obscene as cancer, bitter as the cud
> Of vile, incurable sores on innocent tongues,
> My friend, you would not tell with such high zest
> To children ardent for some desperate glory,
> The old Lie: Dulce et decorum est
> Pro patria mori.

There is a difficulty about drawing from all this a moral for ourselves. I imagine that we agree in our rejection of slavery, eternal damnation, genocide, and uncritical patriotic self-abnegation; so we shall agree that Huck Finn, Jonathan Edwards, Heinrich Himmler, and the poet Horace would all have done well to bring certain of their principles under severe pressure from ordinary human sympathies. But then we can say this because we can say that all those are bad moralities, whereas we cannot look at our own moralities and declare them bad. This is not arrogance: it is obviously incoherent for someone to declare the system of moral principles that he accepts to be *bad,* just as one cannot coherently say of anything that one believes it but it is *false.*

Still, although I can't point to any of my beliefs and say 'That is false', I don't doubt that some of my beliefs are false; and so I should try to remain open to correction. Similarly, I accept every single item in my morality—that is inevitable—but I am sure that my morality could be improved, which is to say that it could undergo changes which I should be glad of once I had made them. So I must try to keep my morality open to revision, exposing it to whatever valid pressures there are—including pressures from my sympathies.

I don't give my sympathies a blank cheque in advance. In a conflict between principle and sympathy, principles ought sometimes to win. For example, I think it was right to take part in the Second World War on the Allied side; there were many ghastly individual incidents which might have led someone to doubt the rightness of his participation in that war; and I think it would have been right for such a person to keep his sympathies in a subordinate place on those occasions, not allowing them to modify his principles in such a way as to make a pacifist of him. Still, one's sympathies should be kept as sharp and sensitive and aware as possible, and not only because they can sometimes affect one's principles or one's conduct or both. Owen, at any rate, says that feelings and sympathies are vital even when they can do nothing but bring pain and distress. In another poem he speaks of the blessings of being numb in one's feelings: 'Happy are the men who yet before they are killed / Can let their veins run cold', he says. These are the ones who do not suffer from any compassion which, as Owen puts it, 'makes their feet / Sore on the alleys cobbled with their brothers'. He contrasts these 'happy' ones, who 'lose imagination', with himself and others 'who with a thought besmirch / Blood over all our soul.' Yet the poem's verdict goes against the 'happy' ones. Owen does not say that they will act worse than the others whose souls are besmirched with blood because of their keen awareness of human suffering. He merely says that they are the losers because they have cut themselves off from the human condition:

By choice they made themselves immune
To pity and whatever moans in man
Before the last sea and the hapless stars;
Whatever mourns when many leave these shores;
Whatever shares
The eternal reciprocity of tears.

EXERCISES

1. Suppose we find that some of our most basic and common moral "intuitions" can be traced deep into our evolutionary history: our history as weak and vulnerable primates who must live in close social groups for protection from fierce predators. If we made such a discovery, would that *weaken* or *strengthen* (or have no effect on) the claim that our intuitions are sources of genuine objective knowledge about moral truths?

2. You are facing a moral quandary, and you want advice. You must choose either of two advisors, but not both. One is Brenda, who is a very clear and careful thinker, but whose feelings and affections seem limited (you sometimes have the impression that she really cares about no one except herself). The other possible source of advice is Brandon: warm and caring, but he quickly becomes muddled when trying to think carefully. Whom would you choose as your moral advisor? Why?

3. If we don't want to make ethical decisions by consulting our feelings of pleasure and pain, and you aren't sure that intuitive feelings are the gold standard of ethical truth, is there any role left for our feelings in ethics? Or should feelings be subjugated by reason, held in check, mistrusted as irrational and misleading distractions from the true moral path?

4. You are a hospital patient, and you have your choice of physicians, both of whom are superbly qualified medical professionals. One is dedicated Dekisha; the other is joyous Christina. Whom would you choose? Does your choice have any relevance for the question of which one is "morally better"?

5. As we discussed in the opening chapter, one basic difference in ethical views is between *transcendent* ethical theories (ethical principles are fixed and absolute and universal) and *contingent* theories (ethics is simply part of our changing natural lives). Intuitionists (like Ross) are generally in the transcendent camp, while those (like Hume) who emphasize feelings usually favor contingent ethics. Does that basic difference in perspectives explain the difference between intuitionists and feelings theorists? That is, do intuitionists and feelings theorists have the *same* experience, but just *interpret* it differently?

6. Plato believed that if you genuinely *know* what is good, then you will do it; that is, all morally bad acts are the product of ignorance of moral truth. Some think that Plato's claim is too strong, but still hold that if you *know*

what is good, then that must involve at least some motive for *doing* what is good or *pursuing* the good; that is, they would say that you cannot *consistently* believe that it is good to help your friends when they are in distress and yet have no inclination whatsoever to aid your distressed friends. *Does* knowing what you ought to do, *knowing* what is right and good, necessarily supply some motivation for action? Can I *genuinely* believe that honesty is good and yet have *no* inclination toward honesty?

7. You have very reliable information that a gang of terrorists is hiding in a small town in New Hampshire (don't worry about *how* you know this; you just know it). These terrorists are masters of secrecy and disguise, and you have no way of discovering who they are, and no way of isolating the town to make sure they do not leave. The gang is planning to release a poison gas that will kill thousands of people in a midwestern city. The *only* way to prevent this attack is to carpet bomb the small New Hampshire town, killing not only the terrorists, but also several hundred innocent people who have no idea there are terrorists in their midst. Would you be morally justified in bombing the town?

   Do you have your answer? Good. I don't want to know what your answer is; keep it to yourself. Instead, look carefully at *how* you reached your answer. Were you guided by reason? Feelings? Both? Or what?

8. You are a member of the university chamber orchestra, which is on a weeklong spring concert tour through several southern cities. One of your friends, J, is not along on the tour. J is not your dearest friend in the world, but is certainly a good friend. J's lover—K—is along on the tour. J and K have been lovers for over a year, and it seems to be a serious relationship; you wouldn't be surprised if they marry next year after they graduate. You and K both play viola in the chamber orchestra, and you've spent a lot of time together on this trip. It's spring, the birds are singing, the bees are buzzing, and after a long cold winter it's great to be soaking up the warmth in the sunny South. As the week wears on, you realize you have become strongly attracted to K, and K apparently feels a reciprocal attraction. You have a private room at the hotel where you are staying, and if you ordered a bottle of champagne and invited K up to your room to watch a movie— well, the outcome is not difficult to imagine. Both you and K are very discreet, and it's unlikely J would learn about it. Would it be *wrong* to have a fling with K?

   Got your answer? Again, I don't want to know what it is. Instead, think again about *how* you reached your answer: through reason, feelings, or what?

   Now *compare* the *process* you followed for answering Questions 7 and 8. Did you follow the same process in both cases? Or did you use different methods? Did your feelings play a larger role in one case than in the other?

   Suppose someone says: "The first type of case must be answered using reason; but the *second* case is better handled through feelings." Would that make sense? Or do all ethical decisions require the same *type* of process (if feelings are important for one ethical question, then must they be important for *all* ethical questions)?

9. If you want to work in the wine industry, you must learn to recognize the delicate nuances and subtle tastes of a variety of wines, and be able to distinguish different qualities of wine; that is, you may need to improve your skills at wine tasting. There are schools for that: if you take the right classes, and work hard at it, you can learn to detect the differences among various types of wine, learn to distinguish between really good wines of each variety and mediocre ones, and learn to detect the many subtle delicate flavors that a very good wine might possess. It takes practice, and hard work, but with the right training you could become very skilled at wine tasting: your sense of taste could become much more perceptive, and you could become much better at distinguishing really good wine from mediocre wine.

   On the sentimentalist view, is there something *analogous* for the moral sentiments? That is, does it make sense to speak of *educating* your moral sentiments so that you detect subtle differences of moral feeling that others might miss? *If* educating the moral sentiments does make sense, then would a proper moral education (according to the sentimentalist) look something like an education in wine tasting?

10. Suppose that you accept the sentimentalist position in ethics; how would that influence your efforts to raise your children to be morally upstanding adults? What kinds of "moral education" or "moral training" would you think essential for the moral development of your children? Or would the sentimentalist regard any efforts at moral education as useless?

11. Every year, thousands of people visit Arches National Park, in Utah; and they stand in awe of the amazing rock structures and the desolate beauty of the deep canyons and sheer cliffs. Three centuries ago, most Europeans would have had a very different reaction: They would have gazed upon a desolate scene of disorder and chaos; rather than a sense of magnificent austere beauty, they would have viewed the scene with disgust, eager to return as swiftly as possible to civilization and its order and regularity: "A proper

English formal garden, with every shrub and flower precisely ordered: now *that* is beautiful; not this wild desolate disorder of rocks and cliffs." So if you find the Utah canyons and cliffs and deserts beautiful, you have a very *different* sense of beauty than that of seventeenth-century Europeans. If that is the case (and if the aesthetic sense is analogous to the moral sense/feeling, as sentimentalists sometimes claim), does that pose a challenge for the sentimentalist view?

12. If there were *no one* capable of appreciating the beauty of a rainbow, would a rainbow still be beautiful? If there were *no one* capable of sensing the goodness of benevolent acts, would benevolent acts still be good?

13. Is loyalty to moral principles a virtue? For example, if we say that Joe has *never wavered* in his commitment to the moral principles he believes in, is that loyalty to his own moral principles *in itself* a virtue? (Racism is surely a morally bad moral view; but is a wishy-washy racist worse than a steadfast racist?)

14. "Acting morally is like swinging a golf club. When it seems easy and natural and comfortable, then you know you have it right." Is that true?

15. "Anyone who genuinely and completely *understands* what is right and what is wrong would never be tempted to do wrong." Is that true?

ADDITIONAL READING

David Hume has two classic works on ethics and emotions (though both works also contain much more). The first is *A Treatise of Human Nature*, originally published in 1738. A good edition is by L. A. Selby-Bigge (Oxford: Clarendon Press, 1978). The second is *An Inquiry Concerning Human Understanding*, originally published in 1751. A good edition is L. A. Selby-Bigge's, *Hume's Enquiries*, 2nd ed. (Oxford: Clarendon Press, 1902).

Kai Nielsen, *Why Be Moral?* (Buffalo, NY: Prometheus Books, 1989) is a very readable defense of nonobjectivist ethics based in emotions.

Mencius was an ancient Confucianist philosopher whose writings promote a very early version of the moral sense theory; see *The Book of Mencius*. Sentimentalism was a major ethical theory in the seventeenth and eighteenth centuries; among its major advocates were Lord Shaftesbury (Anthony Ashley Cooper), in *An Inquiry Concerning Virtue, or Merit*; Francis Hutcheson, in *An Inquiry into the Original of Our Ideas of Beauty and Virtue* and *An Essay on the Nature and Conduct of the Passions and Affections, with Illustrations upon the Moral Sense*; David Hume, in *An Enquiry Concerning the Principles of Morals*; and Adam Smith, *Theory of Moral Sentiments*. Among contemporary advocates of various forms of sentimentalism are Simon Blackburn, in *Spreading the Word* (Oxford: Clarendon Press, 1984), *Essays in Quasi-Realism* (New York: Oxford University Press, 1993), and *Ruling Passions* (New York: Oxford University Press, 1998); Allan Gibbard, in *Wise Choices, Apt Feelings* (Cambridge, MA: Harvard University Press, 1990); and Elizabeth Anderson, *Values in Ethics and Economics* (Cambridge, MA: Harvard University Press, 1993). A good examination of contemporary sentimentalism, and the challenges it faces, can be found in Justin D'Arms and Daniel Jacobson, "Sentiment and Value," *Ethics*, Volume 110 (2000): 722–748.

Among the most important and influential intuitionist writings are G. E. Moore, *Principia Ethica* (New York: Cambridge University Press, 1959); H. A. Prichard, *Moral Obligation* (Oxford: Clarendon Press, 1949); W. D. Ross, *The Right and the Good* (Oxford: Clarendon Press, 1930); W. D. Ross, *Foundations of Ethics* (Oxford: Clarendon Press, 1939); and D. D. Raphael, *The Moral Sense* (London: Oxford University Press, 1957).

Though most intuitionists insist that our genuine intuitions give us *certainty*, Brad Hooker—*Ideal Code, Real World* (Oxford: Oxford University Press, 2000)—has developed a somewhat more modest intuitionist account. Hooker does not regard our intuitive moral convictions as "self-evident" fixed certainties, but he does emphasize the importance of "independently credible" moral beliefs for our reflective development of a system of ethics.

Philip Stratton-Lake has edited an excellent anthology of contemporary work (both pro and con) on intuitionism: *Ethical Intuitionism: Re-evaluations* (Oxford: Oxford University Press, 2002).

NOTES

[1]*The Book of Mencius,* from *A Source Book in Chinese Philosophy,* trans. and comp. by Wing-Tsit Chan (Princeton, NJ: Princeton University Press, 1963), p. 55. Written *c.*350 BCE.

[2]For more detailed discussion of this case, see Jonathan Bennett's superb article, "The Conscience of Huckleberry Finn," *Philosophy,* Volume 49 (1974), 123–134.

[3]David Hume, *A Treatise on Human Nature,* L. A. Selby-Bigge, editor (Clarendon Press: Oxford, 1988), p. 416. First published in 1738.

[4]Hume, p. 414.

[5]W. D. Ross, *The Right and the Good* (Oxford: Clarendon Press, 1930), p. 33.

[6]Ross, pp. 46–47.

4

Ethics and Reason

REASONING ABOUT ETHICS

If you are seeking the surest path to sound moral behavior, you might well decide that *reason* is your best guide. If you favor reason as the right guide to ethics, you are in good company. Throughout the history of ethics, stretching back well over two millennia to Plato and Aristotle in ancient Athens, most philosophers have insisted that careful thought and judicious reasoning are the proper foundation of ethics. Plato believed we know moral truths through the powers of pure reason. Our sensory observations are subject to error and illusion, but the wisdom we acquire through rigorous exercise of reason gives us eternal, unchanging, indubitable truth. Plato compared our situation to that of people in a dark cave. We are trapped on the ledge of a deep cavern, and from our narrow ledge we see only the opposite wall of the cave. Below us there is a fire burning, and someone is holding objects in front of the fire, but all we observe are the flickering shadows on the cave wall. Because we are entrapped and have no other experiences, we take the flickering shadows to be true reality. But if we can escape this world of the senses, and climb out of the cave to the true sunlight of reason, we will recognize how limited and deceptive our early sensory experience was: we were only seeing shadows of objects reflected in firelight, not the true nature of things seen by the light of day, that is, by the light of *reason*. Plato counsels us to abandon the shadowy senses and flickering feelings, and seek instead the wisdom that is revealed only by the bright light of reason. But acquiring that wisdom requires great discipline. In particular, all our desires and passions must be held in tight check, and ruled by our reason.

Reason and Emotions

You may have some doubts about the perfect reliability of reason, but if you are choosing whether to entrust your ethical decisions to your reason or your emotions, most philosophers have believed that reason wins. There are just too many cases where our emotions have led us astray. That emotional decision to buy the flashy new car busted my budget, and the damned thing is always in the shop: I wish I had thought more carefully, and bought a less expensive and more reliable model. My emotions tempt me toward a lunch of chocolate chip cookies washed down with beer, but my reason tells me I'll gain weight, raise my cholesterol, move more slowly when I play tennis, and will be in lousy shape to study for my history exam—a green salad will be a healthier and happier choice. And my emotions send me careening into passionate love affairs that my reason—and my friends—recognize as perfectly disastrous. In his lovely seduction poem, e. e. cummings counsels that "Wholly to be a fool when spring is in the world my blood approves, and kisses are a better fate than wisdom." Sounds good. But reason wisely counsels to think twice before jumping at his offer. At the very least, don't be *wholly* a fool: make sure you have some condoms handy.

So our emotions don't have a great track record as a reliable guide. Besides, for ethical guidance we want something with a bit of constancy and steadiness, and our emotions don't meet that standard. You fall madly in love, and a week later, as the song says, "your perfect lover just looks like a perfect fool." Engineering looked like a fine major—you get to carry a calculator, and you'd look great in one of those hard hats—but reason would have reminded you that you hate math and flunked all your high school science courses. Our emotions don't hold a steady course. Worst of all, they don't set a *reliable* course. Reason seems a better choice for an ethical compass.

Reasoning About an Ethical Issue

Reason may seem a more reliable guide than emotions, but some object that reason simply doesn't apply to ethics. We can reason about math, economic theory, how to build a safe and sturdy bridge across the Hudson River, and how to find a cure for cancer, but ethics is not a subject where we can effectively use reason. That objection raises some large issues about ethics, and we'll be returning to them. But however you resolve those larger issues, it seems clear that we do *some* reasoning about ethical issues. Consider this ethical argument, adapted from a contemporary philosopher Judith Jarvis Thomson. You awaken this morning, ready to leap from your bed and rush to your ethics class. But as you gain consciousness, everything seems wrong. Instead of the sheets you haven't washed in six weeks, you awaken to starched clean white sheets. There are no dirty clothes decorating the room and you can't find your teddy bear. Worst of all, you realize there is a thick double tube attached to your arm, and the tube runs across the room and is attached to the arm of an older woman, apparently fast asleep, lying in another hospital bed.

Just then the door opens, and in walks someone all dressed in white: "Oh, I'm glad you're finally awake," she says. "A terrible thing happened last night. Remember when you stopped by the tavern on your way home from the library? While you were there, someone slipped a delayed-action sleeping potion in your beer, and after you got home and went to bed it caused you to fall into a very deep sleep. The people who drugged you— a nefarious group called the Society of Music Lovers—then kidnapped you, brought you to this hospital, and hooked you up to the woman you see sleeping over there. That's Sarah Sloan, the fabulous violinist. Sarah has acute kidney failure. Her kidneys have completely shut down and the buildup of impurities in her blood would have soon killed her. It turns out that Sarah Sloan has a very rare blood type, and dialysis machines don't work for her. The Society of Music Lovers discovered that you—and you alone—have a matching blood type. So now Sloan's blood is flowing through your body, and your healthy kidneys are purifying her blood as well as your own. Don't worry, it won't cause you any harm. Your kidneys are capable of purifying the blood of several people with no strain. Please understand, we think what the kidnappers did was terribly, egregiously wrong. They had no right to drug you and kidnap you and hook you up to Sarah Sloan, and we at the hospital had no part in that. The first we knew of it was when a nurse came into Sloan's room last night and found you here. But the situation is this: If you unhook yourself from Sarah Sloan, she will die. And so now that you are hooked up to Sloan, you have to *stay* hooked up to her. Not forever, of course. We're building a special dialysis machine that will work for Sarah Sloan's rare blood type, and as soon as that machine is ready we'll detach you and hook Sloan to the machine, and you can go on your merry way. The machine is rather complicated and it will take some time to build: probably about nine months. Until then, you have to stay hooked up to Sloan, because if you unhook yourself then she will die. We can't let her die, so I'm afraid you have no choice in the matter: you must stay hooked up to the violinist."

So what is your reaction to that? What would you say to the people at the hospital?

Most people will be outraged. "It's wrong for you to compel me to stay hooked up to the violinist. I know she will die if I unhook myself; but you have no right to force me to stay hooked up to her. If I decide to stay attached, and save her life, that's one thing. But no one should be able to force me to do that."

Then Thomson gets to the point of this elaborate analogy. If you believe you have a right to unhook yourself from Sarah Sloan, even though she will die, then you must also grant that a woman who is pregnant as a result of rape has a right to an abortion. Even if we grant that the fetus is a person, with all the rights of any other person, then the raped woman still has a right to an abortion, just as you have a right to unhook yourself from Sarah Sloan. The violinist will die when you unhook yourself, and the fetus will die when the woman unhooks herself through abortion. But if you believe you have a right to unhook yourself from the violinist, then that same right extends to the woman who is pregnant as a result of rape. (Thomson is making a very *limited* argument. It is not a case for a general right to elective abortion; rather, she is attempting to demonstrate that even if we grant that the fetus is a person with full rights, there are still circumstances in which a woman would have a right to an abortion.)

There are many ways you might respond to Thomson's analogical argument. Some people find it convincing. Others dispute it. They might claim the analogy is flawed in some way (you aren't related to the violinist, but you are related to the fetus, and that is a morally relevant difference). In any case, we aren't going to settle the question of abortion today—maybe tomorrow. But note this. When you consider Thomson's argument, you are using reason to examine an *ethical* issue. So first off, it is clear you can use reason to examine ethical questions. And second, think about your response to Thomson's argument. You may agree or disagree, you may think it's a bad analogy, you may think the two cases aren't really comparable. But there is one response to the argument that would seem nonsensical to you. Suppose I say: "Look, I certainly do have a right to unhook myself from the violinist; and while the woman who is pregnant as a result of rape is in a situation that is exactly similar to mine in every relevant moral detail, she does *not* have a right to an abortion." You would respond: "That's crazy. If you agree the situations are the same, then you can't say it's right for you and wrong for her. That is self-contradictory, and it makes no sense at all."

So what does Thomson's argument give us? Something like this: *if* you believe you have a right to make decisions about your own body (whether to have surgery, or give blood, or detach yourself from a violinist), then you must believe that others (including a woman who is pregnant as a result of rape) also have that right. Using reason, we have arrived at an ethical conclusion. So it seems that reasoning does have an important role to play in ethics.

Reasoning About Conditional Principles

Actually, very few people would deny that we can reason about ethical issues, as in the previous case. But the issue gets trickier, and considerably more controversial, when we move a step further. What was the conclusion of Thomson's argument? If you believe you have a right to make decisions about your own body, then consistency requires you to believe that others (including a woman who is pregnant as a result of rape) also have that right. That is a *hypothetical* or *conditional* conclusion: if this, then that. Reason seems to be quite useful in helping us with *hypothetical* reasoning, *conditional* goods. *If* you want to build a dam across this river, this is the best point for a dam. *If* we are going to provide everyone in our society with medical care, this is the best means of doing that. *If* you want a really greasy high-fat hamburger, go to Fat Mack's Grill. *If* you want to avoid cheating on the test, then don't look at your neighbor's paper. *If* you have a right to control what happens to your own body, what does that imply about the rights of others to control their own bodies? But we get tougher questions about the role of reason when we consider *categorical* claims, *un*conditional claims, claims with no *ifs* about them.

Kant and Categorical Principles

"Everyone has a right to control what happens to his or her own body." "Cheating is wrong." "Treat all people with respect." "Do not steal." Those are *categorical* statements. It's one thing to say, "*If* you want a good reputation, don't tell lies"; quite another to say, simply and without qualification, "It is wrong to lie." "*If* you value the honor code, you shouldn't cheat" is a much more modest claim than "cheating is wrong." Obviously, reason can help us in dealing with conditionals ("*If* you value trust in your personal relationships, you shouldn't cheat on your lover, because cheating will result in lies and deception and loss of trust"). But can it help if we are seeking unconditional categorical ethical principles ("cheating is wrong")?

Immanuel Kant insisted that reason can indeed supply such absolute categorical ethical principles: ethical principles that reason reveals to be universally true, just as reason reveals universal truths of mathematics. In fact, Kant argues that *only* pure reason could reveal the absolute universal truths of ethics. The facts that we learn from observation and experiment—the number of planets in our solar system, the number of electrons in a nitrogen atom, the speed of light, the cause of AIDS—are all *contingent* truths that might have been otherwise. But truths of ethics must be absolute and universal; that is, they must be *categorical* principles, not conditional. And thus they must come from reason alone.

Kant believes that reason can do much more than merely provide guidance in accomplishing our purposes. According to Kant, reason can actually discover eternal, absolute ethical principles, principles of universal ethical truth that can be known with rational certainty—much as reason can guide us to universal truths of mathematics and geometry. And these are truths we *discover* through reason, not ethical principles of our own making or choosing. Just as the truths of mathematics are equally true in Moscow, Mozambique, and Minneapolis, so also reason reveals ethical truths that are universal. The square root of 16 is 4, without exception—it's 4 whether skies are sunny or gray, and it's 4 whether I like it or not. If I believe the square root of 16 is 5, then I'm not just different: I'm wrong.

Is it possible for reason to supply absolute principles of morality, principles analogous to mathematical truths? Kant assures us that reason, and reason alone, is up to the challenge. Consider a situation you might face: you are the CEO of ABRA Corporation, and you own an enormous amount of ABRA stock. If you manipulate the books a bit—create some subsidiary companies and transfer all the debts to them, and sell some of your assets back and forth between several subsidiary companies and thus show that ABRA has a great cash flow and is turning huge paper profits—then ABRA will look very profitable and the value of your stock will shoot up. Then you can unload your stock while the price is high and pocket a fortune, while telling your investors and employees that everything is going great. When the bubble bursts, you'll be rich. Of course your employees lost their pensions and your stockholders lost their investments, in some cases their entire life savings. Is it legitimate for you to cheat people in this manner to enrich yourself?

Well (Kant would say) *think* about it: Would you think it fair if someone else did this to you? If someone cheated you out of your life savings—or did this to your dear old Mom—would you think it was okay? Of course not. You can't really prefer to be cheated, and you don't approve of a world in which everyone cheats everyone else whenever they have the opportunity. Instead, you want people to deal with you honestly. But there is *no morally relevant difference* between you and the people you are cheating. You can't consistently say it's okay for *me* to cheat others, but it's not alright for others to cheat me. All of you are rational, have your own lives and plans and projects, and are vulnerable to harm. So, if you cannot think it right that someone cheats you—if you cannot genuinely will to be cheated and treated disrespectfully—then simple consistency demands that like cases be treated in a like manner, and so you must conclude that it is not right to cheat others. It is illogical, *irrational* to treat similar cases by different principles. That would be like saying *this* angle is a right angle, but this other identical angle is not, or like saying 2 plus 2 equals 4 for *you*, but for me it totals 5.

Kant's Categorical Imperative

So we arrive, on purely rational grounds, at a basic principle of ethics (Kant's *categorical imperative*): always act in such a way that you could will that your act should be a universal law. This is hardly a new and surprising ethical principle. It is quite similar to what is often called "the golden rule": Do unto others as you would have them do unto you. Or as it is stated in the Jewish tradition: That which is hateful to you, do not unto others. But the difference is that Kant claims the rule can be derived purely from reason, without the aid of either emotions or revelation. Kant's categorical imperative is categorical, not hypothetical or conditional. *Reason requires* that you treat others as you wish to be treated. Kant insists that principle is eternally true, applying equally to Kenyan bankers, Kansas farmers, and Kyoto carpenters (as well as any rational extraterrestrials). It is true whether anyone knows or acknowledges it. And the truth of the principle can be known through pure reason, without the need of experience or observation, and known by any competent reasoner.

Of course not everyone will reason well, or even reason at all. But that does not expose a weakness in Kant's argument. After all, if Steve refuses to consider a mathematical proof, or is simply incapable of reasoning about mathematics, we don't conclude that the mathematical proof is invalidated; rather, we conclude that Steve is closed-minded or stupid or willfully obtuse. Likewise, if Martha refuses to follow the rationally derived principles of ethics, that reveals flaws in Martha, but *not* in the ethical principles.

Kant believes there is a second way of formulating the categorical imperative: always treat all persons as ends in themselves, and never merely as means to our ends. That is, all persons are entitled to be respected as rational beings who are capable of knowing the truths of morality and living by them; anyone who has that special capacity is a moral equal, a member of the kingdom of ends, and cannot legitimately be reduced to a mere means, merely a tool, for someone else's goals. (Of course you can hire a carpenter to build your house, and in so doing you are employing her to accomplish one of your goals. But you cannot legitimately treat her as if she were only a means to your ends. Thus, you cannot cheat her, nor enslave her.) According to Kant, this is just a second way of expressing the same principle. "All persons must be treated as ends in themselves" is essentially the same principle as "always act in such a way that you can will that your act should be a universal law."

Kant's ethics is an example of a *deontological* theory of ethics. "Deontological" comes from the Greek *deon*, meaning that which is binding, in particular a binding duty. According to deontologists, the nature of ethical rules is to bind you to your duty; and that binding is not dependent on consequences. You are duty-bound to keep your promise, even if a better offer comes along. And you are duty-bound, whether the consequences are pleasant or painful. Duty is not based on what is pleasant, beneficial, or advantageous, but rather upon the nature of the obligation itself. Though Kant's rationalist view of ethics is the best known deontological theory, it is not the only one—theological voluntarism (the divine command theory of ethics) is another deontological theory. On the divine command theory, a law is morally binding because God commands it. The consequences of following God's law—whether pleasant or painful—are irrelevant.

Absolute Ethical Principles

On the Kantian view ethics is universal and absolute, and its principles are discovered by the same pure reasoning process that discovers the universal truths of mathematics and geometry. The principles don't depend on observations, experiments, affections, or preferences. When straight lines intersect, they create identical opposite angles. That is true even if there have never been two perfectly straight lines in the world, and it is a truth that cannot be demonstrated by experiments or observations but only by reason. It is true whether it makes you feel warm and fuzzy or cold and upset, and it is true whether you like it or not. Basic ethical principles have exactly the same status. Legend has it that Diogenes walked around the streets of Athens, day and night, carrying a lantern and searching for an honest person, without ever finding one. Perhaps there has never been an honest person in all human history. If so, that does not change the basic ethical fact that honesty is morally right. "Be honest in your dealings with others" is still a true ethical principle. Maybe in our imperfect world honesty is *not* the best policy, and it would create more harm than benefit. That's irrelevant, Kant would insist. The truth of ethical principles doesn't depend on their usefulness or their consequences, but on their rational foundation. Ethical principles are universally and absolutely true, consequences be damned.

Given the exalted status of the moral law, Kant will allow no compromises. The moral law is stern and universal, with no exceptions. It would be irrational to will that it is alright to lie when lying is convenient; instead, we must will a universal principle that shows respect for all persons, and that principle will be: tell the truth. So, when I ask what you think of my expensive new hairstyle, of which I am quite proud but which in fact makes me look like an orangutan on a bad hair day, you cannot tell me it looks great. Respect for the moral law, and for me as a person, requires that you tell the truth. Of course such honesty may damage some of your social relationships, but that is irrelevant. The moral law is universal and absolute, and it requires our singular allegiance, whatever our inclinations and whatever the consequences.

"Morality is not properly the doctrine of how we may make ourselves happy, but how we may make ourselves worthy of happiness." *Immanuel Kant*, Critique of Practical Reason, *1788.*

Kant certainly believes that his austere rational morality *applies* to this world: you *must* follow it in your daily ethical life. But it is not *of* this world: it is not derived by observation or experience, but by pure reason. The truths of rationalist ethics do not depend on God for their justification (though, of course, a rational God would scrupulously follow ethical principles), but this is nonetheless a *transcendent* moral system. It sets up absolute moral principles that cannot be refuted by any worldly events, empirical experiments, or sensory observations. Our affections are part of the natural world, affections that may be felt by other animals, feelings that are apparently variable and changing—witness the amazing speed with which we can fall in love, and how swiftly those feelings of affection can be lost. As part of the natural world, someday these apparently chaotic feelings may be explicable in natural terms (like the apparently lawless wanderings of comets, which Newton and Halley turned into part of a cosmic mechanical clockwork). Kant wants a moral realm that is distinctively human and set apart from the mechanistic natural world, a realm governed by reason and by principles discoverable through pure reason. If human ethics is to be part of that special world, it must be driven by reason, not animal feelings.

ELEMENTS OF KANTIAN ETHICS

Reason and Will

Kant marks the apex of the rationalistic approach to ethics. There are two key elements in Kant's ethical system. First, ethics is based on pure reason: Neither our feelings nor our empirical observations of the world play any part in ethics. Second, the capacity to *follow* the purely rational dictates of the rational moral law must come from the special capacity of the human will (and not from emotions or inclinations). Rationality and willpower are the special glory of humankind. They are the features that justify the claim that we are "made in God's image," and that humans have a special status that sets us apart from and above all other creatures.

Kant's enthusiasm for the purely rational moral law pushes him into a rare burst of poetic exuberance: "two things fill the mind with ever new and increasing admiration and awe . . . : the starry heavens above me and the moral law within me."[1] Note that Kant is speaking of *two* things, both awe-inspiring, but from distinctly different realms. The moral law is based in pure reason, not derived from inclinations nor from observations nor from anything else in the natural world of stars and atoms and animals. And the capacity to follow the dictates of the moral law comes not from our natural capacities—our inclinations, sympathies, and desires—but instead from our special capacity of free will that empowers us to follow the moral law even though all our natural inclinations may work against it. It is this capacity to know the pure moral law and follow its dictates through our power of free will that elevates humans above the world of sense and guarantees our freedom from the mechanism of nature. The mechanistic operations of the starry heavens are awe-inspiring, and properly so—but not more wonderful than the *non*mechanistic power we find within ourselves to know and will the moral law.

Nonnatural Ethics

For Kant, genuine moral acts must stem from our special nonnatural powers of reason and will, not from anything in nature. Thus, if your generous behavior is prompted by your own natural inclinations, then your generous acts have no moral worth. Indeed, your natural inclinations toward kindness and generosity can be an impediment to genuine moral acts: reliance on agreeable and generous dispositions may prevent you from seeking rational principles of moral law and following them through the power of your will. Without such reason-based acts of willpower there is no genuine moral act. Instead there is only behavior from natural inclinations, which may prove beneficial and agreeable but which could just as easily have been vicious and harmful.

Even if you do not agree with Kant that we would be morally better if we entirely banished feelings, you may still grant that strong feelings sometimes obscure our moral outlook. More than one politician wishes his reason had exerted more effective control over his feelings. And strong desires are not the only feelings that can cloud our better judgment. Feelings of kindness and benevolence can also cause problems. In medicine, one of the most severe dangers to patient autonomy is the physician who "feels deeply" that the proposed treatment is really in the best interests of the patient; and so, since she is only working "for the good of the patient," she feels justified in overriding patient choice. Thus, *feeling* that one is striving to provide good care may lead to abuse of the patient's right to choose and control his or her own medical treatment. The harms of such a process are particularly clear in geriatric settings, when caregivers—acting from sincere feelings of kindness and generosity—do things for residents they could do for themselves, and thus

The poet Ogden Nash (in a somewhat whimsical poem entitled "Kind of an Ode to Duty") writes:

> O Duty,
> Why hast thou not the visage of a sweetie or a cutie?

And for most of us—as well as for Aristotle—it would be wonderful if our *duties* had the charms of our desires. If my duty to visit my sick friend were as attractive as my desire to spend the afternoon at the beach, then duty would be a delight. It would be like steamed broccoli having the delightful taste of a hot fudge sundae.

But Kant sees it differently. If duty always matched our desire—if duty had "the visage of a cutie or a sweetie," rather than the stern demeanor of moral demand—then we would merely do right by inclination, rather than through the force and dedication of our wills. And for Kant, acting from inclination has no moral worth at all. For Kant, our uniquely human willpower enables us to overcome desire and follow the demands of the rational moral law, and it is that power which sets humans apart from the mechanical world and gives us our special status.

shape a debilitating sense of helplessness in those they are trying to help. So, whatever the benefits of compassion and care, and whatever the joy of feelings and passions, there is also an important role for reason in ethics. Exactly what is that role? Absolute ethical lawgiver, as Kant maintains? Or menial assistant to the passions, as Hume claimed? Or some other role entirely?

CRITICISMS OF KANTIAN ETHICS

Who Is Excluded from Kant's Kingdom of Ends?

The uncompromising severity of Kant's moral system has prompted criticism of the Kantian model. But there is another basic element of Kantian morality that also raises questions. Kant's ethical system counts all *persons* as moral equals, as members of the moral "kingdom of ends," and in that respect Kant's moral system is wonderfully egalitarian. But to count as a person you must be capable of rationally deliberating about universal moral principles, and must have the special power of will to adhere to those principles. If you are not a member of Kant's kingdom of ends—if you are rationally impaired, or your rational capacities are not sufficient for grasping universal principles—then morally you count for nothing. Thus, for Kant someone suffering severe and irreversible dementia (someone in advanced Alzheimer's, for example) has no moral standing whatsoever. There would be nothing inherently wrong in torturing such an individual, or in inflicting cruelty on dogs, cats, or gerbils. Kant thinks such cruelty is a bad idea, because it may cause those who inflict the torture to become callous, and might lead from abusing puppies to the abuse of rational humans. But apart from such consequences, Kant holds that there is nothing wrong with torturing or otherwise abusing those who are not rational members of the kingdom of ends.

Conflicts among Principles

Some believe there is another problem in Kant's position. Kant's eye is on the awe-inspiring majesty of rational moral principles, and he is perhaps less concerned with the grubby details of moral behavior. But when we endeavor to "act so that our acts might be willed as universal law," we soon generate an abundance of universal laws, and it is difficult to fit them into a consistent whole. Almost any act we are considering can be described in many different ways, and thus can yield many different—and perhaps conflicting—universal laws. Suppose you have a secret basement room, in which you are hiding several Jewish friends from the Nazis. You hear a knock on the door, and you answer it to find storm troopers searching for Jews: "Are there any Jews living here?" What should you do? Kant seems to require that you give an honest answer, though that means the murder of the Jews and likely the murder of you and your family for hiding them. Terrible consequences, certainly; but the rightness or wrongness of an act is not influenced by its consequences. But the problem is that the act you are contemplating can be described in a variety of ways: telling the truth; betraying friends; exposing one's family to harm; or cooperating with a brutally murderous regime. It may be difficult to universalize the principle that we should tell lies, but it is also difficult to universalize the principle that we should betray our friends. Elegant as Kant's system is, it does not always provide clear moral answers to serious moral quandaries.

CONCLUSION

Kant offers a severe and demanding, hard and uncompromising account of morality. Kant would consider that a virtue, rather than a problem. Our capacity to follow the stern dictates of moral principle is what sets us apart from the natural world. We should hardly expect such a model to produce results that are always pleasant and agreeable in the natural world in which we live.

Kant develops a moral system that places morality—and human moral agents—in a distinct and special realm set apart from the natural world. Kantian ethics exists in a realm where desires and feelings and inclinations are excluded, the special powers of reason and free will reign, and the discoveries of the natural sciences cannot encroach. If you feel your cherished sense of the special unique human status threatened by astronomy or biology or psychology, Kant has fashioned a place of refuge.

But if you reject Kant's effort to separate ethics from the natural world, is there anything in Kant you could still find plausible? One need not buy the entire Kantian package in order to appreciate some elements of Kantian ethics. Kant's categorical imperative is in many ways a worthy ideal, and he makes his case for that principle using exclusively the resources of reason. Perhaps Kant's most significant contribution is to show that ethics can effectively employ reason, just as other areas of inquiry do. (Whether Kant places too much emphasis on the role of reason in ethics, and whether reason can establish everything he claims for it in ethics, are vexed questions that will occupy us further.) Reasoning is important in ethics, and it seems obvious that we can reason about ethical issues. After all, whether you agree or disagree with the conclusion of Thomson's violinist analogy, you used *reason* to evaluate her argument. (If I said Thomson's argument must be strong because it feels good to me, you would find that a strange and useless evaluation.) But are there limits to the use of reason in ethics? Can reason supply us with basic categorical principles, as Kant believes? Are feelings also relevant to ethics, or are they—as Kant insists—a distraction and an impediment? In particular, when we get to basic ethical issues, are the justifications for our views based on reason? On feelings? On tradition? *Can* we adequately justify our most fundamental ethical commitments? These are questions we shall examine through the rest of the book, perhaps the rest of our lives.

⇥ FUNDAMENTAL PRINCIPLES OF THE METAPHYSICS OF MORALS ⇥
Immanuel Kant

Immanuel Kant (1724–1804) was one of the greatest philosophers of the Enlightenment. His work had a profound impact on ethics, epistemology, and metaphysics: an impact that is felt to this day. This passage is from Kant's *Fundamental Principles of the Metaphysics of Morals* (1785); it was translated by Thomas K. Abbott.

FIRST SECTION

Transition from the Common Rational Knowledge of Morality to the Philosophical

Nothing can possibly be conceived in the world, or even out of it, which can be called good, without qualification, except a good will. Intelligence, wit, judgement, and the other talents of the mind, however they may be named, or courage, resolution, perseverance, as qualities of temperament, are undoubtedly good and desirable in many respects; but these gifts of nature may also become extremely bad and mischievous if the will which is to make use of them, and which, therefore, constitutes what is called character, is not good. It is the same with the gifts of fortune. Power, riches, honour, even health, and the general well-being and contentment with one's condition which is called happiness, inspire pride, and often presumption, if there is not a good will to correct the influence of these on the mind, and with this also to rectify the whole principle of acting and adapt it to its end. The sight of a being who is not adorned with a single feature of a pure and good will, enjoying unbroken prosperity, can never give pleasure to an impartial rational spectator. Thus a good will appears to constitute the indispensable condition even of being worthy of happiness.

There are even some qualities which are of service to this good will itself and may facilitate its action, yet which have no intrinsic unconditional value, but always presuppose a good will, and this qualifies the esteem that we justly have for them and does not permit us to regard them as absolutely good. Moderation in the affections and passions, self-control, and calm deliberation are not only good in many respects, but even seem to constitute part of the intrinsic worth of the person; but they are far from deserving to be called good without qualification, although they have been so unconditionally praised by the ancients. For without the principles of a good will, they may become extremely bad, and the coolness of a villain not only makes him far more dangerous, but also directly makes him more abominable in our eyes than he would have been without it.

A good will is good not because of what it performs or effects, not by its aptness for the attainment of some proposed end, but simply by virtue of the volition; that is, it is good in itself, and considered by itself is to be esteemed much higher than all that can be brought about by it in favour of any inclination, nay even of the sum total of all inclinations. Even if it should happen that, owing to special disfavour of fortune, or the niggardly provision of a step-motherly nature, this will should wholly lack power to accomplish its purpose, if with its greatest efforts it should yet achieve nothing, and there should remain only the good will (not, to be sure, a mere wish, but the summoning of all means in our power), then, like a jewel, it would still shine by its own light, as a thing which has its whole value in itself. Its usefulness or fruitfulness can neither add nor take away anything from this value. It would be, as it were, only the setting to enable us to handle it the more conveniently in common commerce, or to attract to it the attention of those who are not yet connoisseurs, but not to recommend it to true connoisseurs, or to determine its value.

There is, however, something so strange in this idea of the absolute value of the mere will, in which no account is taken of its utility, that notwithstanding the thorough assent of even common reason to the idea, yet a suspicion must arise that it may perhaps really be the product of mere high-flown fancy, and that we may have misunderstood the purpose of nature in assigning reason as the governor of our will. Therefore we will examine this idea from this point of view.

In the physical constitution of an organized being, that is, a being adapted suitably to the purposes of life, we assume it as a fundamental principle that no organ for any purpose will be found but what is also the fittest and best adapted for that purpose. Now in a being which has reason and a will, if the proper object of nature were its conservation, its welfare, in a word, its happiness, then nature would have hit upon a very bad arrangement in selecting the reason of the creature to carry out this purpose. For all the actions which the creature has to perform with a view to this purpose, and the whole rule of its conduct, would be far more surely prescribed to it by instinct, and that end would have been attained thereby much more certainly than it ever can be by reason. Should reason have been communicated to this favoured creature over and above, it must only have served it to contemplate the happy constitution of its nature, to admire it, to congratulate itself thereon, and to feel thankful for it to the beneficent cause, but not that it should subject its desires to that weak and delusive guidance and meddle bunglingly with the purpose of nature. In a word, nature would have taken care that reason should not break forth into practical exercise, nor have the presumption, with its weak insight, to think out for itself the plan of happiness, and of the means of attaining it. Nature would not only have taken on herself the choice of the ends, but also of the means, and with wise foresight would have entrusted both to instinct.

And, in fact, we find that the more a cultivated reason applies itself with deliberate purpose to the enjoyment of life and happiness, so much the more does the man fail of true satisfaction. And from this circumstance there arises in many, if they are candid enough to confess it, a certain degree of misology, that is, hatred of reason, especially in the case of those who are most experienced in the use of it, because after calculating all the advantages they derive, I do not say from the invention of all the arts of common luxury, but even from the sciences (which seem to them to be after all only a luxury of the understanding), they find that they have, in fact, only brought more trouble on their shoulders. Rather than gained in happiness; and they end by envying, rather than despising, the more common stamp of men who keep closer to the guidance of mere instinct and do not allow their reason much influence on their conduct. And this we must admit, that the judgement of those who would very much lower the lofty eulogies of the advantages which reason gives us in regard to the happiness and satisfaction of life, or who would even reduce them below zero, is by no means morose or ungrateful to the goodness with which the world is governed, but that there lies at the root of these judgements the idea that our existence has a different and far nobler end, for which, and not for happiness, reason is properly intended, and which must, therefore, be regarded as the supreme condition to which the private ends of man must, for the most part, be postponed.

For as reason is not competent to guide the will with certainty in regard to its objects and the satisfaction of all our wants (which it to some extent even multiplies), this being an end to which an implanted instinct would have led with much greater certainty; and since, nevertheless, reason is imparted to us as a practical faculty, i.e., as one which is to have influence on the will, therefore, admitting that nature generally in the distribution of her capacities has adapted the means to the end, its true destination must be to produce a will, not merely good as a means to something else, but good in itself, for which reason was absolutely necessary. This will then, though not indeed the sole and complete good, must be the supreme good and the condition of every other, even of the desire of happiness. Under these circumstances, there is nothing inconsistent with the wisdom of nature in the fact that the cultivation of the reason, which is requisite for the first and unconditional purpose, does in many ways interfere, at least in this life, with the attainment of the second, which is always conditional, namely, happiness. Nay, it may even reduce it to nothing, without nature thereby failing of her purpose. For reason recognizes the establishment of a good will as its highest practical destination, and in attaining this purpose is capable only of a satisfaction of its own proper kind, namely that from the attainment of an end, which end again is determined by reason only, notwithstanding that this may involve many a disappointment to the ends of inclination.

We have then to develop the notion of a will which deserves to be highly esteemed for itself and is good without a view to anything further, a notion which exists already in the sound natural understanding, requiring rather to be cleared up than to be taught, and which in estimating the value of our actions always takes the first place and constitutes the condition of all the rest. In order to do this, we will take the notion of duty, which includes that of a good will, although implying certain subjective restrictions and hindrances. These, however, far from concealing it, or rendering it unrecognizable,

rather bring it out by contrast and make it shine forth so much the brighter.

I omit here all actions which are already recognized as inconsistent with duty, although they may be useful for this or that purpose, for with these the question whether they are done from duty cannot arise at all, since they even conflict with it. I also set aside those actions which really conform to duty, but to which men have no direct inclination, performing them because they are impelled thereto by some other inclination. For in this case we can readily distinguish whether the action which agrees with duty is done from duty, or from a selfish view. It is much harder to make this distinction when the action accords with duty and the subject has besides a direct inclination to it. For example, it is always a matter of duty that a dealer should not over charge an inexperienced purchaser; and wherever there is much commerce the prudent tradesman does not overcharge, but keeps a fixed price for everyone, so that a child buys of him as well as any other. Men are thus honestly served; but this is not enough to make us believe that the tradesman has so acted from duty and from principles of honesty: his own advantage required it; it is out of the question in this case to suppose that he might besides have a direct inclination in favour of the buyers, so that, as it were, from love he should give no advantage to one over another. Accordingly the action was done neither from duty nor from direct inclination, but merely with a selfish view.

On the other hand, it is a duty to maintain one's life; and, in addition, everyone has also a direct inclination to do so. But on this account the anxious care which most men take for it has no intrinsic worth, and their maxim has no moral import. They preserve their life as duty requires, no doubt, but not because duty requires. On the other hand, if adversity and hopeless sorrow have completely taken away the relish for life; if the unfortunate one, strong in mind, indignant at his fate rather than desponding or dejected, wishes for death, and yet preserves his life without loving it—not from inclination or fear, but from duty—then his maxim has a moral worth.

To be beneficent when we can is a duty; and besides this, there are many minds so sympathetically constituted that, without any other motive of vanity or self-interest, they find a pleasure in spreading joy around them and can take delight in the satisfaction of others so far as it is their own work. But I maintain that in such a case an action of this kind, however proper, however amiable it may be, has nevertheless no true moral worth, but is on a level with other inclinations, e.g., the inclination to honour, which, if it is happily directed to that which is in fact of public utility and accordant with duty and consequently honourable, deserves praise and encouragement, but not esteem. For the maxim lacks the moral import, namely, that such actions be done from duty, not from inclination. Put the case that the mind of that philanthropist were clouded by sorrow of his own, extinguishing all sympathy with the lot of others, and that, while he still has the power to benefit others in distress, he is not touched by their trouble because he is absorbed with his own; and now suppose that he tears himself out of this dead insensibility, and performs the action without any inclination to it, but simply from duty, then first has his action its genuine moral worth. Further still; if nature has put little sympathy in the heart of this or that man; if he, supposed to be an upright man, is by temperament cold and indifferent to the sufferings of others, perhaps because in respect of his own he is provided with the special gift of patience and fortitude and supposes, or even requires, that others should have the same—and such a man would certainly not be the meanest product of nature—but if nature had not specially framed him for a philanthropist, would he not still find in himself a source from whence to give himself a far higher worth than that of a good-natured temperament could be? Unquestionably. It is just in this that the moral worth of the character is brought out which is incomparably the highest of all, namely, that he is beneficent, not from inclination, but from duty.

To secure one's own happiness is a duty, at least indirectly; for discontent with one's condition, under a pressure of many anxieties and amidst unsatisfied wants, might easily become a great temptation to transgression of duty. But here again, without looking to duty, all men have already the strongest and most intimate inclination to happiness, because it is just in this idea that all inclinations are combined in one total. But the precept of happiness is often of such a sort that it greatly interferes with some inclinations, and yet a man cannot form any definite and certain conception of the sum of satisfaction of all of them which is called happiness. It is not then to be wondered at that a single inclination, definite both as to what it promises and as to the time within which it can be gratified, is often able to overcome such a fluctuating idea, and that a gouty patient, for instance, can choose to enjoy what he likes, and to suffer what he may, since, according to his calculation, on this occasion at least, he has not sacrificed the enjoyment of the present moment to a possibly mistaken expectation of a happiness which is supposed to be found in health. But even in this case, if the general desire for happiness did not influence his will, and supposing that in his particular case health was not a necessary element in this calculation, there yet remains in this, as in all other cases, this law, namely, that he should promote his happiness not from inclination but from duty, and by this would his conduct first acquire true moral worth.

It is in this manner, undoubtedly, that we are to understand those passages of Scripture also in which we are commanded to love our neighbour, even our enemy. For love, as an affection, cannot be commanded, but beneficence for duty's sake may; even though we are not impelled to it by any inclination—nay, are even repelled by a natural and unconquerable aversion. This is practical love and not pathological—a love which is seated in the will, and not in the propensions of sense—in principles of action and not of tender sympathy; and it is this love alone which can be commanded.

The second proposition is: That an action done from duty derives its moral worth, not from the purpose which is to be attained by it, but from the maxim by which it is determined, and therefore does not depend on the realization of the object of the action, but merely on the principle of volition by which the action has taken place, without regard to any object of desire. It is clear from what precedes that the purposes which we may have in view in our actions, or their effects regarded as ends and springs of the will, cannot give to actions any unconditional or moral worth. In what, then, can their worth lie, if it is not to consist in the will and in reference to its expected effect? It cannot lie anywhere but in the principle of the will without regard to the ends which can be attained by the action. For the will stands between its a priori principle, which is formal, and its a posteriori spring, which is material, as between two roads, and as it must be determined by something, it that it must be determined by the formal principle of volition when an action is done from duty, in which case every material principle has been withdrawn from it.

The third proposition, which is a consequence of the two preceding, I would express thus: Duty is the necessity of acting from respect for the law. I may have inclination for an object as the effect of my proposed action, but I cannot have respect for it, just for this reason, that it is an effect and not an energy of will. Similarly, I cannot have respect for inclination, whether my own or another's; I can at most, if my own, approve it; if another's, sometimes even love it; i.e., look on it as favourable to my own interest. It is only what is connected with my will as a principle, by no means as an effect—what does not subserve my inclination, but overpowers it, or at least in case of choice excludes it from its calculation—in other words, simply the law of itself, which can be an object of respect, and hence a command. Now an action done from duty must wholly exclude the influence of inclination and with it every object of the will, so that nothing remains which can determine the will except objectively the law, and subjectively pure respect for this practical law, and consequently the maxim that I should follow this law even to the thwarting of all my inclinations.

Thus the moral worth of an action does not lie in the effect expected from it, nor in any principle of action which requires to borrow its motive from this expected effect. For all these effects—agreeableness of one's condition and even the promotion of the happiness of others—could have been also brought about by other causes, so that for this there would have been no need of the will of a rational being; whereas it is in this alone that the supreme and unconditional good can be found. The pre-eminent good which we call moral can therefore consist in nothing else than the conception of law in itself, which certainly is only possible in a rational being, in so far as this conception, and not the expected effect, determines the will. This is a good which is already present in the person who acts accordingly, and we have not to wait for it to appear first in the result.

But what sort of law can that be, the conception of which must determine the will, even without paying any regard to the effect expected from it, in order that this will may be called good absolutely and without qualification? As I have deprived the will of every impulse which could arise to it from obedience to any law, there remains nothing but the universal conformity of its actions to law in general, which alone is to serve the will as a principle, i.e., I am never to act otherwise than so that I could also will that my maxim should become a universal law. Here, now, it is the simple conformity to law in general, without assuming any particular law applicable to certain actions, that serves the will as its principle and must so serve it, if duty is not to be a vain delusion and a chimerical notion. The common reason of men in its practical judgements perfectly coincides with this and always has in view the principle here suggested. Let the question be, for example: May I when in distress make a promise with the intention not to keep it? I readily distinguish here between the two significations which the question may have: Whether it is prudent, or whether it is right, to make a false promise? The former may undoubtedly be the case. I see clearly indeed that it is not enough to extricate myself from a present difficulty by means of this subterfuge, but it must be well considered whether there

may not hereafter spring from this lie much greater inconvenience than that from which I now free myself, and as, with all my supposed cunning, the consequences cannot be so easily foreseen but that credit once lost may be much more injurious to me than any mischief which I seek to avoid at present, it should be considered whether it would not be more prudent to act herein according to a universal maxim and to make it a habit to promise nothing except with the intention of keeping it. But it is soon clear to me that such a maxim will still only be based on the fear of consequences. Now it is a wholly different thing to be truthful from duty and to be so from apprehension of injurious consequences. In the first case, the very notion of the action already implies a law for me; in the second case, I must first look about elsewhere to see what results may be combined with it which would affect myself. For to deviate from the principle of duty is beyond all doubt wicked; but to be unfaithful to my maxim of prudence may often be very advantageous to me, although to abide by it is certainly safer. The shortest way, however, and an unerring one, to discover the answer to this question whether a lying promise is consistent with duty, is to ask myself, "Should I be content that my maxim (to extricate myself from difficulty by a false promise) should hold good as a universal law, for myself as well as for others?" and should I be able to say to myself, "Every one may make a deceitful promise when he finds himself in a difficulty from which he cannot otherwise extricate himself?" Then I presently become aware that while I can will the lie, I can by no means will that lying should be a universal law. For with such a law there would be no promises at all, since it would be in vain to allege my intention in regard to my future actions to those who would not believe this allegation, or if they over hastily did so would pay me back in my own coin. Hence my maxim, as soon as it should be made a universal law, would necessarily destroy itself.

I do not, therefore, need any far-reaching penetration to discern what I have to do in order that my will may be morally good. Inexperienced in the course of the world, incapable of being prepared for all its contingencies, I only ask myself: Canst thou also will that thy maxim should be a universal law? If not, then it must be rejected, and that not because of a disadvantage accruing from it to myself or even to others, but because it cannot enter as a principle into a possible universal legislation, and reason extorts from me immediate respect for such legislation. I do not indeed as yet discern on what this respect is based (this the philosopher may inquire), but at least I understand this, that it is an estimation of the worth which far outweighs all worth of what is recommended by inclination, and that the necessity of acting from pure respect for the practical law is what constitutes duty, to which every other motive must give place, because it is the condition of a will being good in itself, and the worth of such a will is above everything.

EXERCISES

1. Children under age 10 are of course of great moral *importance*, and it is a grievous moral wrong to harm them. But can they be moral *actors*? That is, can small children actually commit morally wrong or morally virtuous acts?

2. University professors are usually fairly bright, and they typically hold reason in high regard. But sad to say, university professors are not widely acclaimed as moral models. In fact, academic departments are notorious for being dens of intrigue and betrayal, and squabbling among faculty is common. (Perhaps you are familiar with the saying that university politics is so nasty because the stakes are so low.) If that assessment of the moral status of university faculty is accurate (and it seems clear that university faculty are not morally *better* than average), does that count against the claim that rationality is the core of ethics?

3. Mr. Spock—of Star Trek fame—apparently feels no emotions. Would that make him (in your view) more or less capable of living a morally good life?

4. Kant claims that his categorical imperative is a moral principle that can be known purely by reason, without dependence on any observations or experience. It is a truth of reason that can be established in the same way we work out a proof in mathematics or geometry. If you were proposing a candidate for a moral principle known purely by reason, what do you think would be the best candidate? (You may think it is not possible to know moral truths purely by reason; perhaps you don't think moral truths can be known at all; maybe you doubt that any even exist. No matter. What sort of moral principle do you think would be most plausibly derived by pure reason?)

5. Kant formulates two versions of his categorical imperative, though he claims they are merely different formulations of the same principle. Would it be possible for someone to *consistently* hold the first imperative (always act in such a way that you could will that your act should be a universal law) but *deny* the second imperative (always treat others as ends in themselves, and never merely as means)?

6. In the story of Huck Finn, Huck goes against his moral principles and against his reason (limited and constrained as it is by his racist culture) and refuses to betray his friend, Jim, to the slave catchers. Would a Kantian regard Huck as a *morally better person* if he *had* followed his principles? (Of course a Kantian would regard Huck's basic principle—that slavery is legitimate—as morally awful, and would maintain that Huck had reasoned *badly*. But would the Kantian maintain that Huck ought to follow his own *reasoning*, and not let emotions sway him?)

7. Extraterrestrials arrive, and they are far superior to us in intellect—the most brilliant human thinkers would be regarded as severely mentally deficient among these profoundly rational ETs, and their reasoning processes are far beyond ours: their mediocre high school students offer mathematical insights that astonish and awe our most advanced mathematicians. It turns out that the ethical principles of these super-rational extraterrestrials are *very* different from ours; would a Kantian conclude that we *ought* to adopt their ethical system, even though we can't really understand the reasoning process by which they developed that system?

8. Antonio R. Damasio is a neuropsychologist with a strong interest in the implications of neuropsychological research for questions of philosophy and ethics. In his *Descartes' Error* (New York: G. P. Putnam's Sons, 1994), Damasio describes the 1848 case of Phineas Gage, a pleasant, congenial, hard-working, and very responsible man who suffered a severe brain injury that impaired his capacity to feel emotions. Though his intellectual abilities appeared to remain intact, Gage soon abandoned the positive moral life he had previously lived, becoming abrasive, impulsive, and violent. It's of course difficult to know exactly what happened to Gage, given the fact that his injury occurred over 150 years ago. But *suppose* that this (and other cases Damasio discusses) indicates that when people's emotional capacities are impaired, they generally become incapable of behaving morally. Kant, you remember, maintains that genuine moral behavior does not depend on emotions or feelings. Would such cases refute Kant? Would they provide *any* grounds for doubting Kant's position? How might Kant try to explain such cases?

9. Thomas Nagel, a contemporary Kantian, insists that it would be *irrational* to question our basic moral principles because of some finding in the social sciences: "Someone who abandons or qualifies his basic methods of moral reasoning on historical or anthropological grounds alone is nearly as irrational as someone who abandons a mathematical belief on other than mathematical grounds. . . . Moral considerations occupy a position in the system of thought that makes it illegitimate to subordinate them completely to anything else." According to

Nagel, our mathematical system has its own system of justification and proof; therefore, if someone gave an anthropological account of how our mathematical system originated, that would not give us reason to reject our mathematical beliefs. Likewise, moral reasoning also has its own system of justification; and if someone gave a well-supported anthropological account of our moral principles, that should not cause us to question our moral system. For example, if an anthropologist proved that our cooperative ethical principles had their origins in tribal conflict, that would not be grounds for doubting our ethical views. Do you agree with Nagel? Can you imagine any findings in psychology, anthropology, or biology that would cause you to abandon your *basic* approach to moral reasoning? (Of course if scientists proved to us that trees have complex emotions and intricate systems of reasoning and feel agony when their branches are pruned, that would surely cause us to change *some* of our ethical beliefs: we would begin to consider our treatment of trees an ethical issue. But that wouldn't change our *basic* approach to ethical reasoning; rather, it would just enlarge the boundaries of ethical consideration.) But could *any* discovery in biology, psychology, or anthropology give us good grounds for changing our basic approach to ethics? Or are Nagel and Kant right in maintaining that *no* scientific discovery could give us good grounds for revising our basic methods of ethical thinking?

ADDITIONAL READING

Among Kant's classic works on ethics are *Groundwork of the Metaphysic of Morals*, trans. H. J. Paton, as *The Moral Law* (London: Hutchinson, 1953); *Critique of Practical Reason*, trans. L. W. Beck (Indianapolis, IN: Bobbs-Merrill, 1977); and *Religion Within the Limits of Reason Alone*, trans. T. M. Greene and H. H. Hudson (New York: Harper and Row, 1960).

Excellent works on Kant's ethics include Lewis White Beck's *A Commentary on Kant's Critique of Practical Reason* (Chicago, IL: University of Chicago Press, 1960); and Onora O'Neill, *Constructions of Reason: Explorations of Kant's Practical Philosophy* (Cambridge: Cambridge University Press, 1989). A fascinating brief challenge to Kant's ethical system is Rae Langton's "Maria von Herbert's Challenge to Kant," which can be found in Peter Singer, editor, *Ethics* (Oxford: Oxford University Press, 1994).

Many outstanding contemporary philosophers follow—to at least some degree—the Kantian tradition in ethics. A small sample includes Kurt Baier, *The Moral Point of View* (Ithaca, NY: Cornell University Press, 1958); Marcia W. Baron, *Kantian Ethics Almost Without Apology* (Ithaca, NY: Cornell University Press, 1995); Stephen Darwall, *Impartial Reason* (Ithaca, NY: Cornell University Press, 1983) and *Philosophical Ethics* (Boulder, CO: Westview Press, 1998); Alan Donagan, *The Theory of Morality* (Chicago, IL: University of Chicago Press, 1977); Christine Korsgaard, *Creating the Kingdom of Ends* (Cambridge, MA: Cambridge University Press, 1995); and Thomas Nagel, *The View from Nowhere* (New York: Oxford University Press, 1986).

Kantian ethics can seem cold and austere. For a more engaging experience of Kantian ethics, try some essays by Thomas E. Hill, Jr., who is clearly a Kantian, but writes with grace, charm, and clarity on a variety of ethical issues. See his essays in *Respect, Pluralism, and Justice: Kantian Perspectives* (Oxford: Oxford University Press, 2000); and *Human Welfare and Moral Worth: Kantian Perspectives* (Oxford: Oxford University Press, 2002).

NOTES

[1]Immanuel Kant, *The Critique of Practical Reason and Other Writings in Moral Philosophy*, trans. L. W. Beck (Chicago, IL: University of Chicago Press, 1949), p. 289. First published in 1788.

5

Utilitarian Ethics

Some base ethics on pure reason, while others ground ethics in feelings or intuitions. But from the nineteenth century onward, many have thought that ethics should rest on a different foundation. *Utilitarians* appeal to neither intuition nor abstract reason. Rejecting mysteries or special powers, utilitarians believe that the starting point of ethics is simple and obvious. When we strip away the mysteries and confusions, what do we really want? We want to enjoy pleasures and avoid suffering. This simple truth applies to kings and serfs; rich and poor; butchers, bakers, candlestick makers; humans, chimps, and beagles. Starting from this simple principle, ethics becomes a matter of calculating how to produce the greatest balance of pleasure over suffering. For any act or policy, the question of whether it is ethically right comes down to this: Will it produce the greatest possible balance of pleasure over pain? If so, then it is right. Period.

UTILITARIAN THEORY

Making Utilitarian Calculations

Of course calculating the right act is not always easy. Simple acts may have large and complicated consequences. Telling a lie may seem a small matter, avoiding some immediate problems and not really causing any harm. But you have perhaps discovered from your own experiences the truth of the old dictum: "Oh what a tangled web we weave, when first we practice to deceive." Think of a case that may seem simple. You are a physician, and you discover your patient has an incurable disease that will invariably kill him in one year, but will show few symptoms until near death. Should you tell your patient the awful truth? If you lie to your patient, he will enjoy his remaining year with little worry. If you tell him, he will pass his last year in dread of his approaching death. The utilitarian calculation seems obvious. A year of worry-free enjoyment is a better result than a year of dread and fear, so you should lie to your patient.

But the calculation is not that easy. Your patient may be deprived of the opportunity to do things he had always planned to do: quit work and try writing a novel, visit Paris, or reconcile with his brother. Furthermore, when he finally discovers he has been deceived, he may be profoundly bitter, and feel he was treated like a child rather than an autonomous adult. And others who know the real diagnosis will become enmeshed in the deception, and this may cause them stress. The discomfort of constant deception may also lead them to distance themselves from the patient, and leave him isolated. And there are other consequences, perhaps remote but still serious. If you deceive this patient about his fatal illness, it will undermine the confidence we have in what our doctors tell us. When I go to you for my annual checkup, and you assure me I am perfectly healthy, I will wonder whether you're telling me the truth: "Dr. Jones said I was in good health. However, she told Bill the same thing, and he had a fatal disease and died within a year. I wonder what she's hiding from me."

Taking the Mystery out of Ethics

So making the calculations of pleasure and pain will not be an easy task, but utilitarians are undaunted. They never supposed that ethics would be *easy*, but they do insist ethics is not *mysterious*. Deciding what is right and wrong is not a matter of deep intuition or special mystical insight or ancient rules. It is a difficult but straightforward task of measuring, as best we can, the balance of pleasure over pain that will be produced by a proposed act or policy. The calculations may be challenging, but so are the calculations in plotting the path of Halley's comet. And of course we can make mistakes, just as we do in other calculations. If Halley's comet encounters a passing asteroid we know nothing about, then our calculations will be mistaken. Likewise, if events occur that we could not have anticipated, then our ethical calculations of consequences may also be wrong. But our best chance of plotting the path of Halley's comet is to make the calculations, based on all the information we have. And our best chance of plotting the right ethical behavior is to make our best calculations, based on all the information we can secure. This won't give us ethical infallibility, but it will give us a sound method for pursuing ethics, with *no* appeal to mysteries or intuitions or miracles.

Misconceptions of Utilitarian Ethics

Utilitarian ethics is often reviled, and often misunderstood. Before examining it further, we should clear up a few common misconceptions. First, the utilitarian is not recommending a policy of gross, egoistic, self-centered, short-sighted hedonism. This is not an "eat, drink, and be merry, for tomorrow you die" sort of ethic. What shall I do this evening? Well, I could go out and have a huge steak, a gargantuan chocolate dessert, and then spend the rest of the evening drinking myself into a joyous stupor. Such gluttony has its undeniable charms. But as some of us know from sad experience, it also has its less charming consequences—hours of nausea being only the most immediately obvious. So a good utilitarian—intent on maximizing pleasure, but also concerned about minimizing suffering—would counsel moderation. And when we add in the pleasures one sacrifices while recovering (the joys of philosophy, for example, are strictly incompatible with the suffering of a hangover), clearly moderation is a better course. Besides, there are also the interests of others to calculate: having had too much to drink, my impaired judgment may lead me to drive, and that might cause great suffering for others. And the utilitarian will insist that the joys and sorrows of others must be part of the calculation. *All* pleasures and pains count. My own pleasures and pains are part of the sum, but they count no more and no less than the pleasures and pains of others. (The utilitarian would argue that it is irrational to count my own pleasures as more important than the pleasures of others. After all, I could not possibly have any reasonable grounds for drawing such a distinction—the distinction would be arbitrary. I can of course point out that these pleasures are *mine*, but you can say exactly the same about your pleasures, so that does not justify special preference for my own pleasures.)

Utilitarian ethics is an example of a *teleological* theory of ethics. "Teleological" comes from the Greek word *telos*, meaning end or goal. Such theories are sometimes called *consequentialist* theories, since they base ethical rules and judgments on the *consequences*. Roughly, an act is judged good if it produces good consequences, if it has good results, and if it is productive of worthwhile ends. Utilitarian ethics (the right act is the act that produces the greatest benefits for everyone) is the dominant consequentialist view; but egoism (the right act is the one that produces the greatest benefits for the individual egoist) is also consequentialist. The contrast between teleological and deontological (duty-based) theories is one of the most fundamental divides in ethical theory. Deontologists basically believe that consequences don't matter in ethics; teleologists believe the consequences are the *only* things that matter.

ACT-VERSUS RULE-UTILITARIANS

Act-Utilitarians

Utilitarians aim to maximize pleasure and minimize suffering for everyone. But there are some issues that divide utilitarians. One basic division among utilitarians is between act-utilitarians and rule-utilitarians. Act-utilitarians claim that in determining what we should do, we must consider what *specific act* would produce the best overall consequences. If telling a lie—in this individual instance—would yield the maximum balance of pleasure over pain, then telling a lie is *morally right*. It may well be that in *most* cases telling lies causes more harm than good, but that doesn't matter. We're not concerned with most cases, but with this particular case. In different circumstances, telling a lie would be wrong, because it would not maximize pleasure. But in these circumstances, telling a lie yields the greatest possible balance of pleasure over pain, and so in this situation you *ought* to tell a lie. When we have a new situation, we'll make new calculations.

Rule-Utilitarians

Rule-utilitarians believe that is a superficial way of calculating. In order to determine what really maximizes pleasure and minimizes suffering, we must look more deeply at societal *practices* and *institutions*.

You have promised to meet your philosophy professor for lunch. You know your professor is looking forward to the occasion: you are charming company, and your professor is socially inept and does not often have the pleasure of such a delightful luncheon companion. However, you are likely to find it a rather boring occasion, your professor being fond of long and tedious stories. On the way to the restaurant you encounter the very attractive and fascinating person who sits near you in stats class, who suggests the two of you share lunch. As a good utilitarian, you quickly total up the pleasures and pains. On the one hand, if you keep your promise and meet your professor, then your professor will gain the pleasure of your company. But that has to be balanced against the fact that you will experience suffering—the suffering of listening to your professor's long-winded stories, compounded by the suffering of regret at the delightful lunch date you are passing up, and to that total must be added the suffering your stats classmate will feel when you decline the luncheon invitation. On the other side, if you break your promise to your professor and accept the more attractive offer, then you will gain the pleasure of a more enjoyable lunch and your companion from your stats class will gain the great pleasure of your company. Besides, there's a decent chance that this luncheon engagement might lead to further social relations involving very significant pleasures for you both. Of course your professor will be disappointed at being stood up for your luncheon engagement. But your professor is probably used to such disappointments, and will soon get over it. Before finishing the appetizer, your philosophy professor will probably be lost in thought about some obscure question in medieval philosophy, and so won't suffer for long. Besides, tomorrow in class you can tell your professor you received an emergency call from home, and you are so sorry about missing the luncheon engagement ("I had been looking forward to it all week"), and offer to reschedule the lunch for later. Your professor is quite gullible, and will certainly believe you. When you total it up, it is quickly obvious that a much greater balance of pleasure will result if you break your promise. So it's morally legitimate for you to break your promise in this situation. In fact, for a faithful utilitarian it's morally *obligatory*.

The Rules of Practices

Many utilitarians will applaud your reasoning, and affirm your decision as morally correct. But some utilitarians will disagree. They will insist that your utilitarian calculations have been too narrow. You left out the importance of our *practice* of promise-keeping. If you *promise* to meet me, that doesn't mean you'll meet me unless something better comes along. Of course, if you must be rushed to the hospital for emergency surgery, or take shelter from an approaching tornado, or save the life of a child who is in danger of falling off a cliff—in such cases you are excused from keeping your promise. That is part of the practice of making and keeping promises: in genuine emergency situations, you are excused from keeping your promise. But a more attractive offer from a charming classmate is *not* an emergency, and is *not* a legitimate excuse for breaking your promise. If people could break promises whenever a more appealing or pleasurable option comes along, then the whole purpose and practice of promising would be destroyed. The point of promising is to bind someone to an obligation. "I promise to be faithful to you" does not mean "I promise to be faithful to you unless I meet someone better looking." If you promise to meet me, that means—barring extraordinary events—you will in fact meet me.

Having the practice of promise-keeping is very valuable to us. It enables us to make plans, and it offers an important measure of security and confidence. If having made a promise, we then engaged in utilitarian calculations to determine whether to keep or break the promise, the "promise" would no longer serve its present useful function. If you promise to go to the opera with me, then I can buy the tickets and make dinner reservations and send my jacket to the cleaners. If you can back out should you have a more pleasurable opportunity, I would be foolish to go to such expense. If you are promised a job in Minneapolis—but that promise can be cancelled if a more attractive applicant appears—you cannot confidently sell your house in St. Louis, hire a mover, and make a down payment on a bungalow in the Twin Cities. It might well be that giving the job to the better applicant would result in a greater balance of pleasure over suffering, even when your suffering is figured in the balance. But the whole practice of promising would be lost if we made and kept "promises" by that manner of calculation. Because we value the promise-keeping *practice*, we cannot subject individual promises to utilitarian calculations.

Thus, rule-utilitarians call for a more complicated, double-tiered method of utilitarian calculation. Rather than calculate the aggregate pleasures and pains of a particular act of promise-keeping, rule-utilitarians insist we should *first* calculate the overall pleasures and pains of the practice of promise-keeping. That is, will our society—on an overall long-term utilitarian calculation—gain a greater balance of pleasure over pain by having or not having the practice of promise-keeping? If that utilitarian calculation concludes that the practice of promise-keeping maximizes the overall balance of pleasure, then we should adopt that practice (on utilitarian grounds). Suppose we have adopted the promise-keeping practice, and now we are faced with a specific instance of promising; then as *rule*-utilitarians we must follow the *rules* of the practice. (Of course, if the act does not fall under the rules of any practice favored by utilitarian standards, then we should evaluate the specific act by utilitarian calculations.)

Promise-keeping is perhaps the most obvious candidate for a practice or policy justified by rule-utilitarian calculations, but there may be others as well. Consider a principle that governs our medical research: we should not perform medical experiments on competent persons without their informed consent. That principle offers us important protection and security. When we enter the hospital, we know we can't be used as unwitting guinea pigs in medical experiments. Medical researchers can't go through our records and draft anyone they find particularly useful for medical experimentation. Without that rule we would be very nervous every time we entered the hospital for testing or treatment. But suppose researchers could make an exception and use us in their experiments should they conclude that in *this case* coercing us to be experimental subjects would yield more benefit than harm. Such a utilitarian exception would destroy our sense of security. If we conclude that the practice of requiring consent passes the rule-utilitarian test of producing the maximum balance of pleasure over suffering, we should adopt that practice. We cannot have that practice if we allow exceptions on act-utilitarian grounds.

Consider another candidate for a practice that might be justified by rule-utilitarian calculations: we should not suppress freedom of speech. In a specific instance, it may be that we could achieve a greater balance of pleasure over pain by suppressing speech. For example, pro-Nazi speeches may cause significant pain to many people in our society, and the pleasure taken by neo-Nazis in spewing out their hate-filled diatribes hardly seems to balance out the suffering. But if we find the practice of freedom of speech valuable, we can't decide to suppress that freedom because a specific exercise of free speech causes an overall negative balance of suffering over pleasure. "You have freedom to say whatever you wish, so long as what you say doesn't disturb significantly more people than it pleases": that is *not* freedom of speech.

Some utilitarians—*act*-utilitarians—believe that the rule-utilitarian approach weakens the utilitarian position. According to act-utilitarians, *every* act—from promise-keeping to poetry-writing—should be subjected to utilitarian calculations. Of course as a thorough and careful act-utilitarian, you must consider (when deciding whether to break a promise) what impact that would have on future confidence in promises, and on trust between people. That is an important consideration to add to the calculation, but it's still just one more of the many factors to be considered when calculating what act will produce the greatest overall balance of pleasure over suffering. Which version of utilitarian theory is more plausible remains a vexed question.

UTILITARIANS AND THE QUALITY OF PLEASURES

A second and perhaps even more divisive issue among utilitarians concerns *qualities* of pleasures. Do all pleasures count the same? I derive great pleasure from listening to Britney Spears, while you take delight in Bach and Mozart. There is no doubt that your musical tastes are more sophisticated than mine, and you almost certainly have a deeper understanding and appreciation of music. Still, I derive pleasure from the music I enjoy, just as you do. Is there any difference in our pleasures? If we must choose between satisfying your taste for Bach and my preference for Britney, should we simply flip a coin? That is, should utilitarians further complicate their calculations by factoring in the *qualities* of different pleasures?

Bentham: All Pleasures Are Equal

Jeremy Bentham, who first developed utilitarian ethics, would say there is no difference. Pleasure is pleasure, Bentham asserted. If they give equal pleasure to the participants, then "Pushpin is as good as poetry." The fact that pushpin is a silly game (something like pickup sticks) and poetry is a sublime art makes no difference. There are, of course, some important differences in pleasures. The pleasure derived from overindulgence is a pleasure; but since it carries suffering in its wake, that may make other pleasures a better choice on balance. And my pleasure in the music of Britney Spears is likely to be short-lived, as I soon tire of the repetitive and shallow arrangements, while your pleasure in Mozart and Bach is likely to grow and deepen as your appreciation for the nuances of their music increases. And my pleasure in cheering for the Minnesota Vikings is genuine; but might there be other pleasures that would not also involve so much agony of defeat? Still, according to Bentham, if I get pleasure from playing pinball games, and you take pleasure in poetry, and neither of our pleasurable activities causes harm or suffering to ourselves or others, then my pleasure in pinball is the complete equal of your pleasure in poetry, and there is no reason to favor one over the other on grounds of *quality*.

If we look closely at Bentham's development of utilitarian ethics, it is not difficult to see why he is reluctant to admit differences in qualities of pleasure. Bentham is living in late-eighteenth- to early-nineteenth-century London, and he is appalled at the conditions he sees around him. A few live in great luxury, with huge homes in the city, country estates, and crowds of servants. Many live in desperate poverty, and are forced into theft (punishable by public hanging) or prostitution to survive. Disease is everywhere, and for the impoverished there is little opportunity for an education that might free them from a short, desperate life. When Bentham formulates his utilitarian ethics, he is crafting a tool that can be used for reform. It is obvious that pleasure is good and suffering bad, so we ought to maximize pleasure and minimize suffering for everyone. No doubt Lord Mustard derives great pleasure from taking his carriage up to his country estate for a long weekend. But does it really maximize pleasure for everyone if Lord Mustard has a city mansion and a country estate, while families with small children live in the streets and sleep under bridges? The 12-course feast prepared for Lord Mustard and his guests is a great delight, but does the pleasure of such gluttony outweigh the suffering that could be relieved by feeding several hungry families? If we allow for differences in qualities of pleasures, Lord Mustard has an easy answer: the high quality of pleasures fancied by the aristocracy is so superior to the pleasures pursued by the lower classes that the *quality* of pleasure cancels out the great difference in *quantity*.

Mill and the Qualities of Pleasure

The notion of "higher-quality" pleasures has always been difficult to justify. What it typically means in practice is "the pleasures enjoyed by those in positions of power and privilege." In contemporary society, going to a Shakespeare play is considered a much "higher-quality" pleasure than playing a game of cards; but in Elizabethan London, when Shakespeare was writing his plays, attending one of Shakespeare's plays was regarded as crude, vulgar, and perhaps immoral. The quality of Shakespeare's plays hasn't changed. The people who attend them have. Furthermore, it is difficult to believe that what are regarded as "higher-quality" activities actually provide higher-quality pleasures. Even if we grant that an evening of the Boston Symphony playing Mozart is of higher quality than a Britney Spears concert, it requires a leap of philosophical faith to suppose that the patrons at Symphony Hall are experiencing greater pleasure than are the wildly enthusiastic preteens screaming in ecstasy and singing along with Britney.

John Stuart Mill—a second-generation utilitarian, whose father was a close friend of Jeremy Bentham—would answer that the rock concert no doubt produces greater quantity of pleasure, but the symphony patrons enjoy a much higher quality of pleasure; and for Mill, even small doses of high-quality pleasure easily outweigh mass quantities of lower pleasures. The person of educated and discerning musical tastes may less often find a concert completely satisfying: she detects tiny imperfections that my cruder sensitivities miss. But in Mill's words: "It is better to be a human being dissatisfied than a pig satisfied; better to be Socrates dissatisfied than a fool satisfied."

Mill's version of utilitarianism is certainly more sophisticated than Bentham's. Does it destroy a basic element of utilitarian ethics in exchange for that sophistication? Is pushpin as good as poetry, Britney as good as Bach? That's an issue that still divides utilitarians.

SATISFICING CONSEQUENTIALISM

Utilitarianism is a very demanding ethical theory. If you are a good utilitarian, you must constantly weigh whether your actions produce the greatest possible balance of pleasure over suffering for everyone involved. My evening at the movies with my friends seems a perfectly innocent and morally legitimate activity; but wouldn't we produce a greater balance of pleasure over suffering if we sent the cost of the movie to famine relief, and instead spent our evening helping out at a homeless shelter? Even a quick and rough calculation soon shifts that innocent evening at the movies into the category of moral failure. Indeed, utilitarianism is *such* a demanding theory that various theorists have proposed modifying it into a somewhat less severe form. One of the more interesting models for moderating utilitarian demands was developed by Michael Slote: a theory which he calls "satisficing consequentialism." On the satisficing model, you are not always morally obligated to do whatever would have the *best* overall consequences; instead, your more modest moral obligation is to perform an action that has *good enough* results. Satisficing consequentialism is still a *consequentialist* theory, because it holds that *consequences* are what make acts right or wrong. But it differs from standard utilitarian views because it does not require that the right act must *maximize* beneficial results. As Slote describes it: "Could not someone who held that rightness depended solely on how good an act's consequences were also want to hold that less than the best was sometimes good enough, hold, in other words, than an act might qualify as morally right through having good enough consequences, even though better consequences could have been produced in the circumstances?" (Michael Slote, "Satisficing Consequentialism," *Proceedings of the Aristotelian Society, Supplementary*, Volume 58, 1984: 139–163).

Of course acting in a way that is *good enough*—acting in a way that produces *sufficient* beneficial consequences—may still require a great deal: dropping your spare change in the Salvation Army collection pot once every year is not likely to fulfill your obligation to relieve the suffering of the poor, even under a satisficing standard. But it will certainly require a good deal less than does the standard utilitarian model that requires *always* acting to produce *maximum* benefits for everyone. Slote sees that as an advantage of satisficing consequentialism:

> According to such satisficing act-consequentialism, then, an agent may permissibly choose a course of action that seems to him to do a great deal or a sufficient amount towards the relief of human suffering without considering whether such an action is optimific in the relief of suffering among all the possible courses of action open to him and without the course of action he chooses actually being optimific. . . . such a view of what an agent may permissibly do comes closer to ordinary views about benevolence than the usual forms of optimizing act-consequentialism.

Whether such a *satisficing* form of consequentialism is an improvement over standard utilitarian views is a question you will have to decide. Slote is no doubt correct that satisficing consequentialism "comes closer to ordinary views" of morality than does the standard optimizing view. But that leads to a difficult and divisive question: is an ethical theory better because it is a closer match to our ordinary ethical views? Or should ethical theory function as a corrective guide, showing ways in which our ordinary ethical views fall short? Slote seems to favor the former view, while it seems likely that most utilitarians would see their accounts as a way of revealing the shortcomings in our ordinary beliefs concerning moral obligations.

CRITICISMS OF UTILITARIAN ETHICS

Psychological Criticisms

There have been many criticisms of utilitarian ethics. One important challenge maintains that utilitarianism is psychologically false. No doubt it is true that we sometimes seek pleasure. But is maximizing pleasure and minimizing suffering *always* our primary goal?

Consider our friend Soraya, who is a dedicated mountain climber. She endures grueling training, sore muscles, oxygen deprivation, severe cold, and countless bumps and bruises, all in her quest to scale a challenging mountain face. No doubt there are beautiful vistas to enjoy and the satisfaction of completing a difficult challenge. But to suppose that Soraya climbs mountains for pleasure, or to maximize pleasure over pain, seems clearly false. There are lots of delightful pleasures to be had with much less suffering, and it also seems false to the entire experience. If you suggest to Soraya that she climbs mountains for pleasure, she will reject that as ridiculous. She climbs for the challenge, or to test herself, or "because it's there"—but not to maximize pleasure, and certainly not to minimize pain.

The dedicated utilitarian will reply that in reality, Soraya's mountain climbing is really all about maximizing pleasure: "Soraya gets her pleasures in ways that wouldn't appeal to me; but still, for her the mountain climbing is really just a matter of pleasure. It brings her great pleasure, and that's why she does it. If she could gain more pleasure from playing bridge, she would pursue that." And so it will go with any example we offer: the activity pursued may not be obviously pleasurable to us, but the person doing it must expect to find pleasure in it. Otherwise, why would she do it, rather than pursuing something more enjoyable?

NOZICK'S CHALLENGE TO UTILITARIAN ETHICS

But is it true that our goal, in all our activities, is maximizing pleasure and minimizing suffering? Robert Nozick[1] developed a powerful challenge to that utilitarian claim. Suppose scientists have contrived an amazing "pleasure machine." When you are placed in this machine you have vivid experiences that are complete fantasies, but you are unable to distinguish these fantasies from reality (with "virtual gaming" now available, perhaps this example does not seem so incredible). To make the illusion complete, the machine erases your memory of entering the machine, so that your machine experiences seem to you genuine reality. The machine programmers are generous and trustworthy people, and they offer to place you in the machine and set the machine to provide you with a rich and wonderful and immensely pleasurable life. All your dreams will come true—or at least it will seem to you that they've come true. You will have not a clue that you are living a fantasy, and your pleasure will be maximized. You will win four Olympic gold medals, and be honored with a parade through your hometown. You will win the Nobel Prize for physics, and maybe two years later in literature. You will spend sultry summer nights on the beach with—well, you get the idea. And there will be just enough difficulties to keep things interesting. You will occasionally lose an Olympic event, but then come back four years later with an underdog triumph. None of this will really be happening, of course. But since you won't know that, your pleasure will not be diminished. Would you choose to spend the rest of your life in joyous fantasy inside the pleasure machine?

For an hour it would certainly be tempting. Maybe even for a long weekend. But the rest of your life? Very few people would choose a life of blissfully happy machine-induced fantasy over the often-frustrating realities of life in the real world. But why would you not choose a full life of such fantasy pleasure? You can think of several immediate reasons. Going inside the pleasure machine would take you away from your family and friends, and would cause them unhappiness. Or perhaps you don't really trust the operators of this pleasure machine—maybe their real motive is to perform some ghastly experiment on you. But even if all those problems were solved—your family will not miss you, and the machine operator is absolutely trustworthy—most people still would be reluctant to choose a lifetime of pleasurable fantasy.

If you wouldn't agree to life inside the pleasure machine, then obviously there are things you value *other* than experiencing pleasure and avoiding pain. You take great pleasure in working on problems in physics, and your secret goal is to make a breakthrough discovery in physics and win the Nobel Prize. But if we offer you the pleasure you would gain from your work in physics—as the pleasure machine does—you would quickly decline: "I don't want merely to have the *feeling* of making a great discovery in physics. I want to *make* the discovery. It's true, working on physics problems gives me pleasure. Still, I don't do it for the pleasure, but because I love doing physics."

That brings us to the basic criticism of utilitarian ethics: it confuses (what psychologists call) the positive reinforcer with the behavior shaped by that reinforcer. You gain pleasure from playing chess, and if not you probably would never have become an enthusiastic chess player. You also experience a few frustrations: that stupid move when you lost your bishop and blew a game you should have won still makes you angry. But that is part of what shapes your deep commitment to playing chess: if you always had success, you would enjoy the game but your dedication to chess would not run very deep. If you experience some pleasant success, along with occasional failures, that variable interval schedule of positive reinforcement shapes a deep dedication to the game. You don't play the game for the pleasure, but the pleasure is part of what shapes you to love playing chess. A steady diet of frustrating losses might eventually extinguish your passion for chess. If we didn't gain pleasure and satisfaction from the activity, we probably wouldn't do it; but we aren't doing it *for* the pleasure.

That objection to utilitarian ethics is closely linked to a second. Aiming at pleasure seems a lousy plan for finding happiness. Those who aim at pleasure rarely seem to find it. If you think of people you know who are happy, it's unlikely that your list includes many who focus on the pursuit of pleasure. Instead, the happiest people seem to be those who are pursuing goals and projects they find worthwhile, and happiness comes to them as a bonus.

> "I don't know why we are here, but I'm pretty sure that it is not in order to enjoy ourselves." *Ludwig Wittgenstein, 1889–1951.*

Dostoyevsky's Challenge to Utilitarian Ethics

Finally, few of us can fully embrace utilitarian calculations in making ethical judgments. Russian novelist Fyodor Dostoyevsky poses this powerful challenge:

> Tell me honestly, I challenge you—answer me: imagine that you are charged with building the edifice of human destiny, the ultimate aim of which is to bring people happiness, to give them peace and contentment at last, but that in order to achieve this it is essential and unavoidable to torture just one little speck of creation, that . . . little child beating her chest with her little fists, and imagine that this edifice has to be erected on her unexpiated tears. Would you agree to be the architect under those conditions? Tell me honestly![2]

By utilitarian calculations, the purchase of so much pleasure at the cost of one small child's agony seems a bargain, but very few people could give their moral blessing to such a transaction.

THE USES OF UTILITARIAN ETHICS

Its problems notwithstanding, utilitarianism still has its uses. We might not think that pleasure is our primary goal, and we may have doubts about resolving ethical issues by entering the pleasures and pains in a calculator and pushing the *total* button. Still, we *are* concerned with pleasures and pains. When you consider having minor surgery or a trip to the dentist, you may not think much about the development of effective anesthesia. But if it were not available for the relief of pain, you would certainly think about it a great deal. The pleasures of a good meal may not equal the joys of philosophy, but they are hardly insignificant, and the pain of gnawing hunger can be a sad source of suffering. So even if calculations of pleasures and pains cannot capture everything about ethics, they are still important considerations.

Ironically, for a doctrine that was supposed to yield precise mathematical calculations, utilitarian ethics often works better as a battle axe than a scalpel. Utilitarianism is a blunt instrument, but it has a strong impact, especially in the hands of a contemporary advocate like Peter Singer. As Singer notes, when we test the safety of a new shampoo, we drip the shampoo in concentrated form into the eyes of rabbits, causing them severe pain and probably terror. No doubt a new shampoo that leaves my hair lustrous and manageable has its charms, but are those charms sufficient to justify the infliction of so much suffering? The taste of a char-grilled steak, juicy and tender, is a genuine source of pleasure. But can this gourmet pleasure (which is obviously not essential to sustain our lives, and in fact probably shortens our lives by contributing to higher cholesterol levels) justify the infliction of suffering on cattle that are raised on crowded feedlots and then herded into slaughterhouses? It must be delightful to live in an elegant mansion, richly equipped with jacuzzi and sauna and a master bedroom suite large enough for arena football; but is it really right to spend that much on luxuries that add only a small increase to our pleasure when the same resources could be used to care for many impoverished persons living in hunger and homelessness? If I add a spiffy and expensive new suit to my extensive wardrobe, it will bring me pleasure. But is that small increment of pleasure even remotely comparable to the pleasure and relief of suffering that would result if the same money were used to buy warm winter clothes for a cold and threadbare family? A tummy tuck will certainly improve my sagging appearance, and make me feel better. But the same medical resources could save the lives of many impoverished children who lack adequate health care to prevent and combat their terrible diseases. It doesn't require a careful utilitarian accounting to recognize that spending on such luxuries is hardly the best way to maximize pleasure and minimize suffering.

Utilitarian Ethics and Public Policy

Even if we have doubts about some of the details of utilitarian ethics, we may still find it a helpful general guide when considering what we should do. Furthermore, it may prove quite useful in evaluating social policy. If we are trying to decide whether a new football stadium with luxury boxes for the very rich is a better investment than decent inner-city schools and health care for the very poor, utilitarian calculations might prove their worth. Certainly they are a better guide than whatever politicians are currently using.

OPPOSITION TO UTILITARIANISM

Utilitarian ethics has enduring charms, and many champions. Utilitarians banish mystery from the realm of ethics and are never baffled by an ethical quandary. For utilitarians, ethical questions become engineering problems: They may require difficult calculations, but we have the methods and means to resolve them.

Yet for all its plain charms, utilitarian ethics often inspires deep, visceral, passionate hostility. Dostoyevsky, the great Russian novelist, thought of utilitarianism as a mean-spirited and ignoble ethical counterfeit: ethics is what makes us godlike, and ethical quandaries, though often difficult and sometimes tragic, are the glory of humankind. Utilitarianism turns ethics into a cheap and trivial bookkeeping system. Utilitarianism brings ethics down from the heavens and anchors it squarely to Earth, links ethics closely to basic desires to avoid suffering and secure happiness, dispenses with exalted ethical absolutes, and offers a clear and practical method of resolving ethical issues. But precisely the features that utilitarians find appealing are the features that absolutists find appalling.

Ethical absolutists (such as rationalists and intuitionists) typically find utilitarian theory even more objectionable than the complete denial of moral objectivity. After all, if I deny that there are moral absolutes, at least we're still talking the same language. But if I claim that there is moral objectivity, but insist it's not the objectivity of majestic, absolute, and eternal moral principles but instead the objectivity of contingent practical calculations about how to maximize happiness, that seems to absolutists like a cheapening and demeaning of ethical objectivity. The absolutist hatred of utilitarianism is thus likely to be greater than their hatred of those who deny moral objectivity altogether: It is the intense hatred of the traitor and despoiler, as opposed to the dislike of a clear enemy.

For ethical absolutists, ethics is neither relative to a situation nor contingent upon consequences. Ethics is certainly not about what feels good, or happens to make people happy. Rather, ethics is about principles that are eternally true, principles that demand our unconditional allegiance whether they make us feel good or not. Following the stern dictates of the moral law is not a feel-good enterprise.

William James and Ethical Temperaments

William James, the great American psychologist and pragmatic philosopher of the turn of the twentieth century, maintained that the most basic philosophical issues were decided not by argument or reason, but instead by temperament. According to James, you do not become an absolutist or a utilitarian (or adopt some other ethical stance) because you calmly and objectively evaluate the different views and select the most reasonable alternative. Instead you favor absolutism (or utilitarianism, or whatever) because it just seems right to you: it fits your temperament, it matches the way you live and think, and it fits your view of the world. You don't become a utilitarian because you are persuaded by good reasons to adopt utilitarian ethics; rather, you find the reasons for utilitarianism convincing because the utilitarian perspective fits you. The reasons that justify your utilitarian position are not what convince you to adopt the utilitarian view, but are instead an after-the-fact rationalization or justification of a theory you adopted for the much deeper reasons of temperament and outlook.

Of course most philosophers and ethical theorists would dispute James's account. But it may help make sense of why conflicts between different ethical perspectives—between absolutists and utilitarians, for example—are so enduring and so difficult to resolve. In any case, you might consider how it applies to your own thoughts about ethics. When you encountered utilitarian theory, did it seem to you immediately plausible, or did it seem to you somehow completely wrong? Was that reaction a reflection of your own ethical temperament?

⇌ An Introduction to the Principles of Morals and Legislation ⇌

Jeremy Bentham

Jeremy Bentham lived from 1748 to 1832. He was both a philosopher who set forth the basic principles of utilitarian ethics and a social reformer who worked tirelessly for improvements in British society, especially in the areas of legal, prison, and educational reform. Bentham used the principles of his utilitarian ethics as a blueprint for the reform programs he set in motion, and the political reform movement he helped develop continued long after his death. The following passage was originally published in 1823.

Of the Principle of Utility

1. Nature has placed mankind under the governance of two sovereign masters, *pain* and *pleasure*. It is for them alone to point out what we ought to do, as well as to determine what we shall do. On the one hand the standard of right and wrong, on the other the chain of causes and effects, are fastened to their throne. They govern us in all we do, in all we say, in all we think: every effort we can make to throw off our subjection, will serve but to demonstrate and confirm it. In words, a man may pretend to abjure their empire: but in reality he will remain subject to it all the while. The *principle of utility* recognises this subjection, and assumes it for the foundation of that system, the object of which is to rear the fabric of felicity by the hands of reason and of law. Systems which attempt to question it, deal in sounds instead of sense, in caprice instead of reason, in darkness instead of light.

But enough of metaphor and declamation: it is not by such means that moral science is to be improved.

2. The principle of utility is the foundation of the present work: it will be proper therefore at the outset to give an explicit and determinate account of what is meant by it. By the principle of utility is meant that principle which approves or disapproves of every action whatsoever, according to the tendency which it appears to have to augment or diminish the happiness of the party whose interest is in question: or, what is the same thing in other words, to promote or to oppose that happiness. I say of every action whatsoever; and therefore not only of every action of a private individual, but of every measure of government.

3. By utility is meant that property in any object, whereby it tends to produce benefit, advantage, pleasure, good, or happiness, (all this in the present case comes to the same thing) or (what comes again to the same thing) to prevent the happening of mischief, pain, evil, or unhappiness to the party whose interest is considered: if that party be the community in general, then the happiness of the community: if a particular individual, then the happiness of that individual.

4. The interest of the community is one of the most general expressions that can occur in the phraseology of morals: no wonder that the meaning of it is often lost. When it has a meaning, it is this. The community is a fictitious *body*, composed of the individual persons who are considered as constituting as it were its *members*. The interest of the community then is, what?—the sum of the interests of the several members who compose it.

5. It is in vain to talk of the interest of the community, without understanding what is the interest of the individual. A thing is said to promote the interest, or to be *for* the interest, of an individual, when it tends to add to the sum total of his pleasures: or, what comes to the same thing, to diminish the sum total of his pains.

6. An action then may be said to be conformable to the principle of utility, or, for shortness sake, to utility, (meaning with respect to the community at large) when the tendency it has to augment the happiness of the community is greater than any it has to diminish it.

7. A measure of government (which is but a particular kind of action, performed by a particular person or persons) may be said to be conformable to or dictated by the principle of utility, when in like manner the tendency which it has to augment the happiness of the community is greater than any which it has to diminish it.

8. When an action, or in particular a measure of government, is supposed by a man to be conformable to the principle of utility, it may be convenient, for the purposes of discourse, to imagine a kind of law or dictate, called a law or dictate of utility: and to speak of the action in question, as being conformable to such law or dictate.

9. A man may be said to be a partisan of the principle of utility, when the approbation or disapprobation he annexes to any action, or to any measure, is determined by, and proportioned to the tendency which he conceives it to have to augment or to diminish the happiness of the community: or in other words, to its conformity or unconformity to the laws or dictates of utility.

10. Of an action that is conformable to the principle of utility, one may always say either that it is one that ought to be done, or at least that it is not one that ought not to be done. One may say also, that it is right it should be done; at least that it is not wrong it should be done: that it is a right action; at least that it is not a wrong action. When thus interpreted, the words *ought,* and *right* and *wrong,* and others of that stamp, have a meaning: when otherwise, they have none.

11. Has the rectitude of this principle been ever formally contested? It should seem that it had, by those who have not known what they have been meaning. Is it susceptible of any direct proof? It should seem not: for that which is used to prove every thing else, cannot itself be proved: a chain of proofs must have their commencement somewhere. To give such proof is as impossible as it is needless.

12. Not that there is or ever has been that human creature breathing, however stupid or perverse, who has not on many, perhaps on most occasions of his life, deferred to it. By the natural constitution of the human frame, on most occasions of their lives men in general embrace this principle, without thinking of it: if not for the ordering of their own actions, yet for the trying of their own actions, as well as of those of other men. There have been, at the same time, not many, perhaps, even of the most intelligent, who have been disposed to embrace it purely and without reserve. There are even few who have not taken some occasion or other to quarrel with it, either on account of their not understanding always how to apply it, or on account of some prejudice or other which they were afraid to examine into, or could not bear to part with. For such is the stuff that man is made of: in principle and in practice, in a right track and in a wrong one, the rarest of all human qualities is consistency.

13. When a man attempts to combat the principle of utility, it is with reasons drawn, without his being aware of it, from that very principle itself. His arguments, if they prove any thing, prove not that the principle is *wrong,* but that, according to the applications he supposes to be made of it, it is *misapplied.* Is it possible for a man to move the earth? Yes; but he must first find out another earth to stand upon.

14. To disprove the propriety of it by arguments is impossible; but, from the causes that have been mentioned, or from some confused or partial view of it, a man may happen to be disposed not to relish it. Where this is the case, if he thinks the settling of his opinions on such a subject worth the trouble, let him take the following steps, and at length, perhaps, he may come to reconcile himself to it.

a. Let him settle with himself, whether he would wish to discard this principle altogether; if so, let him consider what it is that all his reasonings (in matters of politics especially) can amount to?

b. If he would, let him settle with himself, whether he would judge and act without any principle, or whether there is any other he would judge and act by?

c. If there be, let him examine and satisfy himself whether the principle he thinks he has found is really any separate intelligible principle; or whether it be not a mere principle in words, a kind of phrase, which at bottom expresses neither more nor less than the mere averment of his own unfounded sentiments; that is, what in another person he might be apt to call *caprice?*

d. If he is inclined to think that his own approbation or disapprobation, annexed to the idea of an act, without any regard to its consequences, is a sufficient foundation for him to judge and act upon, let him ask himself whether his sentiment is to be a standard of right and wrong, with respect to every other man, or whether every man's sentiment has the same privilege of being a standard to itself?

e. In the first case, let him ask himself whether his principle is not despotical, and hostile to all the rest of human race?

f. In the second case, whether it is not anarchical, and whether at this rate there are not as many different standards of right and wrong as there are men? and whether even to the same man, the same thing, which is right today, may not (without the least change in its nature) be wrong to-morrow? and whether the same thing is not right and wrong in the same place at the same time? and in either case, whether all argument is not at an end? and whether, when two men have said, 'I like this', and

'I don't like it', they can (upon such a principle) have any thing more to say?

g. If he should have said to himself, No: for that the sentiment which he proposes as a standard must be grounded on reflection, let him say on what particulars the reflection is to turn? if on particulars having relation to the utility of the act, then let him say whether this is not deserting his own principle, and borrowing assistance from that very one in opposition to which he sets it up: or if not on those particulars, on what other particulars?

h. If he should be for compounding the matter, and adopting his own principle in part, and the principle of utility in part, let him say how far he will adopt it?

i. When he has settled with himself where he will stop, then let him ask himself how he justifies to himself the adopting it so far? and why he will not adopt it any farther?

j. Admitting any other principle than the principle of utility to be a right principle, a principle that it is right for a man to pursue; admitting (what is not true) that the word *right* can have a meaning without reference to utility, let him say whether there is any such thing as a *motive* that a man can have to pursue the dictates of it: if there is, let him say what that motive is, and how it is to be distinguished from those which enforce the dictates of utility: if not, then lastly let him say what it is this other principle can be good for?

⊰⊱ WHAT UTILITARIANISM IS ⊰⊱
John Stuart Mill

John Stuart Mill (1806–1873) was the son of James Mill, a philosopher and economist who was a close friend of Jeremy Bentham. John Stuart Mill grew up surrounded by his father's friends, including Bentham. While he greatly admired Bentham's work, he later proposed a version of utilitarianism that diverged from Bentham's on some key points. He also wrote influential works in logic and economic theory. One of his best-known works is *On Liberty*, a strong defense of freedom and individuality against social and governmental interference.

    The following passage is from the 7th edition of Mill's *Utilitarianism*, published in 1879; the original edition of the work was published in 1861.

The creed which accepts as the foundation of morals, Utility, or the Greatest Happiness Principle, holds that actions are right in proportion as they tend to promote happiness, wrong as they tend to produce the reverse of happiness. By happiness is intended pleasure, and the absence of pain; by unhappiness, pain, and the privation of pleasure. To give a clear view of the moral standard set up by the theory, much more requires to be said; in particular, what things it includes in the ideas of pain and pleasure; and to what extent this is left an open question. But these supplementary explanations do not affect the theory of life on which this theory of morality is grounded—namely, that pleasure, and freedom from pain, are the only things desirable as ends;

and that all desirable things (which are as numerous in the utilitarian as in any other scheme) are desirable either for the pleasure inherent in themselves, or as means to the promotion of pleasure and the prevention of pain.

Now, such a theory of life excites in many minds, and among them in some of the most estimable in feeling and purpose, inveterate dislike. To suppose that life has (as they express it) no higher end than pleasure—no better and nobler object of desire and pursuit—they designate as utterly mean and groveling; as a doctrine worthy only of swine, to whom the followers of Epicurus were, at a very early period, contemptuously likened; and modern holders of the doctrine are occasionally made the subject of equally polite comparisons by its German, French and English assailants.

When thus attacked, the Epicureans have always answered, that it is not they, but their accusers, who represent human nature in a degrading light; since the accusation supposes human beings to be capable of no pleasures except those of which swine are capable. If this supposition were true, the charge could not be gainsaid, but would then be no longer an imputation; for if the sources of pleasure were precisely the same to human beings and to swine, the rule of life which is good enough for the one would be good enough for the other. The comparison of the Epicurean life to that of beasts is felt as degrading, precisely because a beast's pleasures do not satisfy a human being's conceptions of happiness. Human beings have faculties more elevated than the animal appetites, and when once made conscious of them, do not regard anything as happiness which does not include their gratification. I do not, indeed, consider the Epicureans to have been by any means faultless in drawing out their scheme of consequences from the utilitarian principle. To do this in any sufficient manner, many Stoic, as well as Christian elements require to be included. But there is no known Epicurean theory of life which does not assign to the pleasures of the intellect, of the feelings and imagination, and of the moral sentiments, a much higher value as pleasures than to those of mere sensation. It must be admitted, however, that utilitarian writers in general have placed the superiority of mental over bodily pleasures chiefly in the greater permanency, safety, uncostliness, &c., of the former—that is, in their circumstantial advantages rather than in their intrinsic nature. And on all these points utilitarians have fully proved their case; but they might have taken the other, and, as it may be called, higher ground, with entire consistency. It is quite compatible with the principle of utility to recognise the fact, that some *kinds* of pleasure

are more desirable and more valuable than others. It would be absurd that while, in estimating all other things, quality is considered as well as quantity, the estimation of pleasures should be supposed to depend on quantity alone.

If I am asked, what I mean by difference of quality in pleasures, or what makes one pleasure more valuable than another, merely as a pleasure, except its being greater in amount, there is but one possible answer. Of two pleasures, if there be one to which all or almost all who have experience of both give a decided preference, irrespective of any feeling of moral obligation to prefer it, that is the more desirable pleasure. If one of the two is, by those who are competently acquainted with both, placed so far above the other that they prefer it, even though knowing it to be attended with a greater amount of discontent, and would not resign it for any quantity of the other pleasure which their nature is capable of, we are justified in ascribing to the preferred enjoyment a superiority in quality, so far outweighing quantity as to render it, in comparison, of small account.

Now it is an unquestionable fact that those who are equally acquainted with, and equally capable of appreciating and enjoying, both, do give a most marked preference to the manner of existence which employs their higher faculties. Few human creatures would consent to be changed into any of the lower animals, for a promise of the fullest allowance of a beast's pleasures; no intelligent human being would consent to be a fool, no instructed person would be an ignoramus, no person of feeling and conscience would be selfish and base, even though they should be persuaded that the fool, the dunce, or the rascal is better satisfied with his lot than they are with theirs. They would not resign what they possess more than he, for the most complete satisfaction of all the desires which they have in common with him. If they ever fancy they would, it is only in cases of unhappiness so extreme, that to escape from it they would exchange their lot for almost any other, however undesirable in their own eyes. A being of higher faculties requires more to make him happy, is capable probably of more acute suffering, and is certainly accessible to it at more points, than one of an inferior type; but in spite of these liabilities, he can never really wish to sink into what he feels to be a lower grade of existence. We may give what explanation we please of this unwillingness; we may attribute it to pride, a name which is given indiscriminately to some of the most and to some of the least estimable feelings of which mankind are capable; we may refer it to the love of liberty and personal independence, an appeal to which was with the Stoics one of the most effective means for the inculcation of it; to the love of power, or to the love of excitement, both of which do really enter into and contribute to it: but its most appropriate appellation is a sense of dignity, which all human beings possess in one form or other, and in some, though by no means in exact, proportion to their higher faculties, and which is so essential a part of the happiness of those in whom it is strong, that nothing which conflicts with it could be, otherwise than momentarily, an object of desire to them. Whoever supposes that this preference takes place at a sacrifice of happiness—that the superior being, in anything like equal circumstances, is not happier than the inferior—confounds the two very different ideas, of happiness, and content. It is indisputable that the being whose capacities of enjoyment are low, has the greatest chance of having them fully satisfied; and a highly endowed being will always feel that any happiness which he can look for, as the world is constituted, is imperfect. But he can learn to bear its imperfections, if they are at all bearable; and they will not make him envy the being who is indeed unconscious of the imperfections, but only because he feels not at all the good which those imperfections qualify. It is better to be a human being dissatisfied than a pig satisfied; better to be Socrates dissatisfied than a fool satisfied. And if the fool, or the pig, is of a different opinion, it is because they only know their own side of the question. The other party to the comparison knows both sides.

It may be objected, that many who are capable of the higher pleasures, occasionally, under the influence of temptation, postpone them to the lower. But this is quite compatible with a full appreciation of the intrinsic superiority of the higher. Men often, from infirmity of character, make their election for the nearer good, though they know it to be the less valuable; and this no less when the choice is between two bodily pleasures, than when it is between bodily and mental. They pursue sensual indulgences to the injury of health, though perfectly aware that health is the greater good. It may be further objected, that many who begin with youthful enthusiasm for everything noble, as they advance in years sink into indolence and selfishness. But I do not believe that those who undergo this very common change, voluntarily choose the lower description of pleasures in preference to the higher. I believe that before they devote themselves exclusively to the one, they have already become incapable of the other. Capacity for the nobler feelings is in most natures a very tender plant, easily killed, not only by hostile influences, but by mere want of sustenance; and in the majority of young persons it speedily dies away if the occupations to which their position in life has devoted

them, and the society into which it has thrown them, are not favourable to keeping that higher capacity in exercise. Men lose their high aspirations as they lose their intellectual tastes, because they have not time or opportunity for indulging them; and they addict themselves to inferior pleasures, not because they deliberately prefer them, but because they are either the only ones to which they have access, or the only ones which they are any longer capable of enjoying. It may be questioned whether any one who has remained equally susceptible to both classes of pleasures, ever knowingly and calmly preferred the lower; though many, in all ages, have broken down in an ineffectual attempt to combine both.

From this verdict of the only competent judges, I apprehend there can be no appeal. On a question which is the best worth having of two pleasures, or which of two modes of existence is the most grateful to the feelings, apart from its moral attributes and from its consequences, the judgment of those who are qualified by knowledge of both, or, if they differ, that of the majority among them, must be admitted as final. And there needs be the less hesitation to accept this judgment respecting the quality of pleasures, since there is no other tribunal to be referred to even on the question of quantity. What means are there of determining which is the acutest of two pains, or the intensest of two pleasurable sensations, except the general suffrage of those who are familiar with both? Neither pains nor pleasures are homogeneous, and pain is always heterogeneous with pleasure. What is there to decide whether a particular pleasure is worth purchasing at the cost of a particular pain, except the feelings and judgment of the experienced? When, therefore, those feelings and judgment declare the pleasures derived from the higher faculties to be preferable *in kind*, apart from the question of intensity, to those of which the animal nature, disjoined from the higher faculties, is susceptible, they are entitled on this subject to the same regard.

I have dwelt on this point, as being a necessary part of a perfectly just conception of Utility or Happiness, considered as the directive rule of human conduct. But it is by no means an indispensable condition to the acceptance of the utilitarian standard; for that standard is not the agent's own greatest happiness, but the greatest amount of happiness altogether; and if it may possibly be doubted whether a noble character is always the happier for its nobleness, there can be no doubt that it makes other people happier, and that the world in general is immensely a gainer by it. Utilitarianism, therefore, could only attain its end by the general cultivation of nobleness of character, even if each individual were only benefited by the nobleness of others, and his own, so far as happiness is concerned, were a sheer deduction from the benefit. But the bare enunciation of such an absurdity as this last, renders refutation superfluous.

According to the Greatest Happiness Principle, as above explained, the ultimate end, with reference to and for the sake of which all other things are desirable (whether we are considering our own good or that of other people), is an existence exempt as far as possible from pain, and as rich as possible in enjoyments, both in point of quantity and quality; the test of quality, and the rule for measuring it against quantity, being the preference felt by those who, in their opportunities of experience, to which must be added their habits of self-consciousness and self-observation, are best furnished with the means of comparison. This, being, according to the utilitarian opinion, the end of human action, is necessarily also the standard of morality; which may accordingly be defined, the rules and precepts for human conduct, by the observance of which an existence such as has been described might be, to the greatest extent possible, secured to all mankind; and not to them only, but, so far as the nature of things admits, to the whole sentient creation. . . .

I must again repeat, what the assailants of utilitarianism seldom have the justice to acknowledge, that the happiness which forms the utilitarian standard of what is right in conduct, is not the agent's own happiness, but that of all concerned. As between his own happiness and that of others, utilitarianism requires him to be as strictly impartial as a disinterested and benevolent spectator. In the golden rule of Jesus of Nazareth, we read the complete spirit of the ethics of utility. To do as one would be done by, and to love one's neighbour as oneself, constitute the ideal perfection of utilitarian morality. As the means of making the nearest approach to this ideal, utility would enjoin, first, that laws and social arrangements should place the happiness, or (as speaking practically it may be called) the interest, of every individual, as nearly as possible in harmony with the interest of the whole; and secondly, that education and opinion, which have so vast a power over human character, should so use that power as to establish in the mind of every individual an indissoluble association between his own happiness and the good of the whole; especially between his own happiness and the practice of such modes of conduct, negative and positive, as regard for the universal happiness prescribes: so that not only he may be unable to conceive the possibility of happiness to himself, consistently with conduct opposed to the general good, but also that a direct impulse to promote the general good may be in every individual one of the habitual motives of action, and the sentiments connected therewith may fill a large and prominent place in every human being's sentient existence. If the impugners of the utilitarian morality represented it to their own minds in this its true character, I know not what recommendation possessed by any other morality they could possibly affirm to be wanting to it: what more beautiful or more exalted developments of human nature any other ethical system can be supposed to foster, or what springs of action, not accessible to the utilitarian, such systems rely on for giving effect to their mandates.

≈ A CRITIQUE OF UTILITARIANISM ≈
Bernard Williams

Bernard Williams was Monroe Deutsch Professor of Philosophy at the University of California, Berkeley, and a Fellow of All Souls College, Oxford. His work in ethics, epistemology, and many other areas of philosophy has been very influential. The following passage is excerpted from a book that he did with J. J. C. Smart—*Utilitarianism For and Against* (Cambridge: Cambridge University Press, 1973)—in which Smart defended utilitarianism and Williams critiqued utilitarian ethics. Williams' critique is noteworthy for its attention to the personal psychological issues that are involved in adopting a utilitarian ethical stance.

(1) George, who has just taken his Ph.D. in chemistry, finds it extremely difficult to get a job. He is not very robust in health, which cuts down the number of jobs he might be able to do satisfactorily. His wife has to go out to work to keep them, which itself causes a great deal of strain, since they have small children and there are severe problems about looking after them. The results of all this, especially on the children, are damaging. An older chemist, who knows about this situation, says that he can get George a decently paid job in a certain laboratory, which pursues research into chemical and biological warfare. George says that he cannot accept this, since he

is opposed to chemical and biological warfare. The older man replies that he is not too keen on it himself, come to that, but after all George's refusal is not going to make the job or the laboratory go away; what is more, he happens to know that if George refuses the job, it will certainly go to a contemporary of George's who is not inhibited by any such scruples and is likely if appointed to push along the research with greater zeal than George would. Indeed, it is not merely concern for George and his family, but (to speak frankly and in confidence) some alarm about this other man's excess of zeal, which has led the older man to offer to use his influence to get George the job ... George's wife, to whom he is deeply attached, has views (the details of which need not concern us) from which it follows that at least there is nothing particularly wrong with research into CBW. What should he do?

(2) Jim finds himself in the central square of a small South American town. Tied up against the wall are a row of twenty Indians, most terrified, a few defiant, in front of them several armed men in uniform. A heavy man in a sweat-stained khaki shirt turns out to be the captain in charge and, after a good deal of questioning of Jim which establishes that he got there by accident while on a botanical expedition, explains that the Indians are a random group of the inhabitants who, after recent acts of protest against the government, are just about to be killed to remind other possible protestors of the advantages of not protesting. However, since Jim is an honoured visitor from another land, the captain is happy to offer him a guest's privilege of killing one of the Indians himself. If Jim accepts, then as a special mark of the occasion, the other Indians will be let off. Of course, if Jim refuses, then there is no special occasion, and Pedro here will do what he was about to do when Jim arrived, and kill them all. Jim, with some desperate recollection of schoolboy fiction, wonders whether if he got hold of a gun, he could hold the captain, Pedro and the rest of the soldiers to threat, but it is quite clear from the set-up that nothing of that kind is going to work: any attempt at that sort of thing will mean that all the Indians will be killed, and himself. The men against the wall, and the other villagers, understand the situation, and are obviously begging him to accept. What should he do?

To these dilemmas, it seems to me that utilitarianism replies, in the first case, that George should accept the job, and in the second, that Jim should kill the Indian. Not only does utilitarianism give these answers but, if the situations are essentially as described and there are no further special factors, it regards them, it seems to me, as *obviously* the right answers. But many of us would certainly wonder whether, in (1), that could possibly be the right answer at all; and in the case of (2), even one who came to think

that perhaps that was the answer, might well wonder whether it was obviously the answer. Nor is it just a question of the rightness or obviousness of these answers. It is also a question of what sort of considerations come into finding the answer. A feature of utilitarianism is that it cuts out a kind of consideration which for some others makes a difference to what they feel about such cases: a consideration involving the idea, as we might first and very simply put it, that each of us is specially responsible for what *he* does, rather than for what other people do. This is an idea closely connected with the value of integrity. It is often suspected that utilitarianism, at least in its direct forms, makes integrity as a value more or less unintelligible. I shall try to show that this suspicion is correct. Of course, even if that is correct, it would not necessarily follow that we should reject utilitarianism; perhaps, as utilitarians sometimes suggest, we should just forget about integrity, in favour of such things as a concern for the general good. However, if I am right, we cannot merely do that, since the reason why utilitarianism cannot understand integrity is that it cannot coherently describe the relations between a man's projects and his actions.

4. Two Kinds of Remoter Effect

A lot of what we have to say about this question will be about the relations between my projects and other people's projects. But before we get on to that, we should first ask whether we are assuming too hastily what the utilitarian answers to the dilemmas will be. In terms of more direct effects of the possible decisions, there does not indeed seem much doubt about the answer in either case; but it might be said that in terms of more remote or less evident effects counterweights might be found to enter the utilitarian scales. Thus the effect on George of a decision to take the job might be invoked, or its effect on others who might know of his decision. The possibility of there being more beneficent labours in the future from which he might be barred or disqualified, might be mentioned; and so forth. Such effects—in particular, possible effects on the agent's character, and effects on the public at large—are often invoked by utilitarian writers dealing with problems about lying or promise-breaking, and some similar considerations might be invoked here. . . .

I want to consider now two types of effect that are often invoked by utilitarians, and which might be invoked in connexion with these imaginary cases. The attitude or tone involved in invoking these effects may sometimes seem peculiar; but that sort of peculiarity soon becomes familiar in utilitarian discussions, and indeed it can be something of an achievement to retain a sense of it.

First, there is the psychological effect on the agent. Our descriptions of these situations have not so far taken account of how George or Jim will be after they have taken the one course or the other; and it might be said that if they take the course which seemed at first the utilitarian one, the effects on them will be in fact bad enough and extensive enough to cancel out the initial utilitarian advantages of that course. Now there is one version of this effect in which, for a utilitarian, some confusion must be involved, namely that in which the agent feels bad, his subsequent conduct and relations are crippled and so on, *because he thinks that he has done the wrong thing*—for if the balance of outcomes was as it appeared to be *before* invoking this effect, then he has not (from the utilitarian point of view) done the wrong thing. So that version of the effect, for a rational and utilitarian agent, could not possibly make any difference to the assessment of right and wrong. However, perhaps he is not a thoroughly rational agent, and is disposed to have bad feelings, whichever he decided to do. Now such feelings, which are from a strictly utilitarian point of view irrational—nothing, a utilitarian can point out, is advanced by having them—cannot, consistently, have any great weight in a utilitarian calculation. I shall consider in a moment an argument to suggest that they should have no weight at all in it. But short of that, the utilitarian could reasonably say that such feelings should not be encouraged, even if we accept their existence, and that to give them a lot of weight is to encourage them. Or, at the very best, even if they are straightforwardly and without any discount to be put into the calculation, their weight must be small: they are after all (and at best) one man's feelings.

That consideration might seem to have particular force in Jim's case. In George's case, his feelings represent a larger proportion of what is to be weighed, and are more commensurate in character with other items in the calculation. In Jim's case, however, his feelings might seem to be of very little weight compared with other things that are at stake. There is a powerful and recognizable appeal that can be made on this point: as that a refusal by Jim to do what he has been invited to do would be a kind of self-indulgent squeamishness. That is an appeal which can be made by other than utilitarians—indeed, there are some uses of it which cannot be consistently made by utilitarians, as when it essentially involves the idea that there is something dishonourable about such self-indulgence. But in some versions it is a familiar, and it must be said a powerful, weapon of utilitarianism. One must be clear, though, about what it can and cannot accomplish. The most it can do, so far as I can see, is to invite one to consider how seriously, and for what reasons, one feels that what one is invited to do is (in these circumstances) wrong, and in particular, to consider that question from the utilitarian point of view. When the agent is not seeing the situation from a utilitarian point of view, the appeal cannot force him to do so; and if he does come round to seeing it from a utilitarian point of view, there is virtually nothing left for the appeal to do. If he does not see it from a utilitarian point of view, he will not see his resistance to the invitation, and the unpleasant feelings he associates with accepting it, *just* as disagreeable experiences of his; they figure rather as emotional expressions of a thought that to accept would be wrong. He may be asked, as by the appeal, to consider whether he is right, and indeed whether he is fully serious, in thinking that. But the assertion of the appeal, that he is being self-indulgently squeamish, will not itself answer that question, or even help to answer it, since it essentially tells him to regard his feelings just as unpleasant experiences of his, and he cannot, by doing that, answer the question they pose when they are precisely not so regarded, but are regarded as indications of what he thinks is right and wrong. If he does come round fully to the utilitarian point of view then of course he will regard these feelings just as unpleasant experiences of his. And once Jim—at least—has come to see them in that light, there is nothing left for the appeal to do, since *of course* his feelings, so regarded, are of virtually no weight at all in relation to the other things at stake. The 'squeamishness' appeal is not an argument which adds in a hitherto neglected consideration. Rather, it is an invitation to consider the situation, and one's own feelings, from a utilitarian point of view.

The reason why the squeamishness appeal can be very unsettling, and one can be unnerved by the suggestion of self-indulgence in going against utilitarian considerations, is not that we are utilitarians who are uncertain what utilitarian value to attach to our moral feelings, but that we are partially at least not utilitarians, and cannot regard our moral feelings merely as objects of utilitarian value. Because our moral relation to the world is partly given by such feelings, and by a sense of what we can or cannot 'live with', to come to regard those feelings from a purely utilitarian point of view, that is to say, as happenings outside one's moral self, is to lose a sense of one's moral identity; to lose, in the most literal way, one's integrity. At this point utilitarianism alienates one from one's moral feelings. . . .

If, then, one is really going to regard one's feelings from a strictly utilitarian point of view, Jim should give very little weight at all to his; it seems almost indecent, in fact, once one has taken that point of view, to suppose that he should give any at all. In George's case one might feel that things were slightly different. It is interesting, though, that one reason why one might think that—namely that one person principally affected is his wife—is very dubiously available to a utilitarian. George's wife has some reason to be interested in George's integrity and his sense of it; the Indians, quite properly, have no interest in Jim's. But it is not at all clear how utilitarianism would describe that difference.

EXERCISES

1. Suppose for a moment that William James is right, and that the ethical theory one adopts is largely a matter of temperament. If that is the case, how would you go about trying to change someone's views?

2. One objection to utilitarian ethics is that it turns everything into an ethical issue: if I spend an evening at a baseball game, but would have derived more pleasure from going to a concert, then I have committed a moral wrong. Nothing is exempt from moral evaluation. Is that a fair criticism?

3. One evening you get a call from the hospital. Your beloved old philosophy professor Ruth Zeno is near death, and wishes to talk with you. You rush to the hospital. The attending physician confirms that Professor Zeno is indeed in her last hours. When you enter the room, your professor is there alone. She grasps your hand warmly and whispers to you that she has a last request. From her bedside table she pulls out an old shoebox. She opens it, and you discover that it is stuffed with hundred-dollar bills. "There is almost half a million dollars in here," your professor says. "I have no relatives, no debts, no special obligations. The money is rightly mine, saved little by little during the course of my life. All the taxes have been paid. I want you to take this money and build a monument to my favorite racehorse Run Dusty Run in the infield at Pimlico racetrack. I'm certain the officials at Pimlico will give their permission. Run Dusty Run was my favorite racehorse. He wasn't a super horse, and few people remember him. But I cashed a nice bet on him once in Miami, and I loved that horse. He wasn't super fast, but he was always dead game, and he raced his heart out. I want you to take this money—no one else even knows the money exists—and spend every cent of it building a monument for Run Dusty Run. Hire a sculptor and build a beautiful bronze monument in his honor. No tricks, okay? Don't put the money in a savings account, draw out the interest for 50 years, and then finally build the monument. And don't spend just 10 grand on the monument and use the rest for something else. Use *all* the money, as swiftly as possible, to build a monument to Run Dusty Run. I don't have long to live, and I need your answer quickly." Professor Zeno reaches over with her bony fingers and grasps your arm tightly, and her voice becomes raspy. "You were my favorite student, and I have always considered you a friend. Will you *promise* me, now, that you will spend the money and build the monument according to my wishes?"

   Well, it seems a rather silly request. But then your dear old philosophy professor was always a rather strange bird, and you know that she dearly loved playing the ponies. And though her body is swiftly failing, her mind still seems to be clear and sharp. "Okay," you reply. "I promise. I'll build the monument exactly as you wish." Your professor smiles and relaxes her grip on your arm, and after a short conversation about the nature of time—always her favorite philosophical question—she slips into a quiet sleep, and within a few minutes her breathing stops. The doctor comes in and pronounces her dead.

   You take the shoebox, filled with half a million bucks, leave the hospital, and head back to your apartment. "Where am I going to find a sculptor who does monuments for racehorses?" you think to yourself. And then some other thoughts cross your mind. "Nobody else knows about this money. I'm the only one who knows it exists, and I'm the only one who knows about Professor Zeno's weird request. Of course I should keep my promise. . . . Or I *guess* I should keep my promise. . . . Or really, *should* I keep the promise?"

   "Certainly it can't matter any more to Professor Zeno. She's dead. If there is an afterlife, and she's sitting in heaven, then she's already as happy as she can possibly be, and one monument more or less won't change that. If she's in hell, then she's got more to worry about than a stupid monument. And if there's no afterlife, and she's simply dead and gone, then nothing I nor anyone else does will matter to her in the least. It's highly unlikely that Run Dusty Run will be happy about having a monument built in his honor. And as for the horseplayers at Pimlico, all they care about is trying to pick the winner of the next race. You could build an exact replica of the Taj Mahal on the infield of the track, and most of them wouldn't even notice. On the other hand, there's lots of wonderful things that could be done with half a million dollars. It could endow several generous scholarships at Professor Zeno's university. Or maybe add a much needed burn unit at the city hospital. Or start a lead-screening program in the city, and save many children from lead poisoning. That would be nice. We could call it the Zeno Scholarship, or the Zeno Burn Center. Those would be wonderful ways to use the money, ways that would really help people. In fact, it's hard to think of a dumber, more useless way to spend the money than by building that stupid monument.

"Of course, I did promise Professor Zeno, and I would be breaking my promise. But what's the harm in that? Professor Zeno certainly won't mind. And no one else will ever know about the promise (I can just say that Professor Zeno *instructed* the money be used for scholarships for needy philosophy students). So it's not like anyone will lose confidence in promising or the practice of promise-keeping. Of course *I* will know I broke my promise, but that won't make me feel guilty. Instead, I'll feel great about using Professor Zeno's money for a really good purpose. In fact, I would probably feel more guilty if I wasted the money on the stupid monument. So when I think about it carefully, it seems clear that I *ought* to break the deathbed promise I made to Professor Zeno."

Do you agree with that conclusion?

It seems likely the student promiser in this case is an act-utilitarian. But what about *your* answer? Is it based on act-utilitarian ethics? Rule-utilitarian ethics? Kantian ethics? None of the above?

4. Of the three ethical theories mentioned in the final paragraph of the previous question, which of those positions—perhaps none, perhaps more than one—would yield an answer *consistent* with your own answer?

5. What's the difference between a rule-utilitarian and a Kantian? *Is* there really a difference? Can you think of a case in which a rule-utilitarian and a Kantian would reach different conclusions about whether an act is right or wrong? If in *every* case the rule-utilitarian and the Kantian reached the same ethical conclusion, would that mean that there is no significant difference between the two accounts of ethics?

6. There is a spot open in Professor Ponder's film class. Your friends who have taken her class all rave about it: "I really learned to appreciate the artistic potential of films by taking Professor Ponder's class. Before taking the class I liked almost every movie I saw. Now that I have learned from Professor Ponder how to understand and appreciate the fine nuances of the art of film-making, most of the movies I once enjoyed now strike me as stupid and amateurish. But because of my new appreciation of film, I now deeply enjoy a few great movies that otherwise I could never have appreciated. I have gained a depth of enjoyment from those few wonderful films I never dreamed you could get from watching a movie. Of course, it's very rare now that I enjoy going to the movies—most movies I see now strike me as dreadful, even painful to watch. But on the few occasions when I watch a really good movie—wow, that's a great experience. Take Professor Ponder's class: it will change forever your experience of going to the movies." If you think that is likely to be your own result from taking Professor Ponder's class, would you sign up?

7. Suppose that I said, "Look, I'm not personally a utilitarian. I believe that we should be guided by principles, not by consequences. I believe that it is wrong to tell a lie, and I don't need to calculate the consequences of telling lies to know that it's wrong. That's the ethical approach I follow in my personal life. However, I believe that our government should conduct its affairs according to careful utilitarian calculations." Would that be a consistent position? If I am a sincere anti-utilitarian in my personal life, but always vote for politicians who favor utilitarian policies, am I being inconsistent?

8. Suppose that I am a sincere utilitarian; could I consistently believe that it is best to teach my children to live by *principles*, rather than by utilitarian calculations?

9. Utilitarians often view their theories as instruments of social *reform*: it is obvious that the pleasure gained by purchasing a larger yacht is not as great as the suffering that could be relieved by building homes for the homeless; it is obvious that my pleasure in eating veal is overbalanced by the suffering of the farm animals raised and killed to produce that delicacy. Would Michael Slote's satisficing consequentialism be better or worse in promoting social reform?

10. In fall 2003, the Canadian Bar Association was formulating a new code of ethics. One of the issues it was considering was whether lawyers should be barred from sleeping with their clients. The code of ethics for doctors and psychologists prohibits sexual contact between professional and client/patient; should lawyers adopt the same principle?

The Canadian ethical code for lawyers requires that lawyers must always keep their clients' interests paramount. Also, lawyers acknowledge that at least sometimes clients are deeply dependent on their lawyers, and are very vulnerable, so there may exist a significant imbalance of power between lawyer and client. With those things in mind, members of the Canadian Bar Association considered four options. One, they could simply ignore the issue in the new code of ethics. Two, they could prohibit sexual relations in which the lawyer "takes advantage" of the client, by exploiting a difference in power. Three, they could prohibit sexual relations except when a consensual sexual relationship already exists *prior* to the lawyer/client relationship. Or four, they could prohibit *all* sexual relations between lawyer and client.

The Canadian Bar Association asked for advice in dealing with this issue. So give your advice: What rule should be adopted? One of the four? Some other rule?

In making your recommendation, did you roughly follow one of the ethical models (utilitarian, rationalist, Humean) that we have discussed? Did you use a combination of those methods?[3]

11. This case is drawn from J. J. C. Smart, *An Outline of a System of Utilitarian Ethics* (Melbourne: Melbourne University Press and Cambridge, UK: Cambridge University Press, 1961): 16. I came across it in a delightful book by Peg Tittle: *What If . . . Collected Thought Experiments in Philosophy* (New York: Pearson Longman, 2005).

> . . . imagine a universe consisting of one sentient being only, who falsely believes there are other sentient beings and that they are undergoing exquisite torment. So far from being distressed by the thought, he takes a great delight in these imaginary sufferings. Is this better or worse than a universe containing no sentient being at all? Is it worse, again, then a universe containing only one sentient being with the same beliefs as before but who sorrows at the imagined tortures of his fellow creatures?

Smart (a utilitarian) claims that the universe with the mistaken sadist is better than the others. Clearly, Kant would disagree; would you? Or do you agree with Smart?

Could you *consistently* favor a utilitarian view, and still *disagree* with Smart, and insist that the second world is better? Could a utilitarian consistently maintain that the *third* world is better than the first? Better than the second?

ADDITIONAL READING

The classic utilitarian writings are Jeremy Bentham, *An Introduction to the Principles of Morals and Legislation* (London: 1823) and John Stuart Mill, *Utilitarianism* (London: Parker, Son and Bourn, 1863). Perhaps the most influential contemporary utilitarian, and certainly one of the most readable, is Peter Singer. His *Writings on an Ethical Life* (New York: HarperCollins, 2000) is the work of a philosopher thinking carefully about ethical obligations, and also striving to live his life by the right ethical standards. Whatever one thinks of Singer's views—he holds very controversial positions on abortion, animal rights, the obligations of the affluent toward those who are less fortunate, and euthanasia, and has been the target of more protests than any other contemporary philosopher—not even his fiercest critics deny that Singer is an outstanding example of someone who takes ethical issues and living ethically very seriously. Singer's *Writings on an Ethical Life* shows a dedicated utilitarian wrestling honestly with serious ethical issues. See also Singer's *Practical Ethics* (Cambridge, MA: Cambridge University Press, 1979) for his views on a variety of ethical issues.

For a critique of utilitarian ethics, see Samuel Scheffler, *The Rejection of Consequentialism* (Oxford: Clarendon Press, 1982). An excellent debate on utilitarian ethics can be found in J. J. C. Smart and Bernard Williams, *Utilitarianism: For and Against* (Cambridge, MA: Cambridge University Press, 1973). There are several good anthologies that examine a wide range of consequentialist and utilitarian views, including Amartya Sen and Bernard Williams, editors, *Utilitarianism and Beyond* (Cambridge, MA: Cambridge University Press, 1982); Samuel Scheffler, *Consequentialism and Its Critics* (Oxford: Clarendon Press, 1988); Philip Petit, *Consequentialism* (Aldershot, Hants: Dartmouth, 1993); Brad Hooker, Elinor Mason, and Dale E. Miller, *Morality, Rules, and Consequences: A Critical Reader* (Lanham, MD: Rowman & Littlefield, 2000); and Stephen Darwall, *Consequentialism* (Malden, MA: Blackwell, 2003).

Michael Slote's "Satisficing Consequentialism" is found in *Proceedings of the Aristotelian Society, Supplementary Volumes*, Volume 58 (1984): 139–163. A critique of Slote's view is offered by Philip Pettit in the same volume, pages 165–176.

A very good online source for a survey of contemporary consequentialism is Walter Sinnott-Armstrong's article in the online *Stanford Encyclopedia of Philosophy*; go to http://plato.stanford.edu/entries/consequentialism.

NOTES

[1]Robert Nozick, *Anarchy, State and Utopia* (New York: Basic Books, 1974).

[2]The *Karamazov Brothers*, trans. Ignat Avsey (Oxford: Oxford University Press, 1994); first published in 1879–1880.

[3]Information for this case came from *The Gazette*, Montreal, Quebec, August 16, 2003.

6

Pluralism and Pragmatism

VALUE PLURALISM

What is *the* good? What is *the* proper path, the good life, for human beings? What is *the* basic virtue, the *supreme* good, the *summum bonum*, that should guide all our ethical decision making? Philosophers have given a wide variety of answers to those questions. Plato argued that *justice* is the highest good; Aristotle insisted that the life of intellectual virtue is the highest good for humankind; Kant insisted that *the* overriding ethical principle is to follow the *categorical imperative*; for Bentham, the good is striving to produce the greatest balance of pleasure over pain for all. Those, of course, are widely divergent answers. But their enormous differences notwithstanding, they all *agree* on a basic ethical assumption: there is *one* unified overall fundamental good, and that good should organize and direct all our ethical considerations.

That has seemed a natural enough assumption to most philosophers: whatever ethical system we favor, it must be one that is *unified* by a *single* overarching principle, goal, or good. Plato insists that the unifying good is *justice*, Aristotle claims it is *intellectual virtue*, Bentham that the basic good is maximizing the balance of pleasure over suffering, and Nietzsche that we should create a higher being (the Superman or *ubermensch*). But all agree that the goal must be singular and unitary, a goal or end that unites all our ethical considerations into an ordered system. But natural as that assumption may have been to most ethicists, is it a justified assumption?

> There is really no more ground for supposing that all our demands can be accounted for by one universal underlying kind of motive than there is ground for supposing that all physical phenomena are cases of a single law. The elementary forces in ethics are probably as plural as those of physics are. The various ideals have no common character apart from the fact that they are ideals. No single abstract principle can be so used as to yield to the philosopher anything like a scientifically accurate and genuinely useful casuistic [ethical] scale. *William James*, The Moral Philosopher and the Moral Life, *1891*.

There must be a *truth* to ethics, and that means ultimately a unified whole: that was the basic idea behind the common belief in ethical *monism*, behind the belief that there must be a single unifying ethical value. If biology holds a theory that is in conflict with geology, and both are in conflict with physics, then something is *wrong*. In the late nineteenth century, Darwinian biologists insisted that the evolutionary process required hundreds of millions of years; physicists and astronomers insisted that the Earth could not be more than a few million years old (because the Sun would have burned out if it had been burning much longer than that). Both of those views could *not* be right: there cannot be one truth for biologists and a conflicting truth for astronomers and physicists. (The conflict was resolved by the discovery of atomic energy, which explained how a small star could continue releasing enormous amounts of energy for billions of years without burning out). The same idea appeals to ethicists: if there is an ethical *truth*, it must be *unified*: just as the Earth cannot be billions of years old for biologists, and much younger for physicists, so something cannot be the supreme good for you and a less significant good for me; instead, there must be *one* unifying good.

There are, however, dissenters to this ethical orthodoxy. *Value pluralism* (sometimes called ethical pluralism or moral pluralism) is the view that values do *not* have such a unified order: There are multiple values, all of them legitimate and genuine values, they may sometimes be in conflict, and there is no objective way of placing those multiple values in rank order. (In a monarchy, there may be many distinct members of the nobility: the king and queen, the dukes, the earls, the knights, and so on. But there is no question about the *order* of the nobility, with the king and queen at the top. For value pluralists, no such top to bottom ordering is possible among our various values: even *if* it is clear that some values take precedence over others, there are still conflicts among values where no objective ordering is possible.) On the value pluralist view, there are many distinct and different values, and no *supreme* value that orders them all. Or another way of thinking of this: those who favor a unified theory of value may believe that there are many different values, but they all share some defining property (they are all approved by God, they all increase happiness and diminish suffering, or they all contribute to wisdom), whereas value *pluralists* would insist that there is no property that these diverse values have in common, no unifying characteristic.

Value pluralism is a theory about the nature of ethics (values are irreducibly pluralistic); it is *not* the same as *political* pluralism. Political pluralism is the view that citizens of a state should be free to pursue their own values, so long as they do not harm or interfere with other citizens. I may (with Aristotle) reject value pluralism and maintain that the only genuinely good life for humans is one of intellectual virtue, and that pursuit of wisdom is the supreme value; but as a political pluralist, I also hold that you should be free to pursue your own goals and values (goals and values that I regard as *mistaken*), and that the state should not take sides on which personal values are correct. Likewise, I may believe that my religion is the only true religion, yet—as a *political* pluralist—believe that the state should not show preference toward any religion.

Consider a possible example of *value* pluralism. You and I both value liberty, and we both value equal opportunity (if you don't, pretend for a moment that you do). George and Martha are quite wealthy (perhaps you have doubts that their accumulation of wealth is morally legitimate: set that issue aside for the moment). They should have the *liberty* to use their resources as they wish, and they choose to invest a substantial portion of those resources in the education of their daughter, Beverly. They hire tutors to teach Beverly languages at an early age when children are very receptive to learning new languages; they take her on world tours; they hire excellent tutors to help her overcome her early reading problems, and she develops into an excellent reader; they make tutors available for every subject she studies; they send her to the finest and most expensive prep school, where none of her classes have more than a dozen students and she has a full range of AP courses; they spend thousands of dollars on prep courses for her SAT exams. Beverly excels in her studies, makes a splendid SAT score, goes to a top college (her parents happily pay the enormous tuition), and—with this wonderfully advantageous start—goes on to a very successful career. Robert and Alice also have a daughter, Carolyn; but Robert and Alice have little money, both must work to make ends meet, and though they dearly love Carolyn and deeply desire to give her every opportunity, they do not have the resources to provide Carolyn with the special academic advantages enjoyed by Beverly. Carolyn has no tutors, learns no languages; she goes to a large public school that is short on resources, has crowded classrooms and large classes with little individual attention. Carolyn was a good reader in her early years—in fact, considerably better than Beverly at the same age—but with only mediocre reading classes and few books available, Carolyn soon falls behind Beverly in this important area. Carolyn's school has few AP courses, and no tutoring for those courses; and Carolyn's family cannot afford expensive SAT prep courses, much less the high tuition of Beverly's college.

Obviously, Beverly and Carolyn do *not* enjoy equal opportunities. Of course Carolyn may nonetheless go on to a very successful career: many students who start with such disadvantages do manage to overcome them (Supreme Court Justice Sotomayer is a shining example). So, clearly Carolyn does have *some* opportunity; but it would be absurd to suggest that Beverly and Carolyn have *equal* opportunity. Obviously, Carolyn's school should be improved, and (if we *really* believe in equal opportunity) more resources should be devoted to providing a better educational opportunity for Carolyn and her classmates. But we will never have enough resources to provide *all* students with the extraordinary advantages enjoyed by Beverly. Ultimately, the only way we could insure that Beverly and Carolyn have *equal* opportunity is by restricting the resources that George and Martha can devote to Beverly's education; but that would be a restriction on the *liberty* of George and Martha to use their resources as they choose. So this is a genuine conflict among genuine values: a conflict that value pluralists believe cannot be objectively settled. (Of course there might be further debate, even among value pluralists, about whether the equal opportunity/liberty debate is a value conflict that cannot be resolved; for example, some argue that equal opportunity is essential for genuine liberty, and so it must be given precedence even by those—perhaps especially by those—who genuinely value liberty. But value pluralists would still insist that there are at least some conflicts between genuine values that cannot be resolved by such ordering.)

Value pluralism is *not* the view that we simply do not *know* the right order of competing values; rather, value pluralists maintain that there is no *supreme* good to know: there are instead many goods, with no clear order among them. Also, value pluralism is not a nonobjectivist view: pluralists can maintain that the various goods are genuine objective goods (though pluralists *may* also be *nonobjectivists*); however, they insist that there is no objective way of placing all those goods in rank order. (That's not to say that there is *no* rank ordering. My going to a concert may be a good thing, but it is *not* worth running over a crowd of pedestrians in order to get there: preserving the lives of pedestrians is more valuable than my presence at a concert. But if we are instead considering the relative values of equality of opportunity and liberty, the rank ordering may be more difficult; and according to value pluralists, there may be *no* objective way of ordering those values.)

Is there an irreducible plurality of goods? Judith Jarvis Thomson argues that there is, insisting that there are *many* ways of being good, and that those ways do not have a common property. Deborah is a good mother, a good friend, a good soldier, and a good judge; but it is difficult to imagine a "quality of goodness" that makes Deborah *good* in all those distinctive roles. Friendship is a good, along with courage, and open-mindedness, and integrity. But is there a good-making quality common to them all? In some cases, friendship may be threatened by a commitment to integrity; and if that is the case, that raises doubts that they can both be explained by one principle of goodness.

Bernard Williams offers another argument for value pluralism: the argument from regret. You are a very talented violinist, but also very good at biology. You love playing the violin, and you are certain there is genuine value in playing beautiful music and enriching the lives of those who hear you perform; but you are also sure that you would find great satisfaction as a physician, relieving the suffering of those whom you treat. Both careers are very demanding, and you cannot choose both: the demands of medical school and medical practice would not allow you to devote the many hours of practice required to play at the level of a concert violinist. You choose a career as a physician, and you find it worthwhile and satisfying, and you believe you made the right choice, the *better* choice; nonetheless, you occasionally feel a *reasonable* regret that you could not pursue the good of a career as concert violinist. But if good is a unitary whole, such regret would *not* be reasonable: you are confident you made the right choice, and if good is all one, that implies you chose the *greater* good, and it would be unreasonable to *regret* choosing the greater good over the lesser. But your regret *does* seem reasonable—and the most plausible explanation of the reasonableness of that regret is that your choice of a medical career required giving up a *different type* of good, rather than a lesser quantity of general unitary good.

Value pluralism makes ethical judgments more difficult: if there are fundamentally different values—a plurality of values that cannot be placed on a single scale or measured by a single standard—then how can we tell when our value choices are correct? "Always act so as to produce the greatest balance of pleasure over pain." Trying to follow that utilitarian standard is difficult: it is very difficult to determine the larger effects of our acts and policies. But at least utilitarians have a single scale by which to measure all value judgments. For value pluralists, there is no such scale: in trying to choose between loyalty to a friend and commitment to integrity, there may be no workable scale on which to weigh those very different values, and thus there may be no way of being certain we have made the right decision. For value pluralists, ethics is not as neat and measurable as it is for Kantians, utilitarians, or contract theorists. While value *monists* would regard that as a flaw in value pluralism, value pluralists regard it as a more realistic approach to ethics: ethical decision making is *not* (value pluralists sometimes claim) as clear, precise, and easy as ethical theories often imply; instead, ethics is a complex and confusing business, replete with uncertainty and complexity and loose ends.

Do Ethical Obligations Always Come First?

Value pluralists insist that there are multiple values that cannot be measured by a single standard, and thus no decision procedure can be devised that will yield definitive answers about which ethical values should take precedence. But even if we could be clear about our single unitary definitive ethical obligation, there would still be another question: must ethical obligations always take precedence over other interests and goals and goods? In one sense, of course, it is obvious that we always *should* follow our ethical obligation: it is part of the meaning of ethical obligation that you *should* fulfill the obligation. "You ought to keep your promise, but you shouldn't do so." That sounds like nonsense. Of course, one can sensibly say: "You ought to keep your promise, but I *hope* you do not" (you might reasonably say that, for example, if you have learned that your lover has made a promise to meet an old flame for lunch). But the *nature* of ethical obligations is that you *should* fulfill them if you can do so. If Judith says, "I have an ethical obligation to help Allen, but I should not help Allen," then we are justified in concluding that either Judith does not genuinely believe she has an ethical obligation, or that she does not understand the meaning of an ethical obligation. But one *could* say without confusion or misunderstanding: I believe we do have ethical obligations, but I don't believe it is a good idea to always give ethical obligations priority; sometimes life goes better (not *ethically* better, but richer and more satisfying) if we allow other interests and goals to trump our ethical obligations.

Must ethical obligations always take precedence over other interests and goods? Perhaps, ethically speaking, they *should*. But is a life dominated by ethical considerations really the best possible life for humans like ourselves? Before answering that question, it is important to consider what the demands of ethics *are*; and those demands will vary significantly, depending on the account of ethics one holds. If you are a social contract theorist, you probably see the demands of ethics as only moderately burdensome: don't harm others, and follow the basic laws agreed to by the contracting parties. On the other hand, if you are a utilitarian, your ethical system makes much more stringent and comprehensive demands upon you. Indeed, the demands of utilitarian ethics seem to encompass every choice you make, for utilitarian ethics requires that you *always* act in a manner that will produce the greatest balance of pleasure over suffering for everyone. A night at the movies may well give you pleasure, but does it produce the maximum balance of pleasure over suffering for everyone? Couldn't you better use the time spent at the movies to tutor a child who needs help with his early reading skills (wouldn't that be more likely to produce a better overall long-term balance of pleasure over suffering)? And the money spent for movie tickets and popcorn: aren't you obligated, as a good utilitarian, to contribute that money for famine relief? Even if you favor some less demanding ethical theory than classical utilitarianism, the demands of your ethical system are likely to be quite strong. After all, we live in a world in which there is massive poverty, widespread starvation, terrible sickness; and everyday you spend money on inessential goods—a soda or a beer, movie tickets or tennis balls, a new sweater or a magazine—and that money could be used to save the life of someone suffering from starvation or disease in an impoverished country. Most ethical systems would insist that you have an obligation to save another human life when your choice is between saving a life and purchasing a luxury item.

One response to such strong ethical demands is to reject the ethical system that makes those demands: You might favor some ethical theory that makes more modest demands, such as social contract ethics. But there is another alternative: you might conclude that the demands of ethics *are* very strong, but that ethical demands need not always come first. The latter position does not *reject* ethics or its demands—it treats ethical values and ethical obligations as genuine—but it counsels that a full rich human life may include interests and goals that sometimes take precedence over ethical demands and concerns. On this view, ethics remains very important (a life devoid of ethical considerations would be a very poor life indeed); but ethical obligations need not *always* be the *most* important considerations. In the readings which follow, Susan Wolf argues not only that it is legitimate for other considerations to sometimes override ethical obligations; in fact, Wolf maintains that the most satisfactory human life must involve goals and interests that do not always give way before ethical obligations: "I believe that moral perfection, in the sense of moral saintliness, does not constitute a model of personal well-being toward which it would be particularly rational or good or desirable for a human being to strive." Wolf maintains that invariably following the full demands of morality—or always striving for the best possible moral act—would leave us with sadly impoverished lives. Wolf concludes that moral considerations are very important, and perhaps the *most* important elements in living a good life; but they are not the only considerations, and it is quite legitimate, even desirable, to give other considerations and interests room to flourish. As Wolf puts it, there are strong grounds for doubting "the assumption that it is always better to be morally better."

Susan Wolf's view is not without its challengers, of course. Catherine Wilson argues that Wolf's perspective makes us too comfortable with the prevailing standards of our culture of privilege and consumption, and too comfortable with our disproportionate consumption of the world's resources in pursuit of our interests and pleasures. Wilson maintains that Wolf's picture makes the goals and values common in our culture look somewhat more innocent and morally justifiable than they actually are. The question that Wilson brings into focus is the distinction between what is purely a matter of private preference and what is properly within the sphere of public moral concern. Wolf is worried that moral demands might impoverish our private lives and choices, while Wilson notes that our "private choices" may have significant impact on others: particularly if those private choices are purchased at the price of overconsumption of the world's limited resources, support of a world economic system that privileges a few and deprives many, and production of pollution that threatens the well-being of everyone (especially the least privileged).

The demands of morality, and the proper place of those demands, raise difficult issues. Few people will favor an ethics requiring that we sacrifice all feelings, concerns, and interests on the altar of moral principle. On the other hand, if moral behavior seems *too* easy, that might be cause for self-examination. Perhaps you have reached the exalted level of Aristotle's perfectly virtuous person: you have become so thoroughly habituated to doing good acts that you always desire to do what is right. But if you doubt that your moral life has reached such Olympian heights, yet you never feel that the demands of ethics are a bit burdensome, then perhaps you are not giving moral considerations sufficient attention.

PLURALISM AND PRAGMATISM

Pluralists are open to a multiplicity of values, and *pragmatists* favor the testing of various value systems and are ready to consider new approaches to ethics; so there is some natural affinity between the positions. But that affinity should not be overstated. Their common ground notwithstanding, pluralists need not be pragmatists, and pragmatists can certainly reject ethical pluralism. Pragmatists are committed to an *experimental* approach to ethics, in an effort to discover what ethical system works best for human animals. But a pragmatist might believe that her experimental process has yielded a single dominant value as the most plausible and thus reject value pluralism. And from the other side, a value pluralist might believe that there are well-established values, fixed values that are known with certainty, and that because those pluralist values are clearly known, no pragmatic experimentation with values is either needed or justified. So whatever connections we might find among some value pluralists and some ethical pragmatists, we should keep in mind that these are still different and distinct approaches to ethics.

PRAGMATISM

Pragmatists believe that moral principles may indeed be *true*, just as true as scientific principles. But pragmatists insist that our traditional notion of *truth*—in philosophy and ethics as well as in science—is hopelessly muddled. According to the traditional account of truth, a claim is true when it corresponds to reality. Is the Copernican theory true? The traditional correspondence theory of truth counts the theory as true just in case it corresponds to or matches or copies the way the world actually is. The Copernican theory asserts that the Earth orbits the Sun; that theory is true (according to the correspondence account) just in case the Copernican theory corresponds to or maps or copies the planetary reality.

But according to pragmatists, that notion of matching or correspondence just doesn't work. In the first place, it doesn't work because there are many alternative theories that will all fit the data. For example, while the Copernican theory fits all our observations of the solar system, so does the "Yo-Yo theory," which claims that the Earth orbits the Sun until it completes its cycle (which will require another ten million years), and then the Sun will begin to orbit a stationary Earth. The Yo-Yo theory is perfectly silly, of course; but it fits all the data we currently have just as well as does the Copernican theory. So why do we regard the Yo-Yo theory as silly, and the Copernican theory as sober truth? Not (according to the pragmatists) because the latter *corresponds* to reality and the former does not, but rather because the Copernican theory is simpler and more useful and gives us better predictions and control. But that is what truth really consists in: not a correct matching to an external reality, but instead a coherent and workable system that *guides us well* and *works effectively*. (Incidentally, pragmatists are *not* claiming that there is no reality other than our ideas and minds. Pragmatists insist there certainly *is* a reality, and we must strive to understand it. The notion of understanding reality by copying it with our theories is what pragmatists/coherence theorists reject—not the idea of reality itself.)

What is true is not what copies or matches a "reality" independent of our theories and perceptions. That conception of reality is nonsense. It supposes that we can make sense of stepping outside our ideas and perceptions and beliefs and checking some pure "reality-as-it-is-in-itself." But such a "God's-eye view of the world"—or as Thomas Nagel called it, such a "view from nowhere"—is not possible. At the very least, it is not possible for beings like ourselves, animals firmly anchored within the natural world in which we evolved. As William James elegantly states the pragmatist position, "The trail of the human serpent is thus over everything," there is no separating the "real world" from our theories and beliefs and observations. And (pragmatists insist) it's not even clear that we can make sense of the notion of observing the world "as it is in itself," apart from our perceptions and theories. We *always* encounter reality as *part of* that reality, and we approach reality through our perceptions and ideas and theories. We are not "outside observers."

So rather than trying to *match* our theories to "the world as it really and truly is, independently of us," we must instead seek theories that *work best* in the world in which we live. Again, William James: "The true is the name of whatever proves itself to be good in the way of belief, and good, too, for definite, assignable reasons." If a theory works well, guides us effectively, functions well as a *tool* for making predictions and gaining control and living well, then that theory is *true*. It is true in the only sense of being true that makes sense. Of course it is not eternally true or absolutely true; such notions work only in the correspondence theory framework, in which we think of a theory as perfectly true when it is a perfect match for the world (the world "as it truly is," untouched by human hands, human perceptions, or human theories). If a system of physics or astronomy works for us, leads us well into predictions and discoveries, then it is true; if a system of ethics works for us, guides us effectively in how to live successfully as the social animals we are, then it is true.

> But to us pragmatists moral struggle is continuous with the struggle for existence, and no sharp break divides the unjust from the imprudent, the evil from the inexpedient. What matters for pragmatists is devising ways of diminishing human suffering and increasing human equality, increasing the ability of all human children to start life with an equal chance of happiness. This goal is not written in the stars, and is no more an expression of what Kant called "pure practical reason" than it is of the Will of God. It is a goal worth dying for, but it does not require backup from supernatural forces. *Richard Rorty, "The Challenges of Relativism," 1996.*

Pragmatic ethics, then, is an experimentalist approach to ethics, which seeks to find the ethical systems that work best for us, just as physicists and psychologists try to find the theories that work best for those purposes. It's not a social contract theory of ethics: pragmatists maintain that we must *discover* the best ethical theories, not simply choose one. We must discover which ethical systems work best for us, *not* which ethical systems match the "ethical truth" that exists independently of us. Our society might all agree to follow an ethical system that does *not* lead us well; in that case, we would be agreeing to a social contract that is wrong by pragmatic lights. Nor is pragmatism merely a new name for utilitarianism; pragmatists need not believe that an ethical system that maximizes pleasure and minimizes suffering will prove to be the ethical system that leads us best. Perhaps utilitarian ethics will prove itself best, but that is a matter to be decided by ethical experiment and practice, not utilitarian doctrine. And finally, pragmatic ethics is not relativism. Like relativists, pragmatists reject absolute eternal ethical truths that we *discover*; but unless one supposes that the *only* alternative to ethical absolutism is ethical relativism, there seems little reason to classify pragmatists as relativists.

⇒ MORAL SAINTS ⇐
Susan Wolf

Susan Wolf is Edna J. Koury Professor of Philosophy at University of North Carolina at Chapel Hill. She has written fascinating and provocative work on both ethics and free will, including "Moral Saints," which was originally published in 1982 in *Journal of Philosophy* volume 79, number 8.

I don't know whether there are any moral saints. But if there are, I am glad that neither I nor those about whom I care most are among them. By *moral saint* I mean a person whose every action is as morally good as possible, a person, that is, who is as morally worthy as can be. Though I shall in a moment acknowledge the variety of types of person that might be thought to satisfy this description, it seems to me that none of these types serve as unequivocally compelling personal ideals. In other words, I believe that moral perfection, in the sense of moral saintliness, does not constitute a model of personal well-being toward which it would be particularly rational or good or desirable for a human being to strive.

Outside the context of moral discussion, this will strike many as an obvious point. But, within that context, the point, if it be granted, will be granted with some discomfort. For within that context it is generally assumed that one ought to be as morally good as possible and that what limits there are to morality's hold on us are set by features of human nature of which we ought not to be proud. If, as I believe, the ideals that are derivable from common sense and philosophically popular moral theories do not support these assumptions, then something has to change. Either we must change our moral theories in ways that will make them yield more palatable ideals, or, as I shall argue, we must change our conception of what is involved in affirming a moral theory.

In this paper, I wish to examine the notion of a moral saint, first, to understand what a moral saint would be like and why such a being would be unattractive, and, second, to raise some questions about the significance of this paradoxical figure for moral philosophy. I shall look first at the model(s) of moral sainthood that might be extrapolated from the morality or moralities of common sense. Then I shall consider what relations these have to conclusions that can be drawn from utilitarian and Kantian moral theories. Finally, I shall speculate on the implications of these considerations for moral philosophy.

MORAL SAINTS AND COMMON SENSE

Consider first what, pretheoretically, would count for us—contemporary members of Western culture—as a moral saint. A necessary condition of moral sainthood would be that one's life be dominated by a commitment to improving the welfare of others or of society as a whole. As to what role this commitment must play in the individual's motivational system, two contrasting accounts suggest themselves to me which might equally be thought to qualify a person for moral sainthood.

First, a moral saint might be someone whose concern for others plays the role that is played in most of our lives by more selfish, or, at any rate, less morally worthy concerns. For the moral saint, the promotion of the welfare of others might play the role that is played for most of us by the enjoyment of material comforts, the opportunity to engage in the intellectual and physical activities of our choice, and the love, respect, and companionship of people whom we love, respect, and enjoy. The happiness of the moral saint, then, would truly lie in the happiness of others, and so he would devote himself to others gladly, and with a whole and open heart.

On the other hand, a moral saint might be someone for whom the basic ingredients of happiness are not unlike those of most of the rest of us. What makes him a moral saint is rather that he pays little or no attention to his own happiness in light of the overriding importance he gives to the wider concerns of morality. In other words, this person sacrifices his own interests to the interests of others, and feels the sacrifice as such.

Roughly, these two models may be distinguished according to whether one thinks of the moral saint as being a saint out of love or one thinks of the moral saint as being a saint out of duty (or some other intellectual appreciation and recognition of moral principles). We may refer to the first model as the model of the Loving Saint; to the second, as the model of the Rational Saint.

The two models differ considerably with respect to the qualities of the motives of the individuals who conform to them. But this difference would have limited effect on the saints' respective public personalities. The shared content of what these individuals are motivated to be—namely, as morally good as possible—would play the dominant role in the determination of their characters. Of course, just as a variety of large-scale projects, from tending the sick to political campaigning, may be equally and maximally morally worthy, so a variety of characters are compatible with the ideal of moral sainthood. One moral saint may be more or less jovial, more or less garrulous, more or less athletic than another. But, above all, a moral saint must have and cultivate those qualities which are apt to allow him to treat others as justly and kindly as possible. He will have the standard moral virtues to a nonstandard degree. He will be patient, considerate, even-tempered, hospitable, charitable in thought as well as in deed. He will be very reluctant to make negative judgments of other people. He will be careful not to favor some people over others on the basis of properties they could not help but have.

Perhaps what I have already said is enough to make some people begin to regard the absence of moral saints in their lives as a blessing, For there comes a point in the listing of virtues that a moral saint is likely to have where one might naturally begin to wonder whether the moral saint isn't, after all, too good—if not too good for his own good, at least too good for his own well-being. For the moral virtues, given that they are, by hypothesis, *all* present in the same individual, and to an extreme degree, are apt to crowd out the nonmoral virtues, as well as many of the interests and personal characteristics that we generally think contribute to a healthy, well-rounded, richly developed character.

In other words, if the moral saint is devoting all his time to feeding the hungry or healing the sick or raising money for Oxfam, then necessarily he is not reading Victorian novels, playing the oboe, or improving his backhand. Although no one of the interests or tastes in the category containing these latter activities could be claimed to be a necessary element in a life well lived, a life in which *none* of these possible aspects of character are developed may seem to be a life strangely barren. . . .

An interest in something like gourmet cooking will be, for different reasons, difficult for a moral saint to rest easy with. For it seems to me that no plausible argument can justify the use of human resources involved in producing a *paté de canard en croute* against possible alternative beneficent ends to which these resources might be put. If there is a justification for the institution of haute cuisine, it is one which rests on the decision *not* to justify every activity, against morally beneficial alternatives, and this is a decision a moral saint will never make. . . .

A moral saint will have to be very, very nice. It is important that he not be offensive. The worry is that, as a result, he will have to be dull-witted or humorless or bland.

This worry is confirmed when we consider what sorts of characters, taken and refined both from life and from fiction, typically form our ideals. One would hope they would be figures who are morally good—and by this I mean more than just not morally bad—but one would hope, too, that they are *not just* morally good, but talented or accomplished or attractive in nonmoral ways as well. . . . Though there is certainly nothing immoral about the ideal characters or traits I have in mind, they cannot be superimposed upon the ideal of a moral saint. For although it is a part of many of these ideals that the characters set high, and not merely acceptable, moral standards for themselves, it is also essential to their power and attractiveness that the moral strengths go, so to speak, alongside of specific, independently admirable, nonmoral ground projects and dominant personal traits.

When one does finally turn one's eyes toward lives that are dominated by explicitly moral commitments, moreover, one finds oneself relieved at the discovery of idiosyncrasies or eccentricities not quite in line with the picture of moral perfection. . . .

It seems that, as we look in our ideals for people who achieve nonmoral varieties of personal excellence in conjunction with or colored by some version of high moral tone, we look in our paragons of moral excellence for people whose moral achievements occur in conjunction with or colored by some interests or traits that have low moral tone. In other words, there seems to be a limit to how much morality we can stand. . . .

Moreover, there is something odd about the idea of morality itself, or moral goodness, serving as the object of a dominant passion in the way that a more concrete and specific vision of a goal (even a concrete *moral* goal) might be imagined to serve. Morality itself does not seem to be a suitable object of passion. Thus, when one reflects, for example, on the Loving Saint easily and gladly giving up his fishing trip or his stereo or his hot fudge sundae at the drop of the moral hat, one is apt to wonder not at how much he loves morality, but at how little he loves these other things. One thinks that, if he can give these up so easily, he does not know what it *is* to truly love them. There seems, in other words, to be a kind of joy which the Loving Saint, either by nature or by practice, is incapable of experiencing. The Rational Saint, on the other hand, might retain strong nonmoral and concrete desires—he simply denies himself the opportunity to act on them. But this is no less troubling. The Loving Saint one might suspect of missing a piece of perceptual machinery, of being blind to some of what the world has to offer. The Rational Saint, who sees it but foregoes it, one suspects of having a different problem—a pathological fear of damnation, perhaps, or an extreme form of self-hatred that interferes with his ability to enjoy the enjoyable in life.

In other words, the ideal of a life of moral sainthood disturbs not simply because it is an ideal of a life in which morality unduly dominates. The normal person's direct and specific desires for objects, activities, and events that conflict with the attainment of moral perfection are not simply sacrificed but removed, suppressed, or subsumed. The way in which morality, unlike other possible goals, is apt to dominate is particularly disturbing, for it seems to require either the lack or the denial of the existence of an identifiable, personal self. . . .

The moral saint . . . may, by happy accident, find himself with nonmoral virtues on which he can capitalize morally or which make psychological demands to which he has no choice but to attend. The point is that, for a moral saint, the existence of these interests and skills can be given at best the status of happy accidents—they cannot be encouraged for their own sakes as distinct, independent aspects of the realization of human good.

It must be remembered that from the fact that there is a tension between having any of these qualities and being a moral saint it does not follow that having any of these qualities is immoral. For it is not part of common-sense morality that one ought to be a moral saint. Still, if someone just happened to want to be a moral saint, he or she would not have or encourage these qualities, and, on the basis of our common-sense values, this counts as a reason *not to* want to be a moral saint. . . .

The fact that the moral saint would be without qualities which we have and which, indeed, we like to have,

does not in itself provide reason to condemn the ideal of the moral saint. The fact that some of these qualities are good qualities, however, and that they are qualities we *ought* to like, does provide reason to discourage this ideal and to offer other ideals in its place. In other words, some of the qualities the moral saint necessarily lacks are virtues, albeit nonmoral virtues, in the unsaintly characters who have them. . . . In general, the admiration of and striving toward achieving any of a great variety of forms of personal excellence are character traits it is valuable and desirable for people to have. In advocating the development of these varieties of excellence, we advocate nonmoral reasons for acting, and in thinking that it is good for a person to strive for an ideal that gives a substantial role to the interests and values that correspond to these virtues, we implicitly acknowledge the goodness of ideals incompatible with that of the moral saint. Finally, if we think that it is *as* good, or even better for a person to strive for one of these ideals than it is for him or her to strive for and realize the ideal of the moral saint, we express a conviction that it is good not to be a moral saint.

MORAL SAINTS AND MORAL THEORIES

I have tried so far to paint a picture—or, rather, two pictures—of what a moral saint might be like, drawing on what I take to be the attitudes and beliefs about morality prevalent in contemporary, common-sense thought. To my suggestion that common-sense morality generates conceptions of moral saints that are unattractive or otherwise unacceptable, it is open to someone to reply, "so much the worse for common-sense morality." After all, it is often claimed that the goal of moral philosophy is to correct and improve upon common-sense morality, and I have as yet given no attention to the question of what conceptions of moral sainthood, if any, are generated from the leading moral theories of our time.

A quick, breezy reading of utilitarian and Kantian writings will suggest the images, respectively, of the Loving Saint and the Rational Saint. A utilitarian, with his emphasis on happiness, will certainly prefer the Loving Saint to the Rational one, since the Loving Saint will himself be a happier person than the Rational Saint. A Kantian, with his emphasis on reason, on the other hand, will find at least as much to praise in the latter as in the former. Still, both models, drawn as they are from common sense, appeal to an impure mixture of utilitarian and Kantian intuitions. A more careful examination of these moral theories raises questions about whether either model of moral sainthood would really be advocated by a believer in the explicit doctrines associated with either of these views.

Certainly, the utilitarian in no way denies the value of self-realization. He in no way disparages the development of interests, talents, and other personally attractive traits that I have claimed the moral saint would be without. Indeed, since just these features enhance the happiness both of the individuals who possess them and of those with whom they associate, the ability to promote these features both in oneself and in others will have considerable positive weight in utilitarian calculations.

This implies that the utilitarian would not support moral sainthood as a universal ideal. A world in which everyone, or even a large number of people, achieved moral sainthood—even a world in which they *strove* to achieve it—would probably contain less happiness than a world in which people realized a diversity of ideals involving a variety of personal and perfectionist values. More pragmatic considerations also suggest that, if the utilitarian wants to influence more people to achieve more good, then he would do better to encourage them to pursue happiness-producing goals that are more attractive and more within a normal person's reach.

These considerations still leave open, however, the question of what kind of an ideal the committed utilitarian should privately aspire to himself. Utilitarianism requires him to want to achieve the greatest general happiness, and this would seem to commit him to the ideal of the moral saint.

One might try to use the claims I made earlier as a basis for an argument that a utilitarian should choose to give up utilitarianism. If, as I have said, a moral saint would be a less happy person both to be and to be around than many other possible ideals, perhaps one could create more total happiness by not trying too hard to promote the total happiness. But this argument is simply unconvincing in light of the empirical circumstances of our world. The gain in happiness that would accrue to oneself and one's neighbors by a more well-rounded, richer life than that of the moral saint would be pathetically small in comparison to the amount by which one could increase the general happiness if one devoted oneself explicitly to the care of the sick, the downtrodden, the starving, and the homeless. Of course, there may be psychological limits to the extent to which a person can devote himself to such things without going crazy. But the utilitarian's individual limitations would not thereby become a positive feature of his personal ideals. . . .

Still, the criticisms I have raised against the saint of common-sense morality should make some difference to the utilitarian's conception of an ideal which neither requires him to abandon his utilitarian principles nor forces him to fake an interest he does not have or a judgment he does not make. For it may be that a limited and carefully monitored allotment of time and energy to be devoted to the pursuit of some nonmoral interests or to the development of some nonmoral talents would make a person a better contributor to the general welfare than he would be if he allowed himself no indulgences of this sort. The enjoyment of such activities in no way compromises a commitment to utilitarian principles as long as the involvement with these activities is conditioned by a willingness to give them up whenever it is recognized that they cease to be in the general interest.

This will go some way in mitigating the picture of the loving saint that an understanding of utilitarianism will on first impression suggest. But I think it will not go very far. For the limitations on time and energy will have to be rather severe, and the need to monitor will restrict not only the extent but also the quality of one's attachment to these interests and traits. They are only weak and somewhat peculiar sorts of passions to which one can consciously remain so conditionally committed. Moreover, the way in which the utilitarian can enjoy these "extra-curricular" aspects of his life is simply not the way in which these aspects are to be enjoyed insofar as they figure into our less saintly ideals.

The problem is not exactly that the utilitarian values these aspects of his life only as a means to an end, for the enjoyment he and others get from these aspects are not a means to, but a part of, the general happiness. Nonetheless, he values these things only because of and insofar as they *are* a part of the general happiness. He values them, as it were, under the description 'a contribution to the general happiness'. This is to be contrasted with the various ways in which these aspects of life may be valued by nonutilitarians. A person might love literature because of the insights into human nature literature affords. Another might love the cultivation of roses because roses are things of great beauty and delicacy. It may be true that these features of the respective activities also explain why these activities are happiness-producing. But, to the nonutilitarian, this may not be to the point. For if one values these activities in these more direct ways, one may not be willing to exchange them for others that produce an equal, or even a greater amount of happiness. From that point of view, it is not because they produce happiness that these activities are valuable; it is because these activities are valuable in more direct and specific ways that they produce happiness. . . .

The Kantian believes that being morally worthy consists in always acting from maxims that one could will to be universal law, and doing this not out of any pathological desire but out of reverence for the moral law as such. Or, to take a different formulation of the categorical imperative, the Kantian believes that moral action consists in treating other persons always as ends and never as means only. Presumably, and according to Kant himself, the Kantian thereby commits himself to some degree of benevolence as well as to the rules of fair play. But we surely would not will that *every* person become a moral saint, and treating others as ends hardly requires bending over backwards to protect and promote their interests. On one interpretation of Kantian doctrine, then, moral perfection would be achieved simply by unerring obedience to a limited set of side-constraints. On this interpretation, Kantian theory simply does not yield an ideal conception of a person of any fullness comparable to that of the moral saints I have so far been portraying.

On the other hand, Kant does say explicitly that we have a duty of benevolence, a duty not only to allow others to pursue their ends, but to take up their ends as our own. In addition, we have positive duties to ourselves, duties to increase our natural as well as our moral perfection. These duties are unlimited in the degree to which they *may* dominate a life. If action in accordance with and motivated by the thought of these duties is considered virtuous, it is natural to assume that the more one performs such actions, the more virtuous one is. Moreover, of virtue in general Kant says, "it is an ideal which is unattainable while yet our duty is constantly to approximate to it". On this interpretation, then, the Kantian moral saint, like the other moral saints I have been considering, is dominated by the motivation to be moral. . . .

On the second interpretation of Kant, the Kantian moral saint is, not surprisingly, subject to many of the same objections I have been raising against other versions of moral sainthood. Though the Kantian saint may differ from the utilitarian saint as to *which* actions he is bound to perform and which he is bound to refrain from performing, I suspect that the range of activities acceptable to the Kantian saint will remain objectionably restrictive. . . . As the utilitarian could value his activities and character traits only insofar as they fell under the description of 'contributions to the general happiness', the Kantian would have to value his activities and character traits insofar as they were manifestations of respect for the moral law. If the development of our powers to achieve physical, intellectual, or artistic excellence, or the activities directed toward making others happy are to have any moral worth, they must arise from a reverence for the dignity that members of our species have as a result of being endowed

with pure practical reason. This is a good and noble motivation, to be sure. But it is hardly what one expects to be dominantly behind a person's aspirations to dance as well as Fred Astaire, to paint as well as Picasso, or to solve some outstanding problem in abstract algebra, and it is hardly what one hopes to find lying dominantly behind a father's action on behalf of his son or a lover's on behalf of her beloved.

Since the basic problem with any of the models of moral sainthood we have been considering is that they are dominated by a single, all-important value under which all other possible values must be subsumed, it may seem that the alternative interpretation of Kant, as providing a stringent but finite set of obligations and constraints, might provide a more acceptable morality. According to this interpretation of Kant, one is as morally good as can be so long as one devotes some limited portion of one's energies toward altruism and the maintenance of one's physical and spiritual health, and otherwise pursues one's independently motivated interests and values in such a way as to avoid overstepping certain bounds. . . .

Even this more limited understanding of morality, if its connection to Kant's views is to be taken at all seriously, is not likely to give an unqualified seal of approval to the nonmorally directed ideals I have been advocating. For Kant is explicit about what he calls "duties of apathy and self-mastery"—duties to ensure that our passions are never so strong as to interfere with calm, practical deliberation, or so deep as to wrest control from the more disinterested, rational part of ourselves. The tight and self-conscious rein we are thus obliged to keep on our commitments to specific individuals and causes will doubtless restrict our value in these things, assigning them a necessarily attenuated place.

A more interesting objection to this brand of Kantianism, however, comes when we consider the implications of placing the kind of upper bound on moral worthiness which seemed to count in favor of this conception of morality. For to put such a limit on one's capacity to be moral is effectively to deny, not just the moral necessity, but the moral goodness of a devotion to benevolence and the maintenance of justice that passes beyond a certain, required point. It is to deny the possibility of going morally above and beyond the call of a restricted set of duties. Despite my claim that all-consuming moral saintliness is not a particularly healthy and desirable ideal, it seems perverse to insist that, were moral saints to exist, they would not, in their way, be remarkably noble and admirable figures. Despite my conviction that it is as rational and as good for a person to take Katharine Hepburn or Jane Austen as her role model instead of

Mother Theresa, it would be absurd to deny that Mother Theresa is a morally better person. . . .

A moral theory that does not contain the seeds of an all-consuming ideal of moral sainthood seems to place false and unnatural limits on our opportunity to do moral good and our potential to deserve moral praise. Yet the main thrust of the arguments of this paper has been leading to the conclusion that, when such ideals are present, they are not ideals to which it is particularly reasonable or healthy or desirable for human beings to aspire. . . .

If the above remarks are understood to be implicitly critical of the views on the content of morality which seem most popular today, an alternative that naturally suggests itself is that we revise our views about the content of morality. . . . Such a change in approach involves substantially broadening or replacing our contemporary intuitions about which character traits constitute moral virtues and vices and which interests constitute moral interests. If, for example, we include personal bearing, or creativity, or sense of style, as features that contribute to one's *moral* personality, then we can create moral ideals which are incompatible with and probably more attractive than the Kantian and utilitarian ideals I have discussed. Given such an alter-ation of our conception of morality, the figures with which I have been concerned above might, far from being considered to be moral saints, be seen as morally inferior to other more appealing or more interesting models of individuals.

This approach seems unlikely to succeed, if for no other reason, because it is doubtful that any single, or even any reasonably small number of substantial personal ideals could capture the full range of possible ways of realizing human potential or achieving human good which deserve encouragement and praise. Even if we could provide a sufficiently broad characterization of the range of positive ways for human beings to live, however, I think there are strong reasons not to want to incorporate such a characterization more centrally into the framework of morality itself. For, in claiming that a character trait or activity is morally good, one claims that there is a certain kind of reason for devel-oping that trait or engaging in that activity. Yet, lying behind our criticism of more conventional conceptions of moral sainthood, there seems to be a recognition that among the immensely valuable traits and activities that a human life might positively embrace are some of which we hope that, if a person does embrace them, he does so *not* for moral reasons. In other words, no matter how flexible we make the guide to conduct which we choose to label "morality," no matter how rich we

make the life in which perfect obedience to this guide would result, we will have reason to hope that a person does not wholly rule and direct his life by the abstract and impersonal consideration that such a life would be morally good. . . .

If we are not to respond to the unattractiveness of the moral ideals that contemporary theories yield either by offering alternative theories with more palatable ideals or by understanding these theories in such a way as to prevent them from yielding ideals at all, how, then, are we to respond? Simply, I think, by admitting that moral ideals do not, and need not, make the best personal ideals. . . . Given the empirical circumstances of our world, it seems to be an ethical fact that we have unlimited potential to be morally good, and endless opportunity to promote moral interests. But this is not incompatible with the not-so-ethical fact that we have sound, compelling, and not particularly selfish reasons to choose not to devote ourselves univocally to realizing this potential or to taking up this opportunity.

Thus, in one sense at least, I am not really criticizing either Kantianism or utilitarianism. Insofar as the point of view I am offering bears directly on recent work in moral philosophy, in fact, it bears on critics of these theo-ries who, in a spirit not unlike the spirit of most of this paper, point out that the perfect utilitarian would be flawed in this way or the perfect Kantian flawed in that. The assumption lying behind these claims, implicitly or explicitly, has been that the recognition of these flaws shows us something wrong with utilitarianism as opposed to Kantianism, or something wrong with Kantianism as opposed to utilitarianism, or something wrong with both of these theories as opposed to some nameless third alter-native. The claims of this paper suggest, however, that this assumption is unwarranted. The flaws of a perfect master of a moral theory need not reflect flaws in the intramoral content of the theory itself.

MORAL SAINTS AND MORAL PHILOSOPHY

In pointing out the regrettable features and the necessary absence of some desirable features in a moral saint, I have not meant to condemn the moral saint or the person who aspires to become one. Rather, I have meant to insist that the ideal of moral sainthood should not be held as a standard against which any other ideal must be judged or justified, and that the posture we take in response to the recognition that our lives are not as morally good as they might be need not be defensive. It is misleading to insist that one is *permitted* to live a life in which the goals, relationships, activities, and interests that one pursues are not maximally morally good. For our lives are not so comprehensively subject to the requirement that we apply for permission, and our nonmoral reasons for the goals we set ourselves are not excuses, but may rather be positive, good reasons which do not exist *despite* any reasons that might threaten to outweigh them. In other words, a person may be *perfectly wonderful* without being *perfectly moral*. . . .

The claims of this paper do not so much conflict with the content of any particular currently popular moral theory as they call into question a metamoral assumption that implicitly surrounds discussions of moral theory more generally. Specifically, they call into question the assumption that it is always better to be morally better.

The role morality plays in the development of our characters and the shape of our practical deliberations need be neither that of a universal medium into which all other values must be translated nor that of an ever-present filter through which all other values must pass. This is not to say that moral value should not be an important, even the most important, kind of value we attend to in evaluating and improving ourselves and our world. It is to say that our values cannot be fully comprehended on the model of a hierarchical system with morality at the top.

ON SOME ALLEGED LIMITATIONS TO MORAL ENDEAVOR
Catherine Wilson

Catherine Wilson is Regius Professor of Moral Philosophy at University of Aberdeen. She has written extensively on philosophy of science, ethics, and many other areas; her most recent books are *Epicureanism at the Origins of Modernity* (Oxford University Press, 2008) and *Moral Animals: Ideals and Constraints in Moral Theory* (Oxford University Press, 2004). "On Some Alleged Limitations to Moral Endeavor" was originally published in 1993 in *The Journal of Philosophy*, Volume 90, Number 6.

The problem of affluence is neatly summarized by Thomas Nagel. "The bill for two," he observes,

> in a moderately expensive New York restaurant equals the annual per capita income of Bangladesh. Every time I eat out, not because I have to but just because I feel like it, the same money could do noticeably more good if contributed to famine relief. The same could be said of many purchases of clothing, wine, theater tickets, vacations, gifts, books, records, furniture, stemware, etc. It adds up both to a form of life and to quite a lot of money.

Nagel, who has long been concerned with the problem of altruism, confesses that he does not know quite what to make of this observation. He does not believe that his current manner of life can really be justified, and he does not think it is immune from criticism. Yet he also does not think it is obvious that he should not engage in this form of life, or that certain kinds of moral argument have shown that he is in the wrong insofar as he does. Perhaps, he says, he might be converted to another way of living "by a leap of self-transcendence." But because the life after the event would be so different from the life before, it is not, strictly speaking, to be envisioned from his present point of view. . . . Alternatively, he says, one might aim for or hope for a political rather than a personal solution to the problem of unequal distribution of goods.

Although he formulates the problem as an urgent and troubling one, the effect of Nagel's text—in the context of the book of which it is a part—is to diminish its urgency. For Nagel shows himself ready in this book to treat the problem of affluence and responsibility as a particular case of a general nonconvergence between subjective views of the world and an objective view, a nonconvergence to which he assigns a positive rather than a negative value. And here we meet with an extraordinary feature of contemporary moral philosophy: one so striking that it deserves discussion, namely, its thoroughgoing rejection of the idea that philosophical enlightenment entails a detachment from worldly goods and worldly pleasures. . . .

[O]ne reads passages such as the one quoted from Nagel with a sense of unease. It takes only a few degrees of philosophical distance to ask oneself in this connection whether the objects and pursuits deemed meritorious in what Thorstein Veblen referred to almost a century ago as "pecuniary society" really are so; whether the codes of this society correspond to actual meanings? What about those wineglasses and theater tickets? And what are we to say when it is philosophers themselves who implicitly endorse the right to these things and the way of life of which they are part by finding an irreconcilable difference between subjective and objective points of view? Following Karl Mannheim, the founder of the sociology of knowledge, we may well suppose that the intelligentsia of a society, especially its philosophers, are the people whose task it is to produce an interpretation of life for that society, and that what the new moral philosophers are doing is producing such an interpretation. Now, according to Mannheim, an ideology is produced when a "ruling group becomes so interest-bound that they cannot see facts which would undermine their sense of domination; they obscure the real condition of society to themselves and others and thereby stabilize it". . . . We have thus to ask whether the designation of certain spheres of activity and experience as protected regions which are above, beyond, and perhaps beneath the reach of impersonal theories of justice might not constitute an ideology of academicians who are now, in a way they have never been before, part of a materially favored class.

II. THE DECLINE OF IMPERSONAL THEORIES

The earlier trends in ethics to which the work we have been considering may be seen as a response were socio-legal in tenor, broad in scale, and redistributionist in their slant: John Rawls dominated the former era with A Theory of Justice, published in 1971. To show the endpoints of the scale between impartial justice ethics and the ethos of private pursuits which Nagel's passage invokes, we may consider the positions taken by Peter Singer in an article published almost twenty years ago and by Susan Wolf in 1982.

In "Famine, Affluence and Morality," Singer argued that the affluence of the richer nations and their unwillingness to devote more than a fraction of their gross national product—about 1%—to aid to other countries, in which people were suffering from hunger, cold, climactic catastrophes, and overpopulation was wrong. It was also wrong for individuals, not just nations, to devote so little of their own income to charity. The right thing to do, he said, was, in effect, to forgo the glassware, the theater tickets, the new outfits, the vacation, and just give the money one would have spent on those things to a relief organization. It was both possible and morally obligatory to compare the percentage of one's income spent on the non-necessities of life with the percentage spent to provide these necessities for others who do not have them. Psychologically, he admitted, it is difficult to care about people on the other side of the world experiencing a famine or another catastrophe, but it is morally wrong nevertheless to ignore them.

A position orthogonal to this one was adopted by Wolf, who spoke out daringly in favor of private and even wasteful activities. Wolf did not even try to redefine morality in such a way as to make it accord better with experience; she rejected the pursuit of moral perfection in any terms. In "Moral Saints," she considered the appearance of wrongness produced by affluence and argued that it was illusory. She willingly conceded that "no plausible argument can justify the use of human resources involved in producing paté de canard en croûte against possible beneficent ends to which these resources might be put." . . . Yet, she said, it is not right to reproach the diner on paté de canard, and this diner need not maintain a defensive posture with respect to this pleasure. For morality—in the sense in which it would require us to sacrifice ourselves for others— is not the only value, the one to which every other good must be sacrificed. And she went on to describe other projects, which consume time and money, the participation in which precludes the exercise of charity, which are worthy and appropriate for human beings. We need to recognize the value, she insisted, of "the normal person's direct and specific desires for objects, activities, and events that conflict with the attainment of moral perfection." . . .

The unrestrained pursuit of moral excellence would, Wolf said, even make it impossible to be excellent in the broader sense. There were accordingly both positive and negative sides to her paper. Part of it was spent painting sainthood, which she interpreted as the dedication of all one's resources and energies to helping others, in an undesirable light. Saints were portrayed as overly focused, self-righteous, and narrow. The suggestion was that the whole-hearted giving oneself over to projects of relieving other people's suffering would have a strangely dehumanizing effect; we should be in awe of people who managed to do this but it would be unpleasant to be forced into social intimacy with them, for we nonsaints would have no common ground with them. The rest of the article was spent painting a picture of a good or wonderful life. This life is characterized by variety, enjoyment, and the improvement of abilities and talents; the author mentions reading Victorian novels, playing the oboe, improving one's backhand, gourmet cooking, watching old comedies, eating caviar, and cello playing, as its possible constituents. The emphasis here is on pursuits and activities, rather than, as in Nagel's chapter, the accumulation of personal possessions and transitory experiences; however, in both cases, one is not being pejorative in pointing out that some typical enjoyments of upper-middle class people furnish the domain.

The difficulty with Singer's paper, which left it vulnerable to challenges such as Wolf's, was that it seemed to bring us up against the limits of philosophy as a discursive mode. It could not bring about the effect in the reader that its content mandated. Even in the context of the early 1970s concern with social justice, it seemed prophetic, Utopian. The reaction of the reader was to concede that there was a great deal to what Singer had said, that the good arguments were all on his side, but one felt that Singer had claimed the moral high ground and issued an ultimatum, though one without threats or enticements. The paper was, as a text, unpersuasive, for Singer did not even acknowledge our pre-existing local and partialist concerns. In ignoring what people actually care about—the protection of their children and themselves from the more brutal aspects of existence; the cultivation of their talents and interests; and the beautification of themselves, their houses, their environments—he succeeded in portraying only a system of redistribution that could be imposed by a philosopher king. And, like Rawls, he regarded the private emotions of pity and shame as irrelevant to the question of public justice.

Singer's response would have been at the time to say that the philosopher's role is just to point out contradictions and entailments, such as the obligation to charity necessitated by impartialist concepts of justice, which he took for granted. Rhetoric and psychology belong to a different department. Such are the limits of philosophy. Interestingly, Wolf too believes in the limits to philosophy: she does not believe that philosophy can *justify* selfish or inconsequential pursuits, and she claims that justifying them is not what she is doing. Rather, she is taking a meta-ethical stance, and making a meta-ethical claim, viz., that "the posture we take in response to the recognition that our lives are not as morally good as possible need not be defensive." ... According to Wolf, no philosophical theory can tell us how important moral goodness is as against other forms of goodness, or how much time, effort, and money we ought to devote to other-directed moral pursuits as against selfish, pleasurable pursuits. Thus, where Singer failed to take into account some obvious limits of philosophical argument, Wolf seems to be positing and even welcoming the limits to argument.

III. The Fact of Divided Loyalties

One may be convinced by what Wolf says and convinced as a result that Singer's conclusions about what we ought to do are erroneous. In such a case one may nevertheless be dissatisfied with "Moral Saints" for reasons other than the cogency of its argument: one may, for example, believe that asceticism is part of the philosopher's role, and that, whatever she does as a private person, it is wrong for a philosopher to abandon her role in this way. Such disapproval would, however, tend to lend strength to Wolf's implicit contention that the way in which philosophers have often wanted to talk about morality makes them guilty of hypocrisy. Alternatively, however, one might believe that Wolf's claim to be able to speak from outside a moral perspective, from a perspective which recognizes morality as merely one human good among others, is unjustified. If, as I shall try to show, this is in fact the case, then Singer and other philosophers who insist on the need for sweeping revisions to ordinary life in the name of morality have not been answered.

First, though, a word on benign and necessary hypocrisies. In the historian Paul Veyne's illuminating and increasingly cited study of the psychology of divided loyalties—*Did the Greeks Believe in Their Myths?*—he argued that the Greeks did, in some sense, believe in their myths, but that they left off using them where their interest in believing them ended. This pattern of partial allegiance is, he thinks, universal. We live, Veyne argues, in a number of different worlds at once, or rather we live lives that are characterized by various programs—aesthetic, moral, religious, practical, social. Normally, the question of the consistency or inconsistency of these programs does not arise, but sometimes a convulsive effort at consistency is made. (Religious cults provide an obvious example: for the Massachusetts Puritans, for example, constant surveillance and proofing of the thoughts, language, dress, behavior, etc., of oneself, one's children, one's servants, and one's neighbors for their conformity to religious prescripts was an obligation.) But in most places and at most times, life is not like this: our minds are Balkanized but peaceful.

Every special subject—religion, morality, art, and politics—on Veyne's account, has its proponents who claim that it is the alpha and omega of human existence. They argue that it constitutes the highest reality, or the deepest level of analysis, or the most urgent spring of conduct. The moralist says that every human action must be assigned to the category of the morally permitted, obligatory, or proscribed; the theologian says that everything serves and glorifies a god or disobeys his rules. The politician says that all actions are important in so far as they maintain or threaten political ideals and institutions. The aesthete says that only the fascinating, the marvellous, the complicated, or the unfathomable, have enduring value. But whatever these spokespeople say, real life is not like this. At any given moment, each special subject is relatively unimportant; each occupies only a narrow band in the quotidian spectrum.

So it may be that an ethics of the impersonal sort is a cultural icon that serves for cultural orientation without being fully operational at every moment. On parade days—in moments of great indignation or conflict—morality might come, in full dress as it were, into play, and permit the subject to articulate his opposition or think his situation through in a way he could not otherwise. If this is how things are, then the unease prompted by "Moral Saints" is perhaps a function of the fact that, for these worthy cultural icons to serve us well, they cannot be positively identified as such. . . .

IV. IMMANENCE AS A VALUE

. . . . [I]t is one thing to take exception to "Moral Saints" because the author has exposed morality as an idol, thereby producing a general relief, but also a certain discomfort, while failing to give a better foundation for the idea of a wonderful life. It is quite another to take exception to it on the grounds that the literature of partiality and personal projects really constitutes a defense of a life of leisure and privilege, and that part of its constituting such a defense involves the inclusion of a specific statement to the effect that it is not a defense. If it really is a defense posing as a proof that some things need no defense, then, I suggest, it belongs to the category of ideology. For it then shows, even if it does not say that they have them, the rights of the haves against the have-nots, and, by what it excludes, it projects a state of affairs in which the good life described really is an innocent, as opposed to an innocuous life. . . .

Regarded in the value-neutral terms of descriptive sociology, the philosophers we have mentioned can be seen to write without exception from a perspective of choice, plenty, and leisure. The activities and adventures—dining adventures, theatrical adventures, even romantic adventures—which they mention or discuss are plainly bound to an economic context and a milieu that is established in the large or middle-sized cities of the Western industrial democracies. Now, it might be said that it does not matter if the Nagel–Wolf vision of the good life is determined by the culture in which we happen to live; it only matters that other people at other times and in other places should have been allowed to have their particularist ideas of the good life as well. The world of the Thai peasant contains its sensory delights, its music, tastes, colors, and fictions. But the concern here is not that the conception of a good life is narrowly defined or restricted. It is rather that a defense of immanence offered by one who, objectively speaking, enjoys a situation of privilege, is itself an ideology, or, if it is not, nothing has been said to block the charge that it is.

Nagel was troubled by this question: Could a life that is not obviously exploitative and egotistical by the standards of the immediate community nevertheless be criticized from some more detached perspective? His answer, as I read it, is that it *could* be criticized, but that the incommensurability of subjective and objective points of view makes it impossible that this criticism could take the form of a slow, deliberate, willed comparison of one's mode of life with traditional philosophical conceptions of justice: rather, one would have to experience an inner revolution or revelation. The theological motif is further developed by Wolf, who concedes the existence of "saints" who reject the standards of the community. But she assumes the appropriateness of these standards and presents examples of pursuits that are not, in light of those standards, particularly contestable. If an author were to defend the excellence of driving large motorboats, collecting state-of-the-art electronics, and vacationing in resort condominiums, which, in our professional classes, are the primary objects of desire, rather than books and musical instruments, we would have been immediately aware that a certain "lifestyle" was being endorsed. But Wolf's version of the wonderful life is relatively noninvasive and nonaggrandizing. What is hidden, nevertheless, is the underlying excess, waste, and unfairness of the present system of production and distribution which make it possible to live a life of choice and plenty. How could there be a conflict between my playing the oboe and children surviving in drought-stricken Ethiopia when there is not even the slightest hint of a connection between the two? But might it not be the case that the apparent lack of any need for a defense of my oboe playing is a function only of the presentation, not a function of any distinction between public and private life which can be philosophically established?

The tendency in the new morality of private pursuits then is to make goodness more accessible, to relax the standards a person needs to meet to be good, so that a general innocuousness or minimal decency will suffice, so long as the person is achieving something worthwhile in his chosen areas of endeavor. But must we call people who excel at music, gardening, entertaining, the appreciation of literature, or at study, or writing *good*? It is often said or implied that Aristotle would have called them good. And Wolf says that the life she is representing as an ideal is Aristotelian and perhaps even Nietzschean. But it is possible to respond that Aristotle was not dealing with morality as such, and I would call on Nietzsche, who knew that the ancients were dealing with an ethos—an ethos of rank—that they were essentially articulating an idea about what it is to be a *noble* kind of person—to confirm this. Nietzsche's moral antinomianism and his call for a transvaluation of values bear in turn only a superficial relationship to the defense of the sort of life we are considering.

V. Conclusions

One comes away from the best contemporary moral philosophy with three strong impressions. First, one is struck by its desire to replace old-fashioned moral prescriptivism, with its unpleasant tendency to harangue the readership to little avail, with descriptive accounts of what we do care about, and how we in fact establish individual hierarchies of values. Second, one is struck by its perception that, not only is moral theory impoverished by failing to take contingency and partiality into account, but that the value of life is reduced when an effort is made to suppress or exclude them. Third, one is struck by the point that morality cannot, logically, do what it would like to do: draw a sphere around the whole of life and evaluate everything within that sphere in terms of its own requirements. For we have the option, always, simply to pay morality no mind. We may therefore expose ourselves to the condemnation of others; again, however, we have the option, always, to pay those judgments no mind.

The question that has to be faced is whether the resulting award of a philosophically protected status to life as it is lived by a percentage of the population in North America and Britain is not as or more objectionable than the faults ascribed to those impersonal theories of ethics that we are forced to recognize, following Strawson, as revisionary.

Revisionary ethics—ethics which is associated with the fervent wish that people would live differently than they do—is subject to attack on three fronts: on the grounds that the task of philosophy is not to present a Utopian state of affairs and urge its realization but to produce an analysis of moral phenomena as they are actually experienced by us; on the grounds that the ideals it holds up are inhuman; and, finally, on the grounds that the binding character of the moral law of revisionary ethics lies itself in the realm of the imaginary. It is impossible not to feel the force of these criticisms, even when one comes as a nonspecialist to the field. Any honest person must recognize the existence of conflicts in herself, between impartial ideals of justice and the love of ease and luxury; between the desire for purity and integrity and the desire for experience and multiplicity. The world as I found it—as I stumbled into it—and its particular arrangements are not my fault. And though anyone may intone morality to us in the most solemn of accents, it is still up to us to reply that we do not care, or that we care about something else more. Thus, it is absurd to speak of an obligation on our part to be saints. It is even absurd to speak of an obligation to care about morality which philosophy can prove or reveal. But implicit in the practice of philosophy is the recognition of an obligation to criticize that which one is naturally inclined to believe and to do. This applies to the values of immanence as well as to the now more commonly targeted values of abstraction and impersonality.

The contemporary philosophical defense of the plurality of goods, immanence, and contingency contrasts with the historical tendency of moral philosophers to establish a distance between themselves and the values of their culture. The establishment of this distance should not be confused, however, with the establishment of a revisionary moral philosophy that is itself distanced from life and practice. The scrutiny of one's own life for adherence to pecuniary and other culturally determined canons of taste can become but need not be a manifestation of Veyne's neurotic scrupulousness which insists on a perfect obedience to impossible regulations. And the study of the relations between plenitude and choice in an economically dominant society and hardship and confinement in others evinces no hint of an incommensurability between subjective and objective views, no hint of practices or desires so deeply entrenched in our way of life that it is impossible to imagine altering them. Rather, it is by painting a picture of a life in which no re-orientation will occur—unless by a magical act of conversion—because of the very fullness and excellence of that life, that one contributes to occluding the connections that bind the public to the private. Correspondingly, it is by letting the lives of people who do not shop, or travel, or enjoy professional entertainment, make their own impression on us that the perception of a gulf between the private and the public sphere is altered and the superstition that one's own good fortune is either morally deserved, or a highly improbable but lucky accident, undermined.

To the extent that our ordinary way of life does appear immune from criticism and is not perceived as the outcome of those forces which sustain, transmit, and defend privilege, it is, I have suggested, due to the desire that it be made to appear so. When it is suggested that no reconciliation between happiness and charitable practice can be found without a leap into the unknown, or that objective perception will result in the fragmentation of personal integrity, or the loss of one's humanity, or that philosophy, for metatheoretical reasons cannot speak to these issues at all, one can only wonder whether, under the impression that he is showing the hollowness of some cultural icons, the philosopher is not under the spell of some others.

⇌ The Quest for Certainty ⇌
John Dewey

John Dewey (1859–1952) was a leader of the American pragmatist movement in philosophy, writing influential works on ethics, aesthetics, logic, metaphysics, and epistemology. He was also perhaps the most famous "public intellectual" of the first half of the twentieth century: he wrote and lectured on political issues, social debates, economic questions, and many other topics; and he was a leader in promoting new approaches to public education. His work in both philosophy and educational theory continues to exert a powerful influence. The passage below is taken from *The Quest for Certainty*, published in 1929.

. . . . [B]eliefs about values are pretty much in the position in which beliefs about nature were before the scientific revolution. There is either a basic distrust of the capacity of experience to develop its own regulative standards, and an appeal to what philosophers call eternal values, in order to ensure regulation of belief and action; or there is acceptance of enjoyments actually experienced irrespective of the method or operation by which they are brought into existence. Complete bifurcation between rationalistic method and an empirical method has its final and most deeply human significance in the ways in which good and bad are thought of and acted for and upon. . . .

The scientific revolution came about when material of direct and uncontrolled experience was taken as problematic; as supplying material to be transformed by reflective operations into known objects. The contrast between experienced and known objects was found to be a temporal one; namely, one between empirical subject-matters which were had or "given" prior to the acts of experimental variation and redisposition and those which succeeded these acts and issued from them. The notion of an act whether of sense or thought which supplied a valid measure of thought in immediate knowledge was discredited. Consequences of operations became the important thing. The suggestion almost imperatively follows that escape from the defects of transcendental absolutism is not to be had by setting up as values enjoyments that happen anyhow, but in defining value by enjoyments which are the consequences of intelligent action. Without the intervention of thought, enjoyments are not values but problematic goods, becoming values when they re-issue in a changed form from intelligent behavior. The fundamental trouble with the current empirical theory of values is that it merely formulates and justifies the socially prevailing habit of regarding enjoyments as they are actually experienced as values in and of themselves. It completely side-steps the question of regulation of these enjoyments. This issue involves nothing less than the problem of the directed reconstruction of economic, political and religious institutions.

There was seemingly a paradox involved in the notion that if we turned our backs upon the immediately perceived qualities of things, we should be enabled to form valid conceptions of objects, and that these conceptions could be used to bring about a more secure and more significant experience of them. But the method terminated in disclosing the connections or interactions upon which perceived objects, viewed as events, depend. Formal analogy suggests that we regard our direct and original experience of things liked and enjoyed as only *possibilities* of values to be achieved; that enjoyment becomes a value when we discover the relations upon which its presence depends. Such a causal and operational definition gives only a conception of a value, not a value itself. But the utilization of the conception in action results in an object having secure and significant value.

The formal statement may be given concrete content by pointing to the difference between the enjoyed and the enjoyable, the desired and the desirable, the *satisfying* and the *satisfactory*. To say that something is enjoyed is to make a statement about a fact, something already in existence; it is not to judge the value of that fact. There is no difference between such a proposition and one which says that something is sweet or sour, red or black. It is just correct or incorrect and that is the end of the matter. But to call an object a value is to assert that it satisfies or fulfills certain conditions. Function and status in meeting conditions is a different matter from bare existence. The fact that something is desired only raises the *question* of its desirability; it does not settle it. Only a child in the degree of his immaturity thinks to settle the question of desirability by reiterated proclamation: "I want it, I want it, I want it." What is objected to in the current empirical theory of values is not connection of them with desire and enjoyment but failure to distinguish between enjoyments of radically different sorts. There are many common expressions in which the difference of the two kinds is clearly recognized. Take for example the difference between the ideas of "satisfying" and "satisfactory." To say that something satisfies is to report something as an isolated finality. To assert that it is *satisfactory* is to: define it in its connections and interactions. The fact that it pleases or is immediately congenial poses a problem to judgment. How shall the satisfaction be rated? Is it a value or is it not? Is it something to be prized and cherished, *to be* enjoyed? Not stern moralists alone but everyday experience informs us that finding satisfaction in a thing may be a warning, a summons to be on the lookout for consequences. To declare something sat*isfactory* is to assert that it meets specifiable conditions. It is, in effect, a judgment that the thing "will do." It involves a prediction; it contemplates a future in which the thing will continue to serve; it *will* do. It asserts a consequence the thing will actively institute; it will *do*. That it is satisfying is the content of a proposition of fact; that it is satisfactory is a judgment, an estimate, an appraisal. It denotes an attitude *to be* taken, that of striving to perpetuate and to make secure. . . .

Propositions about what is or has been liked are of instrumental value in reaching judgments of value, in as far as the conditions and consequences of the thing liked are thought about. In themselves they make no claims; they put forth no demand upon subsequent attitudes and acts; they profess no authority to direct. If one likes a thing he likes it; that *is* a point about which there can be no dispute:—although it is not so easy to state just *what* is liked as is frequently assumed. A judgment about what

is *to be* desired and enjoyed is, on the other hand, a claim on future action; it possesses *de jure* and not merely *de facto* quality. It is a matter of frequent experience that likings and enjoyments are of all kinds, and that many are such as reflective judgments condemn. By way of self-justification and "rationalization," an enjoyment creates a tendency to assert that the thing enjoyed is a value. This assertion of validity adds authority to the fact. It is a decision that the object has a right to exist and hence a claim upon action to further its existence.

The analogy between the status of the theory of values and the theory of ideas about natural objects before the rise of experimental inquiry may be carried further. The sensationalistic theory of the origin and test of thought evoked, by way of reaction, the transcendental theory of *a priori* ideas. For it failed utterly to account for objective connection, order and regularity in objects observed. Similarly, any doctrine that identifies the mere fact of being liked with the value of the object liked so fails to give direction to conduct when direction is needed that it automatically calls forth the assertion that there are values eternally in Being that are the standards of all judgments and the obligatory ends of all action. Without the introduction of operational thinking, we oscillate between a theory that, in order to save the objectivity of judgments of values, isolates them from experience and nature, and a theory that, in order to save their concrete and human significance, reduces them to mere statements about our own feelings.

Not even the most devoted adherents of the notion that enjoyment and value are equivalent facts would venture to assert that because we have once liked a thing we should go on liking it; they are compelled to introduce the idea that *some* tastes are to be cultivated. Logically, there is no ground for introducing the idea of cultivation; liking is liking, and one is as good as another. If enjoyments *are* values, the judgment of value cannot regulate the form which liking takes; it cannot regulate its own conditions. Desire and purpose, and hence action, are left without guidance, although the question of regulation of their formation is the supreme problem of practical life. Values (to sum up) may be connected inherently with liking, and yet not with *every* liking but only with those that judgment has approved, after examination of the relation upon which the object liked depends. A casual liking is one that happens without knowledge of how it occurs nor to what effect. The difference between it and one which is sought because of a judgment that it is worth having and is to be striven for, makes just the difference between enjoyments which are accidental and enjoyments that have value and hence a claim upon our attitude and conduct. . . .

Thus we are led to our main proposition: *Judgments about values are judgments about the conditions and the results of experienced objects; judgments about that which should regulate the formation of our desires, affections and enjoyments.* For whatever decides their formation will determine the main course of our conduct, personal and social.

If it sounds strange to hear that we should frame our judgments as to what has value by considering the connections in existence of what we like and enjoy, the reply is not far to seek. As long as we do not engage in this inquiry enjoyments (values if we choose to apply that term) are casual; they are given by "nature," not constructed by art. Like natural objects in their qualitative existence, they at most only supply material for elaboration in rational discourse. A *feeling* of good or excellence is as far removed from goodness in fact as a feeling that objects are intellectually thus and so is removed from their being actually so. To recognize that the truth of natural objects can be reached only by the greatest care in selecting and arranging directed operations, and then to suppose that values can be truly determined by the mere fact of liking seems to leave us in an incredible position. All the serious perplexities of life come back to the genuine difficulty of forming a judgment as to the values of the situation; they come back to a conflict of goods. Only dogmatism can suppose that serious moral conflict is between something clearly bad and something known to be good, and that uncertainty lies wholly in the will of the one choosing. Most conflicts of importance are conflicts between things which are or have been satisfying, not between good and evil. And to suppose that we can make a hierarchical table of values at large once for all, a kind of catalogue in which they are arranged in an order of ascending or descending worth, is to indulge in a gloss on our inability to frame intelligent judgments in the concrete. Or else it is to dignify customary choice and prejudice by a title of honor.

The alternative to definition, classification and systematization of satisfactions just as they happen to occur is judgment of them by means of the relations under which they occur. If we know the conditions under which the act of liking, of desire and enjoyment, takes place, we are in a position to know what are the consequences of that act. The difference between the desired and the desirable, admired and the admirable, becomes effective at just this point. Consider the difference between the proposition "That thing has been eaten," and the judgment "That thing is edible." The former statement involves no knowledge of any relation except the one stated; while we are able to judge of the edibility of anything only when we have a knowledge of its interactions with other things sufficient to enable us to foresee its probable effects when it is taken into the organism and produces effects there.

To assume that anything can be known in isolation from its connections with other things is to identify knowing with merely having some object before perception or in feeling, and is thus to lose the key to the traits that distinguish an object as known. It is futile, even silly, to suppose that some quality that is directly present constitutes the whole of the thing presenting the quality. It does not do so when the quality is that of being hot or fluid or heavy, and it does not when the quality is that of giving pleasure, or being enjoyed. Such qualities are, once more, effects, ends in the sense of closing termini of processes involving causal connections. They are something to be investigated, challenges to inquiry and judgment. The more connections and interactions we ascertain, the more we *know* the object in question. Thinking is search for these connections. Heat experienced as a consequence of directed operations has a meaning quite different from the heat that is casually experienced without knowledge of how it came about. The same is true of enjoyments. Enjoyments that issue from conduct directed by insight into relations have a meaning and a validity due to the way in which they are experienced. Such enjoyments are not repented of; they generate no after-taste of bitterness. Even in the midst of direct enjoyment, there is a sense of validity, of authorization, which intensifies the enjoyment. There is solicitude for perpetuation of the *object* having value which is radically different from mere anxiety to perpetuate the *feeling* of enjoyment.

Such statements as we have been making are, therefore, far from implying that there are values apart from things actually enjoyed as good. To find a thing enjoyable is, so to say, a *plus* enjoyment. We saw that it was foolish to treat the scientific object as a rival to or substitute for the perceived object, since the former is intermediate between uncertain and settled situations and those experienced under conditions of greater control. In the same way, judgment of the value of an object to be experienced is instrumental to appreciation of it when it is realized. But the notion that every object that happens to satisfy has an equal claim with every other to be a value is like supposing that every object of perception has the same cognitive force as every other. There is no knowledge without perception; but objects perceived are *known* only when they are determined as consequences of connective operations. There is no value except where there is satisfaction, but there have to be certain conditions fulfilled to transform a satisfaction into a value.

The time will come when it will be found passing strange that we of this age should take such pains to control by every means at command the formation of ideas of physical things, even those most remote from human concern, and yet are content with haphazard beliefs about the qualities of objects that regulate our deepest interests; that we are scrupulous as to methods of forming ideas of natural objects, and either dogmatic or else driven by immediate conditions in framing those about values. There is, by implication, if not explicitly, a prevalent notion that values are already well known and that all which is lacking is the will to cultivate them in the order of their worth. In fact the most profound lack is not the will to act upon goods already known but the will to know what they are. . . .

What difference would it actually make in the arts of conduct, personal and social, if the experimental theory were adopted not as a mere theory, but as a part of the working equipment of habitual attitudes on the part of everyone? It would be impossible, even were time given, to answer the question in adequate detail, just as men could not foretell in advance the consequences for knowledge of adopting the experimental method. It is the nature of the method that it has to be tried. But there are generic lines of difference which, within the limits of time at disposal, may be sketched.

Change from forming ideas and judgments of value on the basis of conformity to antecedent objects, to constructing enjoyable objects directed by knowledge of consequences, is a change from looking to the past to looking to the future. I do not for a moment suppose that the experiences of the past, personal and social, are of no importance. For without them we should not be able to frame any ideas whatever of the conditions under which objects are enjoyed nor any estimate of the consequences of esteeming and liking them. But past experiences are significant in giving us intellectual instrumentalities of judging just these points. They are tools, not finalities. Reflection upon what we have liked and have enjoyed is a necessity. But it tells us nothing about the *value* of these things until enjoyments are themselves reflectively controlled, or, until, as they are recalled, we form the best judgment possible about what led us to like this sort of thing and what has issued from the fact that we liked it.

We are not, then, to get away from enjoyments experienced in the past and from recall of them, but from the notion that they are the arbiters of things to be further enjoyed. At present, the arbiter is found in the past, although there are many ways of interpreting what in the past is authoritative. Nominally, the most influential conception doubtless is that of a revelation once had or a perfect life once lived. Reliance upon precedent, upon institutions created in the past, especially in law, upon rules of morals that have come to us through unexamined customs, upon uncriticized tradition, are other forms of dependence. It is not for a moment suggested that we can get away from customs and established institutions. A mere break would doubtless result simply in chaos. But there is no danger of such a break. Mankind is too inertly conservative both by constitution and by education to give the idea of this danger actuality. What there is genuine danger of is that the force of new conditions will produce disruption externally and mechanically: this is an ever present danger. The prospect is increased, not mitigated, by that conservatism which insists upon the adequacy of old standards to meet new conditions. What is needed is intelligent examination of the consequences that are actually effected by inherited institutions and customs, in order that there may be intelligent consideration of the ways in which they are to be intentionally modified in behalf of generation of different consequences.

This is the significant meaning of transfer of experimental method from the technical field of physical experience to the wider field of human life. We trust the method in forming our beliefs about things not directly connected with human life. In effect, we distrust it in moral, political and economic affairs. In the fine arts, there are many signs of a change. In the past, such a change has often been an omen and precursor of changes in other human attitudes. But, generally speaking, the idea of actively adopting experimental method in social affairs, in the matters deemed of most enduring and ultimate worth, strikes most persons as a surrender of all standards and regulative authority. But in principle, experimental method does not signify random and aimless action; it implies direction by ideas and knowledge. The question at issue is a practical one. Are there in existence the ideas and the knowledge that permit experimental method to be effectively used in social interests and affairs? . . .

Another great difference to be made by carrying the experimental habit into all matter of practice is that it cuts the roots of what is often called subjectivism, but which is better termed egoism. The subjective attitude is much more widespread than would be inferred from the philosophies which have that label attached. It is as rampant in realistic philosophies as in any others, sometimes even more so, although disguised from those who hold these philosophies under the cover of reverence for and enjoyment of ultimate values. For the implication of placing the standard of thought and knowledge in antecedent existence is that our thought makes no difference in what is significantly real. It then affects only our own attitude toward it.

This constant throwing of emphasis back upon a change made in ourselves instead of one made in the world in which we live seems to me the essence of what is objectionable in "subjectivism." Its taint hangs about even Platonic realism with its insistent evangelical dwelling upon the change made within the mind by contemplation of the realm of essence, and its depreciation of action as transient and all but sordid—a concession to the necessities of organic existence. All the theories which put conversion "of the eye of the soul" in the place of a conversion of natural and social objects that modifies goods actually experienced, are a retreat and escape from existence—and this retraction into self is, once more, the heart of subjective egoisms. The typical example is perhaps the other-worldliness found in religions whose chief concern is with the salvation of the personal soul. But other-worldliness is found as well in estheticism and in all seclusion within ivory towers.

It is not in the least implied that change in personal attitudes, in the disposition of the "subject," is not of great importance. Such change, on the contrary, is involved in any attempt to modify the conditions of the environment. But there is a radical difference between a change in the self that is cultivated and valued as an end, and one that is a means to alteration, through action, of objective conditions. The Aristotelian-medieval conviction that highest bliss is found in contemplative possession of ultimate Being presents an ideal attractive to some types of mind; it sets forth a refined sort of enjoyment. It is a doctrine congenial to minds that despair of the effort involved in creation of a better world of daily experience. It is, apart from theological attachments, a doctrine sure to recur when social conditions are so troubled as to make actual endeavor seem hopeless. But the subjectivism so externally marked in modern thought as compared with ancient is either a development of the old doctrine under new conditions or is of merely technical import. The medieval version of the doctrine at least had the active support of a great social institution by means of which man could be brought into the state of mind that prepared him for ultimate enjoyment of eternal Being. It had a certain solidity and depth which is lacking in modern theories that would attain the result by merely emotional or speculative procedures, or by any means not demanding a change in objective existence so as to render objects of value more empirically secure.

The nature in detail of the revolution that would be wrought by carrying into the region of values the principle now embodied in scientific practice cannot be told; to attempt it would violate the fundamental idea that we know only after we have acted and in consequence of the outcome of action. But it would surely effect a transfer of attention and energy from the subjective to the objective. Men would think of themselves as agents not as ends; ends would be found in experienced enjoyment of the fruits of a transforming activity. In as far as the subjectivity of modern thought represents a discovery of the part played by personal responses, organic and acquired, in the causal production of the qualities and values of objects, it marks the possibility of a decisive gain. It puts us in possession of some of the conditions that control the occurrence of experienced objects, and thereby it supplies us with an instrument of regulation. There is something querulous in the sweeping denial that things as experienced, as perceived and enjoyed, in any way depend upon interaction with human selves. The error of doctrines that have exploited the part played by personal and subjective reactions in determining what is perceived and enjoyed lies either in exaggerating this factor of constitution into the sole condition—as happens in subjective idealism—or else in treating it as a finality instead of, as with all knowledge, an instrument in direction of further action.

A third significant change that would issue from carrying over experimental method from physics to man concerns the import of standards, principles, rules. With the transfer, these, and all tenets and creeds about good and goods, would be recognized to be hypotheses. Instead of being rigidly fixed, they would be treated as intellectual instruments to be tested and confirmed—and altered—through consequences effected by acting upon them. They would lose all pretence of finality—the ulterior source of dogmatism. It is both astonishing and depressing that so much of the energy of mankind has gone into fighting for (with weapons of the flesh as well as of the spirit) the truth of creeds, religious, moral and political, as distinct from what has gone into effort to try creeds by putting them to the test of acting upon them. The change would do away with the intolerance and fanaticism that attend the notion that beliefs and judgments are capable of inherent truth and authority; inherent in the sense of being independent of what they lead to when used as directive principles. The transformation does not imply merely that men are responsible for acting upon what they profess to believe; that is an old doctrine. It goes much further. Any belief as such is tentative, hypothetical; it is not just to be acted upon, but is to be *framed* with reference to its office as a guide to action. Consequently, it should be the last thing in the world to be picked up casually and then clung to rigidly. When it is apprehended as a tool and only a tool, an instrumentality of direction, the same scrupulous attention will go to its formation as now goes into the making of instruments of precision in technical fields. Men, instead of being proud of accepting and asserting beliefs and "principles" on the ground of loyalty, will be as ashamed of that procedure as they would now be to confess their assent to a scientific theory out of reverence for Newton or Helmholtz or whomever, without regard to evidence.

If one stops to consider the matter, is there not something strange in the fact that men should consider loyalty to "laws," principles, standards, ideals to be an inherent virtue, accounted unto them for righteousness? It is as if they were making up for some secret sense of weakness by rigidity and intensity of insistent attachment. A moral law, like a law in physics, is not something to swear by and stick to at all hazards; it is a formula of the way to respond when specified conditions present themselves. Its soundness and pertinence are tested by what happens when it is acted upon. Its claim of authority rests finally upon the imperativeness of the situation that has to be dealt with, not upon its own intrinsic nature—as any tool achieves dignity in the measure of needs served by it. The idea that adherence to standards external to experienced objects is the only alternative to confusion and lawlessness was once held in science. But knowledge became steadily progressive when it was abandoned, and clews and tests found within concrete acts and objects were employed. The test of consequences is more exacting than that afforded by fixed general rules. In addition, it secures constant development, for when new acts are tried new results are experienced, while the lauded immutability of eternal ideals and norms is in itself a denial of the possibility of development and improvement.

The various modifications that would result from adoption in social and humane subjects of the experimental way of thinking are perhaps summed up in saying that it would place *method and means* upon the level of importance that has, in the past, been imputed exclusively to ends. Means have been regarded as menial, and the useful as the servile. Means have been treated as poor relations to be endured, but not inherently welcome. The very meaning of the word "ideals" is significant of the divorce which has obtained between means and ends. "Ideals" are thought to be remote and inaccessible of attainment; they are too high and fine to be sullied by realization. They serve vaguely to arouse "aspiration," but they do not evoke and direct strivings for embodiment in actual existence. They hover in an indefinite way over the actual scene; they are expiring ghosts of a once significant kingdom of divine reality whose rule penetrated to every detail of life.

It is impossible to form a just estimate of the paralysis of effort that has been produced by indifference to means. Logically, it is truistic that lack of consideration for means signifies that so-called ends are not taken seriously. It is as if one professed devotion to painting pictures conjoined with contempt for canvas, brush and paints; or love of music on condition that no instruments, whether the voice or something external, be used to make sounds. The good workman in the arts is known by his respect for his tools and by his interest in perfecting his technique. The glorification in the arts of ends at the expense of means would be taken to be a sign of complete insincerity or even insanity. Ends separated from means are either sentimental indulgences or if they happen to exist are merely accidental. The ineffectiveness in action of "ideals" is due precisely to the supposition that means and ends are not on exactly the same level with respect to the attention and care they demand.

It is, however, much easier to point out the formal contradiction implied in ideals that are professed without equal regard for the instruments and techniques of their realization, than it is to appreciate the concrete ways in which belief in their separation has found its way into life and borne corrupt and poisonous fruits. The separation marks the form in which the traditional divorce of theory and practice has expressed itself in actual life. It accounts for the relative impotency of arts concerned with enduring human welfare. Sentimental attachment and subjective eulogy take the place of action. For there is no art without tools and instrumental agencies. But it also explains the fact that in actual behavior, energies devoted to matters nominally thought to be inferior, material and sordid, engross attention and interest. After a polite and pious deference has been paid to "ideals," men feel free to devote themselves to matters which are more immediate and pressing.

It is usual to condemn the amount of attention paid by people in general to material ease, comfort, wealth, and success gained by competition, on the ground that they give to mere means the attention that ought to be given to ends, or that they have taken for ends things which in reality are only means. Criticisms of the place which economic interest and action occupy in present life are full of complaints that men allow lower aims to usurp the place that belongs to higher and ideal values. The final source of the trouble is, however, that moral and spiritual "leaders" have propagated the notion that ideal ends may be cultivated in isolation from "material" means, as if means and material were not synonymous. While they condemn men for giving to means the thought and energy that ought to go to ends, the condemnation should go to them. For they have not taught their followers to think of material and economic activities as *really* means. They have been unwilling to frame their conception of the values that should be regulative of human conduct on the basis of the actual conditions and operations by which alone values can be actualized. . . .

The present state of industrial life seems to give a fair index of the existing separation of means and ends. Isolation of economics from ideal ends, whether of morals or of organized social life, was proclaimed by Aristotle. Certain things, he said, are conditions of a worthy life, personal and social, but are not constituents of it. The economic life of man, concerned with satisfaction of wants, is of this nature. Men have wants and they must be satisfied. But they are only prerequisites of a good life, not intrinsic elements in it. Most philosophers have not been so frank nor perhaps so logical. But upon the whole, economics has been treated as on a lower level than either morals or politics. Yet the life which men, women and children actually lead, the opportunities open to them, the values they are capable of enjoying, their education, their share in all the things of art and science, are mainly determined by economic conditions. Hence we can hardly expect a moral system which ignores economic conditions to be other than remote and empty.

Industrial life is correspondingly brutalized by failure to equate it as the means by which social and cultural values are realized. That the economic life, thus exiled from the pale of higher values, takes revenge by declaring that it is the only social reality, and by means of the doctrine of materialistic determination of institutions and conduct in all fields, denies to deliberate morals and politics any share of causal regulation, is not surprising.

When economists were told that their subject-matter was merely material, they naturally thought they could be "scientific" only by excluding all reference to distinctively human values. Material wants, efforts to satisfy them, even the scientifically regulated technologies highly developed in industrial activity, are then taken to form a complete and closed field. If any reference to social ends and values is introduced, it is by way of an external addition, mainly hortatory. That economic life largely determines the conditions under which mankind has access to concrete values may be recognized or it may not be. In either case, the notion that it is the means to be utilized in order to secure significant values as the common and shared possession of mankind is alien and inoperative. To many persons, the idea that the ends professed by morals are impotent save as they are connected with the working machinery of economic life seems like deflowering the purity of moral values and obligations. . . .

EXERCISES

1. Can you think of a case in which *you* would count two values as *genuine* ethical values although they are in irresolvable conflict?

2. Which sort of world would you *prefer*? A world in which there is a clearly ordered ranking of values, without conflict; or a world in which values genuinely conflict, and no rank ordering is possible?

3. Jesus taught that when someone strikes us, we should "turn the other cheek"; that when someone harms us, we should forgive, and not seek vengeance. In "Honor" cultures and traditions, if someone strikes you or insults you, your personal honor demands that you strike back (at its most extreme, your personal honor would require that you challenge your attacker to a deadly duel). Is this an example of genuine value conflict, between genuine objective values?

4. Susan Wolf notes that a life of "moral sainthood" has its drawbacks. But then, few of us are in any significant danger of becoming moral saints. To the contrary, most of us struggle to be morally decent. Does the fact that we are unlikely to come anywhere close to moral sainthood diminish the significance of Wolf's essay?

5. Catherine Wilson maintains that ethics should make us somewhat uncomfortable with our position of privilege and should challenge our comfortable acceptance of a "lifestyle" of luxurious and aggressive consumption (particularly in light of widespread poverty and misery). *Is* that the proper role of ethics? Or should ethics aim at formulating standards for minimally decent behavior within the culture and cultural values in which we live?

6. Suppose that you adopt Susan Wolf's outlook: moral considerations are important, but they need not always be dominant. How would you decide when and which moral demands could be set aside? For example, suppose you are struggling with the question of whether to buy a Rolex or a less luxurious but perfectly adequate time-piece. You realize that buying the Rolex is a wasteful use of resources that could be turned to morally better uses; but you enjoy having some wasteful flashy luxuries in your life. The question is not whether buying the Rolex is morally wrong (you are a utilitarian, and you have already concluded that it is morally wrong); rather,

the *question* is whether this is an occasion in which you should deny moral considerations a dominant role. *How* could you resolve that question? Would you use *moral* considerations in answering that question? *Could* you use moral considerations in answering that question?

7. William James, one of the best known pragmatists, used his pragmatism to defend belief in God. According to James, belief in God helps some people (including James himself) to live better lives, by giving them greater confidence and more hope for the future; that is, belief in God enables them to *live better*. If that is the case, then belief in God "proves itself to be good in the way of belief, and good, too, for definite, assignable reasons"; and thus belief in God is a *true* belief. James's argument for belief in God has remained controversial to this day (and obviously not all pragmatists agree with it). What do you think of it?

   If you reject James's argument for belief in God, would that mean you must reject the pragmatic account of ethical truth? If you accept his argument, would that imply that you must also accept the pragmatic account of ethical truth?

8. Dewey maintains that we should welcome value experimentation in order to test our ethical views. Obviously, not all value experiments will be acceptable: to take an obvious example, we would not allow value experiments that involve human sacrifice; and the "value experiments" of some religious sects have been banned when they involved the sexual abuse of children. So what sort of limit would you place on "value experimentation"?

9. Have you ever been involved—willingly or unwillingly—in what you would consider a "value experiment"?

ADDITIONAL READING

An excellent general introduction to value pluralism can be found in the "Value Pluralism" article, by Elinor Mason, in the Stanford Encyclopedia of Philosophy; go to http://plato.stanford.edu/entries/value-pluralism.

Among early advocates of value pluralism is William James, in "The Moral Philosopher and the Moral Life"; the essay (which first appeared as an 1891 lecture) can be found in William James, *The Will to Believe* (New York: Dover, 1960). Perhaps the best known contemporary advocate of value pluralism is Isaiah Berlin (whose value pluralism shades into his political pluralism); see his *Four Essays on Liberty* (Oxford: Oxford University Press, 1969). One of the strongest contemporary monistic opponents of value pluralism is Ronald Dworkin, in *Sovereign Virtue* (Cambridge, MA: Harvard University Press, 2000). There are a number of interesting essays on pluralism—with special attention to the pluralistic arguments of Isaiah Berlin, and including a critique by Ronald Dworkin—in *The Legacy of Isaiah Berlin*, edited by Mark Lilla, Ronald Dworkin, and Robert B. Silvers (New York: New York Review of Books, 2001).

Judith Jarvis Thomson's arguments for pluralism can be found in "The Right and the Good," *Journal of Philosophy*, Volume 94 (1997): 273–298. Bernard Williams offers very insightful pluralist arguments in *Problems of the Self* (Cambridge, MA: Cambridge University Press, 1973), and in *Moral Luck* (Cambridge, MA: Cambridge University Press, 1981).

Susan Wolf is well known for her provocative books and articles that cast old questions in a new and interesting light. Her *Freedom within Reason* (New York: Oxford University Press, 1990) is a particularly interesting rationalist account of autonomy. Robert Merrihew Adams develops extensive criticisms of Wolf's "Moral Saints" view from a more religious perspective, in "Saints," *The Journal of Philosophy* (1984): 392–401. Edmund L. Pincoffs argues that virtue ethics can explain how the unrestricted seeking of moral betterment is desirable; see his *Quandaries and Virtues: Against Reductivism in Ethics* (Lawrence, KS: University Press of Kansas, 1986), especially Chapter 6, "A Defense of Perfectionism." Peter Singer argues for ethical demands that require significant changes in our privileged way of life; see his *Writings on an Ethical Life* (New York: HarperCollins, 2000). Robert B. Louden argues that "as concerns morality, more is always better than less," in *Morality and Moral Theory: A Reappraisal and Reaffirmation* (New York: Oxford University Press, 1992); see especially Chapter 3, "Morality and Maximization." Bernard Williams claims that: "Ethical life itself is important, but it can see that things other than itself are important" (p. 184) in *Ethics and the Limits of Philosophy* (Cambridge, MA: Harvard University Press, 1985).

The pragmatist view was developed by Charles S. Peirce, William James, and John Dewey (among others) early in the twentieth century. It remains one of the leading schools of philosophical thought—though its boundaries are not altogether clear, and there is often dispute about who should be considered a pragmatist. For classic pragmatic views of ethics, see William James, *Pragmatism* (originally given as a series of lectures in

1907, it is available in a number of editions). John Dewey was a prolific writer; among his many works are *Ethics*, which he published with James H. Tufts (New York: Holt, 1908); *The Quest for Certainty* (originally given as the Gifford Lectures in 1929, it was published by G. P. Putnam's Sons, New York, in a paperback edition in 1960); and *Human Nature and Conduct* (New York: Henry Holt and Company, 1922). Excellent books on Dewey's work are *Dewey and His Critics*, edited by Sidney Morgenbesser (New York: The Journal of Philosophy, 1977), and *The Philosophy of John Dewey*, edited by Paul Arthur Schilpp and Lewis Edwin Hahn (LaSalle, IL.: Open Court, 1939). For contemporary work on pragmatic ethics, see (in addition to the Rorty citations) Stanley Cavell, *In Quest of the Ordinary* (Chicago, IL: University of Chicago Press, 1988); an excellent brief history and development of the view is Hugh Lafollette's "Pragmatic Ethics," in Hugh LaFollette, editor, *The Blackwell Guide to Ethical Theory* (Oxford: Blackwell Publishers, 2000); and the fascinating "prophetic pragmatism" of Cornel West in *The American Evasion of Philosophy: A Genealogy of Pragmatism* (Madison, WI: University of Wisconsin Press, 1987). The views of Richard Rorty—a leading contemporary pragmatist who is often classified as a relativist, though he himself preferred the title "antidualist" or "antifoundationalist"—can be found in his *Philosophy and the Mirror of Nature* (Princeton, NJ: Princeton University Press, 1979), perhaps his most famous book, though it mentions ethics only briefly; *Contingency, Irony, and Solidarity* (Cambridge, MA: Cambridge University Press, 1989), a very readable book that ranges through literature, social theory, and philosophy—Chapter 9, "Solidarity," contains very interesting elements of his views of ethics; *Truth and Progress: Philosophical Papers,* Volume 3 (Cambridge, MA: Cambridge University Press, 1998); and *Philosophy and Social Hope* (London: Penguin Books, 1999).

7

Social Contract Ethics

We have examined several ethical theories, ranging from Kantian rationalism through sentimentalism and intuitionism to utilitarianism. Though they offer very different views of ethics, they have at least one thing in common: all insist they are explaining how to *find* ethical truth (with the exception of David Hume, who seems to doubt that ethical truth exists). Kant believes you find ethical truth through reason, others believe ethical truth reveals itself through feelings or intuitions, and the utilitarians propose we discover the right act by calculating the balance of pleasure over pain. *Constructivists* take a different approach: ethical principles are *made*, not found. The rules and principles of ethics are not out there, awaiting our discovery, like a distant planet or a new galaxy. According to most moral *realists*, the truths of ethics are true independent of whether anyone acknowledges, pronounces, or recognizes them. In contrast, constructivists insist that "stealing is wrong" is not discovered by utilitarian calculations or empirical research or special insight into ethical truth; instead, "stealing is wrong" becomes an ethical truth when endorsed or pronounced by some particular group or when recognized and affirmed from some special perspective or stance. The best-known constructivist model is the social contract model of ethics. Ethics is *constructed* by social groups, and exists for the benefit of those groups. Social contract theorists insist that the social contract ethical principles are real: they are just as real as chairs and tables. The chair you are sitting in may not exist in nature, and it would not have existed without humans; but it still exists, and it works well. Likewise, we can't discover ethical principles among the stars, but we can *make* an ethical system that works effectively for us.

FRAMING THE SOCIAL CONTRACT

In the "state of nature" there are no rules. As Thomas Hobbes (one of the most famous social contract theorists) describes it, life in a state of nature is a "war of all against all," and in the state of nature life is "solitary, poor, nasty, brutish, and short." You take what you can from me, and I do the same to those who are weaker. And though you are very strong, and thus seem to have great advantages in this war of all against all, you still have to sleep. I'm weak, but deadly if I catch you napping. So no one, however powerful, will ever rest easy. Rather than endure this terrible strife, we decide to *contract* together. And it's not too hard to think of some rules we would adopt. I might find it desirable to kill you and take all your possessions; but since I stand a good chance of being the killee rather than the killer (and if you don't get me, someone else certainly will), it makes more sense to give up my state-of-nature right to kill and steal if everyone agrees not to rob or kill me. And of course we'll need someone to enforce the rules, so a government will have to be formed, with police powers. But its powers are limited, since it would be silly for me to agree to a powerful government that murders me at its whim. I would be better off taking my chances in the state of nature, where at least everyone is roughly equal in strength. So, if the government fails to abide by the contract, then we have a right to overthrow it (governments are not run by "divine right," but instead by the "consent of the governed"). And if I violate the rules, it is legitimate for the government to punish me for breaking my contract.

Social contract theorists construct substantial ethical systems on this modest foundation. Obviously, we will have rules against murder and theft, but they won't end there. Would you want to live in a society in which everyone constantly lied to one another, or constantly cheated one another? Of course not. So it is reasonable for you to renounce lying and cheating, if everyone else also lives by that agreement. Perhaps I would prefer a society in which I am allowed to lie and cheat and you are held to high standards of integrity. But you would never agree to such a contract. So, if I want to live in a society where honesty is the rule—and don't we all prefer that?—then I have to live up to the contract. And the social contract may give us much more. Today you are young and strong and healthy and prosperous, but misfortune may strike any of us, and the infirmities of old age loom in the future. So, we might readily agree that those who suffer misfortunes or illness should be helped by the more fortunate. I may not particularly like giving some of my goods to the sick and infirm, but I'm willing to do so if I gain peace of mind from knowing that when old age weakens me, or misfortune cripples me, I will also receive help.

There are other rules our social contract should contain. For example, I want to be free to practice my religion and suppress all other religions (after all, my religion is the *true* religion, and all others are vile idolatry). But I realize others also have strongly held religious beliefs, and they might gain power, and then my own religion would be banned. I would like to be able to persecute you for practicing a false religion, but I don't want to take a chance of being on the receiving end of the persecution. So I will agree to a freedom of religion rule in our social contract.

Social Contracts and Human Strife

Social contract ethics has solid natural appeal. It constructs ethics with no aid from metaphysics or divinities, bases ethics on agreements requiring neither mysteries nor faith, and places ethics squarely within the natural world. Social contract theory does not depend on any religious sanction or divine human spark or profound rational powers or special intuitions. It makes no assumptions that humans are special beings. To the contrary, social contract theorists often paint a rather gruesome picture of human nature, and still manage to construct a substantial ethical system on that minimalist foundation.

It's no accident that the most rigorous social contract theories tend to develop in times of political and social upheaval. One of the most famous social contract theories was devised by Thomas Hobbes during a time when Europe was racked with war. Protestant armies fought Catholic armies, and the basic rule was simple: if you're not for us, you're against us. Suppose you were trying to live a quiet peaceful life as a baker in a European town under Protestant rule. The Catholic armies sweep in and capture your village—and since you were living there peacefully, that probably means you are a Protestant, and so deserve to die. If somehow you escape death, a few months later a Protestant army arrives on the scene and recaptures your village; and if you survived under Catholic rule, well, that means you must be a Catholic, and thus deserve death. And if you don't get caught in that Protestant–Catholic whipsaw, there is still a good chance that a fervor of witch burning might sweep through your village. With dozens of tortured victims screaming out any names they could think of, the name of the baker might well come to mind, and you could find yourself standing at the stake with a large pile of wood around you and your neighbors eager for your death. And if you somehow survived all those disasters, you are likely to fall victim to the ravages of the terrible Black Death: the bubonic plague, which regularly swept through Europe, killing thousands. Faced with such turmoil, you might begin to wonder if there was any justice or ethics guiding the world's fortunes. God no doubt keeps good order among the angels, and the stars and planets regularly follow their heavenly routes, but if we're going to have peace on Earth we'd better do it ourselves. A social contract seems a good start toward a peaceful and at least minimally harmonious society. And since the contract must govern our vicious natural impulses, it is essential that the government have great power and authority to keep our brutal natural tendencies under control.

Rousseau's Social Contract

On Hobbes's view we need a strong social contract because our *natural* tendencies are toward murder and mayhem and "every man for himself." In our natural state life is nasty and brutish. Only by establishing a powerful governing force can these natural tendencies toward violence and greed be held in check. But not every social contract theorist has had such a negative view of human nature. Jean-Jacques Rousseau, an eighteenth-century philosopher and novelist, was born in Geneva but spent most of his life in France. Rousseau believed the natural state of humankind is basically good. We are all motivated by the emotion of pity:

> Pity is a natural sentiment moderating the action of self-love in each individual and contributing to the mutual preservation of the whole species. It is pity that sends us unreflecting to the aid of those we see suffering; it is pity that in the state of nature takes the place of laws, moral habits, and virtues, with the added benefit that there no one is tempted to disobey its gentle voice . . . [1]

Since Rousseau's state of nature is not so bad—pity holds our self-interests in check, and "will deter a robust savage from robbing a weak child or infirm old person"—we are not so desperate for a social contract that will hold vicious tendencies in check. Instead, we join together in an association in which we all share common goals and principles, and so no one relinquishes any freedom, and no one has greater power than another. John Locke, a British philosopher who lived shortly after Hobbes, also believed in a relatively peaceful and gentle state of nature—and relatively peaceful natural human tendencies—and thus the social contract he proposed was also more limited than that of Hobbes. In particular, Locke insisted on preserving the individual rights of citizens against the temptation of social rulers to become tyrants.

Social Contracts and Human Nature

Social contract theories are sometimes criticized because the notion of persons sitting down together in the "state of nature" and drawing up a careful contract is too implausible. But that's not really a fair criticism: it takes social contract theory much too literally. Social contract theory is not meant to be a historical or anthropological account of how political systems developed. Rather, social contract theory is an examination of the *justice* and *fairness* of political and social and ethical systems. The question is not whether you signed a contract to live under the rules of our society. Obviously you did not. Rather, the important question is whether you *would* sign such a contract if offered the opportunity. If you would, then the system of rules we live under is basically fair, a system we could voluntarily accept. That doesn't mean, of course, that you think every rule we have is a good one. Perhaps you think we should have tighter restrictions on firearms, or a lower legal drinking age, or no laws requiring seat belts. Our social contract is not precisely the one you would draw up if you could arrange all the details. No one thinks the social contract is perfect. The question is whether it is sufficiently fair and decent that we would choose to live under this social contract rather than in a state of nature. If so, then the social contract may not be perfectly fair, but may be fair enough.

Would you prefer to live under our social contract, or in a state of nature? That is how Hobbes framed the question. But that stacks the deck in favor of the social contract. After all, I might prefer a rather lousy society and a seriously unjust government rather than a state of nature in which there is a "war of all against all," and everyone around me is trying to stab me in the back, and life is indeed nasty, brutish, and short. Only a very bad social contract is worse than the state of nature. Of course, that's the way Hobbes wanted it. Having lived through wars and revolutions, Hobbes craved peace. Though he believed people have a right to overthrow their government, he wanted that right exercised only in the most extreme circumstances.

The social contract is a myth: there is no suggestion that warring individuals actually sat down together and drew up a social contract to live by rules and stop attacking one another. Rather, by means of a social contract model we can evaluate the fairness of proposed systems of rules: is this a system you *would* willingly adopt as a rational independent contractor? But in one instance, something very close to the social contract myth actually occurred. In what is now upstate New York, several Indian groups were locked in constant and brutal warfare, until two leaders and peacemakers—Deganawida and Hiawatha— convinced the warring groups to gather together and form a League, with all of the members following "the Great Law of Peace," which developed into an extensive and detailed constitutional agreement. The exact date of this gathering is disputed, but most historians place it between 1450 and 1600. In this agreement, the Seneca, Cayuga, Onondaga, Oneida, and Mohawk peoples agreed to refrain from attacking one another and resolve their differences peacefully. Thus, the Iroquois (or *Haudenosaunee*) nation was formed, and the internal fighting stopped. Ironically, the "savages" of the Americas were often used by European philosophers as the examples of people actually living in a state of nature, while in fact the Iroquois had developed a working social contract—with strong elements of democracy, and substantial respect for the rights of women—during a time when Europeans were living in a situation of almost constant war. Hobbes, for example, writes of "the savage people in many places of America . . . have no government at all; and live at this day in that brutish manner. . . ."

FAIRNESS AND SOCIAL CONTRACT THEORY: JOHN RAWLS

Different social contract theorists start from different views of human nature, and propose a variety of social contracts. One of the best ways of using social contract theory is to compare contract possibilities. Rather than asking whether we prefer our social contract to a war of all against all, we might ask whether we would agree to *this* social contract in preference to some other social contract alternative. If in making that judgment we decide some other social contract would be much fairer, then we might conclude that our social contract is not as fair and just as it could or should be. John Rawls, a contemporary political philosopher, uses social contract theory in just that way. But Rawls adds a special twist. Rather than starting from a state of nature, locked in mortal combat with all around you, instead imagine finding yourself in the midst of a large group of people who have not yet been placed in the world. You might think of this as a group of disembodied spirits, about to be sent to Earth. No one has a gender or a race; you can't tell how tall you will be, how intelligent or dull, how industrious or lethargic; whether you will be fabulously athletic or slow and clumsy; you don't know what religion you will favor, whether you will prefer Wolfgang Mozart or Willie Nelson, nor what political doctrines you will hold. That is, you find yourself behind what Rawls calls "the veil of ignorance." You know nothing about yourself or your abilities, what advantages or disadvantages you will be born with. You know only that you will need food, water, and shelter, that you will be vulnerable to fire, disease, and sharp objects, and that you will have a desire to live and prosper. In short, you know you will be a human, and all your fellow disembodied humans are now meeting to draw up the rules for the human society you are about to create. Under those circumstances, what rules would you adopt?

Behind the Veil of Ignorance

From behind such a veil of ignorance I would never accept a rule that says women should have less opportunity to become president, or that African Americans should have less chance of going to college or be restricted in the places they can live. I wouldn't accept such rules, because there's a chance that I might step out from behind the veil of ignorance and discover that I am an African American woman. So, I would favor setting up a society in which everyone has equal opportunity to compete for everything. And that means real opportunity: not some sham, in which I am sent to inferior schools, suffer lead poisoning in rundown housing and perhaps malnutrition besides, receive substandard or no health care, and then when I turn 18 you announce that now I have the opportunity to "compete equally" with persons who have enjoyed an 18-year head start.

What else would I want in this new society I (whoever "I" turns out to be) am about to enter? I would want a wide range of basic freedoms, such as freedom of speech and freedom of religion. For though it might be great fun to silence those whose views disagree with my own, it would be much more painful to be among those who are silenced—and that's exactly where I might find myself. Besides, from this detached perspective, I can see advantages to allowing the free exchange of ideas, even weird and unpopular ideas (which sometimes turn out to be true, and even if they are false, such challenges stimulate us to think more carefully and critically about why we hold the views we favor). And perhaps I would want some sort of guarantee that if the society I am entering is quite prosperous, then the worst off in that society should have sufficient resources to live a decent life and have genuine opportunities to improve their positions. It's nice to fantasize that I might wake up in this new society and be embodied as a billionaire. But if our society has enormous disparities of wealth, then there's a much better chance of finding myself in poverty. The difference between having a mansion that is 10,000 square feet and one that is 11,000 is not a big deal. I could hardly tell the difference. But the difference between being homeless and having a snug little cottage is enormous. So if I don't know what economic situation I'll be in, I would favor making sure everyone gets at least a comfortable little cottage before anyone builds a ridiculously gargantuan mansion. Everyone must have one bedroom before anyone has 12.

Justice as Fairness

Obviously none of us started as disembodied spirits, floating around in ether drawing up a social contract. Nonetheless, Rawls's model provides a valuable perspective. In particular, it helps us look at our society without the various prejudices and preferences we accumulate because of gender, race, economic class, religion, or political allegiance. His trick of asking us to step behind the "veil of ignorance" is ultimately just a very effective way of asking us to think hard about: How would you like it if *you* were in that position? If we look at a rule of law or a principle of ethics or a social policy in our society, and we can honestly say we would adopt that policy from behind the veil of ignorance, then it is reasonable to conclude that the policy in question is *fair*. If we wouldn't adopt it, then perhaps the policy should be modified.

GAUTHIER'S CONTRACTARIAN ETHICS

David Gauthier has developed a contemporary version of the social contract theory that is quite different from that of Rawls. Rawls's social contract theory is designed to test our basic moral principles and social rules and institutions: from behind the veil of ignorance, stripped of our special interests and biases and privileges, would we regard those rules and structures as *fair* and *just?* Gauthier's social contract theory is designed to provide a rational justification for at least a minimal set of moral principles. Gauthier wants to demonstrate that as rational self-interested beings, there are some moral rules that it makes good sense for us to adopt and follow; and indeed, there are moral rules we rationally *should* follow, even when the rules are not to our immediate advantage. While Rawls uses contract theory to discover or *test* moral systems, Gauthier employs contract theory to show that purely self-interested individuals could and should favor at least a minimally cooperative moral system.

The Prisoner's Dilemma

The basis for Gauthier's social contract system—what Gauthier calls a system of "morals by agreement"—is recent work on game theory, especially related to the famous "prisoner's dilemma." The prisoner's dilemma is an intriguing case that has drawn much attention from economists and sociologists as well as philosophers. Consider the dilemma in its basic form. Susan and Kate are partners in committing a crime, and both have been caught. They are interrogated separately. Both know the police have enough evidence to convict them of burglary, for which they will each receive sentences of 5 years in prison; but they also know the police do *not* have enough evidence to convict them of the bank robbery they also committed. If both continue to deny they were involved in the bank robbery, then neither will be convicted of the bank robbery, and both will serve 5-year sentences for burglary. But if Susan is willing to testify that Kate is guilty of the bank robbery (while Kate continues to deny that either of them were involved in the bank robbery), then the police are willing to give Susan a special deal, and reduce Susan's total sentence to only 2 years. In that case, Kate will get full blame for the bank robbery, and receive a sentence of 12 years, while Susan gets only 2 years. But if *both* Susan and Kate "rat" on one another, then they will both get 10-year sentences. So thinking only of her own rational self-interest, what should Susan do? Of course if she and Kate could get together, they might agree to keep silent, and both serve their 5-year sentences: not a great outcome, but much better than both going up for 10 years, right? But Susan is being questioned separately, and she doesn't know what Kate is going to do, just as Kate doesn't know what Susan will do. As a self-interested rational person, what is Susan's best alternative? Obviously, she should rat on Kate. Suppose that Susan rats on Kate, while Kate says nothing: in that case, Susan will get only a 2-year sentence. (Kate will serve 12 years, but that's her tough luck. Of course we have to assume that Kate doesn't have violent friends who will do serious harm to Susan if Susan rats on her; but let's keep the story relatively simple.) On the other hand, if Kate is over in the other interrogation room ratting on Susan: well, in that case, Susan is still better off ratting on Kate, since Susan will get a 10-year rather than a 12-year sentence. So whatever Kate is doing, Susan is better off ratting on her. Assuming both Susan and Kate are rational self-interested players (and Kate reasons just as Susan did), both will wind up with 10-year prison sentences. But that is a lousy result: though each avoids the 12-year maximum sentence, had both of them kept quiet they would have had 5-year sentences. It would be better for both if they could trust one another to forgo immediate advantages in order to gain greater long-term cooperative benefits.

What's the moral of the story? If people always pursue their interests, they will wind up with results that are less desirable than if they had sacrificed some immediate advantages to cooperate for mutual gains. Thus, a system of *morality* in which we honor agreements and cooperate with others is beneficial for each of us, and it is in my long-term self-interest to honor it. This has wide application. Suppose you and I are neighbors, and we are both building decks. The building projects will go much more efficiently if we work together as a two-person team, rather than individually. If we work individually, it will take each of us approximately 15 hours to build our decks. If we work together, each deck can be completed in 5 hours, and both will be done in 10, and each of us will save 5 hours of labor. So it will be in both our long-term interests to cooperate. I propose we start with my deck, and when that's done we'll do yours. To make this work, you must trust me to honor my commitment, and I must be the sort of person who is trustworthy. Otherwise, you will fear that after you have contributed 5 hours to building my deck, I'll back out of the cooperative agreement and leave you with 15 hours of single-handed deck building. Without a moral system in which promises are kept and cooperation is reciprocated, there can be no mutually beneficial cooperative projects. Committing ourselves to act morally (by cooperating and keeping pledges) when others also act morally fosters the trust essential for mutually beneficial cooperation, and that is enough to establish "morals by agreement." Morality needs no divine or intuitive or mysterious foundation; as rational, self-interested persons we can calculate its advantages for ourselves.

THE SOCIAL CONTRACT MYTH AND ITS UNDERLYING ASSUMPTIONS

Rawls doesn't suppose that we started out as disembodied spirits. And, of course, social contract theorists don't suppose that any group of people living in a brutal war of all against all one day sat down together and signed the social contract: one afternoon we all put down our clubs and spears, sat around the fire and drew up an elaborate social contract. No social contract theorist believes anything like that literally happened. The social contract is a *myth* that social contract theorists use to develop their position. It tells a story that helps us see important truths behind the story. Think of the Jewish creation *myth*. After God created the world, He had all the animals march by, and Adam assigned them names. It's an interesting myth, which signifies the dominion of humans over all animals. (You may not agree with the idea of human dominion expressed by the myth, but that's a different question.) But if you take it as a literal story, it soon becomes a bit silly. It's one thing to think of Adam happily whiling away a few hours naming the big photogenic species. ("I think I'll call that a zebra; you with the long neck, you're a giraffe; and you are going to be named tyrannosaurus rex; and that bird over there will be named robin.") But by the time Adam finished with a few thousand beetle species, he might be getting a bit weary of the game, and he wouldn't even have started on the mollusks, much less the bacteria. Likewise, the social contract myth is not literally true, but the story it tells contains some very important ideas. Whether you agree with those ideas is a question you will have to consider for yourself.

What ideas are presupposed in the social contract myth? The Genesis creation story, in which Adam names all the animals, assumes that Adam is above and over the rest of the animal kingdom, and has control and "dominion" over it. That's important to note, since the assumptions made—but never stated—are often powerful and insidious. We may buy into those assumptions as we listen to the story, and it is sometimes difficult to bring them to the surface and subject them to critical examination. What assumptions are embedded in the social contract myth?

Think about how the social contract comes into being (according to the social contract myth). Each of us was fighting a war of all against all; growing tired of lives that were "nasty, brutish, and short," each of us agreed we would relinquish our state-of-nature rights to commit murder and mayhem in exchange for some peace and security. We each weighed the options, considered what was in our best interests, and signed the contract.

Radical Individualism

There are several underlying assumptions in that story, and perhaps the most basic is this: *each of us, individually,* fought against every other individual in the state of nature, and then we each sat down and individually decided it would be in our best interests to sign the contract. The social contract changes things, bringing order and security. But both as social contractors and state-of-nature warriors we function as distinct units, as isolated individuals fighting for our individual lives and contracting for our individual benefits. Thus, the social contract myth includes a deeply embedded and quite radical assumption of *individuality.* In both the state of nature and under the social contract, the most basic rule appears to be: every woman and man for her or himself. I abide by the contract, but only because it satisfies *my* best interests.

The social contract myth is very powerful and pervasive, and its strong assumption of individualism has had a profound impact. Some of the individualistic emphasis is probably positive. For example, the emphasis on *individual rights* has given us important safeguards against both social and governmental intrusions into our lives. We could certainly make faster medical progress if medical researchers could "draft" a few dozen individuals, infect them with a deadly disease, and then test new drugs in an effort to cure that disease. Of course, some of the drafted research subjects would die. But because we would move faster toward finding a cure, we would ultimately save more lives than are lost. We are morally repulsed at such a plan, the utilitarian benefits notwithstanding. We think it wrong to coercively *use* an individual for the benefit of society: it is a violation of *individual rights.* (Of course we draft people in times of national emergency, and require that they sacrifice their lives in battle for the interests—or the supposed interests—of the community. But that is regarded as a very special case.) Likewise, it might make the community happier if those who champion views we generally find repulsive—racists, religious bigots, neo-Nazis—were silenced. We tolerate their repulsive blather, basically because we strongly believe in the individual rights of free speech and free expression (and we fear that if their unpopular free speech is suppressed, our own individual right of free speech might be next; after all, if you can only espouse views that please the majority, that hardly counts as an individual right of free speech).

So there are clearly some good things in our notion of individual rights. But the radical individualism assumed in the social contract myth is another matter. In the first place, it is biological and anthropological nonsense. We are a profoundly *social* species, and we naturally live in families and societies, and our bonds with family and friends and community run very deep: much deeper than any social contract. We are a rather clever species, but we are neither swift nor strong, we lack sharp teeth for fighting and we have no bony exoskeleton for defense. Besides that, our young are born into years of extreme vulnerability, with few or no resources for protecting themselves. Had we been as radically and ruthlessly individualistic as the social contract myth suggests, we would have died out long before any social contract was drawn up.

While individual rights are very important, the "rugged individual" of social contract myth causes significant problems. It suggests that we must each be totally self-sufficient (though we know that to be false). And it sometimes blinds us to how much we depend on our families and communities in order to live successfully, and thus we are also blinded to the needs of those who fail to receive such support ("*I made it entirely on my own, so she can too*"). As Virginia Held has noted, contract models characterize ethics as an agreement that is mutually advantageous to separated rational individuals of roughly equal strength; but much of life is better modeled in terms of building community and nurturing friendships rather than contractually resolving conflicts. If our model for ethical relationships were one of friendship, or perhaps the relation between mother and child—which is at least as central to our experience as are relations among purely self-interested contractors—then our conception of the good society might be quite different.

Narrow Obligations

The second assumption underlying social contract theory is closely tied to the first. Since we are radically distinct individuals contracting together, the only obligations we incur are those we voluntarily and individually approve. Perhaps that's true. Some people think so. But it is important to note that the assumption is being made, for it is certainly an assumption that is open to question. You "didn't choose to be born," and you didn't choose your parents or your siblings. But most of us believe we have at least some obligations to them. (If you hear of a young man who makes a fortune, but leaves his parents and younger siblings in terrible poverty, most people will have a rather negative moral assessment of this person, whom they will regard as selfish and unfeeling.) And a woman who makes a great fortune, but never "gives back" anything to the community that nurtured her, is regarded as selfish and ungrateful. Social contract theory pulls us in the opposite direction. If you help your aged parents, or contribute to your community, that's nice of you— but not a moral obligation.

Choosing Morality

The third assumption underlying social contract theory is somewhat similar to the second. Just as we "choose" our obligations to others, likewise all moral principles are a matter of "choosing" to accept that moral system. Ethics exists only as a contract among rational parties, each of whom approves the contract as the best deal he or she can get. Thus, ethics is a system we make as a social agreement among reasonable self-interested contractors. If it's not in the contract, then it's not part of the ethical system. And the contract is designed by rational agreement, based on mutual self-interest. Feelings have nothing to do with it.

Outside the Social Contract

A fourth assumption of the social contract myth is perhaps the most subtle. If you can't join in the contract, and you can't live up to the demands of the contract, then you aren't part of the moral community. Those who are weak or infirm, including the very young and at least some of the very old, are not real members of the moral community. Those of us who are full signatories of the social contract may decide to grant them protection, but the protection is given only as a favor, not as a right. Those in that position are at best second-class citizens of the moral community, rather than genuine rights-holding members. As Martha Nussbaum notes (in *Frontiers of Justice*), the logic of social contract theory assumes a second-rate status for those having unusual needs or impairments or disabilities:

> . . . the idea is that people will get together with others and contract for basic political principles only in certain circumstances, circumstances in which they can expect mutual benefit and in which all stand to gain from the cooperation. To include in the initial situation people who are unusually expensive or who can be expected to contribute far less . . . would run contrary to the logic of the whole exercise. If people are making a cooperative arrangement for mutual advantage, they will want to get together with those from cooperation with whom they may expect to gain, not those who will demand unusual and expensive attention without contributing much to the social product, thus depressing the level of society's well-being. . . . This is an unpleasant feature of contract theories that people do not like to mention. (2006, p. 104)

Social contract theory also has strong implications for our model of just punishment. You receive justified punishment if, as a member of the social contracting community, you break the accepted rules.

If you are insane, or so badly damaged in your character formation that you cannot meet the obligations of the social contract, then we may take pity on you and not punish you for the harms you cause. The cost you must pay, however, is the loss of your membership in the moral community: you become something less that a real moral person. That is why some who violate the law—who violate the social contract—prefer even harsh punishment to being "excused" as incompetent. We punish *members* of the moral community who violate the contract. To be excused or exempted from punishment is to be banished from that community. For profoundly social animals like ourselves, that is very harsh punishment indeed.

There are others who also did not sign on to our social contract. People from different cultures, who are not part of our society or our nation, are obviously "outsiders." Under social contract theory, they have no rights, and we have no obligations to them. The most brutal treatment of alien peoples might be regarded as "in bad taste," or "esthetically displeasing," but it is difficult to see how a social contract theorist could condemn it as morally wrong. And the same point applies to nonhuman animals. If they can't understand and accept and follow the rules, then they have no rights and are due no *moral* consideration.

Gauthier's contractarian "morals by agreement" raises disturbing questions of who gets left out of moral consideration. In Gauthier's view, rational self-interested persons will cooperate because they stand to gain more—at least long term—through cooperation. But in cases where we have little to gain through such cooperation (for example, where we have the power to coerce, or when dealing with persons so weak or disabled that they have little to contribute to a cooperative arrangement), Gauthier's purely self-interested individual would have little motive for making the scope of morality broad enough to encompass such persons. On the other hand, Rawls's theory can aid us in thinking more vividly about fair treatment for a wide range of persons: If I were behind the veil of ignorance, and *might* emerge as a severely disabled person, what would I insist upon as fair treatment for persons in my potential condition?

CONCLUSION

Social contract theory forges an ethical system with no help from God or "natural law" or transcendent truths or powers of intuition. It has some definite limits (though dedicated contract theorists may see those limits as legitimate and justifiable), and some of its basic assumptions may not square with what we know about the social nature of human animals. Still, in the hands of a theorist such as John Rawls, social contract theory can push us to think carefully and critically about the moral principles we favor, the society we live in, and the social structures and institutions we support.

⤛ LEVIATHAN ⤜
Thomas Hobbes

Thomas Hobbes was a seventeenth-century British philosopher. The following passage is taken from his most famous work, *Leviathan,* which he published in 1651, two years after the execution of King Charles I. Although Hobbes denied the divine right of kings, he argued that a powerful king is needed to prevent disorder and disaster. His views made him unpopular in England, and he found refuge in France for more than a decade. He was, however, an outspoken enemy of the Catholic Church, and was suspected of atheism, which eventually left him somewhat isolated in France. He returned to England, and with the restoration of Charles II to the monarchy became a favorite at court. Hobbes wrote major works on a wide variety of subjects, including political theory, philosophy, mathematics, history, and optics.

Note that Hobbes's example of people living in a "state of nature" is "the savage people in many places of *America* . . . [who] have no government at all; and live at this day in that brutish manner. . . . " This was a common belief among seventeenth-century Europeans—perhaps a self-serving belief that served to justify the brutal treatment of Native Americans. But at the time Hobbes wrote, the famous

Iroquois Federation (the Five Nations) had been in existence for many years, with such an elaborate system of government that some have suggested the Articles of Confederation of the American colonies were modeled after their rules.

OF THE NATURALL CONDITION OF MANKIND, AS CONCERNING THEIR FELICITY, AND MISERY

Nature hath made men so equall, in the faculties of body, and mind; as that though there bee found one man sometimes manifestly stronger in body, or of quicker mind then another; yet when all is reckoned together, the difference between man, and man, is not so considerable, as that one man can thereupon claim to himselfe any benefit, to which another may not pretend, as well as he. For as to the strength of body, the weakest has strength enough to kill the strongest, either by secret machination, or by confederacy with others, that are in the same danger with himselfe.

And as to the faculties of the mind, (setting aside the arts grounded upon words, and especially that skill of proceeding upon generall, and infallible rules, called Science; which very few have, and but in few things; as being not a native faculty, born with us; nor attained, (as Prudence,) while we look after somewhat els,) I find yet a greater equality amongst men, than that of strength. For Prudence, is but Experience; which equall time, equally bestowes on all men, in those things they equally apply themselves unto. That which may perhaps make such equality incredible, is but a vain conceipt of ones owne wisdome, which almost all men think they have in a greater degree, than the Vulgar; that is, than all men but themselves, and a few others, whom by Fame, or for concurring with themselves, they approve. For such is the nature of men, that howsoever they may acknowledge many others to be more witty, or more eloquent, or more learned; Yet they will hardly believe there be many so wise as themselves: For they see their own wit at hand, and other mens at a distance. But this proveth rather that men are in that point equall, than unequall. For there is not ordinarily a greater signe of the equall distribution of any thing, than that every man is contented with his share.

From this equality of ability, ariseth equality of hope in the attaining of our Ends. And therefore if any two men desire the same thing, which neverthelesse they cannot both enjoy, they become enemies; and in the way to their End, (which is principally their owne conservation, and sometimes their delectation only) endeavour to destroy, or subdue one another. And from hence it comes to passe, that where an Invader hath no more to feare, than another mans single power; if one plant, sow, build, or possesse a convenient Seat, others may probably be expected to come prepared with forces united, to dispossesse, and deprive him, not only of the fruit of his labour, but also of his life, or liberty. And the Invader again is in the like danger of another.

And from this diffidence of one another, there is no way for any man to secure himselfe, so reasonable, as Anticipation; that is, by force, or wiles, to master the persons of all men he can, so long, till he see no other power great enough to endanger him: And this is no more than his own conservation requireth, and is generally allowed. Also because there be some, that taking pleasure in contemplating their own power in the acts of conquest, which they pursue farther than their security requires; if others, that otherwise would be glad to be at ease within modest bounds, should not by invasion increase their power, they would not be able, long time, by standing only on their defence, to subsist. And by consequence, such augmentation of dominion over men, being necessary to a mans conservation, it ought to be allowed him.

Againe, men have no pleasure, (but on the contrary a great deale of griefe) in keeping company, where there is no power able to over-awe them all. For every man looketh that his companion should value him, at the same rate he sets upon himselfe: And upon all signes of contempt, or undervaluing, naturally endeavours, as far as he dares (which amongst them that have no common power, to keep them in quiet, is far enough to make them destroy each other,) to extort a greater value from his contemners, by dommage; and from others, by the example.

So that in the nature of man, we find three principall causes of quarrell. First, Competition; Secondly, Diffidence, Thirdly, Glory.

The first, maketh men invade for Gain; the second, for Safety; and the third, for Reputation. The first use Violence, to make themselves Masters of other mens persons, wives, children, and cattell; the second, to defend them; the third, for trifles, as a word, a smile, a different opinion, and any other signe of undervalue, either direct in their Persons, or by reflexion in their Kindred, their Friends, their Nation, their Profession, or their Name.

Hereby it is manifest, that during the time men live without a common Power to keep them all in awe, they are in that condition which is called Warre; and such a warre, as is of every man, against every man. For WARRE, consisteth not in Battell onely, or the act of fighting; but in a tract of time, wherein the Will to contend by Battell is sufficiently known: and therefore the notion of *Time*, is to be considered in the nature of Warre; as it is in the nature of Weather. For as the nature of Foule weather, lyeth not in a showre or two of rain; but in an inclination thereto of many dayes together: So the nature of War, consisteth not in actuall fighting; but in the known disposition thereto, during all the time there is no assurance to the contrary. All other time is PEACE.

Whatsoever therefore is consequent to a time of Warre, where every man is Enemy to every man; the same is consequent to the time, wherein men live without other security, than what their own strength, and their own invention shall furnish them withall. In such condition, there is no place for Industry; because the fruit thereof is uncertain; and consequently no Culture of the Earth; no Navigation, nor use of the commodities that may be imported by Sea; no commodious Building; no Instruments of moving, and removing such things as require much force; no Knowledge of the face of the Earth; no account of Time; no Arts; no Letters; no Society; and which is worst of all, continuall feare, and danger of violent death; And the life of man, solitary, poore, nasty, brutish, and short.

It may seem strange to some man, that has not well weighed these things; that Nature should thus dissociate, and render men apt to invade, and destroy one another: and he may therefore, not trusting to this Inference, made from the Passions, desire perhaps to have the same confirmed by Experience. Let him therefore consider with himselfe, when taking a journey, he armes himselfe, and seeks to go well accompanied; when going to sleep, he locks his dores; when even in his house he locks his chests; and this when he knows there bee Lawes, and publike Officers, armed, to revenge all injuries shall bee done him; what opinion he has of his fellow subjects, when he rides armed; of his fellow Citizens, when he locks his dores; and of his children, and servants, when he locks his chests. Does he not there as much accuse mankind by his actions, as I do by my words? But neither of us accuse mans nature in it. The Desires, and other Passions of man, are in themselves no Sin. No more are the Actions, that proceed from those Passions, till they know a Law that forbids them: which till Lawes be made they cannot know: nor can

any Law be made, till they have agreed upon the Person that shall make it.

It may peradventure be thought, there was never such a time, nor condition of warre as this; and I believe it was never generally so, over all the world: but there are many places, where they live so now. For the savage people in many places of *America*, except the government of small Families, the concord whereof dependeth on naturall lust, have no government at all; and live at this day in that brutish manner, as I said before. Howsoever, it may be perceived what manner of life there would be, where there were no common Power to feare; by the manner of life, which men that have formerly lived under a peacefull government, use to degenerate into, in a civill Warre.

But though there had never been any time, wherein particular men were in a condition of warre one against another; yet in all times, Kings, and Persons of Soveraigne authority, because of their Independency, are in continuall jealousies, and in the state and posture of Gladiators; having their weapons pointing; and their eyes fixed on one another; that is, their Forts, Garrisons, and Guns upon the Frontiers of their Kingdomes; and continuall Spyes upon their neighbours; which is a posture of War. But because they uphold thereby, the Industry of their Subjects; there does not follow from it, that misery, which accompanies the Liberty of particular men.

To this warre of every man against every man, this also is consequent; that nothing can be Unjust. The notions of Right and Wrong, Justice and Injustice have there no place. Where there is no common Power, there is no Law: where no Law, no Injustice. Force, and Fraud, are in warre the two Cardinall vertues. Justice, and Injustice are none of the Faculties neither of the Body, not Mind. If they were, they might be in a man that were alone in the world, as well as his Senses, and Passions. They are Qualities, that relate to men in Society, not in Solitude. It is consequent also to the same condition, that there be no Propriety, no Dominion, no *Mine* and *Thine* distinct; but onely that to be every mans that he can get; and for so long, as he can keep it. And thus much for the ill condition, which man by meer Nature is actually placed in; though with a possiblity to come out of it, consisting partly in the Passions, partly in his Reason.

The Passions that encline men to Peace, are Feare of Death; Desire of such things as are necessary to commodious living, and a Hope by their Industry to obtain them. And Reason suggesteth convenient Articles of Peace, upon which men may be drawn to agreement. These Articles, are they, which otherwise are called the Lawes of Nature: whereof I shall speak more particularly, in the two following Chapters.

OF THE FIRST AND SECOND NATURALL LAWES, AND OF CONTRACTS

The Right of Nature, which Writers commonly call *Jus Naturale*, is the Liberty each man hath, to use his own power, as he will himselfe, for the preservation of his own Nature; that is to say, of his own Life; and consequently, of doing any thing, which in his own Judgement, and Reason, hee shall conceive to be the aptest means thereunto.

By LIBERTY, is understood, according to the proper signification of the word, the absence of externall Impediments: which Impediments, may oft take away part of a mans power to do what hee would; but cannot hinder him from using the power left him, according as his judgement, and reason shall dictate to him.

A LAW OF NATURE, (*Lex Naturalis*,) is a Precept, or generall Rule, found out by Reason, by which a man is forbidden to do, that, which is destructive of his life, or taketh away the means of preserving the same; and to omit, that, by which he thinketh it may be best preserved. For though they that speak of this subject, use to confound *Jus*, and *Lex*, *Right* and *Law*; yet they ought to be distinguished; because RIGHT, consisteth in liberty to do, or to forbeare; Whereas LAW, determineth, and bindeth to one of them: so that Law, and Right, differ as much, as Obligation, and Liberty; which in one and the same matter are inconsistent.

And because the condition of Man, (as hath been declared in the precedent Chapter) is a condition of Warre of every one against every one; in which case every one is governed by his own Reason; and there is nothing he can make use of, that may not be a help unto him, in preserving his life against his enemyes; It followeth, that in such a condition, every man has a Right to every thing; even to one anothers body. And therefore, as long as this naturall Right of every man to every thing endureth, there can be no security to any man, (how strong or wise soever he be,) of living out the time, which Nature ordinarily alloweth men to live. And consequently it is a precept, or generall rule of Reason, *That every man, ought to endeavour Peace, as farre as he has hope of obtaining it; and when he cannot obtain it, that he may seek, and use, all helps, and advantages of Warre.* The first branch of which Rule, containeth the first, and Fundamentall Law of Nature; which is, *to seek Peace, and follow it.* The Second, the

summe of the Right of Nature; which is, *By all means we can, to defend our selves.*

From this Fundamentall Law of Nature, by which men are commanded to endeavour Peace, is derived this second Law; *That a man be willing, when others are so too, as farre-forth, as for Peace, and defence of himselfe he shall think it necessary, to lay down this right to all things; and be contented with so much liberty against other men, as he would allow other men against himselfe.* For as long as every man holdeth this Right, of doing any thing he liketh; so long are all men in the condition of Warre. But if other men will not lay down their Right, as well as he; then there is no Reason for any one, to devest himselfe of his: For that were to expose himselfe to Prey, (which no man is bound to) rather than to dispose himselfe to Peace. This is that Law of the Gospell; *Whatsoever you require that others should do to you, that do ye to them.* And that Law of all men, *Quod tibi fieri non vis, alteri ne feceris.*

To *lay downe* a mans *Right* to any thing, is to *devest* himselfe of the *Liberty*, of hindring another of the benefit of his own Right to the same. For he that renounceth, or passeth away his Right, giveth not to any other man a Right which he had not before; because there is nothing to which every man had not Right by Nature: but onely standeth out of his way, that he may enjoy his own originall Right, without hindrance from him; not without hindrance from another. So that the effect which redoundeth to one man, by another mans defect of Right, is but so much diminution of impediments to the use of his own Right originall.

OF OTHER LAWES OF NATURE

From that law of Nature, by which we are obliged to transferre to another, such Rights, as being retained, hinder the peace of Mankind, there followeth a Third; which is this, *That men performe their Covenants made:* without which, Covenants are in vain, and but Empty words; and the Right of all men to all things remaining, we are still in the condition of Warre.

And in this law of Nature, consisteth the Fountain and Originall of JUSTICE. For where no Covenant hath preceded, there hath no Right been transferred, and every man has right to every thing; and consequently, no action can be Unjust. But when a Covenant is made, then to break it is *Unjust*; And the definition of INJUSTICE, is no other than *the not Performance of Covenant.* And whatsoever is not Unjust, is *Just.*

⇌ FRONTIERS OF JUSTICE ⇌
Martha Nussbaum

Martha Nussbaum (Ernst Freund Distinguished Service Professor of Law and Ethics at the University of Chicago) develops a powerful critique of the social contract model of ethics, with special attention to the underlying assumptions of that model and to the problem of who is left out of the social contract.

The problem here is not care of the aged, who have paid for their benefits by earlier productive activity. Life-extending therapies do, however, have an ominous redistributive potential. The primary problem is care for the handicapped. Speaking euphemistically of enabling them to live productive lives, when the services required exceed any possible products, conceals an issue which, understandably, no one wants to face.

David Gauthier, *Morals by Agreement*

I. NEEDS FOR CARE, PROBLEMS OF JUSTICE

Sesha, daughter of philosopher Eva Kittay and her husband Jeffrey, is a young woman in her late twenties. Attractive and affectionate, she loves music and pretty dresses. She responds with joy to the affection and admiration of others. Sesha sways to music and hugs her parents. But she will never walk, talk, or read. Because of congenital cerebral palsy and severe mental retardation, she will always be profoundly dependent on others. She needs to be dressed, washed, fed, wheeled out into Central Park. Beyond such minimal custodial care, if she is to flourish in her own way she needs companionship and love, a visible return of the capacities for affection and delight that are her strongest ways of connecting with others. Her parents, busy professionals, both care for Sesha for long hours themselves and pay a full-time caregiver. Still other helpers are needed on the many occasions when Sesha is ill or has seizures, and cannot help by telling where she hurts.

My nephew Arthur is a big good-looking ten-year-old. He loves machines of all sorts, and by now he has impressive knowledge of their workings. I could talk with Arthur all day about the theory of relativity, if I understood it as well as he does. On the phone with Art, it's always "Hi, Aunt Martha," and then right into the latest mechanical or scientific or historical issue that fascinates him. But Art has been unable to learn in a public school classroom, and he cannot be left alone for a minute when he and his mother are out shopping. He has few social skills, and he seems unable to learn them. Affectionate at home, he becomes terrified if a stranger touches him. Unusually large for his age, he is also very clumsy, unable to play games at which most younger children are adept. He also has distracting bodily tics and makes weird noises.

Arthur has both Asperger's syndrome, which is probably a type of high-functioning autism, and Tourette's syndrome. Both of his parents have full-time jobs, and they cannot afford much help. Fortunately his mother's job, as a church organist, allows her to practice at home, and church people don't mind if she brings Arthur to work. More important still, the state in which they live has agreed, after a struggle, to pay for Arthur's education at a private school equipped to handle his combination of gifts and disabilities. None of us knows whether Arthur will be able to live on his own.

Jamie Bérubé loves B. B. King, Bob Marley, and the Beatles. He can imitate a waiter bringing all his favorite foods, and he has a sly sense of verbal humor. Born with Down syndrome, Jamie has been cared for, since his birth, by a wide range of doctors and therapists, not to mention the nonstop care of his parents, literary critics Michael Bérubé and Janet Lyon. In the early days of his life, Jamie had to be fed through a tube inserted into his nose; his oxygen levels were monitored by a blood-gas machine. At the time his father describes him, Jamie is three. A speech therapist works to develop the muscles of his tongue; another teaches him American Sign Language. A massage therapist elongates the shortened muscles of his neck so that his head can sit straighter. Movement therapists work on the low muscle tone that is the main obstacle to both movement and speech in children with Down syndrome. Equally important, a good local preschool in Champaign, Illinois, includes him in a regular classroom, stimulating his curiosity and giving him precious confidence in relationships with other children, who react well to his sweet personality.

Above all, his brother, parents, and friends make a world in which he is not seen as "a child with Down syndrome," far less as "a mongoloid idiot." He is Jamie, a particular child. Jamie will probably be able to live on his own to some extent, and to hold a job. But his parents know that he will, more than many children, need them all his life.

Children and adults with mental impairments are citizens. Any decent society must address their needs for care, education, self-respect, activity, and friendship. Social contract theories, however, imagine the contracting agents who design the basic structure of society as "free, equal, and independent," the citizens whose interests they represent as "fully cooperating members of society over a complete life." They also often imagine them as characterized by a rather idealized rationality. Such approaches do not do well, even with severe cases of physical impairment and disability. It is clear, however, that such theories must handle severe mental impairments and related disabilities as an afterthought, after the basic institutions of society are already designed. Thus, in effect, people with mental impairments are not among those for whom and in reciprocity with whom society's basic institutions are structured.

The failure to deal adequately with the needs of citizens with impairments and disabilities is a serious flaw in modern theories that conceive of basic political principles as the result of a contract for mutual advantage. This flaw goes deep, affecting their adequacy as accounts of human justice more generally. A satisfactory account of human justice requires recognizing the equal citizenship of people with impairments, including mental impairments, and appropriately supporting the labor of caring for and educating them, in such a way as to address the associated disabilities. It also requires recognizing the many varieties of impairment, disability, need, and dependency that "normal" human beings experience, and thus the very great continuity between "normal" lives and those of people with lifelong impairments . . .

. . . . Impairment and disability raise two distinct problems of social justice here, both of them urgent. First, there is the issue of the fair treatment of people with impairments, many of whom need atypical social arrangements, including varieties of care, if they are to live fully integrated and productive lives. In another era, Sesha and Jamie probably would have died in infancy; if they had lived they would have been institutionalized with minimal custodial care, never getting a chance to develop their capacities for love, joy, and, in Jamie's case, substantial cognitive achievement and, probably, active citizenship. Fifteen years ago, before Asperger's syndrome was recognized as a disease, Arthur would have been treated as a smart kid whose parents had messed him up emotionally. He would probably have been institutionalized, with no opportunity to learn, and they would have lived with crushing guilt. A just society, by contrast, would not stigmatize these children and stunt their development; it would support their health, education, and full participation in social and even, when possible, political life.

A just society, we might think, would also look at the other side of the problem, the burdens on people who provide care for dependents. These people need many things: recognition that what they are doing is work; assistance, both human and financial; opportunities for rewarding employment and for participation in social and political life. This issue is closely connected with issues of gender justice, since most care for dependents is provided by women. Moreover, much of the work of caring for a dependent is unpaid and is not recognized by the market as work. And yet it has a large effect on the rest of such a worker's life. My sister could not hold any job that did not allow her long hours at home. That both the Bérubés and Kittays share their child-care responsibilities more equally than is typical among ambitious professionals is made possible only by the extremely flexible schedule of university teaching and writing. They also can afford a lot of help—most of it, as Kittay notes with unease, provided by women who are themselves not paid very highly and not respected by society, as they should be for performing an expert and vital social service.

These problems cannot be ignored or postponed on the grounds that they affect only a small number of people. That would be a bad reason to postpone them anyway, given that they raise pressing issues of equality, just as it would be bad to postpone issues of racial or religious subordination on the ground that they affect only a small minority. But we should acknowledge, as well, that disability and dependency come in many forms. It is not only the wide range of children and adults with lifelong impairments who need extensive and even hourly care from others. The mental, physical, and social impairments that I have just described all have rough parallels in the conditions of the elderly, who are generally even more difficult to care for than children and young adults with disabilities, more angry, defensive, and embittered, less physically pleasant to be with. Washing the body of a child with Down syndrome seems vastly easier to contemplate than washing the incapacitated and incontinent body of a parent who hates being in such a condition, especially when both the washer and the washed remember the parent's prime. So the way we think about the needs of children and adults with impairments and disabilities is not a special department of life, easily cordoned off from the "average case." It also has implications for the way "normals" (people with average flaws and limitations) think about their parents as they age—and about the needs they themselves are likely to have if they live long enough. As the life span increases, the relative independence that many people sometimes enjoy looks more and more like a temporary condition, a phase of life that we move into gradually and all too quickly begin to leave. Even in our prime, many of us encounter shorter or longer periods of extreme dependency on others—after surgery or a severe injury, or during a period of depression or acute mental stress. Although a theoretical analysis may attempt to distinguish phases of a "normal" life from lifelong impairment, the distinction in real life is hard to draw, and is becoming harder all the time.

But if we recognize the continuity between the situation of people with lifelong impairments and phases of "normal" lives, we must also recognize that the problem of respecting and including people with impairments, and the correlative problem of providing care for people with impairments and disabilities, are vast, affecting virtually every family in every society. There are a lot of people whose health, participation, and self-respect are at stake in the choices we make in this area. Meeting these needs in a way that protects the dignity of the recipients would seem to be one of the important jobs of a just society.

At the same time, there is also a vast amount of care work being done, usually without pay and without public recognition that it is work. Arranging for such care in a way that does not exploit the caregiver would also seem to be a central job of a just society: At one time it used to be assumed that all this work would be done by people (specifically, women) who were not full citizens anyway and did not need to work outside the home. Women were not asked whether they would do this work: it was just theirs to do, and it was assumed that they did it by choice, out of love, even though they usually had few choices in the matter. Now we think that women are equal citizens and are entitled to pursue the full range of occupations. We also generally think that they are entitled to a real choice about whether they will do a disproportionate amount of child care or assume the burden of caring for an elderly parent. Nor would most people say, if asked, that the accident of giving birth to a child with severe impairments should blight all prospects, for the parents or one parent, of living a productive personal and social life. But the realities of life in nations that still assume (as to some extent all modern nations do) that this work will be done for free, "out of love," still put enormous burdens on women across the entire economic spectrum, diminishing their productivity and their contribution to civic and political life. Ordinary child care is still disproportionately done by women, since women are far more likely than men to accept part-time work and the career detours it requires. Fathers who agree to help care for a child who will soon go off to school, moreover, are much less likely to shoulder the taxing long-term burden of care for an extremely impaired child or parent. In some nations, a woman who does such work usually can count on some support from an extended family or community network; in others, she cannot.

II. Prudential and Moral Versions of the Contract; Public and Private

What have theories of justice in the social contract tradition said about these problems? Virtually nothing. Nor can the omission be easily corrected, for it is built into the structure of our strongest theories.

Some versions of the social contract (Hobbes, Gauthier) begin from egoistic rationality alone; morality emerges (to the extent that it does) from the constraints of having to bargain with others who are similarly situated. Rawls's version, by contrast, adds a representation of moral impartiality in the form of the Veil of Ignorance, which restricts the parties' information about their place in the future society. Thus, although Rawls's parties themselves pursue their own well-being, with no interest in the interests of others, the parties are explicitly not intended as models of whole people, but only as models of parts of people. The other part, the moral part, is supplied by the informational constraints of the Veil. In both the egoistic and the moralized versions of the social contract, though, the idea that the parties are roughly equal in power and capacity plays a very important structural role in setting up the bargaining situation. As we saw, Rawls called Hume's account of the Circumstances of Justice "the normal conditions under which human cooperation is possible and necessary" (TJ126). He never ceases to endorse Hume's constraint, despite his Kantian focus on fair conditions. His theory is to this extent a hybrid, Kantian in its emphasis on fair conditions and classically contractarian in its emphasis on a "state of nature" and on the goal of mutual advantage.

A rough equality of power and capacity might be modeled in many ways. For example, we could imagine the parties to the social contract as all needy and dependent beings with strong and ineliminable ties to others. But all the major social contract thinkers choose to imagine their parties as rationally competent adults who, as Locke says, are, in the state of nature, "free, equal, and independent." Contemporary contractarians explicitly adopt a related hypothesis. For David Gauthier, people of unusual need or impairment are "not party to the moral relationships grounded by a contractarian theory." Similarly, the parties in Rawls's Original Position know that their abilities, physical and mental, lie within a "normal" range. And citizens in Rawls's Well-Ordered Society, for whom the parties in the Original Position are trustees, are "fully cooperating members of society over a complete life."

This emphasis is built deeply into the logic of the contract situation: the idea is that people will get together with others and contract for basic political principles only in certain circumstances, circumstances in which they can expect mutual benefit and in which all stand to gain from the cooperation. To include in the initial situation people who are unusually expensive or who can be expected to contribute far less than most to the well-being of the group (less than the amount defined by the idea of the "normal," whose use in Rawls we shall study shortly) would run contrary to the logic of the whole exercise. If people are making a cooperative arrangement for mutual advantage, they will want to get together with those from cooperation with whom they may expect to gain, not those who will demand unusual and expensive attention without contributing anything much to the social product, thus depressing the level of society's well-being. As Gauthier frankly acknowledges, this is an unpleasant feature of contract theories that people do not like to mention. Thus the very idea of such a contract leads strongly in the direction of distinguishing between "normal" variations among "normally productive" citizens and the sort of variation that puts some people into a special category of impairment, a move that Rawls explicitly endorses.

Now of course we immediately want to say that people with impairments and related disabilities are not unproductive. They contribute to society in many ways, when society creates conditions in which they may do so. So social contract theorists are just wrong about the facts; if they correct their false factual assumption, they can fully include people with impairments and their unusual needs, mitigating the disabilities associated with these impairments. A defense of social contract theory along these lines is, however, doomed to failure.

Before I turn to a closer consideration of Rawls's theory, let me raise one issue that I shall not treat in full. The very idea of contracting for principles that will govern a public culture is likely to be associated with a neglect of some pressing issues of justice involved in care for dependents, for the following reason. Traditionally, in the history of Western political thought, the realm of contract is taken to be a public realm, characterized by reciprocity among rough equals. This realm is standardly contrasted with another realm, the so-called private realm, or the home, in which people do things out of love and affection rather than mutual respect, contractual relations are not in place, and equality is not a central value. The bonds of family love and the activities that flow from them are imagined as somehow precontractual or natural, not part of what the parties themselves are designing. Even Rawls uses the standard expression "natural affections" to characterize the sentiments that obtain in the family.

By now, however, it is widely acknowledged that the family is itself a political institution that is defined and shaped in fundamental ways by laws and social institutions. Indeed, it should also be clear (and it was already clear to the great John Stuart Mill) that the sentiments it contains are themselves far from natural: they are shaped in many ways by social background conditions and by the expectations and necessities that these impose. None of the thinkers in the social contract tradition gets far in the direction of this insight, however (though in different ways both Hobbes and Rawls have pieces of it). One reason for this failure, I suggest, is the fact that their guiding metaphor for the formation of political principles is the idea of contract, traditionally associated with the ancient distinction between the public and the private realms. There is nothing in the very *idea* of a social contract that would prevent us from using it to think about the design of the family and the work done in the family. Approaches to the family using the ideas of contract and bargain have proven useful in helping us to think about issues of fairness in the relations among family members. One might have thought that Rawls would move in this direction, for he acknowledges that the family is one of the institutions that form part of society's "basic structure," in that it governs people's life chances pervasively, and from the very start of life, and he repudiates the public/private distinction, at least officially. So one might think that he would consider the internal workings of the family as part of what the social compact ought to regulate, although for complex reasons he does not. But, given the history of valuing the family as a realm of private love and affection to be contrasted with the realm of contract, the insight that the family is a political institution is difficult to carry through consistently. None of the theories under consideration treats the family as political in this way. All, in consequence, give very defective guidance concerning problems of justice internal to family life.

EXERCISES

1. Social contract theory is often used to justify punishing those who violate the law (they have accepted the benefits but have broken their agreement to abide by the social contract, and thus the other parties to the contract can legitimately penalize those violators). Jeffrie Murphy has argued that in our society—where there is enormous disparity in wealth, and also huge differences in opportunity (as evidenced by the contrast between urban ghetto schools and suburban schools)—the social contract cannot be used to justify punishment. At least the social contract cannot justify punishing property crimes committed by those in the lowest socioeconomic class, since persons in such circumstances would not likely agree to a contract that would leave them so severely disadvantaged. Of course, there might be other arguments for the justice of punishment; but does Murphy's argument effectively undermine the *social contract* basis for punishment in societies like our own?

2. Though obviously many who commit criminal acts endeavor to escape blame, on some occasions prisoners insist they *should* be punished. In fact, some who seem to be as much victim as criminal are strongest in their insistence that their criminal acts resulted from their own choices and that they are deserving of punishment. John Spenkelink was the first person executed in Florida after that state resumed capital punishment. He had idolized his father, but at age 11 he was the first to find his father's body following his father's suicide. From that time he became involved in a series of petty crimes, drifted around the South, and ultimately murdered a fellow drifter in an argument. Shortly before he was executed he asserted that: "Man is what he chooses to be. He chooses that for himself." Under the social contract model, why might one who commits a crime *insist* he deserves punishment?

3. Social contract theorists generally believe our moral rules are made, rather than discovered. The rules are what we draw up or agree to in our social contract. Yet, a number of social contract theorists—John Locke, for example—also believe there are objective moral truths, factually true moral principles that are just as true as the principles of math or physics. Are those beliefs fundamentally inconsistent, or can they be reconciled? In fact, the U.S. Declaration of Independence obviously contains a social contract view of government, but it starts with the famous pronouncement of *self-evident* ethical truths that do not wait upon social contracts: "We hold these truths to be self-evident: That all men are created equal, and are endowed by their Creator with certain inalienable rights." Is that a *consistent* or a *contradictory* position?

4. Under a strict social contract view of ethics, could we make sense of the notion of "rules of conduct" or "rules of war" between warring nations?

5. Is the United Nations charter an example of a "social contract"?

6. Hobbes suggests that in the "state of nature," "Every man has a right to every thing; even to one another's body." Is it legitimate to speak of "rights" of any kind in the state of nature?

7. Could a social contract theorist be an advocate of animal rights?

8. Could a social contract theorist believe that we have a *moral obligation* to help the impoverished in other countries?

9. Could social contract theory survive the demise of the nation-state?

10. Players in the popular *World of Warcraft* Internet game often form "guilds" or groups that join together in mutual defense and to attack other groups. One dedicated member of such a guild died (in real-life, not in the game), and the members of her guild decided to hold a memorial service for her within the game that she loved. They announced the planned memorial on a World of Warcraft open forum, and one of the members of her guild logged into her account, and placed the deceased woman's character at her favorite game site, a lake. Other game characters from her guild came by the game site to pay their respects and honor their deceased gaming friend. Members of a rival guild, on learning of the planned memorial, organized a "bombing attack" on the memorial service, thus destroying many of their rivals and winning kill points. Those game players who had participated in the memorial service were outraged, and accused the rival guild of being underhanded and disrespectful. *Was* the attack on the memorial service unfair? Was it morally wrong? Was it a violation of the gaming social contract?

    Suppose you have a friend—in real life—who is a member of a rival guild in World of Warcraft. One day he leaves his laptop in the library while he goes to lunch, and you open his WoW account and move his character to a vulnerable location and destroy him. Would that be unfair? Would it be morally wrong?

11. Martha Nussbaum criticizes social contract theory on the grounds that its basic logic requires it to treat "people of unusual need or impairment" as second-class citizens. Is this an implication of social contract theory? Is there any form of social contract theory that could avoid that criticism? That is, could social contract theory be suitably modified to avoid treating such people as second-class citizens, or is that an inevitable part of the theory?

ADDITIONAL READING

The classic sources for social contract theory are Thomas Hobbes's *Leviathan*, John Locke's *Second Treatise on Government*, and Jean-Jacques Rousseau's *Social Contract (Du Contrat Social)*. Hobbes's *Leviathan* is available from Bobbs-Merrill (Indianapolis, IN: 1958); it was originally published in 1651. Locke's *Second Treatise on Government* was originally published in 1690; an accessible edition is from Bobbs-Merrill (Indianapolis, IN: Bobbs-Merrill, Library of Liberal Arts, 1952). Rousseau's *Social Contract* was originally published in 1762; it can be found in an edition edited by R. Masters (New York: St. Martin's Press, 1978).

Discussions of social contract theory tradition include Jean Hampton, *Hobbes and the Social Contract Tradition* (Cambridge, MA: Cambridge University Press, 1986); and P. Riley, *Will and Political Legitimacy: A Critical Exposition of Social Contract Theory in Hobbes, Locke, Rousseau, Kant, and Hegel* (Cambridge, MA: Harvard University Press, 1982).

David Gauthier's version of contractarian theory can be found in *Morals by Agreement* (Oxford: Oxford University Press, 1986) and *Moral Dealing* (Ithaca, NY: Cornell University Press, 1990). For discussion and critique of Gauthier's theory, see Peter Vallentyne, editor, *Contractarianism and Rational Choice* (New York: Cambridge University Press, 1991).

Probably the best-known philosophical book of the late twentieth century presented an updated version of social contract theory: John Rawls, *A Theory of Justice* (London: Oxford University Press, 1971).

Russ Shafer-Landau, in *Moral Realism: A Defense* (Oxford: Clarendon Press, 2003), critiques the general constructivist approach to ethics, including social contract ethics.

A strong critic of the social contract tradition is Martha C. Nussbaum, in *Frontiers of Justice: Disability, Nationality, Species Membership* (Cambridge, MA: Harvard University Press, 2006). Other critics include Carole Pateman, *The Sexual Contract* (Stanford: Stanford University Press, 1988); Virginia Held, *Feminist Morality: Transforming Culture, Society, and Politics* (Chicago, IL: University of Chicago Press, 1993); and Eva Feder Kittay, *Love's Labor* (New York: Routledge, 1999).

Good online sources for material on social contract theory include *Stanford Encyclopedia of Philosophy* at *http://plato.stanford.edu/entries/contractarianism*; and *The Internet Encyclopedia of Philosophy* at *http://www.iep.utm.edu/soc-cont/*.

The constitution of the Iroquois Confederacy can be found at www.constitution.org/cons/iroquois.htm.

NOTE

[1]Jean-Jacques Rousseau, *A Discourse on the Origin of Inequality*, trans. Franklin Philip (Oxford University Press: Oxford, 1994), 36.

8

Virtue Ethics

Our friend Sandra is a brilliant physicist. The physics faculty are in awe of her, the top graduate schools are competing for her, and she seems set to make major scientific discoveries in an outstanding career. Everyone agrees it's just a matter of time before she wins the Nobel Prize for her research. But in addition to physics, Sandra also loves video games; and she surprises everyone by rejecting all graduate school offers, opting instead for a menial job that leaves her free to devote her evenings and weekends to the pursuit of simulated glory. What's our response? We're surprised, certainly, and probably disappointed: Sandra is throwing away a wonderful opportunity—she could have accomplished so much. We think she made a lousy decision. But is Sandra's choice *morally wrong*? Of course we are not going to put Sandra in jail for her choice, and we aren't going to *force* her to go to graduate school; still, is her choice *morally* wrong? Does Sandra's choice fall within the sphere of morality? If Sandra had obligations—say, to support her children—that her video-game playing was causing her to neglect, then she might be violating some special moral obligations. But Sandra is a free agent, unattached, with no dependents. Her choice is disappointing. She is wasting her talents (she is not even designing games, just playing them in blissful isolation). But is her life choice *morally* despicable?

No. Sandra's choice is purely personal. She is hurting no one except herself. This is a private matter, and morality has nothing to do with it. That's certainly one way of looking at it. In fact, that's how we'll see it from the social contract perspective. Ethics is designed to regulate our social behavior, our relations with others. Purely private behavior falls outside the scope of ethical judgment. An argument often made against utilitarians is that they turn everything into an ethical issue and leave no area of nonethical privacy. On the utilitarian view, your act is right if and only if it produces the greatest possible balance of good/pleasure over suffering. Does your Thursday night bowling league pass that test? No; you could accomplish more good by turning it into a Thursday night league for raising funds to eradicate hunger in impoverished countries. So, not a single moment of your life escapes ethical scrutiny. But—so goes the criticism—we want a sphere of life that is private, where ethical evaluations don't intrude. Ethics is great, and moral obligations are important, but they aren't the *whole* of life. Whatever you think of this criticism of utilitarian ethics, it brings to the surface an underlying assumption of many contemporary ethical views: in the purely individual private sphere, ethics doesn't apply. (That means *purely* private, not just the privacy of my own family life. If I abuse my children within the privacy of my own home, that immoral act certainly does have an impact on others.) If the function of ethics is to regulate our social relations for the good and safety of us all, then it is hardly surprising that private, nonsocial matters should fall outside its influence.

But of course from *other* ethical perspectives, Sandra's personal choice may be very much an ethical issue. Kant would have insisted that Sandra has an obligation to develop her talents: she could not will that everyone squander their talents rather than developing them for the common good. For the ancient Greeks and Romans, ethics starts at home: ethics is rooted in personal behavior, in the moral nature of the individual. For example, Plato regarded the state as the "soul writ large." Social ethics derive from individual ethics, not the other way around. Plato would consider Sandra's choice to be governed by her desire for pleasure, rather than controlled by reason, and thus evidence of a disordered and profoundly *immoral* and unjust soul. Aristotle's ethics was quite different from Plato's, but they shared at least one basic premise: both thought that ethics was first and foremost a personal and individual matter. Aristotle focused on how one becomes a good and virtuous person. A society comprised of virtuous persons would be a good society, but the starting point is the personal virtuous life of the individual. The Roman epicureans and stoics were fundamentally opposed in their concept of how to live a good moral life: the epicureans taught that you should seek pleasure (but do so intelligently and prudently, because many apparent pleasures have hidden costs); in contrast, the stoics counseled detachment and the minimization of needs and desires. But both believed that the basic question of ethics is how to live a good and virtuous life.

THE DISTINCTIVE FOCUS OF VIRTUE ETHICS

The ethical views we have examined in earlier chapters focused on what act is right or just or good, or on how—or whether—we can know what act is good. Is theft wrong? Could it ever be right? Is it wrong to lie? How do we know that telling lies is wrong? *Do* we know that telling lies is wrong? Should we share our wealth with those who are less fortunate? Does justice require such benevolence? Is it wrong to inflict suffering on animals to run medical experiments for human benefit?

All of these seem perfectly natural ethical questions; indeed, it may be difficult to imagine any other focus for ethics. But one ethical tradition, which traces its history to ancient Greece but also claims enthusiastic contemporary advocates, would consider such questions a very strange starting point for ethical inquiry. Rather than focusing on right or wrong actions, this tradition concentrates on the *character* of the actor. You can't tell whether an act is right or wrong just by observing the act itself; instead, you must look at the person performing the act.

Considering Character

In some ways, this approach makes perfect sense. After all, if you see me stretch out my hand and rescue a child about to fall from a tall building, you can't tell much about whether the act was good or bad. Of course the act was beneficial, and you're glad I saved the child (you are not some moral monster who delights in watching children plunge from tall buildings). But to know whether my act was actually morally good, you must probe much deeper. *Why* did I stretch out my hand and save the child? If I was having a brief seizure, and my hand shot out and involuntarily closed around the endangered child's arm, then that is certainly fortunate, but it is not morally worthy: an unusually strong gust of wind that blows the child back from the ledge is not a virtuous breeze. Neither the gusting wind nor my grasping seizure even counts as an *act*. And if I had intended to push the child over the ledge, but instead tripped and grasped for something to hold onto, and in so doing inadvertently grabbed the child's arm and pulled it to safety, then again the result is fortunate; but rather than being a good person, I am a moral scoundrel. Fortunately, I am also a clumsy oaf, and so I wound up saving the child instead of murdering it. But my act is nonetheless a vicious act of attempted murder rather than a heroic act of rescue (though I may never admit that). Or suppose I had been sublimely indifferent to the child's peril, caring not at all whether it tumbled or not. Just before the child slipped over the edge, I noticed the winning lottery ticket clutched in its grubby little fist, and so rescued the child strictly in hope of getting a significant share of the winnings. In that case, my act is again beneficial, and certainly better than allowing the child to perish, but it has lost most if not all of its moral luster.

The moral of this story is a simple one: judging an act as either good or bad requires us to examine the *character* and *motives* of the person who performed the act. The starting point for ethics is not the question of what acts are right or wrong, but what *characters* are virtuous or vicious. The virtuous person is not simply one who does the right act; rather, the virtuous person is one who consistently does right acts for the right motives. Aristotle, a virtue ethicist of ancient Athens, states the requirement thus: the virtuous agent first "must have knowledge, second he must choose the acts and choose them for their own sakes, and finally his action must proceed from a firm character."[1] One cannot be virtuous or perform genuinely good acts by accident. It requires deliberate practice and consistent effort at character building. Aristotle believes we aren't naturally virtuous, but we have the capacity to become virtuous by practice: by consistently choosing good acts. And we become vicious in the same manner: by practicing vice, by not consistently making the effort to choose and act well. As you practice, so you become.

Practicing Virtue

Virtue theorists insist that we become good by doing good. If you cut corners in business, you are a shady operator, and you are developing the character of a shady operator. You are becoming practiced at it, it is becoming a habit. And if you tell yourself that you are really an honest and upright person who happens to practice deceit and chicanery in her daily behavior, then you are adding self-deception to the rest of your deceitful character. You are not what you wear, or what you drive, or what you eat; and you are not what you pretend to yourself to be, or wish you were; you are instead what you do. One who lies is a liar, and telling lies entrenches that character trait. If you do less than your best, you develop the habit, and you become— you make yourself—a slothful person. Becoming virtuous is not something we do at some later point when we gain true moral wisdom, or finally reach enlightenment, or have sufficient time for it; becoming virtuous is what we do in the everyday practice of our lives. When you consider whether to lie to your friend, or cut corners on your work, or cheat the newspaper seller, don't ask yourself whether it's right or wrong; rather, ask yourself whether you want to be the sort of person who engages in such behavior and has such a character. The acts you sow shape the character you reap.

> "We are what we repeatedly do. Excellence, then, is not an act, but a habit." *Aristotle*, Nicomachean Ethics.

Virtue and Special Commitments

Virtue theory often appeals to those who set very high standards for themselves. *I* want to be the sort of person who does more than the minimum, who leaves the world a better place than she found it, who has the courage to combat injustice in high places. It's not that I think everyone is obligated to live by such a demanding code, but it's the standard I set for myself, it's who I want to become—and the only way to become that sort of person is by practicing what that sort of person would do, by going the extra mile, by acting bravely, by standing against the crowd or the fashion if that is what justice demands.

THE STRENGTHS OF VIRTUE ETHICS

Virtue theory has some distinct strengths. It emphasizes the strong connection between our acts and our character, and it encourages us to consider our characters as unified wholes rather than viewing each ethical decision in isolation. It reminds us that as moral actors we are more than merely placeholders who perform good or bad acts—that we are persons with histories that shaped us, relations that matter to us, societies we value, and with goals and projects that give our lives meaning and significance.[2] In order to live healthy and satisfying lives, we need commitments. Our commitments should not be *immoral* (if my goal in life is to run a stock scam that will net me $10 million, then virtue is likely to elude me). But neither must our commitments embrace a specifically *moral* goal: the goal of running an outstanding marathon, or composing a superb violin concerto, or discovering a new species of beetle is a legitimate goal. Such projects give my life *integrity*[3]: they are projects with which I identify, and which help to define who I am. Some *moral* ideals may also serve as personal life goals. For example, someone might have a deep commitment to honesty. Even in circumstances when it would be *useful* to fib, even when a lie might do more good than telling the truth, this person's commitment to honesty prevents her from telling a lie. Telling a lie would threaten the integrity and unity of *who she is*, just as for someone else giving up on the project of writing a great novel may undercut her sense of identity. Virtue theory allows space for such commitments. So your personal goals—whether moral (developing integrity) or nonmoral (running a marathon)—are morally relevant to your character development, even though there is more to your character than its moral commitments.

CRITICISMS OF VIRTUE THEORY

What Counts as Virtue?

Its positive features notwithstanding, virtue theory may seem to leave a few loose ends. We become virtuous by practicing virtuous acts. That is inspiring, and it does provide a useful reminder that what we sow is what we reap, and that it is easy to fall into undesirable habits—habits that are not easy to break, character traits that are not easy to change. But we still have the question: If we become virtuous by performing virtuous acts, how do we know which acts are virtuous in the first place? Juanita is a virtuous person because she consistently performs virtuous acts. And her acts count as virtuous because they are the product of a firm virtuous character with settled virtuous motives. But still: *Which* acts are virtuous? Perhaps the answer is that virtuous acts are those done by virtuous persons. We then ask: But how do we recognize genuinely virtuous persons? At that point it will not be helpful to be told that virtuous persons are those who perform virtuous acts. Aristotle tried to escape the circle by suggesting that the genuinely virtuous person is the one who achieves true happiness and genuine satisfaction. But unless we have some independent criterion for "true happiness," we have made little progress.

Some virtue theorists would insist that the demand for "what counts as virtue" is shallow and premature. The goal of virtue theorists is to vividly describe the character traits that are genuinely admirable: ideal characteristics that are worthy of admiration. Virtue theory should not be criticized because it has not completed that project in advance. If we have not given a fully adequate account of genuinely virtuous character (so the virtue theorists would say), at least we have recognized the importance of developing such an account. That is a significant improvement over utilitarian and Kantian ethical theories, which focus too narrowly and superficially on what rules I should follow and acts I should perform, rather than on what I should strive to become and how I can shape a virtuous character.

Another answer offered by some virtue theorists—including Aristotle, and more recently Rosalind Hursthouse and Philippa Foot—is that virtue is what promotes *human flourishing* (or as Aristotle might call it, *true happiness*). Of course, we cannot then say that what constitutes a genuinely happy and flourishing human life is a life in accordance with virtue, for that again spins in a circle. What virtue theorists generally have in mind is a successful life for human beings, for our natural kind. We have some sense of when a deer, or a wolf, or even a tree is *flourishing*; and while it may be more difficult to specify the conditions that result in human flourishing, the question is meaningful and significant, and we can use the resources of psychology, anthropology, biology, and history in seeking an answer. This is not some simplistic question of what makes us *happy*: after all, we can all think of activities that made us (at least temporarily) quite happy, but that certainly did not contribute to our overall flourishing. A flourishing human life must involve joys, pleasures, and happiness; but a stupid and shallow person might live a rather *happy* life that few would count as a genuinely flourishing *human* life. We humans are social beings, who live best in cooperative relations, exercising our distinctive rational capacities. Virtuous acts and virtuous characters are those that contribute to a good, healthy, flourishing life for ourselves, our families, our communities, and our species. Contemporary virtue theorist Rosalind Hursthouse (in *Ethics, Humans, and Other Animals*) uses the human flourishing model to justify some important traditional virtues: "Without honesty, generosity, and loyalty we would miss out on one of our greatest sources of characteristic enjoyment, namely loving relationships; without honesty, we would be unable to cooperate or to acquire knowledge and pass it on to the next generation to build on. And it has long been a commonplace that justice and fidelity to promises enable us to function as a social, cooperating group." Determining what is the best way of living for members of the human species is not an easy question; but it is at least a real question, and seeking to answer it can provide substance and guidance to our account of virtuous character traits. It won't provide easy answers or simple ethical rules, but there is no reason to suppose ethics must be that easy.

Aristotle suggested another guide for what counts as virtuous—a guide that has come to be known as *The Golden Mean*. Aristotle describes it thus:

> Virtue, then, is a state of character concerned with choice, lying in a mean, i.e. the mean relative to us, this being determined by a rational principle, and by that principle by which the man of practical wisdom would determine it. Now it is a mean between two vices, that which depends on excess and that which depends on defect; and again it is a mean because the vices respectively fall short of or exceed what is right in both passions and actions, while virtue both finds and chooses that which is intermediate.[4]

Aristotle's golden mean is sometimes represented as merely "whatever is moderate is right." But that oversimplification turns the doctrine into something ridiculous, as Aristotle himself was well aware. To use Aristotle's own example, it would not be virtuous to commit a moderate number of murders or thefts. As Aristotle says, "they are themselves bad, and not the excesses or deficiencies of them." Furthermore, what counts as moderation may vary. Think of athletic training (another of Aristotle's examples). A moderate training session for a weekend jogger will be quite different from a moderate and well-balanced workout for an Olympic athlete; but both must try to avoid the extremes of overtraining (and wearing themselves down) or neglecting their training (and failing to improve). Trying to strike just the right balance is a difficult task, in both athletics and morality. Spendthrifts are too loose with their money, misers too tight. Bravery is a virtue, and it is the mean between rashness and cowardice. "Discretion is the better part of valor," as the saying goes; the challenge is in knowing exactly where the virtue of discretion ends and the vice of cowardice begins. But Aristotle does not pretend that virtue is easy: "It is no easy task to be good. For in everything it is no easy task to find the middle . . . ; wherefore goodness is both rare and laudable and noble."[5]

Virtue Theory and Situationist Psychology

There is a significant body of psychological research indicating that much of our behavior is *not* the result of our characters, our character traits, and our virtues (as our "common sense" would have it), but instead is controlled or heavily influenced by the *situation* in which the behavior occurs. For example, researchers have found that seemingly trivial influences—such as finding a dime or being prompted to hurry—have a very large influence on whether people stop to help someone with a problem. In one experiment, experimental subjects were divided into two groups. For the first group, a dime was planted where the experimental subject would find it; individuals in the second group did not find a coin. Then a student (who was actually part of the experiment) walked by and dropped some papers. Of 16 individuals who found a dime, 14 stopped to help; of the 25 subjects who did *not* find a dime, only 1 stopped to help. Obviously, finding a dime is not a major event in one's life; but if such trivial circumstances can have such a powerful effect on behavior, that raises serious questions about whether our *characters*—whether vicious or virtuous—play the vitally important role that virtue theory assigns to them. Virtue theorists offer several responses, including claims that the situationist experiments are not the best way of revealing character and that manifestations of character traits are revealed in other circumstances and over longer periods. In any case, the implication of contemporary psychological research for ethical issues remains an important question, and has special relevance for questions of free will and moral responsibility.

Virtue Theory and Individualism

Others have objected that virtue theory may be too individualistic: the focus should be on what acts contribute to the good of all, or at least the good of our society, rather than what acts will allow me to cultivate my own *individual* virtue. One might suggest that the cultivation of individual virtue will invariably contribute to the good of others and to the good of society; but that seems an article of faith, and in imperfect societies that faith may be misplaced. Imagine the following sort of case (which, unfortunately, at one time posed a very real quandary for some persons). It is 1948. You are the black president of a small college deep in the southern United States. Your college is part of the segregated system of higher education in your state: white students attend one set of colleges, and black students attend a different set. Separate but equal, in theory; in practice, the schools are certainly separate, but the white schools receive the lion's share of funds. You are struggling to provide a good education to the students who attend your college, but it's an uphill battle. The students at your college went to segregated elementary and secondary schools, where the same unequal distribution of educational resources meant that they studied in crowded classrooms in dilapidated buildings with inadequate school supplies; and now they have arrived on your campus, with strong goals but weak educational backgrounds, and you are trying to teach them without enough classrooms, in ancient laboratories, with a shortage of faculty, and a host of other problems. You are a shrewd and perceptive college president, and wise to the ways of the segregated state in which you live. You know that if you "play the game" for the exclusively white state legislature—bow and scrape, beg and plead, butter them up with flattery—they will give you the resources you desperately need to provide a good education for the students at your college. If you get those resources, you can educate thousands of young men and women, and give them an opportunity to escape the grinding poverty in which their families live, and an opportunity to eventually challenge and change the racist system in their state. Without such resources, these students have little or no chance of an education or a better life, and without those educated young people it will take much longer to break the ugly grip of racism in the region. But you have no illusions about the cost to you as a person. If you play the game for these racist legislators, you will become a person you detest: a toady to the white power structure, a living embodiment of racial stereotypes. In short, you will accomplish wonderful things, help many young people, and contribute to the overthrow of a vicious apartheid system; but the cost is the sacrifice of your own integrity, your own honor, your own *virtue*. What *should* you do in such circumstances?

There are ways to avoid grappling with this question. You could say that in fact by playing the game for the white legislature, this black college president will *not* make things better, but will in fact delay the needed changes by fostering the racist stereotypes that have hindered progress. Perhaps that's true. That's a question for sociologists. But it's a very difficult question, and it's at least *possible* that in such a vicious system there actually were people whose best way of helping others and bringing change was through obsequious flattery, rather than defiant resistance. That's an ugly thought; but the racist system was an ugly thing. So, even if you think this would not be the best way of helping others in this situation, suspend your doubts for a moment and suppose that you are in a situation where that is the case. (If you believe that there is no conceivable situation when sacrificing your own personal virtue would actually provide better overall results for others, then considering such a situation may be impossible for you. But that is a very strong claim. It strikes me as implausible, and in any case would require substantial argument to support.)

A second way to avoid this question is to claim that by practicing flattery, playing the game, bowing and scraping, one will *not* be sacrificing one's own virtue: it's just a show, a façade, and not what you really are. But if you take this position, you have rejected virtue theory, for virtue theory asserts that you become what you practice: If you practice being a toady to the power system, then you become—you *are*—that sort of person. If we say of someone that "She acts bravely when she is around people weaker than she, but she acts like a coward when she is around powerful people," we are *not* saying that deep down she is really courageous. If I am a soldier who runs away whenever the bullets fly, but insist that deep down I am really very courageous, you will be legitimately skeptical of my bravery.

Henry David Thoreau, in *Walden*, expressed his skepticism about the possibility of *living* one way but actually *being* something else: "As to conformity outwardly, and living your own life inwardly, I have not a very high opinion of that course."

In this case, try to set aside your doubts, and consider what you think the college president—in this horrible but hardly impossible situation—*should* do. Should he sacrifice his virtue for the benefit of his students and their futures? Or should he insist on his own honor, dignity, and integrity, even if the cost is not being able to provide educational resources to young people who desperately need them, and perhaps delaying the overthrow of the oppressive system in which he and his students live?

Don't move on too quickly. Take a few minutes out of your busy life and actually *think* about what this college president *should do*.

Virtue and Society

Some people will favor preserving one's own honor and dignity at all costs: "This above all, to thine own self be true." Others will find that too self-centered, and focus instead on the enormous benefits that might result from better educational resources: young people who otherwise would have been condemned to a life of grinding poverty—perhaps as sharecroppers growing cotton for a wealthy landowner—will instead live satisfying and dignified lives as physicians, lawyers, and engineers. Most of us will agree that the best situation would be one in which we could live honorable, dignified, and virtuous lives and *also* contribute to advancing the welfare of others: Both are good ends. But focus on this question: Which is most basic, the cultivation of your individual virtue or the benefit to the whole? Which is most important? Then we find very different perspectives on what ethics is really about.

Virtue theorists would not all agree on the answer to that question. But many virtue theorists would say that this embattled college president *cannot* live a genuinely virtuous life. Not through any fault of his own, but rather because the full development of a virtuous life requires the support of the right kind of society, a society with a rich tradition of worthwhile values and long-term goals. This man is unlucky: He is living in a society in which living virtuously is not really possible.

But does development of individual virtue really depend on living in the right kind of society? Former U.S. Supreme Court justice Thurgood Marshall lived in precisely the social setting in which our mythical college president is struggling. But he seems to me one of the greatest exemplars of a virtuous person the United States has to offer. Thurgood Marshall devoted his life and his profound intelligence and his outstanding legal skills to challenging the racist laws that shackled African Americans in the mid-twentieth century. He traveled into some of the most dangerous settings, where lynching was a constant threat, and challenged the institutionalized racism of the ruling powers. Marshall was a man of remarkable courage, deep commitment to a noble cause, and extraordinary ability that he used for high purposes. He lived in a vicious society—not a society that supported his development of virtue, but instead a society that he employed his own virtues to change. It is difficult for me to think of anyone who exhibited greater virtue.

Another great example of virtue for many people is Nelson Mandela, a leader in the struggle to overthrow the brutal apartheid system in South Africa: the apartheid society in which Mandela was born and lived. A man of great strength and fortitude, he spent years in the South African prison system—a dangerous place, where South African freedom fighters often "accidentally" died. He refused to give up his struggle for freedom even when offered a release from prison. And yet, when change finally came, and Mandela became the leader of a new South Africa, Mandela refused to seek vengeance and instead worked to heal the scars and suffering and distrust of the past. A remarkable person: very few people in history have combined the virtues of prerevolutionary courage and struggle with postrevolutionary compassion, restraint, and wisdom. Mandela embodied the virtues of both. But the brutal society in which he developed those virtues was certainly not a virtuous society.

It seems doubtful that a good society is an essential condition to the development of virtuous character, since Thurgood Marshall and Nelson Mandela are powerful counterexamples to that claim. Virtue theory nonetheless performs a useful service by emphasizing the importance of community and society in fostering the development of virtue. After all, while the larger society did nothing to help Marshall and Mandela in their development of virtue, surely they were supported by a smaller subsociety (the courageous and committed community of civil rights workers and freedom fighters) that helped shape their characters. In any case, the question of *how* we become virtuous, and how good character is shaped, is an issue often neglected by traditional accounts of ethics. Virtue theory offers a useful focus on that important question.

Are There Multiple Sets of Virtues?

Nelson Mandela is a remarkable and almost unique person. He exhibited outstanding virtue as a revolutionary leader, and he was also wonderful—wise, patient, and forgiving—as the leader of a new country. It is rare to find someone who can do either, and almost unheard of to find someone who excels at both. After all, the virtues required of a revolutionary are hardly the virtues needed as an elected leader. And that raises another important question concerning virtue theory: Are there many *different* and perhaps incompatible sets of virtues? Are there different virtues for different societies, different sets of virtues for various roles in society, or even for different stages of life (are the virtues of youth the same as the virtues of age)? Or does every genuinely virtuous person share a common core of virtue? Though some virtue theorists have argued that there is only one real set of universal virtues, many writers have doubted that there can be a single standard for virtue. Greg Pence offers the following example of radically different virtue sets for distinctly different societies:

> In frontier societies great heroes were often highly intelligent people who functioned beautifully outside the tight bounds of civilized cities with their churches, weddings, schools, lawyers, stores, police, and factories. Such frontier heroes lived by a simple hard code (horse thieves must be caught and killed, 'savages' are the enemy, each person pulls his own weight). When the frontiers became civilized, such heroes often found that their characters did not fit the society they had helped create. Society had required their types, and then moved on.[6]

Of course one might well decide that embodying the "hard code" of the "frontier heroes" is by no means an exercise of virtue: the genocidal murder of "savages" may have been admired in that society, but from a larger perspective it is abominably vicious rather than virtuous behavior. Still, Pence's example does bring out a key question for virtue theories: is virtue universal, or are virtues relative to societies? That is a large and difficult question, essentially the question of whether there are any universal truths of ethics. That's a question that will continue to concern us.

Virtue Theory and Medicine

Whatever the strengths or weaknesses of virtue theory as a general theory of ethics, there are some settings where virtue theory seems particularly helpful. When Aristotle wrote about the virtues almost 2,500 years ago, one of his favorite examples was the practice of medicine. And that still seems a productive setting for virtue theory: it seems especially useful to think about the *virtues* of a good nurse, therapist, or physician. For example, one essential virtue for the practice of medicine is the ability to keep confidences, the ability to maintain confidentiality. People often gossip; it's a minor vice. But if a health professional "gossips" by revealing confidences about his or her patients, that is a betrayal of an essential virtue of medical caregivers. (It is not surprising that virtue theory should have its greatest successes in narrower and more tightly defined realms such as medicine—we have a relatively clear idea of what counts as "good medicine," while we have a much more difficult time agreeing on any *general* idea of human flourishing.)

Medical Beneficence

Another important medical virtue is the commitment to the good of the patient, rather than one's own self-interests. When I buy a used car, I know the salesperson is trying to sell the car for as much as possible. Her primary goal is to maximize her profit on the deal, whether it happens to be in my best interest or not. If I discover I overpaid for the car, I may be somewhat bitter; but (unless there was outright fraud such as rolling back the odometer) I won't blame the salesperson: she has no obligation to place my interests first. When the CEO of a major corporation cheats us we are bitter, but we really didn't expect much: whatever the slick advertising of noble motives, corporations and their officers have a primary commitment to increasing profit, not serving the public welfare (though betraying employees by gutting their pension plans may nonetheless be a special betrayal of trust, or at the very least a violation of a special obligation toward those who made the corporation a success). But if my physician performs unnecessary and dangerous surgery on me in order to put extra money in her own pocket, that's a different matter altogether. Health care workers are supposed to exhibit special virtues, and first among those virtues is a deep commitment to the good of the patient: a commitment to the patient's interests rather than the physician's own benefit. My physician might legitimately refuse to place me on the list for a heart transplant, judging that even though a transplant would benefit me, I can be treated effectively through medication, and other patients with greater need should get priority for the very scarce resource of transplantable hearts. But if my physician gives an available heart to someone else with less medical need but more money (who pays the physician a substantial bonus for the transplant), then I have been betrayed, and the physician has betrayed the virtues of her profession. If a dealer in classic restored cars is selling a beautiful '56 Chevy, and you offer more money than I, the dealer will sell the car to you. I may be disappointed, but the dealer has not failed any principle of virtue. But physicians are members of a profession with a profound tradition of virtue, not dealers of medicine.

When some physicians refused to treat AIDS patients—because it exposed the physician to a very small risk of infection—it was a betrayal of that medical virtue tradition, like a firefighter who only answers the call to "safe" fires or a police officer who pursues only nonviolent criminals. And that is also one of the reasons why profit-making health maintenance organizations (HMOs) have been troubling to many physicians. Physicians have always been concerned with who receives medical benefits: If there is a shortage of a drug, which patients will benefit most from it? If there is a shortage of organs for transplant, which patients are most in need of a transplant, and which ones can be treated by other means? But in an HMO, the physician is expected to make treatment decisions on the basis of cost, rather than what is best for patients. The savings become profits for the HMO and monetary bonuses for the physician, rather than medical benefits for patients with more pressing needs. For many physicians, that threatens a basic value of medicine and undercuts a central virtue of the good physician.

A Virtuous Medical Hero

In 1994 and 1995, there was a terrible ethnic conflict in Rwanda between the Hutu and Tutsi; horrific, genocidal attacks were carried out by both sides. At one point in the conflict there was a hospital that cared for a number of disabled persons from one of the ethnic groups, and the area where the hospital was located was under attack by forces from the opposing group. It was clear the opposing forces would overrun the area within a few days, and would slaughter anyone who remained. A plane was sent in to evacuate the international aid workers who were caring for the disabled patients, but there were no resources for evacuating the patients. There was a young native doctor caring for the patients, and when the international medical workers were evacuated, he was offered the opportunity to escape with them. He refused to go, though staying meant facing a brutal death within a few days. His reason for staying was simple: "I cannot abandon my patients."

Some people regard the behavior of this young doctor as foolish. His patients would soon die anyway, and he could have saved himself and provided medical care for others. His heroic act of caring probably went beyond what a Kantian ethic would require, and far beyond what a utilitarian would think wise. But it was in the virtue tradition of physicians who stayed in quarantined cities to nurse those afflicted with the death-dealing and highly contagious bubonic plague, and typically died with their patients. And it is in the tradition of the heroic firefighters who rushed into the collapsing World Trade Center in a doomed rescue effort. Those who were fleeing that terrible inferno reported their amazement at the firefighters rushing in the opposite direction, toward the collapsing buildings. If we could ask the firefighters who gave their lives in their attempts at rescue, many would no doubt say it was "just part of my job"; but if so, it was part of a "job"—part of a profession—with noble ideals of self-sacrifice, and a deep tradition of heroic virtues. Perhaps the behavior of the young Rwandan doctor does not make utilitarian sense. But it exemplifies an ideal of the medical profession, and physicians and nurses should celebrate him as a hero of a great tradition of virtue. Western doctors who refuse to treat AIDS patients could learn a very important lesson about medical virtues from that young African doctor.

⇒ NICOMACHEAN ETHICS ⇐
Aristotle

Aristotle was a student of Plato, and taught Alexander the Great. He wrote an enormous body of work, doing serious and influential work in almost every subject of knowledge known to the ancient world, ranging from logic to biology, metaphysics to ethics, poetry to rhetoric. His influence throughout the Medieval period was enormous. So great was his fame and authority that for many centuries Christian theologians simply referred to him as "The Philosopher." This translation is by W. D. Ross.

Now that we have spoken of the virtues, the forms of friendship, and the varieties of pleasure, what remains is to discuss in outline the nature of happiness, since this is what we state the end of human nature to be. Our discussion will be the more concise if we first sum up what we have said already. We said, then, that it is not a disposition; for if it were it might belong to some one who was asleep throughout his life, living the life of a plant, or, again, to some one who was suffering the greatest misfortunes. If these implications are unacceptable, and we must rather class happiness as an activity, as we have said before, and if some activities are necessary, and desirable for the sake of something else, while others are so in themselves, evidently happiness must be placed among those desirable in themselves, not among those desirable for the sake of something else; for happiness does not lack anything, but is self-sufficient. Now those activities are desirable in themselves from which nothing is sought beyond the activity. And of this nature virtuous actions are thought to be; for to do noble and good deeds is a thing desirable for its own sake.

Pleasant amusements also are thought to be of this nature; we choose them not for the sake of other things; for we are injured rather than benefited by them, since we are led to neglect our bodies and our property. But most of the people who are deemed happy take refuge in such pastimes, which is the reason why those who are ready-witted at them are highly esteemed at the courts of tyrants; they make themselves pleasant companions in the tyrants' favourite pursuits, and that is the sort of man they want. Now these things are thought to be of the nature of happiness because people in despotic positions spend their leisure in them, but perhaps such people prove nothing; for virtue and reason, from which good activities flow, do not depend on despotic position; nor, if these people, who have never tasted pure and generous pleasure, take refuge in the bodily pleasures, should these for that reason be thought more desirable; for boys, too, think the things that are valued among themselves are the best. It is to be expected, then, that, as different things seem valuable to boys and to men, so they should to bad men and to good. Now, as we have often maintained, those things are both valuable and pleasant which are such to the good man; and to each man the activity in accordance with his own disposition is most desirable, and, therefore, to the good man that which is in accordance with virtue. Happiness, therefore, does not lie in amusement; it would, indeed, be strange if the end were amusement, and one were to take trouble and suffer hardship all one's life in order to amuse oneself. For, in a word, everything that we choose we choose for the sake of something else—except happiness, which is an end. Now to exert oneself and work for the sake of amusement seems silly and utterly childish. But to amuse oneself in order that one may exert oneself, as Anacharsis puts it, seems right; for amusement is a sort of relaxation, and we need relaxation because we cannot work continuously. Relaxation, then, is not an end; for it is taken for the sake of activity. . . .

If happiness is activity in accordance with virtue, it is reasonable that it should be in accordance with the highest virtue; and this will be that of the best thing in us. Whether it be reason or something else that is this element which is thought to be our natural ruler and guide and to take thought of things noble and divine, whether it be itself also divine or only the most divine element in us, the activity of this in accordance with its proper virtue will be perfect happiness. That this activity is contemplative we have already said.

Now this would seem to be in agreement both with what we said before and with the truth. For, firstly, this activity is the best (since not only is reason the best thing in us, but the objects of reason are the best of knowable objects); and, secondly, it is the most continuous, since we can contemplate truth more continuously than we can *do* anything. And we think happiness has pleasure mingled with it, but the activity of philosophic wisdom is admittedly the pleasantest of virtuous activities; at all events the pursuit of it is thought to offer pleasures marvellous for their purity and their enduringness, and it is to be expected that those who know will pass their time more pleasantly than those who inquire. And the self-sufficiency that is spoken of must belong most to the contemplative activity. For while a philosopher, as well as a just man or one possessing any other virtue, needs the necessaries of life, when they are sufficiently equipped with things of that sort the just man needs people towards whom and with whom he shall act justly, and the temperate man, the brave man, and each of the others is in the same case, but the philosopher, even when by himself, can contemplate truth, and the better the wiser he is; he can perhaps do so better if he has fellow-workers, but still he is the most self-sufficient. And this activity alone would seem to be loved for its own sake; for nothing arises from it apart from the contemplating, while from practical activities we gain more or less apart from the action. And happiness is thought to depend on leisure; for we are busy that we may have leisure, and make war that we may live in peace. Now the activity of the practical virtues is exhibited in political or military affairs, but the actions concerned with these seem to be unleisurely. Warlike actions are completely so (for no one chooses to be at war, or provokes war, for the sake of being at war; any one would seem absolutely murderous if he were to make enemies of his friends in order to bring about battle and slaughter); but the action of the statesman is also unleisurely, and—apart from the political action itself—aims at despotic power and honours, or at all events happiness, for him and his fellow citizens—a happiness different from political action, and evidently sought as being different. So if among virtuous actions political and military actions are distinguished by nobility and greatness, and these are unleisurely and aim at an end and are not desirable for their own sake, but the activity of reason, which is contemplative, seems both to be superior in serious worth and to aim at no end beyond itself, and to have its pleasure proper to itself (and this augments the activity), and the self-sufficiency, leisureliness, unweariedness (so far as this is possible for man), and all the other attributes ascribed to the supremely happy man are evidently those connected with this activity, it follows that this will be the complete happiness of man, if it be allowed a complete term of life (for none of the attributes of happiness is *in*complete).

But such a life would be too high for man; for it is not in so far as he is man that he will live so, but in so far as something divine is present in him; and by so much as this is superior to our composite nature is its activity superior to that which is the exercise of the other kind of virtue. If reason is divine, then, in comparison with man, the life according to it is divine in comparison with human life. But we must not follow those who advise us, being men, to think of human things, and, being mortal, of mortal things, but must, so far as we can, make ourselves immortal, and strain every nerve to live in accordance with the best thing in us; for even if it be small in bulk, much more does it in power and worth surpass everything. This would seem, too, to be each man himself, since it is the authoritative and better part of him. It would be strange, then, if he were to choose not the life of his self but that of something else. And what we said before will apply now; that which is proper to each thing is by nature best and most pleasant for each thing; for man, therefore, the life according to reason is best and pleasantest, since reason more than anything else *is* man. This life therefore is also the happiest.

But in a secondary degree the life in accordance with the other kind of virtue is happy; for the activities in accordance with this befit our human estate. Just and brave acts, and other virtuous acts, we do in relation to each other, observing our respective duties with regard to contracts and services and all manner of actions and with regard to passions; and all of these seem to be typically human. Some of them seem even to arise from the body, and virtue of character to be in many ways bound up with the passions. Practical wisdom, too, is linked to virtue of character, and this to practical wisdom, since the principles of practical wisdom are in accordance with the moral virtues and rightness in morals is in accordance with practical wisdom. Being connected with the passions also, the moral virtues must belong to our composite nature; and the virtues of our composite nature are human; so, therefore, are the life and the happiness which correspond to these. The excellence of the reason is a thing apart; we must be content to say this much about it, for to describe it precisely is a task greater than our purpose requires. It would seem, however, also to need external equipment but little, or less than moral virtue does. Grant that both need the necessaries, and do so equally, even if the statesman's work is the more concerned with the body and things of that sort; for there will be little difference there; but in what they need for the exercise of their activities there will be much difference. The liberal man will need money for the doing of his liberal deeds, and the just man too will need it for the returning of services (for wishes are hard to discern, and even people who are not just pretend to wish to act justly); and the brave man will need power if he is to accomplish any of the acts that correspond to his virtue, and the temperate man will need opportunity; for how else is either he or any of the others to be recognized? It is debated, too, whether the will or the deed is more essential to virtue, which is assumed to involve both; it is surely clear that its perfection involves both; but for deeds many things are needed, and more, the greater and nobler the deeds are. But the man who is contemplating the truth needs no such thing, at least with a view to the exercise of his activity; indeed they are, one may say, even hindrances, at all events to his contemplation; but in so far as he is a man and lives with a number of people, he chooses to do virtuous acts; he will therefore need such aids to living a human life.

But that perfect happiness is a contemplative activity will appear from the following consideration as well. We assume the gods to be above all other beings blessed and happy; but what sort of actions must we assign to them? Acts of justice? Will not the gods seem absurd if they make contracts and return deposits, and so on? Acts of a brave man, then, confronting dangers and running risks because it is noble to do so? Or liberal acts? To whom will they give? It will be strange if they are really to have money or anything of the kind. And what would their temperate acts be? Is not such praise tasteless, since they have no bad appetites? If we were to run through them all, the circumstances of action would be found trivial and unworthy of gods. Still, every one supposes that they *live* and therefore that they are active; we cannot suppose them to sleep like Endymion. Now if you take away from a living being action, and still more production, what is left but contemplation? Therefore the activity of God, which surpasses all others in blessedness, must be contemplative; and of human activities, therefore, that which is most akin to this must be most of the nature of happiness.

This is indicated, too, by the fact that the other animals have no share in happiness, being completely deprived of such activity. For while the whole life of the gods is blessed, and that of men too in so far as some likeness of such activity belongs to them, none of the other animals is happy, since they in no way share in contemplation. Happiness extends, then, just so far as contemplation does, and those to whom contemplation more fully belongs are more truly happy, not as a mere concomitant but in virtue of the contemplation; for this is in itself precious. Happiness, therefore, must be some form of contemplation. . . .

Now he who exercises his reason and cultivates it seems to be both in the best state of mind and most dear to the gods. For if the gods have any care for human affairs, as they are thought to have, it would be reasonable both that they should delight in that which was best and most akin to them (i.e. reason) and that they should reward those who love and honour this most, as caring for the things that are dear to them and acting both rightly and nobly. And that all these attributes belong most of all to the philosopher is manifest. He, therefore, is the dearest to the gods. And he who is that will presumably be also the happiest; so that in this way too the philosopher will more than any other be happy.

If these matters and the virtues, and also friendship and pleasure, have been dealt with sufficiently in outline, are we to suppose that our programme has reached its end? Surely, as the saying goes, where there are things to be done the end is not to survey and recognize the various things, but rather to do them; with regard to virtue, then, it is not enough to know, but we must try to have and use it, or try any other way there may be of becoming good. Now if arguments were in themselves enough to make men good, they would justly, as Theognis says, have won very great rewards, and such rewards should have been provided; but as things are, while they seem to have power to encourage and stimulate the generous-minded among our youth, and to make a character which is gently born, and a true lover of what is noble, ready to be possessed by virtue, they are not able to encourage the many to nobility and goodness. For these do not by nature obey the sense of shame, but only fear, and do not abstain from bad acts because of their baseness but through fear of punishment; living by passion they pursue their own pleasures and the means to them, and avoid the opposite pains, and have not even a conception of what is noble and truly pleasant, since they have never tasted it. What argument would remould such people? It is hard, if not impossible, to remove by argument the traits that have long since been incorporated in the character; and perhaps we must be content if, when all the influences by which we are thought to become good are present, we get some tincture of virtue.

Now some think that we are made good by nature, others by habituation, others by teaching. Nature's part evidently does not depend on us, but as a result of some divine causes is present in those who are truly fortunate;

while argument and teaching, we may suspect, are not powerful with all men, but the soul of the student must first have been cultivated by means of habits for noble joy and noble hatred, like earth which is to nourish the seed. For he who lives as passion directs will not hear argument that dissuades him, nor understand it if he does; and how can we persuade one in such a state to change his ways? And in general passion seems to yield not to argument but to force. The character, then, must somehow be there already with a kinship to virtue, loving what is noble and hating what is base.

But it is difficult to get from youth up a right training for virtue if one has not been brought up under right laws; for to live temperately and hardily is not pleasant to most people, especially when they are young. For this reason their nurture and occupations should be fixed by law; for they will not be painful when they have become customary. But it is surely not enough that when they are young they should get the right nurture and attention; since they must, even when they are grown up, practise and be habituated to them, we shall need laws for this as well, and generally speaking to cover the whole of life; for most people obey necessity rather than argument, and punishments rather than the sense of what is noble.

This is why some think that legislators ought to stimulate men to virtue and urge them forward by the motive of the noble, on the assumption that those who have been well advanced by the formation of habits will attend to such influences; and that punishments and penalties should be imposed on those who disobey and are of inferior nature, while the incurably bad should be completely banished. A good man (they think), since he lives with his mind fixed on what is noble, will submit to argument, while a bad man, whose desire is for pleasure, is corrected by pain like a beast of burden. This is, too, why they say the pains inflicted should be those that are most opposed to the pleasures such men love.

However that may be, if (as we have said) the man who is to be good must be well trained and habituated, and go on to spend his time in worthy occupations and neither willingly nor unwillingly do bad actions, and if this can be brought about if men live in accordance with a sort of reason and right order, provided this has force—if this be so, the paternal command indeed has not the required force or compulsive power (nor in general has the command of one man, unless he be a king or something similar), but the law *has* compulsive power, while it is at the same time a rule proceeding from a sort of practical wisdom and reason. And while people hate *men* who oppose their impulses, even if they oppose them rightly, the law in its ordaining of what is good is not burdensome.

EXERCISES

1. Think of a profession you are considering as a career: engineering, or perhaps law or accounting or teaching. Could you develop a distinctive set of virtues for that profession? (That is, are there some virtues that would be particularly important for members of that profession?)

2. You are trying to decide what you should do in a particular case: Say, should I purchase a term paper off the Internet and submit it as my own work? Would it be more helpful to think about that issue in terms of whether the *act* would be right or wrong, or in terms of whether this is contributing to development of the sort of *character* you approve of?

3. Aristotle maintained that only persons of considerable wealth and resources would be able to develop the full range of virtues; Jesus seemed to think that—to the contrary—it was almost impossible for wealthy persons to become genuinely virtuous. Obviously, Aristotle and Jesus had very different concepts of what counts as a virtuous character, but they seemed to agree that one's social setting is very important for the development of virtue. For your own conception of virtue, whatever that may be, would you agree that only in an appropriate society or the right circumstances could one actually live a fully virtuous life?

4. Would it ever be right to sacrifice your own virtue for the good of others?

5. I have lived a dissolute life for many years: a life devoted to excessive eating, heavy drinking, laziness, deceitfulness, and pettiness. At age 45, I awaken one morning in the gutter, painfully sober after a three-day binge, and I resolve to change my ways and pursue virtue. Could I become a virtuous person within an hour? A week? A month? A year? Ever?

6. Dramatist George Bernard Shaw claimed that "Virtue consists, not in abstaining from vice, but in not desiring it." Would Aristotle agree? Would *you* agree?

7. Jeremiah, the great Hebrew prophet, posed this question for God (Jeremiah, Book 12): "Wherefore doth the way of the wicked prosper? Wherefore are all they happy that deal very treacherously?" If God were a virtue theorist, how might God reply to Jeremiah's question? *If* it is true that "the way of the wicked prosper," would that refute virtue theory?

8. Stephen M. Cahn once posed a challenge for virtue theory: he gave an example of a fictitious person, Fred (who Cahn claims is similar to several actual people he has known), who is deceitful, arrogant, and rather lucky, and who gains a reputation for virtuous character, even though he is thoroughly unscrupulous. Fred (according to Cahn) "enjoys great pleasure," and certainly appears to be happy. Can you think of anyone (a public figure, or someone you know) who is similar to Fred, and whom you would regard as *genuinely* happy? If you can, does that count against virtue theory? If you cannot, is that a point in favor of virtue theory? If there are *many* people like Fred, then that will be a severe threat to virtue theory; but if there are only a very few like Fred—and though they are happy, they were very *lucky*, and it was very improbable that they would be happy—would that pose problems for virtue theory?

9. An important distinction for virtue theorists is between people who are *happy* and people who are *flourishing*. Do you know anyone (a public figure or an acquaintance) whom you would count as happy but not flourishing?

10. Could Bentham accept the virtue theory distinction between happy and flourishing? Could Mill?

11. You are a biology professor at the University of Wisconsin. You teach at the medical school, and are well-known for your research: your laboratory has carried out a number of important studies on various drugs. You are approached by ZQZ Pharmaceuticals. The company would like you to run a test on the "off-label" effectiveness of one of its drugs, Zeitelban. Zeitelban has been approved for the treatment of stomach ulcers, but recently some doctors have used it for treatment of high blood pressure (after noticing that ulcer patients treated with Zeitelban sometimes experienced a reduction in blood pressure readings). Such "off-label" treatments are perfectly legal; the problem is that the drug has not really been tested for treatment of hypertension (high blood pressure), and we don't know if it actually works for that. True, a few doctors noticed that their patients experienced lower blood pressure, but we have no idea whether that was caused by the Zeitelban or by something else. Perhaps when their stomach ulcers cleared up that caused them to feel better, reduced their tense worrying about ulcers, and the reduction in tension caused lower blood pressure. Or maybe, the patients started eating less because of their stomach problems, and they lost some weight and that caused the reduction in blood pressure. Or maybe, they stopped smoking, and that was the cause. Without a controlled experiment, we have no idea whether Zeitelban is effective in treating hypertension. Furthermore, since Zeitelban was not tested initially for the treatment of hypertension, we don't know whether it causes problems for patients using it for long-term treatment of hypertension. The initial tests, which led the FDA to approve the drug, were for short-term use with stomach ulcer patients. But treatment of hypertension would involve long-term use, and there might be side effects that the earlier tests did not detect: Zeitelban might cause special problems, even serious dangers, for patients who use it long term. So ZQZ Pharmaceuticals

wants you to run a long-term controlled study on the effectiveness of Zeitelban for the treatment of hypertension. This will be a very large study, and the company will pay you very generously to direct it. Also, with the money you earn for the study you can hire a number of medical students and graduate students at the university, to help you part time and perhaps full time in the summer, and they will also be paid well (and frankly, many of them could really use the money). The grant will also pay for much-needed laboratory equipment, the latest and best. And since this is a major, megabucks grant, the University of Wisconsin will be very happy about it: the dean will probably take you to lunch and lavish praise upon you.

No problems so far. This could be a worthwhile study, and it might provide information to aid in the treatment of hypertension, and thus improve the lives of many people; and it will make your students very happy, since they will make some much-needed extra income. But there's one catch: ZQZ Pharmaceuticals is paying for the study, and it wants control over the publication of any results. The company wants the right to read any research report *before* it is published, and the right to veto publication of your research findings. That is, if your research shows that Zeitelban is useless in the treatment of hypertension, or—even worse— reveals a harmful side effect that earlier studies had not detected, then ZQZ Pharmaceuticals can prevent the publication of your results; indeed, it can require you not to discuss those results with anyone, nor publicize those results in any way. So if your research indicated that use of Zeitelban might cause kidney failure—a potentially lethal side effect—you would be prohibited from publishing that result. Or if your study showed Zeitelban was useless in treating hypertension, but the data from a separate study made by some other laboratory indicated Zeitelban might be an effective hypertension drug, then ZQZ Pharmaceuticals could veto the publication of your results and allow the publication of the other study. Under that condition—ZQZ Pharmaceuticals has veto rights to the publication of your study—would you agree to run the study?

Suppose you want to refuse to run the study under those conditions: you would tell ZQZ Pharmaceuticals you are turning down its megabucks study grant. You are discussing it with one of your fellow researchers, and she wants to accept the grant and run the study. "Look," she says, "I understand your concerns about the publication veto. I feel the same way: I don't like it. But let's be realistic. If we turn down this research contract, they won't have any trouble at all finding another researcher who *will* run the study, and will accept the veto condition; and that researcher may not be quite as good as we are, so the study might not be quite as careful. And that researcher's students will get the money, rather than our students. So the study is going to be run anyway, with the veto condition. Refusing the research contract will just mean our students won't get the research funding, and the study may not be done as well as we could do it. So what will your principled refusal really accomplish? Nothing. At least nothing good. So I say: let's take the contract, and accept the veto power of ZQZ Pharmaceuticals."

What do you think of your colleague's argument? How would that argument look from the perspectives of virtue theory, utilitarian ethics, Humean ethics, and Kantian ethics?

Perhaps you have decided you should accept the research contract; perhaps you've decided you shouldn't. Suppose you *have* decided to accept the contract (maybe ZQZ Pharmaceuticals agreed to drop the veto requirement). The representative from ZQZ Pharmaceuticals drops by with a bottle of champagne to celebrate this wonderful new research partnership between ZQZ Pharmaceuticals and your laboratory, and hands you an envelope. "Look, we at ZQZ Pharmaceuticals consider you part of our family, and we want you to share in any success our company has. These are stock options on ZQZ Pharmaceuticals. Your study will be complete and ready for release next September 15; these options are on $1 million worth of ZQZ Pharmaceuticals stock. These options allow you to purchase ZQZ Pharmaceuticals stock at its September 1 price, and you can exercise the option anytime between September 15 and September 30. It's a pleasure having you as a member of the ZQZ Pharmaceuticals family!" Well, you know what this stock option means. If your research shows that Zeitelban is not effective in treating hypertension, the value of ZQZ Pharmaceuticals stock will not rise, and your stock option will be worthless. But if your research shows Zeitelban *is* safe and effective in treating hypertension, then Zeitelban will be widely sold for hypertension, and ZQZ Pharmaceuticals will make a fortune in profits (there are *huge* numbers of hypertension patients), and the stock price will rise dramatically— and your stock option will be worth a *lot* of money. (Suppose ZQZ Pharmaceuticals stock was at $20 a share on September 1; on September 15, after release of your favorable research on Zeitelban, the stock soars to $40 a share. You can buy a million dollars worth of ZQZ stock at the September 1 price, and immediately sell it for double what you paid: a neat little profit of $1 million, with absolutely no risk. Actually, you would just take the stock option to your broker, and your broker would give you a check.) Sounds peachy. But you know what is really going on: ZQZ Pharmaceuticals is not doing this out of simple kindness; rather, the company is giving you a huge incentive to do a study that shows Zeitelban to be very effective and very safe (the better the drug, the more your stock option is worth). Of course, you are a highly principled researcher, and you would never let that influence you, right? But is it ethically legitimate for you to accept the stock option?

ADDITIONAL READING

The classic source for virtue ethics is Aristotle's *Nicomachean Ethics*. Perhaps the most influential contemporary book on virtue theory is by Alasdair MacIntyre, *After Virtue* (Notre Dame, IN: University of Notre Dame Press, 1981). An excellent exposition of contemporary virtue theory is found in Edmund Pincoffs, *Quandaries and Virtues* (Lawrence, KS: University of Kansas Press, 1986).

An intriguing brief case for virtue theory is presented by novelist and philosopher Iris Murdoch in *The Sovereignty of Good* (New York: Schocken Books, 1971), though Murdoch's work encompasses a great deal more than just a defense of virtue theory. Other influential accounts of virtue theory include Philippa Foot, *Virtues and Vices* (Berkeley, CA: University of California, 1978); Michael Slote, *Goods and Virtues* (New York: Oxford University Press, 1984); and Michael Slote, *From Morality to Virtue* (New York: Oxford University Press, 1992). Major recent works in the virtue theory tradition are Philippa Foot, *Natural Goodness* (Oxford: Oxford University Press, 2001); Rosalind Hursthouse, *On Virtue Ethics* (Oxford: Oxford University Press, 1999); and Michael Slote, *Morals from Motives* (Oxford: Oxford University Press, 2000). An excellent critical review of recent versions of virtue theory is David Copp and David Sobel, "Morality and Virtue: An Assessment of Some Recent Work in Virtue Ethics," *Ethics*, Volume 114 (April 2004), 514–544.

An interesting discussion of virtue theory was prompted by Steven M. Cahn's very brief essay, "The Happy Immoralist." Cahn's essay, together with replies and comments by a number of writers (including several virtue theorists), can be found in *Journal of Social Philosophy*, Volume 35, Number 1 (Spring 2004), 1–20.

The challenge of contemporary situationist psychology for virtue theory is described in Gilbert Harman, "Moral Philosophy Meets Social Psychology: Virtue Ethics and the Fundamental Attribution Error," *Proceedings of the Aristotelian Society*, Volume 99 (1999), 315–332. There have been several responses to this challenge, including James Montmarquet, "Moral Character and Social Science Research," *Philosophy*, Volume 78 (2003), 355–368. An excellent account of situationist psychology and its implications for a number of philosophical questions is by John Doris, *Lack of Character: Personality and Moral Behavior* (Cambridge, MA: Cambridge University Press, 2002).

Good anthologies on virtue ethics include Roger Crisp and Michael Slote, *Virtue Ethics* (Oxford: Oxford University Press, 1997); and Stephen Darwall, *Virtue Ethics* (Oxford: Blackwell, 2003). Good online discussions can be found in the *Stanford Encyclopedia of Philosophy*, at *http://plato.stanford.edu/entries/ethics-virtue*; in *The Internet Encyclopedia of Philosophy* at *http://www.iep.utm.edu/v/virtue.htm*; and in Lawrence Hinman's *Ethics Updates*, at *http://ethics.sandiego.edu/theories/Aristotle/index.asp*

NOTES

[1] Aristotle, *Nichomachean Ethics*, trans. W. D. Ross, p. 1105a.

[2] A point noted by both Susan Wolf, "Moral Saints," *Journal of Philosophy*, 79 (1982), 419–439; and Bernard Williams, "A Critique of Utilitarianism," in J. J. C. Smart and Bernard Williams, *Utilitarianism: For and Against* (Cambridge: Cambridge University Press, 1973).

[3] As Bernard Williams, 1973, describes it.

[4] Aristotle, *Nicomachean Ethics*, trans. W. D. Ross, p. 1107a.

[5] *Ibid.*, p. 1109a.

[6] Greg Pence, "Virtue Theory," in Peter Singer, editor, *A Companion to Ethics* (Oxford: Blackwell, 1991), p. 255.

9

Care Ethics

Men and women are different. Perhaps that's something you already knew. Still, it's worth mentioning, because at times we tend to forget it. For many decades in the United States almost all tests of new drugs were performed on men (often on male college students). And there is some reason for testing on young men, rather than on young women: some drugs may cause severe birth defects if a woman takes the drug early in pregnancy (the thalidomide tragedy is a terrible example); and since a woman might be pregnant without knowing it, testing experimental drugs on women poses special risks to the fetus. There's an easy solution to that problem: test all the new drugs on men.

It was an easy solution, but not a very good one. By testing exclusively on men, we discovered which drugs were safe and effective for men, and at what dosage; but when we prescribed those drugs for women, we had to guess at the correct dosage, and hope that what worked for men would also be safe and effective for women. Sometimes we were right, and sometimes we were wrong. In recent years we have adopted new policies requiring drugs to be tested on both men and women before gaining approval.

THE NEGLECT OF WOMEN'S ETHICAL VIEWS

Until recently, ethical theories—like drugs—were also tested exclusively on men. There were very few women writing about ethics, and many of those who were had been so thoroughly acculturated into a male-dominated philosophical outlook that they adopted the assumptions and perspectives of their male colleagues. Women's voices were largely silent. But this caused little alarm. As in drug testing, the operating assumption was simple: If it works for men, it will work for women. And like the analogous assumption in drug testing, the assumption that male-dominated ethics works universally has been scrutinized and found wanting.

When we recognize the importance of women's contributions to ethical thought, we must avoid the temptation to look for "*the* women's perspective" on ethical questions. That would be as silly and as stereotypical as looking for "*the* African American perspective," or "*the* Arab-American viewpoint," or "*the* Hispanic perspective," or "*the* Irish American ethical position." African American political views range from the leftist thought of Lani Guinier to the far-right position of Clarence Thomas; likewise, there is no single "women's perspective" that can encompass both Nancy Pelosi and Margaret Thatcher. Men have championed such diverse ethical views as utilitarianism, Kantianism, and social contract theory; and women have championed all those views, and more. To avoid supposing that there is a single "women's ethical theory," we'll talk about *care* ethics, rather than *feminist* ethics. Care ethics emphasizes the value of fostering relationships, paying as much attention to personal details as abstract principles, and recognizing the ethical importance of affection and care for others. Not all feminists favor care ethics—in fact, many feminists strongly object to care ethics. And some of the most dedicated advocates of care ethics are men.

Psychological Studies of Ethical Reasoning

The development of feminist/care ethics had important "extra-ethical" scientific influences: the recognition that much of past psychological research was based on a grossly unrepresentative sample that systematically excluded half the population. The result severely undervalued the importance of family and personal relationships in psychological health, misrepresented the process of psychological and moral development, and distorted our perspective of healthy psychological functioning. Contemporary psychological research has endeavored to correct that distortion, and contemporary care ethics has extended that correction to ethics.

In 1982, Harvard psychologist Carol Gilligan published *In a Different Voice,* a very influential study of how women reason about ethical issues. Gilligan had spent years working with Lawrence Kohlberg, a Harvard psychologist, researching the psychological processes involved in moral development. Kohlberg's research tracked a number of children over a period of many years, interviewing them periodically to examine the development of their moral perspectives. In the course of those interviews, Kohlberg posed moral quandaries to his subjects. For example, suppose there is a man, Heinz, whose wife is deathly ill. There is a very expensive drug that will save her life, but Heinz does not have enough money to buy the drug, and has no way of obtaining enough money. The pharmacist will neither give Heinz the drug nor lower the price. The only way Heinz can obtain the drug is by stealing it from the pharmacist. Should Heinz steal the drug?

When confronted with such a case, women often want more details: Why isn't it possible for Heinz to work out an agreement with the pharmacist? Has Heinz really explored every possibility? Is the pharmacist that indifferent to saving Heinz's wife? Also, if Heinz steals (or refuses to steal) the drug, what effect will that have on his relationship with his wife? In contrast, most men are happy to keep the problem at the abstract level: The details about Heinz and his wife and the pharmacist aren't important. It's the principle that counts, principles apply to everyone alike, and thus personal details are irrelevant.

This difference in desire for detail reflects another difference, which Kohlberg thought very significant. Kohlberg was primarily interested in "stages of moral development," and how we make moral progress through those successive stages. We start with self-centered interests, and most of us progress through further stages in which our concerns extend to the welfare of others (Stage 3), then some move forward to the recognition that rules take priority over particular interests (Stage 4), and ultimately a few reach Stages 5 and 6: recognition of abstract principles of universal justice. Women tend to get stuck at level three, focusing on the details of how to maintain relationships and promote the welfare of family and friends. Men are more likely to move on to the abstract principles, and therefore have less concern with the particulars of who is involved.

As Lawrence Kohlberg saw it, this indicated that most women failed to achieve the higher levels of moral development. He thought that might be due to their comparative isolation in the home and the community: maybe when women spend more time dealing with the larger issues of the outside world, they will also make greater moral progress. Carol Gilligan saw it differently. Rather than most women suffering arrested moral development, they tend to have a different perspective on ethics. Abstract principle is useful, but such principles should not be used to the detriment of actual people and their cares and concerns and relationships. As a Jewish carpenter once said, "The law is made for man; not man for the law." From the perspective of Carol Gilligan and many other women (and of course many men as well, including Jesus of Nazareth), abstract principles can lose their usefulness and become harmful if they become ends in themselves that are more important than their actual effects on specific people.

Watching 10-year-old boys play baseball, one might suppose that the best thing about the game is the excuse it gives for extended arguments about rules (and watching 30-year-old fathers arguing about rules at their children's little league games, one might suppose that the boys don't change much as they get older). Sometimes disputes are resolved, and the game continues to the next acrimonious argument; and sometimes the dispute shatters the game and the group, breaking the contestants into divided camps equally certain of their moral superiority and equally aggrieved at the perfidious folly of their former friends.

On the same playground, the girls are also playing games, and they also face disagreements about the rules. But the disagreements are usually settled more quickly, and there is typically more concern with preserving friendships than with following rules. When a disagreement threatens group harmony, the girls are more likely to drop the game and play something else—still playing together—than allow the group to divide into warring factions. This general tendency shouldn't be exaggerated: little girls can be just as principled and unbending as little boys, and little league moms can be just as adamantly obnoxious as little league dads. Still, their general orientations are usually distinctly different: girls focus more on preserving the group, while boys emphasize following the rules.

Philosopher and educator Nel Noddings marks the relevant difference clearly:

> Women, perhaps the majority of women, prefer to discuss moral problems in terms of concrete situations. They approach moral problems not as intellectual problems to be solved by abstract reasoning but as concrete human problems to be lived and to be solved in living. . . .
>
> Faced with a hypothetical moral dilemma, women often ask for more information. It is not the case, certainly, that women cannot arrange principles hierarchically and derive conclusions logically. It is more likely that they see this process as peripheral to or even irrelevant to moral conduct. They want more information, I think, in order to form a picture. Ideally, they need to talk to the participants, to see their eyes and facial expressions, to size up the whole situation. Moral decisions are, after all, made in situations; they are qualitatively different from the solution to geometry problems. Women . . . give reasons for their acts, but the reasons point to feelings, needs, situational conditions, and their sense of personal ideal rather than universal principles and their application.[1]

THE CARE PERSPECTIVE ON ETHICS

The tendency observed on the playground can also be observed in philosophical perspectives on ethics. But the "care" perspective on ethics has larger implications than simply the need to temper principle with concern for particular individuals and their relationships. Annette Baier notes that ethical debate often focuses on the choice between Kantian ethics (with its strong reliance on abstract principle) and utilitarian ethics (with its insistence on calculating consequences). But the emphasis on Kantian versus utilitarian ethics obscures the fact that *both* views share an important basic assumption: the assumption that *reason* is the key to ethical decision making. Kantians reason from abstract principles (the question to be rationally resolved is what those principles are and how any particular act fits under those principles); utilitarians rationally calculate the balance of benefit over harm, and resolve ethical quandaries by adding up the accounts. But for both Kantians and utilitarians the essential element in ethics is the reasoning process.

Baier challenges that assumption. Rules and consequences have obvious importance, and sometimes our feelings must be governed by considerations of rules or consequences (my sympathetic impulse to rescue my toddler from the painful upcoming vaccination may be trumped by rational consideration of the dire consequences that might follow from not having the vaccination). But sympathy is the basic moral capacity, not law-discerning or consequence-calculating reason.

We neglect that to our peril. Teaching doctors, nurses, and physical therapists the "rules" of morality, or how to do utilitarian calculations, may have some benefits. But if this merely coats them with a thin veneer of morality, while leaving them unsympathetic and uncaring and insensitive to the needs and fears and vulnerabilities of their patients, then learning the ethical rules may do more harm than good. Indeed, "ethical codes" more often serve to confer high status on the professionals and protect them from outside criticism ("only doctors are qualified to judge other doctors") rather than encouraging better moral behavior toward actual patients. In medical *care*—with patients who are often frightened and vulnerable— a caring perspective is very valuable.

When I go to my physician, I typically start from a position of grave concern over some health problem I do not understand, and I reveal myself in a way that makes me particularly vulnerable: not only the imperfections in my body but also the flaws in my behavior. In seeking the right diagnosis and treatment, my doctor needs to know that I'm not getting enough exercise, that I occasionally drink too much, that I've been feeling depressed, and that I have very little willpower when tempted by anything like chocolate. The doctor may gently admonish me to give up smoking, or watch my diet, or take my daily medications; but she must avoid any suggestion that she is judging me. She is my confidante, perhaps my partner in seeking restoration of health, a coach who nudges me toward better health habits: but she is not my judge, and not someone who exploits my openness and vulnerability to pass judgment on me. (That is one reason why distributing medical resources on the basis of patient habits and lifestyles—chronic drinkers should be lower on the list for transplants, heavy smokers should have to wait longer for bypass surgery, overeaters should have to pay more for their surgery—is so destructive to medical *care*: it turns doctors into judges, rather than caregiving partners.)

The Relation of Caring to Rules

Important as a care-based perspective is in medicine, there is also a use for rules. My vulnerability may tempt my physician toward a benevolent but destructive paternalism: "This patient is sick, and doesn't really understand what is in his best interests; instead of giving him all this information and letting him make a choice that may be wrong, I'll just choose for him." The motive in this case may be kindness, and it may *feel* like the right thing to do; but most of us would deeply resent being treated in such a paternalistic manner, whatever the motives. It's my body, and I want to make my own decision about what treatments I will and will not have. The doctor's motives may be good, but it's not really a kindness to treat me like a child who is incapable of making his own decisions. Certainly we want our doctors to be caring and concerned, but we also want them to remember the *rule* that every competent person has the right to make his or her own informed decision about medical treatment. There are lots of people who could run my life better than I can, but I still want to run it myself, and I have the basic right to do so.

Trying to balance moral rules and moral feelings is a challenging task. One philosopher who has struggled with that issue is Jonathan Bennett, in an article—which we examined in Chapter 3—titled "The Conscience of Huckleberry Finn." You'll recall that at one point in Mark Twain's novel, Huck Finn is sharing a raft with his friend Jim, an escaped slave. As the raft moves closer and closer to the free states, Jim expresses his deep gratitude to Huck, calling him "the best friend I ever had." Soon Jim will be free, and—he tells Huck—he owes it all to his friend Huck. Without Huck, Jim could never had made the long dangerous trip up the river. As Huck thinks about this, he realizes that what Jim says is true, and Huck begins to feel terrible pangs of conscience. He is helping Jim escape from (what Huck considers) his rightful owner, poor old Miz Watson, who had always been kind to Huck. And Huck is repaying her kindness by practically stealing her property, and he knows what he is doing is wrong. So he resolves to put things right, and turn Jim in to some slave catchers. But when the opportunity comes, Huck is unable to do it: his deep feeling of friendship and affection for Jim outweighs his principled belief that slaves are property that should be returned to their owners.

In this case, Huck's "moral principles" are terribly wrong. Humans cannot be enslaved and treated as property, and we are glad Huck's feelings of affection and friendship triumphed over his flawed principles. But there also may be times when our principles should be a check on our feelings: the benevolent *feeling* of the kindly doctor who wishes to make my decisions for me should be trumped by the *principle* that competent patients have a right to make their own decisions. And if you find clear evidence that your friend has robbed a bank, and some innocent stranger is in the middle of a long prison term after being wrongly convicted of the crime committed by your friend, then probably your principled decision to turn in your friend should not be blocked by your feelings. There are plenty of other examples: a desire for vengeance is surely a natural feeling, but it is far from obvious that it is a reliable moral guide. Our "Founding Fathers" often relied on their visceral "feeling" of revulsion for any skin hue other than pale pink in denying basic rights to those of African descent, and their "feeling" that it was unnatural for women to participate in political life led them to deny rights of self-government to half the population. Rules without feelings leave hollow and sometimes harmful ethics (if you provide for your children from a sense of duty rather than from affection, the result is likely to be resentful and deeply insecure children); but feelings without reflection and rules can produce policies based on the grossest prejudices. If we try to remove feelings and affections from ethics, we are likely to remove the engine that powers ethics, and we shall also destroy some of the most valuable elements of our ethical lives. But we also need to examine our feelings, to root out prejudices and narrow self-serving motives. It is often useful to subject our feelings to careful scrutiny and basic tests. ("Would I think it fair if others treated *me* in that manner? Would I approve of everyone acting this way?

Would I vote for such a rule from behind Rawls's "veil of ignorance"? Will acting on this feeling cause more harm than good?") We can believe in the fundamental ethical importance of feelings without giving our feelings a blank check.

So which should be our moral guide? Our principles, or our feelings of warmth and friendship? That question poses a false dilemma. We need not think of ethics as being either pure principle or pure feeling; rather, the two can both serve useful functions, and they may work well to check and correct each other. My feelings of empathy and care are surely basic to ethics, whatever Kant may claim to the contrary. And rules are not an adequate substitute. When I am ill and frightened and lonely in the hospital, I am greatly cheered by your caring visit; but if I get the impression that you are visiting me purely from a sense of duty, and not out of simple care and affection, that will destroy much if not all of the comfort and pleasure gained from your visit. Even in this case, however, rules and reason may have some use: you are a busy person, with lots of demands on your schedule, and your hospitalized friend is not one of the obvious demands (and going to hospitals is not great fun). Thinking carefully about how your friend has helped and comforted you in the past, and about your duty to reciprocate such kindnesses, may be a useful reminder to buy some flowers and books and stop by the hospital. But a visit done strictly from duty, without genuine care, may be more depressing than uplifting to the patient. Thinking about our duties can certainly be helpful; but acting *purely* from duty—so far from being the ethical ideal that Kant thought it to be—often eviscerates the moral value and benefit of the dutiful act. Useful as such reasoned duty reminders are, they cannot substitute for affection and care.

Caring and Utilitarian Ethics

Care ethics does not ignore or disparage reason, but it does emphasize the importance of empathy and affection, friendships and relationships: elements of ethics (from the perspective of care ethics) Kantian systems woefully neglect. Care ethics also diverges significantly from the impersonal calculations of utilitarianism. By utilitarian standards, my duty is to maximize pleasure and minimize suffering for everyone involved, and the calculations demanded are quite impersonal: I must count my own pleasures and pains and those of my family and friends in the total, but I cannot give those concerns any greater weight than the pleasures and pains of strangers. Such utilitarian concerns have prompted many examples for utilitarian analysis, some of which seem to challenge that basic impersonal utilitarian perspective. One such example is this. My three children are suffering from a deadly disease, and I have just enough medicine to save them (and no possibility of securing more medicine). But across town live four unrelated smaller children who are suffering from the same disease, and the medicine I have would be just enough to save them. Should I save the four strangers or my three children? Simple utilitarian calculations seem to demand that I sacrifice my children to save the four strangers; but for most of us, such behavior would probably not be morally acceptable, much less morally obligatory. If someone sacrificed her three children to save the lives of four strangers, we would be more likely to regard such a person as a moral suspect (will she collect insurance on her children?) rather than a moral hero. She may qualify as a utilitarian saint, but that sort of sainthood strikes many as too cold and impersonal to be a worthy aspiration.

Utilitarians can devise ways of dealing with such examples. Some utilitarians bite the bullet, and insist that saving the four strangers *is* the right act, and our affection for our children should not blind us to the impersonal demands of our duty. Other utilitarians might take a gentler tone: you really *should* save the four strangers rather than your own three children, but that is such a strong ethical demand that you should not be blamed if you cannot meet it. Going still further, some utilitarians may attempt a utilitarian justification of the decision to save your three children in preference to the four strangers: bonds among family and friends are an important source of pleasure, and when we add in the benefits of preserving such relationships, we see that this more comprehensive calculation of the balance of pleasure over suffering would justify saving the lives of the three family members. Perhaps such calculations do add up as the utilitarian suggests; but from the perspective of care ethics, that is still not a satisfactory solution: the bonds of affection and friendship and family must be recognized as an important and distinct ethical element, not just one pleasure calculation among others. Treating our special personal relationships as merely a subset of pleasurable sensations to be entered into the utilitarian calculation seems (to care theorists) an inadequate representation of the basic moral worth of these relations. After all, a very difficult and willful child, who brings more concern than pleasure to her parents, does not for that reason rank lower in ethical consideration or, one hopes, in parental affection.

"Many moral theories . . . employ the assumption that to increase the utility of individuals is a good thing to do. But if asked *why* it is a good thing to increase utility, or satisfy desire, or produce pleasure, or *why* doing so counts as a good reason for something, it is very difficult to answer. The claim is taken as a kind of starting assumption for which no *further* reason can be given. It seems to rest on a view that people seek pleasure, or that we can recognize pleasure as having more intrinsic value. But if women recognize quite different assumptions as more likely to be valid, that would certainly be of importance to ethics. We might then take it as one of our starting assumptions that creating good relations of care and concern and trust between ourselves and our children, and creating social arrangements in which children will be valued and well cared for, are more important than maximizing individual utilities. And the moral theories that might be compatible with such assumptions might be very different from those with which we are familiar." *Virginia Held, "Feminism and Moral Theory," in Eva Feder Kittay and Diana T. Meyers, editors,* Women and Moral Theory *(Totowa, NJ: Rowman and Littlefield, 1987), p. 126.*

Care Ethics and Impersonal Duties

This last point leads to another distinctive feature of care ethics. On Kantian, utilitarian, and social contract views, our duties tend to be *impersonal:* We have duties and obligations to others, of course, but they are duties due to anyone in the same position. On the care view, we may also have impersonal duties, but at least as important are duties of a very personal and individual nature: duties we owe specifically to family or friends, and not to just any generic moral placeholder. These are duties owed not because we are reciprocating benefits we have received but because of our special relations. Furthermore, such duties are typically not based on choices or voluntary contracts. We didn't "ask to be born," nor did we get any choice in our parents or siblings; and come to think of it, probably not a lot of choice in our oldest (and perhaps dearest) childhood friends. But few of us doubt that we have special obligations to them, obligations above and beyond the obligations we have to others generally. Perhaps we could give some sort of justification for those obligations in terms of reciprocating past care and affection; but such justifications are likely to strike us as artificial and unnecessary. If your sister or brother is in need, you feel a strong and special obligation to help. If someone has to stop and calculate that obligation on the basis of rules, and only then recognizes its moral force, we are more likely to think such a person morally impoverished than morally superior. Such basic felt obligations are probably more fundamental than any rule we could devise for their justification. Perhaps in the absence of deep feelings of affection and obligation, adherence to moral rules may serve as a substitute. But it is likely to be a very limited substitute: like a paint-by-number replacement for a work of art.

This is not to suggest that utilitarianism is useless. We may well make some rough utilitarian calculations when we are considering building a mansion for our family, and consider whether some of those resources might better be used to house homeless strangers. But care theorists would insist that we can and should consider such factors, but without reducing our special relations with friends and family to strict impersonal utilitarian calculations of pleasure and pain. Thus, care theorists can find significant uses for moral rules. For example, at times when my affection for family and friends may be at low ebb, bringing a moral rule to mind may be useful. But for care theorists this is a backup system, not the core of morality. While recalling such rules may be useful in those circumstances, the same effect might be achieved though recalling special moments of shared affection and kindness. The care perspective does not deny that moral rules have their uses, but it insists that rules and reason are not the whole—or even the most vital element—of our moral lives.

WOMEN AND ETHICS

Perils of "Feminine" Ethics

Having examined care ethics, are we justified in describing that as "a feminine ethic," in contrast to more masculine Kantian or utilitarian theories? Or more generally, is there a distinctive "feminine" ethic at all? Or is ethics gender neutral? That is a much debated issue, and one on which feminists are deeply divided. That division is not surprising, since the notion of a "distinctly feminine character" has a very mixed history. Women were often oppressed by the "chivalrous" thought systems that glorified their virtue. For example, in 1966 the Mississippi Supreme Court ruled that women could legally be excluded from juries (so much for women defendants having a "jury of their peers"); and the court gave this reason:

> The legislature has a right to exclude women [from jury service] so they may contribute their services as mothers, wives, and homemakers, and also to protect them (in some areas they are still upon a pedestal) from the filth, obscenity, and noxious atmosphere that so often pervades a courtroom during a jury trial.[2]

Their cages (or "pedestals," as the Mississippi judges called them) may have been gilded, but the gilded bars were still there. In 1837, Sarah Grimke gave this analysis of the situation facing women:

> She has surrendered her dearest rights, and been satisfied with the privileges which man has assumed to grant her; she has been amused with the show of power, whilst man has absorbed all the reality into himself. He has adorned the creature whom God gave him as a companion with baubles and gewgaws, turned her attention to personal attractions, offered incense to her vanity, and made her the instrument of his selfish gratification, a plaything to please his eye and amuse his hours of leisure. 'Rule by obedience and by submission sway,' or in other words, study to be a hypocrite, pretend to submit, but gain your point, has been the code of household morality which woman has been taught.[3]

The notion of distinctly masculine/feminine moralities and roles is found in such sayings as "The man is the head, the woman the heart," and "Behind every successful man is a good woman" (far behind, quietly at home, supportive and dependent). And lest one suppose this to be ancient history, there will probably be a wedding in your community this weekend in which the husband promises to love and cherish his wife and the wife promises to love, honor, and *obey* her husband, the head of the household.

Womanly Virtues

Think back to virtue theory. One common question is whether there are *multiple* sets of virtues—perhaps one set of virtues for the old and another for the young. But the one place where the notion of "different sets of virtues" is most prominent is the contrast between *masculine* and *feminine* virtues. A virtuous woman is demure, quiet, modest, and chaste. In fact, "Modesty" and "Chastity" were popular names for girls, not so many years ago. But no boys were named Modesty, because the virtuous male was not modest, but instead proud, ambitious, aggressive, brave, and strong.

> "It would be an endless task to trace the variety of meannesses, cares, and sorrows into which women are plunged by the prevailing opinion that they were created rather to feel than reason, and that all the power they obtain must be obtained by their charms and weaknesses." *Mary Wollstonecraft*, A Vindication of the Rights of Woman, *1792*.

Given the history of a special "feminine morality"—designed to restrict the opportunities and influence of women—it is hardly surprising that most reformers have opposed the notion of "feminine morality." Mary Wollstonecraft (in her famous *Vindication of the Rights of Woman*) argued that there is only one moral system that applies to all: there is no distinctly feminine morality, and no life goals that are peculiarly appropriate for women rather than men.

The Value of Feminist Ethics

On the other side, women have sometimes claimed that the oppressive forms of "feminine morality" notwithstanding, there is a genuine and profoundly valuable feminine consciousness that is rooted in women's social development, a consciousness that must be valued and appreciated. For example, sociologist Ariel Salleh maintains that through "women's lived experience" there is a special connection between woman and nature that offers the best prospect for "a sane, humane, ecological future."[4] But many remain deeply skeptical of such claims about special moral capacities. Jean Grimshaw, for example:

> If ethical concerns and priorities arise from different forms of social life, then those which have emerged from a social system in which women have so often been subordinate to men must be suspect. Supposedly 'female' values are not only the subject of little agreement among women: they are also deeply mired in conceptions of 'the feminine' which depend on the sort of polarization between 'masculine' and 'feminine' which has itself been so closely related to the subordination of women. There is no autonomous realm of female values, or of female activities which can generate 'alternative' values to those of the public sphere; and any conception of a 'female ethic' which depends on these ideas cannot, I think, be a viable one.[5]

This is only the edge of a difficult and ongoing debate. But whatever one's views on the question of whether "care ethics" is distinctly feminine, it is difficult to deny that many of the central themes of care ethics have been ignored or undervalued in Western ethics.

➤ THE NEED FOR MORE THAN JUSTICE ➤
Annette Baier

Annette C. Baier studied philosophy at Somerville College, Oxford, and was Distinguished Service Professor of Philosophy at the University of Pittsburgh before her retirement to her native New Zealand. Though her work is wide-ranging, a central theme is the connection of principles of justice to caring relationships. She is the author of many important philosophical works, including *A Progress of Sentiments: Reflections on Hume's "Treatise,"* *Postures of Mind,* and *Moral Prejudices* (from which this selection is taken).

In recent decades in North American social and moral philosophy, alongside the development and discussion of widely influential theories of justice, taken as John Rawls takes it as the "first virtue of social institutions," there has been a countermovement gathering strength, one coming from some interesting sources. Some of the most outspoken of the diverse group who have in a variety of ways been challenging the assumed supremacy of justice among the moral and social virtues are members of those sections of society whom one might have expected to be especially aware of the supreme importance of justice: blacks and women. Those who have only recently won recognition of their equal rights, who have only recently seen the correction or partial correction of long-standing racist and sexist injustices to their race and sex, are among the philosophers now suggesting that justice is only one virtue among many, and one that may need the presence of the others in order to deliver its own undenied value.

Let me say quite clearly at this early point that there is little disagreement that justice is *a* social value of very great importance, and injustice an evil. Nor would those who have worked on theories of justice want to deny that other things matter besides justice. Rawls, for example, incorporates the value of freedom into his account of

justice, so that denial of basic freedoms counts as injustice. Rawls also leaves room for a wider theory of the right, of which the theory of justice is just a part. Still, he does claim that justice is the "first" virtue of social institutions, and it is only that claim about priority that I think has been challenged. It is easy to exaggerate the differences of view that exist, and I want to avoid that. The differences are as much in emphasis as in substance, or we can say that they are differences in tone of voice. But these differences do tend to make a difference in approaches to a wide range of topics not just in moral theory but in areas such as medical ethics, where the discussion used to be conducted in terms of patients' rights, of informed consent, and so on, but now tends to get conducted in an enlarged moral vocabulary, which draws on what Gilligan calls the ethics of *care* as well as that of *justice*.

"Care" is the new buzzword. It is not, as Shakespeare's Portia demanded, mercy that is to season justice, but a less authoritarian humanitarian supplement, a felt concern for the good of others and for community with them. The "cold jealous virtue of justice" (Hume) is found to be too cold, and it is "warmer," more communitarian virtues and social ideals that are being called in to supplement it. One might say that liberty and equality are being found inadequate without frater-nity, except that "fraternity" will be quite the wrong word if, as Gilligan initially suggested, it is *women* who perceive this value most easily. ("Sorority" will do no better, since it is too exclusive, and English has no gender-neutral word for the mutual concern of siblings.) She has since modified this claim, allowing that there are two perspectives on moral and social issues that we all tend to alternate between, and which are not always easy to combine, one of them what she calls the justice perspective, the other the care perspective. It is increasingly obvious that there are many male philosophical spokespersons for the care perspective (Laurence Thomas, Lawrence Blum, Michael Stocker), so it cannot be the prerogative of women. Nevertheless Gilligan still wants to claim that women are most unlikely to take *only* the justice perspective, as some men are claimed to, at least until some mid-life crisis jolts them into "bifocal" moral vision.

Is justice blind to important social values, or at least only one-eyed? What is it that comes into view from the "care perspective" that is not seen from the "justice perspective"?

Gilligan's position here is most easily described by contrasting it with that of Kohlberg, against which she developed it. Kohlberg, influenced by Jean Piaget and the Kantian philosophical tradition as developed by John Rawls, developed a theory about typical moral development which saw it to progress from a precon-ventional level, where what is seen to matter is pleasing or not offending parental authority figures, through a conventional level in which the child tries to fit in with a group, such as a school community, and to conform to its standards and rules, to a postconventional critical level, in which such conventional rules are subjected to tests and where those tests are of a Utilitarian or, even-tually, a Kantian sort—clear ones that require respect for each person's individual rational will, or autonomy, and conformity to any implicit social contract such wills are deemed to have made or to any hypothetical ones they would make if thinking clearly. What was found when Kohlberg's questionnaires (mostly by verbal response to verbally sketched moral dilemmas) were applied to female as well as male subjects, Gilligan reports, is that the girls and women not only scored generally lower than the boys and men but tended to *revert* to the lower stage of the conventional level even after briefly (usually in adolescence) attaining the postconventional level. Piaget's finding that girls were deficient in "the legal sense" was confirmed.

These results led Gilligan to wonder if there might not be a quite different pattern of development to be discerned, at least in female subjects. She therefore conducted interviews designed to elicit not just how far advanced the subjects were toward an appreciation of the nature and importance of Kantian autonomy but also to find out what the subjects themselves saw as progress or lack of it, what conceptions of moral matu-rity they came to possess by the time they were adults. She found that although the Kohlberg version of moral maturity as respect for fellow persons and for their rights as equals (rights including that of free association) did seem shared by many young men, the women tended to speak in a different voice about morality itself and about moral maturity. To quote Gilligan, "Since the reality of connection is experienced by women as given rather than as freely contracted, they arrive at an under-standing of life that reflects the limits of autonomy and control. As a result, women's development delineates the path not only to a less violent life but also to a maturity realized through interdependence and taking care." She writes that there is evidence that "women perceive and construe social reality differently from men and that these differences center around experiences of attachment and separation . . . because women's sense of integrity appears to be entwined with an ethic of care, so that to see themselves as women is to see themselves in a relationship of connection, the major transitions in women's lives would seem to involve changes in the understanding and activities of care." She contrasts this progressive understanding of care, from merely pleasing others to helping and nurturing, with the sort of pro-gression that is involved in Kohlberg's stages, a progres-sion in the understanding, not of mutual care, but of mutual *respect,* where this has its Kantian overtones of distance, even of some fear for the respected, and where personal autonomy and *in*dependence, rather than more satisfactory interdependence, are the paramount values.

This contrast, one cannot but feel, is one which Gilligan might have used the Marxist language of alienation to make. For the main complaint about the Kantian version of a society with its first virtue justice, construed as respect for equal rights to formal goods such as having contracts kept, due process, equal oppor-tunity including opportunity to participate in political activities leading to policy- and lawmaking, to basic liberties of speech, free association and assembly, and religious worship, is that none of these goods does much to ensure that the people who have and mutually respect such rights will have any other relationships to one another than the minimal relationship needed to keep such a "civil society" going. They may well be lonely, driven to suicide, apathetic about their work and about participation in political processes, find their lives meaningless, and have no wish to leave offspring to face the same meaningless existence. Their rights, and respect for rights, are quite compatible with very great misery, and misery whose causes are not just individual misfortune and psychic sickness but social and moral impoverishment.

Let me try to summarize the main differences, as I see them, between on the one hand Gilligan's version of moral maturity and the sort of social structures that would encourage, express, and protect it and on the other the orthodoxy she sees herself to be challenging. I shall from now on be giving my own interpretation of the significance of her challenges, not merely reporting them. The most obvious point is the challenge to the individualism of the Western tradition, to the fairly entrenched belief in the possibility and desirability of each person pursuing his own good in his own way, constrained only by a minimal formal common good, namely, a working legal apparatus that enforces contracts and protects individuals from undue interference by others. Gilligan reminds us that noninterference can, especially for the relatively powerless, such as the very young, amount to neglect, and even between equals can be isolating and alienating. On her less individualist version of individuality, it becomes defined by responses to dependency and to patterns of interconnection, both chosen and unchosen. It is not something a person *has*, and which she then chooses relationships to suit, but something that develops out of a series of dependencies and interdependencies, and responses to them. This conception of individuality is not flatly at odds with, say, Rawls's Kantian one, but there is at least a difference of tone of voice between speaking as Rawls does of each of us having our own rational life plan, which a just society's moral traffic rules will allow us to follow, and which may or may not include close association with other persons, and speaking as Gilligan does of a satisfactory life as involving the "progress of affiliative relationship" where "the concept of identity expands to include the experience of interconnection." Rawls can allow that progress to Gilligan-style moral maturity may be *a* rational life plan, but not a moral constraint on every life pattern. The trouble is that it will not do just to say "let this version of morality be an optional extra. Let us agree on the essential minimum, that is, on justice and rights, and let whoever wants to go further and cultivate this more demanding ideal of responsibility and care." For, first, the ideal of care cannot be satisfactorily cultivated without closer cooperation from others than respect for rights and justice will ensure, and, second, the encouragement of some to cultivate it while others do not could easily lead to

exploitation of those who do. It obviously *has* suited some in most societies well enough that others take on the responsibilities of care (for the sick, the helpless, the young), leaving them free to pursue their own less altruistic goods. Volunteer forces of those who accept an ethic of care, operating within a society where the power is exercised and the institutions designed, redesigned, or maintained by those who accept a less communal ethic of minimally constrained self-advancement, will not be the solution. The liberal individualists may be able to "tolerate" the more communally minded, if they keep the liberals' rules, but it is not so clear that the more communally minded can be content with just those rules, nor be content to be tolerated and possibly exploited.

For the moral tradition which developed the concept of rights, autonomy, and justice is the same tradition that provided "justifications" of the oppression of those whom the primary rights-holders depended on to do the sort of work they themselves preferred not to do. The domestic work was left to women and slaves, and the liberal morality for rights-holders was surreptitiously supplemented by a different set of demands made on domestic workers. As long as women could be got to assume responsibility for the care of home and children and to train their children to continue the sexist system, the liberal morality could continue to be the official morality, by turning its eyes away from the contribution made by those it excluded. The long unnoticed moral proletariat were the domestic workers, mostly female. Rights have usually been for the privileged. Talking about laws, and the rights those laws recognize and protect, does not in itself ensure that the group of legislators and rights-holders will not be restricted to some elite. Bills of rights have usually been proclamations of the rights of some in-group, barons, landowners, males, whites, nonforeigners. The "justice perspective" and the legal sense that goes with it are shadowed by their patriarchal past. What did Kant, the great prophet of autonomy, say in his moral theory about women? He said they were incapable of legislation, not fit to vote, that they needed the guidance of more "rational" males. Autonomy was not for them; it was only for first-class, really rational, persons. It is ironic that Gilligan's original findings in a way confirm Kant's views—it seems that autonomy really may not be for women. Many of them reject that ideal, and have been found not as good at making rules as are men. But where Kant concludes "so much the worse for women," we can conclude "so much the worse for the male fixation on the special skill of drafting legislation, for the bureaucratic mentality of rule worship, and for the male exaggeration of the importance of independence over mutual interdependence."

It is however also true that the moral theories that made the concept of a person's rights central were not just the instruments for excluding some persons but also the instruments used by those who demanded that more and more persons be included in the favored group. Abolitionists, reformers, women, used the language of rights to assert their claims to inclusion in the group of full members of a community. The tradition of liberal moral theory has in fact developed to include the women it had for so long excluded, to include the poor as well as rich, blacks as well as whites, and so on. Women such as Mary Wollstonecraft used the male moral theories to good purpose. So we should not be wholly ungrateful for those male moral theories, for all their objectionable earlier content. They were undoubtedly patriarchal, but they also contained the seeds of the challenge, or antidote, to this patriarchal poison.

Exploitation aside, why would women, once liberated, not be content to have their version of morality merely tolerated? Why should they not see themselves as voluntarily, for their own reasons, taking on *more* than the liberal rules demand, while having no quarrel with the content of those rules themselves, nor with their remaining the only ones that are expected to be generally obeyed? To see why, we need to move on to three more differences between the Kantian liberals (usually contractarians) and their critics. These concern the relative weight put on relationships between equals, on freedom of choice, and on the authority of intellect over emotions. It is a typical feature of the dominant moral theories and traditions since Kant, or perhaps since Hobbes, that relationships between equals or those who are deemed equal in some important sense have been the relations that morality is primarily concerned to regulate. Relationships between those who are clearly unequal in power, such as parents and children, earlier and later generations in relation to one another, states and citizens, doctors and patients, the well and the ill, large states and small states, have had to be shunted to the bottom of the agenda and then dealt with by some sort of "promotion" of the weaker, so that an appearance of virtual equality is achieved. Citizens collectively become equal to states, children are treated as adults-to-be, the ill and dying are treated as continuers of their earlier more potent selves, so that their "rights" can be seen as the rights of equals. This pretense of an equality that is in fact absent may often lead to desirable protection of the weaker, or more dependent. But it somewhat masks the question of what our moral relationships *are* to those who are our superiors or our inferiors in power. A more realistic acceptance that we begin as

helpless children, that at almost every point of our lives we deal with both the more and the less helpless, that equality of power and interdependency, between two persons or groups, is rare and hard to recognize when it does occur, might lead us to a more direct approach to questions concerning the design of institutions structuring these relationships between unequals (families, schools, hospitals, armies) and of the morality of our dealings with the more and the less powerful. One reason why those who agree with the Gilligan version of what morality is about will not want to agree that the liberals' rules are a good minimal set, the only ones we need pressure *everyone* to obey, is that these rules do little to protect the young or the dying or the starving or any of the relatively powerless against neglect, or to ensure an education that will form persons to be *capable* of conforming to an ethics of care and responsibility. Put baldly, and in a way Gilligan certainly has not put it, the liberal morality, if unsupplemented, may *unfit* people to be anything other than what its justifying theories suppose them to be, ones who have no interest in each other's interests. Yet some must take an interest in the next generation's interests. Women's traditional work, of caring for the less powerful, especially for the young, is obviously socially vital. One cannot regard any version of morality that does not ensure that caring for children gets well done as an adequate "minimal morality," anymore than we could so regard one that left any concern for more distant future generations an optional extra. A moral theory, it can plausibly be claimed, cannot regard concern for new and future persons as an optional charity left for those with a taste for it. If the morality the theory endorses is to sustain itself, it must provide for its own continuers, not just take out a loan on a carefully encouraged maternal instinct or on the enthusiasm of a self-selected group of environmentalists who make it their business or hobby to be concerned with what we are doing to mother earth.

The recognition of the importance for all parties of relations between those who are and cannot but be unequal, and of their effect on personality formation and so on other relationships, goes along with a recognition of the plain fact that not all morally important relationships can or should be freely chosen. So far I have discussed three reasons women have to be not content to pursue their own values within the framework of the liberal morality. The first was its dubious record. The second was its inattention to relations of inequality or its pretense of equality. The third reason is its exaggeration of the scope of choice, or its inattention to unchosen relations. Showing up the partial myth of equality among actual members of a community, and the undesirability of trying to pretend that we are treating all of them as equals, tends to go along with an exposure of the companion myth that moral obligations arise from freely *chosen* associations between such equals. Vulnerable future generations do not choose their dependence on earlier generations. The unequal infant does not choose its place in a family or nation, nor is it treated as free to do as it likes until some association is freely entered into. Nor do parents always choose their parental role or freely assume their parental responsibilities, anymore than we choose our power to affect the conditions in which later generations will live. Gilligan's attention to the version of morality and moral maturity found in women, many of whom had faced a choice of whether or not to have an abortion, and who had at some point become mothers, is attention to the perceived inadequacy of the language of rights to help in such choices or to guide them in their parental role. It would not be much of an exaggeration to call the Gilligan "different voice" the voice of the potential parents. The emphasis on care goes with a recognition of the often unchosen nature of responsibilities of those who give care, both of children who care for their aged or infirm parents and of parents who care for the children they in fact have. Contract soon ceases to seem the paradigm source of moral obligation once we attend to parental responsibility, and justice as a virtue of social institutions will come to seem at best only first equal with the virtue, whatever its name, that ensures that the members of each new generation are made appropriately welcome and prepared for their adult lives.

This all constitutes a belated reminder to Western moral theorists of a fact they have always known, that, as Adam Ferguson and David Hume before him emphasized, we are born into families, and the first society we belong to, one that fits or misfits us for later ones, is the small society of parents (or some sort of child-attendants) and children, exhibiting as it may relationships both of near equality and of inequality in power. This simple reminder, with the fairly considerable implications it can have for the plausibility of contractarian moral theory, is at the same time a reminder of the role of human emotions as much as human reason and will in moral development as it actually comes about. The fourth feature of the Gilligan challenge to liberal orthodoxy is a challenge to its typical *rationalism*, or intellectualism, to its assumption that we need not worry what passions persons have, as long as their rational wills can control them. This Kantian picture of a controlling reason dictating to possibly unruly passions also tends to seem less useful when we are led to consider what sort of person we need to fill the role of parent or, indeed, want in any close relationship. It might be important for father figures to have rational control over their violent urges to beat to death the children whose screams enrage them, but more than control of such nasty passions seems needed in the mother or primary parent, or parent-substitute, according to most psychological theories. Primary parents need to love their children, not just to control their irritation. So the emphasis in Kantian theories on rational control of emotions, rather than on cultivating desirable forms of emotion, is challenged by Gilligan, along with her challenge to the assumption of the centrality of autonomy, or relations between equals, and of freely chosen relations.

It is clear, I think, that the best moral theory has to be a cooperative product of women and men, has to harmonize justice and care. The morality it theorizes about is after all for all persons, for men and for women, and will need their combined insights. As Gilligan said, what we need now is a "marriage" of the old male and the newly articulated female insights. If she is right about the special moral aptitudes of women, then it will most likely be the women who propose the marriage, since they are the ones with the more natural empathy, with the better diplomatic skills, the ones more likely to shoulder responsibility and take moral initiative, and the ones who find it easiest to empathize and care about how the other party feels. Then, once there is this union of male and female moral wisdom, we maybe can teach each other the moral skills each gender currently lacks, so that the gender difference in moral outlook that Gilligan found will slowly become less marked.

EXERCISES

1. On many ethical issues there is a significant difference between men and women. For example, women are more likely than men to oppose capital punishment (of course some women strongly favor capital punishment, and many men fervently oppose it; but on the whole, significantly higher percentages of women oppose capital punishment). Why do you suppose that difference exists?

2. The year was 1984. A middle-aged man named Leroy Reid was arrested in Milwaukee on a weapons violation charge. Reid was a convicted felon who had spent several years in prison. After his release, he had lived for years as a quiet, law-abiding citizen. As was shown at his trial, Reid was a man of very

limited intelligence—a psychologist who testified at the trial said he was not quite in the retarded range, but "substantially below average"—who read at a first-grade level. Reid wanted to find work, and he wanted to do something worthwhile. At some point he saw a magazine advertisement: "Study at home! You can become a private detective!" Reid sent a few dollars to the company, and they sent him a "private detective badge," of which he was very proud. He now believed he was a private detective, and would (as he put it) "be able to help people, like that man on television, the Equalizer." He thought he only needed one more thing to be a private detective: a gun. So he went to a sporting goods shop, and purchased a .22 caliber pistol. (The Brady Bill had not yet been passed, so Reid did not have to undergo a background check.)

Unfortunately for Reid, Wisconsin had recently passed a new law: a law of which Reid had no knowledge. The law made it a crime for a convicted felon to knowingly possess a firearm. One day Reid was hanging around a Milwaukee courtroom, and a sheriff's deputy asked him for identification. Reid proudly showed him the bill of sale for the gun he had purchased, and his "private detective" badge. The deputy asked Reid where the gun was, and Reid said he kept it at home. The deputy told Reid to go and get the gun and bring it to the sheriff's office. Reid did so. When he returned to the sheriff's office, Reid told them he had a gun he wanted to turn in. He was promptly arrested and held in jail until his trial several months later (he could not afford to post bail).

When the case came to trial, the Milwaukee district attorney's office prosecuted the case vigorously. There had recently been a murder of two Milwaukee police officers by a convicted felon who had been carrying a pistol, and the office was eager to prosecute anyone who broke the new law. Reid was defended by a lawyer from the public defender's office, who opened his case with a startling admission: Reid was guilty. Under the law, Reid *was guilty*: He was a convicted felon, he possessed a firearm, and he knew he possessed a firearm. That was all the law required, and there was no doubt on any of those three points. But Reid's lawyer implored the jury not to find Reid guilty: "You've heard all about people getting off on technicalities; this is a case of a man getting nailed on technicalities." True, Reid was guilty under the law. However, he had not intended to break the law (he only wanted a "career opportunity as a private detective" so he could "help people"); and he had no idea he was breaking the law. The prosecutor responded that "ignorance of the law is no excuse": Reid doesn't have to *know* he is breaking the law, or *intend* to break the law. The only requirements are that he be a convicted felon who possesses a firearm and knows he possesses a firearm. Reid meets those conditions; Reid is guilty.

You are on the Milwaukee jury hearing Reid's case. You've heard the evidence and the arguments. What's your verdict? Guilty or not guilty?

3. In the previous case, you thought carefully about what your verdict should be. As you thought, which of the ethical theories—Kantian, Humean, utilitarian, social contract, or care ethics—comes closest to fitting the process by which you reached your verdict? Did you employ more than one?

Second, is the approach you applied the approach you would generally take to ethical issues, or is this a special case? (That is, perhaps you employed a utilitarian approach to this question, but you do not think utilitarian ethics is generally the best method, though it works best in this special case.)

4. It is surely no accident that as more women have gone to law school, and become lawyers and judges and law school professors, there have been some changes in the practice of law. One of the most obvious is the change in the way divorce and child custody cases are handled. Of course many such cases go forward in the traditional manner: each estranged spouse hires the toughest and most battle-hardened lawyer available, and the lawyers fight it out as adversaries, with each side striving to win as much as possible. If there are children, both sides fight to win exclusive custody and limit the opposing spouse to the bare minimum of visiting rights. This makes for exciting adversarial contests, but often the only real winner is the winning lawyer, and the biggest losers are the children, who are largely deprived of one parent. In more and more cases, questions of divorce—and especially questions of child custody arrangements—are settled in special courts that place less emphasis on adversarial victory and more emphasis on reaching a settlement that meets the needs and interests of all the parties involved, especially the children. That is, many of these cases are now settled in settings that aim at cooperative conflict resolution (often including happy reconciliation of the couple that initially consider divorce, and whose tentative early moves in that direction would have been hardened by an adversarial contest) rather than a contest based on rights and principles.

Most people agree that expanding the opportunity for cooperative conflict resolution has been a good thing, and especially beneficial for the children, who are often those who suffer most from divorce. If this is counted as a positive development, and if it has in fact been stimulated by having more women involved in the law (and consequently more people who favor a "care" perspective on ethics), *would* this count as some proof of the legitimacy of care ethics?

5. You are a physician, specializing in the treatment of kidney disease. One of your patients, Alan Durkin, is a relative—a cousin; the two of you share grandparents. Alan is two years younger than you, you have known him since childhood, and you are friends. Alan is not one of your closest friends, but—in addition to now seeing him as your patient for the last three years—you see one another at weddings and funerals and other large family gatherings, maybe two or three times a year. Alan is 45, and his kidney disease has become progressively worse, and now his kidneys have failed to the point that he requires dialysis twice weekly, and soon his need for dialysis will increase to every other day. He can continue with dialysis for some time, and his condition is not immediately life threatening—but a successful kidney transplant would greatly improve his quality of life. Alan is on the waiting list for a kidney transplant, but because his dialysis treatments are relatively successful in purifying his blood, he is not a high-priority transplant candidate. Given the acute shortage of organs available for transplant, you know Alan will not soon receive one of the precious kidneys. But as Alan's physician, you could fudge the data just a little bit—no one would know, and by making his condition look somewhat worse, you could easily bump him higher on the list and greatly improve his chances of receiving a transplant within the next year or so. Of course if you do that, then someone who actually is in greater need for a kidney transplant will be passed over in favor of your cousin Alan. *Should* you fudge the data, or not?

   In attempting to answer that question, which ethical perspective—Kantian, feelings-based, utilitarian, virtue, social contract, or care—is most useful to you?

6. You have finished college, found a good job, and you are now living in a city about a thousand miles from your childhood home, where your widowed mother still lives. One weekend your mother comes to visit you in your new home: she is very proud of you, delighted at your success. It is good to see her, and the two of you reminisce over dinner about events in your childhood. You remember the weekly violin lessons: she drove you there every week, and the two of you always stopped for ice cream on the way home, and how much you enjoyed your conversations on those occasions, and how proud and supportive she was of your violin playing. And your soccer team that almost disbanded because no coach was available, and she stepped in and coached the team—even though she had to study several books on soccer to prepare herself—and the team actually finished second in the league, and how much fun the season was. And how she was always there, cooking a hot breakfast for you every morning, caring for you when you were sick, teaching you to drive, not yelling at you when the fender got smashed, offering a soft shoulder when your first romance fizzled.

   Unfortunately, the next day your mom becomes rather ill; nothing life-threatening, but she needs medical attention. You call your regular doctor, but she's out of town at a medical convention. But she has two other doctors covering her patients in her absence: Dr. Jones and Dr. Smith. Dr. Jones is first on the list, so you take your sick mom to his office. You sign in with the receptionist, and you and your mom settle down in the waiting room to await your turn to see the doctor. As you are waiting, your mom (who is white, and sadly, a racist) notices a picture of Dr. Jones and his staff in the corner of the waiting room; she discovers that Dr. Jones is black. You knew about your mother's racism already: For years it has been one of the few subjects of bitter arguments between you. Your mother immediately demands to leave: She refuses to be treated by a black doctor, and she wants to go to Dr. Smith instead. You find your mother's racist attitudes profoundly repugnant, morally repulsive. But your mother—whom you love, her faults notwithstanding, and who dearly loves you—is sick, and she is deeply disturbed about the prospect of being treated by a Black doctor. You aren't likely to get her past her deep racism in the next few minutes; after all, you've been trying for many years. And she will be much more comfortable seeing a white doctor. You have the car and the keys, and you can force her to see Dr. Jones; or you can agree to take her to Dr. Smith.

   The standard question for such cases is: What should you do? But that is *not* the question being asked here. Instead, think about *how* care theorists would approach this problem: what steps would they take, what process might a care theorist follow? And second, how does the approach of the care theorist *differ* from the approach of some other ethical theorist (of your own choice: say, from a Kantian)?

7. You are a physician at a tissue match laboratory. Ben Thomas makes an appointment to be tested. Ben's daughter, Rebecca, is 25. Rebecca has lost most of the functioning in her kidneys as a result of a severe blow suffered in a bicycle accident. She requires dialysis twice a week, and her health is poor. A kidney transplant would very likely restore her to full health, and she is on a waiting list for a kidney; but the list is long, and Rebecca's chances of getting a kidney are small. Because relatives have the best chance of having a close tissue match (and thus greatly reducing the likelihood of the patient's body *rejecting* the transplanted kidney),

Ben hopes his kidney will be a close match. Ben is in good health, with two healthy kidneys, and if there is a good match, he plans to donate one of his kidneys to Rebecca (an increasingly common procedure). Since Rebecca is on the waiting list for a kidney transplant, you already have complete data on her; you just need to run tests on Ben.

      You run the tests, as Ben requests, and unfortunately the tests show that Ben is not a good tissue match, and cannot contribute a kidney to Rebecca. But the tests also show something else, that neither you nor Ben had anticipated: Ben is not the biological father of Rebecca. Should you tell Ben this additional information? What factors or principles should you weigh in making your decision? Does Ben have a right to this information? Would care theorists and Kantians be likely to reach very different conclusions on this issue? *Must* they reach different conclusions?

8. Suppose someone suggested that "care ethics" is important in the home and among family and friends, but that an ethics of justice must govern our larger and more impersonal ethical lives. What do you think would be Annette Baier's response?

9. Consider the question of "physician-assisted suicide," currently much debated. Those who favor physician-assisted suicide believe that the terminally ill should be able to ask for and receive assistance from their doctors in ending their own lives at the time when they choose to die (the state of Oregon currently allows physician-assisted suicide). Those who oppose physician-assisted suicide believe that doctors should never aid patients in ending their lives, but should instead provide comfort measures until the patient dies naturally. Would a Kantian and a care ethicist be likely to reach different conclusions on the issue of legalizing physician-assisted suicide? Would they *necessarily* reach different conclusions? Might two care ethicists hold differing views on this issue?

10. Care ethics is often described in *contrast* to utilitarian ethics; but is there any form of utilitarian ethics that would be *compatible* with care ethics?

11. Care ethicists are usually fierce critics of social contract ethics; but can you imagine a form of social contract theory (obviously quite different from Hobbes' theory) that a care ethicist might favor?

ADDITIONAL READING

Carol Gilligan, *In a Different Voice: Psychological Theory and Women's Development* (Cambridge, MA: Harvard University Press, 1982), had a powerful impact on the contemporary development of care ethics. Lawrence Kohlberg's account of his research on moral development is in *The Philosophy of Moral Development: Moral Stages and the Idea of Justice* (New York: Harper and Row, 1981). The Gilligan/Kohlberg work has been extensively discussed; see articles by Kohlberg and Owen Flanagan in *Ethics*, Volume 92, Number 3 (April 1982), 499–528; and in *Ethics*, Volume 97 (1987), 622–637; see also Owen Flanagan and Kathryn Jackson, "Justice, Care, and Gender: The Kolhberg-Gilligan Debate Revisited"; and Lawrence Blum, "Gilligan and Kohlberg: Implications for Moral Theory," *Ethics*, Volume 98 (April 1988), 472–491.

      Nel Noddings's work has been influential in both philosophy and education; see her *Caring: A Feminine Approach to Ethics and Moral Education* (Berkeley, CA: University of California Press, 1984); and *Educating Moral People: A Caring Alternative to Character Education* (New York: Teachers College Press, 2002). Annette C. Baier is a clear and cogent writer on this topic, and is particularly insightful in placing care ethics in a larger philosophical perspective. See her *Moral Prejudices* (Cambridge, MA.: Harvard University Press, 1994). Among the best advocates of care ethics is Lawrence A. Blum, *Friendship, Altruism and Morality* (London: Routledge & Kegan Paul, 1980). Viginia Held's edited collection, *Justice and Care* (Boulder, CO: Westview Press, 1995), is an excellent collection of essays on the subject. A very good and wide-ranging anthology is Eva Feder Kittay and Diana Meyers, editors, *Women and Moral Theory* (Totowa, NJ: Rowman & Littlefield, 1987). Other good anthologies are Mary Jeanne Larrabee, *An Ethic of Care: Feminist and Interdisciplinary Perspectives* (New York: Routledge, 1993); James P. Sterba, *Controversies in Feminism* (Lanham, MD: Rowman & Littlefield, 2001); and Samantha Brennan, *Feminist Moral Philosophy* (Calgary, Alberta: University of Calgary Press, 2002).

      Online, see the feminist ethics entry (by Rosemary Tong) in the *Stanford Encyclopedia of Philosophy* at *http://plato.stanford.edu/entries/feminist-ethics*; and in *Ethical Updates* see the Gender and Ethical Theory section at *http://ethics/acusd.edu/theories/Gender/index.html*.

NOTES

[1] Nel Noddings, *Caring: A Feminine Approach to Ethics & Moral Education* (Berkeley, CA: University of California Press, 1984), p. 96.

[2] Quoted in Valerie P. Hans and Neil Vidmar, *Judging the Jury* (New York: Plenum Press, 1986), p. 53.

[3] Sarah Grimke, "The Pastoral Letter of the General Association of Congregational Ministers of Massachusetts, 1837," printed in David A. Hollinger and Charles Capper, editors, *The American Intellectual Tradition,* Volume 1, 4th ed. (New York: Oxford University Press, 2001), p. 274.

[4] Ariel Kay Salleh, "Working with Nature: Reciprocity or Control?" in *Environmental Philosophy: From Animal Rights to Radical Ecology,* 2nd ed., Michael E. Zimmerman, J. Baird Callicott, George Sessions, Karen J. Warren, and John Clark, editors (Upper Saddle River, NJ: Prentice-Hall, 1998), p. 323.

[5] Jean Grimshaw, "The Idea of a Female Ethic," in *A Companion to Ethics,* Peter Singer, editor (Oxford: Blackwell, 1991), p. 498.

10
Ethical Nonobjectivism

We have looked at a variety of ways people have tried to find—or create—ethical standards. Perhaps one of those methods, or some combination of them, or some system we haven't examined will establish ethical truths. But there is another possibility: there are no ethical truths. Science may establish facts, but in ethics there are no facts to discover. There are neither transcendent nor natural moral facts. (Nonobjectivists may allow the possibility of *synthetic* moral facts: that is, the "moral facts" created synthetically by social contracts. We adopt a rule in our contract that it is wrong to steal, so in our society it is wrong to steal. But nonobjectivists would not regard that as an *objective* moral fact. Moral nonobjectivists would say: "True, in your society you have a rule that stealing is wrong; but that doesn't show that stealing is in fact wrong. And if tomorrow you adopted a rule that stealing is right, that would not make the legitimacy of theft a moral fact. You may establish *rules* by force or referendum, but you can't legislate moral *facts* any more than you can legislate biological or astronomical or chemical facts.")

THE NATURE OF ETHICAL NONOBJECTIVISM

Nonobjectivism Is Not Neutral

Note that nonobjectivism is not a neutral position. Nonobjectivists claim that there are *no* objective moral truths. The skeptic maintains that neither side has proved its case, and she can sit quietly, waiting for someone to offer her proof. The nonobjectivist has a case to make, and the case is not an easy one. After all, most people are firmly convinced that there *are* objective moral facts: Slavery is morally wrong, it is and always was and always will be morally wrong. If tomorrow we passed a law making slavery legal, that would not eliminate the moral wrongness of slavery; instead, the moral fact that slavery is wrong would make the new law morally wrong. Bringing books and flowers and encouragement to a hospitalized friend is objectively right. Perhaps in another culture one would bring some other present, or write a poem or sing a song; but caring for a friend—however that care may be manifested in different settings—is morally good, and that's a fact. The nonobjectivist must explain away such supposed moral facts.

Noncognitivism

In recent years many nonobjectivists marched under the banner of *noncognitivism* or *emotivism*. Noncognitivists claimed that such assertions as "stealing is wrong" or "generosity is a virtue" were not real statements at all; that is, they did not make real claims and were not true or false. Instead, such sentences *express* approval or disapproval. They are really saying: "Go generosity!" or "Down with stealing!" Or alternatively, they are imperatives, rather than statements: "Don't steal!" If I say to you "Please close the door," or "Go Steelers," it wouldn't make sense for you to ask: "Is that true?" (You could ask whether I am sincere. Perhaps I really don't like the Steelers, and am simply afraid to cheer for the Browns in the midst of belligerent Steelers fans. But it makes no sense to ask whether "Go Steelers" is *true*.) Likewise (according to the noncognitivists), it makes no sense to ask whether "Honesty is good" is true or false. It expresses feelings of approval, rather than making a claim.

Nonobjectivists are fairly common, but noncognitivists are an endangered philosophical species. However convenient it might be for philosophical theory, it is hard to convince Sarah that when she says, "slavery is wrong," she is merely *expressing* her distaste for slavery. "The hell I am," she will reply. "It's not a matter of taste. Slavery is morally wrong. If you think slavery is okay, that's not like saying you like sushi. I like sushi, you don't; *that's* a matter of taste. When I say I like sushi and you say you don't like sushi, we aren't really in conflict. But when I say slavery is wrong, and you say it's not, we are in deep conflict." If I delight in strawberry ice cream, but hate strawberry shortcake, you may think my tastes a bit unusual, but you will not charge me with inconsistency. However, if I claim all people should be treated as ends in themselves and never merely as means, but then insist there is nothing wrong with slavery, you can correctly point out that my views about slavery are inconsistent with my other moral principles. My moral principle that all persons should be treated as ends in themselves logically implies slavery is wrong. But expressions of feeling don't have logical implications. So whatever status we ascribe to moral principles and moral assertions, it seems implausible to suppose they are merely expressions of feeling.

If we grant that moral claims are genuine statements, that still leaves a lot of questions. In particular, are they statements of *fact*? Are moral statements (such as "stealing is wrong") and moral principles ("you should always treat others as ends in themselves, never merely as means") objectively true, the way "Jupiter is the largest planet in our solar system" is objectively true? Moral objectivists insist that moral statements are true (or at least that we may yet *discover* they are true). Moral nonobjectivists deny that moral statements are true. We may feel strongly about them, and we may be passionately committed to them, and some may be inconsistent with others; but in all that huge class of true statements—"the Earth is the third planet from the Sun," "George Washington was the first president of the United States," or "the Cubs play in Chicago"—moral statements are nowhere to be found.

Arguments for Ethical Nonobjectivism

The Argument from Moral Diversity

The ethical nonobjectivist has a number of arguments for her position. Perhaps the most obvious, and the one most frequently heard, is the argument from the *diversity* of moral views. One needn't go to distant climes and exotic cultures to observe such diversity. We are quite familiar with the bitter differences between those who consider abortion a heinous crime and those who view banning abortion as an egregious violation of women's rights to control their own bodies. And other conflicts are abundant. One group believes capital punishment to be the only morally appropriate punishment for those who commit the most terrible crimes, while the opposing view regards capital punishment as barbaric. Some view sex before marriage as a violation of moral principles, and others regard such lengthy sexual abstinence as a wrongful deprivation of an enjoyable and enriching experience.

Objectivists have two possible answers. First, that the great divergence of moral opinion is more apparent than real. At a deeper level, there is convergence. For example, there is surely deep division concerning the question of abortion, but there are also some important points of growing consensus. Both sides to the dispute tend to agree that women have the right to control over their own bodies (those who oppose abortion believe the rights of the fetus trump the woman's right to control over her own body, but do not eliminate that right). There are those who believe women should be subject to the wills of their husbands, and have no control over anything. But take away the distorting prism of religious zealotry, and few would favor such a view. And of course no moral objectivist would claim that everyone agrees on any moral principle. There is surely consensus among competent astronomers that Jupiter is the planet in our solar system with the greatest mass. But if some astronomers persist in looking through the wrong end of the telescope, or their viewing suffers some other distorting influence, then the fact that they do not agree with this scientific consensus is no reason to think the scientific consensus is wrong. Likewise, moral consensus leaves room for a few dissenters.

That brings us to the second reply objectivists offer to the nonobjectivist argument from moral diversity. That reply is simple: If there is divergence of opinion, it just means that some opinions are wrong. Some people reject Darwin, but that doesn't mean there is no truth in evolutionary theory. And some people approve of child abuse, but that doesn't change the fact that child abuse is wrong. This second answer may be especially attractive to those who claim special access to moral truth (for example, if one believes one has received a special religious revelation, and others have not had that privilege). Even without belief in one's own special knowledge of moral truth, it is quite possible to hope that moral consensus will emerge. It just takes time, and examination of morality has been hamstrung by political and religious oppression. However, we have been making serious inquiries into morality for well over 2,500 years, and there still seem to be precious few points of solid agreement; in any case, significantly fewer than in the sciences. So the nonobjectivist might be justified in asking just how long we are supposed to wait for this emerging moral consensus.

The Argument from the Impossibility of Argument About Ethics

A second argument for moral nonobjectivism was developed by a famous twentieth-century British philosopher A. J. Ayer. He claims that we cannot really argue about ethics, and that the impossibility of ethical argument shows ethics to be nonobjective.

On the surface, Ayer's claim seems bizarre. Go to any clash between pro-lifers and pro-choicers and you will get plenty of arguments about ethics. But Ayer is not impressed by such cases. Look carefully at those "arguments," Ayer would say. For the most part they are just name calling, rather than argument. And when there really is argument, it's not actually about *ethics*. Instead, there are disputes over whether a fetus has consciousness, or whether a fetus has a soul, or whether abortion is "natural," or about the psychological effects on a woman who is forced to carry an unwanted pregnancy to term. But those are questions of biology and theology and psychology, not really questions about ethics. When we encounter a genuine ethical issue—Does the fetus have rights? Does a woman's right to control her own body trump any rights the fetus may have to be born?—then we *cannot argue* about that issue. We might try to discover inconsistencies in the views of the other side, and point out that the position they are holding is inconsistent with some of their other views. For example, the pro-choice group might argue that *if* people maintain that pregnant women should be compelled to give birth because the fetus has "a right to be born," then they ought to also believe that any woman who is not now pregnant should be compelled to implant the excess embryos from fertility clinics, embryos that will die unless they are implanted. But no one believes a woman should be compelled to have an embryo implanted, and so consistency requires that no one be compelled to carry a fetus against her will. The pro-life side might respond that in the case of abortion, one is actively killing the fetus, while in the case of not implanting an embryo, one is simply allowing the embryo to die, but not purposefully killing it. Now the argument turns to the question of whether there is a moral difference between killing and letting die, and again we may turn to examples, but (Ayer would maintain) if we really have a conflict over that *basic ethical* question, we can't argue about that. One group feels strongly one way while the other group feels strongly for the other side, but argument becomes impossible.

Consider an example. Lowell Kleiman is a moral realist who believes in objective moral facts. In support of his moral objectivism, he notes, "cultures that are opposed to genocide, and to killing in general, are more likely to be at peace with their neighbors." From this observation, Kleiman poses the following rhetorical question: "Peace among nations is a moral goal. Why is it difficult to see any moral facts behind the achievement of a moral goal?"[1] And surely for most of us peace *is* a moral goal. But not everyone shares this deeply held value. One of Ezra Pound's poems celebrates "the battle's rejoicing, when our elbows and swords drip the crimson" and pronounces this curse: "May God damn for ever all who cry 'Peace!' " And Pound's warlike values are but an echo of King David's, who sings verses of praise (Psalm 18) to the "God that girdeth me with strength" and "teacheth my hands to war." Most of us will fervently oppose such brutal values, and we will try to convince those who hold them of the error of their ways. "Look, war isn't like the knights of the Round Table. People really get killed, and they suffer terrible injuries, and innocents are caught up in the deadly struggle and are killed or displaced and left homeless, and children die from bombs and land mines and starvation, and the countries engaged in war become more repressive: they lock up citizens suspected of favoring the other side, and rights of free speech are overwhelmed by the demands of propaganda. There's nothing beautiful or glorious about it. In war, life is nasty, brutish, and short." Such points may convince those who held a false picture of what war really involves. During the American Civil War, spectators packed picnic lunches and rode their carriages out to the fields of northern Virginia, near Manassas, to watch the glorious battle unfold, with its stirring music, bright flags, and heroic charges. What they saw instead was a terrible slaughter. Men and horses were blown to bits by rows of cannon and ranks of muskets; confusion and terror reigned on all sides. Many people had their myths about war exploded that day. The reality was very different from what they had fantasized.

But what if someone experiences such brutality and instead finds it thrilling and desirable? "Consider how many innocent people are slaughtered," we say. "That is a small price to pay for the glories of war," is the response. "But if you engage in war, you yourself are likely to meet a swift and brutal end." "Better an hour of war than 70 years of peace," our opponent answers. If someone really holds such a fundamentally different moral outlook from our own, we can certainly *oppose* her, and we may revile her as a moral monster; but can we really *argue* with her? Of course, there are facts we *can* argue about: Is this war necessary to secure a more lasting peace? Is this war essential to preventing other terrible harms? Are there actually lots of civilian casualties in war? Does war in fact make a country more repressive? But suppose our disagreement is not about those issues, but instead about the basic value question: Alice says war, in all its brutal savagery, is good. We say it is morally bad (even if we believe war is sometimes justified, we still believe it to be in itself a bad thing, and something to be avoided when possible). Can we argue with Alice about that *basic* moral issue? Ayer says we cannot; and the impossibility of argument, Ayer maintains, shows that the basic moral issue is not a matter of objective fact.

To answer Ayer's argument, you could go either of two directions. First, you could try to demonstrate that there *is* room for genuine argument on even the most basic ethical issues. Or second, you could accept Ayer's assertion that argument on ethical issues is not possible, but insist that ethics is objective nonetheless: some basic ethical truths are simply known immediately, they are *intuitively* obvious to anyone who thinks clearly and looks objectively at the issue. True, if Alice fails to recognize these basic ethical truths, we cannot argue with her. But that doesn't show that there are no ethical truths. Instead, it reveals that Alice is morally blind.

The Argument from Simplicity: Ockham's Razor

This response to Ayer brings us to a third argument for moral nonobjectivism. It was developed by another twentieth-century British philosopher, J. L. Mackie, and it is known as the "argument from queerness." Mackie argues that belief in moral objectivity would commit us to a very weird sort of thing: moral facts. Moral facts are weird because they combine two distinct properties. First, they must be facts that exist independently of us. They are *objective* facts, which are true whether we recognize them or not. It's an objective fact that Jupiter is the largest planet in our solar system whether I—or anyone else—knows it. (That's why nonobjectivists do not count the rules devised by social contracts as *objective* moral facts.) And second, they must be facts that have the very special and queer property of commanding our approval.

We finally arrive at the basic question that divides objectivists and nonobjectivists. Can we account for ethics and ethical behavior *without* the assumption of objective moral facts? If we can, then a system without moral facts will have the advantage of *simplicity*, and that is a very substantial advantage indeed. "'Tis a blessing to be simple," says the opening line of the famous folk song, and contemporary scientists and philosophers tend to agree. If we favored more complicated explanations over simpler ones, then we could explain anything. But the "explanations" would be quite strange, and they wouldn't offer much help. My watch has stopped. "Must need a new battery," you say. "No," I reply, "it's not the battery; the problem is that my little watch elf is taking a nap, and so he's stopped moving the gears." "There's no watch elf! It's just an old battery." "No, I'll show you." I bang the watch briskly on a table, and the hands start to move again. "You see, I awakened the elf, and he started moving the gears. When the watch soon stops again, it's because the elf returned to slumber." You open the watch, and find no elf. "You see, there's no elf there." "He's there alright," I reply. "But he's very shy, and he hides. Besides, he can make himself invisible." You place a new battery in the watch, and now it runs fine, without stopping. "You see, it's the battery that drives the watch; there's no elf." "There is too an elf," I insist; "but he's a battery-powered elf, and he was getting really run down. That's why he was sleeping so much. Now that he has a new battery, he's back on the job driving the gears and running the watch."

This is a silly dialogue, of course. But it's silly only because of a deeply held principle by which we reason, a principle so common that we hardly know it's there. The principle was formally stated by William of Ockham, back in the early fourteenth century, and we now call it the principle of "Ockham's razor." The principle is this: when giving explanations, don't make assumptions that are not required. Or another way of stating it: when there are competing explanations, both of which give adequate accounts of what is to be explained, then the *simpler* explanation is better; that is, the more *parsimonious* explanation, the *thriftier* explanation, is better. I can "explain" the workings of my watch quite effectively by means of my elf hypothesis. When the watch stops, the elf is asleep. When the watch slows down, the elf is tired. When the watch keeps accurate time, the elf is on top of his game. When the watch is inaccurate, the elf has been drinking. The problem is that this explanation is not as *parsimonious* as the competing explanation. It adds to the explanatory story a very special additional entity: an elf (and not just any elf, but an elf that can make itself invisible). If you let me add elves and ghosts and miracles to my explanatory scheme, then I can "explain" anything; but the explanations violate the principle of Ockham's razor, and are not as efficient and effective as the simpler explanations in terms of rundown batteries and rust.

That's a long detour, but it leads us back to Mackie's argument from queerness. Mackie makes use of Ockham's razor to argue that while moral objectivism might "explain" ethics and ethical behavior, we can give simpler, thriftier, and more parsimonious explanations of the same phenomena *without* appealing to objective moral facts. If we can explain ethical experiences without assuming the existence of objective moral facts, then we have a *better* (because it is simpler) explanation. And like the invisible watch elf, objective moral facts aren't just one more entity in the universe: they are very strange things indeed, and we shouldn't assume they exist unless no simpler explanation is available. Why would objective moral facts be such a strange and exotic addition to the world? As we noted earlier, Mackie claims they must have two distinct properties. First, they must exist in our world (that is a property they share with deck chairs and wombats and rowboats—nothing special about that). Second (and this is the special property), they must automatically and powerfully motivate us. If we recognize that something is *objectively good*, then recognition of that fact motivates us to pursue it. (Of course, something else may block or prevent our pursuit, but recognition of the inherent goodness of the object will nonetheless provide a strong motive for pursuing it.) If I acknowledge that something is in *fact* morally good, but I have no interest in pursuing or preserving that good, then you are justified in concluding that I did not really understand or appreciate its goodness. I'm mouthing the words, but I don't really see the good. Thus, objective moral facts must be very special. They are facts about the world, *and* they automatically arouse in us—in anyone who recognizes them—both approval and motive to pursue. And these special objective moral facts, which are unlike anything else in the world, will also require a special perceptual power if we are to comprehend them. So, the moral objectivist is burdened not only with special strange moral facts but also with special perceptual faculties. Moral objectivism might still be true, but we should not accept such a cumbersome theory if some simpler hypothesis provides a workable alternative account.

How could the moral objectivist attempt to answer Mackie's argument that moral facts are too complicated? One way is to deny that moral facts are as complicated as Mackie suggests. They *are* facts about the world, but they do not necessarily motivate us to *favor* the moral facts. This leads to a spirited debate between "internalists" (who insist that any real moral fact *must* motivate those who recognize the fact), and "externalists" (who hold that the motive to act morally is separate from—external to—the recognition of objective moral facts). It's an interesting debate, but far beyond the scope of this discussion.

In a second possible answer to Mackie's queerness argument, the objectivist might reply that moral facts *are* rather complicated, but not everything is nice and simple. Besides, there are other facts about the world that we recognize as *scientifically* objective that are also quite complicated: consider the many perplexities generated by space and time, not to mention quarks and antimatter. So objective morality is complicated, but that's what morality requires.

But *does* an explanation of morality require something that complicated? That is a very tough and controversial question. If there is a moral *fact*, perhaps the best candidate is something like this: treating others as you would wish to be treated is good. Many different religious traditions, as well as a number of secular philosophical views, have favored this principle—or something quite similar—as the most basic principle of ethics. And even among those who do not think ethics is *objectively true*, most would regard this as good moral guidance. What is the best explanation for the popularity of this moral principle? The explanation favored by the moral objectivists is: there is widespread allegiance to this moral principle because all these various perspectives and cultures and traditions have discovered the same basic moral fact, that it is right and good to treat others as you yourself wish to be treated. That is certainly one possible explanation, and perhaps it is the most satisfactory explanation (though it may involve some rather complicated elements, as we noted before). What *alternative* explanations would be proposed by the nonobjectivists?

Nonobjectivists might hypothesize that any uniformity in moral principles is the result of our common biological heritage. For example, Michael Ruse maintains that our most basic ethical impulses are shaped by our evolutionary history:

> We are what we are because we are recently evolved from savannah-dwelling primates. Suppose that we had evolved from cave-dwellers, or some such thing. We might have as our highest principle of moral obligation the imperative to eat each others' faeces. Not simply the desire, but the obligation.[2]

However plausible or implausible you may find this evolutionary account of our basic values, it does have at least one distinct virtue: it makes no appeal to special ethical powers or complicated moral facts. Instead, this account of ethics is fashioned from materials that are already at hand (our knowledge of evolution). It does not require any special additional resources, and so—by the principle of Ockham's razor—it scores points for simplicity. We do have deep ethical "intuitions," but we don't require special moral facts to account for them.

If the evolutionary explanation does not take your fancy, then you might consider explanations formulated by sociologists and psychologists. We are shaped from an early age to live in at least a minimal degree of harmony with those around us, and we gradually internalize that training. I am happily playing with a bright red shiny fire engine, complete with bell and siren and a nifty ladder. Quite naturally Susie is also attracted to the new toy, and grabs it away. My screams of frustration quickly bring the attention of powerful adults: "No, Susie, he was playing with it first; you can't just take it away from him, that wouldn't be nice." This seems like a peachy result to me, until a few minutes later when the same powerful adult again arrives on the scene: "You've been playing with the fire engine for quite a while. Wouldn't you like to let Susie play with it now?" Well, actually, I wouldn't. I would prefer that Susie go soak her head. But young as I am, I've already learned that this is not really a question about how I feel, but an order—politely phrased, but no less an order—to yield the fire engine to Susie. I can try to hang on to the fire engine at all costs—"Mine! I had it first!"—but I soon discover that is not a very effective strategy: I wind up without the fire engine, sitting in timeout, feeling bitter and powerless. On the other hand, if I cheerfully share the fire engine with that damned Susie, I may get to continue playing with it, and I might even cop an extra cookie or two at snack time. And perhaps best of all, I feel that I am sharing the fire engine with Susie from my own choice: and so I feel powerful rather than powerless, and I also feel like a paragon of virtue. So it's not long before I discover that "treat others as you would like to be treated" has serious benefits. Of course at 4 years old I don't follow it as a moral principle, but I have been effectively shaped into that pattern of behavior. When someone does suggest that principle to me, I am now predisposed to see it as an obvious and basic truth. In different cultures the acculturation process will take somewhat different forms. But we are highly social beings, who live together in close groups. Without some such learning of basic cooperation skills, cooperative projects and harmonious communities would be impossible. So all viable cultures promote the learning of cooperative behavior. And it works a lot better—both socially and psychologically— if that cooperative behavior is *internalized*. I am generous and cooperative with others because I *want* to be, not because I am forced to be. Again, however plausible you find that account, it gets high marks by the standard of Ockham's razor. It is a simple account that requires no additional special resources such as "objective moral facts." (Some moral realists will insist that "cooperative cultures work better" is *itself* a statement of moral fact; but that is a question we'll consider in the next chapter.)

Some might criticize the nonobjectivist explanations provided as somewhat speculative and in any case not so neat and complete as the explanations in terms of special moral faculties that recognize special moral facts. That's a legitimate criticism. The nonobjectivists will answer that their explanations are based on empirical scientific materials from biology, sociology, and psychology and that such explanations are not complete but instead depend on ongoing scientific research. We may not be able to give explanations that are as neat and easy as the moral objectivists offer; but at least we are not appealing to special faculties or special forces or special facts, instead we are trying to give real explanations based on empirical research. It's easy to give neat explanations if you can appeal to moral facts or watch elves, but the *quality*—and particularly the *simplicity*—of the explanations may leave something to be desired.

THE CONTINUING STRUGGLE BETWEEN OBJECTIVISTS AND NONOBJECTIVISTS

So the controversy between moral objectivists and moral nonobjectivists rages on. This is an issue on which you will have to decide for yourself which view is more plausible and more promising. Even though this dispute runs deep, both sides can find some common ground. Whether I think there are objective moral truths or only useful moral guidelines shaped by our cultural or evolutionary history, in either case I think it is important that people cooperate and live in peace. As noted earlier, there *are* people who favor brutal war over peaceful harmony; but fortunately, there are very few—whether objectivists or nonobjectivists—who take that view. For the most part, we prefer to live in communities where people are cooperative and pleasant, kind and considerate. We want to raise our children in such communities, and have them become productive, virtuous members of such communities. Objectivists and nonobjectivists alike tend to share such ideals, so perhaps it doesn't matter so much which side of the divide one falls on.

Still, this is a difference that makes a difference. For example, objectivists and nonobjectivists may have significant differences in the details of how best to shape their children to be cooperative moral citizens. The moral objectivist will aim at placing children in a position to *recognize* the basic moral truths. The nonobjectivist aims at *instilling* or *shaping* a positive moral outlook and desirable moral behavioral patterns. (This is perhaps the source of the controversy between those who believe it is important to reward and reinforce good behavior, and those who believe that such external rewards make it difficult for the child to recognize the intrinsic objective worth of the good behavior.)

Alternatives to Nonobjectivism

If you have always thought of ethics as *transcendent*—perhaps given by God—and you no longer (or perhaps never did) believe in those transcendent sources, then you may suppose that nonobjectivism is the inevitable result. It certainly is one possibility. It is favored by a number of philosophers, and may well be the view you find most plausible. But there are other alternatives to consider. We have already looked at some nontranscendent objectivist views (such as utilitarianism, social contract theory, and pragmatism). The next chapter presents another form of natural moral objectivism—a form of moral realism that was crafted in direct response to some of the nonobjectivist arguments of this chapter.

⟜ LANGUAGE, TRUTH, AND LOGIC ⟜
A. J. Ayer

A. J. Ayer was a very influential twentieth-century British philosopher, who early in his career helped to bring the ideas of the European logical positivists into British, American, and Australian philosophy. Logical positivism was a complex philosophical movement, but among its major goals was making philosophy more scientific and logical, and eliminating from philosophy many of the traditional metaphysical questions that logical positivists regarded as illegitimate *pseudo* questions: questions that had endured for so long because they were either literally nonsensical or because they turned on basic errors in either logic or language. In the following excerpt, Ayer is turning his logical positivist methodology to questions of ethics.

For more details on Ayer's life and work—and on the development of twentieth-century Anglo-American philosophy—see Ayer's fascinating autobiography, *Part of My Life* (London: Collins, 1977; a paperback version was published by Oxford University Press in 1978). It is one of the most honest, revealing, and entertaining autobiographies ever written by a philosopher, as Ayer chronicles the highlights of his love life and his military service with as much enthusiasm as he describes his many philosophical controversies. Another good source for the study of Ayer's work is *The Philosophy of A. J. Ayer*, edited by Lewis Edwin Hahn (LaSalle, IL: Open Court, 1992). For Ayer's later work on moral philosophy—in which he revises some of his earlier views, though he vigorously defends the essentials of his position—see Ayer's *Philosophical Essays* (London: Macmillan, 1969), especially "On the Analysis of Moral Judgments."

It is advisable here to make it plain that it is only normative ethical symbols, and not descriptive ethical symbols, that are held by us to be indefinable in factual terms. There is a danger of confusing these two types of symbols, because they are commonly constituted by signs of the same sensible form. Thus, a complex sign of the form "x is wrong" may constitute a sentence which expresses a moral judgement concerning a certain type of conduct, or it may constitute a sentence which states that a certain type of conduct is repugnant to the moral sense of a particular society. In the latter case, the symbol "wrong" is a descriptive ethical symbol, and the sentence in which it occurs expresses an ordinary sociological proposition; in the former case, the symbol "wrong" is a normative ethical symbol, and the sentence in which it occurs does not, we maintain, express an empirical proposition at all. It is only with normative ethics that we are at present concerned; so that whenever ethical symbols are used in the course of this argument without qualification, they are always to be interpreted as symbols of the normative type.

In admitting that normative ethical concepts are irreducible to empirical concepts, we seem to be leaving the way clear for the "absolutist" view of ethics—that is, the view that statements of value are not controlled by observation, as ordinary empirical propositions are, but only by a mysterious "intellectual intuition." A feature of this theory, which is seldom recognized by its advocates, is that it makes statements of value unverifiable. For it is notorious that what seems intuitively certain to one person may seem doubtful, or even false, to another. So that unless it is possible to provide some criterion by which one may decide between conflicting intuitions, a mere appeal to intuition is worthless as a test of a proposition's validity. But in the case of moral judgements, no such criterion can be given. Some moralists claim to settle the matter by saying that they "know" that their own moral judgements are correct. But such an assertion is of purely psychological interest, and has not the slightest tendency to prove the validity of any moral judgement. For dissentient moralists may equally well "know" that their ethical views are correct. And, as far as subjective certainty goes, there will be nothing to choose between them. When such differences of opinion arise in connection with an ordinary empirical proposition, one may attempt to resolve them by referring to, or actually carrying out, some relevant empirical test. But with regard to ethical statements, there is, on the "absolutist" or "intuitionist" theory, no relevant empirical test. We are therefore justified in saying that on this theory ethical statements are held to be unverifiable. They are, of course, also held to be genuine synthetic propositions.

Considering the use which we have made of the principle that a synthetic proposition is significant only if it is empirically verifiable, it is clear that the acceptance of an "absolutist" theory of ethics would undermine the whole of our main argument. And as we have already rejected the "naturalistic" theories which are commonly supposed to provide the only alternative to "absolutism" in ethics, we seem to have reached a difficult position. We shall meet the difficulty by showing that the correct treatment of ethical statements is afforded by a third theory, which is wholly compatible with our radical empiricism.

We begin by admitting that the fundamental ethical concepts are unanalysable, inasmuch as there is no criterion by which one can test the validity of the judgements in which they occur. So far we are in agreement with the absolutists. But, unlike the absolutists, we are able to give an explanation of this fact about ethical concepts. We say that the reason why they are unanalysable is that they are mere pseudo-concepts. The presence of an ethical symbol in a proposition adds nothing to its factual content. Thus if I say to someone, "You acted wrongly in stealing that money," I am not stating anything more than if I had simply said, "You stole that money." In adding that this action is wrong I am not making any further statement about it. I am simply evincing my moral disapproval of it. It is as if

I had said, "You stole that money," in a peculiar tone of horror, or written it with the addition of some special exclamation marks. The tone, or the exclamation marks, adds nothing to the literal meaning of the sentence. It merely serves to show that the expression of it is attended by certain feelings in the speaker.

If now I generalise my previous statement and say, "Stealing money is wrong," I produce a sentence which has no factual meaning—that is, expresses no proposition which can be either true or false. It is as if I had written "Stealing money!!"—where the shape and thickness of the exclamation marks show, by a suitable convention, that a special sort of moral disapproval is the feeling which is being expressed. It is clear that there is nothing said here which can be true or false. Another man may disagree with me about the wrongness of stealing, in the sense that he may not have the same feelings about stealing as I have, and he may quarrel with me on account of my moral sentiments. But he cannot, strictly speaking, contradict me. For in saying that a certain type of action is right or wrong, I am not making any factual statement, not even a statement about my own state of mind. I am merely expressing certain moral sentiments. And the man who is ostensibly contradicting me is merely expressing his moral sentiments. So that there is plainly no sense in asking which of us is in the right. For neither of us is asserting a genuine proposition.

What we have just been saying about the symbol "wrong" applies to all normative ethical symbols. Sometimes they occur in sentences which record ordinary empirical facts besides expressing ethical feeling about those facts: sometimes they occur in sentences which simply express ethical feeling about a certain type of action, or situation, without making any statement of fact. But in every case in which one would commonly be said to be making an ethical judgement, the function of the relevant ethical word is purely "emotive." It is used to express feeling about certain objects, but not to make any assertion about them.

It is worth mentioning that ethical terms do not serve only to express feeling. They are calculated also to arouse feeling, and so to stimulate action. Indeed some of them are used in such a way as to give the sentences in which they occur the effect of commands. Thus, the sentence "It is your duty to tell the truth" may be regarded both as the expression of a certain sort of ethical feeling about truthfulness and as the expression of the command "Tell the truth." The sentence "You ought to tell the truth" also involves the command "Tell the truth," but here the tone of the command is less emphatic. In the sentence "It is good to tell the truth" the command has become little more than a suggestion. And thus the "meaning" of the word "good," in its ethical usage, is differentiated from that of the word "duty" or the word "ought." In fact we may define the meaning of the various ethical words in terms both of the different feelings they are ordinarily taken to express, and also the different responses which they are calculated to provoke.

We can now see why it is impossible to find a criterion for determining the validity of ethical judgements. It is not because they have an "absolute" validity which is mysteriously independent of ordinary sense-experience, but because they have no objective validity whatsoever. If a sentence makes no statement at all, there is obviously no sense in asking whether what it says is true or false. And we have seen that sentences which simply express moral judgements do not say anything. They are pure expressions of feeling and as such do not come under the category of truth and falsehood. They are unverifiable for the same reason as a cry of pain or a word of command is unverifiable—because they do not express genuine propositions.

Thus, although our theory of ethics might fairly be said to be radically subjectivist, it differs in a very important respect from the orthodox subjectivist theory. For the orthodox subjectivist does not deny, as we do, that the sentences of a moralizer express genuine propositions. All he denies is that they express propositions of a unique non-empirical character. His own view is that they express propositions about the speaker's feelings. If this were so, ethical judgements clearly would be capable of being true or false. They would be true if the speaker had the relevant feelings, and false if he had not. And this is a matter which is, in principle, empirically verifiable. Furthermore they could be significantly contradicted. For if I say, "Tolerance is a virtue," and someone answers, "You don't approve of it," he would, on the ordinary subjectivist theory, be contradicting me. On our theory, he would not be contradicting me, because, in saying that tolerance was a virtue, I should not be making any statement about my own feelings or about anything else. I should simply be evincing my feelings, which is not at all the same thing as saying that I have them.

The distinction between the expression of feeling and the assertion of feeling is complicated by the fact that the assertion that one has a certain feeling often accompanies the expression of that feeling, and is then, indeed, a factor in the expression of that feeling. Thus I may simultaneously express boredom and say that I am bored, and in that case my utterance of the words, "I am bored," is one of the circumstances which make it true to say that I am expressing or evincing boredom. But I can express boredom without actually saying that I am bored. I can express it by my tone and gestures, while making a statement about something wholly unconnected with it, or by an ejaculation, or without uttering any words at all. So that even if the assertion that one has a certain feeling always involves the expression of that feeling, the expression of a feeling assuredly does not always involve the assertion that one has it. And this is the important point to grasp in considering the distinction between our theory and the ordinary subjectivist theory. For whereas the subjectivist holds that ethical statements actually assert the existence of certain feelings, we hold that ethical statements are expressions and excitants of feeling which do not necessarily involve any assertions.

We have already remarked that the main objection to the ordinary subjectivist theory is that the validity of ethical judgements is not determined by the nature of their author's feelings. And this is an objection which our theory escapes. For it does not imply that the existence of any feelings is a necessary and sufficient condition of the validity of an ethical judgement. It implies, on the contrary, that ethical judgements have no validity.

There is, however, a celebrated argument against subjectivist theories which our theory does not escape. It has been pointed out by Moore that if ethical statements were simply statements about the speaker's feelings, it would be impossible to argue about questions of value. To take a typical example: if a man said that thrift was a virtue, and another replied that it was a vice, they would not, on this theory, be disputing with one another. One would be saying that he approved of thrift, and the other that *he* didn't; and there is no reason why both these statements should not be true. Now Moore held it to be obvious that we do dispute about questions of value, and accordingly concluded that the particular form of subjectivism which he was discussing was false.

It is plain that the conclusion that it is impossible to dispute about questions of value follows from our theory also. For as we hold that such sentences as "Thrift is a virtue" and "Thrift is a vice" do not express propositions at all, we clearly cannot hold that they express incompatible propositions. We must therefore admit that if Moore's argument really refutes the ordinary subjectivist theory, it also refutes ours. But, in fact, we deny that it does refute even the ordinary subjectivist theory. For we hold that one really never does dispute about questions of value.

This may seem, at first sight, to be a very paradoxical assertion. For we certainly do engage in disputes which are ordinarily regarded as disputes about questions

of value. But, in all such cases, we find, if we consider the matter closely, that the dispute is not really about a question of value, but about a question of fact. When someone disagrees with us about the moral value of a certain action or type of action, we do admittedly resort to argument in order to win him over to our way of thinking. But we do not attempt to show by our arguments that he has the "wrong" ethical feeling towards a situation whose nature he has correctly apprehended. What we attempt to show is that he is mistaken about the facts of the case. We argue that he has misconceived the agent's motive: or that he has misjudged the effects of the action, or its probable effects in view of the agent's knowledge; or that he has failed to take into account the special circumstances in which the agent was placed. Or else we employ more general arguments about the effects which actions of a certain type tend to produce, or the qualities which are usually manifested in their performance. We do this in the hope that we have only to get our opponent to agree with us about the nature of the empirical facts for him to adopt the same moral attitude towards them as we do. And as the people with whom we argue have generally received the same moral education as ourselves, and live in the same social order, our expectation is usually justified. But if our opponent happens to have undergone a different process of moral "conditioning" from ourselves, so that, even when he acknowledges all the facts, he still disagrees with us about the moral value of the actions under discussion, then we abandon the attempt to convince him by argument. We say that it is impossible to argue with him because he has a distorted or undeveloped moral sense; which signifies merely that he employs a different set of values from our own. We feel that our own system of values is superior, and therefore speak in such derogatory terms of his. But we cannot bring forward any arguments to show that our system is superior. For our judgement that it is so is itself a judgement of value, and accordingly outside the scope of argument. It is because argument fails us when we come to deal with pure questions of value, as distinct from questions of fact, that we finally resort to mere abuse.

In short, we find that argument is possible on moral questions only if some system of values is presupposed. If our opponent concurs with us in expressing moral disapproval of all actions of a given type *t*, then we may get him to condemn a particular action A, by bringing forward arguments to show that A is of type *t*. For the question whether A does or does not belong to that type is a plain question of fact. Given that a man has certain moral principles, we argue that he must, in order to be consistent, react morally to certain things in a certain way. What we do not and cannot argue about is the validity of these moral principles. We merely praise or condemn them in the light of our own feelings.

If anyone doubts the accuracy of this account of moral disputes, let him try to construct even an imaginary argument on a question of value which does not reduce itself to an argument about a question of logic or about an empirical matter of fact. I am confident that he will not succeed in producing a single example. And if that is the case, he must allow that its involving the impossibility of purely ethical arguments is not, as Moore thought, a ground of objection to our theory, but rather a point in favour of it.

Having upheld our theory against the only criticism which appeared to threaten it, we may now use it to define the nature of all ethical enquiries. We find that ethical philosophy consists simply in saying that ethical concepts are pseudo-concepts and therefore unanalysable. The further task of describing the different feelings that the different ethical terms are used to express, and the different reactions that they customarily provoke, is a task for the psychologist. There cannot be such a thing as ethical science, if by ethical science one means the elaboration of a "true" system of morals. For we have seen that, as ethical judgements are mere expressions of feeling, there can be no way of determining the validity of any ethical system, and, indeed, no sense in asking whether any such system is true. All that one may legitimately enquire in this connection is, What are the moral habits of a given person or group of people, and what causes them to have precisely those habits and feelings? And this enquiry falls wholly within the scope of the existing social sciences.

It appears, then, that ethics, as a branch of knowledge, is nothing more than a department of psychology and sociology.

EXERCISES

1. It was suggested that objectivists and nonobjectivists might use different methods in attempting to "morally educate" their children. Are there *other* important differences between the views of objectivists and nonobjectivists? That is, are there other ways in which this difference makes a difference in the way they live?

2. Are your friends moral objectivists or moral nonobjectivists? Perhaps you have discussed this question with some of your friends, and so you have a clear idea of their views. But think of a friend or two with whom you have not had such a discussion. Do you think you could *tell*—from their behavior, or their views on some other issue, or their appearance, or by the clothes they wear, or however—whether they are objectivists?

3. Find someone who disagrees with your views on capital punishment; spend a few minutes trying to convince the person to change his or her mind on this question.

    Certainly you *argued* about the issue. But were any of the arguments genuine *ethical* arguments? For example, if one of you maintained that capital punishment deters crime, and the other insisted that it does not, then you may well have been arguing; but it's an argument about sociology, and not about ethics. If you both simply insisted on the intuitively obvious correctness of your respective positions, then you certainly disagreed, but you didn't really argue about an ethical issue. Was there any point at which you actually argued about values (which Ayer insists is not possible)?

4. In the dispute between objectivists and nonobjectivists, who should have the burden of proof? The nonobjectivist, since she is denying what seems to many quite obvious? Or the objectivist, who is trying to establish the existence of moral truths, something positive? Placing the burden of proof is very important. For example, if I am charged with a crime, the *prosecution*—who is making the claim that I committed the crime—bears the burden of proving it. I don't have to prove my innocence, and that's obviously a good thing. If the burden of proof were reversed, then you could be convicted of all sorts of crimes you did not commit. Where were you on August 25, at 4 A.M., when the State Street Convenience Store was robbed? You say you were home asleep; but can you *prove* that's where you were? Can you prove you did not commit the robbery? Of course not. Fortunately, you don't have to prove you are innocent. The prosecution has the burden of proving you are guilty. So in the case of objectivism versus nonobjectivism: Who has the burden of proof?

5. Ockham's razor—the principle that the simpler explanation is better—is central to the nonobjectivists' arguments against moral objectivism. Suppose an objectivist responded that Ockham's razor is useful in science, but not in ethics. What would you think of that moral objectivist counterargument?

6. Two weeks ago, your good friend Joe spent his entire Saturday helping you move all your stuff into your new apartment. This weekend, Joe is moving into his apartment. You promised to help Joe move. Besides, even if you hadn't promised, you feel that you *ought* to help Joe; after all, he's a good and loyal friend, and he

generously helped you just a couple of weeks ago. Suppose you say: "I know I really ought to keep my promise and help Joe move; but I've got a chance to go to the beach for the weekend, and I really love the beach; so I'm afraid I'm going to skip out on Joe." That's a rotten thing to do to your friend; but still, under strong temptation we've all failed to do the right thing on one or two occasions. But suppose you said: "I know I really ought to keep my promise and help Joe; I *know* it is the right thing to do, and helping Joe would certainly be good. But I have no inclination whatsoever to help Joe. I fully understand that it's the right thing to do, and that helping Joe would be good; but although I *recognize* that helping Joe is good, I am not at all inclined to do the right thing." Would it make *sense* to say that? Suppose one of your friends said: "Look, that's nonsense. You can't say you *know* it would be good to help Joe, and then say that you have *no* inclination to help him. Either you don't *really* think that helping Joe is good, or you are confused about the meanings of the words. If you really *know* that helping Joe is the right thing to do, you must have *some* inclination to do it." Would your friend be right?

7. Whether you are an ethical *objectivist* or an ethical *nonobjectivist*, obviously you believe that the best evidence *supports* your position; otherwise you wouldn't take that position, right? But can you *imagine* evidence that would cause you to change your mind? That is, whether objectivist or nonobjectivist, can you describe *any* evidence which—*if* it existed—would be sufficient grounds for you to switch positions?

ADDITIONAL READING

A number of contemporary philosophers have argued against moral objectivity. Among the most influential are A. J. Ayer, *Language, Truth and Logic* (London: Gollancz, 1970), from which the reading was taken; Gilbert Harman, *The Nature of Morality* (Oxford: Oxford University Press, 1977); John Mackie, *Ethics: Inventing Right and Wrong* (Hammondsworth, UK: Penguin, 1977); C. L. Stevenson, *Ethics and Language* (New Haven, CT: Yale University Press, 1944); and C. L. Stevenson, *Facts and Values* (New Haven, CT: Yale University Press, 1963).

There is a very interesting debate between Richard Rorty (defending a nonobjectivist view) and Hilary Putnam (who favors a moral realist perspective); Rorty's part of the debate can be found in "Putnam and the Relativist Menace," *Journal of Philosophy*, Volume 90 (1993), 443–461. For more on Rorty's views, see the suggested readings at the end of Chapter 6. Putnam's position is elaborated in *Realism with a Human Face* (Cambridge, MA: Harvard University Press, 1990); and *The Many Faces of Realism* (LaSalle, IL: Open Court, 1987).

One of the strongest nonobjectivist writers is Herbert Feigl. See his "Validation and Vindication," in *Readings in Ethical Theory*, C. Sellars and J. Hospers, editors (New York: Appleton-Century-Crofts, 1952); "'De Principiis non Disputandum . . . ?' On the Meaning and the Limits of Justification," in *Philosophical Analysis*, Max Black, editor (Ithaca, NY: Cornell University Press, 1950).

An interesting recent version of nonobjectivism has been proposed by Simon Blackburn; see his *Spreading the Word* (Oxford: Clarendon Press, 1984), *Essays in Quasi-Realism* (New York: Oxford University Press, 1993), and *Ruling Passions* (New York: Oxford University Press, 1998).

NOTES

[1]Lowell Kleiman, "Morality as the Best Explanation," *American Philosophical Quarterly* 26 (1989), 166.

[2]Michael Ruse, *Taking Darwin Seriously* (Oxford: Basil Blackwell, 1986), p. 263.

11

Moral Realism

Moral realism is the position that there are real moral facts, objective moral truths. But exactly what such moral facts are, and how they are known, is a matter of great dispute. Traditionally, moral facts have been very special stuff, known by special faculties. For Plato, moral facts are moral ideals that exist above and beyond our natural world, and are known only through rigorous use of reason. Some have held that moral facts are established by divine will, or through special divine creation, and they are known to us by special revelation or by intuitive powers implanted by God. Kant believed that discovering objective moral truths is analogous to discovering truths of geometry.

CONTEMPORARY MORAL REALISM

The Modesty of Moral Realism

Many people claim to know objective moral facts with absolute certainty: perhaps through reason, or special intuitive powers, or by revelation from a deity. You have heard people (perhaps heard yourself) say: "Everybody knows the difference between right and wrong, I don't care who you are." Such claims usually imply that everyone knows objective moral truths, plain moral facts (though there may be disagreement about whether they are known through reason or intuition or revelation or social training). But in contemporary moral philosophy, the philosophers who march under the banner of "moral realism" mean something much more modest. In fact, many contemporary moral realists would deny that they *know* moral facts at all. However, they do insist that objective moral facts are possible, and that it may be possible to discover them. But moral realists maintain that discovering moral facts is not an easy task—they aren't known through special intuition, or by pure reflective reason. Instead, finding real moral facts (if any exist) will require diligent research, including careful inquiry into the moral lives and moral beliefs of a variety of people and cultures. Maybe such research will yield evidence of real moral facts. Maybe it will not. But we should not decide the question before we do the research. In any case, the existence of objective moral facts is a genuine possibility, which further research might indicate is a reality.

This is not your grandmother's moral realism. And it is certainly not the moral realism of Kant or Plato. First of all, it is a lot less certain of itself. Kant knows moral truths through the exercise of reason, and he has absolutely no doubts about either the existence or the absolute truth of objective moral facts. W. D. Ross intuitively knows the truth of some basic moral principles. The contemporary moral realists, in contrast, champion a more modest thesis: while we are not sure that there are objective moral facts, their existence has not been *dis*proved; and it is possible that careful research will provide reasonable and legitimate grounds for accepting the hypothesis that moral facts exist. So (the moral realists say) let's continue to study the issue with open minds, and see if ultimately the hypothesis of objective moral facts proves more useful and productive and plausible than the hypothesis that there are no such facts. That is about as mild and moderate a claim of moral realism as one can imagine. But it is also a very interesting claim, and it reveals a great deal not only about contemporary ethics but also about contemporary views of science.

Moral Realism and Empirical Research

First of all, contemporary moral realists do not suppose they can drag an objective moral fact out of the bushes, shine a bright light on it for everyone to see, and thus conclusively establish the truth of moral realism. Kant thought he could do that through the use of reason; some believe that intuitions reveal indubitable objective moral truths to those who look carefully; and others announce moral truths carved by God's own finger on tablets of stone (or even gold). But moral realists do not believe the issue will be settled that easily. Instead, contemporary moral realists hold that the existence of moral facts is a complex and challenging issue, requiring both empirical research and a clearer picture of the way facts—whether moral or scientific—are actually established.

Contemporary moral realism is a response to some of the nonobjectivist arguments considered in the previous chapter. Thus, moral realists directly challenge the key nonobjectivist arguments. And contemporary moral realists make no appeal to mysteries or miracles or intuitions, nor to any exalted powers of reason. They argue that moral realism is an empirically and scientifically plausible hypothesis that *may* well be true.

Moral Realism and the Argument from Simplicity

Central to contemporary moral realism is its answer to the *simplicity* argument for nonobjectivism (the argument that nonobjectivism is simpler and thus more scientifically satisfactory than moral objectivism; that is, the argument that the principle of Ockham's razor favors nonobjectivism). Moral realists respond that a more subtle and sophisticated view of science shows that moral realism is not refuted by such accusations of scientific inadequacy. Instead, moral realism remains a scientifically plausible contender for the most satisfactory ethical theory. The following section examines that claim: the claim that contemporary moral realism is compatible with good scientific practice, and that moral realism might prove the most scientifically adequate account of ethics and ethical behavior (or at least might be an important element of such an empirical account).

Establishing Facts

Think for a moment of Nessie, the notoriously shy "Loch Ness Monster" that Scots have been sighting and scientists seeking for many decades. Is there a small herd of fantastic sea creatures that were trapped in Loch Ness many millennia ago and have survived there while the rest of their species and close relatives died out many centuries ago? Well, not so many years ago a fisherman hauled up a very strange-looking fish from a species scientists had believed long extinct. So it's possible that some remnant of a nearly extinct species survives in Loch Ness, however implausible it might be that a sufficiently large breeding population could have survived there this long. Several scientific expeditions have thought it worth examining, and if tomorrow one of those expeditions should entrap Nessie or one of her cousins and bring her to the surface while the television cameras crowd around, then those who believe in Nessie will be proved right. Once the Loch Ness Monster is placed in front of us, and we see it, touch it, and smell it, then that settles the matter. Of course we'll have to check for forgeries. Barnum and Bailey once exhibited a unicorn in their circus, but that didn't establish the existence of unicorns. But barring fraud, this is a straightforward scientific question: Does Nessie exist? If she does, then a species scientists had once thought extinct will be moved to the endangered list, but it will not require a major shakeup of our scientific beliefs.

Not all scientific questions are that simple. Suppose that instead of Nessie, scientists discover a small community of Medusa: people with fierce snakes growing out of their scalps instead of hair. Hitherto we had thought the Medusa a character of Greek mythology, but now we find that they're real. If that happened, scientists wouldn't just add another species, grouped somewhere among the primates.

Scientists already have a niche ready for Nessie, however unlikely it is that Nessie's niche will be filled. But if a Medusa shows up, that would involve a lot more than adding a new branch to the evolutionary tree. It would mean a radical rethinking of our fundamental biological theories. In fact, biologists would spend years looking for the hoax before even considering the possibility that the Medusa is real.

Consider another example. What happens when something burns? Place yourself back in the eighteenth century, sitting comfortably in a Philadelphia tavern and sharing a glass of ale with Benjamin Franklin. Ben pokes a long thin oak splinter in the fireplace, and then lights his clay pipe with the flame. Since you are both fascinated with scientific questions, the discussion soon turns to the nature of fire. What happens when a thick oak log burns in the fireplace? No fair looking through your twenty-first-century science textbook. Look deep into the fire, observe carefully: what do you see? As the fire burns, it consumes the wood, ultimately leaving only the ash and embers. A nice spit of oak burns readily, but the heavy iron grate on which the oak rests does not flame and is not consumed by the flames, though it may glow red-hot. So, what is the scientific explanation? Well, it's fairly obvious, even after an evening sipping ale. The oak logs contain something that is burned, something that the fire consumes: phlogiston. Paper is high in phlogiston, so it burns easily and swiftly and leaves only a small residue of ash. Oak also contains a significant amount of phlogiston, so it burns well. Iron bars, by contrast, contain little or no phlogiston, so they do not burn.

That's a very nice account of burning, and it's certainly the account a good scientist like Ben Franklin would have given in the mid-eighteenth century. Phlogiston theory explains a lot, and it proved valuable for chemists studying the nature of air. Phlogiston can't just disappear when it burns, of course, so it must be absorbed into the air (you can almost see it happen as the smoke rises from the fire). If you light a candle and then place it inside a closed container, the candle soon sputters out: the air has become saturated with phlogiston, and cannot absorb any more, so burning must stop. And if we isolate a type of air in which burning occurs very rapidly and vigorously, then obviously we have found air that contains little or no phlogiston, and thus absorbs phlogiston readily and promotes rapid burning. Joseph Priestley, the great British scientist of the late eighteenth century, called it "dephlogisticated air."

But Antoine Lavoisier, a French contemporary of Priestley's, had different ideas. He called the gas oxygen, and proposed a very different account of burning: an account that turns burning into rapid oxidation, rather than loss of phlogiston. That is, something burns when it reacts rapidly with oxygen.

What will decide the issue between phlogiston and oxidation? It won't be simple; in fact, Priestley died a firm believer in phlogiston, decades after Lavoisier developed his account. The scientific debate over phlogiston and oxygen was not like the scientific discovery of a new species of beetle. Rather, it involved a radical and systematic shift in scientific theory (what Thomas Kuhn called a "paradigm shift"). The traditional phlogiston theory viewed air as a single substance, while the new theory of oxygen divided air into many distinct elements, such as oxygen, nitrogen, and hydrogen. How do we decide which theory is right? The issue won't be settled by one observation, or even one key experiment. Instead, the question is, which theory works best, which theoretical model accounts for more, which theory is less cumbersome, and which theory proves more productive.

Establishing Moral Facts

With our look at Nessie and oxygen in the background, consider now the controversy over moral facts. Opponents of moral realism maintain that we don't need special objective moral facts to account for our ethical data. Of course people feel strongly about lots of moral issues, and have strong convictions about right and wrong; but those phenomena can be explained more simply and productively through examining the cultures that shaped us, and the evolutionary process that formed us. Moral realists propose a radically different explanation, positing a different sort of fact—objective moral facts—that cannot simply be added into the opposing view. That is, objective moral facts are more like the Medusa than Nessie. Should the moral realist view be accepted, or the opposing nonrealist, nonobjectivist position?

Contemporary moral realists believe that this issue is similar to the issue that divided believers in phlogiston from proponents of the new gas theories. Resolving that conflict will require looking not just at the specific event, but at the larger question of what explanatory account ultimately works best for a wide range of questions.

Consider a prime candidate for the status of "objective moral fact." On her way to class, Rita sees a small and overly curious child fall into a flood-swollen river. She does not know the child, nor the child's mother who is screaming for help. At grave risk to her own safety, Rita plunges into the raging maelstrom and rescues the child. Her act is heroic, virtuous, morally good. And moral realists will say that the sentence "Rita performed a morally good act" states a *moral fact*. In contrast, those who deny the existence of moral facts will agree that Rita is heroic and that her heroism warms their hearts and inspires their admiration; but their warm approval of Rita's act notwithstanding, they will deny that it constitutes an objective moral fact. It is simpler (they will say) to explain Rita's act, and our deep approval of her act, in terms of social conditioning and other facts of psychology, biology, and sociology. We don't really require a special category of "moral facts" to make sense of her heroic act, and adding the special category of moral facts makes for a more cumbersome and less economical explanatory scheme. Both the moral realist and her opponent observe the same phenomenon (the heroic rescue), but one observes oxygen while the other sees dephlogisticated air.

MORAL FACTS AND SCIENTIFIC REVOLUTIONS

So what is the *truth* about moral objectivity? Are there real moral facts, or not? According to contemporary moral realists, that is not a simple question, and the verdict isn't in. The verdict will be delivered analogously to the way we get the verdict on the truth of new scientific theories. What happens when a radically new theory is proposed: a theory like the gas theory, which ultimately triumphed over phlogiston? Or Newton's theory, which revolutionized physics? Or Copernicus's theory (the Earth travels around the Sun), which overturned the Ptolemaic theory (the Earth is stationary, and the Sun and all the other planets orbit the Earth)?

Kuhn on the History of Science

Thomas Kuhn, in *The Structure of Scientific Revolutions*, argued that we have a false image of the progress of science. We tend to think that when a new scientific theory is proposed, a crucial experiment is devised to determine whether the old or the new theory is correct, the experiment is carried out, and the old theory survives the challenge or the new theory is proved true. But Kuhn notes that actual scientific practice is not always so neat and clean. Sometimes a new theory does something so impressive that it quickly wins many followers: Halley's prediction of the return of the comet, using Newtonian theory, is a good example of a very impressive scientific prediction. But in that case, most scientists had already adopted Newton's theory years before the comet was sighted, and the failure of the comet to appear would not have caused them to reject Newtonian physics.

Think of the long battle between the Copernicans and followers of Ptolemy. Who is right? Place yourself in the middle of the sixteenth century: you know nothing about gravity, there are no telescopes, there are certainly no space stations. Copernicus proposes a new theory that challenges the longstanding Ptolemaic system. Who is right? How would you decide? Is there some experiment you could do (using only sixteenth-century materials and sixteenth-century science) to decide which theory is true?

Not easy, is it? Well, think about what the two theories claim. Ptolemy claims the Earth is the fixed center of the universe, and everything revolves around it. Copernicus, on the other hand, says the Earth is traveling at a high speed, fast enough to make a complete orbit of the Sun every 365 days: quite a trip. How do we—living in the sixteenth century—decide? Someone devised a brilliant experiment. Suppose that today is the first day of November. According to the Ptolemaic theory, next May the Earth will be exactly where it is right now. But the Copernican theory says that six months from now we'll be a long way from here, all the way over on the other side of the Sun. Suppose Copernicus is right. We make a star sighting tonight, and measure the precise angle between two stars. When we make the same measurement six months from now, the angle should be somewhat different; after all, we are taking measurements from very different locations (on opposite sides of the Sun). The difference between the two angles is called the stellar parallax. The Copernican theory says there should be one; the Ptolemaic theory predicts there will not be one (because the Earth has not moved).

Back in the late 1500s the astronomers got out their instruments, made meticulous observations, and then repeated the process six months later. And they found: no stellar parallax. The crucial experiment was finished. Copernicus lost, the Ptolemaic theory is true. So scientists rejected the Copernican theory, and the Ptolemaic theory triumphed. But of course that wasn't what happened. Many scientists continued to believe in the Copernican theory, even after the crucial stellar parallax experiment seemed to prove the Ptolemaic theory true. Instead of rejecting the Copernican theory, they looked for reasons to explain why the stellar parallax didn't show up. Maybe the measurements weren't accurate. Or maybe the distance to the stars is so enormous (when compared to the distance that the Earth travels around the Sun) that the angle of the stellar parallax is too small to detect with our measuring instruments. (That was the problem. We eventually did develop instruments that could detect the stellar parallax, but centuries later).

So—as Thomas Kuhn notes—the Copernican theory triumphed, despite the fact that a "crucial experiment" went against it. What actually happens, then, when a scientific theory is accepted? It's not a matter of this or that "crucial experiment" (although experiments obviously have great influence). Rather, the scientific community studies the evidence, conducts experiments, debates the competing theories, and revises and amends the competing theories ("The Earth travels around the Sun, *and* the distance between the Sun and the other stars is much greater than we had previously thought"). Eventually, out of this debate there emerges a scientific consensus. Usually the dissenters aren't really converted (the dedicated Ptolemaic theorists don't become Copernicans); instead, the defenders of the losing theory gradually die out, and the winning theory gains the allegiance of future generations of scientists.

Moral Realism and Theoretical Revolution

A similar situation exists in ethics, according to the moral realists. Moral realism is one of the competing theories. There's no "crucial experiment" that will establish either the truth or falsity of moral realism. The question is whether moral realism works better, proves itself more valuable, and whether a consensus forms around our moral judgments in such a way that moral realism emerges as the most plausible explanation. After all, that would be the best evidence we could have for moral realism: we reach some consensus in our moral judgments—we reach general agreement on at least some basic set of moral judgments. If there is such agreement, then the most plausible and productive theory to account for that agreement is that there are *real moral facts* to agree upon.

Two Ways that Moral Realism Might Fail

One: A Better Theory

There are two ways moral realism can fail. First, we might reach some general agreement concerning ethical principles, but some other theory might prove more useful in explaining that agreement: the agreement is not the result of common perception of moral facts, but instead results from a widespread delusion or large-scale social conditioning or a common biological heritage. But we can't know that in advance, so moral realism—at least for the present—remains a viable and plausible ethical theory. It can't be ruled out in advance by skeptical philosophers. Moral realism must have a fair chance to compete.

Two: No Moral Consensus

The second way that moral realism could fail is if there is no general agreement on moral principles. After all, it is precisely that general agreement that the theory of moral realism is designed to explain. (Some moral realists would argue that moral realism is the best explanation for *other* moral phenomena as well, so even without moral consensus moral realism might serve a legitimate explanatory function.) Moral realism is proposed as the most plausible and productive account of moral consensus. But if there is no moral consensus, then there is nothing for moral realism to explain. That being the case, it might appear that moral realism is a nonstarter. After all, isn't it obvious that there is no general moral agreement? (The raging controversies over abortion and capital punishment should swiftly dispel any belief in general moral agreement.)

But the moral realist believes that beneath this troubled and controversial surface, we may find a deep calm of moral consensus. That moral consensus won't be found in the loud confrontations between pro-life and pro-choice demonstrators, nor will it be found in heated dorm room arguments fueled by too much beer and too little sleep; nor should we expect to find moral consensus among politicians jockeying for votes, or among religious zealots who claim the exclusive right to speak for God. But if we put ourselves in a position to think calmly, observe carefully and without prejudice, and consider thoughtfully, then we may find more convergence than we would have thought at first glance.

When we tone down the rhetoric, and sit down and talk calmly together (a rare event in the highly charged abortion controversy), everyone agrees that killing babies is wrong. There is disagreement, obviously, over whether a fetus is a baby; but that disagreement is important precisely because everyone *agrees* that it's wrong to kill babies. Of course there are, tragically, times and places where babies have been killed. A parent sometimes murders a child. But when that happens, we usually find that the murderer was suffering severe depression, or perhaps was unhinged by drugs, or inflamed by wild passions. It was not a case when the parent was guided by cool reason. (Of course there are also cultures in which a baby—especially a baby girl—is sometimes killed shortly after birth. Again, we think that in such circumstances the murderers are not guided by cool collected thought, but instead by religious bigotry or deep biases or cultural pressures.) And while the abortion rhetoric may suggest that pro-lifers have no respect for women's rights to control their own bodies, that again is not really the case. No one on either side believes women should be subject to rape or physical abuse. In fact, both sides agree that women have a basic moral right to control over their own bodies (though one side believes that the right to life of the "unborn baby" trumps the rights of the pregnant woman). Unfortunately, there are cultures that deny women any rights whatsoever. Moral realists believe such cultures have not looked at the question calmly and thoughtfully, but instead are swayed by religious indoctrination. So when we turn down the heat in the struggle over abortion, we find a deep cool reservoir of moral agreement beneath the hot and contentious surface.

Perhaps when we put aside religious fervor, cultural biases, and heated rhetoric, and instead consider calmly and reflectively, then we shall find that there is a substantial area of moral consensus. Or perhaps not. But—so the moral realist insists—the jury is still out. And so the possibility that objective *moral facts* are the best and most plausible explanation remains a legitimate hypothesis, worthy of continued investigation. Contemporary moral realists do not claim certain knowledge of absolute moral truths. Like nonobjectivists, they agree that absolute moral principles are not discoverable through pure reason or God's will or deep emotions. But they insist that the question of objective moral facts remains to be resolved. Maybe such moral facts don't exist. But just because they aren't absolutes dictated by God or pure reason, we shouldn't conclude that the issue is settled.

ᐅᐊ REALISM ᐅᐊ

Michael Smith

Michael Smith, who wrote the essay from which the following passage is excerpted, is a leading contemporary advocate of moral realism. He is the McCosh Professor of Philosophy at Princeton.

Imagine that you are giving the baby a bath. As you do, it begins to scream uncontrollably. Nothing you do seems to help. As you watch it scream, you are overcome with a desire to drown the baby in the bathwater. Certainly you may now be *motivated* to drown the baby. (You may even actually drown it.) But does the mere fact that you have this desire, and are thus motivated, mean that you have a *reason* to drown the baby?

One commonsensical answer is that, since the desire is not *worth* satisfying, it does not provide you with such a reason; that, in this case, you are motivated to do something you have *no* reason to do. However, the standard picture seems utterly unable to accept this answer. After all, your desire to drown the baby need be based on no false belief. As such, it is entirely beyond rational criticism—or so that standard picture tells us.

The problem, here, is that the standard picture gives no special privilege to what we would want if we were 'cool, calm and collected' (to use a flippant phrase). Yet we seem ordinarily to think that not being cool, calm and collected may lead to all sorts of irrational emotional outbursts. Having those desires that we would have if we were cool, calm and collected thus seems to be an independent rational ideal. When cool, calm and collected, you would wish for the baby not to be drowned, no matter how much it screams, and no matter how overcome you may be, in your uncool, uncalm and uncollected state, with a desire to drown it. This is why you have no reason to drown the baby.

Perhaps we have already said enough to reconcile the objectivity of moral judgement with its practicality. Judgements of right and wrong are judgements about what we have reason to do and reason not to do. But what sort of fact is a fact about what we have reason to do? The preceding discussion suggests an answer. It suggests that facts about what we have reason to do are not facts about what we *do* desire, as the standard picture would have it, but are rather facts about what we *would* desire if we were in certain idealized conditions of reflection; if, say, we were well-informed, cool, calm and collected. According to this account then, I have a reason to give to famine relief in my particular circumstances just in case, if I were in such idealized conditions of reflection, I would desire that, even when in my particular circumstances, I give to famine relief. And this sort of fact may certainly be the object of a belief.

Moreover, this account of what it is to have a reason makes it plain why the standard picture of human psychology is wrong to insist that beliefs and desires are altogether distinct; why, on the contrary, having certain beliefs, beliefs about that we have reason to do, does make it rational for us to have certain desires, desires to do what we believe we have reason to do.

In order to see this, suppose I believe that I would desire to give to famine belief if I were cool, calm and collected—i.e. more colloquially, I believe I have a reason to give to famine relief—but, being uncool, uncalm and uncollected, I don't desire to give to famine relief. Am I rationally criticizable for not having the desire? I surely am. After all, from my own point of view my beliefs and desires form a more coherent, and thus a rationally preferable, package if I do in fact desire to do what I believe I would desire to do if I were cool, calm and collected. This is because, since it is an independent rational ideal to have the desires I would have if I were cool, calm and collected, so, from my own point of view, if I believe that I would have a certain desire under such conditions and yet fail to have it, then my beliefs and desires fail to meet this ideal. To believe that I would desire to give to famine relief if I were cool, calm and collected, and yet to fail to desire to give to famine relief, is thus to manifest a commonly recognizable species of rational failure.

If this is right, then it follows that, contrary to the standard picture of human psychology, there is in fact no problem at all in supposing that I may have genuine *beliefs* about what I have reason to do, where having those beliefs makes it rational for me to have the corresponding *desires*. And if there is no problem at all in supposing that this may be so, then there is no problem in reconciling the practicality of moral judgement with the claim that moral judgements express our beliefs about the reasons we have.

However, this doesn't yet suffice to solve the problem facing the moral realist. For moral judgements aren't *just* judgements about the reasons we have. They are judgements about the reasons we have *where those reasons are supposed to be determined entirely by our circumstances*. As I put it earlier, people in the same circumstances face the same moral choice: if they did the same action then either they both acted rightly (they both did what they had reason to do) or they both acted wrongly (they both did what they had reason not to do). Does the account of what it is to have a reason just given entail that this is so?

Suppose our circumstances are identical, and let's ask whether it is right for each of us to give to famine relief: that is, whether we each have a reason to do so. According to the account on offer it is right that I give to famine relief just in case I have a reason to give to famine relief, and I have such a reason just in case, if I were in idealized conditions of reflection—well-informed, cool, calm and collected—I would desire to give to famine relief. And the same is true of you. If our circumstances are the same then, supposedly, we should both have such a reason or both lack such a reason. But do we?

The question is whether, if we were well-informed, cool, calm and collected we would tend to *converge* in the desires we have. Would we converge or would there always be the possibility of some non-rationally-explicable difference in our desires *even under such conditions*? The standard picture of human psychology now returns to centre-stage. For it tells us that there is *always* the possibility of some non-rationally-explicable difference in our desires even under such idealized conditions of reflection. This is the residue of the standard picture's conception of desire as a psychological state that is beyond rational criticism.

If this is right then the moral realist's attempt to combine the objectivity and the practicality of moral judgement must be deemed a failure. We are forced to accept that there is a *fundamental relativity* in the reasons we have. What we have reason to do is relative to what we would desire under certain idealized conditions of reflection, and this may differ from person to person. It is not wholly determined by our circumstances, as moral facts are supposed to be.

Many philosophers accept the standard picture's pronouncement on this point. But accepting there is such a fundamental relativity in our reasons seems altogether premature to me. It puts the cart before the horse. For surely moral practice is itself the forum in which we will *discover* whether there is a fundamental relativity in our reasons.

After all, in moral practice we attempt to change people's moral beliefs by engaging them in rational argument: i.e. by getting their beliefs to approximate those they would have under more idealized conditions of reflection. And sometimes we succeed. When we succeed, other things being equal, we succeed in changing their desires. But if we accept that there is a fundamental relativity in our reasons then we can say, in advance, that this procedure will never result in a massive *convergence* in moral beliefs; for we know in advance that there will never be a convergence in the desires we have under such idealized conditions of reflection. Or rather, and more accurately, if there is a fundamental relativity in our reasons then it follows that any convergence we find in our moral beliefs, and thus in our desires, must be entirely contingent. It could in no way be explained by, or suggestive of, the fact that the desires that emerge have some *privileged* rational status.

My question is: 'Why accept this?' Why not think, instead, that if such a convergence emerged in moral practice then that would itself suggest that these particular moral beliefs, and the corresponding desires, *do* enjoy a privileged rational status? After all, something like such a convergence in mathematical practice lies behind our conviction that mathematical claims enjoy a privileged rational status. So why not think that a like convergence in moral practice would show that moral judgements enjoy the same privileged rational status? At this point, the standard picture's insistence that there is a fundamental relativity in our reasons begins to sound all too much like a hollow dogma.

The kind of moral realism described here endorses a conception of moral facts that is a far cry from the picture presented at the outset: moral facts as queer facts about the universe whose recognition necessarily impacts upon our desires. Instead, the realist has eschewed queer facts about the universe in favour of a more 'subjectivist' conception of moral facts. This emerged in the realist's analysis of what it is to have a reason. The realist's point, however, is that such a conception of moral facts may make them subjective only in the innocuous sense that they are facts about what we would *want* under certain idealized conditions of reflection, where wants are, admittedly, a kind of psychological state enjoyed by subjects. But moral facts remain objective insofar as they are facts about what *we*, not just *you* or *I*, would want under such conditions. The existence of a moral fact—say, the rightness of giving to famine relief in certain circumstances—requires that, under idealized conditions of reflection, rational creatures would *converge* upon a desire to give to famine relief in such circumstances.

Of course, it must be agreed on all sides that moral argument has not yet produced the sort of convergence in our desires that would make the idea of a moral fact—a fact about the reasons we have entirely determined by our circumstances—look plausible. But neither has moral argument had much of a history in times in which we have been able to engage in free reflection unhampered by a false biology (the Aristotelian tradition) or a false belief in God (the Judeo-Christian tradition). It remains to be seen whether sustained moral argument can elicit the requisite convergence in our moral beliefs, and corresponding desires, to make the idea of a moral fact look plausible. The kind of moral realism described here holds out the hope that it will. Only time will tell.

EXERCISES

1. There is a major press conference at the University of Michigan. A group of distinguished researchers from psychology, sociology, philosophy, and biology have all gathered to announce an important discovery: the clear and confirmed discovery of a moral fact. Would you find that more or less plausible than the announcement by a similarly distinguished group of researchers from the physics department that they have discovered a new subatomic particle?

2. Suppose you look at the evidence presented by this distinguished group from the University of Michigan and decide their announced discovery of a moral fact is well supported, reasonable, and very plausible. You are now convinced these researchers have made the confirmed *scientific discovery* of a moral fact. Would that please you or disappoint you?

3. Many moral realists insist that the question of objective moral facts remains an open question, not yet resolved. If that is the case, how long should we wait before deciding that failure to discover an objective moral fact is strong evidence that such facts do not exist?

4. If we never reach moral consensus, might the moral realists still be able to make a case for moral realism?

5. Moral realists claim we are most likely to discover objective moral facts when we think calmly, reflectively, and carefully—and the main reason we haven't reached moral consensus is that we have not thought calmly and carefully. Could the moral realist offer any proof that calm reflection is the best approach to achieving moral consensus?

6. "Cool, calm, reflective thought may work best in scientific inquiry, but ethics is very different. My *ethical* judgments are more reliable when my *feelings* are strongest and hottest." Could the moral realist give a convincing answer to that objection?

7. Contemporary moral realism is a type of moral *objectivism*—along with Kantian and intuitionist theories. But although all three are *objectivist* views, the intuitionist and the Kantian hold very different views from the contemporary moral realist. What would you consider the most *basic* difference between the Kantian and the moral realist? Between the intuitionist and the contemporary moral realist?

8. Consider this objection to moral realism: "Moral realism claims to be a theory about *objective moral facts*; but actually, it's not an objective theory at all: It's subjective, because it depends on the beliefs and desires of people. True, moral realists talk about what *many* people believe and desire under *special* circumstances, but that's still a *subjective* account of ethics." How would the moral realist respond?

9. "Astronomers maintain that black holes exist in our galaxy. A black hole results when a massive star implodes, and all its mass is compressed into a very small volume. This produces an object so dense, and with such powerful gravitational force, that no light can escape. Therefore, you can't really 'see' a black hole; but by making careful observations of the motions of other objects in the vicinity of the black hole, we can reasonably conclude that a black hole exists: it is the *best explanation* for those motions. Likewise, you don't really 'see' a moral fact; but by observing the convergent conclusions and behavior of people who think calmly and carefully about a moral issue, we can conclude that a moral fact exists: It is the *best explanation* for that convergent movement." Is that a good analogy?

ADDITIONAL READING

Geoff Sayre-McCord, *Essays on Moral Realism* (Ithaca, NY: Cornell University Press, 1988) is a superb anthology, bringing together many of the best papers on moral realism. Another excellent anthology—which discusses moral realism and a great deal more—is *Morality, Reason and Truth: New Essays on the Foundations of Ethics*, David Copp and David Zimmerman, editors (Totowa, NJ: Rowman & Allanheld, 1984).

One of the best and clearest accounts of moral realism is a paper by Peter Railton: *The Philosophical Review*, Volume 95 (1986), 163–207. Many of Peter Railton's major papers are collected in his *Facts, Values and Norms: Essays Toward a Morality of Consequence* (Cambridge, MA: Cambridge University Press, 2003). An excellent book-length study of moral realism is David O. Brink's *Moral Realism and the Foundations of Ethics* (Cambridge, MA: Cambridge University Press, 1989). A somewhat different and more traditional perspective on moral realism is championed by Russ Shafer-Landau in *Moral Realism: A Defence* (Oxford: Oxford University Press, 2003).

12

The Scope of Morality

Who counts morally? If a moral code orders "Thou shalt not kill," who is included in the scope of the commandment? That actually involves two questions. First, who is expected to *follow* the order? Second, who is *protected* by the order? Or another way of phrasing those questions: First, what is the scope of moral *agency*? Who are numbered among the moral *actors*? And second, who are the legitimate *subjects* of moral consideration, those to whom moral consideration is owed? To continue with the example, consider the range of that commandment as it is given by the Hebrew God. Obviously, the commandment is to be interpreted quite narrowly, since this same God has just led the children of Israel on a campaign that destroys city after city, and all their inhabitants. So, apparently the commandment applies to the children of Israel: *they* are not to kill one another.

WHO IS DUE MORAL CONSIDERATION?

Social Contract Ethics

For social contract theorists, the answer to who counts morally seems obvious: those who count are those who enter into the contract. If you haven't agreed to the contract, then you are in a state of nature, and you are not covered by any moral rules. Those who *have* agreed to the moral rules—who have agreed to the contract—have obligations toward those who have also accepted the contract, and *no* moral obligations to those who have not. But perhaps the answer is not quite that easy. After all, social contract theorists do not believe that anyone has literally signed the contract. The contract is a myth, a story that offers a model of how morality works: we agree to act decently toward others (not rob from them or kill them) in exchange for such treatment for ourselves. So, on this more sophisticated interpretation of social contract theory, who is—and who is not—covered by the contract? Under the contract model, to qualify as part of the ethical community (and as a moral agent) one must be capable of understanding and following rules. Those who lack that capacity have no moral standing. We might decide to be nice to children, to those who have become childlike due to the infirmities of age or accident, to kittens and puppies—but we have no moral *obligations* to them. (Of course if a full member of our social contract has special interest in and affection for a child, then the other full members should refrain from harming that child. But not because the child is a holder of rights. In a similar manner, other social contractors should not damage your car; but that is because of your interest in the car, not because the car has a right not to be damaged.)

Perhaps social contract theorists can find other ways of dealing with questions regarding what falls outside the scope of the social contract; but the social contract theory itself seems to be of little help for such questions. Contract theorist John Rawls explicitly recognizes this limitation: "We should recall . . . the limits of a theory of justice. Not only are many aspects of morality left aside, but no account can be given of right conduct in regard to animals and the rest of nature."[1]

Kantian Ethics

Under the Kantian model, the requirements for admission to the moral community are even more stringent. To qualify for moral consideration you must be able to use the power of reason to derive and understand the moral law, and you must follow the law *because* you recognize it as a moral imperative (and for no other motive). If you are admitted to the world of moral lawmakers, then you merit very special treatment: you are a member of the kingdom of ends, and you must always be treated as an end, never as merely a means to someone else's ends. But the gatekeeper for this moral community allows very few to pass. And notoriously, Kant has little use for you if you aren't part of the moral community. For example, he thinks there is nothing inherently wrong with torturing dogs: they have no moral standing, and we can do with them as we wish. The only reason for refraining from such acts is that it might cause the torturer to become callous, and that might lead him or her to harm some who *are* members of the moral kingdom of ends. (Consistency would seem to require that Kant also find nothing inherently wrong with torturing small children who have not yet learned to reason, or older people whom age has robbed of the capacity for abstract reason, or the unfortunates who are incapable of such reasoning.)

Tom Regan's Kantian Account of Animal Rights

Kantian ethics appears barren ground in which to sow the idea of animal rights. However, one of the leading proponents of animal rights—Tom Regan—has developed a Kantian argument that fiercely defends the rights of a broad range of nonhuman animals. Not surprisingly, turning Kantian ethics into an animal rights doctrine requires a few modifications, and the most important modification is in who counts as "ends in themselves." For Kant, the only ends in themselves are rational beings who are capable of using reason to ascertain universal ethical principles. It is wrong to treat such rational lawgivers as merely means to someone else's ends, and it is wrong to treat anyone *else* as having inherent value. But Regan claims this sets the bar too high. Why should reason be the distinguishing mark that qualifies you as worthy of moral consideration? According to Kant, reason enables you to recognize and understand the truth of the moral law; but why should it follow that only those capable of such reasoning should be counted as ends in themselves?

The ability to reason about rules and principles is surely a useful capacity, and we are happy to have that ability. But why should anyone suppose that such abstract reasoning ability is the only thing that makes a life worthwhile or valuable in itself? Philosophers might favor abstract reason as the vital element for moral worth; but other equally legitimate candidates are the ability to feel affection, the ability to appreciate beauty, and the ability to wire a house. No doubt some degree of abstract reasoning ability is essential for formulating a system of moral law, but why should it follow that abstract reasoning ability must be the sole criterion for moral worth? Of course, if those who formalize the rules get to choose the rules, then it is not surprising that abstract reasoning ability is chosen as the standard for moral worth. But in the Kantian system, those abstract reasoners who formalize the moral law are supposed to be discovering the moral law, not drawing it up to suit themselves.

Regan proposes that in order to possess inherent worth (and be a member of the "kingdom of ends") you need only be "the subject of a life," not a rational lawmaker. That is, you must be conscious of having a life that can go better or worse. You need not be able to place it on a graph, or reflect deeply about it, or set ultimate goals, or develop rule-governed justifications of your evaluations, or even give a verbal description of the progress of your life. You must *have* a life, and have sufficient self-awareness that you can recognize when things are going well or ill.

If we adopt Regan's revision of Kantian morality, then the moral community becomes considerably more inclusive. Who has a sense of having a life that can go better or worse? Well, you do, of course. If the cafeteria hired Emeril as their head chef, your life would go considerably better. If your lover became madly attracted to your best friend, your life would go much worse. You might or might not spend a lot of time contemplating it, but you would certainly be aware of it. Who else? Obviously, there are humans of all shapes, sizes, genders, and ethnic backgrounds who also meet the standard. But not only humans. Chimpanzees are certainly the subjects of lives that can go better or worse (and in the hands of some researchers, can go considerably worse). Your dog clearly finds life much better when you return home for the summer. Pigs discover that life has taken a turn for the worse when they are squeezed into huge trucks and driven to slaughter. Your gerbils have enjoyed life more since you installed the tunnels and toys for them. And even Perky, your parakeet, is quite delighted to be sitting on your shoulder, and may show clear signs of distress when you leave for the fall semester. Obviously, almost all humans—including most of those who cannot formulate abstract rules—are the subjects of lives, in Regan's sense. So are chimpanzees, gorillas, dogs, mice, and pigs. Crabgrass, bacteria, and viruses are not.

Chimpanzees, humans, dogs, cats, pigs, cows, and laboratory mice have moral standing, according to Regan. They are subjects of lives that can go better or worse. But what animals fall within that range? Are walleye pikes included? Oysters? Spiders? Beetles? Where is the dividing line? That is a very difficult question, and philosophers, psychologists, and biologists might puzzle over it for many years (I think there is likely to be a large area of gray rather than a clear dividing line). But we need no clear line to recognize that the animals we subject to the greatest abuse—the pigs we eat and the chimps and mice we experiment on—fall on this side of the divide. (I can't set a precise moment when day turns into night. That's why we have the notion of twilight. But I know the difference between night and day.) Thus, we have a Kantian (or neo-Kantian) moral obligation to treat many animals we now treat merely as means to our experimental or culinary ends as instead ends in themselves, with their own inherent worth. And we mustn't say that while chimpanzees may have inherent worth, they don't have as *much* inherent worth as we humans do (and thus their rights are not as strong as ours). For if we take the Kantian view, this is not a matter of degree. There are no *degrees* of moral standing. You are smarter, better at abstract reasoning, better looking, warmer and kinder, more imaginative, and more industrious than I; if we are competing for a slot in medical school, you should get it. But there are no second-class members of the kingdom of ends: we are both *equally* entitled to be treated as ends, rather than merely as means to someone else's ends. You don't have greater inherent worth or stronger rights than I just because you are considerably smarter and wiser than I am. My IQ is 85, and yours is twice that; but from a Kantian perspective, you do not have twice the inherent worth I have. We both are entitled to be treated as ends, not merely as means, and we both are entitled to be treated with dignity and respect, rather than *used* as instruments.

Utilitarians and the Moral Community

Though Regan modifies Kantian ethics to encompass concern for nonhuman animals, utilitarian ethics has generally been regarded as a more congenial environment for broadened ethical consideration of other species. Utilitarians have no trouble casting a wide moral net. On the utilitarian view, the morally right act is the act that maximizes pleasure and minimizes pain for *all* who are affected. On this view, minimizing suffering is morally good, whether the suffering afflicts a human, a chimpanzee, or a dog. Even Mill—who rated human pleasures as much higher *quality*, and thus more important, than the pleasures enjoyed by other animals—had no doubt that the pleasures and pains of nonhuman animals were morally significant.

Thus, utilitarians count all suffering and all pleasure as morally significant, regardless of the species of the sufferer. Jeremy Bentham, the modern founder of utilitarian ethics, insisted that it doesn't matter how many legs an animal has. What matters is simply: can it suffer? If it can, it is due *moral* consideration. Suffering is suffering, and the goal of utilitarian ethics is to minimize suffering wherever it is found.

Contemporary utilitarian philosopher Peter Singer takes the same view, and argues that any attempt to count the pleasure and suffering of other species as of less moral significance is gross prejudice. You are considerably smarter, but when it comes to making the moral utilitarian calculation of what policy will minimize suffering and maximize pleasure, your pleasures and pains do not weigh more heavily than mine just because you're smarter, or better looking, or a better athlete. All of those things are (from the utilitarian perspective) irrelevant, since what counts is simply that we suffer or feel pleasure, not how smart or cute we are. If I agree that the policy I am proposing will cause you suffering, but claim your suffering should count for less because you are a woman, that would obviously be rank prejudice: your gender is irrelevant, the only question is whether you are capable of suffering. Likewise, Singer says, if you agree that your proposed policy will cause me suffering, but claim my suffering should count for less because I am not a member of your species, that is just as prejudiced and irrational a conclusion as discounting my suffering because I am of a different gender. So, utilitarianism casts a wide moral net: all who are capable of feeling pleasure or pain must be *counted* in our moral decision making.

Eastern Views

If we are looking for the most *inclusive* moral systems, we must turn to the East. Buddhist morality emphasizes the personal moral development of the individual; but this moral development process requires concern for all in the community, and for Buddhists that community embraces all living things. Perhaps the strongest insistence on moral concern for all living things comes from Jainism, a philosophical system developed around 500 BCE in India by Mahavira. Jainists insist on an uncompromising reverence for all living things, including dogs, cats, pigs, and also insects. In fact, Jainists refuse to eat root crops, such as carrots, because the plant must be killed. (Though this attitude is based on moral reverence for all living things, the concern is not *exclusively* for the living things in their own right. For Jainism, the emphasis is on self-purification, and harming any living being brings harm and corruption on oneself.)

Moral Agents

Kant regards the treatment of animals as morally irrelevant, since nonhuman animals have no moral standing whatsoever. Torturing a stray dog is neither moral nor immoral; rather, for Kant it is *a*moral. Some social contract theorists agree, but most other ethical views—whether neo-Kantian, utilitarian, intuitionist, or emotion-based—would consider the welfare of nonhuman animals at least morally *relevant*. Thus, many ethical views regard nonhuman animals as *subjects* of moral behavior. Could nonhuman animals also count as moral agents? That is, could nonhuman animals act morally or immorally?

If one is a pure Kantian, the answer is easy. Genuine ethical behavior must be driven entirely and exclusively by ethical principles derived from pure reason. No nonhuman animals (and probably very few human animals, for that matter) are capable of such rational devotion to duty, and thus they cannot act morally. But Kant sets very severe standards for what counts as *acting morally*. Kant's standards exclude from the realm of moral action many acts (for example, acts of kindness motivated by sympathy or affection) most of us would count as genuine moral acts. So for those who are not doctrinaire Kantians: What would you count as a moral act? Under what conditions does one qualify as a moral *agent?*

Moral Agency and Intent

"Acting morally" seems to require moral *intent;* but that leads to ambiguity and confusion. I can fully intend to do a generous act without intending to follow a moral rule of generosity. A Boy Scout may specifically intend to do a good deed daily; but you can perform a good deed, and do so *intentionally,* without planning to perform a morally good act. If you misplace your lunch pail, and it is found by a hungry person, then you have fed a hungry person; but it's not at all clear that you performed a moral act, since you didn't *intend* to feed the hungry. But if you see someone who is hungry and give that person your lunch with the purpose of relieving that person's distress, then you have *intentionally* performed a morally worthy act. If we ask you about it later, you may report that you were not intending to perform a morally good act; rather, you were just intending to relieve a hungry person's suffering. But we would still say you intentionally performed what was a morally good act, and for morally worthy reasons (you wanted to relieve suffering). In fact, some might think that one who has to think about some moral rule to "feed the hungry" is not quite as morally upright as is someone who simply strives to relieve suffering (without having to think about what *rule* that falls under). Pure Kantians would not count feeding the hungry as a moral act unless it was done purely from a sense of moral duty and moral principle, but few of us have such a narrow interpretation of moral behavior.

Almost everyone agrees that genuine moral behavior requires more than merely good results. That is a point on which Kantians, utilitarians, care theorists, and virtue ethicists concur. If you save a child from toppling over the ledge, we require further inquiry before judging the act as virtuous. If you are a clumsy would-be murderer who was attempting to shove the child off the ledge, the act was vicious. If your hand stretched out due to a sudden seizure, the motion is fortunate but not morally significant. If you were motivated solely by hope of rich reward, then the act loses its positive moral worth. So, we must look deeper than your extended hand to determine moral worth. But motives—rather than reasons—must be examined, and those motives need not stem from deliberation. If I am a vicious and mercurial but clumsy killer, my spontaneous nondeliberative attempt to shove you from a ledge is morally vicious though it accidentally saves your life. A mother's spontaneous, loving, *un*reflective rescue of her child is morally virtuous: if the act is motivated by affection[2] for the child,[3] the absence of deliberation does not imply absence of moral worth. (That is, *most* would count the mother's loving rescue as a moral act. Kant would not.)

Moral acts such as the rescue of children or friends require the right intent, the proper motive. To act morally I must genuinely *intend* to rescue the child. Giving a verbal account of that intent is a complicated process. *Having* the intent is comparatively simple.

> " . . it is safe to assume that the actions of our ancestors were guided by gratitude, obligation, retribution, and indignation long before they developed enough language capacity for moral discourse." *Frans de Waal,* Good Natured: The Origins of Right and Wrong in Humans and Other Animals (*Cambridge, MA: Harvard University Press, 1996), p. 161.*

Many animals, human and nonhuman, can form and act upon intentions they cannot conceptually order and explain. A hyena intends to feed upon an animal carcass, is threatened by a lion (a lion that intends to chase it away), and quickly revises its intentions in favor of safety. A male chimp carefully searches for heavy stones, weighs each in his hand, and selects the heaviest before carrying it some distance to his rival, where—holding the stone as a potential weapon—the chimp begins the long *intended* intimidation display.[4] A subordinate male chimp *intends* to mate with a female, sees the dominant male in the vicinity, and abruptly changes his intentions. Indeed, there are reports of chimps finding their amorous intentions thwarted by the presence of a dominant male and then *intentionally* feigning the intent to forage in another area in order to draw the desired mate out of the dominant's view.[5] Such intentional deception is not rare: a subordinate chimp amidst dominants may continue to "search" for food after he has found it, and later return alone to claim the treat.[6] (The hard-wired reaction of the robin to a dangerous intruder near its nest—the robin limps away from the nest, and since it appears to be easy prey the predator follows—may be classified as deceptive, but it is certainly not intentional deception; in contrast, the much more variable and flexible deceptive behavior of the chimp is intentional.) It is one thing to question the chimp's conceptual apparatus for distinguishing truth from deception; it is quite another—and much simpler—to conclude that the chimp intends to deceive; and it is simpler still to note that the chimp intends to find food, seek cover, threaten a rival, or rescue a friend.

Rather than verbal conceptualization being a necessary condition of specific intentions, it is probably more common for the manifestation of intentions to serve as the prompt for teaching verbal categorizations of intent. Hearing the sound of breaking glass, I rush to the dining room where my child is playing. He is sitting on the floor, next to a crumpled tablecloth that covers some strange bulges.

"What happened?"

"I don't know, Daddy; there was a crash in the kitchen."

"What's under the tablecloth?"

"Oh, nothing."

When I pick up the cloth I discover a broken lamp, and reprimand my son. "Darling, accidents happen, and I know you didn't mean to pull the tablecloth down and break the lamp. But you shouldn't have tried to deceive me."

"But I wasn't trying to deceive you, Daddy. I was just trying to keep you from finding out I had broken the lamp."

"But that's what deception *is*. When you told me the crash came from the other room and you hid the broken lamp under the tablecloth, you *were* trying to deceive me. You didn't know it was *deception*; but you were intending to mislead me, and that's what it is to intentionally deceive."

In that manner my child may learn to verbally conceptualize and describe intending to deceive. But he needs no instruction in *intending* to deceive: He is quite accomplished at such intentions long before his verbal categorizations match his devious motives.

Limits to the complex conceptualization of intentions are not confined to children and nonhumans, of course. The defendant in a breaking and entering trial may rightly insist he did not intend to commit a felony (a necessary condition for being guilty of breaking and entering); all he intended was to break the window and steal the television set.[7] The defendant may lack the conceptual sophistication to intend the commission of a felony, yet be fully capable of intending and committing one: by intentionally and knowingly stealing another's property. Likewise, a chimp that is incapable of "intending to act morally" may be quite capable of intending a rescue and thereby *intentionally* performing a morally good act.

Michael Bradie claims that "Animals can act on the basis of altruistic motives but they do not and cannot form intentions to so act."[8] But in fact animals—humans and nonhumans—can act on, and intend to act on, altruistic[9] motives as well as hunger and thirst and concupiscence motives. Other animals may not conceptualize their motives quite as elegantly: they may not know they are intending to act altruistically, just as the hapless defendant may not know he intends to commit a felony. That does not bar them from forming and acting on altruistic intentions. Of course, a chimpanzee cannot intend to perform an altruistic act purely because it is in the category "altruistic." That is, a chimp cannot resolve to "do a good (altruistic) deed daily." A chimpanzee can, however, be motivated by affection to *intend* the rescue of a friend. When a human performs such an act for identical motives, we count it as a moral act. Does simple consistency require the same categorization for chimp altruism?

Humans can, as Bradie insists, form intentions to act altruistically in the strong sense of intending to do an altruistic deed *because* it falls under the altruistic classification. Other animals cannot. But that does not preclude other animals from performing genuinely altruistic moral acts. In fact, the wonders of (uniquely human) decisions to do altruistic moral acts because they are altruistic are greatly exaggerated. Humans do occasionally form such intentions—"I will do a good altruistic deed this day"—though such elaborate moral machinations are rare and exotic exceptions among common everyday moral behavior. And except to Kantians, they are not a source of moral delight and wonderment. "Why did you rescue me?" "What a question; you're my friend; when I saw you in danger, my affection for you immediately prompted me to rush to your rescue." Compare that to: "Why did you rescue me?" "It was an act of altruism; and I always strive to do an altruistic deed daily." The latter may be a moral act, but it is not quintessentially moral, and it is certainly not moral to the exclusion of the former. Proper intent is essential for moral behavior; reasoned deliberation is not (unless you are a strict Kantian). If reasoned deliberation were essential for moral behavior, it would indeed exclude nonhumans from moral behavior, along with a substantial part of what we normally consider moral behavior by humans. The Kantian will applaud such narrowing of the moral sphere, but it is not a narrowing required by other views of ethics.

When a bonobo named Kuni saw a starling hit the glass of her enclosure at the Twycross Zoo in Great Britain, she went to comfort it. Picking up the stunned bird, Kuni gently set it on its feet. When it failed to move, she threw it a little, but the bird just fluttered. With the starling in hand, Kuni then climbed to the top of the tallest tree, wrapping her legs around the trunk so that she had both hands free to hold the bird. She carefully unfolded its wings and spread them wide, holding one wing between the fingers of each hand, before sending the bird like a little toy airplane out toward the barrier of her enclosure. But the bird fell short of freedom and landed on the bank of the moat. Kuni climbed down and stood watch over the starling for a long time, protecting it against a curious juvenile. By the end of the day, the recovered bird had flown off safely.

The way Kuni handled the bird was unlike anything she would have done to aid another ape. Instead of following some hardwired pattern of behavior, she tailored her assistance to the specific situation of an animal totally different from herself. The birds passing by her enclosure must have given her an idea of what help was needed. This kind of empathy is almost unheard of in animals since it rests on the ability to imagine the circumstances of another. Adam Smith, the pioneering economist, must have had actions like Kuni's in mind (though not performed by an ape) when, more than two centuries ago, he offered us the most enduring definition of empathy as "changing places in fancy with the sufferer." *Frans de Waal*, Our Inner *Ape (New York: Riverhead Books, 2005), p. 2.*

An Experiment in Moral Agency

Imagine you are imprisoned in a glass cubicle, that you have been deprived of food for a couple of days, and you are desperately hungry. You can see another person who is also imprisoned in another glass cubicle; but apparently you are looking through a one-way mirror, for although you can see and hear this person, he cannot see or hear you, and so you have no means of communicating with him. Finally your jailer brings you food. Indeed, a very attractive and delicious buffet is spread before you. You immediately rush to the table and begin to eat, but you are stopped by a scream coming from the other cubicle. As you started to eat, the person imprisoned in the other cubicle apparently was given a severely painful electrical shock. You take another bite, and the other person again screams in pain. You soon realize that your jailers have arranged things so that if you satisfy your hunger, the stranger in the other cubicle will suffer severe pain during the process. You don't think deeply about it, or formulate a rule, or run a utilitarian calculation; but you put down your plate, and tempting as the food is you refuse to eat more. The food remains before your hungry eyes for many hours, but you never eat. Are you acting morally?

Most of us would say you have indeed acted morally, perhaps even heroically. You did not refuse the food by accident (it wasn't as if you simply never noticed it in your cell). Rather, you purposefully refrained from eating because you did not want someone else to suffer. You didn't base your acts on Kantian reason, or utilitarian calculations, but you purposefully deprived yourself of considerable pleasure (and the relief of your own hunger pains) in order to prevent the suffering of another. And you had no ulterior motive: you weren't expecting to win a gold star for good morality, or a large monetary award from the person you saved from suffering (you don't know the other person, and have no idea whether you will ever encounter that person again). Though a pure Kantian would want to know more before deciding that you acted morally—did you refuse food strictly from duty, or did you instead merely feel sympathy for the other person?—most of us would have no trouble in swiftly concluding that your act was a positive and virtuous *moral act.*

It turns out that this experiment has been done.[10] But the persons involved were rhesus monkeys, rather than humans. And though some hungry monkeys ate the food, a significant number did not. Was the behavior of the rhesus monkeys moral? A *nonreflective human* who refused food under such circumstances—with the intention of preventing the suffering of her fellows—would be considered to have acted morally (by all except the most doctrinaire Kantians). If the cases are analogous, should we draw the same conclusion about the rhesus monkey?

Arguments against Nonhuman Moral Agency

A quick and easy answer to this argument is available: the rhesus monkeys are not humans, so their behavior cannot be moral. That is a quick and easy answer that has (as Bertrand Russell once phrased it) all the advantages of theft over honest labor. The question we are examining is whether nonhuman animals *could* behave morally. Starting with the assumption that they cannot does not take us very far in that inquiry. If we say the rhesus monkeys could *not* act morally, because they are not humans *and* only humans have souls and souls are required for moral behavior, then at least that argument does not beg the question. Still, it does not shed much light on the issue. It is notoriously difficult to get a clear notion of what a soul might be, and in any case, it is not at all clear that if humans have souls then monkeys do not. Neither is it clear why having a soul is a necessity for moral behavior. Perhaps a soul is necessary for immortality, but can only the immortals act morally?

There is another closely related argument against counting nonhuman behavior as moral. If a mother—human, chimp, or feline—caresses a distressed and crying infant, she (most commonly) *intends* to comfort it. Povinelli and Godfrey disparage such comforting as merely the mother seeking relief from the discomfort caused by the infant's crying. For example:

> Chimpanzees show patterns of behavior that appear, from a psychological perspective, only weakly altruistic. Much of what might qualify as chimpanzee altruism may be based on the arousal of feelings of emotional distress in the helper, perhaps through emotional contagion, and the role of social attribution is unclear when helping is prompted by emotional contagion.[11]

But while "feelings of distress" may certainly be aroused in the mother, it is still generally the case that the mother genuinely *intends* to relieve the infant's distress. Were her motive only the relief of her own "emotional contagion" discomfort, the purpose might be achieved more readily by moving out of earshot or tossing the infant from a high branch.

Given the ease of escape from "the emotional contagion" of distress, it is hardly plausible that "apparent altruism" is caused by the "altruistic" helper's self-interest in reducing his or her own suffering. But just as it is invoked by Povinelli and Godfrey to explain away "chimpanzee altruism," so also it has been a favorite psychological explanation for apparent acts of human altruism. Social psychologists call this the "aversive-arousal reduction" account of altruism: a sufferer arouses aversive feelings among those nearby, and in order to reduce their own aroused discomfort they attempt to aid the sufferer. Such aid is (as Batson[12] characterizes it) more "pseudoaltruistic" than genuinely altruistic, since the motive of the aid giver is relief of his or her own distress (when such reduction of aversive stimuli is most conveniently achieved by giving aid).

In a series of cleverly designed experiments, Daniel Batson has demonstrated the implausibility of the popular aversive-arousal reduction account of "altruism." Batson and other researchers have shown that the behavior *predicted* by the aversive-arousal reduction hypothesis simply does not occur. For example, if the hypothesis were correct, then when escape behavior becomes increasingly easy (escape is one way of reducing the supposed aversive arousal from another's suffering) subjects should help less and escape more. But in fact ease of escape has no influence on willingness to help another in distress.[13]

So the aversive-arousal reduction hypothesis fails to account for the altruistic behavior of animals, including human animals. But the fact that it is so readily embraced as an explanation is significant in its own right, for it reveals a good deal about some insidiously influential assumptions. Suppose I am suffering, and that my suffering makes you feel bad (through "emotional contagion"); it need not follow that your efforts to relieve my suffering are directed exclusively at the reduction of your *own* suffering. That may be one of your motives, but another motive—alongside the first, and not in conflict with the first, nor lessened nor cheapened nor "pseudofied" due to the presence of the first—may be the genuinely altruistic motive of relieving *my* suffering. Indeed, it should be rather surprising if in most instances altruistic behavior were motivated purely by either such motive, rather than a combination of the two. Why should there be such a strong temptation—among philosophers, and even among some social psychologists—to draw such a radical distinction between them? The motive of the social psychologist may be innocent enough: setting up artificial distinctions is necessary in order to test competing hypotheses. But why should philosophers assume that being motivated by "emotional contagion" *excludes* the influence of genuine altruism? Lurking in the philosophical shadows is the ghost of Kant. Only from a Kantian assumption that a genuinely moral act must be done *purely* from duty (and not at all from inclination) could it seem that a genuine act of altruistic virtue is fatally contaminated by any taint of pleasure, pain reduction, or inclination for oneself.

The Kantian view is designed to set moral behavior—particularly rule-governed, duty-driven, and human rational moral behavior—dramatically apart from the natural world. It secures for humanity a special godlike sphere *apart* from other animals. But it achieves that radical separation at a high cost. If your motive in rescuing me is purely to perform a dutiful deed, then I may be glad of being rescued, but I shall hardly regard your motives as purer or nobler or more virtuous than the motives of one who rushes to my rescue from immediate affection and heartfelt concern for my welfare, with no dutiful deliberations entering into it.

There is a competitor to the Kantian moral tradition that is more easily accommodated into the natural world and the actual behavior of humans and other animals: to be virtuous is to be moved by the right sorts of concerns, affections, and revulsions. One who takes genuine delight in the pleasures of others and feels deep sympathy with the sufferings of others is a Kantian moral cipher, but perhaps a moral hero for Aristotle or Hume. If you rescue me or feed me or house me because it would cause you great sorrow to know I am suffering, that need not be a "pseudoaltruistic" motive: you are genuinely aiming to relieve *my* suffering. Likewise, if making others happy is a source of genuine joy for you, then you are still striving to make others happy. That your activities also bring you joy does not mean you are primarily seeking your own selfish pleasure, nor does it lessen your genuine striving for the happiness of others. Playing tennis makes me happy, but I don't play tennis in order to be happy. I play tennis because I want to play tennis. If you offered me the happiness, but without the bother of playing tennis, I should think that no bargain. Likewise, a virtuous person who is made happy by bringing joy to others is acting altruistically (not pseudoaltruistically). If she were offered the experience of joy but without the bother of helping others, she would find it a poor and detestable offer. She takes great joy in helping others, but she does not help others in order to make herself joyful. (Of course, should she become depressed, and her kind acts no longer bring her any pleasure, her kind behavior might eventually extinguish; but the fact that her pleasure holds her altruistic behavior steadily in force does *not* imply that her altruism is actually *aimed* at her own pleasure.)

DARWIN AND THE MORAL STATUS OF NONHUMAN ANIMALS

Those who believe animals are moral beings, or at the very least have moral standing (are moral *subjects*), generally oppose the use of animals for research. But that is not because they are "antiresearch," or because they doubt the value of such research. Rather, it is because they believe that the treatment of animals as mere means to our ends is wrong. It would also be valuable to use *humans* any way we wish in conducting scientific research, with no concern for their safety or their interests. That would no doubt be a great benefit for scientific research, but the fact that we would regard such policies as morally loathsome does not imply an antiresearch bias.

Scientists often want to draw a strict line between human research and nonhuman research. Human research must be tightly regulated and restricted: you can't just experiment on a human because you have a special research project you want to pursue, without regard to the interests of the human research subjects, and that rule applies even if the research project is very valuable and beneficial. But such a strict line between humans (who have moral capacities and are ends in themselves) and nonhumans (who are regarded as not themselves moral beings but instead merely as things that may be treated as means to our ends) is inconsistent with contemporary evolutionary science. As Michael Ruse points out:

> Darwinism insists that features evolve gradually, and something as important as morality should have been present in our (very recent) shared ancestors. Furthermore, if morality is as important biologically to humans as is being claimed, it would be odd indeed had all traces now been eliminated from the social interactions of other high-level primates.[14]

Thus, from the perspective of contemporary science, there is no clear moral gap between humans and other species.

If ethics is essentially Kantian, then it is silly to include animals. If ethics is utilitarian, we can include animals as ethical objects, but perhaps not as ethical actors (who make careful calculations). If ethics is a natural, nontranscendent phenomenon, rooted in affections, then its roots are shared with other animals.

⚏ THE DESCENT OF MAN ⚏
Charles Darwin

Charles Darwin lived in England from 1809 to 1892. Though he is often described as having developed "the theory of evolution," in fact there were evolutionary theories (such as LaMarck's) well before Darwin's. His distinctive contribution was his "theory of natural selection," which provided a mechanistic account of how evolution proceeds. He described his theory in two great books, *The Origin of Species* and *The Descent of Man*.

CHAPTER IV. COMPARISON OF THE MENTAL POWERS OF MAN AND THE LOWER ANIMALS—CONTINUED.

I subscribe to the judgment of those writers who maintain that of all the differences between man and the lower animals, the moral sense or conscience is by far the most important. This sense, as Mackintosh remarks, "has a rightful supremacy over every other principle of human action"; it is summed up in that short but imperious word *ought*, so full of high significance. It is the most noble of all the attributes of man, leading him without a moment's hesitation to risk his life for that of a fellow-creature; or after due deliberation, impelled simply by the deep feeling of right or duty, to sacrifice it in some great cause. Immanuel Kant exclaims, "Duty! Wondrous thought, that workest neither by fond insinuation, flattery, nor by any threat, but merely by holding up thy naked law in the soul, and so extorting for thyself always reverence, if not always obedience; before whom all appetites are dumb, however secretly they rebel; whence thy original?"

This great question has been discussed by many writers of consummate ability; and my sole excuse for touching on it, is the impossibility of here passing it over; and because, as far as I know, no one has approached it exclusively from the side of natural history. The investigation possesses, also, some independent interest, as an attempt to see how far the study of the lower animals throws light on one of the highest psychical faculties of man.

The following proposition seems to me in a high degree probable—namely, that any animal what-ever, endowed with well-marked social instincts, the parental and filial affections being here included, would inevitably acquire a moral sense or conscience, as soon as its intellectual powers had become as well, or nearly as well developed, as in man. For, *firstly,* the social instincts lead an animal to take pleasure in the society of its fellows, to feel a certain amount of sympathy with them, and to perform various services for them. The services may be of a definite and evidently instinctive nature; or there may be only a wish and readiness, as with most of the higher social animals, to aid their fellows in certain general ways. But these feelings and services are by no means extended to all the individuals of the same species, only to those of the same association. *Secondly,* as soon as the mental faculties had become highly developed, images of all past actions and motives would be incessantly passing through the brain of each individual: and that feeling of dissatisfaction, or even misery, which invariably results, as we shall hereafter see, from any unsatisfied instinct, would arise, as often as it was perceived that the enduring and always present social instinct had yielded to some other instinct, at the time stronger, but neither enduring in its nature, nor leaving behind it a very vivid impression. It is clear that many instinctive desires, such as that of hunger, are in their nature of short duration; and after being satisfied, are not readily or vividly recalled. *Thirdly,* after the power of language had been acquired, and the wishes of the community could be expressed, the common opinion how each member ought to act for the public good, would naturally become in a paramount degree the guide to action. But it should be borne in mind that however great weight we may attribute to public opinion, our regard for the approbation and disapprobation of our fellows depends on sympathy, which, as we shall see, forms an essential part of the social instinct, and is indeed its foundation-stone. *Lastly,* habit in the individual would ultimately play a very important part in guiding the conduct of each member; for the social instinct, together with sympathy, is, like any other instinct, greatly strengthened by habit, and so consequently would be obedience to the wishes and judgment of the community. These several subordinate propositions must now be discussed, and some of them at considerable length.

It may be well first to premise that I do not wish to maintain that any strictly social animal, if its intellectual faculties were to become as active and as highly developed as in man, would acquire exactly the same moral sense as ours. In the same manner as various animals have some sense of beauty, though they admire widely different objects, so they might have a sense of right and wrong, though led by it to follow widely different lines of conduct. If, for instance, to take an extreme case, men were reared under precisely the same conditions as hive-bees, there can hardly be a doubt that our unmarried females would, like the worker-bees, think it a sacred duty to kill their brothers, and mothers would strive to kill their fertile daughters; and no one would think of interfering. Nevertheless, the bee, or any other social animal, would gain in our supposed case, as it appears to me, some feeling of right or wrong, or a conscience. For each individual would have an inward sense of possessing certain stronger or more enduring instincts, and others less strong or enduring; so that there would often be a struggle as to which impulse should be followed; and satisfaction, dissatisfaction, or even misery would be felt, as past impressions were compared during their incessant passage through the mind. In this case an inward monitor would tell the animal that it would have been better to have followed the one impulse rather than the other. The one course ought to have been followed, and the other ought not; the one would have been right and the other wrong; but to these terms I shall recur.

The more enduring Social Instincts conquer the less persistent Instincts.—We have not, however, as yet considered the main point, on which, from our present point of view, the whole question of the moral sense turns. Why should a man feel that he ought to obey one instinctive desire rather than another? Why is he bitterly regretful, if he has yielded to a strong sense of self-preservation, and has not risked his life to save that of a fellow-creature? or why does he regret having stolen food from hunger?

It is evident in the first place, that with mankind the instinctive impulses have different degrees of strength;

a savage will risk his own life to save that of a member of the same community, but will be wholly indifferent about a stranger: a young and timid mother urged by the maternal instinct will, without a moment's hesitation, run the greatest danger for her own infant, but not for a mere fellow-creature. Nevertheless many a civilized man, or even boy, who never before risked his life for another, but full of courage and sympathy, has disregarded the instinct of self-preservation, and plunged at once into a torrent to save a drowning man, though a stranger. In this case man is impelled by the same instinctive motive, which made the heroic little American monkey, formerly described, save his keeper, by attacking the great and dreaded baboon. Such actions as the above appear to be the simple result of the greater strength of the social or maternal instincts than that of any other instinct or motive; for they are performed too instantaneously for reflection, or for pleasure or pain to be felt at the time; though, if prevented by any cause, distress or even misery might be felt. In a timid man, on the other hand, the instinct of self-preservation might be so strong, that he would be unable to force himself to run any such risk, perhaps not even for his own child.

I am aware that some persons maintain that actions performed impulsively, as in the above cases, do not come under the dominion of the moral sense, and cannot be called moral. They confine this term to actions done deliberately, after a victory over opposing desires, or when prompted by some exalted motive. But it appears scarcely possible to draw any clear line of distinction of this kind. As far as exalted motives are concerned, many instances have been recorded of savages, destitute of any feeling of general benevolence towards mankind, and not guided by any religious motive, who have deliberately sacrificed their lives as prisoners, rather than betray their comrades; and surely their conduct ought to be considered as moral. As far as deliberation, and the victory over opposing motives are concerned, animals may be seen doubting between opposed instincts, in rescuing their offspring or comrades from danger; yet their actions, though done for the good of others, are not called moral. Moreover, anything performed very often by us, will at last be done without deliberation or hesitation, and can then hardly be distinguished from an instinct; yet surely no one will pretend that such an action ceases to be moral. On the contrary, we all feel that an act cannot be considered as perfect, or as performed in the most noble manner, unless it be done impulsively, without deliberation or effort, in the same manner as by a man in whom the requisite qualities are innate.

He who is forced to overcome his fear or want of sympathy before he acts, deserves, however, in one way higher credit than the man whose innate disposition leads him to a good act without effort. As we cannot distinguish between motives, we rank all actions of a certain class as moral, if performed by a moral being. A moral being is one who is capable of comparing his past and future actions or motives, and of approving or disapproving of them. We have no reason to suppose that any of the lower animals have this capacity; therefore, when a Newfoundland dog drags a child out of the water, or a monkey faces danger to rescue its comrade, or takes charge of an orphan monkey, we do not call its conduct moral. But in the case of man, who alone can with certainty be ranked as a moral being, actions of a certain class are called moral, whether performed deliberately, after a struggle with opposing motives, or impulsively through instinct, or from the effects of slowly-gained habit.

But to return to our more immediate subject. Although some instincts are more powerful than others, and thus lead to corresponding actions, yet it is untenable, that in man the social instincts (including the love of praise and fear of blame) possess greater strength, or have, through long habit, acquired greater strength than the instincts of self-preservation, hunger, lust, vengeance, &c. Why then does man regret, even though trying to banish such regret, that he has followed the one natural impulse rather than the other; and why does he further feel that he ought to regret his conduct? Man in this respect differs profoundly from the lower animals. Nevertheless we can, I think, see with some degree of clearness the reason of this difference.

Man, from the activity of his mental faculties, cannot avoid reflection: past impressions and images are incessantly and clearly passing through his mind. Now with those animals which live permanently in a body, the social instincts are ever present and persistent. Such animals are always ready to utter the danger-signal, to defend the community, and to give aid to their fellows in accordance with their habits; they feel at all times, without the stimulus of any special passion or desire, some degree of love and sympathy for them; they are unhappy if long separated from them, and always happy to be again in their company. So it is with ourselves. Even when we are quite alone, how often do we think with pleasure or pain of what others think of us,—of their imagined approbation or disapprobation; and this all follows from sympathy, a fundamental element of the social instincts. A man who possessed no trace of such instincts would be an unnatural monster. On the other hand, the desire to satisfy hunger, or any passion such as vengeance, is in its nature temporary, and can for a time be fully satisfied. Nor is it easy, perhaps hardly possible, to call up with complete vividness the feeling, for instance, of hunger; nor indeed, as has often been remarked, of any suffering. The instinct of self-preservation is not felt except in the presence of danger; and many a coward has thought himself brave until he has met his enemy face to face. The wish for another man's property is perhaps as persistent a desire as any that can be named; but even in this case the satisfaction of actual possession is generally a weaker feeling than the desire: many a thief, if not a habitual one, after success has wondered why he stole some article.

A man cannot prevent past impressions often repassing through his mind; he will thus be driven to make a comparison between the impressions of past hunger, vengeance satisfied, or danger shunned at other men's cost, with the almost ever-present instinct of sympathy, and with his early knowledge of what others consider as praiseworthy or blameable. This knowledge cannot be banished from his mind, and from instinctive sympathy is esteemed of great moment. He will then feel as if he had been baulked in following a present instinct or habit, and this with all animals causes dissatisfaction, or even misery.

At the moment of action, man will no doubt be apt to follow the stronger impulse; and though this may occasionally prompt him to the noblest deeds, it will more commonly lead him to gratify his own desires at the expense of other men. But after their gratification when past and weaker impressions are judged by the ever-enduring social instinct, and by his deep regard for the good opinion of his fellows, retribution will surely come. He will then feel remorse, repentance, regret, or shame; this latter feeling, however, relates almost exclusively to the judgment of others. He will consequently resolve more or less firmly to act differently for the future; and this is conscience; for conscience looks backwards, and serves as a guide for the future.

The nature and strength of the feelings which we call regret, shame, repentance or remorse, depend apparently not only on the strength of the violated instinct, but partly on the strength of the temptation, and often still more on the judgment of our fellows. How far each man values the appreciation of others, depends on the strength of his innate or acquired feeling of sympathy; and on his own capacity for reasoning out the remote consequences of his acts. Another element is most important, although not necessary, the

reverence or fear of the Gods, or Spirits believed in by each man: and this applies especially in cases of remorse. Several critics have objected that though some slight regret or repentance may be explained by the view advocated in this chapter, it is impossible thus to account for the soul-shaking feeling of remorse. But I can see little force in this objection. My critics do not define what they mean by remorse, and I can find no definition implying more than an overwhelming sense of repentance. Remorse seems to bear the same relation to repentance, as rage does to anger, or agony to pain. It is far from strange that an instinct so strong and so generally admired, as maternal love, should, if disobeyed, lead to the deepest misery, as soon as the impression of the past cause of disobedience is weakened. Even when an action is opposed to no special instinct, merely to know that our friends and equals despise us for it is enough to cause great misery.

Man prompted by his conscience, will through long habit acquire such perfect self-command, that his desires and passions will at last yield instantly and without a struggle to his social sympathies and instincts, including his feeling for the judgment of his fellows. The still hungry, or the still revengeful man will not think of stealing food, or of wreaking his vengeance. It is possible, or as we shall hereafter see, even probable, that the habit of self-command may, like other habits, be inherited. Thus at last man comes to feel, through acquired and perhaps inherited habit, that it is best for him to obey his more persistent impulses. The imperious word *ought* seems merely to imply the consciousness of the existence of a rule of conduct, however it may have originated. Formerly it must have been often vehemently urged that an insulted gentleman *ought* to fight a duel. We even say that a pointer *ought* to point, and a retriever to retrieve game. If they fail to do so, they fail in their duty and act wrongly.

If any desire or instinct leading to an action opposed to the good of others still appears, when recalled to mind, as strong as, or stronger than, the social instinct, a man will feel no keen regret at having followed it; but he will be conscious that if his conduct were known to his fellows, it would meet with their disapprobation; and few are so destitute of sympathy as not to feel discomfort when this is realised.

Finally the social instincts, which no doubt were acquired by man as by the lower animals for the good of the community, will from the first have given to him some wish to aid his fellows, some feeling of sympathy, and have compelled him to regard their approbation and disapprobation. Such impulses will have served him at a very early period as a rude rule of right and wrong. But as man gradually advanced in intellectual power, and was enabled to trace the more remote consequences of his actions; as he acquired sufficient knowledge to reject baneful customs and superstitions; as he regarded more and more, not only the welfare, but the happiness of his fellow-men; as from habit, following on beneficial experience, instruction and example, his sympathies became more tender and widely diffused, extending to men of all races, to the imbecile, maimed, and other useless members of society, and finally to the lower animals,—so would the standard of his morality rise higher and higher. And it is admitted by moralists of the derivative school and by some intuitionists, that the standard of morality has risen since an early period in the history of man.

As a struggle may sometimes be seen going on between the various instincts of the lower animals, it is not surprising that there should be a struggle in man between his social instincts, with their derived virtues, and his lower, though momentarily stronger impulses or desires. This, as Mr. Galton has remarked, is all the less surprising, as man has emerged from a state of barbarism within a comparatively recent period. After having yielded to some temptation we feel a sense of dissatisfaction, shame, repentance, or remorse, analogous to the feelings caused by other powerful instincts or desires, when left unsatisfied or baulked. We compare the weakened impression of a past temptation with the ever present social instincts, or with habits, gained in early youth and strengthened during our whole lives, until they have become almost as strong as instincts. If with the temptation still before us we do not yield, it is because either the social instinct or some custom is at the moment predominant, or because we have learnt that it will appear to us hereafter the stronger, when compared with the weakened impression of the temptation, and we realise that its violation would cause us suffering. Looking to future generations, there is no cause to fear that the social instincts will grow weaker, and we may expect that virtuous habits will grow stronger, becoming perhaps fixed by inheritance. In this case the struggle between our higher and lower impulses will be less severe, and virtue will be triumphant.

There can be no doubt that the difference between the mind of the lowest man and that of the highest animal is immense. An anthropomorphous ape, if he could take a dispassionate view of his own case, would admit that though he could form an artful plan to plunder a garden—though he could use stones for fighting or for breaking open nuts, yet that the thought of fashioning a stone into a tool was quite beyond his scope. Still less, as he would admit, could he follow out a train of metaphysical reasoning, or solve a mathematical problem, or reflect on God, or admire a grand natural scene. Some apes, however, would probably declare that they could and did admire the beauty of the coloured skin and fur of their partners in marriage. They would admit, that though they could make other apes understand by cries some of their perceptions and simpler wants, the notion of expressing definite ideas by definite sounds had never crossed their minds. They might insist that they were ready to aid their fellow-apes of the same troop in many ways, to risk their lives for them, and to take charge of their orphans; but they would be forced to acknowledge that disinterested love for all living creatures, the most noble attribute of man, was quite beyond their comprehension.

Nevertheless the difference in mind between man and the higher animals, great as it is, certainly is one of degree and not of kind. We have seen that the senses and intuitions, the various emotions and faculties, such as love, memory, attention, curiosity, imitation, reason, &c., of which man boasts, may be found in an incipient, or even sometimes in a well-developed condition, in the lower animals. They are also capable of some inherited improvement, as we see in the domestic dog compared with the wolf or jackal. If it could be proved that certain high mental powers, such as the formation of general concepts, self-consciousness, &c., were absolutely peculiar to man, which seems extremely doubtful, it is not improbable that these qualities are merely the incidental results of other highly-advanced intellectual faculties; and these again mainly the result of the continued use of a perfect language. At what age does the newborn infant possess the power of abstraction, or become self-conscious, and reflect on its own existence? We cannot answer; nor can we answer in regard to the ascending organic scale. The half-art, half-instinct of language still bears the stamp of its gradual evolution. The ennobling belief in God is not universal with man; and the belief in spiritual agencies naturally follows from other mental powers. The moral sense perhaps affords the best and highest distinction between man and the lower animals; but I need say nothing on this head, as I have so lately endeavoured to show that the social instincts,—the prime principle of man's moral constitution—with the aid of active intellectual powers and the effects of habit, naturally lead to the golden rule, "As ye would that men should do to you, do ye to them likewise"; and this lies at the foundation of morality.

⊷⊷ "The Tower of Morality" from *Primates and Philosophers* ⊷⊷
Frans de Waal

Frans de Waal is an ethologist who has published a number of influential books on primate behavior and social relations. He is currently C. H. Candler Professor of Psychology at Emory University and Director of the Living Links Center at the Yerkes National Primate Center in Atlanta.

Level 1: Building Blocks

Human morality can be divided into three distinct levels, of which the first one-and-a-half seem to have obvious parallels in other primates. Since the upper levels cannot exist without the lower ones, all of human morality is continuous with primate sociality. The first level . . . is the level of moral sentiments, or the psychological "building blocks" of morality. They include empathy and reciprocity, but also retribution, conflict resolution, and a sense of fairness, all of which have been documented in other primates.

In labeling these building blocks, I prefer to employ shared language for humans and apes. . . . If two closely related species act similarly the logical default assumption is that the underlying psychology is similar, too. This holds true regardless of whether we are talking about emotions or cognition, two domains often presented as antithetical even though they are almost impossible to disentangle. The term "anthropomorphic" is unfortunate as it slaps a disapproving label onto shared language. From an evolutionary perspective, we really have no choice other than to use shared language for similar behavioral phenomena in humans and apes. Most likely, they are *homologous*, that is, derived from shared ancestry. The alternative is to classify similar behavior as *analogous*, that is, independently derived. I realize that social scientists comparing human and animal behavior tend to assume analogy, but with respect to closely related species this assumption strikes the biologist as utterly unparsimonious.

Occasionally, we are able to unravel the mechanisms behind behavior. The example Wright offers of reciprocity based on friendly feelings versus cognitive calculations is a case in point. Over the past twenty years, my coworkers and I have collected systematic data and conducted experiments to illuminate the mechanisms behind observed reciprocity. These mechanisms range from simple to complex. . . . Next to humans, chimpanzees appear to show the cognitively most advanced forms of reciprocity.

Level 2: Social Pressure

Whereas the first level of morality seems well developed in our close relatives, at the second level we begin to encounter major differences. This level concerns the social pressure put onto every member of the community to contribute to common goals and uphold agreed-upon social rules. Not that this level is wholly absent in other primates. Chimpanzees do seem to care about the state of affairs within their group and do seem to follow social rules. Recent experiments even indicate conformism. But in relation to morality, the most important feature is the already mentioned *community concern*, reflected in the way high-ranking females bring conflicted parties together after a fight, thus restoring the peace. Here is the original description of this mediation:

> Especially after serious conflicts between two adult males, the two opponents sometimes were brought together by an adult female. The female approached one of the males, kissed or touched him or presented towards him and then slowly walked towards the other male. If the male followed, he did so very close behind her (often inspecting her genitals) and without looking at the other male. On a few occasions the female looked behind at her follower, and sometimes returned to a male that stayed behind to pull at his arm to make him follow. When the female sat down close to the other male, both males started to groom her and they simply continued grooming after she went off. The only difference being that they groomed each other after this moment, and panted, spluttered, and smacked more frequently and loudly than before the female's departure.

Such go-between behavior has been repeatedly observed by my team in a variety of chimpanzee groups. It allows male rivals to approach each other without taking initiative, without making eye contact, and perhaps without losing face. But more importantly: a third party steps in to ameliorate relationships in which she herself is not directly involved.

Policing by high-ranking males shows the same sort of community concern. These males break up fights among others, sometimes standing between them until the conflict calms down. The evenhandedness of male chimpanzees in this role is truly remarkable, as if they place themselves above the contestants. The pacifying effect of this behavior has been documented in both captive and wild chimpanzees.

A recent study of policing in macaques has shown that the entire group benefits. In the temporary absence of the usual performers of policing, the remaining group members see their affiliative networks deteriorate and the opportunities for reciprocal exchange dwindle. It is no exaggeration to say, therefore, that in primate groups a few key players can exert extraordinary influence. The group as a whole benefits from their behavior, which enhances social cohesion and cooperation. How and why policing behavior evolved is a separate issue, but its pervasive effect on group dynamics is undeniable.

The idea that individuals can make a difference for the group has been taken a giant step further in our own species. We actively insist that each individual try to make a difference for the better. We praise deeds that contribute to the greater good and disapprove of deeds that undermine the social fabric. We approve and disapprove even if our immediate interests are not at stake. I will disapprove of individual A stealing from B not only if I am B, or if I am close to B, but even if I have nothing to do with A and B except for being part of the same community. My disapproval reflects concern about what would happen if everyone started acting like A: my long-term interests are not served by rampant stealing. This rather abstract yet still egocentric concern about the quality of life in a community is what underpins the "impartial" and "disinterested" perspective . . . which is at the root of our distinction between right and wrong.

Chimpanzees do distinguish between acceptable and unacceptable behavior, but always closely tied to immediate consequences, especially for themselves. Thus, apes and other highly social animals seem capable of developing prescriptive social rules, of which I will offer just one example:

> One balmy evening at the Arnhem Zoo, when the keeper called the chimps inside, two adolescent females refused to enter the building. The weather was superb. They had the whole island to themselves and they loved it. The rule at the zoo

was that none of the apes would get fed until all of them had moved inside. The obstinate teenagers caused a grumpy mood among the rest. When they finally did come in, several hours late, they were assigned a separate bedroom by the keeper so as to prevent reprisals. This protected them only temporarily, though. The next morning, out on the island, the entire colony vented its frustration about the delayed meal by a mass pursuit ending in a physical beating of the culprits. That evening, they were the first to come in.

However impressive such rule enforcement, our species goes considerably further in this than any other. From very young onwards we are subjected to judgments of right and wrong, which become so much part of how we see the world that all behavior shown and all behavior experienced passes through this filter. We put social thumbscrews on everyone, making sure that their behavior fits expectations. We thus build reputations in the eyes of others, who may reward us through so-called "indirect reciprocity."

Moral systems thus impose myriad constraints. Behavior that promotes a mutually satisfactory group life is generally considered "right" and behavior that undermines it "wrong." Consistent with the biological imperatives of survival and reproduction, morality strengthens a cooperative society from which everyone benefits and to which most are prepared to contribute. In this sense Rawls is on target; morality functions as a social contract.

Level 3: Judgment and Reasoning

The third level of morality goes even further, and at this point comparisons with other animals become scarce indeed. Perhaps this reflects just our current state of knowledge, but I know of no parallels in animals for moral reasoning. We, humans, follow an internal compass, judging ourselves (and others) by evaluating the intentions and beliefs that underlie our own (and their) actions. We also look for logic, such as in the above discussion in which moral inclusion based on sentience clashes with moral duties based on ancient loyalties. The desire for an internally consistent moral framework is uniquely human. We are the only ones to worry about why we think what we think. We may wonder, for example, how to reconcile our stance towards abortion with the one towards the death penalty, or under which circumstances stealing may be justifiable. All of this is far more abstract than the concrete behavioral level at which other animals seem to operate.

This is not to say that moral reasoning is totally disconnected from primate social tendencies. I assume that our internal compass is shaped by the social environment. Everyday, we notice the positive or negative reactions to our behavior, and from this experience we derive the goals of others and the needs of our community. We make these goals and needs our own, a process known as *internalization*. Moral norms and values are not argued from independently derived maxims, therefore, but born from internalized interactions with others. A human being growing up in isolation would never arrive at moral reasoning. Such a "Kaspar Hauser" would lack the experience to be sensitive to others' interests, hence lack the ability to look at the world from any perspective other than his or her own. I thus agree with Darwin . . . that social interaction must be at the root of moral reasoning.

I consider this level of morality, with its desire for consistency and "disinterestedness," and its careful weighing of what one did against what one could or should have done, uniquely human. Even though it never fully transcends primate social motives, our internal dialogue nevertheless lifts moral behavior to a level of abstraction and self-reflection unheard of before our species entered the evolutionary scene. . . .

FACES OF ALTRUISM

Finally, a few words on selfish versus altruistic motives. This seems like a straightforward distinction, but it is confused by the special way in which biologists employ these terms. First, "selfish" is often a shorthand for self-serving or self-interested. Strictly speaking, this is incorrect, as animals show a host of self-serving behaviors without the motives and intentions implied by the term "selfish." For example, to say that spiders build webs for selfish reasons is to assume that a spider, while spinning her web, realizes that she is going to catch flies. More than likely, insects are incapable of such predictions. All we can say is that spiders serve their own interests by building webs.

In the same way, the term "altruism" is defined in biology as behavior costly to the performer and beneficial to the recipient regardless of intentions or motives. A bee stinging me when I get too close to her hive is acting altruistically, since the bee will perish (cost) while protecting her hive (benefit). It is unlikely, however, that the bee knowingly sacrifices herself for the hive. The bee's motivational state is hostile rather than altruistic.

So, we need to distinguish intentional selfishness and intentional altruism from mere functional equivalents of such behavior. . . . Do animals ever intentionally help each other? Do humans?

I add the second question even if most people blindly assume an affirmative answer. We show a host of behavior, though, for which we develop justifications after the fact. It is entirely possible, in my opinion, that we reach out and touch a grieving family member or lift up a fallen elderly person in the street before we fully realize the consequences of our actions. We are excellent at providing *post hoc* explanations for altruistic impulses. We say such things as "I felt I had to do something," whereas in reality our behavior was automatic and intuitive, following the common human pattern that affect precedes cognition. Similarly, it has been argued that much of our moral decision-making is too rapid to be mediated by the cognition and self-reflection often assumed by moral philosophers.

We may therefore be less intentionally altruistic than we like to think. While we are *capable* of intentional altruism, we should be open to the possibility that much of the time we arrive at such behavior through rapid-fire psychological processes similar to those of a chimpanzee reaching out to comfort another or sharing food with a beggar. Our vaunted rationality is partly illusory.

Conversely, when considering the altruism of other primates, we need to be clear on what they are likely to know about the consequences of their behavior. For example, the fact that they usually favor kin and reciprocating individuals is hardly an argument against altruistic motives. This argument would only hold if primates consciously considered the return benefits of their behavior, but more than likely they are blind to these. They may evaluate relationships from time to time with respect to mutual benefits, but to believe that a chimpanzee helps another with the explicit purpose of getting help back in the future is to assume a planning capacity for which there is little evidence. And if future payback does not figure in their motivation, their altruism is as genuine as ours.

If one keeps separate the evolutionary and motivational levels of behavior (known in biology as "ultimate" and "proximate" causes, respectively), it is obvious that animals show altruism at the motivational level. Whether they also do so at the intentional level is harder to determine, since this would require them to know how their behavior impacts the other. . . . The evidence is limited even if not wholly absent for large-brained nonhuman mammals, such as apes, dolphins, and elephants, for which we do have accounts of what I call "targeted helping."

Early human societies must have been optimal breeding grounds for survival-of-the-kindest aimed at family and potential reciprocators. Once this sensibility had come into existence, its range expanded. At some point, sympathy for others became a goal in and of itself: the centerpiece of human morality and an essential aspect of religion. It is good to realize, though, that in stressing kindness, our moral systems are enforcing what is already part of our heritage. They are not turning human behavior around, only underlining preexisting capacities.

CONCLUSION

. . . To neglect the common ground with other primates, and to deny the evolutionary roots of human morality, would be like arriving at the top of a tower to declare that the rest of the building is irrelevant, that the precious concept of "tower" ought to be reserved for its summit. . . . Are animals moral? Let us simply conclude that they occupy several floors of the tower of morality. Rejection of even this modest proposal can only result in an impoverished view of the structure as a whole.

EXERCISES

1. As an intelligent and scientifically literate person, you recognize that the human species is very closely connected to other species. Yet you may be very skeptical of the idea that other species could be ethical actors, and perhaps even skeptical that nonhuman animals have any moral standing whatsoever. If so, what distinct step in the human evolutionary process sets humans apart in their special and unique moral status?

2. Think back to social contract ethics. Is there any plausible way for an animal rights advocate to favor some variety of social contract theory?

3. If studies showed that vegetarians are *healthier*—they live longer and suffer fewer diseases—would that provide any support for the claim that killing animals for food is morally wrong? Would it count against the claim that eating meat is *natural?*

4. The dominant Christian view is that nonhuman animals have no moral standing, and certainly do not qualify as moral agents. But there is one remarkable exception to that rule: St. Francis of Assisi. (St. Francis was such a striking exception that many in the Church campaigned—unsuccessfully—to have him declared a heretic. His views are recognized as part of orthodox Roman Catholic belief, and the Franciscan Order—which he founded—promotes his teachings.) St. Francis was well known for preaching to the birds and animals, and his views are honored in the annual blessing of the animals. One famous event in his life involves a large and ferocious wolf: a wolf that was terrorizing a small village, and had killed a number of its residents. St. Francis spoke to the wolf, the wolf repented of his sinful acts, and was buried in consecrated ground. One may have doubts about some of the details, but the point is that according to this traditional account, the wolf was certainly a moral *agent*: a moral agent who did wrong, and then reformed and lived a good moral life. So, must orthodox Catholics hold that nonhuman animals are not only moral *subjects* but can also —at least in some instances—be moral *agents*?

5. Darwin speaks highly of Kant's writings on ethics; what do you think Kant would say about Darwin's ethical views?

6. At one point de Waal states that "morality functions as a social contract." Given de Waal's views of morality (and of the moral behavior of nonhuman animals), is there some other account of morality that would be *more* congenial to de Waal's perspective?

7. Your friend Joe is a warm and friendly person who is quick to provide aid and comfort to his distressed friends. He becomes angry and resentful when treated unfairly but is well known for being a peacemaker among his friends (he prevents fights and is often successful at reconciling conflicts among his friends). Joe, however, never reflects on his ethical principles or ethical beliefs. It's not that Joe is stupid; it's just that reflective consideration of ethics is something he has never done. When Joe comforts a friend in distress, or prevents a fight, or patches up a conflict, would you count him as acting ethically? Would you count Sam—a chimpanzee who is similar to Joe in comforting friends and preventing conflicts, and who likewise never reflects on his ethical principles or beliefs—as acting ethically?

8. If we became more widely concerned with the rights of nonhuman animals, would that increase, decrease, or have no effect on our concern for humans suffering from dementia (such as from advance Alzheimer's Disease)?

ADDITIONAL READING

A number of excellent books address the implications of Darwinian evolution for ethics, and for our relation to other species. Among the best are: Jeffrie G. Murphy, *Evolution, Morality, and the Meaning of Life* (Totowa, NJ: Rowman and Littlefield, 1982); James Rachels, *Created from Animals: The Moral Implications of Darwinism* (Oxford: Oxford University Press, 1990); Michael Ruse, *Taking Darwin Seriously* (Oxford: Basil Blackwell, 1986); and Peter Singer, *The Expanding Circle* (New York: Farrar, Straus & Giroux, 1981). Good anthologies on the subject include *Evolutionary Ethics*, Matthew H. Nitecki and Doris V. Nitecki, editors (Albany, NY: SUNY Press, 1993); *Issues in Evolutionary Ethics*, Paul Thompson, editor(Albany, NY: SUNY Press, 1995); and *Evolutionary Origins of Morality*, Leonard D. Katz, editor (Thorverton, UK: Exeter Imprint Academic, 2000). Darwin's own ideas can be found in *The Origin of Species* and *The Descent of Man*, both available in many editions.

Frans de Waal has written a number of fascinating books that explore in detail the behavior of other primate species, including the possibility of moral acts by nonhuman primates; see especially his *Chimpanzee Politics* (London: Jonathan Cape, 1982); *Peacemaking Among Primates* (Cambridge, MA: Harvard University Press, 1989); *Good Natured: The Origins of Right and Wrong in Humans and Other Animals* (Cambridge, MA: Harvard University Press, 1996); and *Primates and Philosophers: How Morality Evolved* (Princeton, NJ: Princeton University Press, 2006).

E. O. Wilson is a biologist who is also a superb writer; he has written a number of important works concerning biological influences on behavior, including *Sociobiology: The New Synthesis* (Cambridge, MA: Harvard University Press, 1975); *On Human Nature* (Cambridge, MA: Harvard University Press, 1978); *Biophilia* (Cambridge, MA: Harvard University Press, 1984); and *Consilience* (New York: Alfred A. Knopf, 1998).

NOTES

[1]John Rawls, *A Theory of Justice* (Oxford University Press: Oxford, 1972), p. 512.

[2]Of course there is a "deeper" cause for such solicitude: the preservation of one's genetic legacy. But though that may be the ultimate cause, it does not alter or diminish the genuine selfless concern for the child. Genetic preservation may cause my love, but the rush to rescue is no less motivated by genuine love for the child. (Genetic preservation also fuels my sex drive, but my passion is not directed at the preservation of my genes.) Even if solicitude has its origins in "selfish genes," that does not diminish its genuine moral value. Frans de Waal offers an apt analogy:

> Even if a diamond owes its beauty to millions of years of crushing pressure, we rarely think of this fact when admiring the gem. So why should we let the ruthlessness of natural selection distract from the wonders it has produced? Humans and other animals have been endowed with a capacity for genuine love, sympathy, and care—a fact that can and will one day be fully reconciled with the idea that genetic self-promotion drives the evolutionary process. *Good Natured: The Origins of Right and Wrong in Humans and Other Animals* (Cambridge, MA: Harvard University Press, 1996), pp. 16–17

[3]A similar point is made by Lawrence Blum in his account of "direct altruism":

> The direct altruism view means to express a kind of virtue which does not depend on moral reflectiveness or self-consciousness. It depends only on being responsive to the weal and woe of others. . . . The compassionate or kind person does not necessarily or typically act in order to be virtuous. . . . He need not *aim* at being kind or compassionate. . . . What is necessary is only that he aim to meet the other's need, relieve her suffering, etc. (*Friendship, Altruism and Morality* [London: Routledge & Kegan Paul, 1980], p. 100)

[4]Frans de Waal, *Peacemaking among Primates* (Cambridge, MA: Harvard University Press, 1989), p. 39.

[5]Frans de Waal, *Chimpanzee Politics* (London: Jonathan Cape, 1982), pp. 48ff.

[6]Frans de Waal, 1982, pp. 73–74.

[7]This is an example of the confusions and complications that can grow in contexts of referential opacity; see Willard van Orman Quine, *Word & Object* (Cambridge, MA: MIT Press, 1960).

[8]Michael Bradie, *The Secret Chain: Evolution and Ethics* (Albany, NY: SUNY Press, 1994), p. 136.

[9]Lawrence Blum (1980, pp. 9–10) uses "altruism" in the sense of "a regard for the good of another person for his own sake, or conduct motivated by such a regard." As he notes, this usage does not require that altruism involve self-sacrifice.

[10]The research is described in Jules H. Masserman, Stanley Wechkin, and William Tetris, "'Altruistic' Behavior in Rhesus Monkeys," *American Journal of Psychiatry*, 121, 584–585.

[11]Daniel J. Povinelli and Laurie R. Godfrey, "The Chimpanzee's Mind: How Noble in Reason? How Absent of Ethics?" in *Evolutionary Ethics*, Matthew H. Nitecki and Doris V. Nitecki, editors (Albany, NY: SUNY Press, 1993), p. 310.

[12]C. Daniel Batson, *The Altruism Question: Toward a Social-Psychological Answer* (Hillsdale, NJ: Lawrence Erlbaum, 1991), pp. 43ff.

[13]Batson, 1991, pp. 109–127.

[14]Ruse, 1986, p. 227. Frans de Waal (1996, p. 210) makes a similar point:

> A chimpanzee stroking and patting a victim of attack or sharing her food with a hungry companion shows attitudes that are hard to distinguish from those of a person picking up a crying child, or doing volunteer work in a soup kitchen. To classify the chimpanzee's behavior as based on instinct and the person's behavior as proof of moral decency is misleading, and probably incorrect. First of all, it is uneconomic in that it assumes different processes for similar behavior in two closely related species.

13

Free Will

Questions about free will are closely linked to questions about ethics. But the nature of that link is more controversial. Is free will essential to ethics? What's the relation between free will and moral responsibility? Between moral responsibility and ethics? Before we can examine these issues we must know what free will *is*. That turns out to be a difficult and contentious question.

DETERMINISM

Questions about free will are often prompted by concerns about *determinism*. Determinism is the thesis that for absolutely every event that happens—every leaf that falls, star that explodes, word that is spoken, idea considered, and so on—there is a set of past events that caused it to happen; and given the state of the cosmos at any point in time together with the fixed laws that govern all events, everything that will follow is inevitable. An eighteenth-century French philosopher Pierre Simon de Laplace expressed the idea through the picture of "Laplace's demon": if there were some all-knowing being, who knew the exact state of the entire cosmos at any given time, and all the laws governing the cosmos, then it could predict every detail of the world at any future time. There are two special sources for belief in determinism. One is based in religion, and the other in natural science.

God and Determinism

Consider some of the major characteristics attributed to God by Jews, Christians, and Muslims. God has no limits, and is thus omnipresent. God is not merely very strong, but *all*-powerful: omnipotent. And not just bright, but *all*-knowing: omniscient. This awe-inspiring concept of God also inspires some serious questions. If God knows everything, then God knows everything I have ever done. Furthermore, God knows everything I *will* do, and has known it *forever* (an omniscient God—Who knows *everything*—obviously can't add knowledge as He goes along, because there's no additional knowledge to add). But if a thousand years ago God already knew all my thoughts, choices, and behavior, then am I really acting freely? Am I making genuine choices, or is my life just a script I am destined to follow? And if God has *all* power—not just very strong, but *omni*potent—how can I have independent power to choose and act?

Science and Determinism

So the concept of God as an all-knowing, all-powerful being was one source of determinist belief. A second source was the development of Newtonian physics. Building on the work of Copernicus, Galileo, and Kepler, Isaac Newton developed a system of mathematically precise and elegantly simple laws that explained the motion of the planets, the falling of a rock, the orbit of the Moon, and even the path of a comet. Before Newton, comets were considered strange and inexplicable, bright moving lights with long tails that disrupted the clockwork precision of the starry skies, glowing alien invaders that threatened established order. They were messages from an angry God, or perhaps harbingers of doom. But using Newtonian principles and ancient observations, Edmund Halley predicted the return of the comet that now bears his name: not only its return, but when it would appear, at what point in the sky, and what path it would follow. The British poet Alexander Pope captured the triumphant spirit:

Nature and Nature's laws lay hid in night:
God said, Let Newton be! and all was light.

In the heady excitement of Newtonian physics many wondered if similar laws might be found for other elements of our world. Newtonian physics predicted the paths of comets. Might science also discover precise laws governing the apparent spontaneity and unpredictability of human behavior? Thus, people began to consider the possibility that human behavior (and everything else in the universe) was governed by fixed laws. Those laws might be difficult to discover—after all, human behavior seems at least as complex as the orbit of a comet, and it took many years to understand that—but such explanations may at least be possible. If so, such laws govern a *determined* universe.

> It would be very singular that all nature, all the planets, should obey eternal laws, and that there should be a little animal five foot high, who, in contempt of these laws, could act as he pleases, solely according to his caprice. *Voltaire.*

Hume's Argument for Determinism

David Hume was a strong champion of determinism. Indeed, Hume maintained that determinism is the only reasonable possibility, and that we *all* believe in determinism. Suppose that just now, as you are sitting quietly in your chair contemplating the joys of philosophy, the door to your room very slowly (and rather mysteriously) creaks open. "Why did my door open?" you ask yourself. Probably you don't give it much thought, fascinated as you are by your philosophical inquiries. But concentrate on the opening door for just a moment: Why did it open? "Probably a breeze in the hall," you suggest, but the air is absolutely still. "Maybe the door is not quite level." So you get out your level and check the door—and it turns out to be dead level. "Maybe there was a very small tremor." But seismic reports show that not even the tiniest tremor was recorded. "I'll bet one of my friends is playing a trick on me; there must be some nylon filament attached to the door, and someone is pulling on it." But a careful check reveals no such trickery. The outside door is locked, and there is no one else in the house. You start to get a bit concerned. "Maybe some vile terrorist group is testing a new gamma ray machine, and they are aiming a stream of microparticles at my door." But no such particle stream can be detected. "Well, maybe my room is haunted; perhaps the ghost of some distressed student who perished trying to read philosophy has been troubled by the presence of philosophy books in my room, and opened the door to escape." Okay, I don't know why your door opened, and maybe you won't be able to discover why. But note the process you went through in trying to discover the cause. You looked at air currents, earthquakes, and uneven floors; you considered trickery and terrorist plots; and finally you were driven to a hypothesis about ghosts and goblins. But one explanation never occurred to you at all: There was *no* cause for your door opening; it just happened, with no cause whatsoever. To suppose that doors open without any cause is so alien to your thinking that you will turn instead to terrorist conspiracies and supernatural forces. The cause may be natural or supernatural, mundane or extraordinary, but there *has* to be a cause. Things don't happen without a cause.

The same thinking applies to human behavior. Your friend Nawal has a kind word and a friendly smile for everyone: the most cheerful, warm-hearted person you have ever known. You meet Nawal crossing campus, and bid her good morning. "Go to hell," she replies with a sneer. You are so surprised you drop your books and almost spill your mocha latte. A few seconds later you spot a mutual friend, and you inquire about Nawal's strange behavior: "What's bugging Nawal? She just told me to go to hell." The two of you may consider a variety of explanations for Nawal's unusual cantankerousness. Perhaps she just flunked a calculus exam, or maybe she had a fight with her boyfriend; perhaps her hard drive crashed, or she just left a long and boring philosophy lecture. If no such explanation is available, we may consider other possibilities: her brain has been invaded by space aliens, or the CIA drugged her coffee, or she suffers from demon possession. But again, no matter how far-fetched the causal hypothesis—from space aliens to demon possession—it is still more plausible than concluding that there was no cause, and she just changed from cheerful to cranky with no cause whatsoever. The moral of the story is simple. Whether we are thinking of doors opening, comets orbiting, or people cursing, we believe *everything* that happens has a cause. That is, we all believe in *determinism*. Far from being a strange and exotic doctrine, determinism is—according to Hume—the plainest common sense.

> "Men are deceived if they think themselves free, an opinion which consists only in this, that they are conscious of their actions and ignorant of the causes by which they are determined." *Benedict Spinoza,* Ethics.

Reactions to Determinism

Some see determinism as a doctrine of promise: everything that happens has a cause, and thus it is always worthwhile to examine why events occur. Wars and crime, disease and famine are not random inexplicable mysteries, but instead have definite causes that we might come to understand. By understanding them we may learn to prevent them. And acts of kindness, creations of genius, and periods of social harmony are not just matters of good luck. They are caused, and by understanding their causes we might promote them. In stark contrast, others see determinism as a doctrine of hopelessness and helplessness: determinism means that we are ridiculous puppets whose strings are pulled by forces beyond our understanding, and the *illusion* that we act freely only makes us more absurd.

The negative perspective on determinism was voiced by the American philosopher William Barrett. According to Barrett, determinism conflicts with our "desire for freshness, novelty, genuine creation—in short, an open rather than a closed universe."[1] In Barrett's view, a determined world "would stifle us with boredom."[2]

But why should determinism dictate such boredom? If my life is entirely determined, that does not imply I know the outcome. It's all new and fresh and exciting to me. In theological determinism, God is omniscient and knows everything that will happen. God knows the details of our future lives, but even then we ourselves do not. In natural determinism, every event is determined by natural laws; but obviously we do not know all those laws, and so we cannot even roughly predict the details of our future lives. Either way, the events of our lives remain new and fresh to us. Indeed, they may be new and fresh in the sense that they are original, and have never before occurred (though the conditions that brought them about were already in place).

FATALISM

So if I don't know what will happen, why should determinism frighten me? Why should it threaten me with terrible boredom? Perhaps it is not determinism that is so scary, but a doctrine often confused with determinism: fatalism. Fatalists believe that your "fate" is fixed, your destiny sealed, and struggle as you will there is nothing you can do to change it. Think of a late-night war movie, starring the tough old sergeant with a gruff voice and kind heart. The squad has wandered into an ambush, and is trapped by an enemy machine gun that blocks their advance and prevents their retreat. The sergeant grabs a grenade and prepares to charge the machine gun nest. "You can't go out there, Sarge," pleads the frightened private. "That machine gunner will cut you to ribbons." Sarge tightens his helmet, clutches the grenade, and utters the immortal late-night movie line: "Don't worry, kid. Somewhere out there, there's a bullet with my name on it. When it's my time, that bullet'll catch up with me. And it'll find me whether I'm hiding in a foxhole or charging up a hill. But when that bullet finds me, I'm gonna' be charging straight into it, not hiding in a hole." That's classic fatalism: My ultimate destiny is set, no matter what I do. The trivial details may be up to me—I can charge or cower—but I cannot escape my fate.

"Our hour is marked, and no one can claim a moment of life beyond what fate has predestined." *Napoleon Bonaparte, to Dr. Arnott, April 1821.*

For most of us fatalism prompts a feeling of resentment and helplessness. Some powerful force we cannot understand—a power that seems to delight in toying with us and thwarting our best plans—manipulates our destiny. In ancient Greek drama, Oedipus is fated to murder his father and marry his mother. Oedipus resolves to escape his fate, and so leaves his home and travels to a distant country. There is a battle in which Oedipus kills that country's king, and following local tradition is crowned king and marries the queen. But Oedipus had been adopted as an infant, an event of which he has no memory. The country to which he fled (to escape his fate) is the country of his birth. And as you probably already guessed, the king he killed was his father and the queen was his mother.

Not everyone fears fatalism. To the contrary, some find fatalism comforting. The Roman stoics told the story of a dog tied to a horse-drawn cart that is on its way to market. The dog may fight and bite and struggle and be dragged through the dust behind the cart, or it may trot quietly beside the cart and take what pleasures the day offers. In either case, the dog will arrive at its destiny. The moral is, don't struggle and worry: whatever will be, will be.

Fatalism has its charms, but it seems a very implausible doctrine. It disconnects all our efforts and acts from the system of real causes, and replaces them with a notion of God as a cosmic con man. We feel as if we are having an effect on the world, but the real strings are invisible to us, and are being pulled by a devious deity who thwarts our plans and makes our best efforts work against us. But I see no reason whatsoever to suppose that such a malevolent power exists. Of course, our best laid plans do sometimes go awry, but that sad fact does not imply some diabolical controlling force. As Shakespeare writes in *Julius Caesar:* "Men some time are masters of their fates; the fault, dear Brutus, is not in our stars but in ourselves."

One of the great philosophical poems, *The Rubaiyat of Omar Khayyam*, was written by an eleventh-century Persian poet and astronomer. It was translated (rather loosely) into English by Edward Fitzgerald. One major theme of the poem is fatalism, as indicated by the following two verses:

> Oh, Thou, who didst with pitfall and with gin
> Beset the Road I was to wander in,
>   thou wilt not with Predestined Evil round
> Enmesh, and then impute my Fall to sin!

> Oh, Thou, who Man of baser Earth didst make,
> And ev'n with Paradise devise the Snake:
>   For all the Sin the Face of wretched Man
> Is black with—Man's forgiveness give—and take!

Determinism and Fatalism

If determinism is true, then who we are, what we do, what we think, and what we become are all shaped by—determined by—past causal events in conjunction with complex causal laws. Will you ace your philosophy exam, or bomb it? Will you run a great race on Saturday, or finish far back in the pack? Will your current fling blossom into a great romance, or wither away? Will you join the Green Party? Get into medical school? Move to the coast? Every detail of your life, great and small, is completely determined by past causes. But what distinguishes determinism from fatalism is that those past causes are *not* alien forces that control you against your own will and wishes, forces that thwart your choices and frustrate your efforts. If you are *fated* to slay your father then so it shall be, no matter how hard you struggle: your struggles have nothing to do with it. But determinism is a very different matter. If it is determined that you will run a great race, then given the causes in operation, you will certainly run a great race. But it is not as if you would run a great race even if you were trying to throw the race, or if you did not train hard. For among the key causes that determine your racing success are your own hard training, your fortitude, and your racing skill. Without those key causal factors you would not run well. If determinism is true, then all those factors are determined: you are shaped by your causal history to be a skillful racer, a tireless trainer, and a tough competitor. But those are not *alien* forces that conspire to *make* you run a great race whether you wish it or not. Instead, among the key causal elements are your own efforts, desires, and skills.

DETERMINISM AND FREE WILL

Having distinguished fatalism from determinism, let's look more closely at the latter. For while there seems little reason to believe in fatalism, determinism is a much more serious question. As Hume noted, when something happens we *do* think there must have been some cause. And if we apply that idea universally, determinism is the result. If determinism is true, could we still have free will? Many have answered no. However, there are also many who deny that determinism undercuts free will. They are called *compatibilists*, because they believe free will and determinism are *compatible*; they can peacefully coexist.

Simple Compatibilism

David Hume claimed that all the puzzles and disputes about free will result from sloppy and confused use of language. If we think about it carefully, and avoid verbal entanglements, then free will is a simple and obvious matter, and "all mankind, both learned and ignorant, have always been of the same opinion"[3] about the nature and existence of free will. What does free will mean? Hume answers:

> By liberty [free will] we can only mean a power of acting or not acting according to the determinations of the will; that is, if we choose to remain at rest, we may; if we choose to move, we also may. Now this hypothetical liberty is universally allowed to belong to everyone who is not a prisoner and in chains.[4]

Free will consists in having the power to act in accordance with your own will. If you want to play the oboe, you can play the oboe; if you choose not to attend the anniversary party for Uncle Fred and Aunt Ethyl, then no one will place you in chains and drag you there against your will; if you choose to eat six chocolate chip cookies, then you eat six chocolate chip cookies.

What does it mean for a person to be free? Forget about abstract philosophical principles, and don't be misled by the confusing language philosophers use. We all know what it means to be free: when you can follow your own wishes, make your own plans, pursue your own goals, then you are free. Of course your wishes and desires were shaped by the determining factors in your past, but that doesn't make them any less your own. If you are not being coerced or restrained against your will and against your wishes, then you are free. As we noted, this view of free will is called *compatibilism*: determinism is *compatible* with free will. We'll call Hume's version *simple* compatibilism: doing what *you want* (you are not coerced) is acting freely, and that simple freedom is compatible with your desires and choices and acts being *determined*.

Consider a case of simple compatibilism. The Human Genome Project has finished mapping human genetic structure, and they have discovered a new and interesting gene: the football fan gene. It turns out that all persons who have this gene are dedicated football fans, and persons who lack the football fan gene (geneticists have labeled it the FFG) find football boring. Joline lives and dies with the Green Bay Packers, and sure enough, she tests positive for the FFG. On Sunday morning she is putting on her green and yellow earmuffs, her Packers stocking cap, her Packers mittens, and her heavy Packers coat, and loading her car with beer and a sturdy grill on the way to a tailgate party with her friends at Lambeau Field, to be followed by a football game at which she will yell herself hoarse in support of her beloved Packers. As she rushes around the house, she hums the Packer fight song, interspersed with occasional shouts of "Go to Hell, Bears." She has been looking forward to this game all week, and can hardly wait to get to the stadium. We manage to stop her just long enough to ask a question: "Are you going to the Packers game of your own free will?"

Joline thinks it's the dumbest question she's ever heard. "Of course I'm going of my own free will. Does it look like anyone is forcing me to go to the game? I go because I love football, and I love the Packers. Stop bothering me, I've got to get this bratwurst in the van."

"No, you're mistaken," we reply. "We just got the tests back, and you tested positive for the FFG. You are genetically programmed to love football. Your mom also loved football, didn't she? You probably inherited it from her. So you are going because you have the football fan gene, not because of your own free choice. You may think you are going freely, but in fact you are not."

Joline is not convinced. "Gene-shmeen. So maybe I have the FFG. Or maybe I love football because I was conditioned to love football by my mother: my first toys were a soft green and yellow football and a cuddly teddy bear wearing a Green Bay Packers jersey. Of course there must be causes for why I love football, but whatever *caused* me to love football, that doesn't change the fact that I go to football games because *I like football*. That's how *I choose* to spend my Sunday afternoons. No one forces me to go to football games, I go from my *own free choice*."

Does Joline choose and act freely when she goes to a football game? Let's up the ante. Suppose that given her exact circumstances, she *could not* do otherwise than what she does. Of course, if Joline wanted to spend her afternoon at the movies, she could do so; but given her genetic heritage, she will *not* want to miss the football game. And if there were some special circumstances—one of her friends is deathly ill, and Joline must rush her to the hospital—then Joline would respond to that emergency and skip the football game. But in the circumstances that she is actually in, and being the person she actually is, Joline will inevitably go to the football game. We could predict it with just as much certainty as we can predict the return of Halley's comet: both Joline's path to the football game and the orbit of Halley's comet are completely fixed by natural causes (the natural causes determining Joline's behavior are of course quite different from the natural causes setting the orbit of Halley's comet, but there is no difference in the determined regularity of their movements). If a medical emergency occurs, Joline's path will deviate from the football field; and if a large meteorite collides with Halley's comet, then the comet will deviate from its orbit. But given the *actual circumstances*—no meteorite, and no medical emergency—both will follow their determined natural courses. (And of course, the meteorite and medical emergency would *also* be part of the determined system.) You might wish to dispute that description of Joline's behavior. But suppose you *agree* with that completely naturalistic-deterministic account of Joline's movements. She is still moving due to her *own intentions* (and Halley's comet is not). Is she acting freely? Does she have free will? She certainly thinks she is free. Is her sense of freedom an illusion? Or is the key factor just that she acts from her own intentions (however determined those intentions may be), and so she is still free?

Joline insists that she *is* free. "It's not your genes, nor your early conditioning, nor determinism that destroys freedom. What destroys your freedom is not being allowed to do what you really want to do. I know something about that. When I was a junior in high school, my family moved for a year to a country where women were not allowed to do any athletic activity in public. I love to run, and I love competing in road races. For that whole year, I couldn't go out and run. I was miserable, and had no freedom. Fortunately, now my circumstances allow me to run, and I have good friends who encourage my running, and good safe places to run, and I am able to do what I love to do and freely choose to do. That's freedom, and the fact that you can dig out the determining causes that made me a runner in no way compromises my free will."

Many people will say that Joline has all the freedom anyone could want. She is doing what she wants to do, nobody forces her to act against her own wishes; she is following her own goals and preferences and intentions. Of course, Joline does not *choose* her own genes, nor her own early conditioning; but *those* choices are nonsense. If (before her birth, even before her conception) Joline could choose her own genetic makeup and the environment that would shape her, then *who* would be doing the choosing?

So Joline's behavior is *determined*, in every detail: her genetics and her environmental history shape the person she is. But Joline still acts *freely*, because she follows her own wishes and desires, and can successfully act as she wishes. Her wants and desires and goals are determined by past causes, but they are still her own goals and intentions, and thus she acts freely. Joline's free choices are determined, but not *fated*. Joline goes to the Packers game because that is what she wants: she can successfully pursue her own goals, without some fatalistic trickster intervening to frustrate her plans. If Joline follows her own goals and acts successfully on her own preferences, the fact that her goals and her acts are shaped and *determined* by past causes does not threaten her freedom. That is the view of David Hume and other simple compatibilists.

Deep Compatibilism

Joline goes to Packers games because she *wants* to go. But one October Monday morning, the day after a particularly painful Packer loss, we find Joline in a reflective mood. "I dearly love the Packers, and love going to games. But you know, I wish I didn't. It takes up an enormous amount of time and energy, and for every year of Super Bowl glory there's several years of bitter frustration. I really wish that I didn't care at all about football, and instead loved music. If I liked music as much as I like the Packers, I would have learned a great deal about music, and I would have become a decent musician. Perhaps I would have composed some good songs. That would be very satisfying. It would be better than spending my days waving a green and yellow banner, and I think it would have brought me greater joy. Don't get me wrong, I love cheering for the Packers. But I wish I loved the Packers a lot less and music a lot more."

If Joline loves going to Packers games, but at a deeper reflective level would prefer *not* to have that Packer passion, then is Joline's behavior *free?* A contemporary American philosopher who has worried a great deal about this question is Harry G. Frankfurt. Consider the case of a drug addict (one of Frankfurt's favorite examples). The addict takes drugs because he desires drugs. No one forces him to take drugs; rather, he takes drugs because of his own addictive desire for drugs. (Let's not get bogged down just now in questions about why he started taking drugs. To make the case easier, suppose our addict became addicted to drugs quite innocently, when someone slipped drugs into his morning oatmeal.) The addict certainly has the desire for drugs, and he acts on his own desire, and no one forces him to act on his desire. Yet few of us would call this unfortunate addict free. To the contrary, he seems to be enslaved by his addiction. His enslavement seems worse because it operates internally. It is a terrible thing to be enslaved by some tyrant who holds us in chains; but surely it is just as bad, perhaps even worse, to be enslaved by our own desires.

The drug addict pushes us to think harder about the conditions of genuine freedom. The addict acts on his desires when he consumes drugs, but it is hard to count such acts as genuinely free. Frankfurt proposes that to decide whether the addict is free, we must look deeper into his motivational structure. We might call this *deep* compatibilism, to distinguish it from Hume's *simple* compatibilism. If the addict desires drugs, but experiences that desire as alien and oppressive, then he is not really free: he does not have the will he wants to have. He certainly desires drugs, but at a deeper (or higher-order) level he does not approve of his own desire. Now imagine a very different addict: he desires drugs, and strongly approves of his addictive desire for drugs. He is, in Frankfurt's felicitous phrase, a "willing addict." He has the will he prefers to have, and he can act in accordance with desires he recognizes as his own.

This seems immediately appealing. If I am acting from a will I *approve* and acknowledge as my own, I act freely and have free will. Yet there is something disturbing about counting the willing addict as an exemplar of free will. It's easy to imagine an *unwilling* addict; but who would *willingly* be enslaved to drug addiction?

Consider Sandra, a woman who grows up in an oppressive society in which women are expected to be submissive and subservient. The men make all the decisions, and the women smile sweetly, follow their orders, and praise their wisdom. Sandra doesn't buy it. Sandra believes she has just as much right and certainly as much ability to make decisions, take leadership roles, and choose her own path as does any man. And so Sandra struggles valiantly against the oppressive society that attempts to control and subdue her. But the struggle is long and difficult, Sandra has no support, and she endures constant harsh disapproval. Gradually her spirit and fortitude are worn down, and she begins to submit to the subservient role assigned her. The more she submits, the more approval and affection she receives from those around her. Finally Sandra is broken, and she embraces the rules and roles of her oppressive society. She now sees her earlier struggles as youthful sinful pride, and she is glad that her "willfulness" is gone, and she is grateful to have become a properly subservient woman. She is now submissive, and willingly so. By embracing the culture and rules that subordinate her, she has gained free will. Or so deep compatibilists would say.

But surely not. Sandra didn't have much freedom when she struggled against her oppressive society; but when she *internalizes* the oppressive forces, she does not thereby gain free will. The *unwilling* slave is not free, but the *willing* slave is not freer. To the contrary, the "willingly subservient" Sandra is more deeply oppressed than ever. Or so some might think, in opposition to Frankfurt's account of free will.

So it seems that genuine free will requires more. Sandra has deeply embraced her culture's oppressive rules, and when she thinks about it, she is profoundly grateful to her community for leading her back to the straight and narrow path of submissive righteousness. Otherwise, she might have remained a willful, rebellious, independent woman—and Sandra now sees that as a violation of God's glorious plan, and she is glad to play her own submissive role in God's design. Indeed, she does everything possible to ensure that her own daughters avoid their mother's errors, and she endeavors to raise them as good submissive women. Sandra is deeply, reflectively, and willingly subservient and submissive. Sandra may now be a willing slave, but she hardly seems a free one.

Sandra deeply approves of her subservience. She chooses to be submissive, likes being submissive, and profoundly approves of her desire to be submissive. She acts as she wants to act, and reflectively approves of her wants and desires, and thus has the will she prefers and approves. But in Sandra's case this does not seem to add up to free will. To the contrary, the more profoundly and completely she favors her subservience, the less free she seems. This leads some philosophers to propose stronger conditions for genuine free will. It is not enough that one do what one *wishes* (as Hume's simple compatibilism suggested), nor is it enough that one deeply approve of the wishes and will that one has (as Frankfurt's deep compatibilism demands). Genuine free will requires something more.

Rationalist Compatibilism

So what is this something more that genuine free will requires? Many different proposals have been offered: perhaps all that is required is some capacity to reflect on one's values. But submissive Sandra has that capacity, and it is by no means clear that she enjoys free will. A contemporary American philosopher, Susan Wolf, proposes a very strong additional condition for genuine free will. To have free will you must will the right path, the *truly good*. If you will what is wrong and harmful—an empty life of drug addiction or a life of subservience—then you are not thinking clearly and accurately. To be truly free requires more than just following your own desires (Hume's simple compatibilism), more than following your own *deep* values and preferences (Frankfurt's deep compatibilism). Real freedom requires doing the *right thing* for the *right reason*. Thus, we might call Wolf's version of free will *rationalist* compatibilism.

According to rationalist compatibilism, the genuinely free person is "an agent who can form (and act on) right values because they are right—that is, an agent who is able to 'track' the True and Good in her value judgments. . . . " If a driver is profoundly and unswervingly committed to following a road that will end at a washed out bridge, the driver's dedication to that path does not change the fact that he has chosen the wrong route. His deep dedication to that route looks more like the constraint of obsession than genuine freedom.

In Susan Wolf's view, real freedom does not require open alternatives or the ability to choose otherwise. From Wolf's perspective, that is a false freedom, a capacity to make stupid and arbitrary mistakes. As Wolf sees it, wanting the ability to choose among open alternatives is

> . . . not only to want the ability to make choices even where there is no basis for choice but to want the ability to make choices on no basis even when a basis exists. But the latter ability would seem to be an ability no one could ever have reason to want to exercise. Why would one want the ability to pass up the apple when to do so would merely be unpleasant or arbitrary? Why would one want the ability to stay planted on the sand when to do so would be cowardly or callous?[5]

The ability to pursue open alternatives does not enhance your freedom. To suppose otherwise would be like preferring a train that has the capacity to jump the tracks. True freedom is the capacity to recognize the true track, and then follow it unswervingly. (You do not follow it *mindlessly*, like a puppet or robot; rather, you follow the true path because reason reveals to you what is True and Good, and it is your own rational preference to follow the true path, and you track that path accurately through your own reason and willpower.) This requires strong powers of both reason (to discover what is genuinely good and right) and willpower (to control the passions and inclinations that would lead one astray, and instead follow the stern, narrow path of duty). Those who favor this view (such as Kant) often celebrate the dual powers of reason and will, which enable them to follow the straight and narrow path of the moral law:

> Two things fill the mind with ever new and increasing admiration and awe, the oftener and more steadily they are reflected on: the starry heavens above me and the moral law within me.[6]

Whether you accept or reject Wolf's view, she has (building on the tradition of Plato and Kant) established a philosophical landmark that will help us stay oriented as we explore other views. Whether it is a landmark to guide you on the right path, or a monument to philosophical error, is a question you will have to decide for yourself.

LIBERTARIAN FREE WILL AND THE REJECTION OF DETERMINISM

Libertarian Free Will

As appealing as some find Wolf's rational compatibilist view of freedom—real freedom consists in following a steadfast path, and requires no turnoffs or alternatives—it is vehemently rejected by others. From the opposing perspective, what Wolf leaves out (and what *all* compatibilist accounts of free will lack) is the single most important ingredient in free will: the ability to actually choose, the ability to do otherwise, the opportunity to select among *genuine alternatives*. Even if the one true path is dictated by reason, that will not satisfy the desire for open alternatives and free choices. As Russian novelist Fyodor Dostoyevsky insists in *The Underground Man*:

> What he [humanity] wants to preserve is precisely his noxious fancies and vulgar trivialities, if only to assure himself that men are still men . . . and not piano keys responding to the laws of nature.[7]

And being a highly rational piano key will not satisfy that craving. Instead, real free will is the power to make choices that are not determined by *anything*—not by our genetics, our conditioning, nor even by our reason.

This view of free will has long been popular among philosophers and theologians, as well as among butchers, bakers, and candlestick makers. Roderick Chisholm, a contemporary American philosopher, describes it thus:

> If we are responsible [and Chisholm thinks our power of free will does make us responsible] then we have a prerogative which some would attribute only to God; each of us, when we really act, is a prime mover unmoved. In doing what we do, we cause events to happen, and nothing and no one, except ourselves, causes us to cause those events to happen.[8]

This account of free will is called the *libertarian* position. According to libertarians, free will requires a very special power: the power to choose among genuinely open alternatives, and thus make yourself according to your own plans and preferences.

In the libertarian version of free will, we make ourselves from scratch. That's what Chisholm means by saying that when we act freely we are "unmoved movers": we make free choices that cause things to happen (including causing ourselves to develop our characters and attributes), but those choices are not themselves caused by *anything* other than ourselves (and *we* are not caused by anything outside ourselves to be the way we are). God does not assign us our characters, nature does not shape us, and our genes do not limit us. When we make genuinely free choices, exercising our "special godlike prerogative" of free will, then the causal sequence starts and ends with us. We initiate our free choices, and nothing—neither God nor environment nor genetic heritage—causes us to choose as we do.

Existentialist Versions of Libertarian Free Will

Chisholm celebrates this great self-making and self-choosing power, but no one has endorsed the libertarian view more enthusiastically than Jean-Paul Sartre and the existentialists. Existentialists take their name from their fundamental premise: existence precedes essence. It seems a strange rallying cry, hardly up there with "Remember the Alamo." But for existentialists, "existence precedes essence" is the glorious solution to the problem of free will. We do not have assigned characters, fixed essences, or given natures. We make ourselves by our own self-defining *choices* (we first exist, and then by our *choices* we make our own characters, our own essences, and what we are).

Chisholm explicitly recognizes that this notion of free will grants to humans "a prerogative which some would attribute only to God; each of us, when we really act, is a prime mover unmoved." In the existentialist version humans stake their own claim to this special power of free will. Sartre notes the joys and perils of this extraordinary unconditional freedom:

> Everything is indeed permitted if God does not exist, and man is in consequence forlorn, for he cannot find anything to depend upon either within or outside himself. He discovers forthwith, that he is without excuse. For if indeed existence precedes essence, one will never be able to explain one's action by reference to a given and specific human nature, in other words, there is no determinism—man is free, man *is* freedom. Nor, on the other hand, if God does not exist, are we provided with any values or commands that could legitimize our behavior. Thus we have neither behind us, nor before us in a luminous realm of values, any means of justification or excuse. We are left alone, without excuse. That is what I mean when I say that man is condemned to be free. Condemned, because he did not create himself, yet is nevertheless at liberty, and from the moment that he is thrown into this world he is responsible for everything he does. The existentialist . . . thinks that every man, without any support or help whatever, is condemned at every instant to invent man.[9]

So the free will of the existentialists is a miracle-working power of self-creation. There is no essence to define you, no fixed values to guide you, no causal factors to determine you: you have the godlike power to make yourself, and what you do with this power is completely and inescapably your responsibility. Free will is a miraculous power of self-making and self-transformation.

It's not surprising that many people find this view of free will attractive. In the first place, it ascribes to all who possess free will a remarkable status. Rather than grubby mortal beings shaped out of clay, we are godlike in our power of self-creation. Furthermore, this miracle-working view of free will is appealing because it makes us totally responsible for everything we do. Whatever we accomplish, whatever we become, we did it ourselves with no help from anyone; so we get full credit for what we do, and we don't owe anything to anyone. Since most people who read philosophy have significant accomplishments (you graduated from high school, made it into college, and are enjoying a reasonably successful college career with excellent prospects of success when you graduate), they are happy to believe that they deserve full and absolute credit for whatever they have done with their lives.

The existentialist model of miraculous self-creative free will has some significant advantages. It is a dashing, daring, swashbuckling, swaggering view of free will. It plays well in action movies, but does it hold up under closer scrutiny? Is this radical self-creation view of free will really plausible?

However flattering it may be to think that we have godlike powers of self-creation, in the harsh light of our actual lives it seems a difficult proposition to believe. All of us are well aware—sometimes painfully, sometimes thankfully—of the many forces and influences that shaped us. We may debate the relative impact of "nature" and "nurture": that is, does our genetic legacy have a larger influence on our lives, or does our social and cultural environment carry greater weight? But there is no debate over whether these factors have a profound influence. You have arms instead of wings, and that was set by your genes, not your godlike choice; and you find cannibalism disgusting, a result of cultural shaping rather than an existential choice of your own values. If we "create ourselves" uniquely and entirely, then all the empirical studies of human society, psychology, and biology would seem to be impossible. But given the fact that we know a great deal about how our genetic, social, cultural, and family influences shape us, it is difficult to take seriously the notion that we "make ourselves."

But there is a second problem for the existential notion of self-creation, and it is even more severe. The problem lies in making *sense* of what such self-creation could possibly be. Obviously, the choices you make have a profound influence on your life and your character: your choice to go to college instead of looking for work; your choice to attend a large state university or a small private college; your choice to major in sociology, or secondary education, or civil engineering, or to drop out of college and become a surfer; your choice to live with John, or marry John, or maybe dump John; your choice to work for the small start-up company in Albuquerque or the huge corporation based in Boston. All these choices have a resounding influence on your character, your future, your life, the person you become. So obviously we do, to some extent, make ourselves by our choices. And sometimes those choices seem like pivotal, life-changing choices: the choice to become a musician, rather than joining the wholesale foods company that was founded by your grandfather and where your father has worked his entire career; the choice to renounce your family's religion and become a Taoist; the choice to leave your unhappy marriage. Such choices are important, and they shape our lives and our characters. But *who* is making those choices?

In Sartre's scheme, the self-defining choices are made *before* we have values, preferences, ideals, and characters. We are pure existential points, and the choices we make set the course of how the lines of our character will be drawn. But how is it possible to choose without values, convictions, or preferences? It doesn't seem to be *my* choice at all, but instead just a random, capricious event. I can understand making a choice that reflects my own values and preferences, and I can understand making a choice to reject some of the values I have previously held (because I now hold a different value system). But I can make no sense of what it would be like to choose *before* I have *any* values, direction, or preferences. If I completely "make myself" through my choices, then there seems to be no one originally there to set the choices in motion. The question is not whether Sartre's account is correct; rather, it's a question of whether the account makes enough sense to be *evaluated* for accuracy. Saying that I "make myself through my choices" and that no real self exists prior to those choices (existence precedes essence) leaves a very perplexing question: Who is this "I" who makes the choices?

C. A. Campbell's Libertarian Free Will

Many philosophers like the idea of free choices that are somehow our own choices but are not shaped and determined by who we are. But trying to make *sense* of this libertarian notion of free will has long been a challenge. A common way of trying to make this special model of free choice work is to isolate the choice into as small and unobtrusive a space as possible. One of the most interesting and inventive of those minimizing libertarian approaches to free will is offered by C. A. Campbell.

Campbell acknowledges that our preferences, values, and the largest part of our characters are formed—even determined—by our cultures, genes, and environmental histories. Knowledge of these powerful influences enables us to predict, with considerable accuracy, the future choices and behavior of those we know well. Arthur grew up in a permissive, indulgent environment, and he has developed a strong desire for alcohol. He realizes that he is fast sinking into severe alcohol dependence, and is now trying to avoid drinking. But Arthur is not very strong, and his desire for alcohol is. Thus, we can predict, with some confidence, that Arthur will attend Joe's party, where alcohol will be plentiful; that he will attempt to avoid drinking but will fail; and that he will end the evening passed out on the floor. Carolyn also enjoys parties and having a few drinks. Drinking heavily has some appeal for Carolyn, but the appeal is not very powerful, and Carolyn is a strong and self-disciplined person who sets a careful limit on her alcohol intake and refuses to go beyond that limit. We can confidently predict that Carolyn will end the evening sober, while Arthur will conclude his evening unconscious.

And yet (Campbell claims) our predictions may go wrong. Carolyn's temptation to drink heavily is not very strong, and she has powerful resources for combating that temptation; but tonight she may fail to exercise her willpower, and instead yield to temptation. Arthur confronts the powerful temptation to drink excessively, and his powers of resistance are flabby; but tonight Arthur might rise to the occasion, take courage, and triumph over temptation. We cannot be certain about what Carolyn and Arthur will do, because—according to Campbell—they have a special small domain of "contracausal free will" that enables them to overcome their conditioning and their genes and their social shaping. They have a special power of choice and will that allows them to defy their history and rise to duty and act in a new way (or instead choose to *withhold* the effort of will and follow their desires). C. A. Campbell describes it thus:

> Here, and here alone, so far as I can see, in the act of deciding whether to put forth or withhold the moral effort required to resist temptation and rise to duty, is to be found an act which is free in the sense required for moral responsibility; an act of which the self is sole author, and of which it is true to say that 'it could be' (or, after the event, 'could have been') 'otherwise.'[10]

And Campbell insists that when we observe from "the inner standpoint of the practical consciousness in its actual functioning," we recognize in our moral decisions a "*creative activity*, in which . . . nothing determines the act save the agent's doing of it."[11]

In Campbell's scenario we are not entirely self-made and self-chosen—our desires, affections, and inclinations are the product of our genetic and conditioning histories—but in some of our critical choices (especially choices in which our desire conflicts with our sense of what we should do) we make special free creative choices. This view has several advantages. First and foremost, Campbell's view avoids the existential quandary about who is doing the choosing: *I* make the choice of whether to resist temptation and rise to duty, and the temptation and the duty and the willpower are my own. Second, Campbell's account leaves room for the obvious shaping and conditioning of our characters by our genetic makeup, environmental surroundings, and cultural milieu: these forces shape our desires, our tastes, and perhaps also our sense of duty. And third, the area of free will is a special small niche of willpower, rather than (as in existentialism) the wholesale creation of ourselves. (Of course, existentialists may not see that as an advantage: the idea of totally creating ourselves has a romantic and dashing appeal; as long as we're going to be deities exercising special miraculous creative powers of free will, why be minor deities? Instead of miraculously touching up the details, why not create ourselves from scratch?)

But even Campbell's more modest account of "contracausal free will" raises some serious questions. Suppose that Arthur, our friend who typically drinks himself into oblivion, tonight remains stone sober, resisting all offers of alcoholic refreshment. What shall we say about such a case? And Carolyn, our paragon of self-control, tonight goes on a bender and brings in the dawn dancing on a table, singing Broadway show tunes, and calling for more bourbon. What would you regard as the most plausible account of her unusual behavior?

According to Campbell, Arthur exerted his willpower and rose to duty while Carolyn withheld the effort of will and succumbed to desire. There is nothing more to say, no further explanation is possible. In both cases, it was an act of free choice in which "nothing determines the act save the agent's doing of it." In Arthur's case, the desire was strong and the resources to combat that desire were weak. But it was still *possible* for Arthur to overcome his desire by his choice to exert free will, and that's what happened. For Carolyn, the desire was weak and the powers of self-control were strong, but still Carolyn could and did choose *not* to exert the (comparatively small) amount of willpower necessary to resist temptation.

In neither case is there any question *who* is doing the choosing, who is exercising contracausal free will; but there is a question of *how* such processes occur. Let's look at this more closely. Carolyn *desires* to drink heavily, but she believes she *should not*. Last weekend Carolyn went to a party and drank moderately. This weekend she gets blotto. What happened? On Campbell's libertarian view, there need be no difference in circumstances whatsoever. She might have had exactly the same moral principles, reflectiveness, and willpower; she wasn't feeling sadder, she wasn't feeling more adventurous, and her values hadn't changed. In fact, *everything* might have been exactly the same, molecule for molecule. In precisely the same circumstances, one time she exerted the effort of will to control her drinking and the other time she withheld the effort of will. No further explanation is possible: she just did it. She made her own choices, and in identical circumstances she could have chosen otherwise, and that's all there is to say. (If you think there must have been *some* difference in circumstances to account for the difference in behavior—she was tired, or a bit depressed, or had just broken up with her boyfriend—then you are rejecting Campbell's libertarian view. Of course no two situations will actually be exactly identical. But the point is that on Campbell's view there is nothing in the circumstances or environment that accounts for the different acts; the difference must come *solely* from the contracausal free will.)

Campbell's acts of contracausal free will avoid the existentialist question of who is doing the choosing; but they encounter another version of the same problem, though on a smaller scale. We know *who* is making the choice; but it is difficult to understand *how* the choice is being made. Campbell insists that the moral effort one exerts (or withholds) is the essence of free will: " . . . in moral effort we have something for which a man is responsible *without qualification*, something that is *not* affected by heredity and environment but depends *solely* upon the self itself."[12] No further explanation is possible, but (Campbell claims) no further explanation is needed. To see and understand such acts of free will, you must consult your own personal experience: you must look to the inside, introspect, and observe the internal creative process at work. I can't observe it in you, and you can't observe it in me, and there is no distinctive brain wave pattern that can identify it. But when you look carefully, internally, at your own *creative* process of deciding whether to follow your strongest desire or your sense of duty, then you have the best evidence of this creative free will that anyone could possibly have: your own introspective experience.

So, on Campbell's narrow libertarian view, *why* does Carolyn choose differently this weekend? Not because of differences in her character, or desires, or abilities; not because she desires more, or cares less, or thinks less clearly; rather, because of a special *creative choice*. But if the choice does not come from her own character or desires or moral principles, in what sense is this her choice at all? Obviously, the desires, the moral concerns, and the thinking are Carolyn's own; but if this special creative choice comes from none of those personal characteristics, in what sense does that choice really *belong* to her, rather than being an event that merely *happened* to her? The answer from the libertarians is simple: when you look carefully, when you introspect, you have no doubt that the choice is profoundly your own. You are confident, from your own experience, that such choices exist. No further explanation is possible, and from the perspective of external observation such choices must remain unknowable mysteries. But these ultimate, internal, self-defining choices are the essence of genuine free will.

Whether Campbell's libertarian solution is adequate or inadequate, you will have to decide for yourself. Likewise, you must decide for yourself whether such radical libertarian free will is required for genuine free will, or whether some more modest account offers all you want in the way of free will.

Suppose that we make our own choices, but the choices are not miraculous acts of contracausal self-creation (as the libertarians demand) and neither are they inexorably guided by the True and Good (Wolf's condition for genuine freedom). Instead, we make fallible choices, choices that are sometimes wise and other times stupid, choices that we recognize as being our own. We acknowledge that our choices and our characters were shaped by our rich histories—social, environmental, and genetic. Whatever shaped them, and however good or bad our free choices may be, we recognize them as our own choices, and we find making choices a healthy and desirable element of our lives. In some circumstances our choice-making is so badly restricted and compromised by a harsh background that it hardly qualifies as free choice at all: the woman who is worn down to favor submissiveness, and the child raised in a brutal environment, would be examples of such severe cases that we have doubts about their genuine freedom. But in most cases our histories and opportunities are not so brutally narrow, and the fact that there are causes that shaped our characters and choices is not really troubling. Some will regard such a naturalistic (even deterministic) account of free choice as perfectly adequate for human free will. Others will see it as a sham: real choice and real freedom must transcend such grubby natural boundaries, and be based on special human capacities that have no natural explanation.

There is an interesting parallel between views of free will and views of ethics. Just as some anchor ethics in natural powers (utilitarians and care theorists, for example), others (such as Kantians) insist that real ethical principles must transcend any natural phenomena. Likewise, some place free will squarely within the natural world, growing out of the environments that shaped our characters and choices, while others (libertarians) view free will as our special power to rise above any natural influences. Which view you find most plausible has deep connections to your views on the nature of humans and the nature of the world.

In any case, those are the major competing accounts of free will, and in the next chapter we'll be looking further at some of their ethical implications. If you are not at all sure which of those views is correct, or even which of those views you favor, you're in good company. Debates about the nature of free will, and the plausibility of the competing accounts, have been a major part of the history of philosophy, and the debate goes on.

⇒⊹ ASYMMETRICAL FREEDOM ⊹⇐
Susan Wolf

Susan Wolf, Edna J. Koury Professor of philosophy at the University of North Carolina at Chapel Hill, presents a fascinating version of rationalist free will; and in this essay—"Asymmetrical Freedom," *Journal of Philosophy*, Volume 77 (March 1980): 151–66—she draws out some implications of that view you may find surprising. In addition to her many insightful essays on the subject, her *Freedom Within Reason* (New York: Oxford University Press, 1990) is a rich and very readable study of questions related to both free will and moral responsibility.

In order for a person to be morally responsible, two conditions must be satisfied. First, he must be a free agent—an agent, that is, whose actions are under his own control. For if the actions he performs are not up to him to decide, he deserves no credit or discredit for doing what he does. Second, he must be a moral agent—an agent, that is, to whom moral claims apply. For if the actions he performs can be neither right nor wrong, then there is nothing to credit or discredit him with. I shall call the first condition, *the condition of freedom,* and the second, *the condition of value*. Those who fear that the first condition can never be met worry about the problem of free will. Those who fear that the second condition can never be met worry about the problem of moral skepticism. Many people believe that the condition of value is dependent on the condition of freedom—that moral prescriptions make sense only if the concept of free will is coherent. In what follows, I shall argue that the converse is true—that the condition of freedom depends on the condition of value. Our doubts about the existence of true moral values, however, will have to be left aside.

I shall say that an agent's action is *psychologically determined* if his action is determined by his interests—that is, his values or desires—and his interests are determined by his heredity or environment. If all our actions are so determined, then the thesis of psychological determinism is true. This description is admittedly crude and simplistic. A more plausible description of psychological determination will include among possible determining factors a wider range of psychological states. There are, for example, some beliefs and emotions which cannot be analyzed as values or desires and which clearly play a role in the psychological explanations of why we act as we do. For my purposes, however, it will be easier to leave the description of psychological determinism uncluttered. The context should be sufficient to make the intended application understood.

Many people believe that if psychological determinism is true, the condition of freedom can never be satisfied. For if an agent's interests are determined by heredity and environment, they claim, it is not up to the agent to have the interests he has. And if his actions are determined by his interests as well, then he cannot but perform the actions he performs. In order for an agent to satisfy the condition of freedom, then, his actions must not be psychologically determined. Either his actions must not be determined by his interests, or his interests must not be determined by anything external to himself. They therefore conclude that the condition of freedom requires the absence of psychological determinism. And they think this is what we mean to express when we state the condition of freedom in terms of the requirement that the agent "could have done otherwise."

Let us imagine, however, what an agent who satisfied this condition would have to be like. Consider first what it would mean for the agent's actions not to be determined by his interests—for the agent, in other words, to have the ability to act despite his interests. This would mean, I think, that the agent has the ability to act against everything he believes in and everything

he cares about. It would mean, for example, that if the agent's son were inside a burning building, the agent could just stand there and watch the house go up in flames. Or that the agent, though he thinks his neighbor a fine and agreeable fellow, could just get up one day, ring the doorbell, and punch him in the nose. One might think such pieces of behavior should not be classified as actions at all—that they are rather more like spasms that the agent cannot control. If they are actions, at least, they are very bizarre, and an agent who performed them would have to be insane. Indeed, one might think he would have to be insane if he had even the ability to perform them. For the rationality of an agent who could perform such irrational actions as these must hang by a dangerously thin thread.

So let us assume instead that his actions are determined by his interests, but that his interests are not determined by anything external to himself. Then of any of the interests he happens to have, it must be the case that he does not have to have them. Though perhaps he loves his wife, it must be possible for him not to love her. Though perhaps he cares about people in general, it must be possible for him not to care. This agent, moreover, could not have reasons for his interests—at least no reasons of the sort we normally have. He cannot love his wife, for example, because of the way his wife is—for the way his wife is is not up to him to decide. Such an agent, presumably, could not be much committed to anything; his interests must be something like a matter of whim. Such an agent must be able not to care about the lives of others, and, I suppose, he must be able not to care about his own life as well. An agent who didn't care about these things, one might think, would have to be crazy. And again, one might think he would have to be crazy if he had even the ability not to care.

In any case, it seems, if we require an agent to be psychologically undetermined, we cannot expect him to be a moral agent. For if we require that his actions not be determined by his interests, then *a fortiori* they cannot be determined by his moral interests. And if we require that his interests not be determined by anything else, then *a fortiori* they cannot be determined by his moral reasons.

When we imagine an agent who performs right actions, it seems, we imagine an agent who is rightly determined: whose actions, that is, are determined by the right sorts of interests, and whose interests are determined by the right sorts of reasons. But an agent who is not psychologically determined cannot perform actions that are right in this way. And if his actions can never be appropriately right, then in not performing right actions, he can never be wrong. The problem seems to be that the undetermined agent is so free as to be free *from moral reasons*. So the satisfaction of the condition of freedom seems to rule out the satisfaction of the condition of value.

This suggests that the condition of freedom was previously stated too strongly. When we require that a responsible agent "could have done otherwise" we cannot mean that it was not determined that he did what he did. It has been proposed that 'he could have done otherwise' should be analyzed as a conditional instead. For example, we might say that 'he could have done otherwise' means that he would have done otherwise, if he had tried. Thus the bank robber is responsible for robbing the bank, since he would have restrained himself if he had tried. But the man he locked up is not responsible for letting him escape, since he couldn't have stopped him even if he had tried.

Incompatibilists, however, will quickly point out that such an analysis is insufficient. For an agent who would have done otherwise if he had tried cannot be blamed for his action if he could not have tried. The compatibilist might try to answer this objection with a new conditional analysis of 'he could have tried.' He might say, for example, that 'he could have tried to do otherwise' be interpreted to mean he would have tried to do otherwise, if he had chosen. But the incompatibilist now has a new objection to make: namely, what if the agent could not have chosen?

It should be obvious that this debate might be carried on indefinitely with a proliferation of conditionals and a proliferation of objections. But if an agent is determined, no conditions one suggests will be conditions that an agent could have satisfied.

Thus, any conditional analysis of 'he could have done otherwise' seems too weak to satisfy the condition of freedom. Yet if 'he could have done otherwise' is not a conditional, it seems too strong to allow the satisfaction of the condition of value. We seem to think of ourselves one way when we are thinking about freedom, and to think of ourselves another way when we are thinking about morality. When we are thinking about the condition of freedom, our intuitions suggest that the incompatibilists are right. For they claim that an agent can be free only insofar as his actions are not psychologically determined. But when we are thinking about the condition of value, our intuitions suggest that the compatibilists are right. For they claim that an agent can be moral only insofar as his actions are psychologically determined. If our intuitions require that both these claims are right, then the concept of moral responsibility must be incoherent. For then a free agent can never be moral, and a moral agent can never be free.

In fact, however, I believe that philosophers have generally got our intuitions wrong. There is an asymmetry in our intuitions about freedom which has generally been overlooked. As a result, it has seemed that the answer to the problem of free will can lie in only one of two alternatives: Either the fact that an agent's action was determined is always compatible with his being responsible for it, or the fact that the agent's action was determined will always rule his responsibility out. I shall suggest that the solution lies elsewhere—that both compatibilists and incompatibilists are wrong. What we need in order to be responsible beings, I shall argue, is a suitable combination of determination and indetermination.

When we try to call up our intuitions about freedom, a few stock cases come readily to mind. We think of the heroin addict and the kleptomaniac, of the victim of hypnosis, and the victim of a deprived childhood. These cases, I think, provide forceful support for our incompatibilist intuitions. For of the kleptomaniac it may well be true that he would have done otherwise if he had tried. The kleptomaniac is not responsible because he could not have tried. Of the victim of hypnosis it may well be true that he would have done otherwise if he had chosen. The victim of hypnosis is not responsible because he could not have chosen.

The victim of the deprived childhood who, say, embezzles some money, provides the most poignant example of all. For this agent is not coerced nor overcome by an irresistible impulse. He is in complete possession of normal adult faculties of reason and observation. He seems, indeed, to have as much control over his behavior as we have of ours. He acts on the basis of his choice, and he chooses on the basis of his reasons. If there is any explanation of why this agent is not responsible, it would seem that it must consist simply in the fact that his reasons are determined.

These examples are all peculiar, however, in that they are examples of people doing bad things. If the agents in these cases were responsible for their actions, this would justify the claim that they deserve to be blamed. We seldom look, on the other hand, at examples of agents whose actions are morally good. We rarely ask whether an agent is truly responsible if his being responsible would make him worthy of praise.

There are a few reasons why this might be so which go some way in accounting for the philosophers' neglect. First, acts of moral blame are more connected with punishment than acts of moral praise are connected with reward. So acts of moral blame are likely to be more public, and examples will be readier to hand. Second, and more important, I think, we have stronger reasons for wanting acts of blame to be justified. If we blame someone or punish him, we are likely to be causing him some pain. But if we praise someone or reward him, we will probably only add to his pleasures. To blame someone undeservedly is, in any case, to do him an injustice. Whereas to praise someone undeservedly is apt to be just a harmless mistake. For this reason, I think, our intuitions about praise are weaker and less developed than our intuitions about blame. Still, we do have some intuitions about cases of praise, and it would be a mistake to ignore them entirely.

When we ask whether an agent's action is deserving of praise, it seems we do not require that he could have done otherwise. If an agent does the right thing for just the right reasons, it seems absurd to ask whether he could have done the wrong. "I cannot tell a lie," "He couldn't hurt a fly" are not exemptions from praiseworthiness but testimonies to it. If a friend presents you with a gift and says "I couldn't resist," this suggests the strength of his friendship and not the weakness of his will. If one feels one "has no choice" but to speak out against injustice, one ought not to be upset about the depth of one's commitment. And it seems I should be grateful for the fact that if I were in trouble, my family "could not help" but come to my aid.

Of course, these phrases must be given an appropriate interpretation if they are to indicate that the agent is deserving of praise. "He couldn't hurt a fly" must allude to someone's gentleness—it would be perverse to say this of someone who was in an iron lung. It is not admirable in George Washington that he cannot tell a lie, if it is because he has a tendency to stutter that inhibits his attempts. 'He could not have done otherwise' as it is used in the context of praise, then, must be taken to imply something like 'because he was too good.' An action is praiseworthy only if it is done for the right reasons. So it must be only in light of and because of these reasons that the praiseworthy agent "could not help" but do the right thing.

But when an agent does the right thing for the right reasons, the fact that, having the right reasons, he *must* do the right should surely not lessen the credit he deserves. For presumably the reason he cannot do otherwise is that his virtue is so sure or his moral commitment so strong.

One might fear that if the agent really couldn't have acted differently, his virtue must be *too* sure or his commitment *too* strong. One might think, for example, that if someone literally couldn't resist buying a gift for a friend, his generosity would not be a virtue—it would be an obsession. For one can imagine situations in which it would be better if the agent did resist—if, for example,

the money that was spent on the gift was desperately needed for some other purpose. Presumably, in the original case, though, the money was not desperately needed—we praise the agent for buying a gift for his friend rather than, say, a gift for himself. But from the fact that the man could not resist in this situation it doesn't follow that he couldn't resist in another. For part of the explanation of why he couldn't resist in this situation is that in this situation he has no reason to try to resist. This man, we assume, has a generous nature—a disposition, that is, to perform generous acts. But, then, if he is in a situation that presents a golden opportunity, and has no conflicting motive, how could he act otherwise?

One might still be concerned that if his motives are determined, the man cannot be truly deserving of praise. If he cannot help but have a generous character, then the fact that he is generous is not up to him. If a man's motives are determined, one might think, then *he* cannot control them, so it cannot be to his credit if his motives turn out to be good. But whether a man is in control of his motives cannot be decided so simply. We must know not only whether his motives are determined, but how they are determined as well.

We can imagine, for example, a man with a generous mother who becomes generous as a means of securing her love. He would not have been generous had his mother been different. Had she not admired generosity, he would not have developed this trait. We can imagine further that once this man's character had been developed, he would never subject it to question or change. His character would remain unthinkingly rigid, carried over from a childhood over which he had no control. As he developed a tendency to be generous, let us say, he developed other tendencies—a tendency to brush his teeth twice a day, a tendency to avoid the company of Jews. The explanation for why he developed any one of these traits is more or less the same as the explanation for why he has developed any other. And the explanation for why he has retained any one of these tendencies is more or less the same as the explanation for why he has retained any other. These tendencies are all, for him, merely habits which he has never thought about breaking. Indeed, they are habits which, by hypothesis, it was determined he would never think about breaking. Such a man, perhaps, would not deserve credit for his generosity, for his generosity might be thought to be senseless and blind. But we can imagine a different picture in which no such claim is true, in which a generous character might be determined and yet under the agent's control.

We might start again with a man with a generous mother who starts to develop his generosity out of a desire for her love. But his reasons for developing a generous nature need not be his reasons for retaining it when he grows more mature. He may notice, for example, that his generous acts provide an independent pleasure, connected to the pleasure he gives the person on whom his generosity is bestowed. He may find that being generous promotes a positive fellow feeling and makes it easier for him to make friends than it would otherwise be. Moreover, he appreciates being the object of the generous acts of others, and he is hurt when others go to ungenerous extremes. All in all, his generosity seems to cohere with his other values. It fits in well with his ideals of how one ought to live.

Such a picture, I think, might be as determined as the former one. But it is compatible with the exercise of good sense and an open frame of mind. It is determined, because the agent does not create his new reasons for generosity any more than he created his old ones. He does not *decide* to feel an independent pleasure in performing acts of generosity, or decide that such acts will make it easier for him to make friends. He discovers that these are consequences of a generous nature—and if he is observant and perceptive, he cannot help but discover this. He does not choose to be the object of the generous acts of others, or to be the victim of less generous acts of less virtuous persons. Nor does he choose to be grateful to the one and hurt by the other. He cannot help but have these experiences—they are beyond his control. So it seems that what reasons he *has* for being generous depends on what reasons there *are*.

If the man's character is determined in this way, however, it seems absurd to say that it is not under his control. His character is determined on the basis of his reasons, and his reasons are determined by what reasons there are. What is not under his control, then, is that generosity be a virtue, and it is only because he realizes this that he remains a generous man. But one cannot say for *this* reason that his generosity is not praiseworthy. This is the best reason for being generous that a person could have.

So it seems that an agent can be morally praiseworthy even though he is determined to perform the action he performs. But we have already seen that an agent cannot be morally blameworthy if he is determined to perform the action he performs. Determination, then, is compatible with an agent's responsibility for a good action, but incompatible with an agent's responsibility for a bad action. The metaphysical conditions required for an agent's responsibility will vary according to the value of the action he performs.

The condition of freedom, as it is expressed by the requirement that an agent could have done otherwise,

thus appears to demand a conditional analysis after all. But the condition must be one that separates the good actions from the bad—the condition, that is, must be essentially value-laden. An analysis of the condition of freedom that might do the trick is:

He could have done otherwise if there had been good and sufficient reason.

where the 'could have done otherwise' in the analysis is not a conditional at all. For presumably an action is morally praiseworthy only if there are no good and sufficient reasons to do something else. And an action is morally blameworthy only if there are good and sufficient reasons to do something else. Thus, when an agent performs a good action, the condition of freedom is a counterfactual: though it is required that the agent would have been able to do otherwise *had there been* good and sufficient reason to do so, the situation in which the good-acting agent actually found himself is a situation in which there was no such reason. Thus, it is compatible with the satisfaction of the condition of freedom that the agent in this case could not actually have done other than what he actually did. When an agent performs a bad action, however, the condition of freedom is not a counterfactual. The bad-acting agent does what he does in the face of good and sufficient reasons to do otherwise. Thus the condition of freedom requires that the agent in this case could have done otherwise in just the situation in which he was actually placed. An agent, then, can be determined to perform a good action and still be morally praiseworthy. But if an agent is to be blameworthy, he must unconditionally have been able to do something else.

It may be easier to see how this analysis works, and how it differs from conditional analyses that were suggested before, if we turn back to the case in which these previous analyses failed—namely, the case of the victim of a deprived childhood.

We imagined a case, in particular, of a man who embezzled some money, fully aware of what he was doing. He was neither coerced nor overcome by an irresistible impulse, and he was in complete possession of normal adult faculties of reason and observation. Yet it seems he ought not to be blamed for committing his crime, for, from his point of view, one cannot reasonably expect him to see anything wrong with his action. We may suppose that in his childhood he was given no love—he was beaten by his father, neglected by his mother. And that the people to whom he was exposed when he was growing up gave him examples only of evil and selfishness. From his point of view, it is natural to conclude that respecting other people's property would be foolish. For presumably no one had ever respected his. And it is natural for him to feel that he should treat other people as adversaries.

In light of this, it seems that this man shouldn't be blamed for an action we know to be wrong. For if we had had his childhood, we wouldn't have known it either. Yet this agent seems to have as much control over his life as we are apt to have over ours: he would have done otherwise, if he had tried. He would have tried to do otherwise, if he had chosen. And he would have chosen to do otherwise, if he had had reason. It is because he couldn't have had reason that this agent should not be blamed.

Though this agent's childhood was different from ours, it would seem to be neither more nor less binding. The good fortune of our childhood is no more to our credit than the misfortune of his is to his blame. So if he is not free because of the childhood he had, then it would appear that we are not free either. Thus it seems no conditional analysis of freedom will do—for there is nothing internal to the agent which distinguishes him from us.

My analysis, however, proposes a condition that is not internal to the agent. And it allows us to state the relevant difference: namely that, whereas our childhoods fell within a range of normal decency, his was severely deprived. The consequence this has is that he, unlike us, could not have had reasons even though there were reasons around. The problem is not that his reason was functioning improperly, but that his data were unfortuitously selective. Since the world for him was not suitably cooperating, his reason cannot attain its appropriate goal.

The goal, to put it bluntly, is the True and the Good. The freedom we want is the freedom to find it. But such a freedom requires not only that we, as agents, have the right sorts of abilities—the abilities, that is, to direct and govern our actions by our most fundamental selves. It requires as well that the world cooperate in such a way that our most fundamental selves have the opportunity to develop into the selves they ought to be.

If the freedom necessary for moral responsibility is the freedom to be determined by the True and the Good, then obviously we cannot know whether we have such a freedom unless we know, on the one hand, that there *is* a True and a Good and, on the other, that there *are* capacities for finding them. As a consequence of this, the condition of freedom cannot be stated in purely metaphysical terms. For we cannot know which capacities and circumstances are necessary for freedom unless we know which capacities and circumstances will enable us to form the *right* values and perform the *right*

actions. Strictly speaking, I take it, the capacity to reason is not enough—we need a kind of sensibility and perception as well. But these are capacities, I assume, that most of us have. So when the world co-operates, we are morally responsible.

I have already said that the condition of freedom cannot be stated in purely metaphysical terms. More specifically, the condition of freedom cannot be stated in terms that are value-free. Thus, the problem of free will has been misrepresented insofar as it has been thought to be a purely metaphysical problem. And, perhaps, this is why the problem of free will has seemed for so long to be hopeless.

That the problem should have seemed to be a purely metaphysical problem is not, however, unnatural or surprising. For being determined by the True and the Good is very different from being determined by one's garden variety of causes, and I think it not unnatural to feel as if one rules out the other. For to be determined by the Good is not to be determined by the Past. And to do something because it is the right thing to do is not to do it because one has been taught to do it. One might think, then, that one can be determined only by one thing or the other. For if one is going to do whatever it is right to do, then it seems one will do it whether or not one has been taught. And if one is going to do whatever one has been taught to do, then it seems one will do it whether or not it is right.

In fact, however, such reasoning rests on a category mistake. These two explanations do not necessarily compete, for they are explanations of different kinds. Consider, for example, the following situation: you ask me to name the capital of Nevada, and I reply "Carson City." We can explain why I give the answer I do give in either of the following ways: First, we can point out that when I was in the fifth grade I had to memorize the capitals of the fifty states. I was taught to believe that Carson City was the capital of Nevada, and was subsequently positively reinforced for doing so. Second, we can point out that Carson City *is* the capital of Nevada, and that this was, after all, what you wanted to know. So on the one hand, I gave my answer because I was taught. And on the other, I gave my answer because it was right.

Presumably, these explanations are not unrelated. For if Carson City were not the capital of Nevada, I would not have been taught that it was. And if I hadn't been taught that Carson City was the capital of Nevada, I wouldn't have known that it was. Indeed, one might think that if the answer I gave weren't right, I *couldn't* have given it because I was taught. For no school board would have hired a teacher who got such facts wrong. And if I hadn't been taught that Carson City was the capital of Nevada, perhaps I couldn't have given this answer because it was right. For that Carson City is the capital of Nevada is not something that can be known a priori.

Similarly, we can explain why a person acts justly in either of the following ways: First, we can point out that he was taught to act justly, and was subsequently positively reinforced for doing so. Second, we can point out that it is right to act justly, and go on to say why he knows this is so. Again, these explanations are likely to be related. For if it weren't right to act justly, the person may well not have been taught that it was. And if the person hadn't been taught that he ought to act justly, the person may not have discovered this on his own. Of course, the explanations of both kinds in this case will be more complex than the explanations in the previous case. But what is relevant here is that these explanations are compatible: that one can be determined by the Good and determined by the Past.

In order for an agent to be morally free, then, he must be capable of being determined by the Good. Determination by the Good is, as it were, the goal we need freedom to pursue. We need the freedom *to have* our actions determined by the Good, and the freedom to be or to become the sorts of persons whose actions will continue to be so determined. In light of this, it should be clear that no standard incompatibilist views about the conditions of moral responsibility can be right, for, according to these views, an agent is free only if he is the sort of agent whose actions are not causally determined at all. Thus, an agent's freedom would be incompatible with the realization of the goal for which freedom is required. The agent would be, in the words, though not in the spirit, of Sartre, "condemned to be free"—he could not both be free and realize a moral ideal.

Thus, views that offer conditional analyses of the ability to do otherwise, views that, like mine, take freedom to consist in the ability *to be determined* in a particular way, are generally compatibilist views. For insofar as an agent *is* determined in the right way, the agent can be said to be acting freely. Like the compatibilists, then, I am claiming that whether an agent is morally responsible depends not on whether but on how that agent is determined. My view differs from theirs only in what I take the satisfactory kind of determination to be.

However, since on my view the satisfactory kind of determination is determination by reasons that an agent ought to have, it will follow that an agent can be both determined and responsible only insofar as he performs actions that he ought to perform. If an agent performs a morally bad action, on the other hand, then

his actions can't be determined in the appropriate way. So if an agent is ever to be responsible for a bad action, it must be the case that his action is not psychologically determined at all. According to my view, then, in order for both moral praise and moral blame to be justified, the thesis of psychological determinism must be false.

Is it plausible that this thesis is false? I think so. For though it appears that some of our actions are psychologically determined, it appears that others are not. It appears that some of our actions are not determined by our interests, and some of our interests are not determined at all. That is, it seems that some of our actions are such that no set of psychological facts are sufficient to explain them. There are occasions on which a person takes one action, but there seems to be no reason why he didn't take another.

For example, we sometimes make arbitrary choices—to wear the green shirt rather than the blue, to have coffee rather than tea. We make such choices on the basis of no reason—and it seems that we might, in these cases, have made a different choice instead.

Some less trivial and more considered choices may also be arbitrary. For one may have reasons on both sides which are equally strong. Thus, one may have good reasons to go to graduate school and good reasons not to; good reasons to get married, and good reasons to stay single. Though we might want, in these cases, to choose on the basis of reasons, our reasons simply do not settle the matter for us. Other psychological events may be similarly undetermined, such as the chance occurrence of thoughts and ideas. One is just struck by an idea, but for no particular reason—one might as easily have had another idea or no idea at all. Or one simply forgets an appointment one has made, even though one was not particularly distracted by other things at the time.

On retrospect, some of the appearance of indetermination may turn out to be deceptive. We decide that unconscious motives dictated a choice that seemed at the time to be arbitrary. Or a number of ideas that seemed to occur to us at random reveal a pattern too unusual to be the coincidence we thought. But if some of the appearances of indetermination are deceptive, I see no reason to believe that all of them should be.

Let us turn, then, to instances of immoral behavior, and see what the right kind of indetermination would be. For indetermination, in this context, is indetermination among some number of fairly particular alternatives—and if one's alternatives are not of the appropriate kind, indetermination will not be sufficient to justify moral blame. It is not enough, for example, to know that a criminal who happened to rob a bank might as easily have chosen to hold up a liquor store instead. What we need to know, in particular, is that when an agent performs a wrong action, he could have performed the right action for the right reasons instead. That is, first, the agent could have had the interests that the agent ought to have had, and second, the agent could have acted on the interests on which he ought to have acted.

Corresponding to these two possibilities, we can imagine two sorts of moral failure: the first corresponds to a form of negligence, the second to a form of weakness. Moral negligence consists in a failure to recognize the existence of moral reasons that one ought to have recognized. For example, a person hears that his friend is in the hospital, but fails to attend to this when planning his evening. He doesn't stop to think about how lonely and bored his friend is likely to be—he simply reaches for the *TV Guide* or for his novel instead. If the person could have recognized his friend's sorry predicament, he is guilty of moral negligence. Moral weakness, on the other hand, consists in the failure to act on the reasons that one knows one ought, for moral reasons, to be acting on. For example, a person might go so far as to conclude that he really ought to pay his sick friend a visit, but the thought of the drive across town is enough to convince him to stay at home with his book after all. If the person could have made the visit, he is guilty of moral weakness.

There is, admittedly, some difficulty in establishing that an agent who performs a morally bad action satisfies the condition of freedom. It is hard to know whether an agent who did one thing could have done another instead. But presumably we decide such questions now on the basis of statistical evidence—and, if, in fact, these actions are not determined, this is the best method there can be. We decide, in other words, that an agent could have done otherwise if others in his situation have done otherwise, and these others are like him in all apparently relevant ways. Or we decide that an agent could have done otherwise if he himself has done otherwise in situations that are like this one in all apparently relevant ways.

It should be emphasized that the indetermination with which we are here concerned is indetermination only at the level of psychological explanation. Such indetermination is compatible with determination at other levels of explanation. In particular, a sub-psychological, or physiological, explanation of our behavior may yet be deterministic. Some feel that if this is the case, the nature of psychological explanations of our behavior cannot be relevant to the problem of free will. Though I am inclined to disagree with this view, I have neither the space nor the competence to argue this here.

Restricting the type of explanation in question appropriately, however, it is a consequence of the condition of freedom I have suggested that the explanation for why a responsible agent performs a morally bad action must be, at some level, incomplete. There must be nothing that made the agent perform the action he did, nothing that prevented him from performing a morally better one. It should be noted that there may be praiseworthy actions for which the explanations are similarly incomplete. For the idea that an agent who could have performed a morally bad action actually performs a morally good one is no less plausible than the idea that an agent who could have performed a morally good action actually performs a morally bad one. Presumably, an agent who does the right thing for the right reasons deserves praise for his action whether it was determined or not. But whereas indetermination is compatible with the claim that an agent is deserving of praise, it is essential to the justification of the claim that an agent is deserving of blame.

Seen from a certain perspective, this dealing out of praise and blame may seem unfair. In particular, we might think that if it is truly undetermined whether a given agent in a given situation will perform a good action or a bad one, then it must be a matter of chance that the agent ends up doing what he does. If the action is truly undetermined, then it is not determined by the agent himself. One might think that in this case the agent has no more control over the moral quality of his action than does anything else.

However, the fact that it is not determined whether the agent will perform a good action or a bad one does not imply that which action he performs can properly be regarded as a matter of chance. Of course, in some situations an agent might choose to make it a matter of chance. For example, an agent struggling with the decision between fulfilling a moral obligation and doing something immoral that he very much wants to do might ultimately decide to let the toss of a coin settle the matter for him. But, in normal cases, the way in which the agent makes a decision involves no statistical process or randomizing event. It appears that the claim that there is no complete explanation of why the agent who could have performed a better action performed a worse one or of why the agent who could have performed a worse action performed a better one rules out even the explanation that it was a matter of chance.

In order to have control over the moral quality of his actions, an agent must have certain requisite abilities—in particular, the abilities necessary to see and understand the reasons and interests he ought to see and understand and the abilities necessary to direct his actions in accordance with these reasons and interests. And if, furthermore, there is nothing that interferes with the agent's use of these abilities—that is, no determining cause that prevents him from using them and no statistical process that, as it were, takes out of his hands the control over whether or not he uses them—then it seems that these are all the abilities that the agent needs to have. But it is compatible with the agent's having these abilities and with there being no interferences to their use that it is not determined whether the agent will perform a good action or a bad one. The responsible agent who performs a bad action fails to exercise these abilities sufficiently, though there is no complete explanation of why he fails. The responsible agent who performs a good action does exercise these abilities—it may or may not be the case that it is determined that he exercise them.

The freedom required for moral responsibility, then, is the freedom to be good. Only this kind of freedom will be neither too much nor too little. For then the agent is not so free as to be free from moral reasons, nor so unfree as to make these reasons ineffective.

EXERCISES

1. In the biblical account, the children of Israel are held in slavery in Egypt for many years. At one point Pharaoh apparently considers freeing them, but God "hardened Pharaoh's heart" and thus Pharaoh refused to free the Israeli slaves. Most of us, surely, would say that what Pharaoh did was *morally wrong*: It is wrong to hold slaves in bondage. But if Almighty God *hardened* Pharaoh's heart, then it is difficult to suppose that Pharaoh acted with *free will*. So is free will necessary for performing morally wrong (and morally right) acts? If you still believe that free will is essential for acting wrongly or rightly, how would you explain away this apparent counterexample?

2. If I do something I don't really want to do—such as attending the golden wedding anniversary celebration of Aunt Ethyl and Uncle Fred, or writing a required term paper on "The Accomplishments of Herbert Hoover"—can I still be acting freely?

3. If I give in to temptation, and—against my better judgment and in violation of the diet I'm striving to follow—munch down six large gooey chocolate chip cookies, am I acting freely? Is that an exercise of free will?

4. You are a music major, specializing in oboe performance. Ever since you first heard the oboe, as a small child, you loved the instrument; and as soon as you were old enough for middle school orchestra, you chose the oboe as your instrument. Other kids played soccer; you played oboe. Other kids had favorite rock bands; you had favorite woodwind ensembles.

   Recent research on the human genome reveals an exciting discovery: a profound love of the oboe is caused by a specific gene; and all—and only—those who have that gene really love the oboe. Apparently one can like the oboe without the gene, but all who really love the oboe have the gene; and all who have the gene are deeply and permanently drawn to the oboe immediately upon hearing that instrument. (Of course, if one lives one's entire life isolated deep in a rain forest, and never hears the sweet sound of the oboe, then one will have no passion for the oboe; but all who have the very rare oboe gene, and have an opportunity to hear the oboe, are immediately and passionately dedicated to the oboe.) So your passion for the oboe is genetically programmed. Do you act freely when you practice the oboe? Is your oboe-playing an exercise of free will? Was your choice to study music rather than medicine a free choice?

5. It's quite obvious that most of us prefer to have choices, and to exercise control over our choices. Psychologists have made extensive studies of this preference. (Not everyone prefers to make their own choices; some prefer to have others choose for them, or believe that they cannot really exercise effective control. However, that preference for not making choices is strongly associated with a number of psychological problems: those who do not wish to make their own choices are more likely to become depressed, they suffer pain more acutely, and they generally have less fortitude when working on a difficult project). Could people have a healthy belief in choice-making and their own choice-making effectiveness, and still believe in determinism?

6. Rafia is the youngest vice president at a major financial corporation. She is a brilliant stock analyst, and her future looks bright: gossip around the firm has her on the inside track to become CEO within a decade. But Rafia discovers some deceptive accounting practices that the company has been exploiting to inflate its profits and artificially boost its stock price. When Rafia reports her concerns to the current CEO and to the company's chief financial officer, they tell her not to worry about it, and not to tell anyone: "Nobody outside the company knows about this, and it won't be revealed for many years. By that time we will have sold off our stock and we'll all be very, very rich. The company may go bankrupt, and some stockholders will lose their investments: but that's their tough luck. Lots of companies do this. One of the things you have to learn, as

you climb up the corporate ladder, is how to keep secrets. By keeping this secret, you will become a very successful and wealthy woman." Rafia is appalled. Rafia would love to be rich, and she would love to become a top corporate officer for a major corporation: that's what she went to college for, that's why she has put in incredibly long hours for many years. But the idea of making millions of dollars through fraudulent stock deals while small investors lose their life savings and many employees lose their pension benefits: Rafia believes that is dead wrong, and she refuses to go along. She takes company documents to the Securities and Exchange Commission; the commission investigates, and levies large penalties against Rafia's corporation, and forces them to stop their fraudulent practices. Rafia, however, is fired. Other financial companies see her as a whistle-blowing risk, and refuse to hire her. Rafia winds up in a low-level position working for a small local bank as a loan officer, at a fraction of her former income.

One of Rafia's friends asks her about why she revealed the company fraud: "Rafia, you're smart and savvy. You knew that employees who 'blow the whistle' on their employers usually wind up suffering reprisals, and lose their jobs, and never find jobs that good. You were on the fast track to the very top of the corporate world; it was what you always wanted, it was what you had worked so hard for. Why did you do it?"

"I had to," Rafia replies. "I simply could not go along with that kind of fraud, in which so many people would get hurt. I could never have lived with myself if I had been a party to that. Once I discovered the fraud, I did what I had to do; I simply couldn't have done anything else."

A. Suppose that Rafia, being who she is, and given the deep moral principles she holds, really *could not* do otherwise. Did Rafia act freely?

B. Most of us will find Rafia a morally admirable person. Would she be *more* or *less* admirable if she had wrestled with her conscience, been severely tempted to go along with the fraud and pocket her fortune, agonized over her decision, and after days of indecisiveness decided to reveal the fraud?

C. In what sense, if any, is it true that Rafia "could not do otherwise"? Is *decisive* Rafia more, less, or equally as free as *indecisive* Rafia (of the previous question)?

D. Rafia is planning to take her information to the Securities and Exchange Commission early tomorrow morning: it is the right thing to do, she believes; and she also believes it is what she *must* do; but still, if we ask Rafia, she will tell us she is acting freely. The phone rings. Rafia answers, and finds she is talking to an FBI agent: "We have been investigating the company you work for," the agent tells Rafia, "and we have uncovered evidence of fraud. We know that you made copies of some of the documents that show evidence of the fraudulent practices. Turn those documents in to the Securities and Exchange Commission first thing tomorrow morning, or we will charge you with fraud." "That's exactly what I was planning to do with them," Rafia replies. "Fine," the FBI agent replies; "just be sure that you do, otherwise you'll be arrested." Rafia's resolve to give the documents to the SEC is unchanged; but now she feels that her act is somewhat less free. Is it reasonable for Rafia to feel that the FBI call has somehow diminished her freedom, when the agent is demanding that she do what she had already decided to do anyway?

7. Your friend Saul is the world's greatest procrastinator. If a term paper is due Wednesday at 8 A.M., he *never* starts it before Tuesday night. More likely he will plead for an extension, and start the paper Wednesday afternoon. His ethics term paper is due November 15. On the first day of October, you find Saul at his desk with stacks of ethics books around him, while he works furiously at his keyboard. Looking at the monitor, you discover Saul is on page 12 of the ethics paper that is not due for another six weeks.

You are amazed. "What got into you? That paper isn't due for weeks yet. You *never* work on anything until the very last minute. What's the deal?"

"Nothing happened," Saul replies. "I just exercised my free will and chose to write my term paper punctually, and not procrastinate."

"Yeah, sure," you reply. "I bet your parents threatened to cut off your funds if you flunked another course. Or maybe the dean called you in for a stern lecture. Or, I know, your coach read you the riot act about your low grades. No, I've got it: Allison said she was dumping you if you don't shape up and get your act together. That's got to be it, right?"

"No, nothing like that. I know I have a tendency to procrastinate. And I was sorely tempted to put this paper off until the last minute. But this time I simply chose to do otherwise. It was an act of free will; nothing else has changed; that's the only explanation I can give."

Would you find that a plausible explanation? Or would you suppose that there must be something your friend Saul is not telling you? And what does your answer say about your own view of free will?

8. If psychologists accepted Campbell's libertarian view of free will, would that mean psychology could *never* be a complete science—that there would always be human behavior that would remain completely beyond scientific psychological explanation?

9. Recent neuropsychological studies have shown that when subjects make a choice, characteristic brain activity occurs *before* the subject becomes *aware* of making a choice; that is, when you make a choice, apparently your brain "makes the choice" *prior* to your *awareness* of the choice. Does this research indicate that free will is an illusion? (The research is described in Daniel Wegner, *The Illusion of Conscious Will*.)

ADDITIONAL READING

A number of recent books consider the question of free will in light of recent research in biology and psychology. John M. Doris, in *Lack of Character: Personality and Moral Behavior* (Cambridge, MA: Cambridge University Press, 2002), organizes and reviews several decades of psychological research (particularly social psychology research), and he draws out in detail and depth its philosophical implications in the areas of free will and moral responsibility. One of the most interesting and important books written on free will is by a neuropsychologist, Daniel M. Wegner. *The Illusion of Conscious Will* (Cambridge, MA: Bradford Books, 2002) is a very readable book that draws out the implications of decades of neuropsychological research, and its often surprising results. A superb collection of essays— and commentary—on the implications of contemporary neuroscience for questions of free will can be found in *The Volitional Brain: Towards a Neuroscience of Free Will*, Benjamin Libet, Anthony Freeman, and Keith Sutherland, editors (Thorverton, Exeter UK: Imprint Academic, 1999). Alfred R. Mele, in *Free Will and Luck* (New York: Oxford University Press, 2006) presents an interesting account of free will while also critiquing some of the recent psychological research on the subject; and his *Effective Intentions: The Power of Conscious Will* (New York: Oxford University Press, 2009) is a more detailed critical examination of neuropsychological research and its implications. Bruce N. Waller, *The Natural Selection of Autonomy* (Albany, NY: SUNY Press, 1998) uses recent research in biology and psychology in an attempt to uncover some of the motives common to both libertarian and compatibilist views of free will, and to attack traditional justifications for moral responsibility.

For the best, clearest, and most even-handed guide to the issues surrounding the free will debate (and also for a very creative addition to that debate), see two books by Richard Double: *The Non-Reality of Free Will* (New York: Oxford University Press, 1991), and *Metaphilosophy and Free Will* (New York: Oxford University Press, 1996). A very good presentation of a variety of free will accounts is *Four Views on Free Will*, by John Martin Fischer, Robert Kane, Derk Pereboom, and Manuel Vargas (Oxford: Blackwell, 2007).

For a fascinating libertarian account of free will from the Italian Renaissance, see Giovanni Pico della Mirandola, "The Dignity of Man" (sometimes titled "Oration on the Dignity of Man"); it is available in several renaissance anthologies. C. A. Campbell's *On Selfhood and Godhood* (London: George Allen & Unwin, 1957) is the classic modern source. Randolph K. Clarke offers an excellent detailed study of various versions of libertarian theory in *Libertarian Accounts of Free Will* (New York: Oxford University Press, 2003). Robert Kane has developed what is undoubtedly the most sophisticated and interesting contemporary defense of libertarian free will, in *Free Will and Values* (Albany, NY: SUNY Press, 1985) and *The Significance of Free Will* (Oxford: Oxford University Press, 1996). Kane's edited work, *The Oxford Handbook of Free Will* (Oxford: Oxford University Press, 2002), is a wonderful guide to contemporary thought concerning free will; and his *A Contemporary Introduction to Free Will* (New York: Oxford University Press, 2005) is a good brief introduction to the free will question. Two other influential sources for incompatibilist views of free will are William James, "The Dilemma of Determinism," (1884, available in a number of anthologies); and Jean-Paul Sartre, *Being and Nothingness* (New York: Philosophical Library, 1956).

The classic presentation of both determinism and compatibilism is David Hume, *An Enquiry Concerning Human Understanding*, Section 8, and in his *Treatise of Human Nature*, Book II, Part III. Thomas Hobbes developed an earlier similar account (1651) in *Leviathan*, Chapter 2. A more recent argument for compatibilism can be found in A. J. Ayer, "Freedom and Necessity," in his *Philosophical Essays* (London: Macmillan, 1954). For a delightful critique of compatibilism, presented in a spirited dialogue by an Italian humanist philosopher of the fifteenth century, see Lorenzo Valla, "Dialogue on Free Will." It can be found in *The Renaissance Philosophy of Man*, Ernst Cassirer, Paul Oskar Kristeller, and John Herman Randall, editors (Chicago, IL: The University of Chicago Press, 1948). The book also contains an excellent translation of Giovanni Pico della Mirandola's "The Dignity of Man."

The position we called deep compatibilism is championed by Harry G. Frankfurt. Frankfurt developed his views in a number of essays, all of them collected in *The Importance of What We Care About* (Cambridge, MA: Cambridge University Press, 1988). Another excellent deep compatibilist source is Gerald Dworkin's *The Theory and Practice of Autonomy* (Cambridge, MA: Cambridge University Press, 1988).

Rationalist compatibilism is presented most effectively by Susan Wolf, in *Freedom Within Reason* (New York: Oxford University Press, 1990).

Daniel Dennett has written two very entertaining and readable books that take a compatibilist view on free will: *Elbow Room* (Cambridge, MA: Bradford Books, 1985), and *Freedom Evolves* (New York: Viking, 2003). P. F. Strawson's "Freedom and Resentment" was originally published in 1962; it is now widely anthologized, including in the Gary Watson anthology, *Free Will*, listed here. Strawson's essay has been a very influential compatibilist view, arguing that we simply can't get along without our basic concepts of freedom and responsibility, whatever scientists might discover about determinism.

Philosophers who deny the existence of free will altogether (generally because they favor determinism and believe determinism and free will are incompatible) include Julien Offray de La Mettrie, *Man a Machine* (1747); Baron D'Holbach *The System of Nature* (1770); Arthur Schopenhauer, *Essay on the Freedom of the Will* (first published in 1841, reissued by New York: Liberal Arts Press, 1960). More recently, John Hospers has denied free will (making extensive use of Freudian psychology in his arguments); see "What Means This Freedom," in *Determinism and Freedom in the Age of Modern Science*, Sidney Hook, editor (New York: New York University Press, 1958). B. F. Skinner, in *Beyond Freedom and Dignity* (New York: Alfred A. Knopf, 1971), as well as in his utopian novel, *Walden Two* (first published in 1948; available in paperback, New York: Macmillan, 1976), is often thought to be rejecting free will altogether. In fact, his writings reject *libertarian* free will (and moral responsibility), but he strongly champions compatibilist free will.

There are many excellent free will anthologies; perhaps the best small collection is edited by Gary Watson: *Free Will* (Oxford: Oxford University Press, 1982). There are excellent recent anthologies edited by Laura Waddell Ekstrom, *Agency and Responsibility* (Boulder, CO: Westview Press, 2001); and by Robert Kane, *Free Will* (Malden, MA: Blackwell Publishing, 2002).

Some excellent Web resources are Ted Honderich's *Determinism and Freedom Philosophy Website*, at *http://www.ucl.ac.uk/~uctytho/dfwIntroIndex.htm*; *The Garden of Forking Paths*, at *http://gfp.typepad.com/the_garden_of_forking_pat/*; and the Naturalism.org site at *http://www.naturalism.org/freewill.htm*. Unfortunately, The Garden of Forking Paths site is now inactive (though it still contains a wealth of material); for ongoing discussion of free will and moral responsibility, go to the Flickers of Freedom site, at *http://agencyand responsibility.typepad.com/flickers-of-freedom/*.

NOTES

[1] William Barrett, "Determinism and Novelty," in *Determinism and Freedom in the Age of Modern Science*, Sidney Hook, editor (New York: Collier Books, 1961), p. 46.

[2] Barrett, 1961, pp. 46–47.

[3] David Hume, "Of Liberty and Necessity," *Enquiry Concerning the Human Understanding* (Oxford: Clarendon Press, 1902), p. 80.

[4] Hume, "Of Liberty and Necessity," p. 100.

[5] Susan Wolf, *Freedom Within Reason* (Oxford: Oxford University Press, 990), p. 55.

[6] Kant, 1788, p. 259.

[7] F. Dostoyevsky, *Notes from Underground*, trans. Andrew R. MacAndrew (New York: New American Library, 1961), p. 114. Originally published in 1864.

[8] Roderick Chisholm, "Human Freedom and the Self," The Lindley Lecture, University of Kansas, 1964; reprinted in *Free Will*, Gary Watson, editor (Oxford: Oxford University Press, 1982), 24–35.

[9] Jean-Paul Sartre, "Existentialism Is a Humanism," in *Existentialism from Dostoevsky to Sartre*, W. Kaufmann, editor (New York: New Arena Library, 1975), pp. 352–353. First published in 1946.

[10] C. A. Campbell, *On Selfhood and Godhood* (London: George Allen & Unwin, 1957), p. 163.

[11] Campbell, p. 177.

[12] C. A. Campbell; italics in original.

14

Freedom, Moral Responsibility, and Ethics

The question of free will is closely related to a major ethical issue: Are we *morally responsible* for what we do? Do we justly deserve blame and punishment for our transgressions, and reward for our triumphs? Many philosophers have treated the questions of free will and moral responsibility (or "just deserts") as two sides of a single coin. C. A. Campbell, for example, insists that

> It is not seriously disputable that the kind of freedom in question is the freedom which is commonly recognised to be in some sense a precondition of moral responsibility. Clearly, it is on account of this integral connection with moral responsibility that such exceptional importance has always been felt to attach to the Free Will problem. But in what precise sense is free will a precondition of moral responsibility, and thus a postulate of the moral life in general?[1]

Psychiatrist Willard Gaylin, former director of the Hastings Center for Applied Ethics, sums up his view of the question thus:

> Freedom demands responsibility; autonomy demands culpability.[2]

That's the entire paragraph, and that's all Gaylin has to say on the subject: the connection between freedom (autonomy) and moral responsibility (culpability) is so obvious that it need only be stated.

But the connection has not seemed so obvious to everyone. Some have thought we could be morally responsible (justly deserving of punishment) even though we are not free. For example, Jonathan Edwards (a famous preacher and theologian of colonial New England) denied that humans have free will. God is *omni*potent, *all* powerful, and therefore humans have no power to make choices. Instead a few are saved by the gift of God's grace, and not from their own free choices. But though we are not *free*, we are nonetheless sinful and wicked, and thus God *justly* punishes us. On the other side, some believe we have *free will* (in Hume's compatibilist sense of being free to choose as we wish, though our wishes are determined), but such free will cannot justify moral responsibility. (For moral responsibility we would need *libertarian* free will, and we do not have that.) Thus—on this view—we might have compatibilist free will, but not be morally responsible.

But just as there are differing accounts of free will, there are also many different views of moral responsibility. Before trying to navigate our way through that labyrinth, it is important to be clear on exactly what moral responsibility is.

TYPES OF RESPONSIBILITY

Role Responsibility

Not all responsibility is *moral* responsibility. Moral responsibility is the foundation for judgments that a person justly deserves blame or punishment, praise or reward. There is a very different type of responsibility we might call *role* responsibility,[3] which unfortunately is often confused with moral responsibility. You're planning a picnic with some friends, and it's your job—your responsibility, your *role* responsibility—to bring a keg of beer. Suppose you succeed splendidly, the keg is there on time, nicely chilled, pumping perfectly. Then you have fulfilled your role responsibility. But your *moral* responsibility is another question altogether. It is something very different to suppose that you justly deserve praise or blame, reward or punishment, for how you carry out your role responsibility. Suppose someone says "Susan did a great job providing the keg; she carried out her role splendidly, and deserves our praise." Someone else might deny that Susan deserves any praise for her role responsibility success: "Yeah, Susan provided the keg; but her mom owns the brewery! Susan just told one of the delivery guys when and where to set the keg up, and that's all she had to do. She doesn't deserve any special credit." Maybe Susan does deserve credit, or maybe she doesn't. That is, maybe she is morally responsible for what she did, maybe she is not. But that's a different question from the question of whether she met her role responsibility. If it is clear that she carried out her role responsibility, but her moral responsibility remains in doubt, then obviously these are two different senses of responsibility.

Suppose the opposite occurs: everyone arrives at the picnic, but there's no beer. Susan had the role responsibility for making sure the keg was at the picnic, but she neglected to do it. She failed at her role responsibility. But the question of whether she is morally responsible is quite a different matter. "Susan had role responsibility for the keg, and she blew it. But you can't really blame her: she's been under so much stress from finishing her senior project and waiting to hear from medical schools; it was just more than she could handle." So Susan has *role* responsibility, but it's not at all clear that she also has *moral* responsibility. Again, that marks two distinctly different meanings of responsibility (even if you believe that Susan *is* morally responsible, that is clearly a distinct issue from whether she is role responsible).

Taking Role Responsibility

Another way of marking the distinction between role and moral responsibility is that often one can *take* role responsibility. When we are planning the picnic, Susan can *take* responsibility for bringing a keg, simply by agreeing to do so. But you can't take moral responsibility: if we are debating whether Susan *deserves credit* (is morally responsible) for securing a keg—since her Mom did all the work—Susan can't settle the issue by claiming or taking moral responsibility. Her claim of moral responsibility will not establish that she justly deserves reward. Likewise, if someone claims moral responsibility for a bad act, that will not settle the issue of his actual moral responsibility. John Spenkelink was the first person to be executed by Florida after it reinstated capital punishment. A few days before his execution, Spenkelink *claimed* full moral responsibility for the murder he had committed. What had led him on this path to murder? John had been a well-behaved kid until at age 11 he returned home from school to discover the body of his beloved father, who had committed suicide. After that John lost interest in school, began to get into trouble while skipping school, dropped out, began drinking heavily, and was drifting around the Southeast until he killed a fellow drifter in a violent argument. So was John Spenkelink morally responsible for the path he followed after discovering his father's suicide? Suicide often has a devastating psychological impact on family and friends, and it is hard to imagine the traumatic effect on an adolescent boy who is the first to discover his father's body. Traumatized or not, perhaps John did have full moral responsibility for his further behavior, and for the murder he committed. Perhaps not. But his *claim* of moral responsibility carries no weight in trying to resolve that question. Claiming or taking *role* responsibility is one thing; *moral* responsibility is a different matter.

Role responsibility for a keg at a summer picnic is hardly insignificant. But role responsibility for yourself, and for who you are, and for what you do: that's considerably more important. If I cannot make my own moral decisions, follow my own drummer, and exercise control over my plans and purposes—in short, *take* role responsibility for my own moral life—then I cannot be a full moral being. If you make all my moral decisions for me, usurp my authority, and prevent me from taking responsibility, then I am a puppet rather than a moral agent. I must be able to take responsibility for my own moral life if I am to have a moral life at all. But though I take role responsibility for my own moral life, it is a very different matter to judge that I am *morally responsible*.

Donna makes her own moral decisions, she takes responsibility for them, and she rightly resents interference. But one might acknowledge that Donna takes full role responsibility for her moral life while still questioning whether she justly deserves credit or blame (whether she is *morally* responsible). After all, it is quite legitimate to say: Donna has taken full (role) responsibility for her moral life; but when we understand how vilely she was treated as a child, and how few psychological resources she has for living a virtuous life, we should not blame her for exercising her taken responsibility so miserably.[4] And the same issues arise if Donna lives a life of great moral worth: Donna takes role responsibility for her own moral life and moral decisions; but is she *morally* responsible for her virtuous life, or is she instead lucky to have the early environment and moral fortitude and generous sympathies that enabled her to choose and follow a virtuous life course? (Some will maintain that Donna really is *morally* responsible. But that will be a different issue from judging that she has *taken* responsibility, that she has *role responsibility* for her life.)

Of course, if you are severely incompetent—a small child, or badly brain damaged, or suffering severe dementia—then you are incapable of exercising role responsibility for your life, and someone else has to make decisions for you. But if (perhaps because of an abusive or overindulgent childhood) I am *lousy* at exercising role responsibility for myself (I repeatedly make bad marriage choices and poor career decisions, and I choose impulsively), I may still have *full* role responsibility for my own life. If you try to interfere or offer unsolicited advice, I shall feel resentful. After all, it's *my* life, and I want to make my *own* choices. You may be able to make better choices for me than I could for myself, but I still insist on making my own choices and exercising full role responsibility for my own life. But moral responsibility is quite different. While I may have full role responsibility for running my own life, it does not follow that I am *morally responsible*—that I *justly deserve* reward or punishment—for managing my life well or ill. It makes perfectly good sense to say: "Doug has full role responsibility for his life, he makes his own choices; but (for whatever reason—his early environment or his genetic makeup or his natural impetuosity) Doug is so lousy at exercising responsibility that he deserves no blame for making such a mess of his life." That is, Doug takes role responsibility for his life but may still lack moral responsibility. (You may believe that anyone who exercises role responsibility for her life *is* morally responsible for the choices she makes. Perhaps that's true. The point here is that it is a *separate* issue: the question of whether one is role responsible is not the same as the question of whether one is morally responsible).

In sum, *role* responsibility for yourself and your acts is essential for morality. To live morally, I must make my own choices, rather than being pulled by someone else's strings. But that role responsibility requirement for morality is not *moral* responsibility. So if someone confidently asserts that morality requires responsibility, it is possible he or she is thinking of role responsibility, and then confusing it with moral responsibility.

MORAL RESPONSIBILITY AND THE UTILITY OF PUNISHMENT

When we are considering moral responsibility, the first task is to distinguish it from role responsibility. But with the focus squarely on moral responsibility, there are still serious questions about what justifies claims and ascriptions of moral responsibility. Does Ikram *deserve blame or punishment* (or praise and reward)? That is, is Ikram *morally responsible* for what he did? It is sometimes suggested that this is simply a question of whether it is useful to punish Ikram, but that hardly seems adequate to justify claims of moral responsibility. It's easy to think of cases in which punishment might be *useful*, but would not be justified because the victim of the punishment is not morally responsible: does not justly deserve punishment. For example, suppose that we experience a wave of brutal murders, apparently committed almost randomly by a number of unrelated people, but we have not been able to catch any of the murderers. We become convinced that if one murderer were caught and executed, the others would become frightened and stop their crimes, but unfortunately we cannot apprehend a murderer. However, there is an innocent, harmless, friendless, homeless man roaming the streets, and it would be easy to frame him. So, someone might be tempted to frame this poor innocent and punish him: execute him. And it might even be *useful* to do so (though, of course, there would be great risks of this plot being discovered, with terrible consequences). But however useful it might or might not be, it certainly would not be *just:* the man does not justly deserve punishment. Or consider another case: a person in our community becomes a carrier for a terrible deadly disease, and spreads it to all those with whom she comes in contact. She herself is not affected by the disease, and lives in perfect health while she spreads the disease—unknowingly—to others. When we discover that she is carrying this deadly disease, we will take measures to stop her from spreading this infection. If we cannot destroy the disease in her, we shall have to quarantine her, perhaps even place her in isolation on an island. This will be useful, perhaps even essential; but she certainly does not *deserve* to be placed in solitary confinement.

One more example. A nefarious chemist invents a drug that transforms those who ingest it into violent and dangerous thugs. Our gentle friend Joe is given the drug (the chemist slips it into a glass of orange juice in the cafeteria line, and Joe happens to get that glass). It turns out that the only way to rehabilitate someone who has taken this drug is to punish him severely after he commits a violent act. Most of us will have doubts about Joe *deserving* punishment (Joe merely drew the unlucky juice glass), but the punishment will be quite *useful* if it results in Joe's rehabilitation. In similar manner, when a child touches a hot stove and is burned, it may be a useful learning experience. That does not imply that she justly deserved to be burned. So, genuine moral responsibility cannot be established on the basis of the usefulness of punishment and reward. If a person justly deserves punishment, then that person must be morally responsible for the punished act, and the utility or disutility of the punishment is irrelevant; likewise, if a person justly deserves the reward for winning a race, the fact that more people would be made happy by giving the reward to someone else has no bearing on the winner's just deserts. (Of course, if everyone hates the winner, we might decide to give the award to someone else. But then we will be deciding that there is something more important than just deserts, *not* that the winner does not justly deserve the reward.)

CONDITIONS FOR MORAL RESPONSIBILITY

Moral responsibility, thus, carries very strong conditions. But whatever else moral responsibility may require, *most* have believed that at the very least it requires freedom. I am not morally responsible for shooting someone if I am placed in steel restraints that force my hand to grip a pistol and my finger to close on the trigger. I am not morally responsible for robbing a bank if you have drugged me and turned me into a compulsive bank robber who cannot help robbing banks.

Could You Do Otherwise?

But exactly what sort of freedom—and what sort of free will—does moral responsibility require? C. A. Campbell answers that the only account of free will that can support moral responsibility is the libertarian view, in which you are acting freely (and thus you are morally responsible for your acts) *if and only if* you could have actually done otherwise. So obviously one reason for embracing the rather mysterious, miracle-working model of libertarian free will is because of the libertarian conviction that only such a radical account of free will can make sense of moral responsibility: How could we *blame* someone for doing wrong (or credit someone for doing right) if that person could not have done otherwise?

This question plunges us into a dispute that has raged for many centuries. Consider our profoundly virtuous friend Alexandra. She is a paragon of virtue, who does good joyfully and brushes aside "temptations" easily. Alexandra is offered an opportunity to pick up a huge windfall by profiting on inside information from a corporation CEO: the stock price on Shady Deal Industries is currently very high, but the company's books have been manipulated to hide enormous losses, and when those losses are revealed Shady Deal Industries stock will be almost worthless. Alexandra can sell the stock short, and cash in on a small fortune. There is no way her devious insider trading will be discovered. She will simply look like a shrewd investor who profited by her careful analysis of the market. Alexandra cannot even imagine doing such a thing: "I couldn't possibly do that; it would be unfair to other people who will lose the money I gain through this inside information." Is Alexandra *morally responsible*—does she deserve credit—for her virtuous choice?

Alexandra *cannot* do a devious and dishonest act. Of course she could *if* she wanted to; but given who she is, there is no way she could *want* to do such a thing. (Saying that she could nonetheless do so is just silly; it's like saying that if you had wings, then you could fly—so even though you don't have wings, you could still fly.) So Alexandra cannot consider insider trading. But does it follow that Alexandra deserves no credit, that she is not morally responsible for her virtuous behavior?

It may seem from such examples that one might deserve credit or blame even if one could not do otherwise. But there are cases that seem to lead to the opposite conclusion. Patty Hearst is the daughter of the fabulously wealthy Hearst family. She was kidnapped (and supposedly brainwashed) by a group of revolutionaries calling themselves the Symbionese Liberation Army. She was present and heavily armed during robberies carried out by the Symbionese Liberation Army. At her trial, the prosecution claimed that Patty had been converted to the Symbionese Liberation Army cause, and that she was a willing participant in the robberies. The Hearst case is difficult and controversial, and raises many questions: Was Patty Hearst actually "brainwashed"? Did she genuinely convert to the Symbionese Liberation Army, or was she forced to participate? To avoid those complications, consider a fictional case: Nancy Wurst is a law-abiding college student, the daughter of a wealthy family. She is kidnapped by a band of revolutionaries and bank robbers (the Anarchist Brigade) and *effectively* brainwashed into becoming a dedicated convert to their values (suspend your doubts about whether brainwashing is really possible). She now deeply believes in the values of the Anarchist Brigade, and she robs banks because she *wants* to. She is so profoundly dedicated to the cause that she *cannot* choose otherwise. But she is not some mindless zombie: she discusses the values she now holds, she effectively plans bank robberies, she reads books and watches movies and talks intelligently with her friends. In the course of one of the robberies, Nancy is captured. She remains steadfast in her commitment to the Anarchist Brigade, so we shall certainly have to take steps to protect society from her attacks. But the question is: Does Nancy *deserve punishment*? Is she *morally responsible* for her criminal behavior?

Suppose the Anarchist Brigade has developed *very* effective brainwashing techniques, and they have the ability to convert—brainwash—anyone they capture. Nancy was unlucky: she happened to be the one they caught. Before they kidnapped her, she was just as peaceful and law-abiding as you are (probably more). If you had been the one kidnapped, then you would now be an enthusiastic bank-robbing member of the Anarchist Brigade. Would you deserve punishment for your crimes? That is, would *you* be morally responsible under those circumstances?

The "brainwashing" carried out by the Symbionese Liberation Army on Patty Hearst required several weeks to convert her. The Anarchist Brigade is much better, and they do the job in a couple of days. Suppose they become even more sophisticated, and can do the trick by simply slipping a pill into your coffee, a pill that takes effect in about 30 seconds and radically alters your entire worldview, transforming you into a dedicated disciple of the Anarchist Brigade. The pill was placed in Nancy's coffee while she was having breakfast at the local diner. Several of you were having breakfast together, and she just happened to get the cup with the pill. Does that change anything?

Suppose the process takes a much longer time: not 30 seconds, or 30 days, but about 20 years. That is, suppose that Nancy was born into a family that belonged to the Anarchist Brigade, and the course of her development—her environment together with her genetic heritage—shaped her into a dedicated member of the Brigade. Of course she now robs banks because she *wants* to; she *chooses* to rob banks. But her desires and choices are the determined result of how she was shaped. Like getting the unlucky cup of coffee, Nancy drew the unlucky long-term environment. You, a person who is not tempted to rob banks, drew a more fortunate environmental history. You were lucky, and Nancy unlucky; but can we establish *just deserts* and *moral responsibility* on a foundation of good or bad luck?

If Nancy rejects the Anarchist Brigade (she was a rebellious teenager and rejected her parents' values), then that choice was also the product of her conditioning history. There was some environmental cause that, fortunately, led her to reject a life of bank robbery. Or at least there was such a cause, unless you believe in the special godlike libertarian power to make choices with no causal antecedents. This is not to deny that Nancy makes choices and decisions, follows her own goals, values, and preferences. That may be sufficient to count Nancy and ourselves as *free* (according to compatibilist views of free will). But when we look very closely at the causes that shaped her, and that shape the choices we make and the values we cherish, the notion of *moral responsibility* becomes more problematic. Of course, we can insist that Nancy really *is* a bank robber. That's true, certainly. But the question is whether she *justly deserves punishment* for being a bank robber. Furthermore, Nancy *chooses* to be a bank robber, and she *values* her career of bank robbery. But if those choices and values are the product of her good or bad fortune, there remains the question of whether she is morally responsible for them.

STRAWSON'S SOCIAL JUSTIFICATION OF MORAL RESPONSIBILITY

Peter F. Strawson, in a very influential paper entitled "Freedom and Resentment," proposes a new justification for moral responsibility. Strawson argues that many of our basic social practices and human relations involve (what Strawson calls) the *participant reactive attitudes*: that is, attitudes of natural human social reaction such as resentment, gratitude, forgiveness, anger, and reciprocal love. These reactive attitudes *presuppose* belief in moral responsibility. In contrast to reactive attitudes, we may sometimes take an *objective* stance toward someone. In that case, we treat the individual as *not* being morally responsible, and instead we regard the individual as an object that may potentially cause harm, and which we can try to understand and control—but not as someone we can reason with, or resent, or forgive. You can fear, try to avoid, and attempt to control a madman or a tornado; but you cannot really reason with them, resent them, judge them as morally bad, forgive them, or hold them morally responsible: participant reactive attitudes are not appropriate in those cases. When we regard someone from the objective perspective, that is typically because the individual is demented or severely impaired or in some other way not fully rational, and thus not someone we can regard as an appropriate subject of our reactive attitudes. Strawson insists that we can occasionally regard *some* individuals objectively rather than reactively, but we could not abandon the reactive attitudes altogether, adopting instead a universal objective perspective. Even if we can imagine or speculate about the wholesale rejection of our participant reactive attitudes, it is not realistic: our most basic social relations and interactions require the reactive—rather than objective—attitudes, and these natural human reactions cannot simply be abandoned. Even if some massive psychological and social transformation project made it possible to completely eliminate our reactive attitudes and replace them with objective attitudes, that is certainly not a shift we would endorse. Since we cannot give up those basic social practices or the reactive attitudes involved in them, we cannot really consider giving up belief in moral responsibility (for belief in moral responsibility is an integral element, a precondition, of such reactive attitudes). If you eliminate moral responsibility, you destroy the foundation of our participant reactive attitudes. Perhaps we can't *prove* that there are legitimate grounds for holding people morally responsible; but such proof is not required. Our belief in moral responsibility is demonstrated by our use of social practices for which moral responsibility is an essential element. We cannot give up those social practices, nor would we wish to do so; and so we cannot genuinely consider renouncing belief in moral responsibility.

Strawson's position raises a range of tough questions: If we deny that Joe is morally responsible, can we still regard Joe as rational? As virtuous? As morally bad? Strawson says we cannot, and the entire range of questions is much disputed.

So the question of moral responsibility leaves us with several alternatives. First, we can embrace the libertarian position—a position that strikes some as being hard to swallow, perhaps even incoherent, but which may be the only account that will provide a foundation for moral responsibility. Second, we can try to find a way to justify moral responsibility on compatibilist grounds: Nancy's choices and values and character are the determined product of good or bad fortune, but she still deserves credit or blame for them. Third, we can reject moral responsibility. Or fourth, like Strawson, we can treat moral responsibility as an essential element of our social structure. Philosophers are deeply divided over what alternative is best. You'll have to decide for yourself. But before deciding, you might want to consider how this question is related to your larger views concerning ethics.

MORAL RESPONSIBILITY AND ETHICS

What is the relation between moral responsibility and ethics? Many philosophers believe that without moral responsibility, there could be no real ethics. Libertarian C. A. Campbell insists that denial of justly deserved praise and blame would destroy "the reality of the moral life." You may recall that Susan Wolf is a Kantian, for whom genuine freedom consists in rationally following the True and the Good; but she concurs with Campbell that if we deny moral responsibility, then we must

> . . . stop thinking in terms of what ought and ought not to be. We would have to stop thinking in terms that would allow the possibility that some lives and projects are better than others.[5]

A similar view is voiced by Catholic philosopher F. C. Copleston, who asserts that without moral responsibility "there would be no objective moral distinction between the emperor Nero and St. Francis of Assisi."[6]

ETHICS WITHOUT MORAL RESPONSIBILITY

But would the denial of moral responsibility really mean the end of all morality? Consider morality in its most majestic form: true morality is whatever God pronounces good, and it derives its authority and truth solely from God's holy will. Martin Luther and John Calvin had no difficulty proclaiming such a transcendent moral law while simultaneously rejecting all moral responsibility. God hardens whom He will harden, and shows mercy to whom He will show mercy; and thus, as Paul asserted, "it is not of him that willeth, nor of him that runneth, but of God that showeth mercy." So it is wrong that "any man should boast" of his just deserts; rather, God by His grace makes some righteous while leaving others in depraved wickedness. The virtuous have no grounds for boasting, for they have no moral responsibility for their righteousness. That does not alter the fact that they truly are virtuous (by God's grace) and the wicked are morally loathsome. One may find such moral views repugnant, but it seems clear that Luther and Calvin could consistently champion an *ethical* doctrine and make moral judgments while *rejecting* moral responsibility.

It appears that other ethical systems can also survive without moral responsibility. Suppose Wanda adopts the Kantian view that moral principles are derived from rational deduction, and she deduces that her basic moral obligation is to live by a rule that she could will as a universal law. Wanda further believes that whether one is able to conform one's will to that high rational moral standard is a matter of one's good or bad fortune, and thus we are not morally responsible for either success or failure in our moral lives. It is Wanda's good fortune to have the clear reason and strong willpower required for Kantian moral goodness, but she deserves no credit for her severe moral virtue. Kant himself would agree with Wanda's rationalist ethics, but reject her views on moral responsibility. But it seems that Kantian rationalist ethics does not *require* moral responsibility.

Clearly, if all our acts were purely luck, then morality and moral judgments would be impossible. It's not by *luck* that the Kantian performs a virtuous act: she performs the act purposefully and reflectively, and as a result of her own careful deliberations. But that is consistent with holding that she deserves no *credit* for her purposeful virtuous behavior, since she is ultimately lucky to have developed the capacities for such virtuous rational reflection. Thus, it is not inconsistent to judge her life *virtuous*—by the most severe rationalistic ethical laws—while *denying* that she is morally responsible.[7] They are separate issues, and establishing the existence of moral acts does not automatically entail the existence of moral responsibility.

Moral Judgments and Moral Responsibility

Without moral responsibility, some moral judgments do become impossible. We can no longer say things like Jones justly deserves praise for her virtuous character, and Smith deserves blame for his vicious acts. But that is obviously not the whole of morality. In the absence of moral responsibility, we can continue to judge Jones's character as virtuous and Smith's acts as vicious. And we can strive to shape our children like the virtuous Jones and struggle to eliminate vicious acts in ourselves and others, and thereby consciously shape an environment that maximizes virtue and minimizes vice. Without moral responsibility, there is still a wide range for ethical judgments and behavior and planning.

Consider Ebeneezer Scrooge, the famous Dickens character. Scrooge (pre-ghosts) is the paradigm for a thoroughly greedy and sordid person. Scrooge has sharp intelligence, and he weighs alternatives and makes his own choices, and through his iron self-control he resolutely follows his miserly pattern of life. Scrooge is utterly vile, and his miserly character is thoroughly his own. But is he morally responsible, does he deserve blame for his selfish character and his selfish acts? Dickens shows us how Scrooge's early poverty marked him with a terrible fear of the cruel treatment the world metes out to the impoverished— "there is nothing on which it [the world] is so hard as poverty," Scrooge asserts—and his early love, Belle, describes his resulting character accurately:

> You fear the world too much. . . . All your other hopes have merged into the hope of being beyond the chance of its sordid reproach. I have seen your nobler aspirations fall off one by one, until the master passion, Gain, engrosses you.

But miserliness is a characteristic that Scrooge considers and approves: "What then?" he retorted. "Even if I have grown so much wiser, what then?"

Scrooge is a thoroughly sordid and greedy character. But when Dickens lets us glimpse the grinding poverty that shaped him, we feel less confident that he deserves blame. Certainly, Scrooge has moral faults (such as miserliness) and they are his *own* moral flaws. But does it follow that he is morally responsible for his moral faults? Scrooge intentionally pursues—profoundly and reflectively pursues—a life of greed that enriches himself and impoverishes others. Scrooge is not incompetent, and he follows his own deeply held goal: the goal of accumulating as much wealth as he possibly can, with no regard for who gets hurt or exploited in the process (given the "accounting irregularities" of the past few years, he seems a depressingly familiar figure). Ebeneezer Scrooge is certainly someone most of us would regard as morally loathsome. But is Scrooge morally responsible for his intentional avaricious acts? When we look more deeply into Scrooge's all-consuming and purposeful selfishness, we find a history of desperate deprivation that shaped his greedy character. Scrooge is now a purposefully greedy, cold-hearted, single-minded pursuer of riches, whose acts are morally vicious because his own deepest intentions are vile. But like all of us, he was shaped by forces that made him what he is; and if he has—or lacks—the reflective and self-evaluative[8] capacities to change, then those capacities are themselves the product of forces that were ultimately beyond his control. So, is Scrooge morally responsible for the greedy acts he intentionally performs?

Some answer yes, some no. Clearly, libertarians would reject this account of how Scrooge became what he is. But if you can regard this as even a legitimate *question*, then obviously you believe that judgments of moral responsibility are distinct from moral judgments. If you can judge someone morally bad, and still have some question of whether that morally bad person is *morally responsible*, then you do not believe that morality requires moral responsibility.

Retribution

There is no doubt that retribution is a powerful motive: "revenge is sweet," as the saying goes. When wronged, we desire revenge, and we feel that taking revenge is *just*. Those whose loved ones have been harmed or killed commonly feel that justice requires retribution, and we generally feel that those who work hard and make a contribution justly deserve reward. So obviously we have deep feelings about "retributive justice" and "getting even" and "just rewards." But how reliable are those feelings as moral guides?

That returns us to one of the most basic questions we have examined. Most (Kant is the great exception) believe that our *feelings*, especially our "moral feelings" (such as affection and pity and sympathy), are important. Granted the strength and importance of such feelings, it also seems clear that our feelings can sometimes benefit from guidance. You are walking through the autumn woods with a friend; as you pass along a narrow tree-lined path, your friend holds back a large limb to let you pass—and then just as you draw even, she releases the limb, and it swings back and smacks you in the mouth. You are livid, and every impulse in your being cries out for retribution. But then you discover that your friend suffered a mild stroke, which caused her to lose strength in her arms, and she was unable to hold the branch back. Your improved knowledge of the situation swiftly changes your retributive emotions into feelings of solicitude. Would wider knowledge of the causes of character and behavior have a similar effect on our retributive feelings in other cases? Some say that "To know all is to forgive all." That is, if we really understood what shaped people to be the way they are (if we "walked a mile in their shoes"), we would feel less inclined to demand retribution. Scrooge is a vile and greedy man; but when we look more closely at the harsh forces that shaped him, we perhaps feel less inclined to demand retributive punishment for the wrongs he has committed. We want him to change, of course. We believe that he really is morally bad, and we're glad the ghosts paid him a transforming visit—and in the absence of ghosts, we may seek other means of modifying his character. But we may feel less desire to gain revenge for his miserly treatment of his employees. Or perhaps we still feel a desire for revenge but judge that this is a desire we ought to hold in check (like the desire you sometimes feel to choke the person sitting in the airport lounge talking loudly on his cell phone, or your desire to have a wild fling with your best friend's sweetheart).

CONCLUSION

So we return to the question of the respective roles of feelings and rationality in ethics. As T. S. Eliot says, "in our end is our beginning." Or perhaps we've just been going in circles. Maybe, in the course of examining ethical theories, you have found one that fits perfectly the way you look at ethics. Or possibly you have emerged less certain, and just a bit dizzy, without any clear ethical recipes. If you have also emerged with a better understanding of some of the key issues in ethics, and the connections among those issues, and an interest in those issues, then perhaps that's not a bad thing. One of the most important things in ethics is being sensitive to ethical questions and ethical issues. When people go wrong—they cheat their investors, or abuse their patients, or betray their friends—the problem *may* be that they don't have a clear ethical code to follow. More likely, they didn't really think about what they were doing as having an ethical component at all ("I'm just maximizing profits, there's nothing else to consider"). If we wonder how so many otherwise decent people could have been slaveholders—or more recently, could have supported apartheid in South Africa or the Jim Crow racist oppression of the American South—one likely reason is that they failed to recognize what they were doing as a *moral issue*. Slavery and apartheid were "just the ways things have always worked," or "simply an economic decision." Of course, being bothered by or concerned about ethical issues is not itself sufficient for ethical behavior. (Many slaveholders worried about the moral wrong of enslaving fellow humans, but years and lifetimes passed while they did nothing to correct that wrong.) Still, reflective awareness of ethical issues is an important element of ethical development. So if you are encouraged to think more about ethical issues, and to be more alert to ethical quandaries, then perhaps you've made some ethical gains, even if you are more ethically confused than when you started. And gaining some practice at thinking hard about ethical issues is valuable, even if you are currently confident of your own ethical principles. For new and unsettling ethical issues constantly emerge: Is cloning morally legitimate? Should we allow genetic therapy for human enhancement (to make people taller or faster or smarter, rather than to treat genetic diseases)? Whatever combination of reason, emotion, or intuition comprises your moral capacities, it is important to keep those powers in good working order and give them regular exercise. You're going to need them.

⇒⊶ MORAL LUCK ⊰⇐
Thomas Nagel

Thomas Nagel is a professor of philosophy and law at New York University. Generally recognized as a leading Kantian, he is certainly not doctrinaire in his views. In particular, he is known for raising serious philosophical perplexities to which he offers at most only tentative solutions; and the philosophically famous essay on moral luck, printed here, is a good example. Among Nagel's major works are *The Possibility of Altruism* (Princeton, NJ: Princeton University Press, 1970) *Mortal Questions,* which contains the essay "Moral Luck" (Cambridge, MA: Cambridge University Press, 1979) and *The View from Nowhere* (Oxford: Oxford University Press, 1986). All of Nagel's works are delightful to read; the questions they raise, however, are not easy to answer.

Kant believed that good or bad luck should influence neither our moral judgment of a person and his actions, nor his moral assessment of himself.

The good will is not good because of what it effects or accomplishes or because of its adequacy to achieve some proposed end; it is good only because of its willing, i.e., it is good of itself. And, regarded for itself, it is to be esteemed incomparably higher than anything which could be brought about by it in favor of any inclination or even of the sum total of all inclinations. Even if it should happen that, by a particularly unfortunate fate or by the niggardly provision of a stepmotherly nature, this will should be wholly lacking in power to accomplish its purpose, and if even the greatest effort should not avail it to achieve anything of its end, and if there remained only the good will (not as a mere wish but as the summoning of all the means in our power), it would sparkle like a jewel in its own right, as something that had its full worth in itself. Usefulness or fruitlessness can neither diminish nor augment this worth.

He would presumably have said the same about a bad will: whether it accomplishes its evil purposes is morally irrelevant. And a course of action that would be condemned if it had a bad outcome cannot be vindicated if by luck it turns out well. There cannot be moral risk. This view seems to be wrong, but it arises in response to a fundamental problem about moral responsibility to which we possess no satisfactory solution.

The problem develops out of the ordinary conditions of moral judgment. Prior to reflection it is intuitively plausible that people cannot be morally assessed for what is not their fault, or for what is due to factors beyond their control. Such judgment is different from the evaluation of something as a good or bad thing, or state of affairs. The latter may be present in addition to moral judgment, but when we blame someone for his actions we are not merely saying it is bad that they happened, or bad that he exists: we are judging *him*, saying he is bad, which is different from his being a bad thing. This kind of judgment takes only a certain kind of object. Without being able to explain exactly why, we feel that the appropriateness of moral assessment is easily undermined by the discovery that the act or attribute, no matter how good or bad, is not under the person's control. While other evaluations remain, this one seems to lose its footing. So a clear absence of control, produced by involuntary movement, physical force, or ignorance of the circumstances, excuses what is done from moral judgment. But what we do depends in many more ways than these on what is not under our control—what is not produced by a good or a bad will, in Kant's phrase. And external influences in this broader range are not usually thought to excuse what is done from moral judgment, positive or negative.

Let me give a few examples, beginning with the type of case Kant has in mind. Whether we succeed or fail in what we try to do nearly always depends to some extent on factors beyond our control. This is true of murder, altruism, revolution, the sacrifice of certain interests for the sake of others—almost any morally important act. What has been done, and what is morally judged, is partly determined by external factors. However jewel-like the good will may be in its own right, there is a morally significant difference between rescuing someone from a burning building and dropping him from a twelfth-storey window while trying to rescue him. Similarly, there is a morally significant difference between reckless driving and manslaughter. But whether a reckless driver hits a pedestrian depends on the presence of the pedestrian at the point where he recklessly passes a red light. What we do is also limited by the opportunities and choices with which we are faced, and these are largely determined by factors beyond our control. Someone who was an officer in a concentration camp might have led a quiet and harmless life if the Nazis had never come to power in Germany. And someone who led a quiet and harmless life in Argentina might have become an officer in a concentration camp if he had not left Germany for business reasons in 1930.

I shall say more later about these and other examples. I introduce them here to illustrate a general point. Where a significant aspect of what someone does depends on factors beyond his control, yet we continue to treat him in that respect as an object of moral judgment, it can be called moral luck. Such luck can be good or bad. And the problem posed by this phenomenon, which led Kant to deny its possibility, is that the broad range of external influences here identified seems on close examination to undermine moral assessment as surely as does the narrower range of familiar excusing conditions. If the condition of control is consistently applied, it threatens to erode most of the moral assessments we find it natural to make. The things for which people are morally judged are determined in more ways than we at first realize by what is beyond their control. And when the seemingly natural requirement of fault or responsibility is applied in light of these facts, it leaves few pre-reflective moral judgments intact. Ultimately, nothing or almost nothing about what a person does seems to be under his control.

Why not conclude, then, that the condition of control is false—that it is an initially plausible hypothesis refuted by clear counter-examples? One could in that case look instead for a more refined condition which picked out the *kinds* of lack of control that really undermine certain moral judgments, without yielding the unacceptable conclusion derived from the broader condition, that most or all ordinary moral judgments are illegitimate.

What rules out this escape is that we are dealing not with a theoretical conjecture but with a philosophical problem. The condition of control does not suggest itself merely as a generalization from certain clear cases. It seems *correct* in the further cases to which it is extended beyond the original set. When we undermine moral assessment by considering new ways in which control is absent, we are not just discovering what *would* follow given the general hypothesis, but are actually being persuaded that in itself the absence of control is relevant in these cases too. The erosion of moral judgment emerges not as the absurd consequence of an over-simple theory, but as a natural consequence of the ordinary idea of moral assessment, when it is applied in view of a more complete and precise account of the facts. It would therefore be a mistake to argue from the unacceptability of the conclusions to the need for a different account of the conditions of moral responsibility. The view that moral luck is paradoxical is not a *mistake,* ethical or logical, but a perception of one of the ways in which the intuitively acceptable conditions of moral judgment threaten to undermine it all.

Moral luck is like this because while there are various respects in which the natural objects of moral assessment are out of our control or influenced by what is out of our control, we cannot reflect on these facts without losing our grip on the judgments.

There are roughly four ways in which the natural objects of moral assessment are disturbingly subject to luck. One is the phenomenon of constitutive luck—the kind of person you are, where this is not just a question of what you deliberately do, but of your inclinations, capacities, and temperament. Another category is luck in one's circumstances—the kind of problems and situations one faces. The other two have to do with the causes and effects of action: luck in how one is determined by antecedent circumstances, and luck in the way one's actions and projects turn out. All of them present a common problem. They are all opposed by the idea that one cannot be more culpable or estimable for anything than one is for that fraction of it which is under one's control. It seems irrational to take or dispense credit or blame for matters over which a person has no control, or for their influence on results over which he has partial control. Such things may create the conditions for action, but action can be judged only to the extent that it goes beyond these conditions and does not just result from them.

Let us first consider luck, good and bad, in the way things turn out. Kant, in the above-quoted passage, has one example of this in mind, but the category covers a wide range. It includes the truck driver who accidentally runs over a child, the artist who abandons his wife and five children to devote himself to painting, and other cases in which the possibilities of success and failure are even greater. The driver, if he is entirely without fault, will feel terrible about his role in the

event, but will not have to reproach himself. Therefore this example of agent-regret is not yet a case of *moral* bad luck. However, if the driver was guilty of even a minor degree of negligence—failing to have his brakes checked recently, for example—then if that negligence contributes to the death of the child, he will not merely feel terrible. He will blame himself for the death. And what makes this an example of moral luck is that he would have to blame himself only slightly for the negligence itself if no situation arose which required him to brake suddenly and violently to avoid hitting a child. Yet the *negligence* is the same in both cases, and the driver has no control over whether a child will run into his path.

The same is true at higher levels of negligence. If someone has had too much to drink and his car swerves on to the sidewalk, he can count himself morally lucky if there are no pedestrians in its path. If there were, he would be to blame for their deaths, and would probably be prosecuted for manslaughter. But if he hurts no one, although his recklessness is exactly the same, he is guilty of a far less serious legal offence and will certainly reproach himself and be reproached by others much less severely. To take another legal example, the penalty for attempted murder is less than that for successful murder—however similar the intentions and motives of the assailant may be in the two cases. His degree of culpability can depend, it would seem, on whether the victim happened to be wearing a bullet-proof vest, or whether a bird flew into the path of the bullet—matters beyond his control.

Finally, there are cases of decision under uncertainty—common in public and in private life. Anna Karenina goes off with Vronsky, Gauguin leaves his family, Chamberlain signs the Munich agreement, the Decembrists persuade the troops under their command to revolt against the czar, the American colonies declare their independence from Britain, you introduce two people in an attempt at match-making. It is tempting in all such cases to feel that some decision must be possible, in the light of what is known at the time, which will make reproach unsuitable no matter how things turn out. But this is not true; when someone acts in such ways he takes his life, or his moral position, into his hands, because how things turn out determines what he has done. It is possible *also* to assess the decision from the point of view of what could be known at the time, but this is not the end of the story. If the Decembrists had succeeded in overthrowing Nicholas I in 1825 and establishing a constitutional regime, they would be heroes. As it is, not only did they fail and pay for it, but they bore some responsibility for the terrible punishments meted out to the troops who had been persuaded to follow them. If the American Revolution had been a bloody failure resulting in greater repression, then Jefferson, Franklin and Washington would still have made a noble attempt, and might not even have regretted it on their way to the scaffold, but they would also have had to blame themselves for what they had helped to bring on their compatriots. (Perhaps peaceful efforts at reform would eventually have succeeded.) If Hitler had not overrun Europe and exterminated millions, but instead had died of a heart attack after occupying the Sudetenland, Chamberlain's action at Munich would still have utterly betrayed the Czechs, but it would not be the great moral disaster that has made his name a household word.

In many cases of difficult choice the outcome cannot be foreseen with certainty. One kind of assessment of the choice is possible in advance, but another kind must await the outcome, because the outcome determines what has been done. The same degree of culpability or estimability in intention, motive, or concern is compatible with a wide range of judgments, positive or negative, depending on what happened beyond the point of decision. The *mens rea* which could have existed in the absence of any consequences does not exhaust the grounds of moral judgment. Actual results influence culpability or esteem in a large class of unquestionably ethical cases ranging from negligence through political choice.

That these are genuine moral judgments rather than expressions of temporary attitude is evident from the fact that one can say *in advance* how the moral verdict will depend on the results. If one negligently leaves the bath running with the baby in it, one will realize, as one bounds up the stairs toward the bathroom, that if the baby has drowned one has done something awful, whereas if it has not one has merely been careless. Someone who launches a violent revolution against an authoritarian regime knows that if he fails he will be responsible for much suffering that is in vain, but if he succeeds he will be justified by the outcome. I do not mean that *any* action can be retroactively justified by history. Certain things are so bad in themselves, or so risky, that no results can make them all right. Nevertheless, when moral judgment does depend on the outcome, it is objective and timeless and not dependent on a change of standpoint produced by success or failure. The judgment after the fact follows from an hypothetical judgment that can be made beforehand, and it can be made as easily by someone else as by the agent.

From the point of view which makes responsibility dependent on control, all this seems absurd. How is it possible to be more or less culpable depending on whether a child gets into the path of one's car, or a bird into the path of one's bullet? Perhaps it is true that what is done depends on more than the agent's state of mind or intention. The problem then is, why is it not irrational to base moral assessment on what people do, in this broad sense? It amounts to holding them responsible for the contributions of fate as well as for their own—provided they have made some contribution to begin with. If we look at cases of negligence or attempt, the pattern seems to be that overall culpability corresponds to the product of mental or intentional fault and the seriousness of the outcome. Cases of decision under uncertainty are less easily explained in this way, for it seems that the overall judgment can even shift from positive to negative depending on the outcome. But here too it seems rational to subtract the effects of occurrences subsequent to the choice, that were merely possible at the time, and concentrate moral assessment on the actual decision in light of the probabilities. If the object of moral judgment is the *person*, then to hold him accountable for what he has done in the broader sense is akin to strict liability, which may have its legal uses but seems irrational as a moral position.

The result of such a line of thought is to pare down each act to its morally essential core, an inner act of pure will assessed by motive and intention. Adam Smith advocates such a position in *The Theory of Moral Sentiments,* but notes that it runs contrary to our actual judgments.

> But how well soever we may seem to be persuaded of the truth of this equitable maxim, when we consider it after this manner, in abstract, yet when we come to particular cases, the actual consequences which happen to proceed from any action, have a very great effect upon our sentiments concerning its merit or demerit, and almost always either enhance or diminish our sense of both. Scarce, in any one instance, perhaps, will our sentiments be found, after examination, to be entirely regulated by this rule, which we all acknowledge ought entirely to regulate them.

Joel Feinberg points out further that restricting the domain of moral responsibility to the inner world will not immunize it to luck. Factors beyond the agent's control, like a coughing fit, can interfere with his decisions as surely as they can with the path of a bullet from his gun. Nevertheless the tendency to cut down the scope of moral assessment is pervasive, and does not limit itself to the influence of effects. It attempts to isolate the will from the other direction, so to speak, by separating out constitutive luck. Let us consider that next.

Kant was particularly insistent on the moral irrelevance of qualities of temperament and personality that are not under the control of the will. Such qualities as sympathy or coldness might provide the background against which obedience to moral requirements is more or less difficult, but they could not be objects of moral assessment themselves, and might well interfere with confident assessment of its proper object—the determination of the will by the motive of duty. This rules out moral judgment of many of the virtues and vices, which are states of character that influence choice but are certainly not exhausted by dispositions to act deliberately in certain ways. A person may be greedy, envious, cowardly, cold, ungenerous, unkind, vain, or conceited, but *behave* perfectly by a monumental effort of will. To possess these vices is to be unable to help having certain feelings under certain circumstances, and to have strong spontaneous impulses to act badly. Even if one controls the impulses, one still has the vice. An envious person hates the greater success of others. He can be morally condemned as envious even if he congratulates them cordially and does nothing to denigrate or spoil their success. Conceit, likewise, need not be displayed. It is fully present in someone who cannot help dwelling with secret satisfaction on the superiority of his own achievements, talents, beauty, intelligence, or virtue. To some extent such a quality may be the product of earlier choices; to some extent it may be amenable to change by current actions. But it is largely a matter of constitutive bad fortune. Yet people are morally condemned for such qualities, and esteemed for others equally beyond control of the will: they are assessed for what they are *like*.

To Kant this seems incoherent because virtue is enjoined on everyone and therefore must in principle be possible for everyone. It may be easier for some than for others, but it must be possible to achieve it by making the right choices, against whatever temperamental background. One may want to have a generous spirit, or regret not having one, but it makes no sense to condemn oneself or anyone else for a quality which is not within the control of the will. Condemnation implies that you should not be like that, not that it is unfortunate that you are.

Nevertheless, Kant's conclusion remains intuitively unacceptable. We may be persuaded that these moral judgments are irrational, but they reappear involuntarily as soon as the argument is over. This is the pattern throughout the subject.

The third category to consider is luck in one's circumstances, and I shall mention it briefly. The things we are called upon to do, the moral tests we face, are importantly determined by factors beyond our control. It may be true of someone that in a dangerous situation he would behave in a cowardly or heroic fashion, but if the situation never arises, he will never have the chance to distinguish or disgrace himself in this way, and his moral record will be different.

A conspicuous example of this is political. Ordinary citizens of Nazi Germany had an opportunity to behave heroically by opposing the regime. They also had an opportunity to behave badly, and most of them are culpable for having failed this test. But it is a test to which the citizens of other countries were not subjected, with the result that even if they, or some of them, would have behaved as badly as the Germans in like circumstances, they simply did not and therefore are not similarly culpable. Here again one is morally at the mercy of fate, and it may seem irrational upon reflection, but our ordinary moral attitudes would be unrecognizable without it. We judge people for what they actually do or fail to do, not just for what they would have done if circumstances had been different.

This form of moral determination by the actual is also paradoxical, but we can begin to see how deep in the concept of responsibility the paradox is embedded. A person can be morally responsible only for what he does; but what he does results from a great deal that he does not do; therefore he is not morally responsible for what he is and is not responsible for. (This is not a contradiction, but it is a paradox.)

It should be obvious that there is a connection between these problems about responsibility and control and an even more familiar problem, that of freedom of the will. That is the last type of moral luck I want to take up, though I can do no more within the scope of this essay than indicate its connection with the other types.

If one cannot be responsible for consequences of one's acts due to factors beyond one's control, or for antecedents of one's acts that are properties of temperament not subject to one's will, or for the circumstances that pose one's moral choices, then how can one be responsible even for the stripped-down acts of the will itself, if *they* are the product of antecedent circumstances outside of the will's control?

The area of genuine agency, and therefore of legitimate moral judgment, seems to shrink under this scrutiny to an extensionless point. Everything seems to result from the combined influence of factors, antecedent and posterior to action, that are not within the agent's control. Since he cannot be responsible for them, he cannot be responsible for their results—though it may remain possible to take up the aesthetic or other evaluative analogues of the moral attitudes that are thus displaced.

It is also possible, of course, to brazen it out and refuse to accept the results, which indeed seem unacceptable as soon as we stop thinking about the arguments. Admittedly, if certain surrounding circumstances had been different, then no unfortunate consequences would have followed from a wicked intention, and no seriously culpable act would have been performed; but since the circumstances were *not* different, and the agent *in fact* succeeded in perpetrating a particularly cruel murder, *that* is what he did, and that is what he is responsible for. Similarly, we may admit that if certain antecedent circumstances had been different, the agent would never have developed into the sort of person who would do such a thing; but since he *did* develop (as the inevitable result of those antecedent circumstances) into the sort of swine he is, and into the person who committed such a murder, *that* is what he is blameable for. In both cases one is responsible for what one actually does—even if what one actually does depends in important ways on what is not within one's control. This compatibilist account of our moral judgments would leave room for the ordinary conditions of responsibility—the absence of coercion, ignorance, or involuntary movement—as part of the determination of what someone has done—but it is understood not to exclude the influence of a great deal that he has not done.

The only thing wrong with this solution is its failure to explain how skeptical problems arise. For they arise not from the imposition of an arbitrary external requirement, but from the nature of moral judgment itself. Something in the ordinary idea of what someone does must explain how it can seem necessary to subtract from it anything that merely happens—even though the ultimate consequence of such subtraction is that nothing remains. And something in the ordinary idea of knowledge must explain why it seems to be undermined by any influences on belief not within the control of the subject—so that knowledge seems impossible without an impossible foundation in autonomous reason. But let us leave epistemology aside and concentrate on action, character, and moral assessment.

The problem arises, I believe, because the self which acts and is the object of moral judgment is threatened with dissolution by the absorption of its acts and impulses into the class of events. Moral judgment of a person is judgment not of what happens to him, but of him. It does not say merely that a certain event or state of affairs is fortunate or unfortunate or even terrible. It is not an evaluation of a state of the world, or of an individual as part of the world. We are not thinking just that it would be better if he were different, or did not

exist, or had not done some of the things he has done. We are judging *him*, rather than his existence or characteristics. The effect of concentrating on the influence of what is not under his control is to make this responsible self seem to disappear, swallowed up by the order of mere events.

What, however, do we have in mind that a person must *be* to be the object of these moral attitudes? While the concept of agency is easily undermined, it is very difficult to give it a positive characterization. That is familiar from the literature on Free Will.

I believe that in a sense the problem has no solution, because something in the idea of agency is incompatible with actions being events, or people being things. But as the external determinants of what someone has done are gradually exposed, in their effect on consequences, character, and choice itself, it becomes gradually clear that actions are events and people things. Eventually nothing remains which can be ascribed to the responsible self, and we are left with nothing but a portion of the larger sequence of events, which can be deplored or celebrated, but not blamed or praised.

Though I cannot define the idea of the active self that is thus undermined, it is possible to say something about its sources. There is a close connexion between our feelings about ourselves and our feelings about others. Guilt and indignation, shame and contempt, pride and admiration are internal and external sides of the same moral attitudes. We are unable to view ourselves simply as portions of the world, and from inside we have a rough idea of the boundary between what is us and what is not, what we do and what happens to us, what is our personality and what is an accidental handicap. We apply the same essentially internal conception of the self to others. About ourselves we feel pride, shame, guilt, remorse—and agent-regret. We do not regard our actions and our characters merely as fortunate or unfortunate episodes—though they may also be that. We cannot *simply* take an external evaluative view of ourselves—of what we most essentially are and what we do. And this remains true even when we have seen that we are not responsible for our own existence, or our nature, or the choices we have to make, or the circumstances that give our acts the consequences they have. Those acts remain ours and we remain ourselves, despite the persuasiveness of the reasons that seem to argue us out of existence.

It is this internal view that we extend to others in moral judgment—when we judge *them* rather than their desirability or utility. We extend to others the refusal to limit ourselves to external evaluation, and we accord to them selves like our own. But in both cases this comes up against the brutal inclusion of humans and everything about them in a world from which they cannot be separated and of which they are nothing but contents. The external view forces itself on us at the same time that we resist it. One way this occurs is through the gradual erosion of what we do by the subtraction of what happens.

The inclusion of consequences in the conception of what we have done is an acknowledgment that we are part of the world, but the paradoxical character of moral luck which emerges from this acknowledgment shows that we are unable to operate with such a view, for it leaves us with no one to be. The same thing is revealed in the appearance that determinism obliterates responsibility. Once we see an aspect of what we or someone else does as something that happens, we lose our grip on the idea that it has been done and that we can judge the doer and not just the happening. This explains why the absence of determinism is no

more hospitable to the concept of agency than is its presence—a point that has been noticed often. Either way the act is viewed externally, as part of the course of events.

The problem of moral luck cannot be understood without an account of the internal conception of agency and its special connection with the moral attitudes as opposed to other types of value. I do not have such an account. The degree to which the problem has a solution can be determined only by seeing whether in some degree the incompatibility between this conception and the various ways in which we do not control what we do is only apparent. I have nothing to offer on that topic either. But it is not enough to say merely that our basic moral attitudes toward ourselves and others are determined by what is actual; for they are also threatened by the sources of that actuality, and by the external view of action which forces itself on us when we see how everything we do belongs to a world that we have not created.

EXERCISES

1. If there *are* objective moral facts—suppose, say, that "stealing is wrong" is an objective fact on the same order as "Jupiter is the largest planet in our solar system"—would that *strengthen* human freedom, restrict freedom, or have no bearing on freedom?

2. Suppose that we have two possible prison systems, and you as judge may sentence this convicted bank robber to either: One is Attica, where he will suffer terribly during his eight-year incarceration, and come out unreformed, or maybe worse; the other is Shangrila, where the robber will enjoy interesting work, learn important skills, live a decent and not unpleasant eight years, and will be very unlikely to return to crime. You may think that actually the opposite would result; put that aside for a moment. In this situation, which would you choose for the sentence you impose?

3. All week you have been trying to decide whether to go to the mountains for a Saturday skiing holiday, stay at the university and study for your biology exam, go home to spend the weekend with your family, or volunteer to spend the weekend helping at a homeless shelter. You carefully weigh the benefits and detriments of each course of action, and finally on Friday night—after a week of deliberation—choose to go skiing. On Monday of that week, a close friend, who knows you are trying to decide whether or not to go skiing, confidently writes down what your choice will be, places it in a sealed envelope, and locks it in a safe. As you pack your skiing gear, she hands you the envelope: "I knew all along you would decide to go skiing," she says. Assuming that she really was certain (this is not some "mind-reading" trickery), does this mean that you did not really choose? Does it imply that your choice was not free? Would it lessen or destroy your moral responsibility for that choice?

4. In the previous example, will it make any difference if the reasons that convinced you to go skiing are really good reasons? Will it make any difference if they were *not* good reasons, but were instead the product of elaborate self-deception? (You tell yourself—and convince yourself—that you are going for the exercise, when all your friends know that your real motivation is a glimpse of a ski instructor with whom you once had a passionate relation, but who is now indifferent to you, but for whom you still carry a torch—though you will not admit it to your friends nor even to yourself. You say things like "I wouldn't spend two minutes with that ski instructor, even if she begged me"; meanwhile, your friends exchange knowing smiles.)

5. One fiercely debated philosophical issue is whether *determinism* destroys *reason*. That is, if determinism is true, and everything you do—including your cognitive activities—is determined by past causal events, could you still *reason* about what to do?

   We are spending the afternoon at Saratoga, and I'm trying to pick a horse for the seventh race. God already knows what horse I'll pick (though of course I do not), and the deliberative process I will follow is *determined* by my complex history (what I learned about racehorses from my Aunt Louise, the critical thinking skills I picked up in my logic classes, the statistical analysis I learned from Professor Sykes in my undergraduate stats class, and so on and so forth). I study the racing form carefully, watch the horses and the jockeys in the post parade, check the odds board—and finally settle on Dilapidated Darling, and run up to the window to wager five bucks on her nose. Did I *really* reason about my choice? If the whole process was *determined,* was my "reasoning process" only a sham?

6. Do people really *deserve* punishment for their wrong acts? That is, is it right and fair and just to hold people morally responsible for what they do? Suppose we have been discussing this question for quite some time, and we still disagree: I insist that Arthur *justly deserves* punishment for his bad acts, and you believe that punishment is *not* morally justified. Though we disagree on this fundamental issue, suppose we agree on a number of points: we agree that moral responsibility is different from role responsibility; we agree that punishment is not the best way to reform Arthur and change his bad behavior; and we agree that Arthur's genetics and environment shaped him to be what he is and to act as he does, and given who he is and how he developed, he could not have done otherwise than he did. But even with all these points of *agreement,* our basic *disagreement* over moral responsibility remains: I still believe Arthur *ought* to be punished, and you believe that punishing Arthur is *wrong.* Is there anything further that either of us could do to resolve our conflict, or must we just disagree? Does your answer to that question turn on whether you hold a moral objectivist or nonobjectivist view?

7. Suppose that you totally reject moral responsibility: you firmly believe that *no one*—including yourself—is *ever* morally responsible. Suppose further that you commit an act that *you regard* as morally wrong: for example, your best friend Amanda shared with you a deep secret, and you thoughtlessly revealed it to others, thereby betraying Amanda's confidence and causing her great pain. Could you—as one who *denies* moral responsibility—consistently and sincerely *apologize* for your bad act?

8. If you were convinced that there is no theoretical justification for moral responsibility, would you—as Saul Smilansky recommends—find it plausible and/or desirable to promote widespread *belief* in moral responsibility?

ADDITIONAL READING

H. L. A. Hart draws clear distinctions among types of responsibility in *Punishment and Responsibility* (Oxford: Clarendon Press, 1968).

P. F. Strawson's "Freedom and Resentment" was originally published in 1962 and has been widely anthologized.

Thomas Nagel's "Moral Luck" was a reply to a paper by Bernard Williams; both papers were originally published in 1976, in *Proceedings of the Aristotelian Society.* The paper by Williams can be found in his *Moral Luck* (Cambridge, MA: Cambridge University Press, 1981); and Nagel's paper is in his *Mortal Questions* (Cambridge, MA: Cambridge University Press, 1979). A good collection of papers on the issue of moral luck is Daniel Statman, editor, *Moral Luck* (Albany, NY: SUNY Press, 1993).

The issue of moral responsibility and its implications—and the implications of its denial—have been widely discussed; see, for example, John Martin Fischer and Mark Ravizza, *Responsibility and Control: A Theory of Moral Responsibility* (Cambridge, MA: Cambridge University Press, 1998); John Martin Fischer, *My Way: Essays on Moral Responsibility* (New York: Oxford University Press, 2006); George Sher, *Desert* (Princeton, NJ: Princeton University Press, 1987) and *In Praise of Blame* (New York: Oxford University Press, 2006); Saul Smilansky, *Free Will and Illusion* (New York: Oxford University Press, 2000); R. Jay Wallace, *Responsibility and the Moral Sentiments* (Cambridge, MA: Harvard University Press, 1994); Bruce N. Waller, *Freedom Without Responsibility* (Philadelphia, PA: Temple University Press, 1990); and Michael J. Zimmerman, *An Essay on Moral Responsibility* (Totowa, NJ: Rowman & Littlefield, 1988).

There are many excellent anthologies on moral responsibility, including John Christman, *The Inner Citadel: Essays on Individual Autonomy* (New York: Oxford University Press, 1989); John Martin Fischer, *Moral Responsibility* (Ithaca, NY: Cornell University Press, 1986); John Martin Fischer and Mark Ravizza, *Perspectives on Moral Responsibility* (Ithaca, NY: Cornell University Press, 1993); Ellen Frankel Paul, Fred D. Miller, Jr., and Jeffrey Paul, *Responsibility* (Cambridge, MA: Cambridge University Press, 1999); Ferdinand Schoeman, *Responsibility, Character, and the Emotions: New Essays in Moral Psychology* (Cambridge, MA: Cambridge University Press, 1987); and David Widerker and Michael McKenna, *Moral Responsibility and Alternative Possibilities* (Burlington, VT: Ashgate, 2003).

NOTES

[1]Campbell, 1957, p. 159.

[2]Willard Gaylin, *The Killing of Bonnie Garland* (Hammondsworth, UK: Penguin Books, 1983), p. 338.

[3]Distinguished British legal theorist H. L. A. Hart makes a similar distinction, and first uses the phrase *role* responsibility; see *Punishment and Responsibility* (Oxford: Clarendon Press, 1968).

[4]Just because she does a lousy job at taking responsibility, that does not imply that we should deny her the opportunity. After all, practice at taking responsibility may help her become better at it. And even those of us who are incurably lousy at taking responsibility for ourselves may well prefer our own inept decision making to having someone else make all our decisions for us.

[5]Susan Wolf, "The Importance of Free Will," *Mind*, Volume 90 (1981), 386–405.

[6]F. C. Copleston, "The Existence of God: A Debate," in Paul Edwards and Arthur Pap, editors, *A Modern Introduction to Philosophy*, rev. ed. (New York: The Free Press, 1965), p. 488.

[7]Some claim there can be no real rationality and deliberation if our reasoning is entirely shaped by past causes (if determinism is true). Richard Taylor, for example, makes that the cornerstone of his argument for libertarian free will in *Metaphysics* (Englewood Cliffs, NJ: Prentice-Hall, 1963), pp. 50–55; and many others have made similar claims: Daniel D. Colson, "The Transcendental Argument Against Determinism: A Challenge Yet Unmet," *Southern Journal of Philosophy*, Volume 20 (1982), 15–24; John C. Eccles, "Brain and Free Will," in Gordon Globus, Grover Maxwell, and Irwin Savodnik, editors, *Consciousness and the Brain: A Scientific and Philosophical Inquiry* (New York: Plenum Press, 1976), pp. 101–121; Antony Flew, "Rationality and Unnecessitated Choice," in Newton Garver and Peter H. Hare, editors, *Naturalism and Rationality* (Buffalo, NY: Prometheus Books, 1986), pp. 41–51; J. E. Llewelyn, "The Inconceivability of Pessimistic Determinism," *Analysis*, Volume 27 (1966), 39–44; Alasdair MacIntyre, "Determinism," *Mind*, Volume 66 (1957), 28–41; and Susan Wolf, "The Importance of Free Will," *Mind*, Volume 90 (1981), 386–405. But that cannot account for the consensus philosophical belief that denying moral responsibility entails denying genuine morality; for (although a number of philosophers have claimed that genuine rationality cannot coexist with determinism) rather than being a consensus view (as would be required to support the consensus view that morality requires moral responsibility) it is probably a minority view in contemporary philosophy (opponents include Patricia Churchland, "Is Determinism Self-refuting?" *Mind*, Volume 40 [1981], 99–101; Daniel Dennett, 1984, Chapter 2; Stephen Toulmin, "Reasons and Causes," in Robert Borger and Frank Cioffi, editors, *Explanation in the Behavioural Sciences* [Cambridge, MA: Cambridge University Press, 1970], pp. 1–26; and Bruce N. Waller, "Deliberating About the Inevitable," *Analysis*, Volume 45 [1985], 48–52).

[8]As emphasized by Charles Taylor in "Responsibility for Self," in Amelie Rorty, editor, *Identities of Persons* (Berkeley, CA: University of California Press, 1976), pp. 281–299.

15

The Death Penalty

Though the death penalty has been abolished in most countries, it remains in effect in the United States, and it remains a topic of fierce disagreement. The classic argument for capital punishment is retributive: blood deserves blood, those who commit murder deserve to die, and justice is not done when a murderer is allowed to live. A more sophisticated argument gives capital punishment a symbolic or expressive function: capital punishment is the strongest and most appropriate way for society to express its deep abhorrence of the most awful crimes. The argument that capital punishment is an effective deterrent of crime is perennially popular, though it can offer little empirical support for its claims. Those opposing capital punishment argue that capital punishment may have an expressive function, but that it expresses the wrong message: that killing is a solution, and that reform is impossible. They also argue that capital punishment is a cruel, unusual, and dehumanizing punishment. Among contemporary abolitionists, there are two prominent contemporary arguments: first, that capital punishment is administered in a capricious or arbitrary or racially discriminatory manner; and second, that because of many flaws in our system of justice and the honest mistakes of eyewitnesses, there is grave danger of wrongly executing the innocent.

Louis Pojman's case for capital punishment combines both the retributive and the deterrent arguments; and he insists that even if mistakes are made, we shouldn't give up capital punishment because of a few possible miscarriages of justice in which innocent people are executed. Stephen Bright argues that capital punishment is contrary to the best principles and positive image of the United States, that it is likely to result in executions of the wrongly convicted, and that it is administered in an arbitrary, unfair, and racist manner.

⟨⟨ THE DEATH PENALTY SHOULD BE ABOLISHED ⟩⟩
Stephen B. Bright

Stephen B. Bright is president of the Southern Center for Human Rights and teaches criminal law courses at both Yale and Harvard Law Schools; his essay, "Why the United States Will Join the Rest of the World in Abandoning Capital Punishment," is from *Debating the Death Penalty: Should America Have Capital Punishment?*, edited by Hugo Adam Bedau and Paul G. Cassell (New York: Oxford University Press, 2005), Chapter 6.

The United States will inevitably join other industrialized nations in abandoning the death penalty, just as it has abandoned whipping, the stocks, branding, cutting off appendages, maiming, and other primitive forms of punishment. It remains to be seen how long it will be until the use of the death penalty becomes so infrequent as to be pointless, and it is eventually abandoned. In the meantime, capital punishment is arbitrarily and unfairly imposed, undermines the standing and moral authority of the United States in the community of nations, and diminishes the credibility and legitimacy of the courts within the United States.

Although death may intuitively seem to be an appropriate punishment for a person who kills another person and polls show strong support for the death penalty, most Americans know little about realities of capital punishment, past and present. As Bryan Stevenson describes, the death penalty is a direct descendant of the darkest aspects of American history—slavery, lynching, racial oppression, and perfunctory capital trials known as "legal lynchings"—and racial discrimination remains a prominent feature of capital punishment. The death penalty is not imposed to avenge every killing and—as some contend—to bring "closure" to the family of every victim, but is inflicted in less than 1 percent of all murder cases. Of more than 20,000 murders in the United States annually, an average of fewer than 300 people are sentenced to death, and only 55 are executed each year. Only 19 states actually carried out executions between 1976, when the U.S. Supreme Court authorized the resumption of capital punishment after declaring it unconstitutional in 1972, and the end of 2002. Eighty-six percent of those executions were in the South. Just two states—Texas and Virginia—carried out 45 percent of them.

Any assessment of the death penalty must not be based on abstract theories about how it should work in practice or the experiences of states like Oregon, which seldom impose the death penalty and carry it out even less. To understand the realities of the death penalty, one must look to the states that sentence people to death by the hundreds and have carried out scores of executions. In those states, innocent people have been sentenced to die based on such things as mistaken eyewitness identifications, false confessions, the testimony of partisan experts who render opinions that are not supported by science, failure of police and prosecutors to turn over evidence of innocence, and testimony of prisoners who get their own charges dismissed by testifying that the accused admitted the crime to them. Even the guilty are sentenced to death as opposed to life imprisonment without the possibility of parole not because they committed the worst crimes but because of where they happen to be prosecuted, the incompetence of their court-appointed lawyers, their race, or the race of their victim.

Former Illinois Governor George Ryan is a prominent example of a supporter of capital punishment who, upon close examination of the system, found that it "is haunted by the demon of error—error in determining

guilt, and error in determining who among the guilty deserves to die." As a member of the legislature in 1977, Ryan voted to adopt Illinois's death penalty law and he described himself as a "staunch supporter" of capital punishment until as governor 23 years later, he saw that during that period the state had carried out 12 executions and released from its death row 13 people who had been exonerated. In 2003, Governor Ryan pardoned four people who had been tortured by police until they confessed to crimes they did not commit and commuted the sentences of the remaining 167 people on Illinois's death row. . . .

Further experimentation with lethal punishment after centuries of failure has no place in a conservative society that is wary of too much government power and skeptical of the government's ability to do things well. Further experimentation might be justified if it served some purpose. But capital punishment is not needed to protect society or to punish offenders, as shown by over 100 countries around the world that do not have the death penalty and states such as Michigan and Wisconsin, neither of which have had the death penalty since the mid-1800s. It can be argued that capital punishment was necessary when America was a frontier society and had no prisons. But today the United States has not only maximum security prisons, but "super maximum" prisons where serial killers, mass murderers, and sadistic murderers can be severely punished and completely isolated from guards and other inmates.

Nor is crime deterred by the executions in fewer than half the states of an arbitrarily selected 1 percent of those who commit murders, many of whom are mentally ill or have limited intellectual functioning. The South, which has carried out 85 percent of the nation's executions since 1976, has the highest murder rate of any region of the country. The Northeast, which has the fewest executions by far—only 3 executions between 1976 and the end of 2002—has the lowest murder rate.

The United States does not need to keep this relic of the past to show its abhorrence of murder. As previously noted, 99 percent of the murders in the United States are not punished by death. Even at war crimes trials in The Hague, genocide and other crimes against humanity are not punished with the death penalty. The societies that do not have capital punishment surely abhor murder as much as any other, but they do not find it necessary to engage in killing in order to punish, protect, or show their abhorrence with killing.

Finally, capital punishment has no place in a decent society that places some practices, such as torture, off limits—not because some individuals have not done things so bad that they arguably deserved to be tortured, but because a civilized society simply does not engage in such acts. It can be argued that rapists deserve to be raped, that mutilators deserve to be mutilated. Most societies, however, refrain from responding in this way because the punishment is not only degrading to those on whom it is imposed, but it is also degrading to the society that engages in the same behavior as the criminals. When death sentences are carried out, small groups of people gather in execution chambers and watch as a human being is tied down and put down. Some make no effort to suppress their glee when the sentence is carried out and celebrations occur inside and outside the prison. These celebrations of death reflect the dark side of the human spirit—an arrogant, vengeful, unforgiving, uncaring side that either does not admit the possibility of innocence or redemption or is willing to kill people despite those possibilities.

A HUMAN RIGHTS VIOLATION THAT UNDERMINES THE STANDING AND MORAL AUTHORITY OF THE UNITED STATES

If people were asked 50 years ago which one of the following three countries—Russia, South Africa, or the United States—would be most likely to have the death penalty at the turn of the century, few people would have answered the United States. And yet, the United States was one of four countries that accounted for 90 percent of all the executions in the world in 2001 (the others were China, Iran, and Saudi Arabia), while Russia and South Africa are among the nations that no longer practice capital punishment. Since 1985, over 40 countries have abandoned capital punishment whereas only four countries that did not have it have adopted it. One of those, Nepal, has since abolished it. Turkey abolished the death penalty in 2001 in its efforts to join the European Union, leaving the United States the only NATO country that still has the death penalty.

The United States is also part of a very small minority of nations that allow the execution of children. Twenty-two of the 38 states with death penalty statutes allow the execution of people who were under 18 at the time of their crimes. Between 1990 and the end of 2001, these states put 15 children to death, with Texas carrying out over 60 percent of those executions. The only other countries that executed children during this time were the Congo, Iran, Nigeria, Pakistan, Saudi Arabia, and Yemen. The United States and Somalia are the only two countries that have not ratified the International Covenant on the Rights of the Child, which, among other things, prohibits the execution of people who were children at the time of their crimes.

Being among the world leaders in executions and the leader in execution of children is incompatible with asserting leadership on human rights issues in the world. As Frederick Douglass said over a century ago, "Life is the great primary and most precious and comprehensive of all human rights—[and] whether it be coupled with virtue, honor, and happiness, or with sin, disgrace and misery, . . . [it is not] to be deliberately or voluntarily destroyed, either by individuals separately, or combined in what is called Government."

The retention of capital punishment in the United States draws harsh criticism from throughout the world. . . .

. . . Just as the United States could not assert moral leadership in the world as long as it allowed segregation, it will not be a leader on human rights as long as it allows capital punishment.

ARBITRARY AND UNFAIR INFLICTION

Regardless of the practices of the rest of the world or the morality of capital punishment, the process leading to a death sentence is so unfair and influenced by so many improper factors and the infliction of death sentences is so inconsistent that this punishment should be abandoned.

The exoneration of many people who spent years of their lives in prisons for crimes they did not commit—many of them on death rows—has dramatically brought to light defects in the criminal justice system that have surprised and appalled people who do not observe the system every day and assumed that it was working properly. The average person has little or no contact with the criminal courts, which deal primarily with crimes committed against and by poor people and members of racial minorities. It is a system that is overworked and underfunded, and particularly underfunded when it comes to protecting the rights of those accused.

Law enforcement officers, usually overworked and often under tremendous public pressure to solve terrible crimes, make mistakes, fail to pursue all lines of investigation, and, on occasion, overreach or take shortcuts in pursuing arrests. Prosecutors exercise vast and unchecked discretion in deciding which cases are to be prosecuted as capital cases. The race of the victim and the defendant, political considerations, and other extraneous factors influence whether prosecutors seek the death penalty and whether juries or judges impose it.

A person facing the death penalty usually cannot afford to hire an attorney and is at the mercy of the system to provide a court-appointed lawyer. While many receive adequate representation (and often are not sentenced to death as a result), many others are assigned lawyers who lack the knowledge, skill, resources—and sometimes even the inclination—to handle a serious criminal case. People who would not be sentenced to death if properly represented are sentenced to death because of incompetent court-appointed lawyers. In many communities, racial minorities are still excluded from participation as jurors, judges, prosecutors, and lawyers in the system. In too many cases, defendants are convicted on flimsy evidence, such as eyewitness identifications, which are notoriously unreliable but are seen as very credible by juries; the testimony of convicts who, in exchange for lenient treatment in their own cases, testify that the accused admitted to them that he or she committed the crime; and confessions obtained from people of limited intellect through lengthy and overbearing interrogations.

. . . But these are not minor, isolated incidents; they are long-standing, pervasive, systemic deficiencies in the criminal justice system that are not being corrected and, in some places, are even becoming worse. . . . Law enforcement agencies have been unwilling to videotape interrogations and use identification procedures that are more reliable than those presently employed. People who support capital punishment as a concept are unwilling to spend millions of tax dollars to provide competent legal representation for those accused of crimes. And courts have yet to find ways to overcome centuries of racial discrimination that often influence, consciously or subconsciously, the decisions of prosecutors, judges, and juries.

A Warning That Something Is Terribly Wrong: Innocent People Condemned to Death

Over 100 people condemned to death in the last 30 years have been exonerated and released after new evidence established their innocence or cast such doubt on their guilt that they could not be convicted. The 100th of those people, Ray Krone, was convicted and sentenced to death in Arizona based on the testimony of an expert witness that his teeth matched bite marks on the victim. During the ten years that Krone spent on death row, scientists developed the ability to compare biological evidence recovered at crime scenes with the DNA of suspects. DNA testing established that Krone

was innocent. On Krone's release, the prosecutor said, "[Krone] deserves an apology from us, that's for sure. A mistake was made here. . . . What do you say to him? An injustice was done and we will try to do better. And we're sorry." Although unfortunate to be wrongfully convicted, Krone was very fortunate that there was DNA evidence in his case. In most cases, there is no biological evidence for DNA testing.

Other defendants had their death sentences commuted to life imprisonment without the possibility of parole because of questions about their innocence. For example, in 1994, the governor of Virginia commuted the death sentence of a mentally retarded man, Earl Washington, to life imprisonment without parole because of questions regarding his guilt. Washington, an easily persuaded, somewhat childlike special-education dropout, had been convicted of murder and rape based on a confession he gave to police, even though it was full of inconsistencies. For example, at one point in the confession Washington said that the victim was white and at another that the victim was black. Six years later, DNA evidence—not available at the time of Washington's trial or the commutation—established that Washington was innocent and he was released.

Although DNA testing has been available only in cases where there was biological evidence and the evidence has been preserved, it has established the innocence of many people who were not sentenced to death—more than 100 by the end of 2002. A Michigan judge in 1984 lamented the fact that the state did not have the death penalty, saying that life imprisonment was inadequate for Eddie Joe Lloyd for the rape and murder of a 16-year-old girl. Police had obtained a confession from Lloyd while he was in a mental hospital. Seventeen years later, DNA evidence established that Lloyd did not commit the crime. On his release, Lloyd commented, "If Michigan had the death penalty, I would have been through, the angels would have sung a long time ago."

Sometimes evidence of innocence has surfaced only at the last minute. Anthony Porter, sentenced to death in Illinois, went through all the appeals and review that are available for one so sentenced. Every court upheld his conviction and sentence. As Illinois prepared to put him to death, a question arose as to whether Porter, who was brain damaged and mentally retarded, understood what was happening to him. A person who lacks the mental ability to understand that he is being put to death in punishment for a crime cannot be executed unless he is treated and becomes capable of understanding why he is being executed. Just two days before Porter was to be executed, a court stayed his execution in order to examine his mental condition. After the stay was granted, a journalism class at Northwestern University and a private investigator examined the case and proved that Anthony Porter was innocent. They obtained a confession from the person who committed the crime. Anthony Porter was released, becoming the third person released from Illinois's death row after being proven innocent by a journalism class at Northwestern. . . .

Some proponents of capital punishment argue that the exoneration of Porter and others shows that the system works and that no innocent people have been executed. However, someone spending years on death row for a crime he did not commit is not an example of the system working. When journalism students prove that police, prosecutors, judges, defense lawyers, and the entire legal system failed to discover the perpetrator of a crime and instead condemned the wrong person to die, the system is not working. Porter and others were spared, as Chief Justice Moses Harrison of the Illinois Supreme Court observed, "only because of luck and the dedication of the attorneys, reporters, family members and volunteers who labored to win their release. They survived despite the criminal justice system, not because of it. The truth is that left to the devices of the court system, they would probably have all ended up dead at the hands of the state for crimes they did not commit. One must wonder how many others have not been so fortunate." . . .

Gerald W. Heaney announced, after 30 years of reviewing capital cases as a federal appellate judge, that he was "compelled . . . to conclude that the imposition of the death penalty is arbitrary and capricious." He found that "the decision of who shall live and who shall die for his crime turns less on the nature of the offense and the incorrigibility of the offender and more on inappropriate and indefensible considerations: the political and personal inclinations of prosecutors; the defendant's wealth, race, and intellect; the race and economic status of the victim; the quality of the defendant's counsel; and the resources allocated to defense lawyers." . . .

. . . Even if every single reform were adopted, it would not eliminate the possibility of executing innocent people. As the Canadian Supreme Court recognized in holding that it would not allow the extradition of people to the United States if the death penalty could be imposed, courts will always be fallible and reversible, while death will always be final and irreversible.

The Two Most Important Decisions—Made by Prosecutors

The two most important decisions in every death penalty case are made not by juries or judges, but by prosecutors. No state or federal law ever requires prosecutors to seek the death penalty or take a capital case to trial. A prosecutor has complete discretion in deciding whether to seek the death penalty and, even if death is sought, whether to offer a sentence less than death in exchange for the defendant's guilty plea. The overwhelming majority of all criminal cases, including capital cases, are resolved not by trials but by plea bargains. Whether death is sought or imposed is based on the discretion and proclivities of the thousands of people who occupy the offices of prosecutor in judicial districts throughout the nation. (Texas, for example, has 155 elected prosecutors, Virginia 120, Missouri 115, Illinois 102, Georgia 49, and Alabama 40.) Some prosecutors seek the death penalty at every opportunity, and others never seek it; some seldom seek it; some frequently seek it. There is no requirement that individual prosecutors—who, in most states, are elected by districts—be consistent in their practices in seeking the death penalty.

As a result of this discretion, there are great geographical disparities in where death is imposed within states. Prosecutors in Houston and Philadelphia have sought the death penalty in virtually every case in which it can be imposed. As a result of aggressive prosecutors and inept court-appointed lawyers, Houston and Philadelphia have each condemned over 100 people to death—more than most states. Harris County, which includes Houston, has had more executions in the last 30 years than any *state* except Texas and Virginia. A case is much more likely to be prosecuted capitally in Houston and Philadelphia than in Dallas, Ft. Worth, or Pittsburgh. . . .

Thus, whether the death sentence is imposed may depend more on the personal predilections and politics of local prosecutors than the heinousness of the crime or the incorrigibility of the defendant.

The Role of Racial Bias

The complete discretion given to prosecutors in deciding whether to seek the death penalty and whether to drop the death penalty in exchange for guilty pleas also contributes to racial disparities in the infliction of the death penalty. In the 38 states that have the death penalty, 97.5 percent of the chief prosecutors are white. In 18 of the states, all of the chief prosecutors are white. Even the most conscientious prosecutors who have had little experience with people of other races may be influenced in their decisions by racial stereotypes and attitudes they have developed over their lives.

But the rest of the criminal justice system is almost as unrepresentative of American's racial diversity as prosecutors' offices. In the South, where the death penalty is most often imposed and carried out, over half the victims of crime are people of color, well over 60 percent of the prison population is made up of people of color, and half of those sentenced to death are members of racial minorities. Yet people of color are seldom involved as judges, jurors, prosecutors, and lawyers in the courts.

For example, there is not one African American or Hispanic judge on the nine-member Texas Court of Criminal Appeals, the court of last resort for all criminal cases in that state even though 43 percent of the population of Texas is nonwhite, over 65 percent of the homicide victims are people of color, and nearly 70 percent of the prison population is black, Hispanic, or other nonwhite. This court handles over 10,000 cases each year, most of them involving the lives and liberty of people of color. In Alabama, no African American sits among the nine members of the Alabama Supreme Court or the five members of the Alabama Court of Criminal Appeals—the two courts that review capital cases—even though 26 percent of the population of Alabama is African American, 59 percent of the victims of homicide are African American, and over half those on death row are black. In many courthouses, everything looks the same as it did during the period of Jim Crow justice. The judges are white, the prosecutors are white, the lawyers are white and, even in communities with substantial African American populations, the jury may be all white. In many cases, the only person of color who sits in front of the bar in the courtroom is the person on trial. The legal system remains the institution that has been least affected by the civil rights movement.

Although African Americans constitute only 12 percent of the national population, they are victims of half the murders that are committed in the United States. Yet 80 percent of those on death row were convicted of crimes against white people. The discrepancy is even greater in the Death Belt states of the South. In Georgia and Alabama, for example, African Americans are the victims of 65 percent of the homicides, yet 80 percent of those on death rows are there for crimes against white persons. Studies of capital sentencing have consistently revealed such disparities. . . .

Study after study has confirmed what lawyers practicing in the criminal courts observe every day:

People of color are treated more harshly than white people. A person of color is more likely than a white person to be stopped by the police, to be abused by the police during that stop, to be arrested, to be denied bail when taken to court, to be charged with a serious crime as opposed to a less serious one that could be charged, to be convicted, and to receive a harsher sentence. But a person of color is much *less* likely to be a participant in the criminal justice system as a judge, juror, prosecutor, or lawyer.

It would be quite remarkable if race affected every aspect of the criminal justice system except with regard to the death penalty—the area in which decision makers have the broadest discretion and base their decisions on evidence with tremendous emotional impact. The sad reality is that race continues to influence who is sentenced to death as it has throughout American history.

The Death Sentence for Being Assigned the Worst Lawyer

Capital cases—complex cases with the highest stakes of any in the legal system—should be handled by the most capable lawyers, with the resources to conduct thorough investigations and consult with various experts on everything from the prosecution's scientific evidence to psychologists and psychiatrists to investigate the defendant's mental health. The right to counsel is the most fundamental constitutional right of a person charged with a crime. A person accused of a crime depends on a lawyer to investigate the prosecution's case; to present any facts that may be helpful to the accused and necessary for a fair and reliable determination of guilt or innocence and, if guilty, a proper sentence; and to protect every other right of the accused. However, U.S. Supreme Court Justice Ruth Bader Ginsburg observed in 2001 that she had "yet to see a death case among the dozens coming to the Supreme Court . . . in which the defendant was well represented at trial. People who are well-represented at trial do not get the death penalty."

Those receiving the death penalty are not well represented because many states do not provide the structure, resources, independence, and accountability that is required to insure competent representation in an area of such specialization. . . .

Justice Hugo Black wrote for the U.S. Supreme Court in 1956 that "[t]here can be no equal justice where the kind of trial a [person] gets depends on the amount of money he [or she] has." But today, no one seriously doubts that the kind of trial, and the kind of justice, a person receives depends very much on the amount of money he or she has. The quality of legal representation tolerated by some courts shocks the conscience of a person of average sensibilities. But poor representation resulting from lack of funding and structure has been accepted as the best that can be done with the limited resources available. The commitment of many states to providing lawyers for those who cannot afford them was aptly described by a Chief Justice of the Georgia Supreme Court: "[W]e set our sights on the embarrassing target of mediocrity. I guess that means about halfway. And that raises a question. Are we willing to put up with halfway justice? To my way of thinking, one-half justice must mean one-half injustice, and one-half injustice is no justice at all."

The proponents of capital punishment are always quick to say that people facing the death penalty *should* receive better legal representation. But they . . . do not explain how this is going to be accomplished—whether by a sudden burst of altruism on the part of members of the legal profession, who are going to suddenly start taking capital cases for a fraction of what they can make doing other work; a massive infusion of funding from state legislatures that are searching for revenue for education, transportation, and other areas that have a constituency; or some other miracle. The right to competent representation is celebrated in the abstract, but most states—and most supporters of capital punishment—are unwilling to pay for it. As a result the death penalty will continue to be imposed not upon those who commit the worst crimes, but upon those who have the misfortune to be assigned the worst lawyers.

Death for the Disadvantaged

Capital punishment is inflicted on the weakest and most troubled members of our society such as children, the delusional, the paranoid, the brain-damaged, the chemically imbalanced, those who were abused and neglected as children, and people who endured the most terrible trauma imaginable in military service during war, who came back with post-traumatic stress syndrome, addicted to drugs, with various mental and emotional problems.

Charles Rumbaugh is one of many examples of the execution of the mentally ill. He was only 17 at the time of his crime and suffered from schizophrenia and depression to the point that he repeatedly mutilated himself and attempted suicide. Rumbaugh's parents tried to convince a court not to let him withdraw his appeals. During a hearing, Rumbaugh advanced on a marshal and provoked the marshal to shoot him in the courtroom. He

was taken to the hospital while the hearing continued. He was allowed to withdraw his appeals and was executed by Texas.

Another example is Pernell Ford, who was allowed to discharge his lawyers and represent himself at his capital trial in Alabama in 1984. Ford wore only a sheet to the penalty phase of the trial. He tried to call as witnesses people who were no longer alive. After lawyers appealed his conviction to a federal court, Ford wrote to the court and asked that the petition be dismissed. During a hearing, Ford said that he wanted to die because he was a member of the Holy Trinity, he had supernatural powers that would be enhanced when he died, and he would be able to transfer his soul to people outside the prison. He said that when he died, his 400 thousand wives would receive the millions of dollars he had put in Swiss bank accounts. One psychiatrist who evaluated Ford said that these statements were reflective of Ford's religious beliefs—not evidence of mental illness. Another psychiatrist found that Ford suffered from depression and personality disorder but was still capable of making rational choices. A third psychiatrist found that Ford was incapable of thinking rationally. The court concluded that Ford could give up his appeals because he understood the "bottom line" of his legal situation. Like Charles Rumbaugh, he was allowed to withdraw his appeals. Alabama executed him. . . .

The execution of such severely mentally ill people and treating mentally ill people so that they can be executed should be beneath the American people. Unfortunately, many mentally ill people are left on their own without support and supervision. Society would be better served by providing some care to insure that they take their medications and receive proper treatment to prevent episodes of violence than by executing people who are out of touch with reality. And once a severely mentally ill person has committed a serious crime . . . the appropriate response is to place them in secure mental health facilities, not in execution chambers.

Abandoning fairness, reliability, the quest for racial equality, the rule of law, and the independence and integrity of the judiciary are enormous prices to pay to bring about executions. Some are willing to sacrifice even more—the lives of innocent people. They argue that we are fighting a "war on crime," and, as in any war, there are going to be some innocent casualties. The American notion of justice was once that it was better for ten guilty people to go free than for an innocent person to be convicted. Now, proponents of the death penalty argue it is acceptable to sacrifice more than a few innocent people to wage a war on crime.

CONCLUSION

Courts should not be war zones, but halls of justice. It is time to reexamine the "war on crime"—a war the United States is fighting against its own people, its own children, and the poorest and the most powerless people in society. The American people must ask what kind of society they want to have and what kind of people they want to be. Whether they want a hateful, vengeful society that turns its back on its children and then executes them, that denies its mentally ill the treatment and the medicine they need and then puts them to death when their demons are no longer kept at bay, that gives nothing to the survivors of the victims of the crime except a chance to ask for the maximum sentence and watch an execution.

We should have the humility to admit that the legal system is not infallible and that mistakes are made. We should have the honesty to admit that our society is unwilling to pay the price of providing every poor person with competent legal representation, even in capital cases. We should have the courage to acknowledge the role that race plays in the criminal justice system and make a commitment to do something about it instead of pretending that racial prejudice no longer exists. And we should have the compassion and decency to recognize the dignity of every person, even those who have offended us most grievously. The Constitutional Court of South Africa addressed many of these issues in deciding whether the death penalty violated that country's constitution. Despite a staggering crime rate and a long history of racial violence and oppression, the Court unanimously concluded that in a society in transition from hatred to understanding, from vengeance to reconciliation, there was no place for the death penalty. The American people will ultimately reach the same conclusion, deciding that, like slavery and segregation, the death penalty is a relic of another era, and that this society of such vast wealth is capable of more constructive approaches to crime. And the United States will join the rest of the civilized world in abandoning capital punishment.

THE DEATH PENALTY IS SOMETIMES MORALLY LEGITIMATE
Louis P. Pojman
Why the Death Penalty Is Morally Permissible

Louis P. Pojman (1935–2005) previously taught philosophy at the U.S. Military Academy at West Point; this essay is excerpted from "Why the Death Penalty Is Morally Permissible," in *Debating the Death Penalty: Should America Have Capital Punishment?*, edited by Hugo Adam Bedau and Paul G. Cassell (New York: Oxford University Press, 2005), Chapter 3.

A DEFENSE OF THE DEATH PENALTY
who so sheddeth man's blood, by man shall his blood be shed.
(Genesis 9:6)

There is an ancient tradition, going back to biblical times, but endorsed by the mainstream of philosophers, from Plato to Thomas Aquinas, from Thomas Hobbes to Immanuel Kant, Thomas Jefferson, John Stuart Mill, and C. S. Lewis, that a fitting punishment for murder is the execution of the murderer. One prong of this tradition, the *backward-looking* or deontological position, epitomized in Aquinas and Kant, holds that because human beings, as rational agents, have dignity, one who with malice aforethought kills a human being forfeits his right to life and deserves to die. The other, the *forward-looking* or consequentialist, tradition, exemplified by Jeremy Bentham, Mill, and Ernest van den Haag, holds that punishment ought to serve as a deterrent, and that capital punishment is an adequate deterrent to prospective murderers. Abolitionists like Bedau and Jeffrey Reiman deny both prongs of the traditional case for the death penalty. They hold that long prison sentences are a sufficient retributive response to murder and that the death penalty probably does not serve as a deterrent or is no better deterrent than other forms of punishment. I will argue that both traditional defenses are sound and together they make a strong case for retaining the death penalty. That is, I hold a combined theory of punishment. A backward-looking judgment that the criminal has committed a heinous crime plus a forward-looking judgment that a harsh punishment will deter would-be murderers is sufficient to justify the death penalty. I turn first to the retributivist theory in favor of capital punishment.

RETRIBUTION

> . . . A couple of years ago I spent a long evening with the husband, sister and parents of a fine young woman who had been forced into the trunk of a car in a hospital parking lot. The degenerate who kidnapped her kept her in the trunk, like an ant in a jar, until he got tired of the game. Then he killed her.

Human beings have dignity as self-conscious rational agents who are able to act morally. One could maintain that it is precisely their moral goodness or innocence that bestows dignity and a right to life on them. Intentionally taking the life of an innocent human being is so evil that absent mitigating circumstances, the perpetrator forfeits his own right to life. He or she deserves to die.

The retributivist holds three propositions: (1) that all the guilty deserve to be punished; (2) that only the guilty deserve to be punished; and (3) that the guilty deserve to be punished in proportion to the severity of their crime. . . .

Criminals like Steven Judy, Jeffrey Dahmer, Timothy McVeigh, Ted Bundy (who is reported to have raped and murdered over 100 women), John Mohammed and John Lee Malvo, who murdered 12 people in the killing spree of 2002, . . . have committed capital offenses and deserve nothing less than capital punishment. No doubt malicious acts like the ones committed by these criminals deserve worse punishment than death, and I would be open to suggestions of torture (why not?), but at a minimum, the death penalty seems warranted.

People often confuse *retribution* with *revenge*. Governor George Ryan, who recently commuted the sentences of all the prisoners on death row in the State of Illinois, . . . quotes a letter from the Reverend Desmond Tutu that "to take a life when a life has been lost is revenge, it is not justice." This is simply false. While moral people will feel outrage at acts of heinous crimes, . . . the moral justification of punishment is not *vengeance*, but *desert*. Vengeance signifies inflicting harm on the offender out of anger because of what he has done. Retribution is the rationally supported theory that the criminal deserves a punishment fitting the gravity of his crime.

The nineteenth-century British philosopher James Fitzjames Stephens thought vengeance was a justification for punishment, arguing that punishment should be inflicted "for the sake of ratifying the feeling of hatred—call it revenge, resentment, or what you will—which the contemplation of such [offensive] conduct excites in healthily constituted minds." But retributivism is not based on hatred for the criminal (though a feeling of vengeance may accompany the punishment). Retributivism is the theory that the criminal *deserves* to be punished and deserves to be punished in proportion to the gravity of his or her crime, whether or not the victim or anyone else desires it. We may all deeply regret having to carry out the punishment, but consider it warranted.

On the other hand, people do have a sense of outrage and passion for revenge directed at criminals for their crimes. Imagine that someone in your family was on the receiving end of . . . violent acts. Stephens was correct in asserting that "[t]he criminal law stands to the passion for revenge in much the same relation as marriage to the sexual appetite." Failure to punish would no more lessen our sense of vengeance than the elimination of marriage would lessen our sexual appetite. When a society fails to punish criminals in a way thought to be proportionate to the gravity of the crime, the danger arises that the public would take the law into its own hands, resulting in vigilante justice, lynch mobs, and private acts of retribution. The outcome is likely to be an anarchistic, insecure state of injustice. As such, legal retribution stands as a safeguard for an orderly application of punitive desert.

Our natural instinct is for *vengeance*, but civilization demands that we restrain our anger and go through a legal process, letting the outcome determine whether and to what degree to punish the accused. Civilization demands that we not take the law into our own hands, but it should also satisfy our deepest instincts when they are consonant with reason. Our instincts tell us that some crimes, like McVeigh's, Judy's, and Bundy's, should be severely punished, but we refrain from personally carrying out those punishments, committing ourselves to the legal processes. The death penalty is supported by our gut animal instincts as well as our sense of justice as desert.

The death penalty reminds us that there are consequences to our actions, that we are responsible for what we do, so that dire consequences for immoral actions are eminently appropriate. The death penalty is such a fitting response to evil.

DETERRENCE

The second tradition justifying the death penalty is the utilitarian theory of deterrence. This holds that by executing convicted murderers we will deter would-be murderers from killing innocent people. The evidence for deterrence is controversial. Some scholars, like Thornstein Sellin and Bedau, argue that the death penalty is not a deterrent of homicides superior to long-term imprisonment. Others, such as Isaac Ehrlich, make a case for the death penalty as a significant deterrent. Granted that the evidence is ambiguous, and honest scholars can differ on the results. However, one often hears abolitionists claiming the evidence shows that the death penalty fails to deter homicide. This is too strong a claim. The sociological evidence doesn't show either that the death penalty deters or that it fails to deter. The evidence is simply inconclusive. But a commonsense case can be made for deterrence.

Imagine that every time someone intentionally killed an innocent person he was immediately struck down by lightning. When mugger Mike slashed his knife into the neck of the elderly pensioner, lightning struck, killing Mike. His fellow muggers witnessed the sequence of events. When burglar Bob pulled his pistol out and shot the bank teller through her breast, a bolt leveled Bob, his compatriots beholding the spectacle. Soon men with their guns lying next to them were found all across the world in proximity to the corpses of their presumed victims. Do you think that the evidence of cosmic retribution would go unheeded?

We can imagine the murder rate in the United States and everywhere else plummeting. The close correlation between murder and cosmic retribution would serve as a deterrent to would-be murderers. If this thought experiment is sound, we have a prima facie argument for the deterrent effect of capital punishment. In its ideal, prompt performance, the death penalty would likely deter most rational criminally minded from committing murder. The question then becomes how do we institute the death penalty so as to have the maximal deterrent effect without violating the rights of the accused.

We would have to bring the accused to trial more quickly and limit the appeals process of those found guilty "beyond reasonable doubt." Having DNA evidence should make this more feasible than hitherto. Furthermore, public executions of the convicted murderer would serve as a reminder that crime does not pay. Public executions of criminals seem an efficient way to communicate the message that if you shed innocent blood, you will pay a high price. . . .

Former Prosecuting Attorney for the State of Florida, Richard Gernstein, has set forth the common-sense case for deterrence. First of all, he claims, the death penalty certainly deters the murderer from any further murders, including those he or she might commit within the prison where he is confined. Second, statistics cannot tell us how many potential criminals have refrained from taking another's life through fear of the death penalty. He quotes Judge Hyman Barshay of New York: "The death penalty is a warning, just like a lighthouse throwing its beams out to sea. We hear about shipwrecks, but we do not hear about the ships the lighthouse guides safely on their way. We do not have proof of the number of ships it saves, but we do not tear the lighthouse down."

Some of the commonsense evidence is anecdotal, as the following quotation shows. British member of Parliament Arthur Lewis explains how he was converted from an abolitionist to a supporter of the death penalty:

> One reason that has stuck in my mind, and which has proved [deterrence] to me beyond question, is that there was once a professional burglar in [my] constituency who consistently boasted of the fact that he had spent about one-third of his life in prison. . . . He said to me "I am a professional burglar. Before we go out on a job we plan it down to every detail. Before we go into the boozer to have a drink we say 'Don't forget, no shooters'—shooters being guns." He adds "We did our job and didn't have shooters because at that time there was capital punishment. Our wives, girlfriends and our mums said, 'Whatever you do, do not carry a shooter because if you are caught you might be topped [executed].' If you do away with capital punishment they will all be carrying shooters."

It is difficult to know how widespread this reasoning is. My own experience corroborates this testimony. Growing up in the infamous Cicero, Illinois, home of Al Capone and the Mafia, I had friends who went into crime, mainly burglary and larceny. It was common knowledge that one stopped short of killing in the act of robbery. A prison sentence could be dealt with—especially with a good lawyer—but being convicted of murder, which at that time included a reasonable chance of being electrocuted, was an altogether different matter. No doubt exists in my mind that the threat of the electric chair saved the lives of some of those who were robbed in my town. No doubt some crimes are committed in the heat of passion or by the temporarily (or permanently) insane, but some are committed through a process of risk assessment. Burglars, kidnappers, traitors and vindictive people will sometimes be restrained by the threat of death. We simply don't know how much capital punishment deters, but this sort of commonsense, anecdotal evidence must be taken into account in assessing the institution of capital punishment. . . .

Gernstein quotes the British Royal Commission on Capital Punishment (1949–53), which is one of the most thorough studies on the subject and which concluded that there was evidence that the death penalty has some deterrent effect on normal human beings. Some of its evidence in favor of the deterrence effect includes these points:

1. Criminals who have committed an offense punishable by life imprisonment, when faced with capture, refrained from killing their captor though by killing, escape seemed probable. When asked why they refrained from the homicide, quick responses indicated a willingness to serve life sentence, but not risk the death penalty.
2. Criminals about to commit certain offenses refrained from carrying deadly weapons. Upon apprehension, answers to questions concerning absence of such weapons indicated a desire to avoid more serious punishment by carrying a deadly weapon, and also to avoid use of the weapon which could result in imposition of the death penalty.
3. Victims have been removed from a capital punishment State to a non-capital punishment State to allow the murderer opportunity for homicide without threat to his own life. This in itself demonstrates that the death penalty is considered by some would-be-killers.

Gernstein then quotes former District Attorney of New York, Frank S. Hogan, representing himself and his associates:

We are satisfied from our experience that the deterrent effect is both real and substantial . . . for example, from time to time accomplices in felony murder state with apparent truthfulness that in the planning of the felony they strongly urged the killer not to resort to violence. From the context of these utterances, it is apparent that they were led to these warnings to the killer by fear of the death penalty which they realized might follow the taking of life. Moreover, victims of hold-ups have occasionally reported that one of the robbers expressed a desire to kill them and was dissuaded from so doing by a confederate. Once again, we

think it not unreasonable to suggest that fear of the death penalty played a role in some of these intercessions.

On a number of occasions, defendants being questioned in connection with homicide have shown a striking terror of the death penalty. While these persons have in fact perpetrated homicide, we think that their terror of the death penalty must be symptomatic of the attitude of many others of their type, as a result of which many lives have been spared.

. . . Gernstein notes:

The commissioner of Police of London, England, in his evidence before the Royal Commission on Capital Punishment, told of a gang of armed robbers who continued operations after one of their members was sentenced to death and his sentence commuted to penal servitude, but the same gang disbanded and disappeared when, on a later occasion, two others were convicted of murder and hanged.

Gernstein sums up his data: "Surely it is a common sense argument, based on what is known of human nature, that the death penalty has a deterrent effect particularly for certain kinds of murderers. Furthermore, as the Royal Commission opined, the death penalty helps to educate the conscience of the whole community, and it arouses among many people a quasi-religious sense of awe. In the mind of the public there remains a strong association between murder and the penalty of death. Certainly one of the factors which restrains some people from murder is fear of punishment and surely, since people fear death more than anything else, the death penalty is the most effective deterrent."

I should also point out that *given the retributivist argument* for the death penalty, based on desert, the retentionist does not have to prove that the death penalty deters *better* than long prison sentences, but if the death penalty is deemed at least as effective as its major alternative, it would be justified. If evidence existed that life imprisonment were a *more effective* deterrent, the retentionist might be hard pressed to defend it on retributivist lines alone. My view is that the desert argument plus the commonsense evidence—being bolstered by the following argument, the Best Bet Argument, strongly supports retention of the death penalty.

The late Ernest van den Haag has set forth what he called the Best Bet Argument. He argued that even though we don't know for certain whether the death penalty deters or prevents other murders, we should bet that it does. Indeed, due to our ignorance, any social policy we take is a gamble. Not to choose capital punishment for first-degree murder is as much a bet that capital punishment doesn't deter as choosing the policy is a bet that it does. There is a significant difference in the betting, however, in that to bet against capital punishment is to bet against the innocent and for the murderer, while to bet for it is to bet against the murderer and for the innocent.

The point is this: We are accountable for what we let happen, as well as for what we actually do. If I fail to bring up my children properly so that they are a menace to society, I am to some extent responsible for their bad behavior. I could have caused it to be somewhat better. If I have good evidence that a bomb will blow up the building you are working in and fail to notify you (assuming I can), I am partly responsible for your death, if and when the bomb explodes. So we are responsible for what we omit doing, as well as for what we do. Purposefully to refrain from a lesser evil which we know will allow a greater evil to occur is to be at least partially responsible for the greater evil. This responsibility for our omissions underlies van den Haag's argument, to which we now return.

Suppose that we choose a policy of capital punishment for capital crimes. In this case we are betting that the death of some murderers will be more than compensated for by the lives of some innocents not being murdered (either by these murderers or others who would have murdered). If we're right, we have saved the lives of the innocent. If we're wrong, unfortunately, we've sacrificed the lives of some murderers. But say we choose not to have a social policy of capital punishment. If capital punishment doesn't work as a deterrent, we've come out ahead, but if it does work, then we've missed an opportunity to save innocent lives. If we value the saving of innocent lives more highly than the loss of the guilty, then to bet on a policy of capital punishment turns out to be rational. Since the innocent have a greater right to life than the guilty, it is our moral duty to adopt a policy that has a chance of protecting them from potential murderers. . . .

If the Best Bet Argument is sound, or if the death penalty does deter would-be murderers, as common sense suggests, then we should support some uses of the death penalty. It should be used for those who commit first-degree murder, for whom no mitigating factors are present, and especially for those who murder police officers, prison guards, and political leaders. Many states rightly favor it for those who murder while committing another crime, such as burglary or rape. It should be used in cases of treason and terrorist bombings. It should also be considered for the perpetrators of egregious white collar crimes such as bank managers embezzling the savings of the public. The savings and loan scandals of the 1980s, involving wealthy bank officials absconding with the investments of elderly pensioners and others, ruined the lives of many people. This gross violation of the public trust warrants the electric chair. Such punishment would meet the two conditions set forth in this paper. The punishment would be deserved and it would likely deter future crimes by people in the public trust. It would also make the death penalty more egalitarian, applicable to the rich as well as the poor.

Let me consider two objections often made to the implementation of the death penalty: that it sometimes leads to the death of innocents and that it discriminates against blacks.

Objection 1: Miscarriages of justice occur. Capital punishment is to be rejected because of human fallibility in convicting innocent parties and sentencing them to death. In a survey done in 1985 Hugo Adam Bedau and Michael Radelet found that of the 7,000 persons executed in the United States between 1900 and 1985, 25 were innocent of capital crimes. While some compensation is available to those unjustly imprisoned, the death sentence is irrevocable. We can't compensate the dead. As John Maxton, a member of the British Parliament puts it, "If we allow one innocent person to be executed, morally we are committing the same, or, in some ways, a worse crime than the person who committed the murder."

Response: Mr. Maxton is incorrect in saying that mistaken judicial execution is morally the same as or worse than murder, for a deliberate intention to kill the innocent occurs in a murder, whereas no such intention occurs in wrongful capital punishment.

Sometimes the objection is framed this way: It is better to let ten criminals go free than to execute one innocent person. If this dictum is a call for safeguards, then it is well taken; but somewhere there seems to be a limit on the tolerance of society toward capital offenses. Would these abolitionists argue that it is better that 50 or 100 or 1,000 murderers go free than that one innocent person be executed? Society has a right to protect itself from capital offenses even if this means taking a finite chance of executing an innocent person. If the basic activity or process is justified, then it is regrettable, but morally acceptable, that some mistakes are made. Fire trucks occasionally kill innocent pedestrians while racing to fires, but we accept these losses as justified by the greater good of the activity of using fire trucks. We judge the use of automobiles to be acceptable even though such use causes an average of 50,000 traffic fatalities each year. We accept the morality of a defensive war even though it will result in our troops accidentally or mistakenly killing innocent people.

The fact that we can err in applying the death penalty should give us pause and cause us to build a better appeals process into the judicial system. Such a process is already in most places in the American and British legal systems. That an occasional error may be made, regrettable though this is, is not a sufficient reason for us to refuse to use the death penalty, if on balance it serves a just and useful function.

Furthermore, abolitionists are simply misguided in thinking that prison sentences are a satisfactory alternative here. It's not clear that we can always or typically compensate innocent parties who waste away in prison. . . .

The abolitionist is incorrect in arguing that death is different from long-term prison sentences because it is irrevocable. Imprisonment also takes good things away from us that may never be returned. We cannot restore to the inmate the freedom or opportunities he or she lost. Suppose an innocent 25-year-old man is given a life sentence for murder. Thirty years later the error is discovered and he is set free. Suppose he values three years of freedom to every one year of life. That is, he would rather live 10 years as a free man than 30 as a prisoner. Given this man's values, the criminal justice system has taken the equivalent of 10 years of life from him. If he lives until he is 65, he has, as far as his estimation is concerned, lost 10 years, so that he may be said to have lived only 55 years.

The numbers in this example are arbitrary, but the basic point is sound. Most of us would prefer a shorter life of higher quality to a longer one of low quality. Death prevents all subsequent quality, but imprisonment also irrevocably harms one by diminishing the quality of life of the prisoner.

Objection 2: The second objection . . . made against the death penalty is that it is unjust because it discriminates against the poor and minorities, particularly African Americans, over rich people and whites. Stephen B. Bright makes this objection. . . . Former Supreme Court Justice William Douglas wrote that "a law which reaches that [discriminatory] result in practice has no more sanctity than a law, which in terms provides the same." . . .

Response: First of all, it is not true that a law that is applied in a discriminatory manner is unjust. Unequal justice is no less justice, however uneven its application. The discriminatory application, not the law itself, is unjust. A just law is still just even if it is not applied consistently. For example, a friend once got two speeding tickets during a 100-mile trip (having borrowed my car).

He complained to the police officer who gave him his second ticket that many drivers were driving faster than he was at the time. They had escaped detection, he argued, so it wasn't fair for him to get two tickets on one trip. The officer acknowledged the imperfections of the system but, justifiably, had no qualms about giving him the second ticket. Unequal justice is still justice, however regrettable. So Justice Douglas is wrong in asserting that discriminatory results invalidate the law itself. Discriminatory practices should be reformed, and in many cases they can be. But imperfect practices in themselves do not entail that the laws engendering these practices themselves are unjust. . . .

. . . If we concluded that we should abolish a rule or practice, unless we treated everyone exactly by the same rules all the time, we would have to abolish, for example, traffic laws and laws against imprisonment for rape, theft, and even murder. Carried to its logical limits, we would also have to refrain from saving drowning victims if a number of people were drowning but we could only save a few of them. Imperfect justice is the best that we humans can attain. We should reform our practices as much as possible to eradicate unjust discrimination wherever we can, but if we are not allowed to have a law without perfect application, we will be forced to have no laws at all.

Nathanson . . . argues that the case of death is different. "Because of its finality and extreme severity of the death penalty, we need to be more scrupulous in applying it as punishment than is necessary with any other punishment." The retentionist agrees that the death penalty is a severe punishment and that we need to be scrupulous in applying it. The difference between the abolitionist and the retentionist seems to lie in whether we are wise and committed enough as a nation to reform our institutions so that they approximate fairness. Apparently, Nathanson is pessimistic here, whereas I have faith in our ability to learn from our mistakes and reform our systems. If we can't reform our legal system, what hope is there for us?

More specifically, the charge that a higher percentage of blacks than whites are executed was once true but is no longer so. Many states have made significant changes in sentencing procedures, with the result that currently whites convicted of first-degree murder are sentenced to death at a higher rate than blacks.

One must be careful in reading too much into these statistics. While great disparities in statistics should cause us to examine our judicial procedures, they do not in themselves prove injustice. For example, more males than females are convicted of violent crimes (almost 90% of those convicted of violent crimes are males—a virtually universal statistic), but this is not strong evidence that the law is unfair, for there are biological/psychological explanations for the disparity in convictions. Males are on average and by nature more aggressive (usually tied to testosterone) than females. Simply having a Y chromosome predisposes them to greater violence. Nevertheless, we hold male criminals responsible for their violence and expect them to control themselves. Likewise, there may be good explanations why people of one ethnic group commit more crimes than those of other groups, explanations that do not impugn the processes of the judicial system nor absolve rational people of their moral responsibility.

Recently, Governor George Ryan of Illinois, the state of my childhood and youth, commuted the sentences of over 150 death row inmates. Apparently, some of those convicted were convicted on insufficient evidence. If so, their sentences should have been commuted and the prisoners compensated. Such decisions should be done on a case-by-case basis. If capital punishment is justified, its application should be confined to clear cases in which the guilt of the criminal is "beyond reasonable doubt." But to overthrow the whole system because of a few possible miscarriages is as unwarranted as it is a loss of faith in our system of criminal justice. No one would abolish the use of fire engines and ambulances because occasionally they kill innocent pedestrians while carrying out their mission.

Abolitionists often make the complaint that only the poor get death sentences for murder. If their trials are fair, then they deserve the death penalty, but rich murderers may be equally deserving. At the moment only first-degree murder and treason are crimes deemed worthy of the death penalty. Perhaps our notion of treason should be expanded to include those who betray the trust of the public: corporation executives who have the trust of ordinary people, but who, through selfish and dishonest practices, ruin their lives. As noted above, my

proposal is to consider broadening, not narrowing, the scope of capital punishment, to include business personnel who unfairly harm the public. The executives in the recent corporation scandals who bailed out of sinking corporations with golden, million-dollar lifeboats while the pension plans of thousands of employees went to the bottom of the economic ocean, may deserve severe punishment, and if convicted, they should receive what they deserve. My guess is that the threat of the death sentence would have a deterrent effect here. Whether it is feasible to apply the death penalty for horrendous white-collar crimes is debatable. But there is something to be said in its favor. It would remove the impression that only the poor get executed.

CONCLUSION

. . . A cogent case can be made for retaining the death penalty for serious crimes, such as first-degree murder and treason. The case primarily rests on a notion of justice as desert but is strengthened by utilitarian arguments involving deterrence. It is not because retentionists disvalue life that we defend the use of the death penalty. Rather, it is because we value human life as highly as we do that we support its continued use. The combined argument based on both backward-looking and forward-looking considerations justifies use of the death penalty. I have suggested that the application of the death penalty include not only first-degree murder but also treason (willful betrayal of one's country), including the treasonous behavior of business executives who violate the public trust.

The abolitionists . . . point out the problems in applying the death penalty. We can concede that there are problems and reform is constantly needed, but since the death penalty is justified in principle, we should seek to improve its application rather than abolish a just institution. We ought not throw out the baby with the dirty bathwater.

EXERCISES

1. Pojman notes that abolitionists often make the complaint that only the poor get death sentences for murder. In response, he suggests that the death penalty might also be appropriate for white-collar criminals who steal millions of dollars from the pension plans of their employees. Is that an answer to the abolitionists' complaint?
2. The classic argument for capital punishment is retributive: blood deserves blood, those who commit murder deserve to die, and justice is not done when a murderer is allowed to live. The retributive view is stated plainly by Igor Primoratz:

> Capital punishment ought to be retained where it obtains, and reintroduced in those jurisdictions that have abolished it, although we have no reason to believe that, as a matter of deterrence, it is any better than a very long prison term. It ought to be retained, or reintroduced, for one simple reason: that justice be done in cases of murder, that murderers be punished according to their just deserts.

Many people (including, of course, Primoratz) regard that as a clear and certain truth. But what is the *basis* for the claim that murderers *justly deserve* to be executed? Is it a gut feeling? A matter of religious faith? An instinct?

3. Walter Berns—a supporter of capital punishment—insists that "the criminal law must be made awful, by which I mean 'inspiring, or commanding profound respect or reverential fear.' It must remind us of the moral order by which alone we can live as *human* beings, and in America . . . the only punishment that can do this is capital punishment." Assuming that the death penalty does command reverential fear, is that an appropriate goal for a democratic society to have toward its laws, or is it more appropriate for a monarchical or tyrannical society?

4. In ancient Greece, condemned prisoners (such as Socrates) were given a poison (hemlock) that they could take, by their own hand, at any time during the appointed day of execution. Would that be a better form of execution than the current system of "lethal injection"?

5. Pojman and Bright obviously have fundamental disagreements on the capital punishment issue; however, are there any important points on which they *agree*?

6. Since the development of DNA testing of evidence, 17 people who were convicted of capital crimes and were on death row (for a total of 187 years) have been proved not guilty and released (for details, see Innocenceproject.com); and since DNA evidence is available only in a comparatively small number of cases, it is likely that several times that number who are awaiting execution or have already been executed were in fact innocent. Louis Pojman does not regard that as a sufficient reason to abolish capital punishment; if you *agree* with Pojman, what specific changes would you require (if any) to reduce the *likelihood* of wrongful executions?

7. In 2004, the state of Texas executed Cameron Willingham by lethal injection; Willingham had been convicted of the arson murder of his two young daughters. Following his conviction, there was extensive further investigation of the fire in which the children died, by some of the top arson investigators in the United States. The conclusion of those expert investigators was that the fire was in fact an accident, and not a case of arson at all. A noted fire expert, Gerald Hurst, sent a report to Governor Rick Perry prior to the execution; Hurst stated that not "a single piece of evidence supports a finding of arson." Governor Perry apparently ignored all the dissenting expert evidence that showed there was no crime of arson, and approved Willingham's execution. Would it be just to charge Governor Perry with negligent homicide? (Details of the Willingham case can be found in an essay by David Grann in the Sept. 7, 2009, issue of *The New Yorker*.)

ADDITIONAL READING

Among the important U.S. Supreme Court cases on capital punishment are *Gregg v. Georgia* (see especially Justice Thurgood Marshall's dissent) and *Furman v. Georgia*. Full transcripts of all U.S. Supreme Court cases dealing with capital punishment can be found at http://www.Oyez.org. For further study of key Supreme Court death penalty cases, a good source is Barry Latzer, *Death Penalty Cases: Leading U.S. Supreme Court Cases on Capital Punishment* (Woburn, MA: Butterworth-Heinemann, 1997).

Franklin E. Zimring and Gordon Hawkins, *Capital Punishment and the American Agenda* (Cambridge, MA: Cambridge University Press, 1986), place capital punishment within a world setting and draw the historical and sociological background for use of capital punishment in the United States. A recent issue of *The Journal of Criminal Law & Criminology*, Volume 95, Number 2 (2005) is devoted to articles discussing the death penalty.

For arguments opposing capital punishment, see Stephen Nathanson, "The Death Penalty as a Symbolic Issue," Chapter 11 of his book, *An Eye for an Eye? The Morality of Punishing by Death* (Totowa, NJ: Rowman & Littlefield, 1987), pp. 131–146; Charles Black, *Capital Punishment: The Inevitability of Caprice and Mistake*, 2nd ed. (New York: W. W. Norton, 1976); and Thomas W. Clark, "Crime and Causality: Do Killers Deserve to Die?" *Free Inquiry* (February/March 2005): 34–37. The view in favor of capital punishment can be found in Walter Berns, *For Capital Punishment: Crime and the Morality of the Death Penalty* (New York: Basic Books, 1979); and Ernest van den Haag, "In Defense of the Death Penalty: A Legal-Practical-Moral Analysis," *Criminal Law Bulletin*, Volume 14 (1978): 51–68.

Michael A. Mello, *Dead Wrong: A Death Row Lawyer Speaks out Against Capital Punishment* (Madison: The University of Wisconsin Press, 1997), is very readable. A recent book by David R. Dow, *Executed on a Technicality: Lethal Injustice on America's Death Row* (Boston, MA: Beacon Press, 2005), uncovers basic injustices committed in the prosecution of many now on death row. Barry Scheck, Peter Neufeld, and Jim Dwyer, *Actual Innocence* (New York: Doubleday, 2000), provide a particularly good examination of the death penalty in light of the many mistaken convictions that have recently been overturned (often through analysis of DNA evidence).

Three books offer interesting debates on the subject. E. Van den Haag and J. P. Conrad, *The Death Penalty: A Debate* (New York: Plenum, 1983); Louis P. Pojman and Jeffrey Reiman in *The Death Penalty: For and Against* (Lanham, MD: Rowman & Littlefield, 1998); and (in a much larger context) Jean Hampton and Jeffrie Murphy, *Forgiveness and Mercy* (Cambridge, MA: Cambridge University Press, 1988).

Among the many anthologies are Hugo Adam Bedau and Paul G. Cassell, *Debating the Death Penalty: Should America Have Capital Punishment?* (New York: Oxford University Press, 2005); Carol Wekesser, *The Death Penalty: Opposing Viewpoints* (San Diego, CA: Greenhaven Press, 1991); Robert M. Baird and Stuart E. Rosenbaum, *Punishment and the Death Penalty: The Current Debate* (Amherst, NY: Prometheus Books, 1995); James R. Acker, Robert M. Bohm, and Charles S. Lanier, *America's Experiment with Capital Punishment* (Durham, NC: Carolina Academic Press, 1998); Austin Sarat, *The Killing State: Capital Punishment in Law, Politics, and Culture* (New York: Oxford University Press, 1999); and Austin Sarat, *The Death Penalty: Influences and Outcomes*, Volume 1 (Aldershot, UK: Ashgate, 2005).

The Ethics Updates Web site has links to other sites (see especially the link to the documentary series *Frontline*), as well as several full-text articles, recordings of discussions and debates, and video discussions; go to *http://ethics.sandiego.edu/Applied/DeathPenalty*.

16

Abortion

Arguments concerning abortion are concentrated around three distinct issues. First, what is the status of the fetus (or as pro-life forces prefer, the unborn child)? This issue is formulated in many different ways: at what point does the fetus gain consciousness, at what point is the fetus viable (at what point could it survive outside the womb), when—if ever—does the fetus become a person, when is the fetus a living being, and (an issue that traditional Catholic theology found important) when does the fetus gain a soul (at what point does ensoulment occur)? Second, what are the rights of the woman who is carrying the fetus, and when (if ever) do they trump the rights of the fetus (if the fetus has rights)? And third, what would be the effects of making abortion illegal? Would abortions still occur, but at greatly increased risk to the life and health of the woman? Would safe abortions be available only to the wealthy and well-connected?

⊨ ABORTION IS IMMORAL ⊨
Don Marquis

Don Marquis is Professor of Philosophy at University of Kansas; this essay is an excerpt from his "Why Abortion Is Immoral," *Journal of Philosophy,* Volume 86 (April 1989).

The view that abortion is, with rare exceptions, seriously immoral has received little support in the recent philosophical literature. No doubt most philosophers affiliated with secular institutions of higher education believe that the anti-abortion position is either a symptom of irrational religious dogma or a conclusion generated by seriously confused philosophical argument. The purpose of this essay is to undermine this general belief. This essay sets out an argument that purports to show, as well as any argument in ethics can show, that abortion is, except possibly in rare cases, seriously immoral, that it is in the same moral category as killing an innocent adult human being.

The argument is based on a major assumption. Many of the most insightful and careful writers on the ethics of abortion . . . believe that whether or not abortion is morally permissible stands or falls on whether or not a fetus is the sort of being whose life it is seriously wrong to end. The argument of this essay will assume, but not argue, that they are correct.

Also, this essay will neglect issues of great importance to a complete ethics of abortion. Some anti-abortionists will allow that certain abortions, such as abortion before implantation or abortion when the life of a woman is threatened by a pregnancy or abortion after rape, may be morally permissible. This essay will not explore the casuistry of these hard cases. The purpose of this essay is to develop a general argument for the claim that the overwhelming majority of deliberate abortions are seriously immoral.

I.

. . . If the generalization a partisan in the abortion dispute adopts were derived from the reason why ending the life of a human being is wrong, then there could not be exceptions to that generalization unless some special case obtains in which there are even more powerful countervailing reasons. Such generalizations would not be merely accidental generalizations; they would point to, or be based upon, the essence of the wrongness of killing, what it is that makes killing wrong. All this suggests that a necessary condition of resolving the abortion controversy is a more theoretical account of the wrongness of killing. After all, if we merely believe, but do not understand, why killing adult human beings such as ourselves is wrong, how could we conceivably show that abortion is either immoral or permissible?

II.

In order to develop such an account, we can start from the following unproblematic assumption concerning our own case: it is wrong to kill *us*. Why is it wrong? Some answers can be easily eliminated. It might be said that what makes killing us wrong is that a killing brutalizes the one who kills. But the brutalization consists of being inured to the performance of an act that is hideously immoral; hence, the brutalization does not explain the immorality. It might be said that what makes killing us wrong is the great loss others would experience due to our absence. Although such hubris is understandable, such an explanation does not account for the wrongness of killing hermits, or those whose lives are relatively independent and whose friends find it easy to make new friends.

A more obvious answer is better. What primarily makes killing wrong is neither its effect on the murderer nor its effect on the victim's friends and relatives, but its effect on the victim. The loss of one's life is one of the greatest losses one can suffer. The loss of one's life deprives one of all the experiences, activities, projects, and enjoyments that would otherwise have constituted one's future. Therefore, killing someone is wrong, primarily because the killing inflicts (one of) the greatest possible losses on the victim. To describe this as the loss of life can be misleading, however. The change in my biological state does not by itself make killing me wrong. The effect of the loss of my biological life is the loss to me of all those activities, projects, experiences, and enjoyments which would otherwise have constituted my future personal life. These activities, projects, experiences, and enjoyments are either valuable for their own sakes or are means to something else that is valuable for its own sake. Some parts of my future are not valued by me now, but will come to be valued by me as I grow older and as my values and capacities change. When I am killed, I am deprived both of what I now value which would have been part of my future personal life, but also what I would come to value. Therefore, when I die, I am deprived of all of the value of my future. Inflicting this loss on me is ultimately what makes killing me wrong. This being the case, it would seem that what makes killing *any* adult human being prima facie seriously wrong is the loss of his or her future.

How should this rudimentary theory of the wrongness of killing be evaluated? It cannot be faulted for deriving an 'ought' from an 'is', for it does not. The analysis assumes that killing me (or you, reader) is prima facie seriously wrong. The point of the analysis is to establish which natural property ultimately explains the wrongness of the killing, given that it is wrong. A natural property will ultimately explain the wrongness of killing, only if (1) the explanation fits with our intuitions about the matter and (2) there is no other natural property that provides the basis for a better explanation of the wrongness of killing. This analysis rests on the intuition that what makes killing a particular human or animal wrong is what it does to that particular human or animal. What makes killing wrong is some natural effect or other of the killing . . . .

The claim that what makes killing wrong is the loss of the victim's future is directly supported by two considerations. In the first place, this theory explains why we regard killing as one of the worst of crimes. Killing is especially wrong, because it deprives the victim of more than perhaps any other crime. In the second place, people with AIDS or cancer who know they are dying believe, of course, that dying is a very bad thing for them. They believe that the loss of a future to them that they would otherwise have experienced is what makes their premature death a very bad thing for them. A better theory of the wrongness of killing would require a different natural property associated with killing which better fits with the attitudes of the dying. What could it be?

The view that what makes killing wrong is the loss to the victim of the value of the victim's future gains additional support when some of its implications are examined. In the first place, it is incompatible with the view that it is wrong to kill only beings who are biologically human. It is possible that there exists a different species from another planet whose members have a future like ours. Since having a future like that is what makes killing someone wrong, this theory entails that it would be wrong to kill members of such a species. Hence, this theory is opposed to the claim that only life that is biologically human has great moral worth, a claim which many antiabortionists have seemed to adopt. This opposition, which this theory has in common with personhood theories, seems to be a merit of the theory.

In the second place, the claim that the loss of one's future is the wrong-making feature of one's being killed entails the possibility that the futures of some actual nonhuman mammals on our own planet are sufficiently like ours that it is seriously wrong to kill them also. Whether some animals do have the same right to life as human beings depends on adding to the account of the wrongness of killing some additional account of just what it is about my future or the futures of other adult human beings which makes it wrong to kill us. No such additional account will be offered in this essay. Undoubtedly, the provision of such an account would be a very difficult matter. Undoubtedly, any such account would be quite controversial. Hence, it surely should not reflect badly on this sketch of an elementary theory of the wrongness of killing that it is indeterminate with respect to some very difficult issues regarding animal rights.

In the third place, the claim that the loss of one's future is the wrong-making feature of one's being killed does not entail, as sanctity of human life theories do, that active euthanasia is wrong. Persons who are severely and incurably ill, who face a future of pain and despair, and who wish to die will not have suffered a loss if they are killed. It is, strictly speaking, the value of a human's future which makes killing wrong in this theory. This being so, killing does not necessarily wrong some persons who are sick and dying. Of course, there may be other reasons for a prohibition of active euthanasia, but that is another matter. Sanctity-of-human-life theories seem to hold that active euthanasia is seriously wrong even in an individual case where there seems to be good reason for it independently of public policy considerations. This consequence is most implausible, and it is a plus for the claim that the loss of a future of value is what makes killing wrong that it does not share this consequence.

In the fourth place, the account of the wrongness of killing defended in this essay does straightforwardly entail that it is prima facie seriously wrong to kill children and infants, for we do presume that they have futures of value. Since we do believe that it is wrong to kill defenseless little babies, it is important that a theory of the wrongness of killing easily account for this. Personhood theories of the wrongness of killing, on the other hand, cannot straightforwardly account for the wrongness of killing infants and young children. Hence, such theories must add special ad hoc accounts of the wrongness of killing the young. The plausibility of such ad hoc theories seems to be a function of how desperately one wants such theories to work. The claim that the primary wrong-making feature of a killing is the loss to the victim of the value of its future accounts for the wrongness of killing young children and infants directly, it makes the wrongness of such acts as obvious as we actually think it is. This is a further merit of this theory. Accordingly, it seems that this value of a future-like-ours theory of the wrongness of killing shares strengths of both sanctity-of-life and personhood accounts while avoiding weaknesses of both. In addition, it meshes with a central intuition concerning what makes killing wrong.

The claim that the primary wrong-making feature of a killing is the loss to the victim of the value of its future has obvious consequences for the ethics of abortion. The future of a standard fetus includes a set of experiences, projects, activities, and such which are identical with the futures of adult human beings and are identical with the futures of young children. Since the reason that is sufficient to explain why it is wrong to kill human beings after the time of birth is a reason that also applies to fetuses, it follows that abortion is prima facie seriously morally wrong.

This argument does not rely on the invalid inference that, since it is wrong to kill persons, it is wrong to kill potential persons also. The category that is morally central to this analysis is the category of having a valuable future like ours; it is not the category of personhood. The argument to the conclusion that abortion is prima facie seriously morally wrong proceeded independently of the notion of person or potential person or any equivalent. Someone may wish to start with this analysis in terms of the value of a human future, conclude that abortion is, except perhaps in rare circumstances, seriously morally wrong, infer that fetuses have the right to life, and then call fetuses "persons" as a result of their having the right to life. Clearly, in this case, the category of person is being used to state the *conclusion* of the analysis rather than to generate the *argument* of the analysis.

The structure of this anti-abortion argument can be both illuminated and defended by comparing it to what appears to be the best argument for the wrongness of the wanton infliction of pain on animals. This latter argument is based on the assumption that it is prima facie wrong to inflict pain on me (or you, reader). What is the natural property associated with the infliction of pain which makes such infliction wrong? The obvious answer seems to be that the infliction of pain causes suffering and that suffering is a misfortune. The suffering caused by the infliction of pain is what makes the wanton infliction of pain on me wrong. The wanton infliction of pain on other adult humans causes suffering. The wanton infliction of pain on animals causes suffering. Since causing suffering is what makes the wanton infliction of pain wrong and since the wanton infliction of pain on animals causes suffering, it follows that the wanton infliction of pain on animals is wrong.

This argument for the wrongness of the wanton infliction of pain on animals shares a number of structural features with the argument for the serious prima facie wrongness of abortion. Both arguments start with an obvious assumption concerning what it is wrong to do to me (or you, reader). Both then look for the characteristic or the consequence of the wrong action which makes the action wrong. Both recognize that the wrong-making feature of these immoral actions is a property of actions sometimes directed at individuals other than postnatal human beings. If the structure of the argument for the wrongness of the wanton infliction of pain on animals is sound, then the structure of the argument for the prima facie serious wrongness of abortion is also sound, for the structure of the two arguments is the same. The structure common to both is the key to the explanation of how the wrongness of abortion can be demonstrated without recourse to the category of person. In neither argument is that category crucial . . . .

Of course, this value of a future-like-ours argument, if sound, shows only that abortion is prima facie wrong, not that it is wrong in any and all circumstances. Since the loss of the future to a standard fetus, if killed, is, however, at least as great a loss as the loss of the future to a standard adult human being who is killed, abortion, like ordinary killing, could be justified only by the most compelling reasons. The loss of one's life is almost the greatest misfortune that can happen to one. Presumably abortion could be justified in some circumstances, only if the loss consequent on failing to abort would be at least as great. Accordingly, morally permissible abortions will be rare indeed unless, perhaps, they occur so early in pregnancy that a fetus is not yet definitely an individual. Hence, this argument should be taken as showing that abortion is presumptively very seriously

wrong, where the presumption is very strong—as strong as the presumption that killing another adult human being is wrong.

III.

How complete an account of the wrongness of killing does the value of a future-like-ours account have to be in order that the wrongness of abortion is a consequence? This account does not have to be an account of the necessary conditions for the wrongness of killing. Some persons in nursing homes may lack valuable human futures, yet it may be wrong to kill them for other reasons. Furthermore, this account does not obviously have to be the sole reason killing is wrong where the victim did have a valuable future. This analysis claims only that, for any killing where the victim did have a valuable future like ours, having that future by itself is sufficient to create the strong presumption that the killing is seriously wrong. . . .

V.

In this essay, it has been argued that the correct ethic of the wrongness of killing can be extended to fetal life and used to show that there is a strong presumption that any abortion is morally impermissible. If the ethic of killing adopted here entails, however, that contraception is also seriously immoral, then there would appear to be a difficulty with the analysis of this essay.

But this analysis does not entail that contraception is wrong. Of course, contraception prevents the actualization of a possible future of value. Hence, it follows from the claim that futures of value should be maximized that contraception is prima facie immoral. This obligation to maximize does not exist, however; furthermore, nothing in the ethics of killing in this paper entails that it does. The ethics of killing in this essay would entail that contraception is wrong only if something were denied a human future of value by contraception. Nothing at all is denied such a future by contraception, however.

Candidates for a subject of harm by contraception fall into four categories: (1) some sperm or other, (2) some ovum or other, (3) a sperm and an ovum separately, and (4) a sperm and an ovum together. Assigning the harm to some sperm is utterly arbitrary, for no reason can be given for making a sperm the subject of harm rather than an ovum. Assigning the harm to some ovum is utterly arbitrary, for no reason can be given for making an ovum the subject of harm rather than a sperm. One might attempt to avoid these problems by insisting that contraception deprives both the sperm and the ovum separately of a valuable future like ours. On this alternative, too many futures are lost. Contraception was supposed to be wrong, because it deprived us of one future of value, not two. One might attempt to avoid this problem by holding that contraception deprives the combination of sperm and ovum of a valuable future like ours. But here the definite article misleads. At the time of contraception, there are hundreds of millions of sperm, one (released) ovum and millions of possible combinations of all of these. There is no actual combination at all. Is the subject of the loss to be a merely possible combination? Which one? This alternative does not yield an actual subject of harm either. Accordingly, the immorality of contraception is not entailed by the loss of a future-like-ours argument simply because there is no nonarbitrarily identifiable subject of the loss in the case of contraception.

VI.

The purpose of this essay has been to set out an argument for the serious presumptive wrongness of abortion subject to the assumption that the moral permissibility of abortion stands or falls on the moral status of the fetus. Since a fetus possesses a property, the possession of which in adult human beings is sufficient to make killing an adult human being wrong, abortion is wrong. This way of dealing with the problem of abortion seems superior to other approaches to the ethics of abortion, because it rests on an ethics of killing which is close to self-evident, because the crucial morally relevant property clearly applies to fetuses, and because the argument avoids the usual equivocations on 'human life', 'human being', or 'person.' The argument rests neither on religious claims nor on Papal dogma. It is not subject to the objection of "speciesism." Its soundness is compatible with the moral permissibility of euthanasia and contraception. It deals with our intuitions concerning young children.

Finally, this analysis can be viewed as resolving a standard problem—indeed, *the* standard problem—concerning the ethics of abortion. Clearly, it is wrong to kill adult human beings. Clearly, it is not wrong to end the life of some arbitrarily chosen single human cell. Fetuses seem to be like arbitrarily chosen human cells in some respects and like adult humans in other respects. The problem of the ethics of abortion is the problem of determining the fetal property that settles this moral controversy. The thesis of this essay is that the problem of the ethics of abortion, so understood, is solvable.

⇒ MOST ABORTIONS ARE MORALLY LEGITIMATE ⇒
Bonnie Steinbock

Bonnie Steinbock is Professor of Philosophy at University at Albany, SUNY; this is part of her article, "Why Most Abortions Are Not Wrong," *Advances in Bioethics*, Volume 5 (1999), 245–267.

I. INTRODUCTION

. . . My belief that abortion is not wrong is based on two considerations: the moral status of the embryo and fetus and the burdens imposed by pregnancy and childbirth on women. I begin by presenting briefly the view of moral status that I take to be correct, that is, the interest view. The interest view limits moral status to beings who have interests and restricts the possession of interests to conscious, sentient beings. The implication for abortion is that it is not seriously wrong to kill a nonconscious, nonsentient fetus where there is an adequate reason for doing so, such as not wanting to be pregnant. Next I discuss Don Marquis' challenge to the interest view. According to Marquis, killing is prima facie wrong when it deprives a being of a valuable future like ours. If a being has a valuable future, the fact that it is now nonconscious and nonsentient is irrelevant. Marquis' account of the wrongness of killing implies that abortion is almost always wrong. I try to show that his view has serious problems, in particular, that it applies to gametes as well as fetuses, and it makes contraception as well as abortion seriously wrong . . . .

II. THE MORAL STATUS OF THE FETUS

I use the term "fetus" to refer to the unborn at all stages of pregnancy, even though this is not, strictly speaking, correct. Between conception and 8 weeks, the correct term is "embryo"; the term "fetus" is correctly used between 8 weeks gestation age and birth. I will use the term "fetus" throughout, both in order to avoid the inconvenience of the phrase "embryo or fetus" and because using the term "embryo," which refers to the earliest weeks of pregnancy, might convey an unfair advantage to my argument. Everything I have to say about abortion in this essay applies as much to a 12-week-old fetus as it does to a newly fertilized egg.

I will not discuss the morality of abortion beyond the first trimester of pregnancy (approximately 12 weeks long) since the vast majority of abortions (approximately 90 percent) take place by then. I am quite willing to accept that late abortions, especially those that occur after 24 weeks, are morally problematic; but since these are quite rare (about 1 percent of all abortions) and almost always done for very serious moral reasons such as to preserve the life or health of the mother or to prevent the birth of an infant with a serious disability, I will not discuss these abortions. Instead, I will focus on so-called elective abortions, those chosen to avoid the burdens of pregnancy, childbearing, and childrearing.

Most opponents of abortion say that abortion is wrong because it is the killing of an innocent human being. They see no morally relevant difference between an early gestation fetus and a newborn baby. If it would be wrong to kill a newborn because it is unwanted (something on which there is virtually unanimous agreement), then, according to this thinking, it is equally wrong to perform an abortion, which deliberately kills the fetus.

The question, then, is whether an early gestation fetus (or simply "fetus" as I will say from now on) is morally equivalent to a newborn baby. This seems to me completely implausible. A newborn can feel, react, and perceive. It cries when it is hungry or stuck with needles. Very soon after birth it cries from boredom or loneliness as well and can be soothed by being rocked and held. By contrast, the first-trimester fetus cannot think, feel, or perceive anything. It is certainly alive and human, but it feels and is aware of nothing; it is more like a gamete (a sperm or an ovum), which is also alive and human, than a baby. While early abortion is not the psychological equivalent of contraception, it is morally closer to contraception than to homicide.

My thesis is that killing fetuses is morally different from killing babies because fetuses are not, and babies are, sentient. By sentience, I mean the ability to experience pain and pleasure. But what is the moral significance of sentience? I have argued that sentience is important because nonsentient beings, whether mere things (e.g., cars and rocks and works of art) or living things without nervous systems (e.g., plants), lack interests of their own. Therefore, nonsentient beings are not among those beings whose interests we are required to

consider. To put it another way, nonsentient beings lack moral status. I refer to this view of moral status as "the interest view."

Critics of the interest view ask why a being has to feel or experience anything to have interests. Leaving a bicycle out in the rain will cause it to rust, affecting adversely both its appearance and its performance. Why can we not say that this is contrary to its interests? Stripping the bark off a tree will cause it to die. Why can't we say that this is against the tree's interest? Limiting interests to sentient beings (namely, animals—human and otherwise) seems to limit unduly the arena of our concern. What about rivers and forests and mountains? What about the environment?

However, this objection misconceives the interest view. The claim is not that we should be concerned to protect and preserve only sentient beings, but rather that only sentient beings can have an interest or a stake in their own existence. It is only sentient beings to whom anything matters, which is quite different from saying that only sentient beings matter. The interest view can acknowledge the value of many nonsentient beings, from works of art to wilderness areas. It recognizes that we have all kinds of reasons—economic, aesthetic, symbolic, even moral reasons—to protect or preserve nonsentient beings. The difference between sentient and nonsentient beings is not that sentient beings have value and nonsentient ones lack value. Rather, it is that since nonsentient beings cannot be hurt or made to suffer, it does not matter *to them* what is done to them. In deciding what we should do, we cannot consider *their* interests since they do not have any. It might be wrong to deface a work of art or to burn a flag, but it is not a wrong *to* the painting or the flag. Put another way "golden rule"–type reasons do not apply to nonsentient beings. That is, no one would explain opposition to burning the flag of the United States of America by saying, "How would you like it if you were a flag and someone burned you?" Instead, such opposition would have to be based on the symbolic importance of the flag and the message that is conveyed when it is burned in a political demonstration. (I am not saying that flag-burning *is* wrong, only contrasting an intelligible reason for opposing flag-burning, based on the symbolic value of the flag, with an absurd reason.)

The interest view is a general theory about moral status, but it has implications for the morality of abortion. During early gestation, fetuses are nonsentient beings and, as such, they do not have interests. Scientists do not agree on precisely when fetuses become sentient, but most agree that first-trimester fetuses are not sentient. The reason is that, in the first trimester, the fetal nervous system is not sufficiently developed to transmit pain messages to the brain. Since the brain cannot receive pain messages, the first-trimester fetus is not sentient; it cannot feel anything. The synaptic connections necessary for pain perception are established in the fetal brain between 20 and 24 weeks of gestation. This means not only that premature infants *are* capable of experiencing pain—something that doctors rejected until very recently—but also that, throughout the first and most of the second trimester, fetuses do not experience pain or any other sensation. Despite the claims of propaganda films like *The Silent Scream*, first-trimester fetuses do not suffer when they are aborted.

Prolifers may think that I have missed the point of their opposition to abortion. They need not claim that abortion *hurts* the fetus, or causes it to experience pain, but rather that abortion deprives the fetus of its *life*. I quite agree that this is the important issue, but I maintain that a nonsentient being is not deprived of anything by being killed. In an important sense, it does not have a life to lose.

Now this claim may strike some people as odd. If the fetus is alive, then surely it has a life to lose? But this is just what I am denying. It seems to me that unless there is conscious awareness of some kind, a being does not have a life to lose. Consider all the living cells in our bodies which die or are killed. Surely it would be absurd to speak of all of them as losing their lives or being deprived of their lives. Or consider those in a state of permanent unconsciousness, with no hope of regaining consciousness. I would say that such persons have already lost their lives in any sense that matters, even though they are still biologically alive. It is not biological life that matters, but rather conscious existence. Killing the fetus before it becomes conscious and aware deprives it of nothing. To put it another way, the first-trimester fetus has a biological life, but its biographical life has not yet begun. The interest view suggests that it is *prima facie* wrong to deprive beings of their biographical lives, but not wrong to end merely biological lives, at least where there are good reasons for doing so, such as not wanting to bear a child.

III. The Argument from Potential

Of course, there is one difference between a human fetus and any other living, nonsentient being, namely, that if the fetus is not killed, but allowed to develop and grow, it will become a person, just like you or me. Some opponents of abortion cite the potential of the fetus to become a sentient being, with interests and a welfare of its own, as the reason for ascribing to it the moral status belonging to sentient beings. Equally, on this view, the potential of the fetus to become a person gives it the same rights as other persons, including the right to life.

The potentiality principle has been criticized on several grounds. Firstly, it does not follow from the fact that something is a potential *x* that it should be treated as an actual *x*. This is often called "the logical problem with potentiality." As John Harris puts it, we're all potentially dead, but that's no reason to treat living people as if they were corpses. Secondly, it is not clear why potential personhood attaches only to the fertilized egg. Why aren't unfertilized eggs and sperm also potential people? If certain things happen to them (like meeting a gamete) and certain other things do not (like meeting a contraceptive), they too will develop into people. Admittedly, the chance of any particular sperm becoming a person is absurdly low, but why should that negate its potential? Isn't every player a potential winner in a state lottery, even though the chances of winning are infinitesmal? We should not confuse potentialities with probabilities. So if abortion is wrong because it kills a potential person, then using a spermicide as a contraceptive is equally wrong because it also kills a potential person. Few opponents of abortion are willing to accept this conclusion, which means either giving up the argument from potential or finding a way to differentiate morally between gametes and embryos.

IV. Marquis' Argument

Don Marquis argues that traditional arguments on abortion, both those of opponents of abortion and those of proponents of a woman's right to choose, are seriously flawed. His argument against abortion derives from a general principle about the wrongness of killing. Killing adult human beings is *prima facie* wrong because it deprives them of their worthwhile future. Marquis writes:

> The loss of one's life is one of the greatest losses one can suffer. The loss of one's life deprives one of all the experiences, activities, projects, and enjoyments that would otherwise have constituted one's future. Therefore, killing someone is wrong, primarily because the killing inflicts (one of) the greatest possible losses on the victim . . . . When I am killed, I am deprived both of what I now value which would have been part of my future personal life, but also what I would come to value. Therefore, when I die, I am deprived of all of the value of my future. Inflicting this loss on me is ultimately what makes killing me wrong. This being the case, it would seem that what makes killing *any* adult human being *prima facie* seriously wrong is the loss of his or her future.

This argument for the wrongness of killing applies only to those who in fact have a future with experiences, activities, projects, and enjoyments. In Marquis' view, it might not be wrong to kill someone in a persistent vegetative state (PVS), for example, who will never regain consciousness, because such a person no longer has a valuable future. (There might be other reasons against killing PVS patients, but these would not refer to the loss inflicted on the patient.) Similarly, persons who are severely and incurably ill and who face a future of pain and despair and who wish to die may not be wronged if they are killed, because the future of which they are deprived is not considered by them to be a valuable one. However, most fetuses (leaving aside those with serious anomalies) do have valuable futures. If they are not aborted, they will come to have lives they will value and enjoy, just as you and I value and enjoy our lives. Therefore, abortion is seriously wrong for the same reason that killing an innocent adult human being is seriously wrong: it deprives the victim of his or her valuable future.

Marquis' argument against abortion is similar to arguments based on the principle of potentiality in that the wrongness of killing is derived from the loss of the valuable future the fetus will have, if allowed to grow and develop, rather than being based on any characteristic, such as genetic humanity, the fetus now has. However, Marquis' view differs from traditional potentiality arguments in two ways. Firstly, most arguments from potential maintain that it is wrong not only to kill persons, but also to kill potential persons. Though a human fetus is not now a person, it will develop into one if allowed to grow and develop. By contrast, Marquis' argument says nothing about the wrongness of killing persons and therefore nothing about the wrongness of killing potential persons. Marquis is explicit about his argument not necessarily being limited to persons but applying to any beings who have valuable futures like ours. Some nonpersons (e.g., some animals) also might have such futures, and so it might be wrong to kill them in Marquis' account. Admittedly, the concept of a person is not coextensive with the capacity to have a valuable future, and there are heated debates about what it is to be a person. However, if we use the term "person" simply to mean an individual with a valuable future like ours and hence one it would be seriously wrong to kill, we can reword Marquis' account in terms of the wrongness of killing persons.

Another way in which Marquis differs from potentiality theorists is that his argument is not based on the potential of the fetus to become something different

from what it is now. Rather, it is wrong to kill a fetus because killing it deprives it of its valuable future—the very same reason why it is wrong to kill you or me. Thus, although Marquis focuses on a certain kind of potential, namely, the fetus's potential to have experiences in the future, this potential is no different from the potential that any born human being has to have future experiences. Thus, he cannot be accused of basing the wrongness of killing born human beings on a feature that we actually possess, while basing the wrongness of abortion on a (merely) potential feature of the fetus.

Marquis thinks that his view is superior to other accounts of moral status in that it is able to explain what is wrong with killing people who are temporarily unconscious, something the interest view seems incapable of doing. If it is morally permissible to kill nonsentient beings, why is it wrong to kill someone in a reversible coma? Such a person is not now conscious or sentient. And if we appeal to his future conscious states, the same argument seems to apply to the fetus, who will become conscious and sentient if we just leave it alone.

Two responses can be made to this objection to the interest view. The first is to note an important difference between a temporarily unconscious person and a fetus. The difference is that the person who is now unconscious has had experiences, plans, beliefs, desires, etc. in the past. These past experiences are relevant because they form the basis for saying that the comatose person wants not to be killed while unconscious. "He valued his life," we might say. "Of course he would not want to be killed." This desire or preference is the basis for saying that the temporarily unconscious person has an interest in not being killed. But the same cannot be said of a nonsentient fetus. A nonsentient fetus cannot be said to want anything, and so cannot be said to want not to be killed. By contrast, if I am killed while sleeping or temporarily comatose, I am deprived of something I want very much, namely, to go on living. This is not an *occurrent* desire; that is, it is rarely if ever a desire of which I am consciously aware, but it is certainly one of my desires. We have all sorts of desires of which we are not at any particular moment consciously aware, and it would be absurd to limit our desires to what we are actually thinking about. Nor do our desires, plans, and goals, or the interests composing them, vanish when we fall into dreamless sleep.

However, our interests are not limited to what we take an interest in, as Tom Regan has correctly noted. Our interests also include what is *in* our interest, whether or not we are interested in it. For example, getting enough sleep, eating moderately, and foregoing tobacco might be in the interest of a person who has no interest in following such a regime. Now even if the nonconscious fetus is not interested in continuing to live, could we not say that continued existence is *in* its interest? If the fetus will go on to have a valuable future, is not that future in its interest?

The issue raised here is whether the future the fetus will go on to have is in an important sense *its* future. Marquis considers the existence of past experiences to be entirely irrelevant to the question of whether an entity can be deprived of its future. But this is not at all clear. Killing embryos or early gestation fetuses differs from killing adult human beings because adult human beings have a life that they (ordinarily) value and which they would prefer not to lose: a biographical as opposed to merely biological life. How might the idea of having a biographical life be connected with the possibility of having a personal future, a future of one's own? In an unpublished manuscript, "The Future-Like-Ours Argument Against Abortion and The Problem of Personal Identity," David Boonin-Vail uses a plausible theory of personal identity—the psychological continuity account—to argue that nonsentient fetuses do not have a personal future. According to the psychological continuity account of personal identity, having a certain set of past experiences is what makes me the person I am, and the experiences that I have, *my* experiences. What makes experiences at two different times experiences of the same person is that they are appropriately related by a chain of memories, desires, intentions, and the like. So an individual's past experiences are not, as Marquis claims, otiose to an account of the value of his future; indeed, they are precisely what makes his future *his*.

On this account of personal identity, then, there is an important difference between someone who is temporarily unconscious and a fetus. The difference is this: when the unconscious person regains consciousness, "there will be a relationship of continuity involving memories, intentions, character traits, and so on between his subsequent experiences and those which he had before he lapsed into the coma."

This is what makes his future experiences (those he will have if he is not killed) *his*. The situation of the preconscious fetus is quite different.

When he gains (rather than regains) consciousness, there will be no relationship of continuity involving memories, intentions, character traits, and so on between his subsequent experiences and those which he had before he gained consciousness precisely because he *had* no experiences before he

gained consciousness. This is what permits us to say of the preconscious fetus that it is not he who will have these later experiences if he is not killed. And this, in turn, is what permits us to deny that *he* will be harmed if we prevent those experiences from occurring.

If we accept the psychological continuity account of personal identity, then past experiences do matter because without past experiences there is no one with a personal future. This is not to say that this provides us with a reason to kill the presentient fetus but rather that we lack the strong reason for not killing it that we have in the case of people like you and me. The justificatory reason for killing the fetus stems from the woman's rights to bodily autonomy and self-determination, to which I will return in the next section.

However, perhaps the psychological continuity account is wrong. Perhaps personal identity is better based on physical continuity. In that case, even if the born human being has no memories connecting her to the fetal stage, we can still say that she is the same individual because there is physical continuity between the born human and the fetal human.

There are certain advantages to a physical continuity account of personal identity. It allows us to say of someone who develops total amnesia that he has a history of which he has absolutely no memory, and this seems to be a plain statement of fact. Similarly, most people have very few memories about anything that occurred before the ages of four or five; yet most of us are convinced that we are the same individuals we were when very young. Of course, there could be psychological connections of which we have no memory. For example, providing an infant with secure, loving experiences as opposed to terrifying or traumatic ones is likely to affect the psychological development of the eventual adult, whether or not she remembers what happened. So it may be that a more sophisticated psychological account, one that is not entirely dependent on memory, is the better account of identity, but I will not pursue that issue.

Boonin-Vail argues that the trouble with basing identity on physical continuity is that this implies that contraception is as wrong as abortion, something most people, including Marquis, want to reject. Thus, the claim that contraception prevents a gamete from enjoying a future like ours takes the form of a *reductio ad absurdum*: the argument (allegedly) commits one to an absurd (or at least unacceptable) conclusion. A physical continuity account of personal identity is vulnerable to the objection that it makes contraception as wrong as abortion because there seems to be no reason why embryos have and gametes do not have valuable futures. For the embryo does not appear *ex nihilo*. Its physical history goes back to the conjoining of the sperm and ovum. Thus, if you prevent the sperm and ovum from conjoining, you deprive each of them of the future they would have had if fertilization had taken place.

Marquis says that his view does not apply to contraception because, prior to fertilization, there is no entity that has a future. It is only after fertilization, when there is a being with a specific genetic code, that there is an individual with a future who can be deprived of that future by being killed. But why should this be so? Admittedly, neither gamete can have a future all by itself, but that is also true of the embryo, which cannot develop all by itself. It needs a uterus and adequate nutrients to develop into a fetus and a baby. Admittedly, the future the sperm will have is not its future alone; it shares its future with the ovum it fertilizes. This makes the situation of gametes unusual, perhaps unique, but does not seem to provide a reason why gametes cannot have futures if the criterion of identity is physical continuity.

Sometimes it is said that a sperm is not a unique individual in the way that a fetus is. For who the sperm turns out to be depends on which ovum it unites with. Why, however, should this lack of uniqueness deprive the sperm of being a potential person, or to use Marquis' language, why should its lack of uniqueness prevent it from having "a future like ours"? Although we cannot specify which future existence the sperm will have, if it is allowed to fertilize an egg, it will become *somebody* and that somebody will have a valuable future.

I think the reason we do not usually think of sperm as having futures is that, in the ordinary reproductive context, literally millions of sperm are released, and only one can fertilize the egg. The rest are doomed. So it seems implausible to say that by killing sperm, we are depriving them of a future. Still, *one* of them might fertilize the egg, even though we cannot say which one it will be, and that one sperm will not get to develop into an embryo and eventual person if it is killed before conception occurs.

Moreover, assisted reproductive technology (ART) facilitates the tracing of an embryo back to its constituent gametes in a way never before possible. In the context of *in vitro* fertilization (IVF), where an egg and sperm are placed in a petri dish for fertilization to occur, we *can* identify the particular gametes who might unite. If dumping out the contents of the petri dish after fertilization has occurred would be immoral because doing that deprives the fertilized egg of "a future like ours,"

why is it not equally wrong to dump out the contents of the petri dish seconds before fertilization occurs? The ability to identify which gametes make up the embryo is even greater in the micromanipulation technique known as intracytoplasmic sperm injection (ICSI). The ICSI technique enables patients with male factor infertility, where not enough motile sperm can be recovered for ordinary *in vitro* fertilization (IVF), to be considered for assisted reproductive intervention. In ICSI, a single sperm is injected directly into the egg. The isolation of a single sperm makes it possible for us to identify with certainty which sperm conjoined with the egg in the resultant embryo. Thus, the individual who comes to be after fertilization is physically continuous with the sperm in the pipette and the egg in the petri dish. Killing the gametes before fertilization deprives both of them of the future they would have had.

Marquis might respond to the ART examples by maintaining, in his account, that embryos *in vitro* do not have valuable futures like ours. It is only after implantation, when twinning is no longer possible, that we have an individual who can be said to have a personal future. Thus, Marquis need not be backed into claiming a moral difference between dumping out a petri dish just before or just after conception. Equally, his view is compatible with allowing contraceptives and abortifacients that kill the embryo before implantation occurs. These are seen as importantly morally different from terminating a clinical pregnancy, that is, after implantation occurs. Certainly most of us do regard abortion, even in the first trimester, as morally different from contraception or even a morning after pill. It seems to me, however, that the reason is not that the status of the embryo radically changes with implantation. Rather, it is that most people have very different feelings toward the termination of a pregnancy than they have toward the prevention of pregnancy . . . .

In any event, I do not think Marquis has adequately explained why embryos have valuable futures and gametes do not. For this reason, I consider his account of why abortion is immoral to be vulnerable to the usual objection to potentiality arguments, namely, that they make contraception seriously wrong. The interest view avoids this difficulty. As for its alleged difficulty with explaining why it is wrong to kill sleeping and temporarily comatose people, I maintain that this can be explained in terms of the interests of the nonconscious person, interests that a fetus does not yet have. For these reasons, the interest view seems to me a better account of moral status than the future-like-ours account.

EXERCISES

1. Don Marquis starts from the basic premise that what makes killing wrong is that the individual who is killed is deprived of the value of his or her future. Based on that premise he concludes that abortion is wrong, but he also draws out some implications that are not usually associated with the pro-life view. What views does Marquis hold that *most* pro-life theorists would not share?

2. Marquis claims that his argument against abortion is *analogous* (structurally similar) to a strong argument against inflicting suffering on animals; and that since the latter argument is sound, that is good reason for thinking the former argument, against abortion, is also sound. Is the comparison a good one?

3. Marquis claims that his argument shows that morally permissible abortions will be rare indeed, unless, perhaps, they occur so early in pregnancy that a fetus is not yet definitely an individual. That is certainly an exception that most advocates of the pro-life position would *not* make. Is it an exception required by Marquis's position? Does it provide any possibility of finding common ground between Marquis and Steinbock?

4. Bonnie Steinbock bases her view of which individuals have moal status (are due moral consideration) on whether the individual is *sentient*; Marquis bases his arguments on whether an individual has a future that will have value for that individual. Arguing from very different starting points, they wind up with very different conclusions. Is there any objective way of deciding which starting point is *better*, or which is *correct*?

5. We all believe that it is wrong to kill humans who are temporarily unconscious. Marquis believes that his account gives the best explanation of this belief, while Steinbock maintains that the account given by her explanation is better. This is an interesting test case. Which account do you find more plausible?

6. There is no more heated issue in American society than the issue of abortion. We are not likely to reach agreement on the abortion question in the near future, perhaps not ever. Without resolving that issue, is there anyway we might make the controversy less heated, less acrimonious?

7. You may have very strong feelings about the question of abortion, whichever side you favor. That being so, you probably have a very negative opinion of many of those who hold the position opposing your own. Still, perhaps you are willing to admit that at least *some* of the people on the other side are not completely evil. Can you think of at least *some* good characteristics of *some* of your opponents?

ADDITIONAL READING

Among the anthologies on abortion is Susan Dwyer and Joel Feinberg's *The Problem of Abortion*, 3rd ed. (Belmont, CA: Wadsworth, 1997). An anthology that compares competing views on a number of issues related to the abortion controversy is Charles P. Cozic and Stacey L. Tipp, *Abortion: Opposing Viewpoints* (San Diego, CA: Greenhaven Press, 1991). An anthology edited by William B. Bondeson, H. Tristram Engelhardt, Jr., Stuart F. Spicker, and Daniel H. Winship, *Abortion and the Status of the Fetus* (Dordrecht, Holland: D. Reidel Publishing, 1984), contains very interesting articles concerning the physical and moral status of the fetus, and a fascinating historical introduction by H. Tristram Engelhardt, Jr.

Bryan Hilliard, *The U.S. Supreme Court and Medical Ethics* (St. Paul, MN: Paragon House, 2004), provides a clear analysis of the key Supreme Court cases related to abortion. Judith Jarvis Thomson's "In Defense of Abortion" remains the classic pro-choice argument, though it is very limited in scope. It originally appeared in *Philosophy & Public Affairs*, Volume 1, Number 1 (1971), and is now widely anthologized. Another well-known pro-choice essay is by Mary Anne Warren: "On the Moral and Legal Status of Abortion," *The Monist*, Volume 57, Number 1 (1973).

Ronald Dworkin's *Life's Dominion: An Argument About Abortion, Euthanasia, and Individual Freedom* (New York: Alfred A. Knopf, 1993) treats the issue very carefully, showing respect for both sides of this deeply contentious issue. Frances Myrna Kamm, *Creation and Abortion: A Study in Moral and Legal Philosophy* (New York: Oxford University Press, 1992), is another excellent and thoughtful book on the subject. Laurence Tribe, *Abortion: The Clash of Absolutes* (New York: W. W. Norton, 1990), is the work of a distinguished legal scholar who seeks some common ground on the question.

For a superb and even-handed resource on the abortion controversy, including many links to other sites as well as to videos, recorded radio discussions, and a wide variety of full-text articles, go to Ethics Updates at *http://ethics.sandiego.edu/*.

17

Should the Police Use Deceit in Interrogations?

There are some clear boundaries that police investigations are not supposed to cross. For example, police cannot "entrap" suspects into committing a crime: police can set up a sting operation, in which they pose as drug dealers or prostitutes and arrest those who seek them out; but they cannot seek out citizens and entice them into illegal acts. An undercover officer cannot offer a citizen a thousand dollars to make a drug delivery, and then arrest the citizen for drug dealing; in that case, the idea for the criminal act comes from the police, and there is no reason to suppose that the entrapped citizen was eager to become a drug dealer. And, of course, there are other restrictions: the police cannot legitimately beat a confession out of you, or obtain a confession by threats, or refuse to allow a suspect access to his/her lawyer, or subject the suspect to such severe and prolonged questioning that the suspect becomes psychologically disoriented and physically exhausted. But beyond such obviously coercive measures, the lines governing legitimate police interrogation techniques become rather blurred, and *almost* anything goes. As Jerome H. Skolnick and Richard A. Leo note:

> Contemporary police interrogation is routinely deceptive. As it is taught and practiced today, interrogation is shot through with deception. Police are instructed to, are authorized to—and do—trick, lie, and cajole to elicit so-called "voluntary" confessions.

Among the routine deceptive techniques practiced during interrogation are misrepresentation of the seriousness of an offense (a suspect might be told he is being charged with murder, when in fact the crime victim's injuries were not lethal), making false promises to the defendant (such as promises of leniency), and pretending to have evidence (such as fingerprints or the confessions of other members of the group). Are such deceptive techniques legitimate methods of police investigation? Should there be tighter restrictions on police methods of interrogation?

⇒✢ SOME POLICE DECEIT AND TRICKERY ✢⇐ IS LEGITIMATE

Christopher Slobogin

Christopher Slobogin holds the Milton Underwood Chair in Law at Vanderbilt University, where he is also a Professor of Psychiatry and Director of the Criminal Justice Program. Professor Slobogin agrees with a general prohibition against lying, but he believes that deception by police—though it causes some serious harms—can be justified as a special exception: lies to publicly identified enemies are legitimate, and criminals are enemies of society. But this requires, Slobogin insists, that the process be public and that those suspected of criminal behavior recognize that the police view them as enemies. This essay is excerpted from "Deceit, Pretext, and Trickery: Investigative Lies by the Police," *Oregon Law Review*, volume 76, Winter 1997.

A lie is a statement meant to deceive. Many police, like many other people, lie occasionally, and some police, like some other people, lie routinely and pervasively. Police lie to protect innocent victims, as in hostage situations, and they tell "placebo lies" to assure or placate worried citizens. They tell lies to project nonexistent authority, and they lie to suspects in the hopes of gathering evidence of crime. They also lie under oath, to convict the guilty, protect the guilty, or frame the innocent.

Some of these lies are justifiable. Some are reprehensible. Lying under oath is perjury and thus rarely permissible. On the other hand, lying that is necessary to save a life may not only be acceptable but is generally applauded (even if it constitutes perjury). Most types of police lies are of murkier morality, however. In particular, considerable disagreement exists over the permissibility of lying to suspects as a means of gathering evidence. If the police want to uncover a conspiracy, search a house, or obtain a confession, may they lie in an effort to do so? . . .

I

The Nature of Investigative Lies and Why They Occur

Of the many varieties of lies police tell, the most prevalent type is probably the lie told to catch a criminal, if only because apprehending perpetrators of crime is a primary job of the police. Of course, lies to catch criminals can be directed at nonsuspects whom the police believe have useful information. Most, however, are aimed at the suspects themselves and occur in one of three contexts: undercover work, searches and seizures, or interrogation. In each of these three contexts, the following discussion borrows from the sociological literature in exploring the nature and causes of police lies and then briefly reviews the law's (usually accommodating) response to them.

A. Undercover Work   Undercover work is by definition *deceptive*. It normally involves outright lies. Typically, an undercover agent gives or presents a fake identity and a fabricated history, denies any involvement with the police, and engages in any number of other lies. For example, an agent might pose as a lover, a prisoner, a priest, or a member of the Mafia; in playing such roles, lying is inevitable and extensive.

Law enforcement's justification for this type of deception is twofold. First, certain types of crime—for instance, so-called "victimless crime," fraud, narcotics sales, organized crime, and terrorism—are considered difficult to detect or prevent through other means. Second, independently from solving a particular crime, undercover agents and informants gather general information about criminal activity and the key figures in it that is thought to be otherwise inaccessible. These objectives have led every major police department to devote significant resources to undercover work by police officers and by "snitches" recruited to work for the police.

The Supreme Court has given wide leeway to this type of deceptive activity. Indeed, even the Warren Court—popularly perceived as the most liberal group of justices in the Court's history on the subject of criminal suspects' rights—expressed a strong aversion to regulating undercover work. The established basis for this stance, found in a number of Court decisions, is that one assumes the risk that one's acquaintances are government agents; any expectation to the contrary is unreasonable and therefore not protected by the Fourth Amendment. Accordingly, as a constitutional matter, police need neither a warrant nor any level of suspicion before engaging in undercover operations. . . .

B. Searches and Seizures   Lying meant to effectuate a search or a seizure is routine practice for many police officers. Such lies come in at least two varieties. The first involves lying about police authority to conduct the search or seizure. For instance, police may state that they do not need a warrant when they know the law requires they have one, assert they have a warrant when they do not, or state they can get a warrant when in fact they know they can not. This last ruse, designed to encourage acquiescence from an otherwise unwilling person, is one among many deceitful ways of obtaining consent; police have also been known, for instance, to get motorists to sign a consent form for a car search by misrepresenting the form as a ticket. Finally, the police may simply make up a reason for conducting a search and seizure, such as when they fabricate a traffic violation as a ground for stopping a car.

The second type of lie misrepresents the police's purpose, not the police's authority. These so-called "pretextual" actions arise in a number of contexts. For instance, the police might ask for permission to enter a house for some innocuous purpose (such as investigation of a nonexistent burglary), when their actual intent is to conduct a search of its interior once inside. A similar, extremely common ruse is an effort to get a better look at a car's occupants and contents by stopping the car for a traffic violation, one which is not made up (as described in the preceding paragraph) but which is never or rarely enforced except in pretextual situations. In the same pretextual vein is a lie to get a suspect to "come quietly" rather than risk a violent arrest or a police "suggestion" that a person have a "short chat" with officers, whose real intentions are to seize the individual for a much longer period of time. In all of these situations, the police have the technical legal authority to engage in the act based on consent or some minor violation of the law but are dissembling their purpose.

As with undercover work, the primary police justification for both types of deceptive searches and seizures is their efficacy at catching criminals. According to Jerome Skolnick, a veteran observer of the police, the typical police officer believes that he has "the ability to distinguish between guilt and innocence" and that once he has decided that someone is guilty (or suspicious), he "ought to be free to employ the techniques of his trade." Skolnick implies that lies to suspects about police authority or purpose are, as far as the police are concerned, "techniques of the trade" that should be fostered rather than criticized.

This assertion is borne out by the observations of sociologists Thomas Barker and David Carter, who also conclude that many police endorse an "end justifies the means" approach to deception. One statement they report seems particularly illuminative on this score. Told that his description of police methods for obtaining consent sounded like "a lot of lies," one officer responded: "It is not police lying; it is an art. After all the criminal has constitutional protection. He can lie through his teeth. Why not us? What is fair is fair."

The sentiment that "it takes a liar to catch a liar" apparently resonates with many police officers. Particularly interesting is the officer's reference to police lying as an "art," which dovetails with Skolnick's observation that police see fabrication as part of their craft. It suggests that, in this investigative context, police do not think they are "lying" at all; they are merely playing a role.

In short, police view deceitful searches and seizures as a professional investigative tool—the moral equivalent to undercover investigation. While courts presumably disagree with this stance when the lies are about police authority (because if the claimed authority did not exist, then the Fourth Amendment is violated), most have put their imprimatur on the much larger category of pretextual searches and seizures. After intimating it would do so on more than one occasion, the Supreme Court itself recently affirmed that the typical pretextual police action does not violate the U.S. Constitution. In *Whren v. United States*, which explicitly upheld a concededly pretextual traffic stop, the Court stressed that the subjective mental state of the police is irrelevant to Fourth Amendment analysis in most situations. As a result of decisions like these, the police know that as long as they have a legal explanation for their action, any duly limited entry, stop or seizure will usually be considered constitutional regardless of the hidden agenda.

C. Interrogation   As with undercover work, fabrication in the interrogation context is openly acknowledged by the police today. Indeed, the leading interrogation manual, authored by Inbau, Reid, and Buckley, continues to preach vigorously the merits of deceptive interrogation techniques, despite the Supreme Court's implicit criticism of one of its earlier incarnations in *Miranda v. Arizona*. The techniques they espouse include: (1) showing fake sympathy for the suspect by becoming his "friend" (e.g., by falsely telling a person suspected of rape that the interrogator himself had "roughed it up" with a girl in an attempt to have intercourse with her); (2) reducing feelings of guilt through lies (e.g., by telling a person suspected of killing his wife that he was not as "lucky" as the interrogator, who had recently been on the verge of seriously harming his nagging wife when the doorbell rang); (3) exaggerating the crime in an effort to prod the suspect into negotiating or in hopes of obtaining a denial which will indirectly inculpate the suspect (e.g., accusing the suspect of stealing $40,000 when only $20,000 was involved); (4) lying that suggests the futility of denying the truth (e.g., statements that sufficient evidence already exists to convict when it does not); and (5) playing one codefendant against another (e.g., leading one to believe the other has confessed when no confession has occurred).

Many other deceptive techniques, somewhat less openly acknowledged, are associated with giving the warnings mandated by Miranda. For instance, police might tell the suspect that "whatever you say may be used for or against you in a court of law," despite the fact that police are extremely unlikely to testify for the defense in any subsequent prosecution. They might also mislead the suspect into believing that only written statements are admissible or that a state-paid attorney will be provided only once the individual is in court.

As with the other investigative lies discussed, the police believe these techniques are necessary to catch criminals, in this situation because of the suspect's natural reluctance to respond to direct questions and the general prohibition on physically coercive interrogation practices. . . .

II

Which Police Lies Are OK?

In recent times, probably the best known treatment of lying and its justification is the work by the moral philosopher Sissela Bok. Because her framework for evaluating deception throws considerable light on the nature and moral viability of police lying, this Article will rely primarily on her work. . . .

A. Bok's Framework   Bok begins by asserting that lies require a reason. They require a reason because, more so than truth, they have routine deleterious effects on the hearer of the statement, the maker of the statement, and society at large. The duped, she notes, often "feel wronged . . . [and] are wary of new overtures." Their autonomy is also denigrated by the lying, because they have been deprived of the ability "to make choices for themselves according to the most adequate information available." As to the negative effects of lying on those who perpetrate the lie, Bok points out how lying can become an intrinsic part of one's personality: "psychological barriers wear down; lies seem more necessary, less reprehensible; the ability to make moral distinctions can coarsen; the liar's perception of his chances of being caught may warp." Further, others will trust the liar less. Also, "paradoxically, once his word is no longer trusted, he will be left with greatly decreased power—even though a lie often does bring at least a short-term gain in power over those deceived." Finally, lying harms society:

> The veneer of social trust is often thin. As lies spread—by imitation, or in retaliation, or to forestall suspected deception—trust is damaged. Yet trust is a social good to be protected just as much as the air we breathe or the water we drink. When it is damaged, the community as a whole suffers; and when it is destroyed, societies falter and collapse. . . .

Bok next postulates an apparatus for assessing the reasons that might be given for lying. Her principal assertion here is that lies that cannot be justified publicly are not justifiable. Furthermore, she asserts, the "public" which assesses the lie must be composed of "reasonable persons" taken from all walks of life, including "those representing the deceived or others affected by the lie"; this public assessment is particularly important where lying by the government is involved. Finally, she develops three steps these reasonable persons should pursue in assessing the worth of the lie.

First, those who evaluate the lie must "look carefully for any alternatives of a non-deceptive nature available to the liar." They should only begin to consider excuses for a lie after determining that no truthful statement would do.

If no such alternatives present themselves, the second step involves "weighing . . . the moral reasons for and against the lie." Bok identifies four conceivable justifications for lying: (1) preventing harm; (2) producing benefit; (3) fairness, which includes giving people what they deserve, correcting injustice, and simple revenge; and (4) veracity itself, in the sense that telling a lie may protect the truth. However, Bok is very leary of any of these justifications, given the ease with which a liar can manipulate these concepts to justify any lie. Thus, she emphasizes that reasonable persons evaluating a lie should "share the perspective of the deceived and those affected by lies." They should "be much more cautious than those with the optimistic perspective of the liar [and] value veracity and accountability more highly than would individual liars or their apologists."

Third, in evaluating the moral reasons for and against the lie, reasonable persons should be particularly attentive to identifying its potential ill effects on those not directly involved in the lie:

> Under all circumstances, these reasonable persons would need to be very wary because of the great susceptibility of deception to spread, to be abused, and to give rise to even more undesirable practices . . . . Spread multiplies the harm resulting from lies; abuse increases the damage for each and every instance. Both spread and abuse result in part from the lack of clear-cut standards as to what is acceptable. In the absence of such standards, instances of deception can and will increase, bringing distrust and thus more deception, loss of personal standards on the part of liars and so yet more deception, imitation by those who witness deception and the rewards it can bring, and once again more deception.

The potential for spread and abuse, Bok writes, is particularly likely when the lies are told by people in power. Thus, she concludes, reasonable persons need to construct the "clearest possible standards and safeguards in order to prevent these [government] liars from drifting into more and more damaging practices—through misunderstanding, carelessness, or abuse."

B. Bok's Lying Scenarios   . . . Of all lies, Bok finds lies in a crisis to be the most justifiable. The classic crisis, of course, occurs when life is imminently threatened. Telling a lie to prevent such harm is justifiable because little time exists to consider alternatives, the negative effects of the lie are outweighed by the fact that an innocent life will be saved, and those effects are negligible in any event. Lies of this type are so extraordinary that they "would neither be likely to encourage others to lie nor make it much more likely that the person who lied to save a life might come to lie more easily or more often." Whether lies could be told to avert less immediate or less significant harms would depend upon a number of factors, especially whether the use of force is the only alternative. In general, however, Bok resists enlarging this exception without a careful public assessment of the claim of crisis from the perspective of the deceived. Liars making this claim, she cautions, can be counted upon to exaggerate the threat, its immediacy, or its need.

Put in terms of Bok's four possible excuses for lies, lying in a crisis is best seen as a way of preventing harm and to a lesser extent as a means of producing benefit. In contrast, Bok says that the claim that lying to liars is permissible derives primarily from a fairness or "just deserts" excuse. . . . As Bok says, to justify lying simply because the recipient is a liar "would be to make oneself entirely dependent on the character deficiencies in others, and to stoop always to the lowest common denominator in reciprocating lies for lies." Further, of course, we may be wrong about when someone is lying. For this reason, lying to people we think are liars is "likely to invite vast increases in actual deception and to escalate the seriousness of lies told in retaliation, . . . a notion [that] would not stand up well under the test of publicity."

Lying to a liar might also be grounded on the veracity excuse to the extent lying is meant to reveal the mendacity of the recipient of the lie. Here again, Bok agrees with St. Augustine, who stated that "mendacity is best rebutted, not imitated." Truthful alternatives generally exist for exposing a lie. Even if there are none, the damage caused to the character of the liar and society at large by routinely lying to people thought to be liars out-weighs the veracity excuse.

The claim that lying to enemies is justifiable is closely related to the previous two types of claims. An enemy often precipitates crises and will often lie to win. In terms of excuses, lying to an enemy might both prevent harm and promote fairness. While Bok is more hospitable to this claim, she again argues for caution. Both the fairness and prevention of harm excuses are, in her mind, very prone to abuse.

As Bok notes, the fairness excuse takes on added allure here because not only is an enemy usually a liar but he is also perceived as bad—outside the "social contract" as Bok puts it and thus arguably less worthy of truthfulness. Yet, as Bok points out, the identification of enemies, like the identification of liars, is a treacherous task, easily tainted by bias and prejudice. Further, many liars invoking this excuse tend to avoid the public scrutiny necessary to justify the lie. For these people, "paranoia governs them to such an extent that they imagine that the public itself constitutes the conspiracy they combat."

Lying to enemies to prevent harm raises the same types of concerns. To the liar, enemies are too readily perceived. Furthermore, even when enemies are clearly identified, lies to them may be heard by and can deceive friends as well, with a consequent serious loss of trust when the deception is unveiled. In particular, Bok points out that "when a government is known to practice deception, the results are self-defeating and erosive." Here she quotes Hannah Arendt, the astute observer of totalitarian states, who argues that government deceit over the long run results in "the absolute refusal to believe in the truth of anything, no matter how well it may be established." Eventually, it destroys "the sense by which we take our bearings in the real world."

Bok does concede, consistent with the discussion on lies in a crisis, that "whenever it is right to resist an assault or a threat by force, it must then be allowable to do so by guile." Thus, says Bok, deceiving a kidnapper may be justifiable when deceiving enemies in business is not.

Moreover, in a passage that has direct implications for police lying, Bok is willing to countenance lying to an enemy in one nonemergency situation: when a public declaration of hostilities against the alleged enemy is made. She reasons that:

> Such open declarations lessen the probability of error and of purely personal spite, so long as they are open to questioning and requests for accountability. . . . The more openly and clearly the adversaries, such as criminals, can be pinpointed, and the more justifiable, therefore, the criteria for regarding them as hostile, the more excusable will it be to lie to them if honesty is of no avail.

She goes on to say:

> If the designation of a foe is open, as in a declaration of war, deception is likely to be expected on all sides. While it can hardly be said to be consented to, it is at least known and often acquiesced in. But

the more secret the choice and pursuit of foes, the more corruptible the entire process, as all the secret police systems of the world testify. There is, then, no public control over who counts as an adversary nor over what can be done to him. The categories of enemies swell, and their treatment grows increasingly inhumane.

Even with such an open declaration, however, Bok worries that the public will be swept up by the mere fact that hostilities have been declared and not remain reasonable and objective in evaluating whether lying is permissible. Because such declarations do not "lessen the possibility of joint discrimination by members of a group or society [they] ought therefore to function only in combination with a strong protection of civil rights."

C. Bok and the Police   Overall, Bok makes a provocative case against lying in most instances. Except for lying in imminent crises and lying to publicly declared enemies, most lying is to be avoided. Unfortunately, Bok only fleetingly reflects on the applicability of these conclusions to lying by the police. . . . Nonetheless, . . . her analysis is rich in implications for police deceit, and in particular investigative lying. . . .

First, we must inquire into whether the reasons for Bok's general injunction against lying make sense in the law enforcement context. Bok's premise that lying should generally be avoided is based on the assertion that deceit harms the dupe, the liar, and society. That assertion tends to be borne out by social science research indicating that in many situations trust is crucial to one's own sense of self-worth and the formation of relationships. But does investigative lying by the police produce these three harms to any significant extent?

Very likely it does, even when one focuses solely on investigative lying that is viewed as necessary because truthful, noncoercive alternatives are not available. First, almost by definition, deception during undercover operations, searches and seizures, and interrogation diminishes the dignity and autonomy of the dupe. In each of these situations, the dupe will be making decisions about whether to disclose embarrassing or incriminating knowledge or whether to allow access to private areas while lacking information that is potentially highly relevant to such decisions (e.g., the identity or motives of the liar or the scope of one's rights).

To a Kantian, this fact alone might justify a ban or substantial limitations on investigative lying. To one of a more utilitarian bent, however, greater harm from investigative lying will probably need to be identified to outweigh the benefit that comes from deceitful police

work that is necessary (i.e., for which there is no truthful, noncoercive alternative). In other words, the assessment of costs associated with investigative lying must focus on the second and third potential harms Bok identifies—those inflicted on the liars (in this case the police) and on society at large.

The latter costs are likely to be the heaviest. There is no doubt, for instance, that the deceit connected with covert investigation can undermine trust in government not only in those who are targets of the deceit but among those duped by it. Typically, undercover work is relegated to the underworld and is rarely exposed to the rest of us. When it is, however, the feeling of betrayal can be significant. For example, when citizens of a mid-size midwestern community discovered that a local executive had been an undercover spy for an FBI investigation of his company, many were outraged. As a reverend stated in explaining the reactions of his congregation to the news:

> The biggest feeling here right now is a sense of being violated. It's as though I became a good friend of your family, came over to your house all the time, then started rifling through your drawers . . . . It's not an intruder, though. It's someone who's trusted—by a company and by an entire community.

A member of the same church condemned the federal government with the words "they're about as underhanded as anybody."

Knowledge of undercover work not only undermines trust in government but can be deeply inimical to a democratic society. Carried to its "Big Brother" extreme, as it has been in some countries, government snooping chills speech, association, and the general openness of society. Although the possibility that one's acquaintance is a government agent is a risk the Supreme Court tells us we must assume, empirical research strongly suggests that it is not a risk most people want to assume.

Just as clear is the sense of betrayal, as well as outright hostility, on the part of those subjected to pretextual police actions, reactions which again lead to antipathy not only toward police but also the government they represent. Perhaps one of the most damning examples of this phenomenon is the fact that African Americans in Los Angeles and other urban areas cynically joke about the "offense" of "driving while black." As one court bluntly described the inherent risk of pretextual actions:

> Some police officers will use the pretext of traffic violations or other minor infractions to harass

members of groups identified by factors that are totally impermissible as a basis for law enforcement activity—factors such as race or ethnic origin, or simply appearances that some police officers do not like, such as young men with long hair, heavy jewelry, and flashy clothing.

The belief that police lie during interrogation can also have harmful effects. As several commentators have pointed out, betrayal in the interrogation room might not only taint the police and society generally but also undermines the effectiveness of interrogation itself. A suspect's discovery that a promise or statement is false might lead to subsequent resistance even to legitimate offers, thus possibly resulting in loss of a confession. On a more systemic level, knowledge that police interrogators lie may make all suspects more reluctant to talk, for fear that police importunings are based on fabrication. A general distrust of police interrogators might even create an unwillingness on the part of nonsuspects to cooperate with authorities.

As a general summary of these points, Maurice Punch's observations are apt:

> [Police] deviance elicits a special feeling of betrayal. In a sense, they are doubly condemned; that is, not just for the infringement itself but even more for the breach of trust involved. Something extra is involved when public officials in general and policemen in particular deviate from accepted norms: "That something more is the violation of a fiduciary relationship, the corruption of a public trust, of public virtue."

These effects of police deceit are especially likely in communities which routinely interact with the police.

Perhaps less obvious than its effects on the duped and on society is the insidious impact of investigative lying on the police themselves. For the reasons discussed in Part I, police may genuinely believe that this type of lying is morally justified. However, as Klockars has pointed out, "as the police officer becomes comfortable with lies and their moral justification, he or she is apt to become casual with both." Thus, as Bok would predict, police lying feeds on itself. It can also lead to other effects. Barker and Carter assert that "police lying contributes to police misconduct and corruption and undermines the organizatio[n's] discipline system." In the undercover context, Marx has documented even more dramatic impacts, including accounts of officers whose undercover role is so all-consuming that they become

criminals themselves. Police clearly are not immune from the corrupting influence of deceit that Bok describes.

In short, investigative lying can produce significant negative consequences of the type hypothesized by Bok and should therefore, under Bok's scheme, presumptively be avoided even if truthful alternatives are not available. However, this conclusion does not mean that such lying is impermissible in all instances. Recall that the two scenarios in which Bok is most likely to countenance lying involve lies in "crisis" and lying to publicly declared "enemies." Both might occur during police investigation, the first occasionally, the second with some regularity.

The crisis exception might apply, for instance, when police believe they need information to avert harm to themselves or someone else (e.g., a kidnapping situation). Indeed, given the general maxim about the relationship of force and deception subscribed to by Bok, lying would be permissible in any situation in which the police are authorized to use physical coercion (e.g., lying to get a suspect to "come in quietly"). At the same time, the crisis exception should not be stretched to cover every effort to apprehend criminals who might harm another. Bok, at least, would require some showing of imminent danger to another person's interests before recognizing a crisis. In many cases in which lying to catch a criminal is practiced, police are not even sure their prey is a criminal, much less that harm is imminent.

Of considerably more significance to investigative lying is Bok's "open declaration of hostilities" scenario, the primary exception to the notion that lying to liars and to enemies in noncrisis situations is unjustifiable. As indicated above, Bok herself uses criminals as an example of an "enemy," who if openly pinpointed as such, can be foiled through lying, at least if truthful alternatives do not exist. However, unless applied with caution, this exception too could easily swallow the rule against lying. Recall that, according to Bok, identification of the person as a criminal must be a public enterprise, so as to minimize the possibility that he will be the target of personal spite or prejudice. Simply asserting that there is a "war on crime" and handing over to the police discretion to decide who is the enemy in that war (and who is lying about not being one) obviously does not meet Bok's demands in this regard; as she notes, discrimination can only be combatted by removing that discretion through public evaluation. The issue thus becomes how to effectuate this public identification of the criminal.

III

Implementing the Public Identification Predicate

Based on Bok's work, the principle most relevant to analyzing investigative lying seems to be the moral need to identify publicly the "enemy"—the criminal—before engaging in deception. If this public identification occurs, investigative deception that has no good, truthful alternative can be used against the person so identified. If it does not, deception is much less likely to be morally justifiable under Bok's scheme.

The difficulty arises in operationalizing the public identification idea in the investigative context. Of course, the legislature, presumably through public debate, has already identified the conduct that is criminal (and is therefore "enemy") conduct. However, as suggested in Part II, a public vote authorizing police to use deception to "apprehend criminals" is insufficient because it begs the all-important question of who (as opposed to what) is criminal. At the same time, public debate about the criminality of particular individuals would not only be cumbersome but counterproductive; it would alert the targets to the fact they are under suspicion. The best compromise between these two positions is a requirement of ex ante review by a judge, analogous to what occurs in the warrant process. After explaining this conclusion, the rest of this Article applies it to deception used in undercover operations, searches and seizures, and interrogation.

A. The Case for Judicial Review as a Proxy

One way to avoid the inefficiency and counterproductiveness of a public debate about particular suspects is to focus the discussion on particular police "practices." This is, in fact, the approach Bok suggests with respect to use of unmarked police cars. She asserts that the propriety of this investigative technique should be publicly debated and that it should be permitted only if a consensus develops in its favor. If the technique is eventually adopted, not only does the public debate enhance its acceptability, but it ensures that "those who still choose to break the speed laws will be aware of the deceptive practice and can decide whether to take their chances or not."

However, in contrast to use of unmarked police cars, many deceptive police practices cannot be discussed without reference to what the police know about the target of the practice. The public's response to decoy stings, pretextual stops, or trickery during interrogation is likely to vary greatly depending upon whether these practices are used randomly or aimed at people thought to be guilty. Should the police be able to pose as door-to-door encyclopedia salespeople? The answer might be yes if they use the ruse to gain entry into the house of a person suspected of kidnapping children but no if they simply go door-to-door to see what they can find. Should the police be able to stop a car for violation of a minor traffic law that is usually not enforced to get a peak into the backseat or consent to a full search? The answer might be yes if the police suspect the car driver of being a drug courier but no if the police stop any violators they "feel like" stopping. Should police be able to lie to someone about finding his fingerprints at the scene of the crime to scare him into confessing? The answer might be yes if he's arrested but no if investigators with few or no leads come to the person's house and make the statement simply to see how he'll respond.

To the extent the public cares about all its members (including, as Bok requires, those who will be duped), it will want to take steps that limit investigative lying to those likely to be criminals. If a "practice" can be defined to meet that goal, then no further guidance is necessary. If, on the other hand, the practice as defined could be used against anyone, then some further effort at ensuring that it will be employed only against authentic suspects should be attempted.

One method of doing so would be to say to the police: "Make sure you use this technique only against suspects." However, leaving identification of the criminal up to the police—those who will do the lying—violates Bok's notion of public debate among reasonable persons. This would be so even if we added a requirement that the individual officer seek a second opinion from another officer. As she notes, "more than [mere] consultation with chosen peers is needed whenever crucial interests are . . . at stake." People of all allegiances should be consulted so as to avoid the impact of prejudice and personal spite on the decision to deceive.

We are thus again back to the original dilemma: how to obtain public input about who is to be considered a criminal-enemy, when public input would be cumbersome and might alert the enemy. Another answer is to appoint a proxy for the public, who would act as a check on police discretion on the public's behalf. Although not an entirely satisfactory solution, the proposition defended here is that the magistrate—the person who, in our current system, makes probable cause decisions and issues search and arrest warrants—can fulfill this role. . . .

The assumption I will make, then, is that the judicial or "official" identification of a person as a criminal is both necessary and sufficient to meet Bok's demand for public debate as to whether a person is an "enemy." If this official identification occurs (the cause showing), then the police are morally justified in using deceit to gather evidence from the identified individual, at least when good truthful alternatives are not available (the necessity showing). If, on the other hand, the judge is not willing to label the person a suspect, or finds that deceit isn't necessary to investigate him further, then deception would not be permissible. The concrete implications of this official-identification predicate are several.

B. Distinguishing Passive and Active Undercover Work

Consider first the implications of the official identification idea for undercover work. To understand these implications, it is useful to divide covert investigative techniques into two types; passive and active. Passive covert investigation would not require judicial authorization, whereas active undercover work would.

Passive undercover operations are those which merely provide people with the opportunity to commit the crime, without importuning any particular person. Posing on a street corner as a prostitute waiting for a john is an example of a passive operation, as is putting out the word that cocaine can be bought in a particular alley or that stolen property can be sold at a specified location. These types of passive-undercover operations can be meaningfully debated in the abstract: should citizens be tempted by police posing as prostitutes, drug dealers, or fences? If it were determined, after such debate, that a certain kind of baiting operation is or may be efficacious, any particular operation of that kind need not be preceded by judicial authorization, since people who take the bait are likely to be criminals. Like the use of an unmarked police car to catch speeders, the only people against whom the police intervene are those they know to be committing crime. Abuse of discretion and the potential for betraying innocent people and damaging citizen trust in government are minimized.

These potential harms are much greater, however, when the undercover operation takes on an active mode by going after a specific target or targets thought to be criminal rather than seeking to lure criminals out of the general population. The propriety of infiltrating a particular organization or establishing an intimate relationship with a particular individual *cannot* be the subject of an abstract public debate. Moreover, there is no guarantee that the direct impact of such covert deception will be visited only on those who are clearly criminals, making the potential for the discrimination that Bok fears much greater. Thus, where active undercover operations are contemplated, judicial authorization should be obtained. The police should not be able to use such techniques unless the public, in the form of the judge, decides that good reason to do so exists and that more straightforward methods are not likely to work. . . .

C. Curtailing Pretextual Actions

Ex ante judicial authorization would also be required for deceptive searches and seizures. As with active undercover operations, a search or seizure requires the police to target a particular individual. Thus, police should not be able to use deception to effectuate such an action unless the target has been identified as a potential criminal by the public's proxy, the judge.

This second proposal is in some ways more radical than the previous one, since in effect it would eliminate almost all deception in connection with overt searches and seizures. In situations in which the police misrepresent their authority (e.g., by saying they do not need a warrant when in fact they do), they usually lack sufficient suspicion to authorize their action. Assuming so, a judge is unlikely to find the target is a criminal-enemy to whom police can lie. Pretextual actions misrepresenting the motivations of the police would also be significantly curtailed. Because the latter are also usually based on hunches rather than articulable suspicion approval of a pretextual action would seldom be sought and, if sought, would seldom be granted. . . .

D. Trickery during Interrogation: Pre- and Post-Arrest

. . . In contrast to the typical undercover operation or search and seizure, most interrogation in which deceit is practiced takes place after a person has been taken into custody. It thus follows either an indictment, a judicially issued arrest warrant, or a formal assertion by the police that they believe the interrogated person is a criminal, an assertion they know will be tested in front of a judge within a short timespan. As a result, the public declaration that is the cornerstone of Bok's enemy exception either precedes or hangs over the typical interrogation process, at least if one accepts the notion of the judge acting as the public's proxy. Furthermore, . . . the official identification here is overt. Thus, as Bok would prefer, the person subjected to interrogation is on notice that the police view him or her as an enemy. . . .

In short, under Bok's framework as interpreted in this article, a good case can be made for the proposition that postarrest trickery is permissible. Because the arrest threshold both limits police deception to openly identified "enemies" and alerts the potential dupe to the adversarial relationship, such trickery is not inherently immoral, at least when, as will often be the case, a colorable claim can be made that direct questions will not obtain the desired information. . . .

Two . . . caveats to this discussion of interrogation trickery must be made. First, Bok's admonition that deceptive practices should be publicly debated is especially pertinent here. Although the official identification of particular individuals as enemies probably must, by default, fall on judges, various interrogation practices can also be the subject of scrutiny in the abstract. Indeed, the public could decide, contrary to what has been argued to this point, that all deception during interrogation is improper. Certainly, plausible arguments have been advanced in this regard. More specifically, public debate might focus on certain types of practices. For instance, one deceptive technique that has occasioned much comment involves a police officer posing as another type of professional, say the defendant's court-appointed lawyer, a clergyperson, or a psychiatrist. As Joseph Grano has argued, the virtually universal legislative recognition of lawyer–client and psychiatrist–patient privileges could be construed to stand for a decision by the public that statements made to these individuals are confidential and that therefore police cannot learn of them through deception. Public debate might also address whether prosecutors, as distinct from the police, can ever lie to suspects. Perhaps, as officers of the court and members of the bar, they should be prohibited from doing so. Obviously, a number of other general issues of this sort can and should be debated.

A final consideration in determining what types of deception, if any, might be permitted during interrogation is the degree of coercion created by the deceptive practice. The Supreme Court itself has recognized that certain types of deceit can render a confession involuntary. Bok also notes that deception can create coercive circumstances, particularly when it limits knowledge of one's alternatives. . . .

CONCLUSION

A central lesson of Sissela Bok's analysis is that, once lying becomes a practice, it is rarely justifiable. Routine deceit coarsens the liar, increases the likelihood of exposure, and when exposed, maximizes the loss of trust. When the deceptive practice is carried out by an agent of the government, it is even more reprehensible, both because the liar wields tremendous power and because government requires trust to be effective. Thus, limitations on police lying are justifiable and perhaps necessary. . . .

The extrapolation of Bok's analysis developed in this Article suggests that once an individual has been identified as a suspect through the public proxy of a judge, noncoercive deception in the investigative setting is often permissible. On the other hand, in the absence of such an identification, or when deception leads the dupe to believe he has no choice but to provide the sought-after evidence, investigative lying is wrong and should be prohibited. On this premise, warrantless "active" undercover operations and pretextual police actions are improper, unless necessary to save a life or useful as a substitute for legitimate use of force. On the other hand, deception associated with passive, bait-type stings is proper, so long as the general propriety of the sting has been subject to public debate. Trickery in connection with postarrest, precharge interrogation is also proper, so long as it does not coerce the dupe.

⨯ LYING BY POLICE SHOULD BE ⨯ GENERALLY PROHIBITED
Margaret L. Paris

Margaret L. Paris is Professor and Philip H. Knight Dean at the University of Oregon School of Law. Paris welcomes Slobogin's concern over the proper limits of deceptive police interrogation, but believes that he does not go far enough. Because of the destructive consequences of police deception, Paris would allow deceptive interrogations only in the most extreme and extraordinary circumstances: when such deception is the only possible means of saving lives. Her arguments are taken from "Lying to Ourselves," *Oregon Law Review*, volume 76, Winter 1997.

Christopher Slobogin's article contributes to the emerging dialogue regarding police lying in two important ways. First, the article challenges us to categorize and morally evaluate the lies in which police engage during investigations. The article's focus on moral questions is a welcome change from the "ends-justifies-the-means" approach of some current criminal procedure scholarship that advocates the lifting of restrictions on police conduct on the basis of a questionable belief that fewer restrictions mean more convictions. Second, the article appears to invite legislatures and rulemaking bodies to debate the morality of police lying. Historically, legislatures and rulemaking bodies have left it to the courts to regulate police lying and other forms of police misconduct. Slobogin points out, however, that courts applying constitutional law have "acquiesced in, if not affirmatively sanctioned," police lying. Because constitutional law permits courts little room to impose meaningful restrictions on police lying, those of us desiring to address that social ill must not only oppose any further erosion of current doctrine in the courts, but also must affirmatively address the problem of police lying in legislative and administrative forums. I hope that Slobogin's article and the accompanying responses are read broadly by police, legislators, administrators, and other rulemakers, to whom the responsibility of tackling the issue falls.

I am also enthusiastic about Slobogin's project because I agree with his tentative conclusion that police lies are often unjustifiable. I would, however, go farther than Slobogin . . . and prohibit all police lying except when necessary to save lives. Slobogin employs Bok's evaluative method to suggest that police may justifiably lie to suspects who have been publicly identified as criminals even in noncrisis situations—that is, even in situations in which lives are not at stake. According to Slobogin, Bok acknowledges that an otherwise unjustified lie might be justifiable if it is told to an enemy to avert a crisis, and criminal suspects can be considered "enemies," as that term is used by Bok. Slobogin advances this rationale to justify police lies to suspects undergoing custodial interrogation as well as deceptive undercover techniques used against people "likely to be criminals" or those about whom judicial authorization to lie has been obtained. I will focus specifically on Slobogin's discussion of lies during interrogation . . . because I tend to think lying during interrogation is more damaging than other types of deception.

Working within Bok's framework, I disagree with Slobogin's proposal to permit lies during interrogation on two grounds. Bok disapproves of all lies except those that can be publicly justified. According to Bok, lies can be publicly justified when: (1) there are no alternatives to lying (the necessity principle); and (2) lying would produce a surfeit of benefits versus harms (the utility principle). While Bok suggests that lies to enemies sometimes pass these tests, Slobogin's equation of arrested suspects with "enemies" does not meet these tests. Slobogin's proposal to permit lies during interrogation condones unnecessary lying because truthful alternatives exist. Slobogin's proposal also creates negative consequences that will likely outweigh the benefits, although costs and benefits are difficult to quantify in this context.

Before I address these issues, however, I will explore whether Slobogin's proposal to permit lying during interrogation is capable of public justification, an important predicate to Bok's "lying to enemies" exception.

I

Public Justification

Bok generally finds lies justifiable only if they are told to avert a crisis. However, Bok does seem to acknowledge, in principle, a "narrow justification" for deception in noncrisis situations involving self-defense against enemies, and Bok indicates several times that "criminals" are among those to whom the label "enemy" would apply. Bok stresses that one of the more critical features of this justification is public identification of the enemy.

Slobogin uses Bok's passages referring to criminals as enemies to construct a rule permitting police to lie to persons who have been identified as criminals. He proposes several limitations on this license. First, Slobogin would not permit police to lie to suspects who are interrogated before arrest because the police at that stage might not have probable cause to believe those suspects are guilty of criminal behavior. Slobogin would not consider those suspects to be "enemies" until police have developed probable cause to support an arrest. For the same reason, Slobogin would not permit lying to nonsuspects and witnesses. Second, Slobogin proposes that we permit police to lie only before formal charges have been lodged against suspects. Slobogin imposes this limit because criminal charges usually are initiated only when the prosecution has sufficient evidence to proceed. After that point, it would be unnecessary to extract a confession by lying or, presumably, any other means. Third, Slobogin would prohibit "coercive" lying, which he considers immoral because it limits suspects' knowledge of alternatives.

Despite these limitations, Slobogin's proposal would permit lying in the vast majority of custodial interrogations. I believe that Bok would reject Slobogin's proposal because the generous permission to lie would soon overwhelm the limits that Slobogin advocates. Bok's language is susceptible to more than one interpretation, but nowhere does Bok state that lying to enemies is justifiable on a broad scale. To the contrary, she argues that deception is analogous to violence and that, while both are justifiable in principle when used in preemptive strikes against enemies, they are, in practice, unrestrainable in such a context. Because the practical application of justificatory schemes is of great importance to Bok, she ultimately suggests that we should resort to deception and violence only in crisis situations.

It is worthwhile to explore why Bok predicts that, as a practical matter, if deception (and violence) against enemies are condoned they are likely to proliferate. Those reasons are especially pertinent in the context of Slobogin's proposal to permit lying during interrogation. Bok believes that all significant lies (including lies told by those, like police, who occupy positions of trust) must stand up to the scrutiny of unbiased, reasonable people. Bok argues that public justification avoids the malleability of the liar's own conscience, which would all too easily assess the balance in favor of the lie. Public justification brings objectivity and wisdom, eliminates bias, challenges assumptions, and exposes fallacious reasoning. Bok asserts that a necessary part of public justification is the ability of the public to "adopt the perspective not only of liars but of those lied to; and not only of particular persons but of all those affected by lies—the collective perspective of reasonable persons seen as potentially deceived." The importance of the public's objectivity cannot be overstated: Bok rejects lies in situations in which the public justification test cannot function in an unbiased manner.

According to Bok, in situations involving enemies, the public justification test will inevitably break down as the public's reasonableness and objectivity disappears. When the public perceives an enemy, it will react with hostility, precluding the kind of balanced, perspective-shifting analysis that the public justification test requires. Bok states that if the public has been "whipped into a frenzy of hostility, one cannot speak of 'publicity' in the sense in which it has been used up to now in this book." Because the public cannot put itself in the enemy's shoes, Bok ultimately concludes that deceptive schemes based on the "lying to enemies" justification should not be sanctioned. Even deceptive practices that are carefully circumscribed at the outset will eventually expand beyond reasonable limits because the public's hostility will prevent it from objectively maintaining limits on lying. Bok explains that, in practice, neither deception nor violence can "be contained within . . . narrow boundaries; they end up growing, perpetuating themselves, multiplying, and feeding on one another, to produce the very opposite of increased safety."

If Bok were asked to comment on Slobogin's use of the "lying to enemies" justification to support police lying during interrogations, I believe she would point out that her public-justification test cannot function well in the atmosphere of public hostility that surrounds crime, and that public sympathies will inevitably allow deceptive police practices to expand beyond the limits

proposed by Slobogin. For this practical reason, I believe Bok would not agree that lying during interrogation can be justified by reference to her narrow "lying to enemies" exception.

The problem of maintaining public objectivity in the "enemies" context might be alleviated if the parameters on police lying that Slobogin proposes were defined in legislation or administrative rules. It is not clear, however, that legislative or administrative bodies are capable of maintaining greater objectivity than the general public when it comes to crime and police lying or that those politically accountable bodies can avoid endless tinkering with Slobogin's parameters if the public demands change. There have been few intelligent public discussions of issues related to crime or law enforcement since the presidential election of 1968, when national politicians began inciting a public panic about crime. The political dangers inherent in advocating limits on police lying may mean that the issues cannot be fully aired. On the other hand, a few productive national conversations about law enforcement have occurred recently in connection with situations such as Waco and Ruby Ridge, in which relatively large numbers of the public were able to empathize with the suspects. These dialogues provide at least a glimmer of hope that the public may be capable of critically examining law enforcement practices and maintaining reasonable limits on deception. The malleability of public opinion of law enforcement suggests to me (as I believe it would to Bok) that the wisest course would be to enact a nearly absolute prohibition on police lying. An absolute rule would have a better chance of long-term survival than a nuanced one.

I would like to see Slobogin address in more detail Bok's reservations about the practical problems of implementing a limited "lying to enemies" exception to the general presumption against lying. The present article does not explain adequately how those problems could be overcome. Even if Slobogin were able to convince me that the limitations of his proposed "license to lie" would not be lifted quickly, however, I would still oppose his approach because he does not demonstrate that police lying during interrogations is either necessary or beneficial, both of which are required before a lie can be justified under Bok's method. The next section addresses those points in turn.

II

The Necessity and Utility of Lying

Bok acknowledges that lies to avoid a crisis with an enemy may sometimes be necessary, but she nevertheless requires an exacting search for truthful alternatives, even when an enemy is involved. Despite Bok's exhortation that alternatives must be sought before lying can be justified, Slobogin does not explore the alternatives to lying during interrogation. If Slobogin had examined the alternatives, he would have perceived an obvious one: police can interrogate truthfully. Of course, to be considered a viable alternative, truthfulness would have to advance the goals sought during interrogation. Slobogin does not clearly articulate the goals of interrogation, but he appears to assume that gathering information from suspects is the chief objective. I would add another objective: interrogations provide important opportunities for police to distribute information to suspects (and more indirectly, the public) about such things as integrity, honest dialogue, and trustworthiness. The dissemination of this kind of information is essential to a successfully functioning criminal justice system. Because this information is transmitted in large part by exemplification, it cannot be conveyed through deceit.

Even if we focus exclusively on the information-gathering objective of interrogations, we must recognize the possibility that truthful interrogations can produce confessions or useful information. It is far from clear that the amount of information derived from interrogations would be significantly reduced if police were required to tell the truth. Certainly, interrogators, who place great stock in the tools of manipulation and deception, would argue that their effectiveness would be jeopardized. However, the fact that professional interrogators believe deceit to be essential is not persuasive. There is no evidence that those in the law enforcement business have seriously considered, much less tried, the alternative.

Even if lying increases confession rates, it is not certain whether confession rates affect conviction rates. Professor Paul Cassell has attempted to establish a relationship between confessions and convictions in his efforts to compute the cost of Miranda, estimating that Miranda has resulted in lost convictions in 3.8% of all serious criminal cases and concluding that such a loss amounts to a significant social cost. Other scholars disagree with both his estimate and his conclusion, however. For example, Professor Stephen Schulhofer argues that Miranda affected fewer than one percent of all cases in the period shortly after the Court issued that decision, its "net damage to law enforcement is zero," and even if Cassell's 3.8% figure is accurate, that figure represents a small cost.

In addition, both Slobogin and Cassell overestimate the utility of confessions. Both assume that deception is successful if it produces confessions. Confessions are of limited use, however, if they are ruled inadmissible. Slobogin admits that lies can sometimes cause a court to

rule a confession inadmissible on voluntariness grounds. Lies might also produce statements that run afoul of the corpus delicti rule, which excludes confessions unless they are supported by independent evidence of guilt. The corpus delicti rule represents a judicial determination that confessions are of questionable reliability—a determination that casts doubt on the utility of obtaining a confession through any means. In fact, wrongful convictions based on erroneous deception-induced confessions must be considered a cost of, not a benefit from, those confessions. It is not mere speculation that lies might induce untruthful statements. Psychological and sociological studies indicate that suspects are susceptible to police pressure and sometimes confess even when they are innocent. The vulnerability of suspects and the possibility that they might confess even when innocent are magnified in the hands of an interrogator well-versed in deceit and other interrogation techniques. Even "experienced" suspects are vulnerable to sophisticated interrogation techniques. Thus, although a broad rule permitting lies during postarrest, precharge interrogations might facilitate confessions, some of those confessions would be inadmissible and some would undermine the accuracy of the criminal justice system.

Slobogin acknowledges that there is conflicting research on whether confession rates affect conviction rates, and he acknowledges that a relationship between the two is necessary to his analysis. He nevertheless assumes that postarrest, precharge deceit is necessary to obtain convictions. Slobogin's failure to seriously consider the alternative of being truthful in interrogations and to demonstrate any conclusive link between confessions and convictions undercuts his conclusion that lying in interrogations is necessary and useful.

If we take Bok's test seriously, then, we would have to reject Slobogin's conclusion that lying in postarrest, precharge settings is justifiable. There are alternatives to lying, and the benefits of lying are not clear. Slobogin might fine tune his proposal by limiting lying to situations in which a judicial officer has found no viable alternative to lying and has concluded that lying is likely to produce useful information or admissible evidence. Moreover, the judicial officer would have to determine that the benefits from lying outweigh the harms caused by lying. The time and effort involved in that kind of judicial oversight, however, would make lying too expensive in all but the most pressing circumstances.

In my discussion of the benefits and costs of lying, I have saved for last the special harm that police lying causes. As I explain in the next section, those harms, while difficult to quantify, are substantial.

III

Special Harms

Bok's evaluative method for determining when lying may be justified requires a careful assessment of the harms that lying causes and a rejection of lies whose harms outweigh the benefits to be gained. Bok stresses that lying damages the liar, the dupe, and society in general. Slobogin acknowledges the nature of some of those damages in the criminal investigation context. He and I differ, though, in the weight we assign to those harms. This kind of disagreement may be intractable because the relative weights of benefits and harms is a very subjective matter. Nevertheless, a few brief points might help to highlight the nature of our disagreement.

First, lies harm the liars. Slobogin acknowledges that lying has an "insidious impact" on police themselves, and he is particularly aware of the danger that lying in the interrogation context may lead to police perjury under oath. This, of course, is a widespread harm that also damages the dupe and society in general. Given Slobogin's concern for "testilying," I would have thought that he would seek to reduce the sheer number of lies that police tell. Yet his rule permitting lies during interrogation would mean that police would continue to lie extensively and presumably would continue to incur the kinds of damages that he describes so well. Slobogin explains his acceptance of lying during postarrest, precharge interrogations in part by the fact that arrested suspects are likely to be guilty. He may reason from this that police would have difficulty complying with a rule forbidding them from lying to guilty people and would therefore lie twice as much as they do now to cover up what happened during interrogations. I agree that this could be a problem, but presumably sufficiently strict sanctions for lying would correct the problem. I also would expect cover-ups to diminish if lying becomes generally unacceptable among police.

Slobogin also underestimates the damage that lying does to subjects of interrogation, although he acknowledges that some damage occurs. Slobogin's willingness to characterize arrested suspects as "enemies" helps mask the damage caused by lying because the word "enemies" implies hostile outsiders—persons outside our social or national connections, whose loyalty and trust we do not seek. I might (but only might) agree that we need not worry as much about the damage caused by lying when we deal with true outsiders because we are not so concerned about maintaining social bonds with them. But when it comes to persons in this country who are suspected (or even convicted) of criminal behavior, we ignore at our own peril the damage caused by lying. As the commentators to whom Slobogin refers have argued, the loyalty and trust of "suspects" are of great concern to us because they will continue to live among us or will return to us after a period of incarceration, unless they are locked up for life without the possibility of parole. As a result, it is important that we behave honorably and truthfully with them to initiate, maintain, or renew their loyalty and trust and to exemplify appropriate behavior.

Slobogin suggests that those who are probably innocent should fare better in our calculations than those who are probably guilty, but this distinction conceals many troubling subtleties that make it unworkable in practice. For example, I am not certain how Slobogin would view the suspect whose behavior might ultimately be determined to have been lawful based on self-defense or some other excuse or justification and who might therefore be legally innocent although appearing guilty to police at the outset. In the same way, it would be useful to know how Slobogin would deal with the suspect whose crime was minor and nonviolent, the first-time offender, the suspect whose behavior might be decriminalized, or the offender whose behavior was previously acceptable but has been recently criminalized. Suspects in each of these categories would enjoy more sympathy than the violent criminal, and they probably make up a larger portion of criminal suspects than violent offenders. Add to these complexities the pervasive nature of racial, ethnic, and class bias in the criminal justice system, and an outright prohibition on all interrogation lying seems far preferable to a rule with a rationale that depends on a simplistic distinction between innocence and guilt.

Finally, there are the social costs of Slobogin's proposal. It harms a society when the officers who enforce its laws behave like the worst used car salesmen. That harm is compounded because deceptive tactics employed by police to obtain evidence reflect poorly on courts that supervise the admission of that evidence. The U.S. Supreme Court used these harms to justify the Fourth Amendment exclusionary rule, although more recently it has abandoned the "judicial integrity" rationale in favor of deterrence of police misconduct alone. These unquantifiable but very real harms deserve renewed attention and increased weight in the emerging dialogue about police lying. Unfortunately, Slobogin gives them short shrift when he evaluates the morality of lying during interrogations.

CONCLUSION

Professor Slobogin's article initiates an important discussion about the morality of police lying. Nevertheless, Slobogin's approach falls short when it evaluates police lying during interrogations. Police lying is unjustifiable in that context because it is unnecessary and harmful as well as impossible to restrain within reasonable limits. A thorough moral evaluation of police lying suggests that all police lying should be prohibited, except that which is necessary to save lives.

EXERCISES

1. One recommendation for dealing with the problem of deceptive interrogation techniques is to videotape all interrogation sessions, so that the jury could judge whether confessions were genuine, and a judge could decide whether a confession was obtained under coercive circumstances (and so should not be admitted as evidence). Should videotaping be required? Would that solve the problem?

2. In one of the most common forms of deception employed by police interrogators, the interrogator pretends to be deeply concerned for the welfare of the suspect, and tries to convince the suspect—under the guise of concerned friendship—that confession would be of great benefit to the suspect (the District Attorney would think more kindly of you, you could explain why you were justified in committing the crime and make people understand your situation, etc.). Under Slobogin's model of what counts as acceptable deceptive interrogation, would that sort of deceptive practice be prohibited?

3. A common concern about the practice of police deception in interrogation is that it is difficult to prevent the further spread of such deception: If we become accustomed to lying and faking evidence in interrogations, wouldn't that make it too easy to take the next step and actually fabricate evidence (if we're "certain" that this suspect is guilty); or perhaps go from lying to the suspect to lying to a jury during the trial? Is that a realistic concern?

4. Paris asserts that "It harms a society when the officers who enforce its laws behave like the worst used car salesmen." Paris does not note any specific harms that are caused to society from such police behavior; would it be possible to list such specific harms?

ADDITIONAL READING

Sissela Bok, *Lying: Moral Choice in Public and Private Life* (1978), is an important examination of lying and its effects; Christopher Slobogin refers to Bok's book at several points in his article.

Wesley G. Skogan and Tracey L. Meares, "Lawful Policing," *Annals, AAPSS*, Volume 593 (May 2004): 66–83, review research on police adherence to laws and rules; they note the difficulty in determining the degree to which police are following or violating the rules, and argue that internal processes are the best means of improving compliance. Jerome H. Skolnick and Richard A. Leo, "The Ethics of Deceptive Interrogation," *Criminal Justice Ethics*, Volume 11, Number 1 (Winter/Spring 1992): 3–12, examine the legal history of deceptive interrogation, explore various types of police deception, and warn of its dangers; the quotation in the introduction to this debate is from their article. An essay by Welsh S. White, "Deceptive Police Interrogation Practices: How Far Is Too Far?: Miranda's Failure to Restrain Pernicious Interrogation Practices," *Michigan Law Review*, Volume 99 (2001): 1211–1247, examines deceptive interrogation techniques in the context of false confessions and legal protection for the rights of suspects.

A classic manual for police interrogation, which coaches interrogators in the use of deceptive techniques, is Fred E. Inbau and John E. Reid, *Criminal Investigation and Criminal Interrogation*, 3rd ed. (Baltimore, MD: Williams and Wilkins Co., 1962), which expands their earlier *Lie Detection and Criminal Investigation*, 3rd ed. (Baltimore, MD: Williams and Wilkins Co., 1953); its most recent edition is *Criminal Interrogation and Confessions* (Boston, MA: Jones & Bartlett Publishers, 2004). Another standard manual advocating deceptive techniques is Charles E. O'Hara and Gregory L. O'Hara, *Fundamentals of Criminal Investigation*, 7th ed. (2003). An incisive critique of Inbau's manual can be found in Yale Kamisar, "What Is an 'Involuntary' Confession? Some Comments on Inbau and Reid's *Criminal Interrogation and Confessions*," *Rutgers Law Review*, Volume 17 (1963). Fred Inbau gives arguments in favor of deceptive interrogation techniques in "Law and Police Practice: Restrictions in the Law of Interrogation and Confessions," *Northwestern University Law Review*, Volume 52 (1957); and "Police Interrogation: A Practical Necessity," in the *Journal of Criminal Law, Criminology, and Police Science*, Volume 52 (1961). (Inbau's enthusiasm for deceptive interrogation methods may well seem excessive by contemporary standards; however, when evaluating Inbau's work, it should be remembered that when he originally developed his interrogation model in the early 1950s, Inbau was attempting to move police interrogation practices away from methods of violent coercion: the beating and threatening of suspects was not an uncommon interrogation technique, and Inbau was campaigning to abolish that method. Whatever one thinks of the deceptive techniques advocated by Inbau, they are surely an improvement over police torture of suspects.)

Paul Cassell voices doubts concerning false confessions in "The Guilty and the 'Innocent': An Examination of Alleged Cases of Wrongful Conviction from False Confessions," *Harvard Journal of Law and Public Policy*, Volume 22 (1999). Concern about false confessions and the techniques that induce them is voiced by Miriam S. Gohara, "A Lie for a Lie: False Confessions and the Case for Reconsidering the Legality of Deceptive Interrogation Techniques," *Fordham Urban Law Journal*, Volume 33 (March 2006): 791–842; she also examines the law concerning deceptive interrogation techniques. Other good examinations of psychological techniques leading to false confessions are Richard A. Leo and Richard J. Ofshe, "The Consequences of False Confessions: Deprivations of Liberty and Miscarriages of Justice in the Age of Psychological Interrogation," *Journal of Criminal Law and Criminology*, Volume 88 (1998); and Hollida Wakefield and Ralph Underwager, "Coerced or Nonvoluntary Confessions," *Behavioral Sciences and the Law*, Volume 16 (1998): 423–440. Psychological examinations of why innocent persons might confess to crimes—especially when confronted with deceptive interrogation techniques, including fake fingerprint or DNA identifications—include Richard J. Ofshe and Richard A. Leo, "The Decision to Confess Falsely: Rational Choice and Irrational Action," *Denver University Law Review*, Volume 74 (1997); and two articles by Saul M. Kassin: "The Psychology of Confession Evidence," *American Psychologist*, Volume 52 (1997), and "On the Psychology of Confessions: Does Innocence Put Innocents at Risk?" *American Psychologist*, Volume 60 (2005).

18

Homosexual Sex

Homosexual rights, gay marriage, gays in the military: these issues evoke strong feelings. Though some societies have been quite tolerant, perhaps favorable, toward homosexual relations (the ancient Greeks and Romans, for example), there is no doubt that homosexuals have suffered severe persecution. Homosexuals face imprisonment and even capital punishment in many cultures, and social ostracism, abuse, and violent assaults are far from uncommon. The U.S. military policy under which homosexuals are allowed to serve in the military so long as they keep their sexual activities and identities hidden was perhaps well intentioned, but ultimately it satisfies no one. "You can join us, so long as you constantly pretend to be someone else," is not a very welcoming invitation. Conservative icon and decorated air force pilot Senator Barry Goldwater was a strong advocate for open admission of homosexuals into the armed forces, and he stated his view with characteristic bluntness: "Everyone knows that gays have served honorably in the military since at least the time of Julius Caesar. They'll still be serving long after we're all dead and buried. That should not surprise anyone. . . . You don't need to be straight to fight and die for your country. You just need to shoot straight" (*Washington Post*, June 10, 1993).

In order to examine the question fairly, it is necessary to set aside some of the hot-button controversies and concentrate on the specific issue: Is homosexuality immoral? Many other issues are too easily conflated with that one. First, this is not a question of whether child sexual abuse is immoral. Sexual abuse is wrong whether the abuser is heterosexual or homosexual. After all, most cases of child sexual abuse are committed by heterosexuals, which does not imply that heterosexuality itself is morally wrong. Second, this is not a question of sexual promiscuity. Both heterosexual and homosexual relationships can be monogamous, and both homosexuals and heterosexuals are sometimes promiscuous (as anyone who lives in a college community is well aware). Third, this is not a question of whether some religion approves of or condemns homosexuality. That some religious traditions have condemned homosexuality is clear (though there is considerable dispute about whether Judeo-Christian doctrines should be interpreted as condemning homosexuality). And fourth, this is not a debate about the legal status of homosexual acts: one might believe that homosexual acts are wrong, but that in a free society people's private lives should not be under the control of law (just as one might believe that heterosexual oral sex is wrong, or that drinking alcohol is wrong, but believe that they should not be legally prohibited). Or one might believe that the moral status of homosexuality is irrelevant to the question of legality, since the government should not legislate morality; again, Barry Goldwater:

> The conservative movement, to which I subscribe, has as one of its basic tenets the belief that government should stay out of people's private lives. Government governs best when it governs least—and stays out of the impossible task of legislating morality. But legislating someone's version of morality is exactly what we do by perpetuating discrimination against gays. (*Washington Post*, June 10, 1993)

The question at issue here is whether homosexual acts between consenting adults are morally wrong, and in that controversy one of the contested issues is the question of what is natural. That question leads to two more: First, how do we define natural? And second, what reasons are there for considering what is natural as good and anything unnatural bad? The question of what is "natural" is of central importance to the "natural law" tradition of ethics: a tradition that has its roots in some remarks by Aristotle, and that became a central part of the Roman Catholic ethical tradition through the work of Thomas Aquinas in the fifteenth century. Though a popular view for many centuries, natural law ethics faced severe challenges as science rejected "purposeful" models of explanation in favor of more "mechanical" models; and—except among Catholic theologians—natural law ethics was largely abandoned. Recently, several writers (including John Finnis) have attempted to revive the natural law position, applying it to ethics as well as to legal issues.

There is now considerable dispute about exactly what counts as "natural law ethics"; but the natural law tradition generally involves several basic ideas: human acts (and the laws and principles governing them) are morally good when they promote the development of our true human nature; our human nature and its proper development is assigned by God; and the key element of our human nature is our rationality.

⇒ HOMOSEXUAL SEX IS WRONG ⇐
John M. Finnis

John Finnis, Professor of Law and Legal Philosophy at Oxford and Biolchini Professor of Law at the University of Notre Dame, is a leader of the new natural lawyers who advocate natural law ethics; his remarks are excerpted from his "Law, Morality, and Sexual Orientation," *Notre Dame Journal of Law, Ethics, and Public Policy*, Volume 9, 1995.

During the past thirty years there has emerged in Europe a standard form of legal regulation of sexual conduct. This standard form or scheme, which I shall call the "standard modern [European] position," is accepted by the European Court of Human Rights and the European Commission of Human Rights (the two supra-national judicial and quasi-judicial institutions of the European Convention for the Protection of Human Rights and Fundamental Freedoms (1950), to which almost all European states are party, whether or not they are also party to the European [Economic] Community now known as the European Union). The standard modern European position has two limbs. On the one hand, the state is not authorized to, and does not, make it a punishable offence for adult consenting persons to engage, in private, in immoral sexual acts (for example, homosexual acts). On the other hand, states do have the authority to discourage, say, homosexual conduct and "orientation" (i.e. overtly manifested active willingness to engage in homosexual conduct). And typically, though not universally, they do so. That is to say, they maintain various criminal and administrative laws and policies which have as part of their purpose the discouraging of such conduct. Many of these laws, regulations, and policies discriminate (i.e.

distinguish) between heterosexual and homosexual conduct adversely to the latter. . . .

The standard modern [European] position is consistent with the view that (apart perhaps from special cases and contexts) it is unjust for **A** to impose any kind of disadvantage on **B** simply because **A** believes (perhaps correctly) that **B** has sexual inclinations (which he may or may not act on) towards persons of the same sex. . . . The position does not give **B** the widest conceivable legal protection against such unjust discrimination (just as it generally does not give wide protection against needless acts of adverse private discrimination in housing or employment to people with unpopular or eccentric political views). But the position does not itself encourage, sponsor or impose any such unjust burden. (And it is accompanied by many legal protections for homosexual persons with respect to assaults, threats, unreasonable discrimination by public bodies and officials, etc.)

The concern of the standard modern position itself is not with inclinations but entirely with certain *decisions* to *express or manifest* deliberate promotion of, or readiness to engage in, homosexual *activity* or *conduct,* including promotion of forms of life (e.g. purportedly marital cohabitation) which both encourage.

such activity and present it as a valid or acceptable alternative to the committed heterosexual union which the state recognizes as marriage. Subject only to the written or unwritten constitutional requirement of freedom of discussion of ideas, the state laws and state policies which I have outlined are intended to discourage decisions which are thus deliberately oriented towards homosexual conduct and are manifested in public ways.

The standard modern position differs from the position which it replaced, which made adult consensual sodomy and like acts crimes per se. States which adhere to the standard modern position make it clear by laws and policies such as I have referred to that the state has by no means renounced its legitimate concern with public morality and the education of children and young people towards truly worthwhile and against alluring but bad forms of conduct and life. Nor have such states renounced the judgment that a life involving homosexual conduct is bad even for anyone unfortunate enough to have innate or quasi-innate homosexual inclinations.

The difference between the standard modern position and the position it has replaced can be expressed as follows. The standard modern position considers that the state's proper responsibility for upholding true worth (morality) is a responsibility *subsidiary* (auxiliary) to the *primary* responsibility of parents and non-political voluntary associations. The subsidiary character of government is widely emphasized and increasingly accepted, at least in principle, in contemporary European politics. (It was, for example, a cornerstone of the Treaty of Maastricht of 1992.) This conception of the proper role of government has been taken to exclude the state from assuming a directly parental disciplinary role in relation to consenting *adults*. That role was one which political theory and practice formerly ascribed to the state on the assumption that the role followed by logical necessity, from the truth that the state should encourage true worth and discourage immorality. That assumption is now judged to be mistaken (a judgment for which I shall argue in the final part of this lecture).

So the modern theory and practice draws a distinction not drawn in the former legal arrangements—a distinction between (a) supervising the truly private conduct of adults and (b) supervising the *public realm or environment*. The importance of the latter includes the following considerations: (1) this is the environment or public realm in which young people (of whatever sexual inclination) are educated; (2) it is the context in which and by which everyone with responsibility for the well-being of young people is helped or hindered in assisting them to avoid bad forms of life; (3) it is the milieu in

which and by which all citizens are encouraged and helped, or discouraged and undermined, in their own resistance to being lured by temptation into falling away from their own aspirations to be people of integrated good character, and to be autonomous, self-controlled persons rather than slaves to impulse and sensual gratification.

While the type (a) supervision of truly private adult consensual conduct is now considered to be outside the state's normally proper role (with exceptions such as sado-masochistic bodily damage, and assistance in suicide), type (b) supervision of the moral-cultural-educational environment is maintained as a very important part of the state's justification for claiming legitimately the loyalty of its decent citizen. . . .

The standard modern position involves a number of explicit or implicit judgments about the proper role of law and the compelling interests of political communities, and about the evil of homosexual conduct. Can these be defended by reflective, critical, publicly intelligible and rational arguments? I believe they can. Since, even the advocates of "gay rights" do not seriously assert that the state can never have any compelling interests in public morality or the moral formation of its young people or the moral environment in which parents, other educators, and young people themselves must undertake this formation, I shall in this lecture focus rather on the underlying issue which receives far too little public discussion: What is wrong with homosexual conduct? Is the judgment that it is morally wrong inevitably a manifestation either of mere hostility to a hated minority, or of purely religious, theological, and sectarian belief which can ground no constitutionally valid determination disadvantaging those who do not conform to it?

I have been using and shall continue to use the terms "homosexual activity," "homosexual acts" and "homosexual conduct" synonymously, to refer to bodily acts, on the body of a person of the same sex, which are engaged in with a view to securing orgasmic sexual satisfaction for one or more of the parties. . . .

At the heart of the Platonic-Aristotelian and later ancient philosophical rejections of all homosexual conduct, and thus of the modern "gay" ideology, are three fundamental theses: (1) The commitment of a man and woman to each other in the sexual union of marriage is intrinsically good and reasonable, and is incompatible with sexual relations outside marriage. (2) Homosexual acts are radically and peculiarly non-marital, and for that reason intrinsically unreasonable and unnatural. (3) Furthermore, according to Plato, if not Aristotle, homosexual acts have a special similarity to solitary masturbation, and both types of radically non-marital act are manifestly unworthy of the human being and immoral.

I want now to offer an interpretation of these three theses which articulates them more clearly. . . . My account also articulates thoughts which have historically been implicit in the judgments of many non-philosophical people, and which have been held to justify the laws adopted in many nations and states both before and after the period when Christian beliefs as such were politically and socially dominant. And it is an application of the theory of morality and natural law developed over the past thirty years by Germain Grisez and others. . . .

Plato's mature concern, in the *Laws*, for familiarity, affection and love between spouses in a chastely exclusive marriage, Aristotle's representation of marriage as an intrinsically desirable friendship between quasi-equals, and as a state of life even more natural to human beings than political life, and Musonius Rufus's conception of the inseparable double goods of marriage, all find expression in Plutarch's celebration of marriage—as a union not of mere instinct but of reasonable love, and not merely for procreation but for mutual help, goodwill and cooperation for their own sake. Plutarch's severe critiques of homosexual conduct (and of the disparagement of women implicit in homosexual ideology), develop Plato's critique of homosexual and all other extra-marital sexual conduct. Like Musonius Rufus, Plutarch does so by bringing much closer to explicit articulation the following thought. Genital intercourse between spouses enables them to actualize and experience (and in that sense express) their marriage itself, as a single reality with two blessings (children and mutual affection). Non-marital intercourse, especially but not only homosexual, has no such point and therefore is unacceptable.

The core of this argument can be clarified by comparing it with Saint Augustine's treatment of marriage in his *De Bono Coniugali*. The good of marital communion is here an instrumental good, in the service of the procreation and education of children so that the intrinsic, non-instrumental good of friendship will be promoted and realized by the propagation of the human race, and the intrinsic good of inner integration be promoted and realized by the "remedying" of the disordered desires of concupiscence. Now, when considering sterile marriages, Augustine had identified a further good of marriage, the natural *societas* (companionship) of the two sexes. Had he truly integrated this into his synthesis, he would have recognized that in sterile and fertile marriages alike, the communion, companionship, *societas* and *amicilia* of the spouses—their being

married—*is* the very good of marriage, and is an intrinsic, basic human good, not merely instrumental to any other good. And this communion of married life, this integral amalgamation of the lives of the two persons (as Plutarch put it before John Paul II), has as its intrinsic elements, as essential *parts* of one and the same good, the goods and ends to which the theological tradition, following Augustine, for a long time subordinated that communion. It took a long and gradual process of development of doctrine, through the Catechism of the Council of Trent, the teachings of Pius XI and Pius XII, and eventually those of Vatican II—a process brilliantly illuminated by Germain Grisez—to bring the tradition to the position that procreation and children are neither the *end* (whether primary or secondary) to which marriage is instrumental (as Augustine taught), nor instrumental to the good of the spouses (as much secular and "liberal Christian" thought supposes), but rather: Parenthood and children and family are the intrinsic fulfillment of a communion which, because it is not merely instrumental, can exist and fulfill the spouses even if procreation happens to be impossible for them.

Now if, as the recent encyclical on the foundations of morality, *Veritatis Splendor*, teaches, "the communion of persons in marriage" which is violated by every act of adultery is itself a "fundamental human good," there fall into place not only the elements of the classic philosophical judgments on non-marital sexual conduct but also the similar judgments reached about such conduct by decent people who cannot articulate explanatory premises for those judgments, which they reach rather by an insight into what is and is not *consistent with* realities whose goodness they experience and understand at least sufficiently to will and choose. In particular, there fall into place the elements of an answer to the question: Why cannot non-marital friendship be promoted and expressed by sexual acts? Why is the attempt to express affection by orgasmic non-marital sex the pursuit of an illusion? Why did Plato and Socrates, Xenophon, Aristotle, Musonius Rufus, and Plutarch, right at the heart of their reflections on the homoerotic culture around them, make the very deliberate and careful judgment that homosexual *conduct* (and indeed all extra-marital sexual gratification) is radically incapable of participating in, actualizing, the common good of friendship?

Implicit in the philosophical and common-sense rejection of extra-marital sex is the answer: The union of the reproductive organs of husband and wife really unites them biologically (and their biological reality is part of, not merely an instrument of, their *personal* reality); reproduction is one function and so, in respect of that function, the spouses are indeed one reality, and their sexual union therefore can *actualize* and allow them to *experience* their *real common good—their marriage* with the two goods, parenthood and friendship, which (leaving aside the order of grace) are the parts of its wholeness as an intelligible common good even if, independently of what the spouses will, their capacity for biological parenthood will not be fulfilled by that act of genital union. But the common good of friends who are not and cannot be married (for example, man and man, man and boy, woman and woman) has nothing to do with their having children by each other, and their reproductive organs cannot make them a biological (and therefore personal) unit. So their sexual acts together cannot do what they may hope and imagine. Because their activation of one or even each of their reproductive organs cannot be an actualizing and experiencing of the *marital* good—as marital intercourse (intercourse between spouses in a marital way) can, even between spouses who *happen* to be sterile—it can do no more than provide each partner with an individual gratification. For want of a *common good* that could be actualized and experienced *by and in this bodily union*, that conduct involves the partners in treating their bodies as instruments to be used in the service of their consciously experiencing selves; their choice to engage in such conduct thus disintegrates each of them precisely as acting persons.

Reality is known in judgment, not in emotion, and *in reality*, whatever the generous hopes and dreams and thoughts of *giving* with which some same-sex partners may surround their sexual acts, those acts cannot express or do more than is expressed or done if two strangers engage in such activity to give each other pleasure, or a prostitute pleasures a client to give him pleasure in return for money, or (say) a man masturbates to give himself pleasure and a fantasy of more human relationships after a gruelling day on the assembly line. This is, I believe, the substance of Plato's judgment—at that moment in the *Gorgias* which is also decisive for the moral and political philosophical critique of hedonism—that there is no important distinction in essential moral worthlessness between solitary masturbation, being sodomized as a prostitute, and being sodomized for the pleasure of it. Sexual acts cannot *in reality* be self-giving unless they are acts by which a man and a woman actualize and experience sexually the real giving of themselves to each other—in biological, affective and volitional union in mutual commitment, both open-ended and exclusive—which like Plato and Aristotle and most peoples we call marriage.

In short, sexual acts are not unitive in their significance unless they are marital (actualizing the all-level unity of marriage) and (since the common good of marriage has two aspects) they are not marital unless they have not only the generosity of acts of friendship but also the procreative significance, not necessarily of being intended to generate or capable in the circumstances of generating but at least of being, as human conduct, acts of the reproductive kind—actualizations, so far as the spouses then and there can, of the reproductive function in which they are biologically and thus personally one.

The ancient philosophers do not much discuss the case of sterile marriages, or the fact (well known to them) that for long periods of time (e.g. throughout pregnancy) the sexual acts of a married couple are naturally incapable of resulting in reproduction. They appear to take for granted what the subsequent Christian tradition certainly did, that such sterility does not render the conjugal sexual acts of the spouses non-marital. (Plutarch indicates that intercourse with a sterile spouse is a desirable mark of marital esteem and affection.) For: A husband and wife who unite their reproductive organs in an act of sexual intercourse which, so far as they then can make it, is of a kind suitable for generation, do function as a biological (and thus personal) unit and thus can be actualizing and experiencing the two-in-one-flesh common good and reality of marriage, even when some biological condition happens to prevent that unity resulting in generation of a child. Their conduct thus differs radically from the acts of a husband and wife whose intercourse is masturbatory, for example sodomitic or by fellatio or coitus interruptus. In law such acts do not consummate a marriage, because in reality (whatever the couple's illusions of intimacy and self-giving in such acts) they do not actualize the one-flesh, two-part marital good.

Does this account seek to "make moral judgments based on natural facts"? Yes and no. No, in the sense that it does not seek to infer normative conclusions or theses from non-normative (natural-fact) premises. Nor does it appeal to any norm of the form "Respect natural facts or natural functions." But yes, it does apply the relevant practical reasons (especially that marriage and inner integrity are basic human goods) and moral principles (especially that one may never *intend* to destroy, damage, impede, or violate any basic human good, or prefer an illusory instantiation of a basic human good to a real instantiation of that or some other human good) to facts about the human personal organism.

Societies such as classical Athens and contemporary England (and virtually every other) draw a distinction between behavior found merely (perhaps extremely) offensive (such as eating excrement), and behavior to be repudiated as destructive of human character and relationships. Copulation of humans with animals is repudiated because it treats human sexual activity and satisfaction as something appropriately sought in a manner as divorced from the actualizing of an intelligible common good as is the instinctive coupling of beasts—and so treats human bodily life, in one of its most intense activities, as appropriately lived as merely animal. The deliberate genital coupling of persons of the same sex is repudiated for a very similar reason. It is not simply that it is sterile and disposes the participants to an abdication of responsibility for the future of humankind. Nor is it simply that it cannot *really* actualize the mutual devotion which some homosexual persons hope to manifest and experience by it, and that it harms the personalities of its participants by its disintegrative manipulation of different parts of their one personal reality. It is also that it treats human sexual capacities in a way which is deeply hostile to the self-understanding of those members of the community who are willing to commit themselves to real marriage in the understanding that its sexual joys are not mere instruments or accompaniments to, or mere compensations for, the accomplishment of marriage's responsibilities, but rather enable the spouses to *actualize and experience* their intelligent commitment to share in those responsibilities, in that genuine self-giving.

Now, as I have said before, "homosexual orientation," in one of the two main senses of that highly equivocal term, is precisely the deliberate willingness to promote and engage in homosexual acts—the state of mind, will, and character whose self-interpretation came to be expressed in the deplorable but helpfully revealing name "gay." So this willingness, and the whole "gay" ideology, treats human sexual capacities in a way which is deeply hostile to the self-understanding of those members of the community who are willing to commit themselves to real marriage.

Homosexual orientation in this sense is, in fact, a standing denial of the intrinsic aptness of sexual intercourse to actualize and in that sense give expression to the exclusiveness and open-ended commitment of marriage as something good in itself. All who accept that homosexual acts can be a humanly appropriate use of sexual capacities must, if consistent, regard sexual capacities, organs and acts as instruments for gratifying the individual "selves" who have them. Such an acceptance is commonly (and in my opinion rightly) judged to be an active threat to the stability of existing and future marriages; it makes nonsense, for example, of the view that adultery is per se (and not merely because it may involve deception), and in an important way, inconsistent with conjugal love. A political community which judges that the stability and protective and educative generosity of family life is of fundamental importance to that community's present and future can rightly judge that it has a compelling interest in denying that homosexual conduct—a "gay lifestyle"—is a valid, humanly acceptable choice and form of life, and in doing whatever it *properly* can, as a community with uniquely wide but still subsidiary functions, to discourage such conduct.

HOMOSEXUAL RELATIONS ARE MORALLY LEGITIMATE
John Corvino

John Corvino, Professor of Philosophy at Wayne State University, specializes in ethical theory and applied ethics, and is a well-known lecturer on topics related to homosexuality; the following is drawn from "Why Shouldn't Tommy and Jim Have Sex? A Defense of Homosexuality," from *Same Sex: Debating the Ethics, Science, and Culture of Homosexuality* (Lanham, MD: Rowman & Littlefield, 1997).

Tommy and Jim are a homosexual couple I know. Tommy is an accountant; Jim is a botany professor. They are in their forties and have been together fourteen years, the last five of which they've lived in a Victorian house that they've lovingly restored. Although their relationship has had its challenges, each has made sacrifices for the sake of the other's happiness and the relationship's long-term success.

I assume that Tommy and Jim have sex with each other (although I've never bothered to ask). Furthermore, I contend that they probably *should* have sex with each other. For one thing, sex is pleasurable. But it is also much more than that: a sexual relationship can unite two people in a way that virtually nothing else can. It can be an avenue of growth, of communication, and of lasting interpersonal fulfillment. These are reasons why most heterosexual couples have sex even if they don't want children, don't want children yet, or don't want additional children. And if these reasons are good enough for most heterosexual couples, then they should be good enough for Tommy and Jim.

Of course, having a reason to do something does not preclude there being an even better reason for not doing it. Tommy might have a good reason for drinking orange juice (it's tasty and nutritious) but an even better reason for not doing so (he's allergic). The point is that one would need a pretty good reason for denying a sexual relationship to Tommy and Jim, given the intense benefits widely associated with such relationships. The question I shall consider in this paper is thus quite simple: Why shouldn't Tommy and Jim have sex?

Homosexual Sex Is "Unnatural"

Many contend that homosexual sex is "unnatural." But what does that mean? Many things that people value—clothing, houses, medicine, and government, for example—are unnatural in some sense. On the other hand, many things that people detest—disease, suffering, and death, for example—are "natural" in the sense that they occur "in nature." If the unnaturalness charge is to be more than empty rhetorical flourish, those who levy it must specify what they mean. Borrowing from Burton Leiser, I will examine several possible meanings of "unnatural."

What Is Unusual or Abnormal Is Unnatural

One meaning of "unnatural" refers to that which deviates from the norm, that is, from what most people do. Obviously, most people engage in heterosexual relationships. But does it follow that it is wrong to engage in homosexual relationships? Relatively few people read Sanskrit, pilot ships, play the mandolin, breed goats, or write with both hands, yet none of these activities is immoral simply because it is unusual. As the Ramsey Colloquium, a group of Jewish and Christian scholars who oppose homosexuality, writes, "The statistical frequency of an act does not determine its moral status." So while homosexuality might be unnatural in the sense of being unusual, that fact is morally irrelevant.

What Is Not Practiced by Other Animals Is Unnatural

Some people argue, "Even animals know better than to behave homosexually; homosexuality must be wrong." This argument is doubly flawed. First, it rests on a false premise. Numerous studies—including Anne Perkins's study of "gay" sheep and George and Molly Hunt's study of "lesbian" sea-gulls—have shown that some animals do form homosexual pair-bonds. Second, even if animals did not behave homosexually, that fact would not prove that homosexuality is immoral. After all, animals don't cook their food, brush their teeth, participate in religious worship, or attend college; human beings do all of these without moral censure. Indeed, the idea that animals could provide us with our standards—especially our sexual standards—is simply amusing.

What Does Not Proceed from Innate Desires Is Unnatural

Recent studies suggesting a biological basis for homosexuality have resulted in two popular positions. One side proposes that homosexual people are "born that way" and that it is therefore natural (and thus good) for them to form homosexual relationships. The other side maintains that homosexuality is a lifestyle choice, which is therefore unnatural (and thus wrong). Both sides assume a connection between the origin of homosexual orientation, on the one hand, and the moral value of homosexual activity, on the other. And insofar as they share that assumption, both sides are wrong.

Consider first the pro-homosexual side: "They are born that way; therefore it's natural and good." This inference assumes that all innate desires are good ones (i.e., that they should be acted upon). But that assumption is clearly false. Research suggests that some people are born with a predisposition toward violence, but such people have no more right to strangle their neighbors than anyone else. So while people like Tommy and Jim may be born with homosexual tendencies, it doesn't follow that they ought to act on them. Nor does it follow that they ought *not* to act on them, even if the tendencies are not innate. I probably do not have any innate tendency to write with my left hand (since I, like everyone else in my family, have always been right-handed), but it doesn't follow that it would be immoral for me to do so. So simply asserting that homosexuality is a lifestyle choice will not show that it is an immoral lifestyle choice.

Do people "choose" to be homosexual? People certainly don't seem to choose their sexual *feelings*, at least not in any direct or obvious way. (Do you? Think about it.) Rather, they find certain people attractive and certain activities arousing, whether they "decide" to or not. Indeed, most people at some point in their lives wish that they could control their feelings more— for example, in situations of unrequited love—and find it frustrating that they cannot. What they *can* control to a considerable degree is how and when they act upon those feelings. In that sense, both homosexuality and heterosexuality involve lifestyle choices. But in either case, determining the origin of the feelings will not determine whether it is moral to act on them.

What Violates an Organ's Principal Purpose Is Unnatural

Perhaps when people claim that homosexual sex is unnatural they mean that it cannot result in procreation. The idea behind the argument is that human organs have various natural purposes: eyes are for seeing, ears are for hearing, genitals are for procreating. According to this argument, it is immoral to use an organ in a way that violates its particular purpose.

Many of our organs, however, have multiple purposes. Tommy can use his mouth for talking, eating, breathing, licking stamps, chewing gum, kissing women, or kissing Jim; and it seems rather arbitrary to claim that all but the last use are "natural." (And if we say that some of the other uses are "unnatural, but not immoral," we have failed to specify a morally relevant sense of the term "natural.")

Just because people can and do use their sexual organs to procreate, it does not follow that they should not use them for other purposes. Sexual organs seem very well suited for expressing love, for giving and receiving pleasure, and for celebrating, replenishing, and enhancing a relationship—even when procreation is not a factor. Unless opponents of homosexuality are prepared to condemn heterosexual couples who use contraception or individuals who masturbate, they must abandon this version of the unnaturalness argument. Indeed, even the Roman Catholic Church, which forbids contraception and masturbation, approves of sex for sterile couples and of sex during pregnancy, neither of which can lead to procreation. The Church concedes here that intimacy and pleasure are morally legitimate purposes for sex, even in cases where procreation is impossible. But since homosexual sex can achieve these purposes as well, it is inconsistent for the Church to condemn it on the grounds that it is not procreative.

One might object that sterile heterosexual couples do not *intentionally* turn away from procreation, whereas homosexual couples do. But this distinction doesn't hold.

It is no more possible for Tommy to procreate with a woman whose uterus has been removed than it is for him to procreate with Jim. By having sex with either one, he is intentionally engaging in a nonprocreative sexual act.

Yet one might press the objection further and insist that Tommy and the woman *could* produce children if the woman were fertile: whereas homosexual relationships are essentially infertile, heterosexual relationships are only incidentally so. But what does that prove? Granted, it might require less of a miracle for a woman without a uterus to become pregnant than for Jim to become pregnant, but it would require a miracle nonetheless. Thus it seems that the real difference here is not that one couple is fertile and the other not, nor that one couple "could" be fertile (with the help of a miracle) and the other not, but rather that one couple is male-female and the other male-male. In other words, sex between Tommy and Jim is wrong because it's male-male—i.e., because it's homosexual. But that, of course, is no argument at all.

What Is Disgusting or Offensive Is Unnatural

It often seems that when people call homosexuality "unnatural" they really just mean that it's disgusting. But plenty of morally neutral activities—handling snakes, eating snails, performing autopsies, cleaning toilets, and so on—disgust people. Indeed, for centuries, most people found interracial relationships disgusting, yet that feeling—which has by no means disappeared— hardly proves that such relationships are wrong. In sum, the charge that homosexuality is unnatural, at least in its most common forms, is longer on rhetorical flourish than on philosophical cogency. At best it expresses an aesthetic judgment, not a moral judgment.

HOMOSEXUAL SEX IS HARMFUL

One might instead argue that homosexuality is harmful. The Ramsey Colloquium, for instance, argues that homosexuality leads to the breakdown of the family and, ultimately, of human society, and it points to the "alarming rates of sexual promiscuity, depression, and suicide and the ominous presence of AIDS within the homosexual subculture." Thomas Schmidt marshals copious statistics to show that homosexual activity undermines physical and psychological health. Such charges, if correct, would seem to provide strong evidence against homosexuality. But are the charges correct? And do they prove what they purport to prove?

One obvious (and obviously problematic) way to answer the first question is to ask people like Tommy and Jim. It would appear that no one is in a better position to judge the homosexual lifestyle than those who know it firsthand. Yet it is unlikely that critics would trust their testimony. Indeed, the more homosexual people try to explain their lives, the more critics accuse them of deceitfully promoting an agenda. (It's like trying to prove that you're not crazy. The more you object, the more people think, "That's exactly what a crazy person would say.")

One might instead turn to statistics. An obvious problem with this tack is that both sides of the debate bring forth extensive statistics and "expert" testimony, leaving the average observer confused. There is a more subtle problem as well. Because of widespread antigay sentiment, many homosexual people won't acknowledge their romantic feelings to themselves, much less to researchers. I have known a number of gay men who did not "come out" until their forties and fifties, and no amount of professional competence on the part of interviewers would have been likely to open their closets sooner. Such problems compound the usual difficulties of finding representative population samples for statistical study.

Yet even if the statistical claims of gay rights opponents were true, they would not prove what they purport to prove, for several reasons. First, as any good statistician realizes, correlation does not equal cause. Even if homosexual people were more likely to commit suicide, be promiscuous, or contract AIDS than the general population, it would not follow that their homosexuality causes them to do these things. An alternative—and very plausible—explanation is that these phenomena, like the disproportionately high crime rates among African Americans, are at least partly a function of society's treatment of the group in question. Suppose you were told from a very early age that the romantic feelings that you experienced were sick, unnatural, and disgusting. Suppose further that expressing these feelings put you at risk of social ostracism or, worse yet, physical violence. Is it not plausible that you would, for instance, be more inclined to depression than you would be without such obstacles? And that such depression could, in its extreme forms, lead to suicide or other self-destructive behaviors? (It is indeed remarkable that couples like Tommy and Jim continue to flourish in the face of such obstacles.)

A similar explanation can be given for the alleged promiscuity of homosexuals. The denial of legal marriage, the pressure to remain in the closet, and the overt hostility toward homosexual relationships are all more conducive to transient, clandestine encounters than they are to long-term unions. As a result, that which is challenging enough for heterosexual couples—settling down and building a life together—becomes far more challenging for homosexual couples.

Indeed, there is an interesting tension in the critics' position here. Opponents of homosexuality commonly claim that "marriage and the family . . . are fragile institutions in need of careful and continuing support." And they point to the increasing prevalence of divorce and premarital sex among heterosexuals as evidence that such support is declining. Yet they refuse to concede that the complete absence of similar support for homosexual relationships might explain many of the alleged problems of homosexuals. The critics can't have it both ways: if heterosexual marriages are in trouble despite the various social, economic, and legal incentives for keeping them together, society should be little surprised that homosexual relationships—which not only lack such supports, but face overt hostility—are difficult to maintain. . . .

Of course, there's more to a flourishing life than avoiding harm. One might argue that even if Tommy and Jim are not harming each other by their relationship, they are still failing to achieve the higher level of fulfillment possible in a heterosexual relationship, which is rooted in the complementarity of male and female. But this argument just ignores the facts: Tommy and Jim are homosexual *precisely because* they find relationships with men (and, in particular, with each other) more fulfilling than relationships with women. Even evangelicals (who have long advocated "faith healing" for homosexuals) are beginning to acknowledge that the choice for most homosexual people is not between homosexual relationships and heterosexual relationships, but rather between homosexual relationships and celibacy. What the critics need to show, therefore, is that no matter how loving, committed, mutual, generous, and fulfilling the relationship may be, Tommy and Jim would flourish more if they were celibate. Given the evidence of their lives (and of others like them), this is a formidable task indeed. . . .

But doesn't homosexuality threaten society? A Roman Catholic priest once put the argument to me as follows: "Of course homosexuality is bad for society. If everyone were homosexual, there would be no society." Perhaps it is true that if everyone were homosexual, there would be no society. But if everyone were a celibate priest, society would collapse just as surely, and my friend the priest didn't seem to think that he was doing anything wrong simply by failing to procreate. Jeremy Bentham made the point somewhat more acerbically roughly 200 years ago: "If then merely out of regard to population it were right that [homosexuals] should be burnt alive, monks ought to be roasted alive by a slow fire."

From the fact that the continuation of society requires procreation, it does not follow that *everyone* must procreate. Moreover, even if such an obligation existed, it would not preclude homosexuality. At best, it would preclude *exclusive* homosexuality: homosexual people who occasionally have heterosexual sex can procreate just fine. And given artificial insemination, even those who are exclusively homosexual can procreate. In short, the priest's claim—if everyone were homosexual, there would be no society—is false; and even if it were true, it would not establish that homosexuality is immoral.

The Ramsey Colloquium commits a similar fallacy. Noting (correctly) that heterosexual marriage promotes the continuation of human life, it then infers that homosexuality is immoral because it fails to accomplish the same. But from the fact that procreation is good, it does not follow that childlessness is bad—a point that the members of the colloquium, several of whom are Roman Catholic priests, should readily concede.

I have argued that Tommy and Jim's sexual relationship harms neither them nor society. On the contrary, it benefits both. It benefits them because it makes them happier—not merely in a short-term, hedonistic sense, but in a long-term, "big picture" sort of way. And, in turn, it benefits society, since it makes Tommy and Jim more stable, more productive, and more generous than they would otherwise be. In short, their relationship—including its sexual component—provides the same kinds of benefits that infertile heterosexual relationships provide (and perhaps other benefits as well). Nor should we fear that accepting their relationship and others like it will cause people to flee in droves from the institution of heterosexual marriage. After all, as Thomas Williams points out, the usual response to a gay person is not "How come *he* gets to be gay and I don't?"

HOMOSEXUALITY VIOLATES BIBLICAL TEACHING

At this point in the discussion, many people turn to religion. "If the secular arguments fail to prove that homosexuality is wrong," they say, "so much the worse for secular ethics. This failure only proves that we need God for morality." Since people often justify their moral beliefs by appeal to religion, I will briefly consider the biblical position.

At first glance, the Bible's condemnation of homosexual activity seems unequivocal. Consider, for example, the following two passages, one from the "Old" Testament and one from the "New":

You shall not lie with a male as with a woman; it is an abomination. (Lev. 18:22)

For this reason God gave them up to degrading passions. Their women exchanged natural intercourse for unnatural, and in the same way also the men, giving up natural intercourse with women, were consumed with passion for one another. Men committed shameless acts with men and received in their own persons the due penalty for their error. (Rom. 1:26–27)

Note, however, that these passages are surrounded by other passages that relatively few people consider binding. For example, Leviticus also declares,

The pig . . . is unclean for you. Of their flesh you shall not eat, and their carcasses you shall not touch; they are unclean for you. (11:7–8)

Taken literally, this passage not only prohibits eating pork, but also playing football, since footballs are made of pigskin. (Can you believe that the University of Notre Dame so flagrantly violates Levitical teaching?)

Similarly, St. Paul, author of the Romans passage, also writes, "Slaves, obey your earthly masters with fear and trembling, in singleness of heart, as you obey Christ" (Eph. 6:5)—morally problematic advice if there ever were any. Should we interpret this passage (as Southern plantation owners once did) as implying that it is immoral for slaves to escape? After all, God himself says in Leviticus,

[Y]ou may acquire male and female slaves . . . from among the aliens residing with you, and from their families that are with you, who have been born in your land; and they may be your property. You may keep them as a possession for your children after you, for them to inherit as property. (25:44–46)

How can people maintain the inerrancy of the Bible in light of such passages? The answer, I think, is that they learn to interpret the passages *in their historical context.*

Consider the Bible's position on usury, the lending of money for interest (for *any* interest, not just excessive interest). The Bible condemns this practice in no uncertain terms. In Exodus God says that "if you lend money to my people, to the poor among you, you shall not exact interest from them" (22:25). Psalm 15 says that those who lend at interest may not abide in the Lord's tent or dwell on his holy hill (1–5). Ezekiel calls usury "abominable"; compares it to adultery, robbery, idolatry, and bribery; and states that anyone who "takes advanced or accrued interest . . . shall surely die; his blood shall be upon himself" (18:13).

Should believers therefore close their savings accounts? Not necessarily. According to orthodox Christian teaching, the biblical prohibition against usury no longer applies. The reason is that economic conditions have changed substantially since biblical times, such that usury no longer has the same negative consequences it had when the prohibitions were issued. Thus, the practice that was condemned by the Bible differs from contemporary interest banking in morally relevant ways.

Yet are we not in a similar position regarding homosexuality? Virtually all scholars agree that homosexual relations during biblical times were vastly different from relationships like Tommy and Jim's. Often such relations were integral to pagan practices. In Greek society, they typically involved older men and younger boys. If those are the kinds of features that the biblical authors had in mind when they issued their condemnations, and such features are no longer typical, then the biblical condemnations no longer apply. As with usury, substantial changes in cultural context have altered the meaning and consequences—and thus the moral value—of the practice in question. Put another way, using the Bible's condemnations of homosexuality against contemporary homosexuality is like using its condemnations of usury against contemporary banking.

Let me be clear about what I am *not* claiming here. First, I am not claiming that the Bible has been wrong before and therefore may be wrong this time. The Bible may indeed be wrong on some matters, but for the purpose of this argument I am assuming its infallibility. Nor am I claiming that the Bible's age renders it entirely inapplicable to today's issues. Rather, I am claiming that when we do apply it, *we must pay attention to morally relevant cultural differences between biblical times and today.* Such attention will help us distinguish between specific time-bound prohibitions (e.g., laws against usury or homosexual relations) and the enduring moral values they represent (e.g., generosity or respect for persons). And as the above argument shows, my claim is not very controversial. Indeed, to deny it is to commit oneself to some rather strange views on slavery, usury, women's roles, astronomy, evolution, and the like.

Here, one might also make an appeal to religious pluralism. Given the wide variety of religious beliefs (e.g., the Muslim belief that women should cover their faces, the Orthodox Jewish belief against working on Saturday, the Hindu belief that cows are sacred and should not be eaten), each of us inevitably violates the religious beliefs of others. But we normally don't view such violations as occasions for moral censure, since we distinguish between beliefs that depend on particular revelations and beliefs that can be justified independently (e.g., that stealing is wrong). Without an independent justification for condemning homosexuality, the best one can say is, "My religion says so." But in a society that cherishes religious freedom, that reason alone does not normally provide grounds for moral or legal sanctions. That people still fall back on that reason in discussions of homosexuality suggests that they may not have much of a case otherwise.

CONCLUSION

As a last resort, opponents of homosexuality typically change the subject: "But what about incest, polygamy, and bestiality? If we accept Tommy and Jim's sexual relationship, why shouldn't we accept those as well?" Opponents of interracial marriage used a similar slippery-slope argument in the 1960s when the Supreme Court struck down antimiscegenation laws. It was a bad argument then, and it is a bad argument now.

Just because there are no good reasons to oppose interracial or homosexual relationships, it does not follow that there are no good reasons to oppose incestuous, polygamous, or bestial relationships. One might argue, for instance, that incestuous relationships threaten delicate familial bonds, or that polygamous relationships result in unhealthy jealousies (and sexism), or that bestial relationships—do I need to say it?—aren't really "relationships" at all, at least not in the sense we've been discussing. Perhaps even better arguments could be offered (given much more space than I have here). The point is that there is no logical connection between homosexuality, on the one hand, and incest, polygamy, and bestiality, on the other.

Why, then, do critics continue to push this objection? Perhaps it's because accepting homosexuality requires them to give up one of their favorite arguments: "It's wrong because we've always been taught that it's wrong." This argument—call it the argument from tradition—has an obvious appeal: people reasonably favor tried-and-true ideas over unfamiliar ones, and they recognize the foolishness of trying to invent morality from scratch. But the argument from tradition is also a dangerous argument, as any honest look at history will reveal.

I conclude that Tommy and Jim's relationship, far from being a moral abomination, is exactly what it appears to be to those who know them: a morally positive influence on their lives and on others. Accepting this conclusion takes courage, since it entails that our moral traditions are fallible. But when these traditions interfere with people's happiness for no sound reason, they defeat what is arguably the very point of morality: promoting individual and communal well-being. To put the argument simply, Tommy and Jim's relationship makes them better people. And that's not just good for Tommy and Jim: that's good for everyone.

EXERCISES

1. Why does Finnis regard heterosexual relations within marriage as a special good?

2. In what way does Finnis regard his argument as based on natural facts?

3. Of the various accounts of "unnatural" that Corvino gives, which is closest to the way that Finnis thinks of homosexuality as unnatural?

4. Corvino states that for homosexuals, the choice is not between homosexual relations and heterosexual relations but between homosexual relations and celibacy; and he suggests that no matter what one thinks about whether heterosexual relations are more fulfilling than homosexual relations, clearly homosexual relations are more fulfilling than celibacy, and thus homosexual relations should not be condemned. Could Finnis agree with that conclusion?

5. Do contemporary Darwinian accounts of evolution pose a problem for natural law ethics?

6. Could an atheist consistently favor a form of natural law ethics?

7. Barry Goldwater is often described as the "father of conservatism," and certainly he was one of the most influential conservative political leaders in twentieth-century American politics. His basic conservative principle was that people should be left alone to do as they wish—without governmental interference—so long as they do not harm others. Following that principle, Goldwater believed that there should be no discrimination against homosexuals: consenting homosexual adults should be able to live their lives as they wish, subject only to the condition—which applies to homosexuals and heterosexuals alike—that they do not harm others. Among contemporary American conservatives, however, opposition to homosexual rights is very common: conservative Republicans are typically the leaders in efforts to deny consenting homosexuals the right to live as they wish, without harming others. These conservatives champion "traditional values" (and they see homosexual rights as contrary to those traditional values); and that allegiance to "traditional values" pushes aside the older conservative Goldwater principle that "people should be free to do as they wish, without interference, so long as they do not harm others." Which of these "conservative" views has a better claim on the "conservative" banner?

8. Could a *natural* tendency (such as the widespread human tendency to submit to higher authority) be morally bad?

9. Suppose we discovered that sexism is *natural* in males; would that tell us anything about the moral status of sexism?

ADDITIONAL READING

A superb anthology is edited by John Corvino, *Same Sex: Debating the Ethics, Science, and Culture of Homosexuality* (Lanham, MD: Rowman & Littlefield, 1997). Another excellent anthology is Robert M. Baird and M. Katherine Baird, *Homosexuality: Debating the Issues* (Amherst, NY: Prometheus Books, 1995).

For a sympathetic approach to homosexual rights, see Richard D. Mohr's *Gays/Justice: A Study of Ethics, Society, and Law* (New York: Columbia University Press, 1988). For the opposing view, see Roger Scruton, *Sexual Desire* (London: Weidenfeld and Nicolson, 1985).

Michael Ruse offers a powerful critique of the claim that homosexuality is unnatural in "The Morality of Homosexuality," in Robert Baker and Frederick Elliston, editors, *Philosophy and Sex*, rev. ed. (Buffalo, NY: Prometheus Books, 1984).

Linda J. Tessier, *Dancing After the Whirlwind: Feminist Reflections on Sex, Denial, and Spiritual Transformation* (Boston, MA: Beacon Press, 1997), combines philosophy, religion, psychology, and poetry into a unique exploration of the rich structure of lesbian relations.

A remarkable online source for more information is Professor Lawrence Hinman's *Ethics Updates*. Go to *http://ethics.sandiego.edu*, and under the applied heading click on "Sexual Orientation."

The classic source for natural law theory is Thomas Aquinas, *Summa Theologiae*. Contemporary versions of natural law ethics can be found in John Finnis, *Natural Law and Natural Rights* (Oxford: Oxford University Press, 1980); John Finnis, *Fundamentals of Ethics* (Oxford: Oxford University Press, 1983); and Germain Grisez, *Life and Death with Liberty and Justice* (Notre Dame, IN: University of Notre Dame Press, 1979).

A good general account of natural law ethics is "Natural Law," by Stephen Buckle, in Peter Singer, editor, *A Companion to Ethics* (Oxford: Blackwell Publishers, 1991).

19

Should Performance-Enhancing Drugs Be Banned from Athletics?

The most common argument for banning performance-enhancing drugs is that they are too dangerous and harmful to athletes. Whether such paternalism is ever justified and whether it is justified in special limited cases are long-debated questions, but paternalism is not a special issue for athletics. If you think paternalism is legitimate, there is no problem extending such paternalism to athletes. If you reject paternalism but still wish to ban the athletic use of performance-enhancing drugs, then you will need nonpaternalistic grounds for such a ban.

One line of nonpaternalistic argument against performance-enhancing drugs is based on the essential elements of human athletic competition. In athletic competition, we are not interested in how fast a mile can be traversed, but in how fast a human athlete can do it. There is nothing wrong with competitions in which giant mechanical contraptions hurl pumpkins a mile or more, and nothing wrong with seeing how far such a mechanical marvel might throw a discus or javelin. Likewise, we might find a bionic man competition entertaining: how well can clever scientists engineer a human form that is designed to run very fast, lift enormous weights and leap tall buildings in a single bound, all within the confines of a human skin? It might well become a great favorite on cable television, but it would not be a human athletic competition.

Another argument is based on fairness: the wealthy nations hire great trainers and contrive optimum diets but their best athletes are still outrun by the swift Kenyans, who have gloried in long-distance racing since childhood. And that is an element that most people want in sport: the outcome ultimately depending on athletic skill and training, and perhaps a lucky bounce, rather than by which side has hired the most creative drug designer or the most ambitious genetic enhancer. The "integrity of sport" aside, much of the joy and satisfaction that people take in sports would be lost if sporting ability could be produced in a laboratory and injected into athletes. Simon develops his argument for restrictions on performance-enhancing drugs along these lines.

There is another fairness line of argument: If drug enhancement becomes common in a sport, then persons who prefer not to use the drugs will be forced out of the highest level of competition. If steroid use becomes commonplace among football linemen, then those who do not use steroids will be placed at a great disadvantage and be unable to compete at the top levels. Many people find that unfair, but others challenge that conclusion.

PERFORMANCE-ENHANCING DRUGS SHOULD BE BANNED FROM ATHLETICS

Robert L. Simon

Robert L. Simon is Marjorie and Robert W. McEwen Professor of Philosophy at Hamilton College, coach of the Hamilton College varsity golf team from 1986 to 2000, a past president of the Philosophic Society for the Study of Sport, and a member of the editorial board for the *Journal of the Philosophy of Sport*. His essay excerpted here is from "Good Competition and Drug-Enhanced Performance," *Journal of the Philosophy of Sport*, volume 11 (1984), pp. 6–13.

Competition in sport frequently has been defended in terms of the search for excellence in performance. Top athletes, whether their motivation arises from adherence to the internal values of competition or desire for external reward, are willing to pay a heavy price in time and effort in order to achieve competitive success. When this price consists of time spent in hard practice, we are prepared to praise the athlete as a worker and true competitor. But when athletes attempt to achieve excellence through the use of performance-enhancing drugs, there is widespread condemnation. Is such condemnation justified? What is wrong with the use of drugs to achieve excellence in sport? Is prohibiting the use of performance-enhancing drugs in athletic competition justified?

The relatively widespread use of such drugs as anabolic steroids to enhance performance dates back at least to the Olympics of the 1960s, although broad public awareness of such drug use seems relatively recent. Anabolic steroids are drugs, synthetic derivatives of the male hormone testosterone, which are claimed to stimulate muscle growth and tissue repair. While claims about possible bad consequences of steroid use are controversial, the American College of Sports Medicine warns against serious side effects. These are believed to include liver damage, artherosclerosis, hypertension, personality changes, a lowered sperm count in males, and masculinization in females. Particularly frightening is that world-class athletes are reportedly taking steroids at many times the recommended medical dosage—at levels so high that, as Thomas Murray has pointed out, under "current federal regulations governing human subjects . . . no institutional review board would approve a research design that entailed giving subjects anywhere near the levels . . . used by the athletes."

The use of such high levels of a drug raises complex empirical as well as ethical issues. For example, even if steroid use at a low level does not actually enhance athletic performance, as some authorities claim, it is far from clear whether heavy use produces any positive effects on performance. At the very least, athletes who believe in the positive effects of heavy doses of steroids are not likely to be convinced by data based on more moderate intake.

As interesting as these issues are, it will be assumed in what follows that the use of certain drugs does enhance athletic performance and does carry with it some significant risk to the athlete. Although each of these assumptions may be controversial, by granting them, the discussion can concentrate on the ethical issues raised by use of performance-enhancing drugs.

I. WHAT IS A PERFORMANCE-ENHANCING DRUG?

If we are to discuss the ethics of using drugs to enhance athletic performance, we should begin with a clear account of what counts as such a drug. Unfortunately, a formal definition is exceedingly hard to come by, precisely because it is unclear to what substances such a definition ought to apply.

If it is held to be impermissible to take steroids or amphetamines to enhance performance, what about special diets, the use of coffee to promote alertness, or the bizarre practice of "blood doping," by which runners store their own blood in a frozen state and then return it to their body before a major meet in order to increase the oxygen sent to the muscles?

It is clear that the concept of an "unnatural" or "artificial" substance will not take us very far here, since testosterone hardly is unnatural. Similarly, it is difficult to see how one's own blood can be considered artificial. In addition, we should not include on any list of forbidden substances the use of medication for legitimate reasons of health.

Moreover, what counts as a performance-enhancing drug will vary from sport to sport. For example, drinking alcohol normally will hurt performance. However, in some sports, such as riflery, it can help. This is because as a depressant, alcohol will slow down one's heart rate and allow for a steadier stance and aim.

Rather than spend considerable time and effort in what is likely to be a fruitless search for necessary conditions, we would do better to ignore borderline cases and focus on such clear drugs of concern as amphetamines and steroids. If we can understand the ethical issues that apply to use of such drugs, we might then be in a better position to handle borderline cases as well. However, it does seem that paradigm cases of the drugs that are of concern satisfy at least some of the following criteria.

1. If the user did not believe that use of the substance in the amount ingested would increase the chances of enhanced athletic performance, that substance would not be taken.
2. The substance, in the amount ingested, is believed to carry significant risk to the user.
3. The substance, in the amount ingested, is not prescribed medication taken to relieve an illness or injury.

These criteria raise no concern about the normal ingestion of such drugs as caffeine in coffee or tea, or about medication since drugs used for medicinal purposes would not fall under them (1). The use of amphetamines and steroids, on the other hand, do fall under the criteria . . . .

Why should the use of possibly harmful drugs solely for the purpose of enhancing athletic performance be regarded as impermissible? In particular, why shouldn't individual athletes be left at liberty to pursue excellence by any means they freely choose?

II. PERFORMANCE-ENHANCING DRUGS, COERCION, AND THE HARM PRINCIPLE

One argument frequently advanced against the use of such performance-enhancing drugs as steroids is based on our second criterion of harm to the user. Since use of such drugs is harmful to the user, it ought to be prohibited.

However, if we accept the "harm principle," which is defended by such writers as J.S. Mill, paternalistic interference with the freedom of others is ruled out. According to the harm principle, we are entitled to interfere with the behavior of competent, consenting adults only to prevent harm to others. After all, if athletes prefer the gains that the use of drugs' provide along with possible side effects to the alternative of less risk but worse performance, external interference with their freedom of choice seems unwarranted.

However, at least two possible justifications of paternalistic interference are compatible with the harm principle. First, we can argue that athletes do not give informed consent to the use of performance-enhancing drugs. Second, we can argue that the use of drugs by some athletes does harm other competitors. Let us consider each response in turn.

Informed Consent

Do athletes freely choose to use such performance-enhancing drugs as anabolic steroids? Consider, for example, professional athletes whose livelihood may depend on the quality of their performance. Athletes whose performance does not remain at peak levels may not be employed for very long. As Carolyn Thomas maintains, "the onus is on the athlete to . . . consent to things that he or she would not otherwise consent to . . . Coercion, however, makes the athlete vulnerable. It also takes away the athlete's ability to act and choose freely with regard to informed consent." Since pressures on top amateur athletes in national and world-class competition may be at least as great as pressures on professionals, a comparable argument can be extended to cover them as well.

However, while this point is not without some force, we need to be careful about applying the notion of coercion too loosely. After all, no one is forced to try to become a top athlete. The reason for saying top athletes are "coerced" is that if they don't use performance-enhancing drugs, they may not get what they want. But they still have the choice of settling for less. Indeed, to take another position is to virtually deny the competence of top athletes to give consent in a variety of sports related areas including adoption of training regimens and scheduling. Are we to say, for example, that coaches coerce athletes into training and professors coerce students into doing work for their courses? Just as students can choose not to take a college degree, so too can athletes revise their goals. It is also to suggest that *any* individual who strives for great reward is not competent to give consent, since the fear of losing such a reward amounts to a coercive pressure.

While the issue of coercion and the distinction between threats and offers is highly complex, I would suggest that talk of coercion is problematic as long as the athlete has an acceptable alternative to continued participation in highly competitive sport. While coercion may indeed be a real problem in special cases, the burden of proof would seem to be on those who deny that top athletes *generally* are in a position to consent to practices affecting performance.

Harm to Others

This rejoinder might be satisfactory, critics will object, if athletes made their choices in total isolation. The competitive realities are different, however. If some athletes use drugs, others—who on their own might refrain from becoming users—are "forced" to indulge just to remain competitive. As Manhattan track coach Fred Dwyer points out, "The result is that athletes—none of whom understandingly, are willing to settle for second place—feel that 'if my opponent is going to get for himself that little extra, then I'm a fool not to.'" Athletes may feel trapped into using drugs in order to stay competitive. According to this argument, then, the user of performance-enhancing drugs is harming others by coercing them into becoming users as well.

While the competitive pressures to use performance-enhancing drugs undoubtedly are real, it is far from clear that they are unfair or improperly imposed. Suppose, for example, that some athletes embark on an especially heavy program of weight training. Are they coercing other athletes into training just as hard in order to compete? If not, why are those athletes who use steroids "coercing" others into going along? Thus, if performance-enhancing drugs were available to all, no one would cheat by using them; for all would have the same opportunity and, so it would be argued, no one would be forced into drug use any more than top athletes are forced to embark on rigorous training programs.

Perhaps what bothers us about the use of drugs is that the user may be endangering his or her health. But why isn't the choice about whether the risk is worth the gain left to the individual athlete to make? After all, we don't always prohibit new training techniques just because they carry along with them some risk to health. Perhaps the stress generated by a particularly arduous training routine is more dangerous to some athletes than the possible side effects of drugs are to others?

Arguably, the charge that drug users create unfair pressures on other competitors begs the very question at issue. That is, it presupposes that such pressures are morally suspect in ways that other competitive pressures are not, when the very point at issue is whether that is the case. What is needed is some principled basis for asserting that certain competitive pressures—those

generated by the use of performance enhancing drugs—are illegitimately imposed while other competitive pressures—such as those generated by hard training—are legitimate and proper. It will not do to point out that the former pressures are generated by drug use. What is needed is an explanation of why the use of performance enhancing drugs should be prohibited in the first place.

While such arguments, which describe a position we might call a libertarianism of sports, raise important issues, they may seem to be open to clear counter-example when applied in nonathletic contexts. Suppose for example that your co-workers choose to put in many extra hours on the job. That may put pressure on you to work overtime as well, if only to show your employer that you are just as dedicated as your colleagues. But now, suppose your fellow workers start taking dangerous stimulants to enable them to put even more hours into their jobs. Your employer then asks why you are working less than they are. You reply that you can keep up the pace only by taking dangerous drugs. Is the employer's reply, "Well, no one is forcing you to stay on the job, but if you do you had better put in as many hours as the others" really acceptable?

However, even here, intuitions are not a particularly reliable guide to principle. Suppose you have other less stressful alternatives for employment and that the extra hours the others originally work without aid of drugs generate far more harmful stress than the risk generated by the use of the stimulant? Perhaps in that case your employer is not speaking impermissibly in telling you to work harder. If not, just why does the situation change when the harmful effects are generated by drugs rather than stress? Alternatively, if we think there should be limits both on the stress generated by pressures from overtime *and* the risks created by drug use, why not treat similar risks alike, regardless of source? Similarly, in the context of sport, if our goal is to lower risk, it is far from clear that the risks imposed by performance-enhancing drugs are so great as to warrant total prohibition, while the sometimes equal risks imposed by severe training regimens are left untouched.

Harm and the Protection of the Young

Even if athletes at top levels of competition can give informed consent to the use of performance-enhancing drugs, and even if users do not place unfair or coercive competitive pressures on others, the harm principle may still support prohibition.

Consider, for example, the influence of the behavior of star athletes on youngsters. Might not impressionable boys and girls below the age of consent be driven to use performance-enhancing drugs in an effort to emulate top stars? Might not high school athletes turn to performance-enhancing drugs to please coaches, parents, and fans?

Unfortunately, consideration of such remote effects of drug use is far from conclusive. After all, other training techniques such as strict weight programs also may be dangerous if adopted by young athletes who are too physically immature to take the stress such programs generate. Again, what is needed is not simply a statement that a practice imposes some risk on others. Also needed is a justification for saying the risk is improperly imposed. Why restrict the freedom of top athletes rather than increase the responsibility for supervision of youngsters assigned to coaches, teachers, and parents? After all, we don't restrict the freedom of adults in numerous other areas where they may set bad examples for the young.

III: Drugs and the Ideal of Competitive Sport
Our discussion so far suggests that although the charges that use of performance-enhancing drugs by some athletes harms others do warrant further examination, they amount to less than a determinative case against such drug use. However, they may have additional force when supported by an account of competitive sport which implies a distinction between appropriate and inappropriate competitive pressures. What we need, then, is an account of when risk is improperly imposed on others in sport. While I am unable to provide a full theory here, I do want to suggest a principled basis, grounded on an ethic of athletic competition, for prohibition of paradigm performance-enhancing drugs.

My suggestion, which I can only outline here, is that competition in athletics is best thought of as a mutual quest for excellence through challenge. Competitors are obliged to do their best so as to bring out the best in their opponents. Competitors are to present challenges to one another within the constitutive rules of the sport being played. Such an account may avoid the charges, often directed against competitive sports, that they are zero-sum games which encourage the selfish and egotistical desire to promote oneself by imposing losses on others.

In addition, the ideal of sport as a *mutual* quest for excellence brings out the crucial point that a sports contest is a competition between *persons*. Within the competitive framework, each participant must respond to the choices, acts, and abilities of others—which in turn manifest past decisions about what one's priorities should be and how one's skills are to be developed. The good competitor, then, does not see opponents as things to be overcome and beaten down but rather sees them as persons whose acts call for appropriate, mutually acceptable responses. On this view, athletic competition, rather than being incompatible with respect for our opponents as persons, actually presupposes it.

However, when use of drugs leads to improved play, it is natural to say that it is not athletic ability that determines outcome but rather the efficiency with which the athlete's body reacts to the performance enhancer. But the whole point of athletic competition is to test the athletic ability of persons, not the way bodies react to drugs. In the latter case, it is not the athlete who is responsible for the gain. Enhanced performance does not result from the qualities of the athlete *qua* person, such as dedication, motivation, or courage. It does not result from innate or developed ability, of which it is the point of competition to test. Rather, it results from an external factor, the ability of one's body to efficiently utilize a drug, a factor which has only a contingent and fortuitous relationship to athletic ability.

Critics may react to this approach in at least two different ways. First, they may deny that drug use radically changes the point of athletic competition, which presumably is to test the physical and mental qualities of athletes in their sport. Second, they may assert that by allowing the use of performance-enhancing drugs, we expand the point of athletic competition in desirable ways. That is, they may question whether the paradigm of athletic competition to which I have appealed has any privileged moral standing. It may well be an accepted paradigm, but what makes it acceptable?

Drugs and Tests of Ability

Clearly, drugs such as steroids are not magic pills that guarantee success regardless of the qualities of the users. Athletes using steroids must practice just as hard as others to attain what may be only marginal benefits from use. If performance enhancers were available to all competitors, it would still be the qualities of athletes that determined the results.

While this point is not without force, neither is it decisive. Even if all athletes used drugs, they might not react to them equally. The difference in reaction might determine the difference between competitive success and failure. Hence, outcomes would be determined not by the relevant qualities of the athletes themselves but rather by the natural capacity of their bodies to react to the drug of choice.

Is this any different, the critic may reply, from other innate differences in athletes which might enable them to benefit more than others from weight training or to run faster or swing harder than others? Isn't it inconsistent to allow some kinds of innate differences to affect outcomes but not the others?

Such an objection, however, seems to ignore the point of athletic competition. The point of such competition is to select those who do run the fastest, swing the hardest, or jump the farthest. The idea is not for all to come out equally, but for differences in outcome to correlate with differences in ability and motivation. Likewise, while some athletes may be predisposed to benefit more from a given amount of weight training than others, this trait seems relevant to selection of the best athlete. Capacity to benefit from training techniques seems part of what makes one a superior athlete in a way that capacity to benefit from a drug does not.

Competition and Respect for Persons

At this point, a proponent of the use of performance-enhancing drugs might acknowledge that use of such drugs falls outside the prevailing paradigm of athletic competition. However, such a proponent might ask, "What is the *moral* force of such a conclusion?" Unless we assume that the accepted paradigm not only is acceptable, but in addition that deviance from it should be prohibited, nothing follows about the ethics of the use of performance-enhancing drugs.

Indeed, some writers seem to suggest that we consider new paradigms compatible with greater freedom for athletes, including freedom to experiment with performance-enhancing drugs. W.M. Brown seems to advocate such a view when he writes,

> Won't it [drug use] change the nature of our sports and ourselves? Yes. . . . But then people can choose, as they always have, to compete with those similar to themselves or those different. . . . I can still make my actions an 'adventure in freedom' and 'explore the limits of my strength' however I choose to develop it.

I believe Brown has raised a point of fundamental significance here. I wish I had a fully satisfactory response to it. Since I don't, perhaps the best I can do is indicate the lines of a reply I think is worth considering, in the hope that it will stimulate further discussion and evaluation.

Where athletic competition is concerned, if all we are interested in is better and better performance, we could design robots to "run" the hundred yards in 3 seconds or hit a golf ball 500 hundred yards when necessary. But it isn't just enhanced performance that we are after. In addition, we want athletic competition to be a test of *persons*. It is not only raw ability we are testing for; it is what people do with their ability that counts at least as much. In competition itself, each competitor is reacting to the choices, strategies, and valued abilities of the other, which in turn are affected by past decisions and commitments. Arguably, athletic competition is a paradigm example of an area in which each individual competitor respects the other competitors as persons. That is, each reacts to the intelligent choices and valued characteristics of the other. These characteristics include motivation, courage, intelligence, and what might be called the metachoice of which talents and capacities are to assume priority over others for a given stage of the individual's life.

However, if outcomes are significantly affected not by such features but instead by the capacity of the body to benefit physiologically from drugs, athletes are no longer reacting to each other as persons but rather become more like competing bodies. It becomes more and more appropriate to see the opposition as things to be overcome—as mere means to be overcome in the name of victory—rather than as persons posing valuable challenges. So, insofar as the requirement that we respect each other as persons is ethically fundamental, the prevailing paradigm does enjoy a privileged perspective from the moral point of view.

It is of course true that the choice to develop one's capacity through drugs is a choice a person might make. Doesn't respect for persons require that we respect the choice to use performance enhancers as much as any other? The difficulty, I suggest, is the effect that such a choice has on the process of athletic competition itself. The use of performance-enhancing drugs in sports restricts the area in which we can be respected as persons. Although individual athletes certainly can make such a choice, there is a justification inherent in the nature of good competition for prohibiting participation by those who make such a decision. Accordingly, the use of performance-enhancing drugs should be prohibited in the name of the value of respect for persons itself.

ATHLETES SHOULD BE ALLOWED TO USE PERFORMANCE-ENHANCING DRUGS
W. M. Brown

W. M. Brown is a philosophy professor at Trinity College, Hartford, Connecticut, and dean of the faculty. He has written extensively in philosophy of science and the philosophy of sport. His arguments are from "As American as Gatorade and Apple Pie: Performance Drugs and Sports," in Joram Graf Haber, editor, *Ethics for Today and Tomorrow* (Sudbury, Mass.: Jones and Bartlett, 1997), pp. 324–341.

As long as people have played at sports they have tried to develop their skills and capacities with all the means at their disposal. In recent years, public discussion of such efforts has focused on the use of performance-enhancing drugs, in part because we are caught up in a quagmire of issues relating to illegal drug use, and in part because we are perplexed by ethical and practical issues relating to developments in biotechnology. Our sports have changed and our attitudes toward them and the athletes who perform in them are undergoing similar changes. By and large, the controversies over professionalism and race in sport are over, those over sex and gender are passing, but the controversy over performance drugs is unresolved.

This paper is a critique of a number of arguments that are frequently made to resolve that controversy by showing why performance drugs should be forbidden to all athletes participating in organized sports such as amateur and professional leagues and international competitions like the Olympic Games. The arguments have moral as well as practical aspects, focusing as they do on athletes' rights and principles of liberty or of avoiding harm. Surprisingly, perhaps, one of the most curious aspects of the controversy is what people mean when they argue about drugs in sports.

One reason for this is that much of the notoriety of drug use in sports is related to athletes' use of recreational drugs: cocaine, alcohol, and tobacco, for example. Few of these drugs are thought by anyone to enhance athletic performance. Indeed, aside from the illegality of some of them, they are deplored because they diminish one's skills and produce aberrant behavior on and off the playing fields. Another reason is that many of the substances used to enhance athletic performance are not usually thought of as drugs at all, for example an athlete's own blood, or hormones, or widely used food products like caffeine or sugar. And finally, there is puzzlement over the availability of synthetically produced substances that naturally occur in the human body such as testosterone, human growth hormone, and erythropoietin which have widespread therapeutic uses and even uses for otherwise healthy individuals coping with the processes of aging.

But having mentioned a few, I will not catalogue the list of substances that are used to enhance athletic performance or seek to define them. The issues I will discuss cut across such lists and concern more general views about fairness, health, consensus, autonomy, and the nature of sports as they are brought to bear on the practice of enhancing athletic performance. Nor will the arguments I will consider hinge on the effectiveness of such substances. No one really knows whether many of these products are effective at all or in what ways or with what risks. Virtually no serious major studies of their use by athletes have been made, and most of our evidence is speculative and anecdotal, extrapolated from very different contexts or reported by journalists. So I will assume that some performance drugs are effective and some are not, that some are risky and some are safe, and proceed to explore what conclusions we can reach about their use by athletes.

1. FAIRNESS

Perhaps the most frequently cited issue concerning drugs and sports is that of fairness. The claim is that taking "performance drugs" is a form of cheating, that it is therefore fundamentally unfair. After all, if some athletes are using something that gives them a decisive advantage, it is argued, it is unfair to the basic premise of competition in sports (whether competition against present opponents or competition for records). Competition in sports (as opposed to competition in love and war) assumes some basic similarities among all participants so that contests are close and, therefore, both bring out the best in the competitors and are exciting to watch. Such a situation also, it is claimed (rightly, it seems to me), makes it more likely that the contest will be won in the margin where various factors come into play that are dear to our traditions: effort, will, determination, fortitude, and courage, among others.

And it is true: when an athlete breaks the rules, such as those banning the use of performance drugs, that is clearly a form of cheating, and its practice introduces an aspect of unfairness into the sport. But in an important way this argument misses the point. The ethical issue we are addressing is precisely that of the value of such rules, of the wisdom or justification of prohibiting the use of performance drugs. It therefore begs the question to stress that such drugs are forbidden and so it is wrong to use them.

There is a version of this argument that seems to acknowledge this point, but goes on to claim that when some athletes use drugs and others do not (for whatever reason other than that they are banned), an inequality is introduced that renders competition unfair, not because of any cheating, but because of the discrepancy in performance that drug use may introduce. The short answer to this argument is that there are always likely to be differences among athletes (even if they are clones) and that these differences are (to mention a particular sport) what makes for horse racing. Without them, sports competition would surely hold little interest for us. Competition would resemble the predicament of Buridan's ass with unresolveable stalemates or contests won by random chance.

A more persuasive version of this argument is to note that in highly competitive sports where there are many pressures from family, coaches, teammates, managers, and owners, there can be no free choice to use performance drugs. At best it is a subtle form of coercion, a "forced choice," that produces for some athletes an unhappy dilemma: don't compete or take drugs. We can acknowledge the crucial premise that individual autonomy is a central value. (Indeed, it is one I will employ frequently.) The additional factual premise that no one can be expected to withstand such pressures is more problematic. For one thing, it is clear that although many athletes now use performance drugs, many do not, and the latter are among the finest and most successful athletes now performing. But for another, every innovation or change in training, techniques, and equipment places similar pressure on athletes to adopt the changes or lose a competitive edge (assuming also that the changes are really effective in enhancing performance). The charge of coercion hinges on the prior assumption that the choice to use performance drugs is deeply objectionable and therefore many people would not want to use them. Of course, if their use is illegal or harmful, many athletes will be reluctant to use them. So athletes who choose not to use drugs are at an unfair advantage only if there is a good reason not to use them. And that, of course, is just the issue at stake. But these reasons need to be assessed. Someone might complain that he can be a boxer only if competitors are allowed to punch the head, and since that is very dangerous, he is unfairly forced to choose between boxing and getting his head punched (and punching others in the head) or not competing at all. The wise choice may be switch to swimming, but the choice is not in any interesting sense coerced. . . .

In the discussion to follow, various additional arguments concerning the use of performance drugs are examined to assess their cogency and persuasiveness.

2. HEALTH

Performance drugs are dangerous, so this argument goes, and banning their use is a way of protecting athletes from their own ill-conceived acts. The danger lies in the injuries that the use of performance drugs may cause. Recently, this case has been made most vociferously in regard to anabolic steroids, the drug of choice for athletes seeking to increase muscle mass useful for various sports ranging from football to track to gymnastics. But many other drugs are also available, including beta-blockers, growth hormones, and food ingredients such as caffeine; presumably the argument can be made in regard to them as well.

There are, however, two issues that need to be separated in this regard. One is an empirical issue concerning the actual harms likely to be caused by performance drug use. The other is the ethical issue of paternalism, the justification of restricting the actions of others ostensibly for their own good. A by-product of this argument is what appears to be a remarkable case of hypocrisy.

As for the first issue, there is some evidence that the use of some performance drugs carries risks of injury to the users. But the evidence is remarkably sparse and, of course, differs for different drugs. Much of it is anecdotal—the lore of boxing and weight-lifting aficionados, the stuff of locker room banter. Such research-based evidence as is available is often inconclusive. Some studies suggest that steroids are effective in enhancing performance; others claim there is no significant enhancing effect. Athletes tend to discount the extreme claims of risk of injury because their own experience has not confirmed them; and much of the research evidence has been based not on studies of efforts to enhance athletic performance but rather on cases of medical therapy and extrapolation to nonmedical circumstances. What this suggests is that the factual claims concerning performance drugs remain significantly unsubstantiated both in regard to drug risks and in regard to performance enhancement. The sensible thing to do would surely be to find out who is right by encouraging careful and competent research into both kinds of claims.

But this would not be the end of it. It seems likely that some substances or procedures would be relatively dangerous and others relatively risk-free; some would be relatively effective, others ineffective. In this case, it could be argued that dangerous ones especially should be carefully used, if effective, to eliminate or minimize their side effects, but that all performance drugs should be studied and the results be widely and publicly available to athletes and their coaches and physicians. The goal should be to eliminate or reduce the likelihood of harm to athletes, as it is for other risks in sport.

A brief comment is in order about relative risk. In many sports, the activities of the sports themselves are far more dangerous than the use of any of the performance drugs that have even a bare chance of being effective. Deaths and injuries due to the use of performance drugs are rare. Scarcely more than a dozen deaths are noted by some authorities, and most of these can be attributed not to performance drugs, but to recreational drugs like cocaine and alcohol used off the playing fields and unconnected to competitive efforts. But deaths and serious injuries due to the sports themselves number in the hundreds in sports like football, boxing, mountain climbing, hockey, cycling, and skiing. Where the sports themselves are far more dangerous than anything risked by using performance drugs, one can only wonder at the hypocrisy that prompts the extraordinary tirades directed at the latter but seldom at the former. The most vociferous criticism of performance drugs seems far more closely linked to our national hysteria about illicit drugs in general than to the health of our athletes.

Still, if we assume that there are dangers in using performance drugs, and clearly there are some even if their use is monitored by knowledgeable physicians, should we prohibit them on the grounds that athletes cannot be expected to make rational choices about their use and hence are at risk of excessive injury to their health? I have argued elsewhere that child athletes should be prohibited on paternalistic grounds from using such drugs. But the issue is not so clear with adult athletes. Unlike airline pilots or subway train drivers, for example, athletes who use performance drugs pose no obvious dangers to others. Nor are the drugs in question related to diminished performance, but rather to enhanced and improved performance. So concerns

about athletes' health are paternalistic in the strong sense of being directed not toward preventing harm to others, but to the drug users themselves. There often seems to be a discrepancy between concerns about athletes' health and safety in general and concerns about risks of using performance drugs. In any case, one could equally well argue that making their use safer while preserving the autonomy and freedom of choice of the athletes is a far preferable approach. If there are effective performance-enhancing drugs (and there seem to be some), and if they are or could be relatively safe to use (and some are), then the health argument, as I have called it, seems ineffective as a general argument against their use.

One final note. Hormonal supplements for healthy adults are not a new item in the pharmacopoeia. More recently men and women are being given sex hormones and growth hormone supplements to offset the effects of aging, apparently with favorable results. Women have taken estrogen for years to offset the effects of menopause. The World Health Organization is currently administering steroids as a male contraceptive in doses greater than those said to have been used by Ben Johnson when he was disqualified after his victory at the Seoul Olympics. It is hard to argue in light of such practices that the use of performance drugs, even the most risky kinds, including steroids, should have no place in the training or performance of athletes.

3. NATURALNESS AND NORMALITY

The argument shifts at this point, therefore, to the claim that performance drugs are unnatural additives to the athlete's training or performance regimen. Even if their careful use is relatively harmless, the argument goes, they are objectionable because they are artificial and unnatural additives to sporting activities. There are two versions of this argument. One is that it is the drugs that are unnatural; the other is that it is the athletes who use them who are unnatural or abnormal.

The first version is the less plausible. The reason is that many of the drugs used to enhance performance are as natural as testosterone, caffeine, or an athlete's own blood. True, some drugs are the product of manufacturing processes or are administered using medical technologies. But, of course, so are many of our foods, vitamins, and medicines, all routine parts of the athlete's regimen. If by *natural* one means not artificially synthesized or processed, or known to occur in nature independent of human intervention, few of the nutritional and medical resources available to athletes today would be allowed. Performance drugs, therefore, cannot be identified or forbidden under this rubric without taking many things we find indispensable down the drain with them.

The claim for abnormality may be a bit stronger. After all, to the extent that performance drugs work effectively at all, they are designed to render their users superior in ability and rates of success beyond what we would expect otherwise. And this, the argument concludes, renders them abnormal. Of course, this is in one sense true. If normality is defined in terms of statistical frequencies, then highly effective athletes are abnormal by definition. Such people are already abnormal if compared with the rest of us; their reflexes, coordination, neuromuscular development, and fitness levels already place them far to the right on the bell-shaped curves showing the range of human capacities and performance. Performance drugs are scarcely needed to place them among the abnormal, that is, the statistically rare individuals who can run a mile under 3:50, accomplish a gymnastic routine, slam dunk a basketball, or climb Mt. Everest without canisters of extra oxygen. Looked at another way, however, athletes are probably the most natural components of their sports; their efforts reveal to all of us various ranges of human abilities as currently manifested under the very artificial and unnatural constraints of our present-day sports and their assortment of bats, balls, rules, shoes, training techniques, and ideologies.

Surely, however, those who make this argument know this. Perhaps they are using the word *abnormal* in its other sense of connoting what is bad or undesirable, and since they can't quite articulate what is so bad about performance drugs, they rely on the claim of abnormality or unnaturalness to carry the weight of their condemnation. Here again, then, we need to move on to other arguments that may make the case more substantively and effectively, or at least make clearer what it is about the use of performance drugs that seems to some critics so deplorable. . . .

5. THE NATURE OF SPORT

Some claim that there are central characteristics of sports that mitigate against the use of performance drugs. I want to consider one such claim, formulated by Alasdair MacIntyre, and developed by others. The claim is that sports are practices, coherent forms of organized social activity that create certain goods and values intrinsic to them and which are attained by performing in accordance with the standards of excellence integral to the practices. This characterization of practices gives rise to a distinction between those goods that are internal to the practices and those that are external to it. Internal goods arise out of the exercise of skills developed to fulfill the defining goals of the activities; external goods are rewards typically offered by institutions that support the practices but also tend to exploit them for reasons of their own that are unconnected with the practices' own immediate activities. Thus a well-thrown pitch, a stolen base, and a perfect bunt are exercises of skill within the practice of baseball and offer their own rewards. The fame, salaries, and trophies that are also rewarded are external to the game and provided by institutions not directly involved in the practice itself.

There is much to be said for this conception of sports. It highlights some of the features of a favorite view of them: the virtuous and innocent player motivated by the love of the game; the power and skill of the practitioner, a thing of beauty and grace; the corrupt and venal exploiters of youth and innocence for worldly gain. But it divides motives and satisfactions too neatly, borrowing the metaphor of inside and outside to suggest that practices are like the bodies of the players themselves, inwardly pure and driven by their own dynamics, confronted by external forces of corruption and greed. The idea is that performance drugs, like an invading microorganism, infiltrate from the outside to foul the internal workings of sports, the athletes themselves, distorting their skills, depriving them of the internal goods of the sports, and motivating them toward the external rewards of larger social institutions. The argument then goes something like this. Performance drugs are not relevant to the internal goods of sports which derive from "achieving those standards of excellence" characteristic of the practice. Their use tends rather to be driven by external goals of winning and victory and the fame or riches attendant on them.

But this argument is unpersuasive for several reasons. The first is that the basic distinction between internal and external goods, though serviceable for some purposes, blurs at crucial places. For example, there are clearly satisfactions to be gained from the exercise of the skills one develops in sport. Such skills are largely specific to given sports: taking a turn on a 400m track and other tactical skills in a foot race, for example, are not easily carried over to golf or basketball. This is due by and large to the arbitrary character of sports, their curious separateness from the skills of the workplace and home. Nevertheless, such skills are sometimes carried over to other sports. And in sports where many diverse skills are called for—in the biathlon, triathlon, and decathlon, for example—skills developed in one sport are transferable to others. No matter that the combination often limits performance to less than that of the specialist; the satisfaction of each skill's development, not just in their combination, is still present. But now such skills and their attendant satisfactions must be both internal and external to specific sports, and if transferable to practices other than the sports themselves—as are the skills, many argue, of teamwork, cooperativeness, and planning—are doubly external.

Or take the good of winning. Winning it is said is an external good of sports and as such would seem to cut across various sports. But winning in one sport is surely not the same as winning in another, and winning at one level of competition is surely different from winning at another. Indeed winning surely emerges as the final, overall configuration of the game itself, internal to the dynamics of the play, its culmination, not an externally imposed determination by those external to the activity. Even in those rare cases where controversial results lead to reviews by others, they are decided by the internal constraints of the sport, not by external institutional needs. And the rewards of winning may be internal or external. True, fortune is usually introduced from outside sports these days, but fame and admiration run deep within the sports themselves and are not just the province of institutional or social renown.

Health and fitness would seem to be external goods imposed on sports, as we have seen in our earlier discussion of the effects of performance drugs. But both are elusive. Fitness is to sports as intelligence is to tests: both seem specific to the ways in which they are measured, by essentially arbitrary cultural norms. Just as there seems no clear way to measure a general intelligence or IQ, so there seems no way to measure general fitness beyond capabilities developed in specific sports or other activities. (Questions like, "Are musicians smarter than lawyers?" give place to "Are basketball players more fit than swimmers?") Health is a notoriously slippery concept. Indeed, it is an uneasy companion of sports like boxing, mountain climbing, football, and many others, which carry with them inherent risks of injury that may be reduced but not eliminated: those risks are integral to the sports themselves and help define the excitement and challenge that are among their internal goods.

So little is to be gained for our purposes from the distinction between internal and external goods. And this is brought out by the second reason, that performance drugs are intended to enhance performance, as measured by the sports' own activities and standards, their own internal goods. Schneider and Butcher have argued that such enhancement is tantamount to changing the skills required by a sport and thus "changes the sport." But this claim is implausible. Training at high altitude greatly enhances the oxygen transport capacity of long-distance runners, but few would argue that it changes the skills required to run a marathon or changes the sport itself. The jump shot, a basketball skill first performed in the late 1940s, changed the sport only in the sense that it added excitement and challenge to the game. Indeed, Schneider and Butcher emphasize this point themselves. And to the extent that performance drugs could enhance performance, they would contribute to the exercise of skills at a higher level where the challenges and satisfactions might be all the greater.

Surely this is the reason why athletes have always tried to better their opponents, to find ways to excel, in spite of the fact that no one doubts that their secrets to success will soon be out. No one would seek to ignore a new training technique, equipment modification, or diet on the grounds that since one's opponents will soon catch on, the discovery will just escalate the competition, soon making it harder than ever to win. To this extent, sports recapitulate life and reflect a constant striving to win and enjoy, to compete and share in the competition of the game. In this sense, performance drugs may be as relevant to sports and their internal goods as any other way of enhancing one's performance. . . .

7. Slippery Slopes

Another way, I think, of expressing worries that some have about performance drugs is by seeing their claims as slippery slope arguments. I have considerable sympathy for such arguments because they force us to consider longer-range consequences of proposals and to factor in both the past history of human folly and the broad outlines of human behavior as telling evidence for prospects of the future. I have touched on this kind of argument by noting that we might imagine that performance drugs were highly significant factors in athletic achievements rather than marginal or sometimes even negative ones as they now in fact seem to be. In such imaginary circumstances, it is probable that our sports would change. Certainly high-performance sports or professional sports might well come to seem far different for us as spectators from the everyday variety of sports that most of us participate in as amateurs. But in many ways, this is already true. Few of us play basketball or tennis or swim in ways that even our fantasies can liken to professional or even collegiate athletics. So such changes are not necessarily ones we need deplore. The range of abilities and achievements in sports is already enormous and provides niches for us all to enjoy our various skills and interests.

Furthermore, performances in sports have changed in astonishing ways over the last century independently of what we now think of as performance drugs. Training methods, diet, equipment, and above all the selection of the most gifted potential athletes from larger pools have all contributed to these changes that are, I suspect, far greater than any we might expect by the use of performance drugs even in the distant future. . . .

But if performance drugs are allowed, what's next? Aren't there further ways in which athletic performance could be enhanced? And are we to tolerate these, too, in the name of personal choice and autonomy on the part of athletes? For example, some years ago someone invented a mechanical device for moving one's legs fast enough to enable one to run at record-breaking speed. We need only recall the fictional "bionic man" of television to imagine more sophisticated aids to physical activity. Such cases seem to challenge our very conception of athletic endeavor. As Robert Simon noted, "If all we are interested in is better and better performance, we could design robots" to do it for us. But, of course, what we are interested in is human performance, our own and that of those we watch as spectators, though we can easily imagine interest in android or robot performance, too, just as we acknowledge our interest in competition among other animals in dog and horse racing, for example. But the issue here is the limits of human performance, even the limits of what is to count as human for purposes of sport. So let's consider whether there are some reasonable stopping places on the slippery slope.

One place is the body's own basic boundary, the skin (though it is a porous and partial boundary at best). The differences between sports that are most evident are the differences in equipment and technical aids: the balls, bats, padding, skates, skis, cars, spikes, and other paraphernalia that define different sports, even the other animals who are used sometimes to augment human efforts. Changing the type of equipment in effect changes the identity of the sport. Changing the quality of the equipment also changes the sport, but not its identity, though it complicates efforts to compare performances across such equipment changes and sometimes requires minor changes in the rules. So where the slippery slope involves modifications of equipment, we can easily accept the new technologies as changing the sport.

The problem with performance drugs is that they are integrated into the body's own biosynthetic and metabolic pathways and so are intended to change the performance quality of the athlete, not the circumstances of the sport as defined by its goals, equipment, and rules. Here the slippery slope may yield the more difficult case where the last two possibilities come together, integration into the body of nonbiological technologies. If we condone the use of performance drugs, why not also the use of bionic implants, of artificial bones or organs? Most of the surgery available today for athletes is restorative, repairing the ravages of sports injuries. But not all. Some surgery may enhance performance, allowing greater muscle development or range of movement. And if this were possible on a wider scale, would we consider it, like performance drugs, to be liable to control? Should tissue implants to increase metabolic activity be forbidden? Should surgically improved visual acuity be outlawed? These are the stuff of science fiction for the most part, but we can begin to see the possibility of such procedures.

To some extent, we are at a loss to answer these questions, and not just for sports. Our fears about such changes run deep. Would such procedures be fraught with severe side effects that would make their transient benefits pale by adverse comparison? Do they finally threaten our sense of human identity to a degree that we would find intolerable? Do they hold out the prospects of further divisions among us, not only by wealth, race, and belief, but also by health, talent, and access to biotechnology? I do not have adequate answers to these questions. Even after we satisfy ourselves of the reasonable safety of performance drugs or other performance enhancers (assuming that we could do that), many of these other questions would remain. But they are not limited to the case of sports. These fundamental issues are the spawn of biological technology in general and its possible future impact on our society. It is probably impossible to decide them in advance of the actual development of our knowledge and technology.

8. PERSONHOOD

I want now to look at an argument that . . . performance drugs, by stressing the physical competence of athletes, detract from their qualities as persons and hence corrupt the ideal of sport as competition among persons. The gist of the argument seems to be that performance drugs somehow provide a physical boost to athletic ability that is totally separate from the personal qualities we often cherish in athletes, such as perseverance, good judgment, sportsmanship, grace under pressure, and a striving for excellence. Sometimes, the argument goes further in stressing that when some athletes use performance drugs, they force others to use them, contrary to their desires and hence can corrupt their autonomy and freedom as persons.

These are serious claims, but are they cogent? Two considerations suggest that they are not. One is that the use of performance drugs is no different in these effects than are other ways that athletes develop their skills and capacities or enhance their competitive performance. The other is that none of these approaches to developing their excellence need undermine the athletes' qualities as persons. Consider the first of these two points. Athletes use a variety of means to improve their skills and extend their capacities to perform in their chosen sports. Training methods and diets are obvious ones, but many other techniques are common including psychological counseling and, above all, practice and competition which can develop mental toughness and tactical acuity. Performance drugs can also be used to promote training and the development of athletic skills. They are never a substitute for the hard work of general athletic preparation, and, if they are useful at all, are helpful in enhancing the effects of that work, not in substituting for it. Living at high altitude promotes the body's production of red blood cells, but it is worth little if training is absent. The same is true in actual performance. Performance drugs do not provide skill, stamina, and knowledge; at most, they give a boost to those already developed.

So far, then, performance drugs seem no more a threat to an athlete's "personhood" than any other technique of training or performance. Little is to be gained by stressing that performance drugs have effects on one's body: that's the point of them, as it is of most athletic training and practice. But it is worth noting that there are few other experiences in life outside of sports where we feel so unified in mind and body, where the distinction between being persons and having bodies seems so fatuous. And nothing, so far as I can see, in the use of performance drugs need threaten the development of those personal qualities that we often value in athletes. If it is true that some performance drugs can alter mood and outlook, then careful study is needed to determine how these can affect one's personality. But pep talks, rivalries, and counseling can also affect mood and attitude, as can the sports themselves and are indeed relied on to do so as teams and individuals gear up for tough competition. If we are worried about performance drugs affecting moods, then we must also consider other tried and true methods for doing the same thing. Presumably it is only some moods, perhaps aggressive ones, that are said to be objectionable. If so, then much in the way certain sports are played and

their players are developed must be changed as well. Performance drugs, like other athletic techniques, work primarily to enhance what is already there.

Again, it is said that athletes are coerced into choosing to use performance drugs, a curious contradictory claim in itself, by the fact that if some competitors use them, others must use them as well in order to compete successfully. But this is surely true of all changes in technique or training or tactics that athletes develop, as I have already noted. No one can introduce a successful change without others adopting it if they wish to compete successfully. We do not usually suggest that this denies athletes their autonomy. If you can't develop a good jump shot, or move to Colorado to train in the mountains, or develop a new tactical ploy, it is not your autonomy or free choice that is threatened. There may be an element of unfairness when the adoption of new techniques depends on wealth or special knowledge. But this may be the case for many features of dynamic and changing sports, not just for the use of performance drugs. The remedy would seem to be openness and research, not banning and secrecy. . . .

Our sports have changed over the years. The days of the leisured amateur performing with elegant insouciance seem quaint and puzzling in an age of professionalism and "high-performance" skills driven by commerce and nationalism. There is much to deplore in these changes, but much also to commend. We have seen the end to racism in American sport and positive efforts to resolve the problems of full participation in sports for women. Amateur and school sports flourish as never before. But because sports present so visibly to us a view of what it is to be human (though to be sure in only one of the many ways we understand ourselves), they are a focus of the concerns we have about the impact on human life of modern technologies, especially biomedical technologies. We should not, I believe, either reject or embrace these technologies uncritically, but study and reflect on the way they are changing our lives and our conceptions of who we are. They will continue to change us and our sports. I have argued not so much for the use of performance drugs as for the flourishing in sports of a critical exploration of their use and its impact on how we understand our skills and achievements.

EXERCISES

1. Genetic scientists have discovered that injecting specific genetic materials cause mice to increase muscle density by an average of 25 percent and the mice don't have to lift weights to achieve the increase. Leaving aside the very substantial health risks, suppose that we gave such injections to all NFL players, who by next season had added an extra 25 percent muscle density (the 240 pound running back end is now about

300 pounds of super dense muscle). Suppose that this innovation were used by *everyone* in the league. From the perspective of the fan watching the game: Would that make NFL football better, or worse, or would it have no effect?

2. I have a special drug, and it will turn you into a brilliant musician (or novelist, physicist, philosopher, or gymnast—take your choice). Your candle will burn very bright but briefly: the drug will cut your life expectancy in half. The question is not whether you would choose to take the drug; rather, should you have the *choice* to take such a drug, or should it be banned?

3. Following up on the previous question: Suppose that this new drug enhances musical performance to such a degree that those not taking the drug cannot compete, and all opportunities for professional musical performance are monopolized by those taking the drug. Would those who desire a career in musical performance but do not wish to take this dangerous drug have grounds for complaint?

4. One key point on which Robert Simon and W. M. Brown disagree is whether drug-enhanced athletic performance is a threat to the athlete's "personhood": as Simon puts it, if athletic performance is drug-enhanced, the result may be that "athletes are no longer reacting to each other as persons but rather become more like competing bodies." How strong is this objection? Is it possible to formulate this objection more precisely than Simon does? Does Brown have an adequate response?

5. Appearing before a San Francisco grand jury investigating drug use in baseball, Gary Roberts—a Tulane University expert in sports law—testified that "For all we know, the American public may not give a damn. They may be happy if all their gladiators were stoked up on steroids and hitting 500 home runs." *Should* sports *fans* have a voice in this issue?

6. While drug- or steroid-enhanced athletic performance and blood doping have received lots of attention (cases from the Olympics, Major League Baseball, and NFL Football spring to mind), many scientists believe we are only at the earliest stages of artificially enhancing athletic performance, and that in the near future there will be genetic enhancement techniques that would produce much more dramatic effects, with perhaps considerably greater dangers to the athletes, and that such genetic enhancement will be remarkably expensive. Should genetic enhancement be treated differently from performance-enhancing drugs? That is, could you consistently favor allowing performance-enhancing drugs but ban genetic enhancement?

7. "Tommy John" surgery (doctors call it UCL, or ulnar collateral ligament reconstruction) often makes baseball pitchers *more* effective than they were prior to their injury and surgery. If UCL surgery reached a level at which it could reliably improve one's pitching ability, would it be legitimate for athletes to have such surgery when they had suffered no prior injury? Would it be ethically legitimate for a surgeon to perform such surgery (on players without injuries) or would that violate the principles of medical ethics?

ADDITIONAL READING

John Hoberman, "Listening to Steroids," offers an interesting history of the issue, with particular attention to the tension between the desire for drugs that enhance, restore, and rejuvenate and, on the other side, the widespread distrust of pharmacological solutions to our problems. Hoberman also examines the contrast between our negative attitude toward using drugs for athletic enhancement and our at least tacit approval of drug use for enhancement of musical performances. The article, along with many others on a variety of topics, can be found in an excellent anthology edited by William J. Morgan, Klaus V. Meier, and Angela J. Schneider, *Ethics in Sport* (Champaign, IL.: Human Kinetics, 1991).

Dr. Robert Voy, the former Chief Medical Officer for the United States Olympic Committee, is opposed to the use of drugs to enhance athletic performance and is disturbed by the extent to which drugs are currently involved in sports. His book, *Drugs, Sport, and Politics* (Champaign, IL: Leisure Press, 1991), gives an interesting inside view of the problems, as well as his proposals for reform.

An interesting discussion of some of the changes in sport driven by professionalism and commercialism can be found in William Morgan, *Leftist Theories of Sport: A Critique and Reconstruction* (Urbana and Chicago, IL: University of Illinois Press, 1994).

An excellent general collection on ethics and sports is Jan Boxill, editor, *Sports Ethics* (Oxford: Blackwell Publishing, 2003). Another good anthology, with an excellent collection of articles on athletics and drugs, is William J. Morgan and Klaus V. Meier, Editors, *Philosophic Inquiry in Sport*, 2nd ed. (Champaign, IL: Human Kinetics, 1995).

20

Can Terrorism Ever Be Justified?

It is always important to have clear definitions that do not prejudge important ethical issues, but it is particularly important when dealing with terrorism. Suppose that a government directed its armed forces to make a missile attack against an office building in another country; would that count as a terrorist attack? There is no reason to believe that the Saudi government had any knowledge of or involvement in the attack on the Twin Towers; but *if* the Saudi citizens who hijacked the airliners and attacked the Twin Towers had been military personnel acting under orders of the Saudi government, would that still have been a terrorist attack? The answers to those questions will depend, obviously, on how terrorism is defined. And definitions are not always neutral: under the preferred U.S. State Department definition of terrorism, official acts by states can never count as terrorist acts.

Terrorism often involves the killing of innocent people. Is terrorism, then, always an unjustified wrong? That conclusion is not quite so obvious. After all, we know that making war on a country will involve the killing of innocents; but most people believe that war is sometimes justified. If it is sometimes acceptable to kill innocents for the political purposes of war, why would it never be acceptable to kill innocents for the political purposes of a terrorist group (for example, if the terrorist group is seeking recognition of what it regards as its legitimate claim for territorial independence as a sovereign country)? Or suppose a country is under foreign occupation, perhaps a very brutal occupation. Those who want to throw off the occupation typically cannot declare war against their occupiers: they have no resources for raising or equipping armies. If it is wrong for them to plant a bomb in a city of the occupying country in a terrorist strike aimed at forcing the occupier to leave, how could it be right for a nation to bomb the city of an enemy that is attempting to forcibly conquer and occupy that nation?

⇥ TERRORISM IS ALWAYS WRONG ⇤
C. A. J. (Tony) Coady

C. A. J. (Tony) Coady is Australian Research Council Senior Research Fellow in Philosophy at the University of Melbourne; this essay is excerpted from "Terrorism, Just War and Supreme Emergency," in C. A. J. (Tony) Coady and Michael O'Keefe, editors, *Terrorism and Justice: Moral Argument in a Threatened World* (Melbourne University Press, 2002).

What Is Terrorism?

Defining terrorism is a hazardous task. It has been estimated that there are well over one hundred different definitions of terrorism in the scholarly literature. This disarray reflects the highly polemical contexts in which the term is used so that the act of defining can become a move in a campaign rather than an aid to thought. Consider some influential definitions picked out by the Terrorism Research Center in the United States.

1. 'Terrorism is the use or threatened use of force designed to bring about political change.'
2. 'Terrorism constitutes the illegitimate use of force to achieve a political objective when innocent people are targeted.'
3. 'Terrorism is the premeditated, deliberate, systematic murder, mayhem, and threatening of the innocent to create fear and intimidation in order to gain a political or tactical advantage, usually to influence an audience.'
4. 'Terrorism is the unlawful use or threat of violence against persons or property to further political or social objectives. It is usually intended to intimidate or coerce a government, individuals or groups, or to modify their behaviour or politics.'
5. 'Terrorism is the unlawful use of force or violence against persons or property to intimidate or coerce a government, the civilian population, or any segment thereof, in furtherance of political or social objectives.'

We might note that . . . [the first] definition has the consequence that all forms of war are terrorist. Whatever verdict we give on war, it is surely just confusing to equate all forms of it, including the armed resistance to Hitler, with terrorism. More interestingly, several of the definitions make use of the idea of unlawful or illegitimate violence, but this seems to fudge too many questions about what is wrong with terrorism. The idea of the illegal simply raises the issue of what and whose laws are being broken—armed internal resistance to Hitler by German citizens would arguably have been justified, yet it would certainly have been against German law. And the adjective illegitimate needs unpacking in terms of what makes this or that use of force illegitimate.

Rather than further reviewing the varieties of definition, I propose to concentrate on one key element in common responses to and fears about terrorism, namely the idea that it involves 'innocent' victims. This element features in several of the quoted definitions. It was recently overtly invoked by Yasser Arafat's

condemnation of terrorism when he said: 'no degree of oppression and no level of desperation can ever justify the killing of innocent civilians. I condemn terrorism, I condemn the killing of innocent civilians, whether they are Israeli, American or Palestinian.' It also usefully provides a point of connection with the moral apparatus of just war theory, specifically the principle of discrimination and its requirement of non-combatant immunity. Of course, terrorism does not always take place in the context of all-out international war, but it usually has a warlike dimension. I will define it as follows: 'the organised use of violence to target non-combatants ("innocents" in a special sense) for political purposes.'

This definition has several contentious consequences. One is that states can themselves use terrorism, another is that much political violence by non-state agents will not be terrorist. As to the former, there is a tendency, especially among the representatives of states, to restrict the possibility of terrorist acts to non-state agents. But if we think of terrorism, in the light of the definition above, as a tactic rather than an ideology, this tendency should be resisted, since states can and do use the tactic of attacking the innocent. This is why allegations of terrorism against Israeli government forces in parts of Palestine during the anti-terrorist campaign in 2002 made perfect sense, even if the truth of the claims was contentious.

Some theorists who think terrorism cannot be perpetrated by governments are not so much confused as operating with a different definition. They define terrorism, somewhat in the spirit of the FBI definition, as the use of political violence by non-state agents against the state. Some would restrict it to violence against a democratic state. This is the way many political scientists view terrorism. Call this the political definition to contrast with the tactical definition.

A further consequence of the tactical definition is that it implies a degree of purposiveness that terrorism is thought to lack. Some theorists have claimed that terrorism is essentially 'random,' others that it is essentially 'expressive.' In both cases, the claim is that a reference to political purposes is inappropriate. In reply, it can be argued that talk of terrorism as random is generated by the genuine perception that it does not restrict its targets to the obvious military ones, but this does not mean that it is wild and purposeless. Indeed, most terrorists think that the best way to get certain political effects is to aim at 'soft' non-combatant targets. Similarly, there can be no doubt that many terrorist attacks are expressive and symbolic, involving the affirmation of the attitude: 'We are still here; take notice of us.' Yet the expressive need not exclude the purposive. So terrorist acts can be, and usually are, both expressive and politically purposive. It is a further question whether these purposes are particularly realistic. The idea that terrorist acts are merely expressive is partly sustained by the belief that when viewed as purposive the acts are basically futile. The futility is often real enough, but purposive acts abound that are in fact futile. Note that I am not *defining* terrorism as immoral: it needs discussion and some background moral theory to show that it is immoral.

The Just War Tradition

It is time to say a few words about the just war tradition that provides much of that background. In the just war tradition, this account has two key divisions—the *jus ad bellum* and the *jus in bello*. The former tells us the conditions under which it can be right to resort to war, the latter is concerned to guide us in the permissible methods by which we should wage a legitimate war.

Under the *jus ad bellum* it is common to list the following conditions:

1. War must be declared and waged by legitimate authority.
2. There must be a just cause for going to war.
3. War must be a last resort.
4. There must be reasonable prospect of success.
5. The violence used must be proportional to the wrong being resisted.

Under the *jus in bello* there are basically two governing principles:

1. *The Principle of Discrimination*—this limits the kind of violence that can be used, principally by placing restrictions on what count as legitimate targets.
2. *The Principle of Proportionality*—this limits the degree of response by requiring that the violent methods used do not inflict more damage than the original offence could require.

There are clearly many difficulties with these conditions, but equally clearly they make initial intuitive sense. In this brief discussion, I shall concentrate on the Principle of Discrimination since it is the principle most relevant to my approach to terrorism.

Moral restrictions on how one conducts oneself in war are apt to be met with incredulity. 'You do what needs to be done to win' is a common response. There is a certain appeal in this pragmatic outlook, but it flies in the face not only of just war thinking but of many common human responses to war. The concept of an

atrocity, for instance, has a deep place in our thinking. Even that very tough warrior, the US war ace General Chuck Yeager writes in his memoirs that he suffered genuine moral revulsion at orders to commit 'atrocities' that he was given and complied with in World War II. He was especially 'not proud' of his part in the indiscriminate strafing of a 50 square mile area of Germany that included mainly non-combatants.

A major part of the discrimination principle concerns the immunity of non-combatants from direct attack.

Various questions have been raised about the making of the combatant/non-combatant distinction in the context of modern war. The first point of clarification is that when we classify people as non-combatants or innocents we do not mean that they have no evil in their hearts, nor do we mean that combatants are necessarily full of evil thoughts. The classification is concerned with the role the individual plays in the chain of agency directing the aggression or wrongdoing. And it is agency, not mere cause, that is important since the soldier's aged parents may be part of the causal chain that results in his being available to fight without their having any agent responsibility for what the soldier is doing. The combatant may be coerced to fight, but is still prosecuting the war, even if the greater blame lies with those who coerce. On the other hand, young school children may be enthusiastic about their country's war, but are not prosecuting it. Neither are the farmers whose products feed the troops, for they would feed them (if they'd buy) whatever their role. It should be added that the combatant/non-combatant distinction is not equivalent to the soldier/civilian distinction even though they overlap considerably. Some civilians, such as political leaders and senior public servants, will be legitimate targets if they are actively directing or promoting unjust violence whether or not they wear uniforms or bear arms.

But even when these distinctions are made there seems room not only for doubt about the application of the distinction to various difficult categories of person such as slave labourers coerced to work in munitions factories but also its applicability at all to the highly integrated citizenry of modern states. Some people say that it is surely anachronistic to think of contemporary war as waged between armies; it is really nation against nation, economy against economy, peoples against peoples. But although modern war has many unusual features, its 'total' nature is more an imposed construction than a necessary reflection of changed reality. Even in World War II not every enemy citizen was a combatant. In any war, there remain millions of people who are not plausibly seen as involved in the enemy's lethal chain of agency. There are, for instance, infants, young children, the elderly and infirm, lots of tradespeople and workers, not to mention dissidents and conscientious objectors. This challenge to the distinction requires there to be no serious moral difference between shooting a soldier who is shooting at you and gunning down a defenceless child who is a member of the same nation as the soldier. The conclusion is perhaps sufficiently absurd or obscene to discredit the argument.

In fact, there has been a remarkable change on this issue in the strategic doctrine and military outlook of many major powers since the end of the Cold War. It is now common to pay at least lip service to the principle, as evidenced by certain restraint shown or announced during the Gulf War, and the bombing of Serbia, and by the widespread condemnation of Russian brutality in Chechnya. The rhetoric, at least, of the recent US-led war in Afghanistan is also respectful of the distinction. The real question is not so much whether it is immoral to target non-combatants (it is), but how 'collateral' damage and death to non-combatants can be defended. The conduct of war in contemporary circumstances is morally impossible unless the activities of warriors are allowed to put non-combatants at risk in certain circumstances. Some modification to the immunity principle to allow indirect harming seems to be in line with commonsense morality in other areas of life, and to be necessitated by the circumstances of war. If it is not available, then pacifism, as Holmes has argued, seems the only moral option.

The tactical definition of terrorism faces the problems already discussed concerning the meaning of the term 'non-combatant,' but even more acutely. In guerilla war, for instance, insurgents may not be easily identifiable as combatants, and will seek to enlist or involve the villagers and local inhabitants in the campaign, thereby blurring their status as non-combatants. On the other hand, many state officials who are not directly prosecuting the campaign against the insurgents may be plausibly viewed as implicated in the grievances the revolutionaries are seeking to redress. There are certainly problems here, but they do not seem insurmountable. In the heat and confusion of battle, it may be difficult and dangerous to treat even children as non-combatants, especially where children are coerced or seduced into combatant roles (as is common in many contemporary conflicts). Nonetheless, a premeditated campaign of bombing regional hospitals to induce civilian lack of cooperation with rebels is in palpable violation of the *jus in bello*. So are the murder of infants, and the targeting of state officials, such as water authorities

or traffic police, whose roles are usually tangentially related to the causes of the conflict. It is true that some ideologies purport to have enemies so comprehensive as to make even small children and helpless adults 'combatants.' Western advocates of strategic bombing of cities in the name of 'total war' share with the Islamic fanatics who incorporate American air travellers and sundry citizens of Manhattan into their holy targets a simplistic and Manichaean vision of the world. This vision is at odds with the just war tradition's attempt to bring some moral sanity to bear upon the use of political violence.

WAR, TERRORISM AND 'SUPREME EMERGENCY'

Is terrorism wrong? Given just war theory and the tactical definition, the answer is clearly yes. And if one takes the principle of non-combatant immunity to invoke an absolute moral prohibition, as just war thinkers have commonly done, then it is always wrong. Yet many contemporary moral philosophers, sympathetic to just war thinking, are wary of moral absolutes. They would treat the prohibition as expressing a very strong moral presumption against terrorism and the targeting of non-combatants, but allow for exceptions in extreme circumstances. So, Michael Walzer thinks that in conditions of 'supreme emergency' the violation of the normal immunity is permissible in warfare, though only with a heavy burden of remorse. He thinks the Allied terror bombing of German cities in World War II (in the early stages) was legitimated by the enormity of the Nazi threat. John Rawls has recently endorsed this view while condemning the bombings of Hiroshima and Nagasaki. If this concession is allowed to states, it seems mere consistency to allow it to non-state agents on the same terms. The general reluctance to do so suggests that such categories as 'supreme emergency' may mask contestable political judgements.

The basic idea, we may here take from the tradition, plausibly traceable to Machiavelli, is that certain necessities of life may require the overriding of profound and otherwise 'absolute' moral prohibitions in extreme situations. Walzer's defence of the terror bombing of German cities in World War II in terms of 'supreme emergency' is clearly in the tradition, and provides a useful focus for discussing its relevance to terrorism. Walzer does not defend the bombing unequivocally. He thinks that, though it was morally wrong as a violation of the principle of discrimination, it was justified by the plea of supreme emergency in the early stages of the war. In the later stages, however, it was just plain morally criminal, since an Allied victory could be reasonably foreseen on the basis of morally legitimate targeting and fighting. The bombing of Dresden was therefore an outright atrocity, though the bombing of other German cities up to 1942 was not. He is clear that the bombing in this earlier phase was a violation of the principle of discrimination, and at one point calls it 'terrorism.' It was morally wrong, and implies guilt, but had to be done.

Walzer's use of the category 'supreme emergency' here is based on the idea that the need to defeat Nazi Germany was no ordinary necessity. Hitler's victory would have been a dire blow to civilisation. The enormity of his regime and its practices was such that his extended empire would have been a disaster for most of the people living under its sway. In addition, the threat of Hitler's victory was present and urgent, and the bombing of German cities aimed directly at the civilian populations was the only offensive weapon the British had.

A CRITIQUE OF THE SUPREME EMERGENCY DEFENCE

A . . . curiosity of Walzer's argument is that it is presented primarily as an argument available to states and their representatives. But, if we think only of the connotations of 'supreme emergency,' it is not at all obvious that the issue can be so restricted. Palestinian resistance groups, for example, can mount a powerful case that they face a hostile power bent upon subordination and dispossession to a degree that threatens not only their lives but their way of life. Even the various groups around Osama bin Laden may well see themselves as qualifying for this exemption. No doubt it can be argued that there are various delusions and mistakes in their outlooks, but the history of warfare is replete with similar delusions and mistakes.

My own view is that the supreme emergency story suffers from grave defects whether it is offered as an exemption on behalf of a state, or some less established political community, or a group claiming to represent either. The first problem is that it undervalues the depth and centrality of the prohibition on killing the innocent. In spite of Walzer's agonising about the need to acknowledge that we have violated an important moral restraint by our bombing or other terror tactic, he locates the prohibition on attacking non-combatants within what he calls 'the war convention.' Although, there is some unclarity about what he means by this, the terminology suggests that the prohibition is itself somehow merely conventional. On the contrary, it is, as I have argued, basic to what makes it legitimate to wage a just war at all. More generally, the prohibition on

intentionally killing innocent people functions in our moral thinking as a sort of touchstone of moral and intellectual health. To suspend this, because of necessity or supreme emergency, is to bring about an upheaval in the moral perspective.

My second point is that the primacy of the political community that lies behind much of the dirty hands debate is highly suspect. Walzer admits of individuals that they can never attack innocent people to aid their self-defence. He then adds: 'But communities, in emergencies, seem to have different and larger prerogatives. I am not sure that I can account for the difference, without ascribing to communal life a land of transcendence that I don't believe it to have.' Walzer goes on to try to locate the 'difference' in the supposed fact that 'the survival and freedom of political communities . . . are the highest values of international society.' Maybe they are the highest values of international society, but this is hardly surprising if one construes international society as a society of political communities, namely recognised states. What is needed, at the very least, is an argument that locates the survival and freedom of political communities as the highest *human* value, and one that is capable of justifying the overriding that 'supreme emergency' requires. I doubt that any such argument exists. Certainly, it is not enough to point to the undoubted value of political life for there are many other values that are equally, if not more, significant.

A third consideration against the dirty hands story in its 'supreme emergency' form is that admission of this exemption is likely to generate widespread misuse of it. On Walzer's own account the 'legitimate' resort to terror in the early stages of World War II led rapidly to its illegitimate use thereafter. It is surely plain enough that the widespread resort to state terror in various contexts has been justified in ways that parallel Walzer's apologetic, and non-state agents are not slow to follow suit. We surely do better to condemn the resort to terrorism outright with no leeway for exemptions, be they for states, revolutionaries or religious zealots.

MORAL RESPONSE

Finally what sorts of violent responses to terrorism can be morally legitimate? The first thing to say of this is that the use of terrorism to combat terrorism should be ruled out. Attacking the innocent is illicit when used by non-state groups and it is wrong when used by states in response. Two wrongs do not make a right. Second, the use of violence to capture or even kill terrorists is legitimate if it accords with the conditions of the *jus ad bellum* that govern the morality of resort to war. One of the crucial conditions most relevant here, and especially relevant to the present 'war against terrorism,' is whether the exercise is likely to achieve success. Here it is difficult to know what success amounts to. Venting of rage or grief is hardly sufficient. Bringing the agents of terrorist attack to justice or destroying them would seem a legitimate aim, as would diminishing the future prospect of terrorist attacks. At the time of writing, it is unclear whether the war in Afghanistan has fulfilled these aims. A further campaign of violence against the nations classified by President Bush as forming an 'axis of evil' looks even more problematic from this point of view. It is also doubtful whether it would satisfy the conditions of last resort and proportionality. Finally, and more generally, massive aerial bombardments to aid the military overthrow of ugly regimes is likely to be politically and morally inadequate as a response to terrorism. The paradigm of state-against-state warfare is ill adapted to the threat of terrorists like al-Qaeda since such terrorists are not state-based, are relatively independent of the host nations they infest, and breed on the oppression and injustice in the international order that remain unaddressed by campaigns of violence. Bombing campaigns like that in Afghanistan inevitably produce alarmingly high numbers of non-combatant casualties and damage to civilian infrastructure. Even where these are not directly intended their scale can betray an immoral indifference to innocent life.

⇒ TERRORISM MIGHT SOMETIMES BE JUSTIFIED ⇐
Gabriel Palmer-Fernandez

Gabriel Palmer-Fernandez is a professor in the Department of Philosophy and Religion and Director of the Dale Ethics Center at Youngstown State University; the reading is excerpted from his "Terrorism, Innocence, and Justice," *Philosophy & Public Policy Quarterly* (Spring 2005).

On May 21, 1856, proslavery forces from Missouri attacked the antislavery town of Lawrence, Kansas. They looted stores, burned buildings, and assaulted residents. Three days later, John Brown, proclaiming himself the servant of the Lord, and his group of antislavery fighters sought revenge by killing five proslavery farmers along the Pottawatomie Creek. At the Doyle farm, James and his two sons were hacked to death. Mrs. Doyle, a daughter, and a fourteen-year-old son were spared. Brown and his fighters then moved on to a second farm, where Allen Wilkinson was taken prisoner, and finally to a third where William Sherman was executed. The attack on Lawrence and the killings at Pottawatomie Creek sparked a guerilla war between proslavery and antislavery forces in Missouri and Kansas. It lasted several months and cost nearly two hundred lives.

Brown's campaign against slavery won him many supporters in the North, particularly among a group of wealthy New Englanders. With their help, Brown moved to Virginia where he hoped to start a slave rebellion. In 1859 he raided the United States armory in Harper's Ferry and held some sixty hostages. He was defeated, arrested and charged with inciting a slave insurrection, murder, and treason. In a plea for Brown's life, Henry David Thoreau said, Brown "was like the best of those who stood on Concord Bridge . . . . You who pretend to care for Christ crucified, consider what you are about to do to him who offered himself to be the savior of four millions of men." On December 1859, Brown was hanged. But in the North, church services and public meetings glorified his deeds. Ralph Waldo Emerson, for example, said that Brown's execution would "make the gallows glorious as the cross." Some years later, in an address given at Harper's Ferry, Frederick Douglass praised Brown's unequalled dedication to the cause of abolition by saying, "I could live for the slave, but he could die for him."

The activities of John Brown and his militia have been repeated countless times throughout the world, particularly in the past few decades. Men and women organize themselves into a group and engage in acts of violence for a political objective. Sometimes they wish to have their own separate homeland or defeat a foreign aggressor—the IRA in Ireland, ETA in Spain, Irgun in Israel, Tamil Tigers in Sri Lanka, FLN in Algeria, Hezbollah in Palestine. At other times they wish to overturn an unjust, tyrannical government and establish, as the Constitution of the United States declares, a "more perfect union." Such violence is almost always illegal. No state or system of law could long endure should it tolerate private violence, even for an important political objective. By almost all accounts, it is irregular violence, like vigilante justice, often biased in its own favor. Even when it elicits our sympathies, we regret if not fear this kind of violence. How, then, shall we think of John Brown? Was he a criminal, murderer, traitor, a religious zealot who killed and held hostage ordinary people? Was he a martyr whose selfless sacrifice contributed to the liberation of millions of children, women, and men from slavery?

I. TERRORISM

One response is that John Brown killed innocent civilians. That makes him a murderer. It doesn't matter that he was motivated by a strong sense of justice, abolishing that horrible institution of slavery. That is a view that is well established in international law and that long tradition of moral reasoning called the just war theory. Among the important provisions of that theory is the principle of noncombatant immunity. It says that civilians are innocent and on that account they are to be spared the ravages of war. They are immune from deliberate attack and killing them is, as Elizabeth Anscombe puts it, "always murder." But what is the meaning of innocence in war? Why may we kill soldiers but never the ordinary citizen? Were Douglass, Thoreau and Emerson wrong about making Brown's "gallows glorious as the cross"? Was Brown, in today's language, a terrorist or a freedom fighter?

We do well first to come to some conceptual understanding of terrorism. What is it? How does it differ from other forms of political violence? When we define terrorism we need to be careful not to confuse the conceptual with the moral issues. Some writers do just that, giving a definition of terrorism that makes terrorism always by its very nature an immoral activity. This makes any disagreement about the morality of terrorism a disagreement about its nature. Although it is difficult, we can distinguish one from the other.

In a recent article, C. A. J. Coady gives the following definition: terrorism is "the organized use of violence to target noncombatants ('innocents' in a special sense) for a political objective." At first sight this seems a very useful definition. It covers a broad range of relevant phenomena and allows us to distinguish political from criminal violence, and more important to recognize that terrorism is a tactic used not only by nonstate groups (Aum Shinrikyo, al-Qaida, KKK), but also by states themselves as a way of governing their citizens. Such an understanding is compatible with much of the history of terrorism. For example, the first English-language use of the word dates from 1795 and, like the French use that

appeared a few years earlier, describes a mode of governing aimed to suppress political dissent. Examples of state terrorism abound: the mass-drowning and massacre of helpless prisoners during The Reign of Terror under Robespierre in France; executions in the former Soviet Union under Stalin and in Haiti under "Papa Doc" Duvalier; the killing fields under Pol Pot in Cambodia; or the recent wave of torture, rapes, and arbitrary arrests in Equatorial Guinea, to name a few.

Coady's definition captures this important dimension of terrorism. However, there are a few problems with it. First, it does not address an important development in the history of terrorism. The emergence of anarchist movements in Russia, France, Spain, Italy, and the United States in the 19th century brought a new type of violence not by states but, as we say today, "from below," intended to bring about political change. Terrorism in this period referred to a way of fighting rather than governing and was largely restricted to the assassination of high political figures. There was during this period hardly a trace of indiscriminate violence or the desire to intimidate and create fear in a civilian population for a political objective. On the contrary, a crucial feature of terrorism during this period was the attempt to arouse the spirit of revolt by highly selective violence and assassinations. This understanding of terrorism continued well into the twentieth century. For example, in Hardman's entry in the *Encyclopedia of the Social Sciences,* published in 1934, indiscriminate violence was not yet a defining feature of terrorism: "Terrorist acts are directed against persons who as individuals, agents or representatives of authority interfere with the consummation of the objectives of group."

Now, contemporary terrorism differs from its predecessors in an important way. Perhaps as early as 1940, it emerged as a way of fighting by acts of indiscriminate violence with the goal of intimidating, creating fear, and undermining the morale of a population. The paradigm case is the intentional indiscriminate aerial bombardment of German cities during World War II, where it was thought that subjecting large segments of the population to the terror of aerial bombardment would produce domestic unrest and widespread opposition to the war. The use of terror by revolutionary or insurgent groups (as some in Iraq today) differs from indiscriminate aerial bombardment only in degree, not in kind. Both aim for the same objective, to undermine civilian morale for the sake of arousing political opposition, and employ the same means, random killing and other acts of indiscriminate violence.

Second, contemporary terrorism is not restricted solely to targeting persons. Several groups have emerged in the past decades that strike only at property. Radical elements of the environmental and animal rights movements have engaged in a wide range of violent actions aimed to change social policies and practices that pollute water and air, and destroy forests and animal species. In the 1980s, for example, some of these groups spiked trees in public lands in Maine, Maryland, and North Carolina, others firebombed research facilities at Oregon State, Michigan State and Washington State Universities, and still others sabotaged and sunk whaling vessels in Iceland.

The above concerns can easily be incorporated in Coady's definition. However, it has a further problem: by his account, terrorism targets the noncombatant—the ordinary civilian. This is problematic because there are many cases of killing soldiers that have a strong resemblance to terrorism. Consider the suicide bombing on October 1983 in Beirut that killed 241 American soldiers and 58 French paratroopers, or the identical attack on the U.S. military barracks at Khobar Towers in Saudi Arabia on June 1996. What about killing soldiers on leave as they dine with their families, or go to the grocery store, or drink a beer at the local bar? Or soldiers sent on humanitarian missions after natural disasters, like the recent tsunami in South Asia? Not the happiest way of putting it, but perhaps if we distinguish between soldiers, who are military personnel not in a condition of war, and combatants who are soldiers in war, we can understand why killing the French paratrooper or American soldier in Beirut and killing him on the battlefield are very different things. Combatants are soldiers in war. They are legitimate targets and killing them is an act of war. But soldiers (not in war) are much closer to civilians and killing them is an act of terror.

I propose, then, the following definition of the core feature of terrorism. Terrorism is the organized use of violence against civilians or their property, the political leadership of a nation, or soldiers (who are not combatants in a war) for political purposes. On this account, Robespierre, Stalin, Pol Pot, the radical environmentalists, the suicide bombers in Beirut and Saudi Arabia were terrorists. So, too, was John Brown. They killed civilians or destroyed their property or held hostages for a political purpose. We need now to determine whether what John Brown and other terrorists do is immoral. To do so, I first take up the question of innocence.

II. INNOCENCE

For Coady and many other writers, terrorism is immoral because it deliberately kills persons who are illegitimate targets, persons who are, Coady says, innocent in

a special sense, and those persons who are innocent in a special sense are the noncombatants. But these terms—illegitimate targets, innocence, and noncombatants—do not jibe. Furthermore, conflating them, as Coady does, confuses the conceptual and moral issues in terrorism. It smuggles the moral appraisal of terrorism into its definition, motivating the unavoidable conclusion that terrorism is, by definition, immoral.

The distinction between legitimate and illegitimate targets of attack has a long history. For example, the Hebrew Bible contains at least one passage that spares children and women from death in war, as well as livestock and fruit-bearing trees (Deuteronomy 20). The 14th century text by Honoré Bonet, *Tree of Battles*, explicitly prohibits the killing of ploughmen, laborers, pilgrims, and clerics (so, too the ox and the ass) because, Bonet writes, "they have no concern with war."

When Coady says that noncombatants are innocent in a "special sense," . . . innocence refers to the role one plays in the prosecution of a war. Noncombatants are innocent in the special sense that they do not bear arms, are not directly engaged in the prosecution of a war, and do not pose a danger of imminent death to enemy combatants. But this notion of innocence makes no moral sense, for at least two reasons. First, it assumes that the role of the civilian is much like that of the medieval serf who toils the soil now for this lord and later for another, as the knightly class competed for honor, status, glory, and land. If there is any moral sense to the notion of innocent civilian it is here that we find it: harmless persons alienated from the source of political power lacking any responsibility for the war. Under the political conditions of the time, there were no conscripts, volunteers, or citizen-soldiers. Armies consisted of hired guns of foreign mercenaries with little if any loyalty to a nation, but to the spoils and other material rewards of war. For them, war was not a political act or a form of public service. Civilians were immune from war only because they would later provide the source of labor the victor would need to profit from the newly conquered land. They were property, much like Bonet's ox and ass.

But the nature of war changed dramatically with the French Revolution. Political power went from the monarchy to the people. Consequently, war was no longer the king's or the knight's concern. It became the people's business. "The young men shall fight," the French National Convention declared in 1793, "married men shall forge weapons and transport supplies; women will make tents and clothes and will serve in the hospitals; the children will make up old linen into lint; the old men will have themselves carried into the public square to rouse the courage of the fighting men, to preach hatred of kings and the unity of the Republic." To assume that civilians are passive bystanders who, as Bonet puts it, "have no concern with war," fails to recognize that for modern democracies war is a complex institution in which civilians play a crucial role. They provide not only the public spirit essential for war, but also the material necessities for success.

Second, if civilians cannot be killed in war because they are innocent, we must recognize that innocents are always killed in war—not civilians, but morally innocent soldiers. Coady alludes to this point when he says that what is important is "the role the individual plays in the chain of agency directing the aggression or wrongdoing." Those who are in that chain directing aggression or wrongdoing are guilty and may (perhaps must) be killed. Some soldiers will surely be in that chain. But others fighting on behalf of justice and acting in self-defense are innocent and morally may not be killed. Suppose you unjustly attack me and I defend myself. Though I use lethal force against you, I am innocent of any aggression or wrongdoing. You do not have open to you to say that because I employ lethal force against you, you may do likewise and that killing me would not be wrong. Now, there are many soldiers who fit this description—innocent combatants fighting a war of self-defense. There will also likely be very many innocent combatants in totalitarian regimes whose leadership is guilty of aggression or wrongdoing, for example, forced conscripts in Baathist Iraq under Hussein in the 1991 Persian Gulf War. They were more cannon fodder than anything else. Combatants of totalitarian states hardly have any responsibility for the wars they fight and even when they fight an unjust war (like Hussein's aggression against Kuwait in 1990) seem more like Bonet's serf, ox or ass having no responsibility for the war. But civilians of democratic nations are not like Bonet's serf, mere property used now by this lord and then the other, or combatants of totalitarian regimes removed from the source of political power. Citizens of democratic states fighting an unjust war have a measure of responsibility for the injustice. Are they, therefore, legitimate targets of attack?

III. Justice

There are many things any one of us may not have caused but which were nonetheless under our power to influence or control. Insofar as such things were under our power, we share some responsibility for them. And if such things bring harm to others, we are (partially) responsible for the harm. Suppose you endorse

a political candidate by voting for him. This candidate declares that once elected he'll balance the federal budget by (among other things) slashing college financial aid, adversely affecting, discriminating against, harming, say, Chicanos and African-Americans, but not white Americans. Are you by voting for that candidate responsible for discrimination, for the harm? Surely not, you will say, since you did not cause the policy nor wish to discriminate against Chicanos or African-Americans. But still you support him. He's your man in Washington. Four more years! That view of responsibility is very short sighted. It fails to see that government policies in a democracy are joint ventures. They are never the result of any one individual, but of many acting in concert for a common purpose. In such ventures, individuals play a necessary role by endorsing, contributing, or participating in them. By playing a necessary role in any one of those ways, each individual shares responsibility for the venture.

Those statements invite some general queries: What is the responsibility of citizens for their government's actions? Suppose a democratic regime, like ours, wages an unjust war. Just who is responsible? Are we morally responsible for the injustice of that war? Are we legitimate targets of deliberate attack? Would killing any one of us be an act of injustice?

Coady, the law of war, and the just war theory are firm in the opinion that regardless of the injustice of a government's actions, civilians are immune from deliberate attack. Individuals can lose their immunity in a number of ways, for example, by becoming soldiers, working for the war machine, or bearing arms. War is, however, never an individual, private, or personal enterprise. It is not something you or I do, but something we do together for a common purpose. It is a joint venture, a national activity. If we are engaged in grave injustice, say, a war of aggression, do those who endorse, contribute, or participate in the venture, as soldiers or civilians, lose their immunity from attack? How shall we think about this?

Suppose there is a gang of thieves headed by George and Tony in competition for territory and resources with another gang, headed by Boris and Jose. George and Tony decide to eliminate the competition and send their best hit men to kill Boris and Jose. Of course, Boris and Jose can defend themselves by killing the hit men, who are engaged in a criminal, immoral activity. But may they also kill those who sent them, George and Tony? After all, the hit men can botch their mission and then George and Tony will send their second best. Would it not be preferable for Boris and Jose to remove the danger by killing George and Tony rather than the hit men? Or do we say that since George and Tony are not bearing arms only the hit men may be killed? Who is responsible for the danger imposed on Boris and Jose?

In a democratic system like ours, given the possibility of free action, civilians bear a high burden of responsibility. When we support an unjust war, does it really make any sense to say that we are immune from attack because we are not bearing arms? Do we say only our soldiers can be killed, even when we, and not they, are responsible for an illegal and unjust proceeding? Are those who support an unjust war really innocent?

The fact is that not everyone will support an unjust war. And so, we have to distinguish between those who do and are therefore morally responsible, like George and Tony, and those who do not, who may not be killed because they are innocent of injustice. But it seems correct to say that George and Tony along with those who support, encourage, and send out the troops to wage an illegal and unjust war may morally be killed. If we take the idea of democratic popular sovereignty really seriously, then it is difficult to avoid that conclusion.

But there's at least one problem here: those who would attack a people waging an unjust war may kill only the guilty, otherwise they commit murder. Yet, there is no practical way by which one can do that. Bombs and bullets cannot read the bumper stickers on our cars that say "Not In My Name" and "Regime Change Begins At Home"; bombs and bullets do not know that some of us have organized anti-war demonstrations and that we know and have declared that this is an immoral, illegal, and criminal war. Nonetheless, suppose in some (very rare) circumstances the guilty can be distinguished from the innocent. When possible, then, the guilty may morally be killed.

We might, however, retreat from this view, even when we agree that it is correct. Perhaps morality is not always the best guide. Sometimes it demands too much. In the present case, it demands (at least permits) killing those responsible for grave injustice, the guilty. Of them, there will be very many and most of them will be found among the civilian population. But for the sake of reducing the carnage of war, we might let most of the guilty go free and restrict legitimate targets of attack to soldiers in war. But we do so not because civilians are innocent. Rather we do so because without limiting the range of legitimate targets to soldiers, there would be no room for war in this world. That might be a very good thing. But in the world as I know it, we must make some room for various forms of political violence as they can secure important moral goods—insurrection and revolution, for example, to free the slave and defeat tyrants, and war to defend the nation against those who would unjustly attack us.

EXERCISES

1. Could any act of the revolutionary insurgents of the American colonies against the British occupation legitimately be classified as terrorist by the British?

2. Suppose two terrorist groups make similar attacks against similar targets: both destroy office buildings containing government and military offices, along with civilian offices, and both attacks kill government officials, military officers, and civilians. One attack is aimed at a brutal occupying regime that is carrying out mass murder, while the latter attack is aimed at an occupying regime following more humane practices. On your view, *might* the former attack be justified while the latter is wrong? Or must they be considered morally equal, because both involve the killing of innocents?

3. For many years Nicaragua was ruled by a family of brutal dictators, the Somoza family, who tortured and killed many Nicaraguan citizens and ruled Nicaragua with an iron hand. Many U.S. corporations (especially agricultural corporations) had good relations with the Somoza dictatorship, and they made enormous profits in their dealings with the Somoza family (as did the Somoza family itself). The United States provided significant support, both militarily and economically, to the Somoza dictatorship. In 1979 a revolutionary movement within Nicaragua finally succeeded in overthrowing the Somoza regime and installing a new government that gave more power and resources to the Nicaraguan people, particularly the peasantry. The Reagan administration—which took power in 1980—regarded the new government as a threat to U.S. economic interests. Though there was no declaration of war against Nicaragua, the Reagan administration ordered the CIA to secretly mine several Nicaraguan harbors. The mining severely damaged Nicaraguan shipping and the Nicaraguan economy, and placed those using the harbors at grave risk—several freighters and small fishing boats were damaged by the mines, and a number of fishermen were killed. Was the CIA mining a terrorist act?

4. Suppose that a *dictatorship* wages an aggressive and unjust war against the peaceful country of Tranqua; and from the other side Tranqua is unjustly attacked by a *democracy*. Would people in Tranqua be more

justified in launching terrorist attacks against the citizens of the democracy than against the citizens of the dictatorship?

5. Imagine that in 1840, Great Britain turned its military might against a comparatively weak United States, overwhelmed the United States and occupied it, and placed the entire country under British military rule. If a U.S. civilian (there is no longer a U.S. military) threw a bomb at a British military patrol, would that be a terrorist act? Would the act be morally justified? Suppose that the bomb were thrown at a food supply center in Philadelphia, which is run by British civilians and is supplying food to occupying British troops. Would that be a terrorist act? Would it be justified? What if the bomb were thrown into a bank in London? Would any of your answers change if the goal of the British military occupation was not the military domination and exploitation of the United States, but was instead the sincere desire to abolish slavery in the United States?

ADDITIONAL READING

A good starting point for the examination of terrorism and related issues is Michael Walzer, *Just and Unjust Wars: A Moral Argument with Historical Illustrations*, 3rd ed. (New York: Basic Books, 2000).

A number of distinguished philosophers grapple with the issues related to terrorism in R. G. Frey and Christopher W. Morris, editors, *Violence, Terrorism, and Justice* (Cambridge, MA: Cambridge University Press, 1991). Walter Reich, editor, *Origins of Terrorism: Psychologies, Ideologies, Theologies, States of Mind* (Cambridge, MA: Cambridge University Press, 1990), contains interesting perspectives, including an essay by psychologist Albert Bandura. *Ethics in International Affairs*, edited by Andrew Valls (Lanham, MD: Rowman & Littlefield, 2000), has excellent articles on terrorism as well as on just war theory and global justice. Catherine Besteman's *Violence: A Reader* (New York: New York University Press, 2002) contains some good pieces not found elsewhere. The essays in James P. Sterba, editor, *Terrorism and International Justice* (New York: Oxford University Press, 2003), place the issue of terrorism in a larger global context. C. A. J. (Tony) Coady and Michael O'Keefe, eds., *Terrorism and Justice: Moral Argument in a Threatened World* (Melbourne University Press, 2002), is a particularly good collection.

Igor Primoratz, "The Morality of Terrorism," in *Journal of Applied Philosophy*, Volume 14, Number 3 (1997), 221–233, examines the issue of terrorism in the context of larger ethical theories.

A remarkable Web site on terrorism is the University of Michigan Documents Center site, America's War Against Terrorism: World Trade Center/Pentagon Terrorism and the Aftermath, at *http://www.lib.umich.edu/govdocs/usterror.html.* Another good online resource is the Terrorism Research Center, at *http://www.terrorism.com.*

Credits

Page 11: James Rachels, "God and Human Attitudes." *Religious Studies*, volume 7, 1971: 325–337. Reprinted with permission of Cambridge University Press.

Page 24: Bernard Williams, "Relativism, History and the Existence of Value," pp. 106–107 in Joseph Raz, *The Practice of Value*, edited by R. Jay Wallace (Oxford: The Clarendon Press, 2003) (210 words out of 900)

Page 28: Bishop Butler, from Fifteen Sermons Preached 11 of "Fifteen Sermons Preached at the Rolls Chapel." *Journal of Anthropological Research*, Vol. 53, No. 3, Universal Human Rights versus Cultural Relativity (Autumn 1997), pp. 371–381. University of New Mexico.

Page 30: Elvin Hatch, "The Good Side of Relativism." *Journal of Anthropological Research*, Vol. 53, No. 3, Universal Human Rights versus Cultural Relativity (Autumn 1997), pp. 371–381. With permission of the *Journal of Anthropological Research*, University of New Mexico, Albuquerque, NM. USA.

Page 45: Simon Blackburn, "we sentimentalists . . . " from "Must We Weep for Sentimentalism" in James Dreier, editor, *Contemporary Debates in Moral Theory* (Oxford: Blackwell Publishing, 2006).

Page 50: Four lines from T.S. Eliot's "Little Gidding" from *Four Quartets*. Faber & Faber Ltd. Reprinted by permission.

Page 54: David Hume, "A Treatise of Human Nature."

Page 57: Adam Smith, "Theory of Moral Sentiments."

Page 61: Jonathan Bennett, "The Conscience of Huckleberry Finn." *Originally published in Philosophy*, volume 49, 1974. Copyright 1974 by the Royal Institute of Philosophy. Reprinted by permission of the author.

Page 66: Extracts from "Dulce et Decorum Est" and "Insensibility" are from *The Collected Poems of Wilfred Owen*, edited by C. Day Lewis. Copyright Chatto & Windus Ltd. 1946, copyright 1963. Reprinted by permission of the Owen Estate, Chatto & Windus Ltd., and New Directions Publishing Corporation.

Page 67: Extracts from "Dulce et Decorum Est" and "Insensibility" are from *The Collected Poems of Wilfred Owen*, edited by C. Day Lewis. Copyright Chatto & Windus Ltd. 1946, copyright 1963. Reprinted by permission of The Owen Estate, Chatto & Windus Ltd., and New Directions Publishing Corporation.

Page 78: Immanuel Kant, "Fundamental Principles of the Metaphysics of Morals."

Page 94: Jeremy Bentham, "An Introduction to the Principles of Morals and Legislation."

Page 96: John Stuart Mill, "Utilitarianism"

Page 99: Bernard Williams, excerpt from "A Critique of Utilitarianism," from J. J. C. Smart and Bernard Williams, *Utilitarianism: For and Against* (Cambridge: Cambridge University Press, 1973). pp. 97–100, 101–104.

Page 111: Susan Wolf, "Moral Saints," *The Journal of Philosophy*, volume 79, number 8, August 1982, pp. 419–439. Reprinted by permission.

Page 117: Catherine Wilson, "On Some Alleged Limitations to Moral Endeavor." [Adapted] *The Journal of Philosophy*, Vol. 90, No. 6 (June 1993): 275–289. Reprinted by permission.

Page 122: John Dewey, Excerpt from "The Construction of Good," from *The Quest for Certainty*. Center for Dewey Studies, Southern Illinois University. Reprinted by permission.

Page 138: "Disabilities and the Social Contract," reprinted by permission of the publisher from *Frontiers of Justice: Disability, Nationality, Species Membership* by Martha C. Nussbaum, pp. 96–154. Cambridge, Mass: The Belknap Press of Harvard University Press, Copyright (c) 2006 by the President and Fellows of Harvard College.

Page 139: Thomas Hobbes, *The Leviathan*

Page 157: Aristotle, "Nichomachean Ethics," Trans. by W. D. Ross, p. 1107, 1109

Page 171: Annette C. Baier, "The Need for More Than Justice," *Canadian Journal of Philosophy*, suppl. Vol. on Science, Ethics, and Feminism, edited by Marsha Hanen and Kai Nielsen, vol. 13 (1987). Copyright (c) 1987. Reprinted by permission of the University of Calgary Press.

Page 186: Reprinted Alfred Jules Ayer, *Language, Truth and Logic*. Copyright (c) 1952 Dover Publications. Used with permission.

Page 197: Michael Smith, Excerpt from "Realism." Peter Singer (ed.), *A Companion to Ethics*. Blackwell, 1990, pp. 399–410. Reprinted by permission. Charles Darwin, *The Descent of Man*, 2nd ed. (London: John Murray, 1875), p. 99. First published in 1871.

Page 214: de Waal, Frans, *Primates and Philosophers*. (c) 2006 by Princeton University Press. Reprinted by permission of Princeton University Press.

Page 232: Susan Wolf, "Asymmetrical Freedom." *Journal of Philosophy* LXXVII, 3, March 1980, pp. 151–66. Copyright (c) 1980. Reprinted by permission.

Page 252: Thomas Nagel, "Moral Luck" pp. 24–38 in Mortal Questions. Copyright © 1979. Cambridge University Press. Reprinted with permission of Cambridge University Press.

Page 261: Stephen B. Bright, "Why the United States Will Join the Rest of the World in Abandoning Capital Punishment" from *Debating the Death Penalty: Should America Have Capital Punishment?* Eds., Hugo Adam Bedau & Paul Cassell, pp. 152–182. Copyright © 2005. Reprinted by permission of Oxford University Press.

Page 268: Louis P. Pojman and Jeffrey Reiman, "The Death Penalty: For and Against," as seen in *Debating the Death Penalty: Should America Have Capital Punishment?* Eds. Hugo Adam Bedau and Paul Cassell, pp. 51–75. Reprinted by permission of Rowman & Littlefield.

Page 277: Don Marquis, "Abortion is Immoral" *Journal of Philosophy*. LXXXVI, 4 (April 1989); 183–202. Copyright © 1989. Reprinted by permission.

Page 281: Bonnie Steinbock, "Why Most Abortions are Not Wrong." *Advances in Bioethics*, vol. 5, 1999, pp. 245–268. Copyright © 1999 with permission from Emerald Group Publishing Limited.

Page 288: Christopher Slobogin, Excerpt from "Deceit, Pretext and Trickery: Investigative Lies by the Police." *Oregon Law Review*, Winter 1997. Reprinted by permission of the author.

Page 297: Margaret L. Paris, "Lying by Police Should be Generally Prohibited." From "Lying to Ourselves" *Oregon Law Review*, Vol. 76, Winter 1997. Reprinted by permission of the author.

Page 305: John M. Finnis, "Homosexual Sex is Wrong" from "Law, Morality, and Sexual Orientation," *Notre Dame Journal of Law, Ethics, and Public Policy*, Volume 9, 1995. Reprinted by permission of the author.

Page 309: John Corvino, "Why Shouldn't Tommy and Jim Have Sex?" pp. 3–16 from *Same Sex: Debating the Ethics, Science and Culture of Homosexuality*. Copyright (c) 1997 Rowman & Littlefield. Reprinted by permission.

Page 317: Robert L. Simon, "Performance-Enhancing Drugs Should be Banned from Athletics." From "Good Competition and Drug-Enhanced Competition," *Journal of the Philosophy of Sport*, vol. 11 (1984), pp. 6–13.

Page 322: From HABER 0 7637 02269. *Ethics for Today and Tomorrow*, 1E. © 1997 Wadsworth, a part of Cengage Learning, Inc. Reproduced by permission. www.cengage.com/permissions

Page 330: C.A.J. Coady, "Terrorism, Just War and Supreme Emergency," in C.A. J. (Tony) Coady and Michael O'Keefe, eds., *Terrorism and Justice: Moral Argument in a Threatened World*. Copyright © 2002 Melbourne University Press. Used with permission.

Page 335: Gabriel Palmer-Fernandez, "Terrorism Might Sometimes Be Justified." From "Terrorism, Innocence, and Justice," *Philosophy & Public Policy Quarterly* (Spring 2005). Reprinted by permission of the author.

Glossary

Act-utilitarianism: A version of utilitarian ethics in which the rightness or wrongness of all acts is judged by whether they maximize pleasure and minimize suffering.

Ad hominem argument: *Ad hominem* literally means "to the person." An ad hominem argument is an argument that focuses on a person (or group of people), typically attacking the person. For example, "Joe is a liar," "Sandra is a hypocrite," "Republicans are cold-hearted." Ad hominem arguments are *fallacious* only when they attack the source of an *argument* in order to discredit the argument; for example, "Joe's argument against drinking and driving doesn't carry much weight, because Joe himself is a lush." When *not* attacking the source of an *argument,* ad hominem arguments do *not* commit the ad hominem *fallacy,* and can often be valuable and legitimate arguments. For example, an ad hominem attack on someone giving *testimony* ("Don't believe Sally's testimony, she's a notorious liar") is relevant, and *not* an ad hominem fallacy; likewise, it is a legitimate use of ad hominemargument (*not* an ad hominem *fallacy*) if you are attacking a job applicant ("Don't hire Bruce; he's a crook"), a politician ("Don't vote for Sandra; she's in the pocket of the tobacco industry"), and in many other circumstances ("Don't go out with Bill, he's a cheat and a creep").

Ad hominem fallacy: *See* Ad hominem argument.

Argument from simplicity: *See* Ockham's Razor.

Care ethics: The ethical perspective that emphasizes the ethical importance of personal relations and affections and friendships; it holds that such relationships have been neglected and undervalued in traditional ethical theories.

Categorical Imperative, Kant's: In Kantian ethics, the principle that one should always act in such a manner that one could will that one's act should be a universal law. (Kant claims that a second way of stating the same principle is that one should always treat other persons as ends-in-themselves, never as merely means to an end.)

Categorical principles: Principles that hold without qualification and in all circumstances; absolute principles, in contrast to *conditional* principles.

Compatibilism: The view that determinism is compatible with free will; we can have free will even if determinism is true.

Conditional principles: Principles that apply only under specified conditions (in contrast to *categorical* principles); for example, "*If* you want to be trusted, then you should tell the truth" is a conditional principle, in contrast to the categorical principle "Tell the truth."

Consequentialism: Any ethical theory that judges the rightness or wrongness of an act on the basis of its consequences, rather than on the basis of what principle the act falls under; contrasted with *deontological* ethics.

Cultural relativism: The ethical theory which asserts that ethical principles are relative to cultures; what is right or wrong is determined by the specific culture, and moral practices will differ from culture to culture.

Deontological ethics: Any ethical system that judges right and wrong acts in terms of principles or duties, rather than on the basis of the consequences of the acts; contrasted with *consequentialism.*

Determinism: The view that, given the state of the universe at any point, all future events are fixed by casual laws, and only one future course is genuinely possible.

Divine Command ethics: The view that all values and ethical principles are established by God's command or by God's will; also known as theological voluntarism.

Egoism: *See* Ethical egoism; Psychological egoism.

Ethical egoism: The view that the right act is the act that benefits the individual actor; that is, the ethical view that every person ought to act strictly for his or her own benefit.

Existentialism: The philosophical position based on the claim that "existence precedes essence"—that is, the view that we make and define ourselves by our own choices, rather than being determined or limited by our given characters or histories or natures.

Fallacy: A standard argument error or deception; usually one that is so common that it has been given a special name.

Fatalism: The view that the most significant events in our lives (such as our key successes or failures, as well as our deaths) are fixed by fate, and we can do nothing to alter our fates; we may be able to make some choices of details, but our larger fate is inescapable.

Golden Mean: The moderate or balanced position that—according to Aristotle's virtue ethics—is usually where virtue resides and is thus an appropriate target for behavior.

Intuitionism: The view that ethical truths or principles are known by special powers of intuition.

Libertarian: One who holds that we have a special power of free will that is strictly incompatible with determinism.

Moral agent: One who is capable of performing a good or bad moral act.

Moral realism: In its contemporary form, the view that objective moral facts will prove to be the best possible explanation for our experiences of moral phenomena.

Moral responsibility: A condition in which one justly deserves punishment or reward, praise or blame; one has moral responsibility in circumstances when it is appropriate that one receive "just deserts" for one's acts.

Natural law ethics: An ethical theory that counts human acts (and the laws and principles governing them) as morally good when they promote the development of our true human nature; maintains that our human nature and its proper development is assigned by God; and holds that the key element of our human nature is our God-given rationality.

Noncognitivism: A form of ethical nonobjectivism according to which all value assertions are actually disguised commands or expressions of emotion; value assertions and ethical assertions do not make real statements and are neither true nor false; sometimes called emotivism.

Nonobjectivism: The view that in ethics there is no truth and no objective facts.

Objectivism: The view that there are genuine objective ethical facts; ethical claims are factually true or false.

Ockham's Razor: A principle of scientific and explanatory methodology holding that when evaluating explanations, the simpler explanation is (all else being equal) to be preferred to more complicated explanations; alternatively, the principle that "we should not multiply entities beyond necessity," or that explanations should not posit the existence of more entities or objects than are strictly required for a satisfactory explanation.

Pragmatism: The view that there are no fixed absolute truths, and true beliefs are not those that accurately copy an independent detached reality; rather, true beliefs are tools that guide us effectively in our tasks and inquiries.

Prisoners' Dilemma: In game theory, any situation in which players can gain more through cooperation than by each one directly pursuing his or her individual interests.

Psychological egoism: The empirical psychological (not ethical) claim that every individual does in fact always act for his or her own benefit.

Relativism: *See* Cultural relativism and sociological relativism.

Retribution: Punishment justly inflicted on one who has harmed another, for the purposes of restoring moral balance rather than for any other social or individual good.

Role responsibility: Responsibility for a task or project, or responsibility that is attached to a particular role (such as the responsibility of a doctor to her patients); distinguished from *moral* responsibility.

Rule-utilitarianism: A version of utilitarian ethics according to which rules and institutions are judged by utilitarian standards (do they maximize pleasure and minimize suffering?) and the rightness or wrongness of individual acts is determined by whether they fit under the rules of beneficial institutions and practices.

Satisficing consequentialism: A version of consequentialist ethics that holds that an act can be good *enough*—can produce ethically satisfactory results—even if it does not produce the best possible consequences.

Sentimentalism: In ethics, the view that feelings/sentiments are essential to gaining knowledge of ethical truths. (The term is used in literature with a different meaning; in literature, "sentimentalism" refers either to the excessive use of sentiment or to an emphasis on the natural goodness of humankind.)

Situationism: In social psychological research, situationism is the view that human behavior is heavily influenced by the perceived situation of the person; that is, the view that situational circumstances often have greater influence on behavior than does personal character.

Social contract theory: A type of ethical or political theory that starts from the perspective of what system of rules or ethical principles would be favored by those drawing up a mutual agreement for governing themselves.

Sociological relativism: The sociological (not ethical) observation that cultures differ in rules and practices.

State of nature: In social contract theory, the mythical situation prior to any social contract; in Hobbes' theory, a state of war of all against all, with no rules.

Strawman fallacy: The fallacy of distorting, exaggerating, or misrepresenting an opponent's position in order to make it easier to attack.

Theological voluntarism: *See* Divine Command ethics.

Utilitarian ethics: The ethical theory that judges the rightness or wrongness of an act in terms of its consequences—in particular, whether it produces the greatest balance of pleasure over suffering for everyone involved.

Value pluralism: (sometimes called ethical pluralism or moral pluralism) It is the view that there is not a single highest value, and that values do not have a unified order: There are multiple values, all of them legitimate and genuine values; those values may sometimes be in conflict; and there is no objective way of placing those multiple values in rank order.

Veil of ignorance: In the work of philosopher John Rawls, the "veil of ignorance" is an imaginative device for considering what counts as just and fair in a state or society. Suppose a group of people were planning to form a society, but none of them know anything at all about their own conditions in the society (no one knows his or her race, gender, or ethnic group; whether he or she would be strong or weak, healthy or chronically ill, industrious or lethargic, smart or dull); then from that condition of profound ignorance of their own positions or places in the society (from behind that "veil of ignorance") the rules and principles they would agree upon to govern the society would be rules that are fair and just (because free of biases and special interests).

Virtue ethics: An approach to ethics that focuses on the character of the ethical actor and on how good character develops, rather than on duties, rules, and determination of the right act in a specific situation.

Index